S0-BMW-523

DATE DUE   8

Demco

MILITARY
MEDICINE

MILITARY MEDICINE

From Ancient Times to the 21st Century

Jack E. McCallum

A B C CLIO

Santa Barbara, California • Denver, Colorado • Oxford, England

Library of Congress Cataloging-in-Publication Data
McCallum, Jack Edward, 1945–
    Military medicine : from ancient times to the 21st century / Jack E. McCallum.
        p. ; cm.
    Includes bibliographical references and index.
    ISBN 978-1-85109-693-0 (hardcover : alk. paper)
    1. Medicine, Military—History—Encyclopedias. I. Title.
    [DNLM: 1. Military Medicine—History—Handbooks. WZ 80 M4892m 2008]

    UH215.M36 2008
    616.9'802309—dc22

                                                              2007045470

12 11 10 09 08   1 2 3 4 5 6 7 8 9 10

This book is also available on the World Wide Web as an ebook. Visit www.abc-clio
.com for details.

ABC-CLIO, Inc.
130 Cremona Drive, P.O. Box 1911
Santa Barbara, California 93116–1911

Senior Production Editor: Cami Cacciatore
Production Manager: Don Schmidt
Media Manager: Caroline Price
Media Editor: Ellen Rasmussen
File Management Coordinator: Paula Gerard

This book is printed on acid-free paper. ∞
Manufactured in the United States of America

To Spencer Tucker, who guided me through my studies in history and who remains a constant source of wisdom and inspiration.

CONTENTS

INTRODUCTION

Overview of the Evolution of Military Medicine

Deciphering archeological remains, observing nonhuman primates, and studying the few remaining hunter-gatherer societies drives one to the unsettling conclusion that there has never been a time when humans did not devote a large portion of their energies to injuring one another. It is also evident that, for almost as long as some have specialized in carnage, others have struggled to fix its damage.

Military medicine is, however, much more than just repairing wounds. When armies congregate, they subject their bodies to the stress and deprivation of campaigns, they occasionally try to poison each other, and they regularly share their infestations. Caring for soldiers, then, requires the skill of both the physician and the surgeon, and it is impossible to understand the history of either medicine or surgery without recognizing the contributions that came from providing that care.

Can we really prove that organized aggression predated the ability of humans to record it? Perhaps. Primatologists have seen chimpanzees sharpen sticks and use them to attack smaller apes. Sociologists living with Amazonian and South Pacific forest tribes witnessed lives defined by constant intertribal conflict. Prehistoric skulls, dented from being beaten with clubs, have holes scraped and drilled alongside the fractures. One can easily envision a prehistoric surgeon working his way through the broken bone in an effort to mend the brain injury below. In fact, prehistoric neurosurgery was surprisingly common. Intentionally punctured skulls have been found in considerable numbers and across a broad geography; perforated crania have been unearthed in France, Great Britain, the Netherlands, Germany, Peru, the United States, Algeria, Zimbabwe, and a number of Pacific Islands.

Medicine in Prerecorded Historical Times

At the close of the last ice age—about 10,000 years ago—the nomads who had roamed the savannas of Africa and Asia learned to cultivate grains and husband animals and settled in the great river valleys of North Africa and the Middle East (along the Nile and the Tigris and Euphrates rivers),

India (the Ganges and Indus rivers), and China (the Yellow and Yang-tze rivers). People who congregated and farmed were better able to feed themselves, but they also put themselves in the food chain for microorganisms that, benefiting from their physical proximity, could more readily pass from animal to man or from man to man. A few examples include the pox virus that infects both cattle and humans, canine distemper which is a first cousin of human measles, and influenza that travels between birds and humans in annual waves. Even though most epidemics eventually result in immunity that blunts the disease, infections were the principal threat to aggregated populations and remained so until the very recent understanding of microbiology and resultant techniques of treatment and prevention brought them under partial control.

The !Kung San people of Africa's Kalahari Desert give us a hint of the devastating effect infections had on Neolithic populations. Infectious disease is still responsible for 70 to 80 percent of deaths in those nomads (Cohen 1989, 109). Since virtually everything we know about controlling infections that makes our risk less than theirs was learned in the last 150 years, their susceptibility to infectious disease is typical of almost the whole of human history.

When people strayed out of their areas of cultivation to trade or—more pertinent to our topic—to make war, they took their infections with them and inflicted them on populations that, because they had never encountered those diseases, had no immunity to them. The history of epidemic disease is inseparable from the history of war.

People want to control their own destinies, and attempts to treat disease must be ancient indeed. Unfortunately, the lack of a written record blinds us to what the earliest therapies might have been. Unlike the intentionally perforated skulls, soft tissue leaves no trace when it decays, and evidence of treatment vanishes with it. All we have for evidence of the majority of injuries and illnesses and their treatment is the occasional icon. A French cave painting dating from around 15,000 B.C. may be the oldest such record. A dancer, his head sheathed with that of an animal, could easily be a present-day shaman casting spells for his isolated Amazonian tribe.

Shamanism and medical magic point to the importance of the equation of disease and injury that, in various disguises, persists and is surprisingly pervasive, even in otherwise sophisticated societies. Prior to the classical Greeks, all societies saw illness and injury as one and the same. The only difference between them was that injury was directly inflicted by some identifiable act, like a fall or a blow from a club, whereas illness was inflicted either by an enemy's curse or by the maleficence of a god; but it was still an injury. The belief that illness was just supernaturally inflicted injury was the defining concept of medical treatment for millennia. To the earliest physicians (who, not surprisingly, doubled as priests) it seemed obvious that those who would treat disease should direct their energies toward the cause. If the cause was a man or one of his deities, magic—or religion—aimed at negating the evil influence was not just reasonable, it was required. Any attempt to alter the course of the disease by treating it was at best futile and at worst sacrilegious. For the first 3,000 years of which we have written records, technicians treated wounds. Priests treated diseases.

Needless to say, infection is not the only thing—although until quite recently it was the main thing—that kills people at war. The story of military surgery parallels the evolution of military technology. Not long after settling into the riverine civilizations, men learned to make weapons that were more effective than wooden spears and stone axes, and, by the time writing emerged around 5000 B.C., the Sumerians of lower Mesopotamia had already moved beyond simply crushing, slashing, and poking with a stick or a stone. They had learned to harden copper into bronze that would hold an edge sharp enough to slice skin and muscle and could, when mounted at the tip of a spear, penetrate any protection that was not metal itself. They also learned to use bows, first simple wooden arcs and then compound recurved models, to kill from a distance. When wild asses and horses were harnessed to light vehicles with axled, spoked wheels, the weapons and those who wielded them were able to travel long distances at prodigious speed. Of course, the same chariots that were so good at transporting weapons and warriors were equally effective at transporting microbes and diseases.

Ancient Egyptian and Greek Military Medicine

Better weapons caused worse injuries and worse injuries necessitated better wound care. The record of some early advances in trauma management survives in a handful of stunning papyruses from the Middle Kingdom including those carrying the names of Egyptologists Georg Ebers and Edwin Smith. Both documents date from the 18th Dynasty (roughly the first half of the 16th century B.C.), were at one time owned by Edwin Smith (although Ebers bought his in 1873), and may have actually come from the same excavation. But there the similarity ends.

The Smith papyrus (which was brilliantly translated and turned into a beautiful elephant folio edition by James Breasted in 1922) is composed almost entirely of the "Book on Wounds" and may have been a manual of military surgery. It proceeds in an orderly fashion down the body, starting with the head, and is rich with details of diagnosis, treatment, and prognosis. The scribe copying the papyrus, however, got only as far as the thorax. For reasons we will never know, he stopped his work in the middle of a sentence and never came back to it. The Smith papyrus perpetuates knowledge that had existed for at least a millennium and makes an important point. Until very recently, the pace of medical change was glacial, and the bulk of medical practice was based on theories that might have been unchallenged and unchanged for centuries.

The Ebers document (translated in 1937 by B. Ebell) brings up again the dichotomy between treatments based on observation and experience (empiricism) that was often left to surgery and the magic that pervaded medical therapies. The papyrus is a catalogue of drugs and potions but it is also laden with spells and incantations. It is worth pointing out that the damage done by conflating medicine and magic lies not just in its ineffectiveness. Making medicine a function of the supernatural removes the need for—and often even the possibility of—questioning and research.

Greek military medicine, like the rest of Greek history, can be divided into two broad eras—the ancient and the classical. The ancient Greeks shared the ethnic origin and a good deal of the civilization and technology of their Minoan predecessors. War was a seasonal but endemic activity in the islands and city-states of the eastern Mediterranean, but the means of inflicting and treating injury were virtually indistinguishable from those used in Egypt and Sumeria for the previous 2,000 years. Disease was still seen as injury inflicted by the gods or a magically adept enemy, and its treatment was almost entirely a matter of imprecation and incantation. Empirical (as opposed to magical) medicine concerned itself almost entirely with the treatment of wounds. However, the ancient Greeks were first storytellers and later story writers, and Homer's *Iliad* and *Odyssey* are our earliest clear picture of wartime injuries and their treatment. Homer's limitations as a medical resource are, however, considerable. German historian and physician Franz Frölich tallied the types and mortality of the 147 injuries in the *Iliad*, but there is almost no further detail. It does appear that very little organized medical care was delivered to the wounded on either side during the Trojan War. Greek military leaders occasionally doubled as wound surgeons, and the few actual surgeons who accompanied the army doubled as military leaders. That their surgery was almost entirely confined to repair of wounds is reflected in the fact that *iatros*, the Greek word for physician, literally means "remover of arrows."

Classical Greek Military Medicine

During the 500 years between Homer and Hippocrates, almost nothing new developed in Greek military medicine. That changed with the compilation of knowledge from the library on the island of Cos for which Hippocrates is given credit although it is almost certainly the product of a number of inquiring minds. For the first time, human injury and disease were subjected to systematic observation and categorization. Hippocratic surgery was the repair of wounds supplemented with a smattering of orthopedics, and Hippocrates was clear that surgery and war went hand in hand. He advised that anyone who would become a surgeon should find himself an army and follow it.

A number of reasonably detailed accounts of the travails and treatment of Greek and Persian armies on campaign survive. The descriptions of Herodotus and Xenophon stand out in that regard. Because Greeks fought not only their neighboring city-states but also went to war with and for other powers, their military medicine spread through much of the ancient world. Late in Hellenic history, Philip of Macedon and his son Alexander actually began taking military surgeons on their campaigns and elevated those practitioners to a status they would not enjoy again for centuries. After Alexander's death, respect for Greek military surgeons went into steep decline as did the art they practiced.

Roman Military Medicine

In the first several hundred years after the 753 B.C. founding of the republic, Roman medicine in general and military medicine specifically were accorded little interest and were practiced at a generally low standard. Early republican armies fought in phalanges indistinguishable from those of Athens and Sparta, and the wounds inflicted by them were similar. Medical practice was mostly the province of Greek slaves who, in the best of cases, were viewed as marginally competent and, in the worst, were suspected of actively trying to kill their patients. That attitude changed around 91 B.C. and was marked by the arrival in Rome of Asclepiades of Bithynia, whose talent and reputation helped improve the status of medicine under the empire.

By the time of the Punic Wars, the phalanx had evolved into more maneuverable three-deep maniples and then into cohorts of professional infantry welded into tightly organized 6,000-man legions. Rome and its opponents could field armies approaching 100,000 men comprised of both armored troops and lance-bearing cavalry. The large, well-armed forces brought a commensurate increase in both injury and disease.

In addition, Roman generals and emperors realized that a soldier who knew his wounds would be looked after was more likely to fight. Military medicine became a state obligation, and the status of military surgeons improved commensurately. To lure physicians to Rome, Julius Caesar offered them citizenship, and Germanicus paid his military surgeons from his own pocket. By the time of Trajan (A.D. 98–138), every legion and every Roman naval vessel had its own surgeons, holding a rank equivalent to noncommissioned officers and who were excused from combat and routine camp duties.

As the empire expanded beyond the Italian peninsula, the sick and wounded could no longer be cared for in private homes. Other arrangements had to be made in the far-flung reaches of the empire, so the imperial forces established a network of military hospitals (*valetudinaria*) built with a sophistication and attention to sanitation that would not be seen again for almost 2,000 years.

Roman advances in the practice of military medicine were, however, almost entirely organizational. The actual practice of medicine and surgery were, even when not directly in the hands of Greek immigrants, derived almost entirely from classical Greek works. It is telling that one of two most frequently cited Roman medical authors, Aulus Cornelius Celsus, was an encyclopedist and not a physician at all. Still, Roman military medicine represented an apex destined to precede a 1,000-year decline.

Military Medicine in the Middle Ages

Historians often define the Middle Ages as the time between the fall of Rome in A.D. 476 and the fall of the Eastern Empire in 1453, and those dates have some logic with regard to military medicine. The fall of the empire marked an end to organized care of fighting forces, and Constantinople's fall and the consequent flood of physician refugees was a proximate cause of the dispersion of classical learning that reawakened medicine in Western Europe. Those physicians had read the Greek authorities and many had served in the Eastern Empire's armies, which were the only ones that had preserved organized military medicine. Perhaps a more specific date—the publication in 1543 of Andreas Vesalius's anatomical studies that finally supplanted those of Galen—better serves as the end of the medical Middle Ages.

For almost a millennium after Rome's demise, no organized military existed in Western Europe; warfare was the province of bands of isolated horsemen. What medical care was practiced fell to the religious orders—at least until a 13th-century papal decree barred monks from exposing themselves to human blood.

The Crusades saw aggregations of fighting men but not organized national armies, and essentially no medical care was provided for the soldiers. Nestorian refugees from Constantinople had fled to Edessa in Asia Minor with their libraries and had subsequently passed the classical Greek texts to Arabs, who translated and preserved them. The Crusaders, however, failed to learn from their Arab opponents and brought nothing of medical usefulness home except the refugee Teutonic knights and Hospitallers and a few facilities dedicated to caring for the sick and wounded.

Developments in Military Medicine in the 14th through 17th Centuries

Change in both military tactics and military medicine came in the early years of the 14th century. The Swiss rediscovered the phalanx and the long pike and, at the Battle of Paupen in 1339, proved that a well-organized force on foot could defeat armored horsemen. At Crécy seven years later,

English bowmen again demonstrated the vulnerability of armored knights. Western Europe had rediscovered Macedonian and Roman methods of combating cavalry, and the use of masses of foot soldiers led directly to the reappearance of military medicine. At first, that reappearance was mostly a "top down" phenomenon: Henry V took a physician, a surgeon, and several assistants with him to Agincourt, but they were available to only a handful of nobles. The bulk of the English army remained without medical care. The Swiss were an exception; they were the first nation-state since the fall of Rome to make care of armies and their dependents a state responsibility.

Medical care of soldiers in the 14th century was severely hampered by the fact that medicine had divorced itself from surgery and relegated the latter to poorly trained and largely illiterate itinerant practitioners. For soldiers, surgery consisted entirely of removing sharp objects and dressing wounds. Since those who did surgery were ignorant of infection and uninterested in sanitation, what they did to wounds was almost always worse than simply leaving them alone. It would be another 200 years before surgeons learned that what they were doing was harmful, and 300 more before that knowledge actually changed practice.

Physicians in the 14th century had rediscovered the fact that some diseases spread from person to person, although they still had no idea how that happened. They recognized eight contagious illnesses—plague, phthisis, epilepsy, scabies (which included syphilis), erysipelas, anthrax, trachoma, and leprosy—and attempted to control them with various degrees of quarantine. That practice became a matter of maritime routine and national policy with the repeated waves of bubonic plague after 1346.

The 15th century saw three signal events in the history of military medicine: widespread use of gunpowder weapons, the rise of standing armies, and the printing press. Gunpowder had been used sporadically in Europe since the 1200s (and in China for a good deal longer), but it became a practical weapon in the 1400s with the development of metal casting techniques capable of producing relatively durable cannon barrels and with the matchlock musket, a weapon which could be carried by an infantryman. Unlike blades and points, which penetrated the skin but seldom broke bones, these weapons created fractures below open wounds leaving the damaged bone exposed and contaminated. Inflammation and infection were so common that most military surgeons were convinced that gunpowder itself was poisonous, and they embarked on a variety of gruesome and universally harmful methods of "detoxifying" the wounds, most of which involved probing with unwashed hands or instruments and irrigating with some boiling, noxious concoction often devised by the operator. Their dismal results convinced military surgeons that the only reliable way to prevent death from a compound fracture was to remove the extremity altogether;

that conviction resulted in an epidemic of military amputations that lasted until the end of the 19th century.

Charles VII of France (1422–1461) with his *compagnies d'ordonance*, and Holy Roman Emperor Maximilian I (1459–1519) with his *Landesknecht*, had the first standing armies responsible to the state rather than to the local nobility since the Roman legions. Neither had a formal medical service, but Maximillian's troops did pay at least a modicum of attention to sanitation while on campaign and included an assortment of barbers and wound dressers among their camp followers. In 1480, Isabella of Castille spent her own funds to establish field hospitals and transportation for those wounded while fighting to expel the Moors from Iberia.

The first printed book appeared in 1454, and, in spite of futile German attempts to maintain a monopoly on the technology, presses sprang up in cities across Europe before the century was out. Initially, almost all the medical books printed were in Latin or Greek and were reproductions of heavily redacted manuscripts that had survived in either Arab or Byzantine libraries. Books with new information printed in languages accessible to the ordinary practitioner did not become common until almost a century later.

Physicians in the 16th century finally left Galen and Hippocrates behind. Andreas Vesalius began dissecting human cadavers in Padua and, with the help of Titian's student Jan Van Calcar, produced atlases that corrected a plethora of misconceptions that had plagued medicine since the time of the ancient Greeks. William Harvey took the new knowledge of anatomy and applied it to physiology. He was able to demonstrate that blood circulated through the body and explained (for the most part) how that happened. On the battlefield, Ambroise Paré serendipitously discovered that gunshot wounds left alone healed better than those inflicted with hot cauteries and boiling oil. He also showed that bleeding could be stopped more effectively by tying arteries above a wound than by burning the tissue around it. These were the first halting steps toward actually making military surgery more beneficial than harmful to its subjects.

The 1500s also were a time in which the concept of standing armies, like those in France and the Holy Roman Empire, spread across Europe. Those large, organized forces necessitated integral structures for transportation and medical care of the wounded.

The next century proved to be one of almost constant warfare fought on a scale without precedent, particularly in the religious wars of Central Europe and the civil war in England. Gustavus Adolphus of Sweden and his astoundingly complex "order of fire" ("manual of arms") made muskets an effective weapon and rendered pike men all but obsolete. Meanwhile, cavalrymen replaced their lances with pistols and swords. Continued improvements in metallurgy and casting led to artillery powerful enough to eventually beat down most walled fortifications, and, consequently, siege warfare became common. When armies stayed in one place for long periods of time, sanitation suffered and infectious diseases proliferated. When a siege broke and the armies moved, they trailed typhus, dysentery, plague, and pox—both great and small—behind them.

Although medical scientists were learning a great deal about human anatomy and physiology, another two centuries would pass before that information was translated into clinically useful techniques. On a practical level, medicine and surgery continued the separation that had started in the Middle Ages. Physicians had only a handful of useful drugs—opiates and quinine being the best—and a large number of harmful ones. They did not know what caused contagious diseases and would not have been able to treat them if they had known.

Eighteenth century standing armies most often included both regimental physicians and surgeons, but their usefulness was marginal at best. Military surgery remained the province of barbers, whose rank was a bit above that of a drummer but below that of a clerk and far below that of their medical counterparts. Treatment of wounds consisted of probing for bullets with dirty fingers, dressing with foul ointments, and amputation.

Although it was marked by periodic dynastic conflicts and two revolutions that occasioned immense exchanges of territory between governments, the 18th century was, at least to an extent, a respite sandwiched between religious wars and those of Napoleon. Armies became better organized and muskets easier to load and fire, giving rise to set-piece battles in which lines of riflemen faced one another and shot until one side ran out of either courage or men.

Military Medicine in the 18th and 19th Centuries

The science of military medicine in the 18th century saw the first medically mediated defeat of a nutritional disease (scurvy) and an infectious disease (smallpox). The century also produced important works on military and naval sanitation by the likes of John Pringle and James Lind. Wound care continued to be hampered by a commitment to inducing "laudable pus." Harm done in the belief that suppuration was necessary to healing was compounded by use of "heroic" but useless therapies employing strychnine, arsenic, and venesection. On the positive side of the ledger, the training, qualifications, and status of military physicians and surgeons improved. Surgeons were finally allowed to wear their regiment's uniform, and, by the end of the century, most had attained officer rank. Military medical practitioners were required to pass standardized examinations, and regulations were published regarding organization and operation of their hospitals. The first military medical schools were chartered in France in 1775, and the first journal devoted to military medicine (the *Journal de médicine militaire*) was launched in 1782.

As had been the case in prior centuries, military medicine in the 1800s followed a path furrowed on one side by advances in the technology of war and on the other by the scientific understanding of the human body. The ruts were seldom parallel, and medicine lurched along sometimes directed by one and sometimes by the other.

Military medicine in the Napoleonic Wars was at once a story of the disastrous effects of amassing previously unheard of numbers of combatants and of the benefits of early treatment and evacuation of those wounded in battle. The giant armies created by drafting the civilian population in a *levée en masse* were inevitably subject to parasites and their diseases, especially typhus. Perhaps the brightest spot in the management of infectious disease in the late 1700s and early 1800s was the general control of smallpox that began with inoculation with live virus mandated by George Washington during the American Revolution and evolving to general use of Edward Jenner's cowpox vaccine which virtually eliminated what had long been a recurring plague.

When governments sent thousands of men out to live off the land or on the sea in whatever climate extremes they might find, those men were inevitably exposed to diseases of dietary deficiency and environmental exposure such as scurvy and frostbite. The Royal Navy conquered the first, while the French Army succumbed to the second.

The mid-19th-century Crimean War again exposed soldiers to cold and infection (primarily dysentery), but, this time, immediate and graphic communication between the battlefield and the domestic press cast a harsh light on military medicine's shortcomings. That exposure led to recruitment of female nurses which in turn resulted in a dramatic improvement in hospital care for the sick and wounded. Surgical anesthesia was tried in the Crimea, but the real benefit from being able to operate on an unconscious patient would have to wait another 30 years since bacteria still had the final say in the outcome.

Although anesthesia was commonly used in the American Civil War, there was still no control of operative infection and surgical results remained dismal. That conflict saw huge masses of men thrown at the muzzles of weapons too powerful and too accurate for the offensive tactics of set-piece battle. Terrible wounds were common, and those that could not be managed by either simple dressing or amputation were generally beyond help. Even so, as in Napoleonic Europe and the Crimea, disease was more lethal than trauma. Ignorance of the causes of disease and lack of even the most basic sanitation left both sides subject to the ravages of malaria, typhoid, typhus, and dysentery.

The real breakthroughs in medicine—attributable in no small part to military physicians—began in the 1860s when Louis Pasteur and Robert Koch proved that one disease after another was caused by microorganisms.

When British army surgeon Ronald Ross unraveled the complex life cycle of the plasmodium, he proved that the mosquito was the key to malaria transmission. This discovery was followed soon after by conquest of an even uglier, deadlier, and more frightening insect-borne epidemic disease—yellow fever. And, again, the triumph belonged to military surgeons; Walter Reed and his Yellow Fever Commission combined Cuban physician Carlos Finlay's insight with a series of brilliantly designed (if ethically questionable) experiments to document the first known viral causation of a human disease and its transmission by the *Aedes aegyptii* mosquito. Vector management was added to quarantine, sanitation, and vaccination in the armamentarium for combating infectious diseases.

The triumph over yellow fever following the Spanish-American War (1898) belied the otherwise dismal experience with infectious disease during that conflict. So many men died of typhoid in training camps in the American South that the postwar Dodge Commission demanded a complete overhaul of the U.S. Army Medical Department. Although the price in lost lives was high, the resulting reorganization meant the Army would have more surgeons, a nurse corps, and better supplies when the next war started. The Spanish-American War also saw limited use of X-ray and general adoption of surgical asepsis, although the number of injuries was perhaps too small to adequately demonstrate an effect. That proof would have to wait for a larger conflict and more injuries, but the wait would not be a long one.

The 20th and 21st Centuries: Dramatic Change in Military Medicine Procedures

The 20th century witnessed advances in military medicine that, measured in numbers of saved limbs and lives, dwarfed the cumulative achievements of all the rest of history. During World War I, monitored, safe anesthesia and aseptic surgery made wounds that had previously been uniformly fatal treatable. A new vaccine virtually eliminated tetanus on the Western Front. Better sanitation at least limited typhus and dysentery, although again more effectively on the Western Front than in Eastern Europe and the Middle East. On the other side of the scale, land mines, machine guns, barbed wire, submarines, airborne bombs, and chemical warfare combined with armies that were an order of magnitude larger than those of the prior century. That combination kept the ability to kill and maim well ahead of the ability to treat and cure.

Between the world wars, chemicals and biological agents that were specifically effective against bacterial infections were discovered. Because infection could be controlled, surgeons could operate on injuries to parts of the body previously entered only at great peril. Chest, head, and abdominal injuries could be surgically repaired with at least reasonable hope of success. Malaria could be prevented as long as soldiers could be convinced to take the prophylactic drugs. With the exception of viral disease, military epidemics appeared to be things of the past. But, as in the prior world war, World War II proved that man's ability to inflict harm could still outstrip his talents for repairing it. Aerial bombing, particularly with incendiaries, produced civilian injuries on a scale and of a severity never before experienced, and the closing days of the war added radiation injury to the list of military medical concerns.

Perhaps most disturbing was the participation of the medical establishments of Germany and Japan in unconscionable (and generally unproductive) experiments on civilian and military prisoners. Active participation by physicians and scientists in those experiments led to an explicit set of rules and restrictions that have—although with increasingly frequent exceptions—governed medical research since the 1940s. The Nuremberg Code's restrictions on human experimentation came directly from malfeasance in military medicine, and military physicians have been involved in a number of its subsequent infringements.

The wars of the second half of the 20th century and the beginning of the 21st have been of a smaller scale than those of the first half of the 20th century. Nations have so far refrained from use of nuclear weapons and have, with rare exceptions, not used either biological or chemical weapons. Mass casualties from large battles have not occurred. On the other hand, hardly a year has passed without conflict somewhere in the world, and asymmetric warfare (a euphemism for terrorism) has made blasts from improvised explosive devices a dominant mode of injury. In addition, better transport and truly phenomenal advances in surgery performed within hours of injury have saved the lives of large numbers of combatants who would have died only a few years ago. An unfortunate consequence of that success is the growing number of survivors with extensive and often incapacitating injuries. Control of infections has, for the first time in history, made disease a minor contributor to military morbidity and mortality.

Perhaps the most striking aspect of the history of military medicine is how slowly it progressed for the first 4,900 years of recorded history and how quickly it has progressed in the last 100 years. What follows is a topic-by-topic consideration of some of the people, diseases, and techniques that have contributed to that story.

References

Breasted, James Henry. *The Edwin Smith Surgical Papyrus Published in Facsimile and Hieroglyphic Transliteration with Translation and Commentary in Two Volumes.* Chicago: University of Chicago Press, 1930.

Cohen, Mark N. *Health & the Rise of Civilization.* New Haven, CT: Yale University Press, 1989.

Abdominal Injuries in War

Because of the risk of damage to multiple organs, penetrating injuries of the abdomen have been a major cause of battlefield death and have a greater impact than any other injury on overall survival.

Prior to the 16th century, most such injuries were caused by bladed weapons that could perforate the digestive tract; major blood vessels; or solid viscera such as the kidney, liver, or spleen. The advent of gunpowder weapons made penetrating abdominal injuries more common and more lethal.

Prior to the 18th century, patients with penetrating abdominal injuries were essentially untreatable, and most died from their injuries. A common course involved penetration of the intestine, and spillage of feces into the peritoneal cavity followed—often after days of excruciating pain—by sepsis and death. In the late 1700s, scattered reports of exploration and repair of punctured viscera, especially the stomach, appeared. Perhaps the most famous such case was that which American army surgeon William Beaumont described in his land-

mark study of gastric physiology based on observations of Canadian voyageur Alexis St. Martin's gastric fistula that resulted from a shotgun blast to the abdomen.

The advent of anesthesia and antiseptic technique made surgical exploration and repair of damaged organs practical and gave surgery for intra-abdominal trauma a reasonable chance of success. In 1881, American gynecologist James Marion Sims, a medical volunteer in the Franco-Prussian War, recommended early operation for all abdominal penetrations. In the absence of antibiotics, however, the death rate from secondary infection caused by fecal spillage from the perforated bowel remained high. In a monograph describing his experience with abdominal wounds in the Boer War, George Makins persisted in recommending nonoperative management, although 33 percent of the patients who survived long enough to come under his care still died. Nicholas Senn had a similar experience with American soldiers at Santiago during the Spanish-American War in 1898.

During the Russo-Japanese War of 1905, Russian princess and surgeon Vera

Ignatievna Gedroitz brought her own ambulance train with a surgical suite to the line of battle, where she could operate on patients with abdominal injuries soon after they were wounded. Her results were said to be better than those of her colleagues who either did not operate or operated after the delay necessary to move the men to rear-area hospitals.

At the onset of World War I, there was still a debate as to whether patients with abdominal wounds were more likely to survive with or without exploratory surgery. The English tended to be conservative, while the Germans were more inclined to operate. Mortality from abdominal wounds in that war was an estimated 53 percent. In World War II, even with the advent of antibiotics, mortality ranged from 18 to 36 percent. In a series of soldiers wounded in Viet Nam, mortality was said to have been 10 percent, but if one includes all patients who did not live to come to the hospital, the estimate ranges as high as 42 percent. Of those who died, 60 percent succumbed to hemorrhage; 25 percent died from sepsis; and 15 percent died in pulmonary failure (presumably related to shock).

In recent conflicts in southeastern Europe and in the Middle East, an estimated 20 percent of battle casualties had an abdominal wound, and approximately half of those died. Because infection is most often averted with early surgery or controlled with broad-spectrum antibiotics, sepsis has become a relatively rare cause of death after abdominal wounds. Most deaths are now due to blood loss and its complications.

See also Beaumont, William; Russo-Japanese War; Spanish-American War; Viet Nam War; World War I Medicine; World War II Medicine

References
Coupland, R. 1996. "Abdominal Wounds in War." *British Journal of Surgery* 83: 1505–1511.
Makins, George. *Surgical Experiences in South Africa, 1899–1900*. Philadelphia: Blakiston, 1900.
Rignault, Daniel. 1992. "Abdominal Trauma in War." *World Journal of Surgery* 16 (September): 940–946.
Senn, Nicholas. *Medico-surgical Aspects of the Spanish American War*. Chicago: AMA Press, 1900.
Wangensteen, Owen, and Sarah Wangensteen. *The Rise of Surgery from Empiric Craft to Scientific Discipline*. Minneapolis: University of Minnesota Press, 1978.

Acquired Immune Deficiency Syndrome (AIDS)

Acquired immune deficiency syndrome (AIDS) is a disease caused by human immunodeficiency virus type 1 (HIV-1), which attacks the lymphocytes that protect against infection and malignancy.

The disease probably came to humans from the chimpanzee *Pan troglodytes troglodytes* and was first recognized in 1981, although it may have been sporadically present for many years prior to that. The AIDS pandemic was first seen in male homosexuals and recipients of multiple blood transfusions and subsequently spread to users of intravenous drugs. As the disease became more prevalent, its means of spread changed. According to the World Health Organization, by 2003 the most common method of spreading HIV/AIDS was heterosexual sex.

By the end of 2003, an estimated 40 million people were living with HIV infection, and an estimated 20 million had died of AIDS. About two-thirds of the cases have occurred in sub-Saharan Africa with another one-fifth in South Asia. Recently, the disease has become much more common in Russia, China, and India. About 1.1 percent of the world's population between ages 15 and 49 are infected with the virus. AIDS is the world's fourth leading cause of death, and 1998 estimates indicate that 16,000 new infections a day were occurring, 95 percent of which were in developing countries.

The AIDS pandemic is militarily significant for two reasons: The affected population is in the same age group as that from which military forces are drawn, and the demographic and economic effects of the disease are likely to alter some nations' ability to field armies for use outside their borders or even to maintain internal order. In sub-Saharan Africa, AIDS has already profoundly affected the military. In 2002, 23 percent of the South African National Defense Force was infected with the virus and seven of 10 deaths in that country's military were AIDS related. South Africa is the only country in its region capable of foreign military operations, and that ability has been significantly impaired by AIDS. Similar rates of infection have been seen in Zambia, Thailand, and Cambodia, where HIV infection rates in the military are two to five times that in the civilian population.

Although Africa and Southeast Asia are the regions most affected by AIDS/HIV at present, the disease is rapidly spreading through Eurasia, especially in Russia, China, and India. Eurasia has five-eighths of the world's population, four of its five million-man armies, and five of its eight declared nuclear states. In 2001, there were an estimated 7 to 12 million AIDS cases in Eurasia; 66 million new cases and 43 million deaths from the disease are predicted over the next half century in Russia, China, and India alone. The demographic effects of that rate of infection would be profound. It is estimated that, by mid-century, Russia's population, which was 144 million in 2003, could shrink to less than 100 million if AIDS continues to spread at the current rate and continues to be incurable. Because the deaths would primarily occur in the young adult population, the effects would be particularly evident in the economic and military spheres. Russia's real gross national product could decline by as much as 40 percent, while India and China could see zero growth by 2025.

See also Syphilis

References
Eberstadt, Nicholas. 2002. "The Future of AIDS." *Foreign Affairs* 81 (November/December): 22–44.

Fauci, Anthony S. 1999. "The AIDS Epidemic: Considerations for the 21st Century." *New England Journal of Medicine* 341 (September 30): 1046–1050.

Field, Mark G. 2004. "HIV and AIDS in the Former Soviet Bloc." *New England Journal of Medicine* 351 (July 8): 117–120.

Steinbrook, Robert. 2004. "The AIDS Epidemic in 2004." *New England Journal of Medicine* 351 (8): 115–117.

Yeager, Roger. 2000. "AIDS Brief: Military Populations." Prepared for the Sectoral AIDS Briefs Series, U.S. Agency for International Development, World Health Organization, Washington, D.C.

Aeromedical Evacuation

Evacuation of the sick and wounded by either fixed-wing or rotary aircraft is known as aeromedical evacuation.

Attempts to create a military air ambulance date to 1910, when Capt. George Gosman of the U.S. Army Medical Corps built an

An H-5 helicopter of the Third Air Rescue Squadron transports a wounded soldier in a litter capsule during the Korean War. The tough terrain in Korea made air transport the primary form of medical evacuation. (National Archives)

airplane with a stretcher at an airfield near Pensacola, Florida. His invention was not used because the War Department refused to fund further development. The French modified six aircraft to carry three litters each during World War I, and Serbia used standard service aircraft to transport up to 12 casualties starting in 1915. In 1918, Maj. Nelson E. Driver of the U.S. Army Medical Corps and Capt. William Ocker of the American Air Service modified a JN-4 airplane to carry a litter in the rear cockpit, but it was 1920 before the first American military aircraft specifically designed as an air ambulance was deployed. The British Royal Air Force transported casualties by air during a campaign in Somaliland in 1919 and moved 359 wounded by air in 1923 in Kurdistan.

The Germans used aeromedical evacuation extensively between 1936 and 1938 in the Spanish Civil War, moving sick and wounded soldiers back to Germany in JU-52s altered to carry 10 litters and as many as eight ambulatory patients. The trip took up to 10 hours at altitudes that required heated cabins and supplemental oxygen.

By World War II, fixed-wing transport of the sick and wounded was standard military procedure. In 1942 the Fifth Air Force evacuated 13,000 patients from New Guinea to Australia, and 383,676 patients were air evacuated from Europe in the last six months of the war. In 1943 a Sikorsky R-6 helicopter, the first rotorcraft used for air evacuation, was modified to carry a pilot and a medic inside the aircraft and two patients in litters attached to the outside.

When the Military Air Transport Service was chartered after World War II, patient transport was one of its designated missions. In 1949, the secretary of defense declared air transport the method of choice for moving those injured in battle. At the onset of the Korean Conflict, the rough terrain and inadequate land transport facilities on the peninsula and the need to transport patients to remote specialized medical facilities proved this decision to have been a good one and hastened its implementation.

Late in July 1950 a helicopter detachment of the 3rd Air Rescue Squadron under Capt. Oscar N. Tibbetts was sent to Korea to retrieve downed pilots. Because United Nations forces' air superiority was established early in the war, the unit was underutilized, and Col. Chauncey Dovell, commander of the Eighth Army Medical Services, requisitioned the helicopters to transport the sick and wounded. The first trial flight (with the portly Dovell as a passenger) took off from a school yard in Taegu and landed at the 8054th Evacuation Hospital at Pusan on August 3, 1950. After the Chinese offensive of November 1950, Gen. Douglas MacArthur decided helicopters should be a routine part of his medical units' equipment, and he convinced the surgeon general to establish and equip two helicopter ambulance companies of 24 craft each.. The Marines began using helicopter evacuation that month and it was routine in the Army by January 1951.

Sikorsky H-5 helicopters were the most popular for air evacuation from the beginning, but they were fragile, and, because they were no longer in production, parts were scarce. For these reasons, they were initially reserved to move patients from aid stations to mobile army surgical hospitals (M.A.S.H. units) and were used only for those patients deemed unlikely to survive without air transport. As the Korean Conflict progressed and the H-5s' unique suitability to their mission became clear, helicopters were used closer to the front lines and for less urgent cases. Ultimately, helicopter transport from the site of trauma to an appropriate treatment facility became a standard of care not only in the military but also in the transport of civilian trauma victims.

U.S. Navy physicians realized that air transport to rear-area hospitals was faster and more efficient than transport by sea. As a consequence, ships which had initially been earmarked to transport and treat patients became floating stationary hospitals with helipads to receive the wounded.

Single-engine, fixed-wing aircraft were also used to move patients. The L5-B could carry one litter and one ambulatory patient, and the C-64 could carry three litters and two ambulatory patients. Transport from Pusan to Japan and on to the United States was principally carried out by aircraft of World War II vintage: the C-47 (which could carry 18 to 24 litters or 25 ambulatory patients), the C-54 (18 to 36 litters or 31 to 45 ambulatory patients), the C-46 (24 litters and 9 ambulatory patients or 37 ambulatory patients), and the C-87 (14 litters and six ambulatory patients or 19 ambulatory patients). Late in the Korean Conflict, the newer C-119 and C-124 became available. The C-124 could be configured to carry 136 litters,

35 medical personnel, and a portable operating facility. Its lack of soundproofing and insulation and the length of time required to load and unload such a large contingent limited its usefulness in combat situations but did not seriously detract from its ability to transport stable patients the long distance from Japan to the United States.

In the U.S. operations in Iraq and Afghanistan starting in 2001, high-speed jet transports have been used to carry patients whose surgery had been partially completed in field hospitals to base hospitals as far away as Europe to have their operations completed.

See also Korean Conflict; Viet Nam War; World War I Medicine; World War II Medicine

References

Cleaver, Frederick. *U.S. Army Battle Casualties in Korea*. Chevy Chase, MD: Operations Research Office, 1956.

Cowdrey, Albert E. *United States Army in the Korean War: The Medic's War*. Washington, D.C.: Center of Military History, United States Army, 1987.

Naval Aerospace Medical Institute. *U.S. Naval Flight Surgeon's Manual*. Washington D.C.: Bureau of Medicine and Surgery, Department of the Navy, 1989.

Smith, Allen D. 1953. "Air Evacuation—Medical Obligation and Military Necessity." *Air University Quarterly* 6: 98–111.

Aesculapius (Asclepias in the Greek Form)

Aesculapius was a semi-mythical figure possibly based on an 11th-century B.C. Thessalonian healer whose cult remained popular for seven hundred years.

Aesculapius was said to have been the son of Apollo—also known as Apollo Alexikakos (averter of ills)—physician to the gods and thought to be able to start epidemics with arrows from his bow or avert them with his benevolence. His mother was said to have been the nymph Coronis, a princess of Thessaly. She died when Aesculapius was an infant, and he was raised by Chiron, the benevolent centaur who taught him (and other Greek heroes including Jason, Achilles, and Hercules) the art of healing.

Tradition had it that Aesculapius's skill in surgery and medicine was so great that he transgressed the laws of nature by restoring life to the dead, causing Pluto, the god of the underworld, to complain that Hades was becoming depopulated. In response, Zeus killed Aesculapius with a thunder bolt.

Aesculapius's children included his daughters Hygeia, the goddess of health, and Panacea, the goddess of healing. His legend blends with that of the Egyptian Imhotep, another probably historical figure elevated to divine status.

More than 100 shrines and temples to Aesculapius were erected throughout the Greek peninsula and the surrounding islands. Most were in the midst of pleasant groves of trees, and many were augmented with theaters and spas. Most sufferers came to an Asclepiad facility after treatments by empirical physicians had failed. Therapeutic regimens at the temples tended toward prayers and incantations, but patients were also given sedatives and directed to sleep in the temple and report on their dreams, which were taken as messages from the gods that would direct appropriate cures.

Snakes, considered symbols of regeneration because they could shed their skin and grow a new one each year, were sacred to Aesculapius and were frequent denizens of his temples. The ancient Greek physician was often portrayed bare chested, carrying a single wooden staff with a coiled snake similar to the caduceus that became the symbol of medicine in later millennia. Asclepiad priests were careful to collect reports of successfully treated cases on marble votive tablets, and the collation of these reports were a foundation of later Hippocratic medicine.

See also Classical Greek Military Medicine; Hippocrates of Cos; Minoan and Ancient Greek Military Medicine

Reference
Garrison, Fielding. *An Introduction to the History of Medicine*. Philadelphia: W. B. Saunders Co., 1929.

Albucasis
(936–1013 or 1013–1106)

Islamic physician of the Cordovan Caliphate and the most frequently cited surgical authority of the Middle Ages, Albucasis is also know as Abulkasim or Al-Zahrawi Abul-Oasim.

Albucasis was born in the Spanish village of Medinat al-Zahra near Cordova, where he spent his professional life. He was an active practitioner who was said to have left his doors open day and night and whose courtyard was reputed to have been perennially overflowing with the poor patients for whom he cared as a charitable obligation.

His *Altaserif* (variously translated as *Praxis*, *The Method*, or *The Collection*) comprised 30 volumes and was a virtually encyclopedic treatment of 11th-century medical knowledge. It was completed in A.D. 1000 and reflected Albucasis's nearly 50 years of study and practice. Although Albucasis was even more respected in the Orient than in Europe, French physician Guy de Chauliac referred to him more than 200 times in his own surgical treatise, and, through the 12th century, he was considered part of a classical triumvirate with Hippocrates and Galen.

The last volume of the *Altaserif* was dedicated to surgery and was divided into three parts. The first part dealt in detail with use of the cautery; the second with lithotomy, wound care, and amputation for gangrene; and the third with fractures and dislocations, including an excellent description of paralysis from spinal trauma. Albucasis's surgical treatise is notable for its pictures of surgical instruments beside the text describing their use, and it contains a section dedicated to military medicine.

Albucasis based his surgical works on the sixth book of Paul of Aegina's compendium but emphasized that great care should be used in deciding to perform an operation and that good results could only be achieved by surgeons with a detailed knowledge of anatomy. His descriptions of removing arrows, based on details of actual cases, were particularly useful. Albucasis described ligating severed arteries well before Ambroise Paré wrote about the procedure, although the latter is widely credited with the technique. It is fair to consider Albucasis the first to treat surgery as a science based on anatomy rather than merely as a craft.

See also Amputation; Cauterization; Chauliac, Guy de; Islamic Military Medicine; Ligature; Medieval Military Medicine; Paré, Ambroise

References
LeClerc, Lucien. *Histoire de la Médecine Arabe*. New York: Burt Franklin, 1971 (originally published 1876).
Spink, M. S. *Albucasis on Surgery and Instruments*. London: Wellcome Institute, 1973.
Zimmerman, Leo, and Ilza Veith. *Great Ideas in the History of Surgery*. Baltimore: Williams & Wilkins Co., 1961.

Alcoholism

Although alcohol use by soldiers and sailors has surely occurred throughout recorded history, the attitude toward excessive drinking and the idea of alcoholism as either a disease or a moral failure appeared only in the latter half of the 19th century.

Beer and wine were standard parts of military rations for centuries and were treated as both stimulants and medication. Military commanders often took the point of view that alcohol prior to battle boosted their troops' courage while military physicians held that alcohol helped protect personnel from both heat and cold.

A change in military use of alcohol occurred when rum began to replace beer and wine in both the British Army and Navy in the 18th century. Rum was notoriously inexpensive in the Caribbean, had a higher alcohol content than beer or wine, and, consequently, required less storage space. Prior to the 1700s, a standard Royal Navy ration included either a pint of wine or one-half pint of brandy daily, although, on short voyages, a gallon of beer was occasionally substituted. After introduction of rum, British Army authorities estimated that an army of 36,000 would require 550,000 gallons a year of the liquor for standard rations with extra allotments before battles or during celebrations. In areas outside North America, spirits other than rum—arrack in South Asia, whiskey in Ireland, and gin in the Far East—were substituted.

Chronically underpaid British soldiers often worked part time at hired labor and were frequently paid in alcohol rather than money. Sutlers and the soldiers' wives freely purveyed spirits as well. Alcohol's ready availability, together with the fact that troops were typically billeted rather than being housed in barracks, where their behavior might have been more easily controlled, led to an epidemic of alcohol abuse in the British Army during the 19th century. By mid-century, the majority of British soldiers were habitual drunkards. The problem was

compounded by the fact that civilian alcohol use had also increased dramatically, and inebriation was viewed more as normal social activity than as either sin or sickness.

British military surgeons had, however, begun to notice that alcohol abuse was having a serious adverse effect on soldiers' health, and their commanders simultaneously noticed an erosion of military effectiveness. John Bell calculated that the deaths among troops in Jamaica numbered eight times that among troops in Germany during the Seven Years War (1756–1763) and blamed rum for the disparity.

Thomas Trotter was among the first physicians to view excessive alcohol use as a disease, a point of view contrary to that of the general population that he first put forth in his doctoral dissertation and repeated in his 1804 essay "On Drunkenness." The attitude was hardly universal even among physicians. John Pringle and Donald Monro both favored military use of liquor as an aid to stamina and as protection against the elements. James Lind agreed, although his fellow naval surgeon Gilbert Blane opposed including grog in sailors' rations. The argument was complicated by the fact that the military had begun adding Peruvian bark (cinchona or quinine) to wine, rum, or gin as antimalarials, and surgeons used alcohol as an anesthetic during battlefield surgery.

After the middle of the 19th century, Trotter's attitude was more generally accepted. That altered view, combined with moving troops to barracks and the evangelical temperance movement, came together to result in a dramatic decrease in military alcohol abuse. After 1848, even army canteens were forbidden to sell alcohol.

Alcohol abuse was not a major problem among the Entente and American armies during World War I. In fact, beer was frowned on as a German vice, and alcohol production was seen as an unnecessary diversion of scarce grain supplies that could be better used for food. American ethanol production dropped during the war while U.S. troops were regularly treated to lectures extolling the virtues of temperance.

In World War II, however, alcohol abuse again became common among American troops although it was generally treated more as a disease than as a disciplinary problem. Alcoholism was diagnosed in 42,420 members of the U.S. Army in 1944 and 1945 alone and accounted for 42,044 hospital admissions among those troops between 1942 and 1945.

The attitude toward alcoholism in the military changed again during the Viet Nam War. Drunkenness was quietly tolerated and was probably seen as preferable to the widespread abuse of other drugs. Hospitalization for "simple drunkenness" was forbidden by regulation. In fact, a belief was generally held that self-medication with alcohol was a reasonable and possibly effective treatment for posttraumatic stress disorder.

Alcoholism among veterans of both the Korean and Viet Nam wars has emerged as a serious public health problem. As many as 75 percent of Viet Nam veterans diagnosed with posttraumatic stress disorder have had alcohol problems at some time in their lives, and 25 percent of veterans of Korea and Viet Nam continued to drink excessively 10 years after discharge.

Alcohol abuse has persisted in the more limited military actions of the late 20th and early 21st centuries. Among Norwegian United Nations peacekeepers sent to South Lebanon, 43 percent reported increased alcohol use during their deployment.

See also Blane, Sir Gilbert; Drug Addiction; Lind, James; Naval Medicine; Pringle, Sir John; Trotter, Thomas; Viet Nam War

References
Branchey, L., W. Davis, and C. S. Lieber. 1984. "Alcoholism in Vietnam and Korea Veterans: A Long Term Follow-Up." *Alcoholism Clinics and Experimental Research* 8 (November/December): 572–575.
Kopperman, Paul. 1966. "'The Cheapest Pay' Alcohol Abuse in the Eighteenth Century British Army." *Journal of Military History* 60 (May): 445–470.
Op den Velde, Wybrand, P. G. Aarts, P. R. Falger, J. E. Hovens, H. Van Duijn, J. H. De Groen, and M. A. Van Duijn. 2002. "Alcohol Use, Cigarette Consumption and Chronic Posttraumatic Stress Disorder." *Alcohol and Alcoholism* 37: 355–361.

Ambulances and Transport

"Ambulance" derives from the Latin *ambulare*, meaning to walk or move from place to place, and was modified by French surgeon Dominique-Jean Larrey to *hôpital ambulante*, referring to his hospitals that moved with a traveling army.

Until World War I, "ambulance" referred to the hospital itself, although the British and Americans occasionally extended the definition to include the various means of transport to those treatment facilities.

Descriptions of transporting wounded from the battlefield date to around 1000 B.C. in Homer's *Iliad*, but transport of the wounded consisted primarily of being carried by horses or in the arms or on the backs of one's comrades through the Crusades. Wheeled ambulances became a formal part of a standing army for the first time when Queen Isabella of Castille donated 400 wagons to carry her sick and wounded troops in 1487.

During his service as surgeon to Gen. Adam-Philippe de Custine's Army of the Rhine in 1792, Larrey revolutionized the

French surgeon Dominique-Jean Larrey's horse-drawn ambulance, introduced during the French Revolutionary Wars. (National Library of Medicine)

practice of military medicine by adopting a system of emergency treatment in the field followed by removal to rear-area hospitals. The transport was accomplished in two- or four-wheeled horse-drawn carts that operated just behind the front line during battle. The wagons had spring suspensions to make the ride more tolerable for injured soldiers. Larrey attached 340 men and a chief surgeon to each 10,000 soldiers, and his system of stretcher bearers, ambulance wagons, and mobile hospitals demonstrably decreased battlefield mortality in Napoleon's armies.

Larrey's improvements were not, however, immediately adopted by other military medical corps. The British took only a few wagons to the Crimea in 1854, and those were too large to be pulled by the available undersized Bulgarian horses. The resulting poor transport played a major role in the medical service's dismal performance in that war.

U.S. Army regulations of 1814 provided for two-wheeled carts to carry the wounded, but only when they were not needed to carry baggage or supplies. This regulation was revised in 1821 to allow an unspecified number of light wagons manned by civilian contract labor to move the wounded. The first formal American ambulance system came with the establishment of the U.S. Army Medical Board in 1859, at which time a combination of four-wheeled Tripler (after Charles S. Tripler) and two-wheeled Finley (after Clement Finley) and Coolidge (after Richard H. Coolidge) wagons were bought. The Finleys had no springs and were said to be so uncomfortable that no soldier was willing to ride in one twice. The Triplers could carry four men on two tiers of spring mattresses and an additional six "sitters," but their inordinate weight necessitated a team of four horses. During the American Civil War, the Rosecrans ambulance, which had spring suspension and could carry up to 12 men, became the most popular conveyance. All of these vehicles still doubled as baggage carriers in the war's early years.

Changes were instituted in July 1862 when Surgeon General William Hammond appointed Jonathan Letterman to succeed Tripler as medical director of the Army of the Potomac. Letterman, under the August 1862 General Orders No. 147, adopted Larrey's system of dedicated stretcher bearers and carts used only to transport the wounded. The effectiveness of Letterman's system was first demonstrated at the Battle of Antietam, where the field was entirely cleared of 12,410 casualties in less than 48 hours. The system was extended to the rest of the Union Army and, by the Wilderness Campaign (May–June 1864), Northern forces were equipped with one ambulance wagon for every 150 combatants.

The Confederate Army never developed an ambulance corps, relying throughout the war on whatever wagons were not otherwise occupied to move the wounded.

A combination of technological advances changed ambulance transport in the latter half of the 19th century. Increased firing distance of both artillery and small arms necessitated moving field hospitals as much as 2,000 yards behind the front lines, and that shift meant the wounded had to be carried much longer distances before they could be treated. In addition, advances in antisepsis and anesthesia made it possible to effectively treat more men and gave transport a new significance. Finally, armies had exploded in size since Napoleon's *levée en masse*, and battles with tens of thousands of wounded in a single day became commonplace.

A partial solution to these problems came with the advent of the motor vehicle. In 1898, the French Army experimented with a steam-powered medical wagon, and, in 1901, Kaiser Wilhelm offered a prize for

the best motorized military ambulance. In 1906, the British Army adopted the Straker-Squire ambulance van, and, by 1913, the French Army deployed a motorized surgical unit built on the chassis of a Paris bus. The vehicle had a fully equipped operating room with electric lights and tents that folded from its sides into receiving areas and recovery wards.

The British Army entered World War I with only 950 lorries and 250 motor cars, and the need for motor ambulances was acute from the war's onset. By November 1914, both the French and the British were commandeering or borrowing every available private vehicle, making the early military ambulance service a conglomeration of virtually every make of automobile on the road. Even Renault taxis were pressed into service.

American volunteer troops introduced the rugged Ford Model T to the French front in 1915, and the small car with a plywood box capable of carrying three litters bolted to the chassis became a favorite. Ultimately, Ford crated and shipped 3,805 cars for assembly in France, and, after the United States entered the war in 1917, General Motors supplied another 3,070 cars. In general, the Fords were lighter and more maneuverable and were primarily used near the front. The General Motors cars were larger, more comfortable, and more commonly used for longer transports in the rear. The other common ambulance on the Western Front was the French Kellner, with a canvas body and hangers for six stretchers.

In the years between World War I and World War II, military surgeons turned their attention to more rapid means of moving the wounded, leading first to evacuation in fixed-wing aircraft and then helicopter evacuation, and motor transport assumed a secondary role.

See also Aeromedical Evacuation; American
    Field Service and Other World War I
    Volunteer Ambulance Services; Civil
    War in the United States; Crimean War;
    Larrey, Baron Dominique-Jean; Letterman,
    Jonathan; Napoleonic Wars; Stretchers and
    Litters; World War I Medicine

References
American Ambulance Field Service. *Friends
    of France: The Field Service of the American
    Ambulance Described by Its Members*. Boston:
    Houghton Mifflin, 1916.
American Ambulance Field Service. *History of
    the American Field Service in France: "Friends
    of France," 1914–1917*. Boston: Houghton
    Mifflin, 1920.
Barkley, Katherine T. *The Ambulance: The Story
    of Emergency Transportation of Sick and
    Wounded through the Centuries*. Hicksville,
    NY: Exposition Press, 1978.
Gillet, Mary, *The Army Medical Department,
    1818–1865*. Washington, D.C.: Center of
    Military History, 1987.
Haller, John S. *Farmcarts to Fords: A History of the
    Military Ambulance, 1790–1925*. Carbondale:
    Southern Illinois University Press, 1992.

American Field Service and Other World War I Volunteer Ambulance Services

A group of volunteers, the best known of
which was the American Field Service,
played a significant role in evacuation of
the wounded on the Western Front and
comprised the first organized American
presence during World War I.

At the outset of the war, the French ambulance service was primarily composed
of horse-drawn wagons; with only 40 motorized medical transports, the Allies were
desperately short of both cars and drivers.
Within weeks of the war's onset, H. Herman
Harjes, an American partner in the Paris
banking firm Morgan-Harjes, collected five
Packards and a group of volunteer drivers
and began moving French wounded from
rear-area receiving points to various hospitals, primarily in and around Paris.

By October 9, 1914, Harjes had added
his own hospital in a chateau in the village
of Ricquebourg, between Compiègne and
Montdidier, to the transport service, but
the rapid increase in the number of French
evacuation hospitals rendered his facility
redundant. The need for his cars, however,
persisted, and Harjes concentrated his efforts in building an ambulance service that
eventually came under the aegis of the
American Red Cross.

At about the same time, Richard Norton,
a young aesthete with a Harvard doctorate, set up a similar volunteer corps for the
British expeditionary force. Norton, son of
the famous Boston academic Charles Eliot
Norton, was an amateur archaeologist and
sometime art smuggler with a wide circle
of wealthy, influential friends and an im-
perious personality. He and his brother
managed to garner significant donations
of money and equipment and to recruit a
broad range of primarily upper-class volunteers, including John Dos Passos, e. e.
cummings, and Charles Nordhoff, all of
whom later wrote about their experience
in what became the Anglo-American Volunteer Motor-Ambulance Corps. Norton's
corps was temporarily subsumed under
the British Red Cross and was supported
by the St. John Ambulance Association. By
1916, Norton found himself at odds with
the British Red Cross and merged with
Harjes into the unit that bore both their
names and was assigned to the American
Red Cross. When the unit dissolved in
1917, it comprised 13 sections with more
than 100 cars and in excess of 200 drivers
and mechanics.

The best known of the American volunteer units was the American Field Ambulance Service (later shortened to American Field Service, or AFS), organized and directed by Abram Piatt Andrew, a Princeton doctoral graduate, former Harvard professor, and recent assistant secretary of the treasury. In 1914, fresh from defeat in a Congressional primary election, Andrew, a dedicated Francophile, decided to go to Paris to offer whatever help he could to the war effort.

The venerable American Hospital in the upper-class Paris suburb of Neuilly had established an ancillary military hospital in a partially finished school building. Like other volunteer hospitals, the Neuilly facility, whose directors realized they could not get patients without the transport to bring them in, had formed its own motor ambulance corps. (The French term *ambulance* actually referred to the entire organization rather than just to the vehicles that brought the wounded to the hospital.) Andrew took over that service and, with the help of his friend Henry Sleeper, who was associated with the Boston banking firm Lee Higginson & Co., began soliciting money and volunteers.

The initial AFS volunteers came overwhelmingly from among Sleeper's and Andrew's Ivy League circle of friends and were predominantly undergraduates from Harvard and Yale Universities. Later volunteers included undergraduates and recent alumni of other New England colleges as well as from Stanford University; the Universities of California, Chicago, Michigan, Wisconsin, and Illinois; and Washington University in St. Louis.

Unlike Norton and Harjes, who used whatever donated vehicles they could get, Andrew decided early on that efficiency dictated use of a uniform car, and he settled on converted Model T Fords. The first American Hospital Fords were donated by Harold White, manager of Ford Motor Company's Paris assembly plant. Canvas-covered wooden frames were bolted to the back of the chassis for carrying the *blessés* while the windshieldless driver's compartment was left open to the air. Henry Ford, a dedicated pacifist, refused to contribute to the war effort in any way and, throughout almost all of the AFS's short life, Andrew and Sleeper were forced to buy their Fords and their replacement parts at retail prices. The $360 cost was small enough and donations were large enough that they were able to accumulate several hundred vehicles. The chassis were bought in Detroit and shipped to France in wooden crates for local assembly, and the wood from the crates was salvaged to build the ambulance bodies.

The Fords proved a fortuitous choice for more than just reasons of economy. They were easy to assemble and simple enough mechanically that even the inexperienced American volunteers became adequate mechanics. The cars used either gravity or a splash system instead of fuel, water, and oil pumps, which were more likely to break down. Most of the parts were interchangeable, and the frame was built of remarkably durable vanadium steel. The engine was a single block with the pistons and valves mounted on top where they could be easily removed and cleaned or replaced. Although they could only carry two to six wounded (depending on whether they sat or required stretchers), the Fords were more maneuverable and took up less road space than the larger Packards, Cadillacs, Peugeots, and Bentleys used by other units. The semi-elliptical rear springs gave the ambulances a comparatively smooth ride and made them a favorite of the French soldiers.

Like Norton's and Harjes's units, the AFS cars initially operated as behind-the-lines transports, but all the Americans wanted to be more closely involved in the actual war. In April 1915, Andrew convinced the French general staff to allow his cars to go to the *postes de secours*—collecting stations just behind the lines—so they could move the wounded from the actual front to evacuation hospitals. What began as an experiment proved so effective that Andrew's cars and the Norton-Harjes units became the sole transport in parts of the front from Amiens to the Vosges.

Andrew eventually separated himself from the American Hospital in a dispute over allocation of donated funds, and the AFS continued as an independent effort until the United States entered the war in April 1917. The U.S. Army decided from the time of American entry into the war that the volunteer ambulance units would be under control of the Army Medical Corps, and they assigned Col. Jefferson Randolph Keen to effect that change. Norton and virtually all his drivers refused to be "militarized," but Andrew accepted a commission as major in the U.S. Army and, with a majority of his drivers, submitted to military control. The AFS role was expanded to include transport of military materiel as well as the wounded, and the Ford Model A replaced the little "flivvers" on the Western Front.

Norton, disillusioned and intensely disliked by Gen. John J. Pershing, left France. While passing through London on his way home, he succumbed to meningitis at the age of 46 on August 2, 1918. Herman Harjes joined the U.S. Army and became Pershing's liaison to the French. He returned to banking in Paris after the war and died at 51 in 1926 from injuries sustained in a fall during a polo match. Andrew returned to Glouces-

ter, Massachusetts, and replaced Augustus Gardner (the man who had defeated him in his prewar campaign) as that district's Republican congressman, a seat he held for seven terms. He became a close friend and confidant of Gardner's flamboyant art-collecting and museum-founding mother, Isabella Stewart Gardner. Andrew died at his seaside home in 1936 at the age of 63.

Unspent donations to the AFS, augmented by the proceeds from Georges Clemenceau's postwar American speaking tour, were used to fund travel scholarships for American and European secondary school students that have persisted with the same name as a New York-based organization that arranges international student exchanges.

See also Ambulances and Transport; World War I Medicine

References
Hansen, Arlen J. *Gentlemen Volunteers: The Story of the American Ambulance Drivers in the Great War, August 1914–September 1918.* New York: Arcade Publishing, 1996.
History of the American Field Service in France "Friends of France" 1914–1917. Told by its Members. Boston: Houghton Mifflin Co., 1920.
Morse, Edwin. *The Vanguard of American Volunteers: In the Fighting Lines and in Humanitarian Service, August 1914–April 1917.* New York: Charles Scribner's Sons, 1919.

American Revolutionary War

The American Revolution marked the beginning of organized medicine in the United States and the first institutional use of preventive medicine in the new country.

When the war started, approximately 3,500 physicians were practicing in the colonies, but only about 200 had medical degrees, the rest having been trained in apprenticeships, many of which involved only a year studying with an apothecary. The oldest American medical school had functioned for only 20 years, and most practitioners had gotten their degrees in England, Scotland, or France. In spite of academic inconsistency, physicians, along with ministers and lawyers, were usually the best-educated men in the community, and, as with their fellow professionals, most were sympathetic to the revolution. During the war, medical practitioners played leading roles not only in professional but also in governmental and military spheres. Physicians signed the Declaration of Independence and served as governors, state legislators, congressmen, senators, and judges. Eight doctors were generals, and two later served as secretaries of the War Department.

The Revolutionary War began without any provision for medical care of sick and wounded Continental soldiers. Gen. Horatio Gates, presuming that death and suffering were inevitable concomitants of battle, left wounded men lying in the field for up to three days after the Battle of Bunker Hill. Outraged when men lucky enough to be retrieved were forced to pay exorbitant fees for quarters in which to convalesce, the Massachusetts Provincial Congress mandated establishment of military hospitals to be staffed by surgeons and surgeon's mates and ordered that the colonel of each regiment appoint one surgeon and two mates to serve with his unit. Each regiment had its own "hospital," provided a suitable house could be found to serve that purpose. Orderlies and male nurses, usually unwilling members of the regiment, were detailed for 24 hours at a time to tend the patients. Occasionally a female housekeeper or servant was hired to feed and wash the sick and

wounded. This regimental staffing, patterned after that of the British Army, was adopted by the rest of the colonies but resulted in care that was at best inconsistent and often disastrously inadequate.

In the winter of 1776, pneumonia, dysentery, small pox, malnutrition, and frostbite were rife in the army. Gen. George Washington, alarmed at the dismal medical service, petitioned the Continental Congress to establish a general medical corps (confusingly termed "the Hospital"). This first national military medical organization, established July 27, 1775, was staffed to serve an anticipated army of 20,000 with a director general, a chief physician, four surgeons, an apothecary, 20 surgeon's mates, one clerk, a storekeeper, and one nurse for every 10 patients. General hospitals were established, and the regimental hospitals were reduced to little more than dispensaries. Hospital surgeons were paid $1-2/3 a day, $1/3 more than their regimental counterparts, although surgeons still ranked below the lowest ensign or quartermaster.

Benjamin Church, the first director general, lasted only until October 1775, when he was charged with treason and cashiered. When John Morgan of Philadelphia succeeded Church, he inherited a sick, scattered army with so few medical supplies that he was forced to appeal to the public for such necessities as blankets and bandages. Morgan attempted to strengthen the centrally controlled Hospital, provoking the ire of regimental surgeons who correctly perceived a diminution in their status and a loss of access to government funds and supplies. He lost the ensuing political battle and was replaced by William Shippen, Jr. Under Shippen, the medical service was again reorganized on April 7, 1777. The colonies were divided into four military districts

(North, East of the Hudson, the Hudson to the Potomac, and Southern to be activated if needed), each with its own director general who was responsible for hospitals, medical supplies, and the care of the sick and wounded in his area. The director general appointed a physician general and a surgeon general to whom both the regimental surgeons and the Hospital would report. He was to recruit matrons and nurses and to supply wagons and litters to transport the wounded. Like Morgan, Shippen made enemies and was accused of malpractice and financial mismanagement by both Morgan and famous Philadelphia physician and signer of the Declaration of Independence Benjamin Rush. Shippen was tried and acquitted of those charges, but was censured, and retired in 1780. He was replaced by John Cochran, who served until the war ended.

Medical affairs were conducted under the Medical Committee of the Congress until the War Department was formed in February 1781, after which time the director general reported to the secretary of war. Medical care in the Continental Army was never adequate. Although 1,200 physicians eventually served (only 100 of whom had degrees), death rates were astronomical. Roughly 250,000 men fought on the American side, 25,000 of whom died in service. There were 6,500 battle deaths and 10,000 deaths in hospital. Wounded were usually transported in open carts, and fully 25 percent of those who reached the hospital died, usually of infection. A 50 percent mortality rate for a mid-thigh amputation brought the paradoxical benefit of a decrease in the frequency of an operation that had surely been overused as the war progressed.

As bad as care was for the wounded, it was worse for the sick. Smallpox and typhoid decimated Benedict Arnold's army during the siege of Quebec City in early 1776, and disease forced abandonment of the Canadian invasion. Edward Jenner had not yet shown that cowpox vaccination afforded protection from smallpox, and variolation—intentionally exposing those who were previously uninfected to material from persons afflicted with mild cases of actual smallpox—was the only available alternative. Variolation with its 10 percent mortality was controversial, but Washington boldly required that both his soldiers and local citizens to whom they were exposed be inoculated. In the first American use of institutional preventive medicine, Washington ordered immunization of all new recruits.

Attempts to control venereal disease, a pervasive problem, tended to be punitive rather than therapeutic. Each officer hospitalized with a venereal infection had $10 deducted from his pay and each enlisted man $4, the proceeds going to buy bedding and clothes for the sick. Treatment of most diseases was ineffective at best and often harmful. The colonial physician's medicine chest often had only herbals. Quinine and opium were sporadically available to treat pain and fever, but the pharmacologic armamentarium was heavily weighted toward purgatives like ipecac and toxic compounds such as mercurials.

Medical care in the European armies that fought in the revolution was generally better than its American counterpart, although still poor. British military surgeons, attached to individual regiments, were paid one shilling a day plus one penny a week of each man's pay to cover the cost of supplies, with any surplus staying with the doctor. The British military physician was assisted by surgeon's mates and barber-surgeons. The barber-surgeons, who ranked below even fifers and drummers, were responsible for reducing fractures, cauterizing wounds, probing for bullets, and amputations.

French military medicine was traditionally the best on the Continent, although when French troops under Lt. Gen. the Comte de Rochambeau arrived in Newport in 1780, 1,600 soldiers had to be immediately hospitalized for scurvy, and one-tenth of the rest were ill with dysentery. The French did send 50 physicians, surgeons, and pharmacists with their 5,000 troops, and they established hospitals at Boston; Newport and Providence, Rhode Island; Williamsburg, Virginia; and Savannah, Georgia.

After the war, the medical service, along with the rest of the American army, was disbanded. Only a small contingent was retained to guard the frontier forts, and each regiment was again made responsible for its own medical care. High death and complication rates among Continental soldiers did lead to widespread demands for better medical training after the war and directly contributed to formation of a number of new American medical schools.

See also Church, Benjamin; Cochran, John; Rush, Benjamin; Shippen, William, Jr.; Smallpox; Syphilis

References

Ashburn, P. M. *A History of the Medical Department of the United States Army*. Boston: Houghton Mifflin Co., 1929.

Packard, Francis. *A History of Medicine in the United States*. New York: Paul B. Hoeber, Inc., 1931.

Reiss, Oscar. *Medicine and the American Revolution*. Jefferson, NC: McFarland & Co., Inc., 1998.

Amputation

The term "amputation" generally refers to the removal of all or part of an extremity which has been deemed impossible to save either because of the extent of injury or the risk of spreading disease such as infection or tumor from the injured limb to the rest of the body.

After dressing of wounds and removal of foreign bodies, amputation was the military surgeon's most important operation from ancient times until well into the 19th century. In the days before transfusion, anesthesia, and antisepsis, the surgeon's speed was the primary determinant of a patient's survival, and operating times of three to four minutes for amputation through the thigh were typical. Early amputations were performed with a single sweeping, circular cut through the skin, muscle, tendons, nerves, and vessels, followed by a quick transection of the bone with a specially designed saw. The inevitable hemorrhage was then controlled by applying hot pitch or oil and a pressure dressing.

The earliest surviving detailed description of amputation is from the Roman Aulus Cornelius Celsus and dates to the first century A.D. and was used to stop the spread of infection from gangrene. Celsus stressed the importance of avoiding undue blood loss, of making the incision well within the margin of healthy tissue and never through a joint, and of leaving enough skin to cover the end of the remaining extremity. Leaving healthy skin over the stump allowed fitting of effective prostheses, so the Romans developed elegant wooden extremities that were often covered with thin brass plates. Galen described ligating vessels, but finding and tying a bleeding artery took time. Since speed was essential in operations being done without anesthesia, hot oil remained the preferred method of hemostasis for almost 500 more years.

The technique of amputation changed little between Galen and the mid-19th century,

Illustration of an amputation, from Hans von Gersdorff's Feldtbuch der Wundartzney, *first published in 1517. (National Library of Medicine)*

and most military physicians considered it an operation best done with only three instruments: a scalpel to cut the skin; a long, double-edged amputation knife to cut the muscle, tendons, vessels, and nerves; and a sharp saw to cut the bone. The sole exception to this approach was Ambroise Paré's reintroduction of the ligature for hemostasis in the late 16th century. Napoleon's surgeon, Baron Dominique-Jean Larrey, brought amputation directly to the battlefield, arguing that shock from the initial injury lessened the pain of surgery and that patients had better chance of recovery if they were not allowed to lose large amounts of blood during transport to a hospital for surgery.

Speed remained the cardinal consideration well into the 1800s, and English surgeon Robert Liston became world famous for his ability to amputate a limb in an astoundingly short time. He was said to be able to remove a leg in 25 seconds using his gigantic left hand as a tourniquet while he cut and sewed with his right, although he inadvertently removed one of his patient's testicles and two of his assistant's fingers during a bravura performance. Liston was also the first to use anesthesia for amputation. He referred to the technique as a "Yankee dodge" but was ultimately forced to admit it was an irreplaceable advance. Anesthesia may have removed the suffering from the operation, but the death rate from postoperative infection following amputation still approached 60 percent, and it would not be until Joseph Lister's introduction of antisepsis late in the 19th century that amputation would finally become both tolerable and safe.

In fact, with the advent of anesthesia and antisepsis, most limbs that had previously required amputation could be saved, and the importance of the operation faded. Since the early 20th century, even limbs beyond salvage usually heal better after carefully controlled amputation and are more amenable to prosthesis. Death from the procedure is now rare.

See also Celsus, Aulus Cornelius; Larrey, Baron Dominique-Jean; Saw; Scalpel

References
Bennion, Elisabeth. *Antique Medical Instruments*. Berkeley: University of California Press, 1979.
Sachs, Michael, Jorg Bojunga, and Albrecht Encke. 1999. "Historical Evolution of Limb Amputation." *World Journal of Surgery* 23: 1088–1093.
Thompson, C. J. S. *The History and Evolution of Surgical Instruments*. New York: Schuman's, 1942.

Anesthesiology

Anesthesiology is the physiologic and pharmacologic management of patients during surgery.

Use of drugs to relieve the pain and anxiety of surgery dates to prehistory; seeds of the opium poppy have been found in the ruins of Swiss lakeside villages occupied in the third millennium B.C., and the Egyptians were using opium extracted from those seeds by 1591 B.C. In the first century A.D., Roman physician and herbalist Dioscorides used mandragora bark to induce sleep, to which compound his contemporary Aulus Cornelius Celsus recommended adding hyoscyamus seed and extract of opium poppies to relieve pain. These drugs continued as standards recommended by Avicenna in the 10th century and into the 13th century when Ugo de Lucca combined them with mulberry, flax, hemlock, lapathum, ivy, and lettuce seed and dried them in a sponge that could be moistened when needed and either inhaled or ingested.

Valerius Cardus synthesized ether (which he called sweet oil of vitriol) in 1540, although it remained a recreational drug particularly popular among medical students for the next three centuries. Andreas Vesalius introduced endotracheal ventilation when he placed a hollow reed in a pig's trachea and blew into it to keep the animal's lungs inflated while he opened the chest and examined the beating heart. In 1667, Robert Hooke used tracheal insufflation of air to keep a dog with an open chest alive for an hour. Joseph Priestly discovered nitrous oxide in 1772, and, at his recommendation, Humphrey Davy experimented with it on animals and humans, including himself, and suggested it could be used in surgery, but it remained for Hartford, Connecticut, dentist Horace Wells to actually use it for that purpose in 1845.

In 1659, Christopher Wren suggested to Robert Boyle that he might introduce opium directly into the bloodstream through a hollow quill. When Boyle used this approach on a dog, the animal became instantly comatose. Johann Major of Kiel repeated the experiment on a man in 1667, but the idea then went dormant until 1874, when Pierre Oré used intravenous chloral hydrate to anesthetize a patient. Intravenous anesthesia became a standard with the invention of barbiturates in the 1920s. Baron Dominique-Jean Larrey and his contemporaries used alcohol liberally as a sedative. In 1859, Albert Niemann isolated cocaine from the Peruvian coca leaf and, in 1884, Carl Koller began using the drug as a local anesthetic.

Alexander Monro secundus (son of Alexander Monro primus) recommended phlebotomy with removal of blood until the patient became flaccid and unconscious as an aid to reducing dislocated joints and in delivering babies, a practice that persisted into the early 1800s.

True surgical anesthesia began in 1842 when Georgia physician Crawford W. Long, who had participated in "ether frolics" as a medical student, tried the gas occasionally when operating on patients. He did not, however, publish his findings, claiming he had been too busy practicing to write journal articles. On October 16, 1846, Boston dentist William T. G. Morton, who had successfully used the drug in several tooth extractions, convinced John Collins Warren, the direct descendant of American Revolutionary War military surgeons John and Joseph Warren, to anesthetize a patient during a public operation at Massachusetts General Hospital. The demonstration was a stunning success, and ether anesthesia became a surgical standard in the United States and Europe within months.

James Simpson of Edinburgh was dissatisfied with ether's side effects and replaced it with chloroform, which became popular in England. It was especially prevalent in obstetric practice after Queen Victoria delivered her eighth child with its assistance over the objections of church officials, who contended relieving pain during childbirth violated the will of God.

The first wartime use of anesthesia for surgery was by American surgeon Edward H. Barton in 1847 during the Mexican-American War.

Anesthesia during surgery remained a delicate balance between having the patient too awake and dying from apnea and anoxia. In 1903, Harvey Cushing and George Crile brought the Riva-Rocci blood pressure monitoring device to Boston from Europe and recommended its routine use during surgery, but the Harvard University Medical School faculty, after careful consideration, decided that routine monitoring during anesthesia was an unnecessary inconvenience. The first orotracheal intubation for surgical anesthesia was done in 1894 by William Macewen.

Military practice played a major role in the evolution of anesthesia from an adjunct managed primarily by nurses and medical students into a medical specialty. Ether anesthesia, although complicated by tracheal irritation or aspiration of vomited stomach contents far more often than was desirable, was considered by Americans too simple a process to warrant expending the resources of a trained physician. The British, however, took a different view, and London physician John Snow became the first professional anesthesiologist in 1847.

World War II brought dramatic changes to anesthetic practice for a number of reasons. First, more complicated surgical procedures on more severely wounded people required better intraoperative care. Second, women, who had been primarily responsible for anesthesia, were not in the draft pool, so the military was forced to train men to do the job. Third, American military physicians were exposed to the British system in which doctors rather than nurses did the bulk of anesthesia. Finally, in an effort to attract workers during a period of frozen wages, American companies began offering health insurance, which made it possible for civilians to pay for expensive operations and the ancillary personnel necessary to perform them.

The U.S. Army instituted a series of 12-week training courses for general practitioners to turn them into anesthesiologists. These men were routinely available at the field hospital and specialty hospital level. Early in the war, spinal anesthesia and open-drop ether were common, but, as the war progressed and as American surgeons became more adept at handling critically injured soldiers, endotracheal intubation and complex monitoring became standard.

During the Korean and Viet Nam conflicts, more rapid transportation of the wounded and improvement in surgical technique and in resuscitation brought progressively less stable patients to the operating room. By the Viet Nam War, the combination of barbiturate induction and halothane, nitrous oxide, and oxygen anesthesia, frequently combined with prolonged artificial ventilation, had become standard. Techniques of managing shock and severe trauma moved from military to civilian practice in the latter decades of the 20th century.

Surgical and anesthetic practice changed somewhat in the Afghanistan and Iraq conflicts of the late 20th and early 21st centuries in that emphasis was placed on rapid stabilization near the front and early transport of the wounded to specialized rear-area facilities. Forward-area mobile hospitals composed of two tents and supplies carried on six Humvees could be set up in less than an hour wherever the troops happened to be. Procedures in those facilities were generally kept under two hours. Bleeding was stopped and patients were stabilized before being moved—often without closing their incisions—to larger hospitals, some of which were hundreds or even thousands of miles away. Whereas it took an average of 45 days for a wounded soldier in Viet Nam to be transferred to the United States, it took only an average of four days in the Iraq War and could be as little as 36 hours. During transport, the patient remained sedated and ventilated, resulting essentially in a very prolonged anesthetic. These techniques have resulted in a dramatically lower death-due-to-injury rate than in previous conflicts and in saving lives that would have inevitably been lost in earlier conflicts.

See also Field Hospitals; Iraq and Afghan Wars; Korean Conflict; Mexican-American War; Morphine; Shock; Triage; Viet Nam War; World War II Medicine

References
Aldrete, J. A., G. M. Marron, and A. J. Wright. 1984. "The First Administration of Anesthesia in Military Surgery: On Occasion of the Mexican-American War." *Anesthesiology* 61 (November): 585–588.

Gawande, Atul. 2004. "Casualties of War—Military Care for the Wounded in Iraq and Afghanistan." *New England Journal of Medicine* 351 (December 9): 2471–2480.

Metzler, Samuel, and John Auer. 1909. "Continuous Respiration without Respiratory Movements." *Journal of Experimental Medicine* 11: 622–625.

Morton, William T. G. *Remarks on the Proper Mode of Administering Sulphuric Ether by Inhalation*. Boston: Dutton and Wentworth, 1847.

Waisel, David. 2001. "The Role of World War II and the European Theater of Operations in the Development of Anesthesiology as a Physician Specialty in the U.S.A." *Anesthesiology* 94: 907–914.

Wangensteen, Owen H., and Sarah D. Wangensteen. *The Rise of Surgery from Empiric Craft to Scientific Discipline*. Minneapolis: University of Minnesota Press, 1978.

Anthrax

Anthrax is a bacterial infection primarily resident in cattle and, to a lesser extent, in sheep, goats, horses, and pigs.

Anthrax is caused by *Bacillus anthracis*, a large, gram-positive, rod-shaped organism that is capable of forming spores that can survive in the soil for many years. The organism produces two toxins: one that causes local tissue swelling, and one that causes cell death and is highly lethal. Human anthrax occurs in three forms: a cutaneous form, in which the organism usually enters through a cut or scrape and causes an erosive, poorly healing, but rarely fatal ulcer; a gastrointestinal form, in which the organism is ingested and in which 25–75 percent of victims die; and an extremely deadly pulmonary form, in which the organism is inhaled and which carries a 90–100 percent mortality from respiratory failure. Human-to-human transfer does not occur in either the gastrointestinal or respiratory forms of the disease and is rare in the cutaneous form.

Anthrax has been recognized for millennia; the plague that decimated Pharaoh's cattle described in the ninth chapter of Exodus was, in all likelihood, anthrax. Woolsorters' and ragpickers' diseases of the mid-19th century were inhalation anthrax acquired from cloth contaminated by anthrax spores. Anthrax was the first bacterium visualized

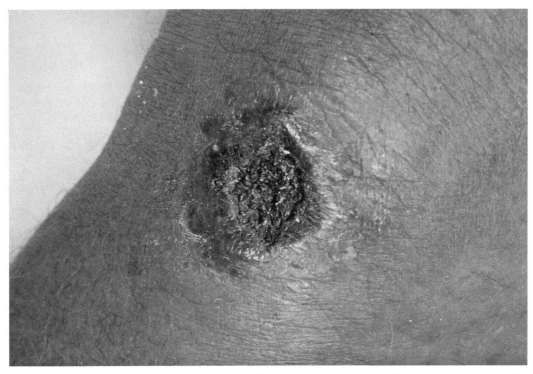

Lesion caused by the bacterium Bacillus anthracis. *The lesion has begun to turn black, hence the origin of the name "Anthrax," after the Greek name for coal. (Centers for Disease Control/James H. Steele)*

under a microscope, and Louis Pasteur developed the first animal vaccine against the disease in 1881.

Anthrax's potential as a weapon was recognized before World War II. It takes only 8,000 to 10,000 spores to kill 50 percent of people exposed to airborne anthrax, and its use as a biological weapon has the potential military advantage of removing a human population without associated property damage. The Japanese Imperial Army used the organism in China and later experimented with it in prisoners of war held in its Unit 731. The unit director, Shiro Ishii, escaped prosecution for war crimes in return for supplying records of his experiments to American military biologists. After World War II, American scientists working on

Project St. Joe released noninfectious aerosols in St. Louis; Winnipeg, Manitoba, Canada; and Minneapolis to evaluate anthrax's potential as a weapon.

The Soviet Union, in violation of the 1972 Biological Weapons Convention which specifically bans research with offensive bioweapons (although it permits research into defense against those weapons), conducted large-scale biological warfare research and development. On April 2, 1979, anthrax spores were inadvertently released from its facility at Sverdlovsk resulting in approximately 1,000 civilian deaths. At their Stepnogorsk facility, the Soviets developed anthrax strains roughly three times as lethal as those released at Sverdlovsk. In 1991 Iraq admitted to having large stockpiles of weaponized anthrax, a claim that contributed to the United States prosecuting the first Gulf War. The terrorist group Aum Shinrikyo, which caused 12 deaths by releasing sarin gas in a Tokyo subway station in 1995, also dispersed aerosols of anthrax and botulinum toxin in that city on at least eight occasions. The fact that those efforts failed to cause any deaths calls into question the potency of their preparations. The World Health Organization has estimated that an airborne release of 50 grams of anthrax over an urban population center of 5 million would infect 250,000 people and kill approximately 100,000. The U.S. Congressional Office of Technology Assessment estimated that release of 100 kilograms of anthrax over Washington, D.C., would result in between 130,000 and 3 million deaths.

Inhalation anthrax typically begins with fever and malaise followed by a "honeymoon" period in which the patient temporarily improves prior to the rapid onset of shortness of breath, bloody cough, respiratory failure, and death. Anthrax vaccine combined with a four-week course of either ciprofloxacin or doxycycline results in an approximately 90 percent survival rate. Prior to the Gulf War, 150,000–200,000 allied soldiers were vaccinated against anthrax, and it is to be assumed that such inoculations will be an integral part of future military actions. Environmental Protection Agency air quality monitoring stations have recently been equipped to detect airborne anthrax and smallpox under the assumption that these organisms might be a preferred method of terrorist attack. In addition, under the auspices of Project BioShield, an $878 million contract has been awarded to VaxGen Inc. of Brisbane, California, to develop a recombinant anthrax vaccine.

A fatal case of anthrax due to bioterrorism in which the organism was used to contaminate mail handled by the U.S. Postal Service occurred in October 2001. Letters delivered to cities on the East Coast and to congressional offices in Washington, D.C., resulted in a total of 22 cases of human anthrax. The source remains unidentified.

See also Biblical Military Medicine; Chemical and Biological Warfare; Iraq and Afghan Wars; Unit 731; World War II Medicine

References
Bush, Larry, Barry Abrams, Anne Beall, and Caroline Johnson. 2001. "Index Case of Fatal Inhalational Anthrax Due to Bioterrorism in the United States." *New England Journal of Medicine* 22 (November 29): 1607–1610.
Inglesby, T., D. Henderson, J. Bartlett, M. S. Ascher, E. Eitzen, A. M. Friedlander, J. Hauer, J. McDade, M. T. Osterholm, T. O'Toole, G. Parker, T. M. Perl, P. K. Russell, K. Tonat, and the Working Group on Civilian Biodefense. 1999. "Anthrax as a Biological Weapon: Medical and Public Health Management." *Journal of the American Medical Association* 281 (May 12): 1735–1745.
Miller, Judith, Stephen Engelberg, and William Broad. *Germs: Biological Weapons and America's Secret War.* New York: Simon & Schuster, Inc., 2001.
Zajtchuk, Russ, and Ronald Bellamy, eds. *Textbook of Military Medicine: Medical Aspects of Chemical and Biological Warfare.* Washington, D.C.: Office of the Surgeon General, U.S. Department of the Army, 1997.

Antisepsis

Antisepsis is the use of chemicals to retard growth of bacteria and decrease the risk of wound infection.

Its practice is as old as recorded medical history; about one-third of all prescriptions in the 1550 B.C. Ebers papyrus contained honey, most likely for an antiseptic purpose. The biblical Good Samaritan poured oil and wine into the wounds of the man injured by thieves on the road to Jericho, and Homeric Greeks emphasized washing wounds with water or wine after removing enemy arrows. Besides those relatively benign substances, ancient physicians also irrigated wounds with turpentine, pitch, tar, and olive oil in an effort to forestall suppuration.

The Roman medical writer Aulus Cornelius Celsus recommended myrrh and frankincense dissolved in alcohol to clean wounds and noted that, in addition to decreasing inflammation, the combination decreased blood loss by enhancing the tendency of blood to clot. Styrax and benzoin, derived from similar Southeast Asian trees, persisted as favorites of Napoleonic surgeon Baron Dominique-Jean Larrey, and the latter remains in regular use for wound dressings in modern operating rooms. Balsam of Peru came to Europe as the second Incan wonder drug (cinchona or quinine being the first) in 1553 and continued in use through World War I.

The term "antisepsis" first appeared in the 1721 London pamphlet "An Hypothetical Notion of the Plague, and some out-of-the-way thoughts about it," by Pierre S. de la Place, in which various chemicals were recommended to stop putrefaction and "generation of Insects." In 1752, Sir John Pringle conducted a series of ingenious experiments in which he used various acids to retard decomposition in freshly killed animals. Unfortunately, although he was able to confirm that antiseptics slowed postmortem putrefaction, he failed to extend his findings to wound treatment.

An effective means of decontaminating wounds became more important with the introduction of gunpowder weapons. The nearly universal occurrence of infection after gunshot wounds, which we now understand to be related to foreign material carried into the wound with the projectile, was initially thought to be caused by gunpowder, leading to the erroneous conclusion that the powder was poisonous.

Oakum—the threads of tarred rope unraveled and wadded up for packing into wounds—was a popular disinfectant in 17th- and 18th-century navies and remained in regular use through the American Civil War. Even Lord Joseph Lister, the father of surgical antisepsis, recommended it as an adjunct to be used after washing with carbolic acid. In fact, Lister's recommendation has been at least partially vindicated by a recent demonstration that growth of *Staphylococcus aureus* is significantly slowed in dilute solutions of pine tar.

Various forms of alcohol were preferred antiseptics from the time of the Romans, when Celsus used wine in addition to the previously mentioned tincture of myrrh. This recommendation was carried forward through the Middle Ages by Hugh of Lucca, Henri de Mondeville, Lanfranc of Milan, and Guglielmo Salicetti. Guy de Chauliac used distilled spirits to irrigate wounds, and Ambroise Paré did the same with *aqua vit*. In 1863, Auguste Nélaton of Paris reduced his operative infection rate to less than 2 percent by filling the open wounds with large alcohol-soaked packs. The practice was, however, rejected by Nélaton's colleagues because it impeded the formation of the "laudable pus," which they believed was necessary to healing.

Once European physicians accepted Ignaz Semmelweis's and Louis Pasteur's demonstrations that wound contamination caused infection and Lord Lister's application of that work to surgery, a rush to identify effective antiseptics ensued. Mercuric chloride dissolved in alcohol (corrosive sublimate) had been used since the 15th century and was brought back as a hand wash and wound irrigant and remained in common use until the 1890s. Silver nitrate had also been used since the 1400s and remained especially popular for eye injuries.

Chlorine had been discovered in 1774, and the French had used it to disinfect stables, cemeteries, and dissecting rooms. As *eau de Javelle*, hypochlorite was used to disinfect military hospitals. Semmelweis had used hypochlorite as a hand wash, and it remained as the basis of the Carrel-Dakin irrigation technique in World War I. Napoleon Bonaparte hired Bernard Courtois to create artificial nitrates for explosives, but, in 1811, the chemist discovered bromine instead. British surgeon John Davis recommended the new gas for wound irrigation in 1839, and it was widely used to disinfect Union hospitals during the American Civil War.

Creosote, from the Greek for "I preserve flesh," is distilled from beech wood tar and was produced in 1832 by German chemist Karl Reichenbach, who immediately enlisted a local physician to try it as a wound disinfectant. Carbolic acid, or phenol, had been discovered in 1834 and, by mid-century, was recognized as an aid in wound healing. In 1867, Lord Lister recommended it first for treatment of open fractures, which had, on account of their high rate of infection, been the primary cause of amputation. It was so effective that it became the antiseptic of choice for the balance of the century and was used as a hand wash, an irrigant, a soak for instruments, and a spray in the operating theater.

Hospital gangrene (*pourriture d'hôpital*) in the Crimea led to use of ferric chloride, camphorated vinegar, lead acetate, and sulphates of zinc and aluminum as disinfectants. Nitric acid was used for the same purpose in American Civil War hospitals.

After his battlefield experience in World War I, Alexander Fleming led a campaign against routine use of disinfectants, arguing that their irritant properties outweighed their benefit. The argument went on for most of the interwar years but, ironically, was settled when Fleming himself discovered penicillin and antibiotics displaced antiseptics as the primary method of bacterial control.

See also Carrel-Dakin Irrigation; Classical Greek Military Medicine; Egyptian Military Medicine; Fleming, Sir Alexander; Lister, Lord Joseph; Medieval Military Medicine; Pasteur, Louis; Roman Military Medicine; World War I Medicine

References
Fleming, Alexander. 1919. "The Action of Chemical and Physiological Antiseptics in a Septic Wound." *British Journal of Surgery* 7: 99–129.
Kelly, Francis. 1961. "Iodine in Medicine and Pharmacy." *Proceedings of the Royal Society of Medicine* 54: 831–836.
Wangensteen, Owen, and Sarah Wangensteen. *The Rise of Surgery from Empiric Craft to Scientific Discipline.* Minneapolis: University of Minnesota Press, 1978.

Archigenes of Apamea (ca. 75–129)

Archigenes of Apamea (Syria) was said to have been the most influential of the Eclectic physicians and was the primary inspiration for the works of Aretaeus and Aetius.

Archigenes dismissed the Humoralism of Aristotle and the Solidism of Asclepiades in favor of a theory that vital air was drawn into the lungs to remove heat generated by the heart and that blood was formed in the liver. This "pneumatism" had originated with Athenaeus of Attalia, who taught Claudius Agathinas of Sparta who, in turn, taught Archigenes.

Archigenes wrote a long dissertation on the pulse that, although it contained many mistakes and a good deal of fancy, inspired Galen's work on the same subject. Archigenes practiced in Rome during the emperor Trajan's reign and was the first to treat dental infections by drilling out the infected parts of the tooth. He recommended filling the resultant cavity with a paste made of roasted earthworms, the herb spikenard, and crushed spider's eggs. Archigenes wrote 11 books describing various remedies including an entire volume on the medicinal uses of beaver testicles. His major contributions to military medicine were treatises on amputation describing both tourniquets and ligatures to limit blood loss and on plastic reconstruction of facial wounds.

See also Amputation; Rehabilitation and Reconstructive Surgery; Roman Military Medicine

References

Lascaratos, John, Mimis Cohen, and Dionyssios Voros. 1998. "Plastic Surgery of the Face in Byzantium in the Fourth Century." *Plastic and Reconstructive Surgery* 102 (September): 1274–1280.
LeClerc, Daniel. *History of Physick.* London: D. Brown, 1699.

Asclepiades of Bithynia (ca. 124–40 B.C.)

Asclepiades was a Syrian-born physician who, as a result of his skill and personality, played a major role in establishing Greek medicine in Rome.

Asclepiades was born in the Middle Eastern village of Bithynia and moved to Rome, where he established a widely respected practice based on promoting a healthy lifestyle rather than use of chemical remedies preferred by his contemporaries. He also brought no fewer than nine ways to set a fractured or dislocated shoulder to the city. Prior to that, Roman practitioners had relied on splints made of green reeds and imprecations to the gods to treat those injuries.

Asclepiades's works occupy the foggy borderland between philosophy and physic. He scorned Aristotelian humoralism in favor of a concept of disease based on Democritus's theory that matter was made up of small, indivisible particles—atoms. Asclepiades was a categorizer, and he devised a system in which all disease was presumed to be caused by the body's particles not being held together correctly. In that system, illnesses were divided into *status strictus* (too tightly held), *status laxus* (too loosely held), or *status mixtus* (presumably a bit of each).

Like Hippocrates, Asclepiades thought most diseases could be treated by good air, abundant sunlight, good diet, and a combination of water therapy and massage. He avoided most drugs but advised wine and music for insomnia. He condensed his ideas in the Latin phrase *cito tuto jucunde*, or "swiftly, safely, and sweetly."

Asclepiades was said to have brought life back to a man already in his coffin using only vigorous massage. His regimens of physical exercise, diet, and sanitation were particularly well received in Roman gymnasium society and in the military. He gave the first good description of tracheotomy, although the procedure was not widely adopted and Caelius Aurelianus dismissed it as a futile and irresponsible idea. Asclepiades was also attacked by Galen in *On the Natural Faculties*. As only fragments of Asclepiades's writings survive, most of what we know of his work is derived from references by other authors.

Asclepiades lived a long and comfortable life and, according to the historian Pliny, died in his dotage from a fall down a flight of stairs.

See also Galen of Pergamum; Roman Military Medicine; Tracheotomy

Reference
Vallance, J. T. *The Lost Theory of Asclepiades of Bithynia*. Oxford, UK: Clarendon Press, 1990.

Asepsis

Asepsis is the attempt to prevent bacteria from entering a surgical wound, as opposed to antisepsis, which concentrates on killing organisms already present.

In 1878, Robert Koch demonstrated that he could cause infections in rabbits by injecting bacteria under their skin, and, by the mid-1880s, the bacterial theory of wound infection had been generally accepted in Europe and the United States. The practice of surgical asepsis actually can be traced to the work of Ignaz Semmelweis, who had demonstrated that "childbed fever" was caused by medical students going directly from contaminated dissecting rooms to the delivery room. Aseptic techniques in abdominal surgery were used by Alfred Heger of Freiberg in 1876 and in cranial surgery by Ian Macewen (who combined asepsis and anesthesia for the first time while operating on a fractured skull) in 1879.

By 1882, Ernst von Bergmann of Berlin's Ziegelstrasse Clinic summed up the decade's major surgical advance with the terse statement that now surgeons washed their hands *before* operations. In fact, the clinic used a complicated procedure in which fat and debris were removed from the patient's skin, which was then scrubbed with a stiff brush, soap, and water as hot as could be tolerated, and finally cleansed with alcohol followed by sublimate of mercury. The surgeon used a metal scraper to remove loose skin and dirt under the nails and then put his hands through the same process.

Surgical gloves were first suggested in the 1830s, but they were intended to protect the surgeon from syphilis rather than to protect the patient from infection. The latter development came in the late 1890s from William Halsted's service at Johns Hopkins University and was precipitated by the fact that his scrub nurse and future wife Caroline Hampton was sensitive to disinfectants and got a severe rash when she used them to clean her hands.

Heat sterilization of surgical instruments was suggested by Koch and by Lord Joseph Lister's student Charles Chamberland and, by the mid-1880s, had been generally adopted in Europe and the United States. Felix Würtz suggested it was best for doctors not to breathe into wounds in 1563, but surgical face masks did not come into general use until Carl Flügge proved that droplets from speech carried bacteria and Johann Mikulicz-Radecki took that information to the operating room in 1897.

Actually, complete asepsis is impossible, and the effort to achieve it stalled during World War I when a large proportion of the wounds coming to military surgeons were hopelessly contaminated with bacteria that had been allowed to multiply for hours prior to treatment. Surgeons fell back on chemical disinfection in spite of British bacteriologist Alexander Fleming's repeated warnings about the adverse effects of those substances on wound healing.

Development of surgical implants, particularly for orthopedic and cardiovascular injuries, has led to renewed attention to decreasing surgical wound contamination.

In 1956, Stephen Eck demonstrated that, although intradermally injected doses of up to 10,000 staphylococcal organisms might not lead to infection in an otherwise uncompromised wound, the combination of a single silk suture and as few as 100 organisms could result in infection. The infection risk posed by implants has led to widespread use of prophylactic antibiotics and to technical advances such as new chemical disinfectants, better barrier substances for drapes and gowns, surgical "space suits" to reduce bacteria shed from the operating team, and directed air flow in surgical suites to blow bacteria away from the surgical field. Evolution of antibiotic-resistant bacteria and subviral microorganisms resistant to steam sterilization has further complicated surgical asepsis.

See also Antisepsis; Fleming, Sir Alexander; Koch, Robert; Lister, Lord Joseph; Surgical Gloves; World War I Medicine

References
Greenblatt, Samuel H., ed. *A History of Neurosurgery in Its Scientific and Professional Contexts*. Park Ridge, IL: American Association of Neurological Surgeons, 1997.
Keen, William Williams. *Surgery: Its Principles and Practice*. Philadelphia: W. B. Saunders Co., 1908.
Wangensteen, Owen, and Sarah D. Wangensteen. *The Rise of Surgery from Empiric Craft to Scientific Discipline*. Minneapolis: University of Minnesota Press, 1978.

Atabrine

The trade name for quinacrine hydrochloride, Atabrine is a yellow powder developed in the 1920s by German chemical company I. G. Farben as a substitute for quinine in the treatment of malaria.

Atabrine became an essential treatment for malaria after 1942 when the Japanese seized the Dutch East Indies, which had, up to that time, been the source of more than 90 percent of the world's supply of the cinchona bark used in making quinine. When American forces were deployed in the South Pacific, prophylactic treatment for malaria was necessary. American laboratories embarked on studies of more than 14,000 compounds that might be effective, and almost 100 of those were ultimately tested on humans. Many of the tests, including those involving Atabrine, were carried out on prisoners in state and federal penitentiaries in the United States in experiments that were later cited by defense attorneys in the Nuremberg war crimes trials as justifications for human experimentation in German concentration camps.

Atabrine has a number of unpleasant side effects, including discoloration of the skin, muscle aches, and occasional psychosis. In 1943, it was found that these side effects could be lessened by giving a single large dose followed by much smaller maintenance amounts, a practice that had the additional benefit of requiring less of the scarce drug. Atabrine was subsequently replaced by chloroquine and primaquine, both of which are more effective and have fewer side effects.

See also Human Experimentation; Malaria; Quinine; World War II Medicine

References
Greiber, Marvin. 1947. "Psychosis Associated with the Administration of Atabrine." *American Journal of Psychiatry* 104 (November): 306–314.
Haynes, William. *The Chemical Front*. New York: Alfred A. Knopf, 1944.
Pullman, Theodore. 1948. "Comparison of Chloroquine, Quinacrine (Atabrine), and

Quinine in the Treatment of Acute Attacks of Sporozoite-Induced Vivax Malaria (Chesson Strain)." *Journal of Clinical Investigation* 27 (May): 46–50.

Athens, Great Plague of

The Great Plague of Athens was an epidemic that occurred during a Spartan siege of that city in 430–429 B.C.

The plague, which was meticulously documented by the Greek historian Thucydides, killed a quarter of the Athenian population and a number of important leaders, including Pericles. It contributed significantly to Sparta's defeat of the Delian League in the Peloponnesian War and the subsequent decline of Athenian civilization.

Thucydides says the disease arose in Ethiopia, spread to Egypt and Libya, and entered Athens through the port city of Piraeus. Further, he reports that people who were in perfect health suddenly and without any apparent reason got high fevers, red eyes, and foul breath. Victims' skin became so hot they jumped into cisterns for relief. These symptoms were followed by vomiting, convulsions, and death. Spartans outside the city's walls remained entirely free of disease.

A number of diseases, including Ebola, typhus, plague, smallpox, measles, yellow fever, scarlet fever, ergot poisoning, and Riff Valley fever, have been suggested as causing the plague, but none of those hypotheses has been proven and none of those diseases precisely fits Thucydides's description. The episode remains one of the earliest documented examples of the disastrous effect an infectious illness can have on a population with no prior exposure to that disease.

See also Classical Greek Military Medicine

References
Langmuir, A. D., T. D. Worthen, J. Solomon, and E. Petersen. 1985. "The Thucydides Syndrome. A New Hypothesis for the Cause of the Plague of Athens." *New England Journal of Medicine* 313 (October 17): 1027–1030.
Morgan, Thomas E. 1979. "Plague or Poetry? Thucydides on the Epidemic at Athens." *Transactions of the American Philological Association* 124 (April): 536–537.

Atropine

Atropine is an alkaloid extracted from the *Atropa belladonna* or deadly nightshade plant.

Atropine was first purified in 1836 when Philipp L. Geiger isolated it from its parent plant, but the drug's physiologic effects—both toxic and beneficial—have been known for centuries. Atropine specifically blocks the muscarinic acetylcholine receptors that are central to transmission in the parasympathetic nervous system. The drug causes dilatation of the pupils (thus the term "belladonna," or beautiful lady, from the fact that Venetian women used it to make their eyes large and black), dry mouth, cessation of sweating, retention of urine, slow heart beat, and disorders of mentation. Because organophosphate nerve gases such as sarin act by overstimulation of the cholinergic receptors, atropine is a specific antidote for those gases.

Romans mixed belladonna alkaloids with wine as recreational hallucinogens, and Plutarch of Chaeronea described their use to poison Mark Antony's troops during the Parthian Wars. The "dwale" given the Danes by Macbeth and described in the Shakespearean play was also belladonna based.

Introduction of nerve gases to warfare has made atropine a key method of defense in situations where chemical attack is a risk. Preloaded, autoinjection syringes are now standard pieces of equipment for combat troops.

See also Chemical and Biological Warfare

Reference
Holzman, R. S. 1998. "The Legacy of Atropos, the Fate Who Cut the Thread of Life." *Anesthesiology* 89 (July): 241–249.

Aviation Medicine

From its beginnings, manned flight has been inextricably linked with human physiology, and, since much of the evolution of aviation technology is driven by the military, flight surgeons have played a major role in aeronautical research.

Aviation began on June 5, 1783, when French paper makers Jacques and Joseph Montgolfier first publicly flew a 33-foot-diameter paper balloon filled with air heated by a wool and straw fire in the village of Vidalon-les-Annonay. The unmanned vehicle rose an estimated 6,000 feet before sinking back to earth. On August 28 of that year, another pair of French brothers, Charles and Marie-Noel Robert, filled an unmanned balloon with hydrogen and flew it more than 15 miles. The following month, the Montgolfiers sent a sheep, a duck, and a rooster 1,700 feet in the air in a demonstration for King Louis XVI that lasted eight minutes.

On November 21, 1783, French surgeon Pilatre de Rozier and the Marquis d'Arlandes became the first men to fly in a Montgolfier balloon, which stayed aloft for 25 minutes. Ten days later, the Robert brothers flew a hydrogen-filled balloon to an altitude of 9,000 feet and stayed aloft for 27 minutes. American Benjamin Frank-lin witnessed both flights. Charles Robert suffered the first recorded aviation-related medical problem when he had acute pain above his jaw that he correctly attributed to changes in air pressure in the middle ear.

The first flight over open water came in 1785 when American physician John Jeffries paid the £700 cost to have French balloonist Jean-Pierre Blanchard fly him across the English Channel. Blanchard subsequently came to the United States where, in 1793, he conducted a demonstration flight for President George Washington.

As flying became more popular, fledgling aviators began testing the limits of human endurance at altitude. In 1804, three Italians accidentally went too high and suffered both hypothermia and hypoxia. Their balloon crashed in the Adriatic Sea and, although all three were retrieved and survived, one of the men lost all ten of his fingers from frostbite. Prior to that experience, scientists had been unaware of the ambient temperature drop of 3.5°C for every 1,000-foot increase in altitude.

In April 1875, Joseph Croce-Spinelli, Théodore Sivel, and Gaston Tissandier set out to test the limits to which humans could ascend. Croce-Spinelli and Sivel had worked with French physiologist Paul Bert who understood that oxygen tension decreased with increasing altitude. Bert, who has been called the father of aviation medicine, had previously built a pressure chamber and experimented on himself, and his 1878 *La Presion Barométrique: Récherches de la Physiologie Experimentale* remained a standard text until World War I. The three French pilots carried bags of oxygen but exhausted their supply on their ascent to 28,000 feet, and only Tissandier survived the flight. The other two, lovers as well as fellow pilots, were buried in Paris's Pére Lachaise cemetery beneath a re-

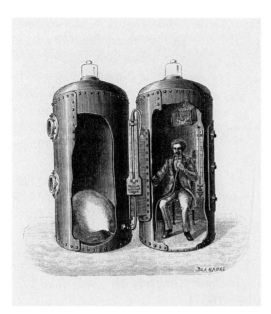

Cross-section illustration of French physiologist Paul Bert seated in his pressure chamber breathing oxygen-enriched air, 1878. (National Library of Medicine)

cumbent statue in which, covered by only a sculpted blanket, each holds the other's hand and a bouquet of flowers. Bert, although he was not present for the flight, publicly accepted responsibility for the deaths.

Actually, the physiologic effects of altitude were not new information. Aristotle had said it was impossible for humans to survive on top of 10,000-foot Mount Olympus without breathing through a wet sponge. Joseph de Acosta, in 1588, gave a detailed description of the adverse effects of climbing into the higher elevations in the Andes Mountains.

Even with supplementary oxygen, ascent beyond 40,000 feet remained impossible until Auguste Picard and Paul Kipfer created a sealed capsule that supplied oxygen under pressure, removed carbon dioxide, and maintained a tolerable temperature. This first "space capsule" reached 51,795 feet on

May 27, 1931. The American military also sponsored experimental flights through the 1930s, studying the physiology of high altitude with special attention to effects of radiation and finally reaching 72,395 feet in the Explorer series of flights. In 1947, mice were carried to more than 100,000 feet, but World War II had largely diverted attention from studies of altitude to other aspects of aviation physiology such as gravitation and hypothermia.

The U.S. Army ordered its first airplane in 1908 and, four years later, established minimum physical qualifications for pilots. Germany, which had done the same two years earlier, actually deserves credit for starting military aviation medicine. Combat flight medicine began in 1916 when the airplane was recognized as an effective weapon. The U.S. Army established a group under Lt. Col. Theodore Charles Lyster to formally examine prospective pilots and started a school for flight surgeons. In 1919, Dr. H. Graeme Anderson of the Royal Air Force published the first text devoted entirely to aviation medicine, *The Medical and Surgical Aspects of Aviation*. Between the world wars, Germany developed an extensive experimental program in aviation medicine. The Luftwaffe's Dr. Heinz von Diringshofen built an experimental centrifuge and showed that vision begins to disappear at acceleration five times the force of gravity (or 5 Gs) and that consciousness was lost if acceleration was maintained at 6 Gs for 10 to 15 seconds. His *Medical Guide for Flying Personnel* was translated into English and was used by both sides during World War II. The Luftwaffe also experimented on explosive decompression and the effects of prolonged cold, initially using their own personnel but later changing to concentration camp inmates as experimental subjects.

Both the Russian and American air forces experimented with pressure suits between the world wars. Wiley Post, with the assistance of the Goodyear Tire Company, built the first self-contained pressure suit in 1934 and tested it to a pressure differential of five pounds per square inch before its seams failed. A subsequent device pressurized with liquid oxygen was, however, successful. The Russians also tested pressure suits built by Dr. Vladislav A. Spasskiy beginning in 1934. Canadian Dr. W. R. Franks built the first G suit to ameliorate the cardiovascular effects of rapid acceleration in 1940. The suit was used by the Fleet Air Arm of the Royal Navy in North Africa in 1942. Flak suits, constructed with overlapping plates of one-millimeter-thick manganese steel by the Wilkinson Sword Company for B-17 crews of the American Eighth Air Force in 1942, offered the first protection from ground fire.

After World War II, experiments in aeronautical physiology turned to space flight. Skeptics who had doubted that man could withstand the acceleration necessary to escape Earth's atmosphere were proven wrong when Russian Yuri Gagarin became the first man in space on April 12, 1961. The first physician in space was Russian Boris G. Yegorov, who flew on Voskhod I on October 12, 1964. American Neil Armstrong was the first man to step on the moon on July 20, 1969.

See also Cold Injury and Frostbite; Human Experimentation; World War I Medicine; World War II Medicine

References

Beavers, C. L. 1938. "A Chronological History of Aviation Medicine." *Flight Surgeons Topics* 2: 185–206.
Benford, Robert. *Doctors in the Sky*. Springfield, Ill: Charles C. Thomas, 1955.
Engle, Eloise, and Arnold S. Lott. *Man in Flight: Biomedical Achievements in Aerospace.* Annapolis, MD: Leeward Publications, Inc., 1979.
N.a. 1883. "The Sivel and Croce-Spinelli Ascension." *Manufacturers and Builders* 15 (April): 88.
Ricketts, Henry. "Aviation Medicine." In William Taliaferro, *Medicine and the War.* Chicago: University of Chicago Press, 1944.
West, John. 2004. "Paralysis and Blindness during a Balloon Ascent to High Altitude." *High Altitude Medicine & Biology* 5 (December): 453–456.

Avicenna (Ibn Sena) (980–1037)

Court physician and vizier to the caliph of Baghdad, Avicenna was referred to as the "prince of physicians."

Avicenna was born in the village of Afchana near the city of Bouhkara. The proximity of his birthplace to the ancient Silk Road gave him unusual access to learning from China and South Asia. He was a child prodigy who mastered the Koran at age 10, began studying medicine at 16, and was treating the royal family by 18. He remained a successful court physician and also served the caliph as vizier, or adviser. He was chief physician to the largest and most important hospital at Baghdad and wrote more than 100 books. Avicenna was a polymath who, in addition to his medical works, authored the world's first comprehensive text on geology. By preserving the Greek medical tradition housed in Baghdad's libraries and augmenting it with learning from Persia and India, he joined the other two great Islamic physicians, Rhazes and Albucasis, in making Arab medicine the most advanced of its time.

Avicenna's *Canon* was an encyclopedic work that attempted to collect and arrange the entire corpus of existing medical knowledge and relate that knowledge to the writings of Galen and Aristotle. The *Canon* remained a primary reference for European physicians through the Middle Ages.

Avicenna described reduction of spinal fractures. He recommended irrigation with wine to sterilize wounds and knew that diabetic urine tasted sweet. He described anthrax, which he called Persian fire, and he generally considered surgery to be inferior to other, less invasive, forms of treatment. In common with other Islamic physicians, Avicenna preferred, when he was forced to operate, to use the cautery rather than the knife. That technique actually hampered wound healing and its general acceptance set surgery back for centuries. The *Canon's* section on military surgery has little that is original and is mostly derived from Book Six of Paul of Aegina's compendium.

Although Avicenna was an occasional experimenter and scientist, he was primarily an organizer and a philosopher. He served his caliph well and was well rewarded for that service. He was able to afford a lifelong devotion to wine and women and his luxurious lifestyle may well have contributed to his early death.

See also Albucasis; Cauterization; Islamic Military Medicine; Rhazes (Abu Bakr Mohammed ben Zakariah)

Reference
LeClerc, Lucien. *Histoire de la Médecine Arabe.* New York: Franklin Burt, 1971 (originally published 1876).

B

Bandaging and Wound Dressing

Bandaging and wound dressing comprise the techniques for protecting and stabilizing wounds.

The art of bandaging dates at least as far back as ancient Egypt, where mummy dressers used up to 1,000 yards of linen soaked in resins, pitch, and liquid naphtha to wrap their charges. There is virtually no bandaging technique that was not used by those skilled embalmers. Many of their salves had antiseptic properties, and it is likely that their postmortem dressing techniques were translated directly to antimortem medicine.

While patients and their families see and appreciate an artfully applied bandage, they are seldom aware of the skill exercised in the tissues beneath it. That perception may well account for the disproportionately high number of early medical images that deal with wound dressing. Ancient Greeks were, like the Egyptians, given to impregnating their bandages with various balms, although Hippocrates, in the fifth century B.C., pointedly recommended rinsing wounds with clean water or wine and avoiding greasy dressings.

Roman armies were the first to include designated battlefield surgeons. Those surgeons' primary duties were first aid mostly consisting of application of bandages to stop bleeding and to prevent further damage to traumatized tissue. It is rumored that Emperor Trajan tore up his own toga when cloth for bandages ran short during battle. At the beginning of the Christian era, Galen made complex bandages a major part of the system, which held sway through the Middle Ages.

The Italian School of Salerno (which was founded in A.D. 900 and was flourishing by 1100) taught surgery as a separate discipline and bandaging as a primary skill. The Salernitans anticipated casting when they advocated cloth bandages hardened with a flour and egg solution.

In the 13th century, Theodoric raised the issue of cleanliness with the recommendation that wounds be dressed early with the cleanest available cloth and then left undisturbed until they healed. His suggestion lost out to the fallacious theory that wounds would not heal properly in the absence of "laudable pus." The question of clean bandages took on renewed importance in the

16th century with the advent of gunpowder weapons. Cannonballs created wide, deep, contaminated wounds unlike anything found in Galen's descriptions, and they proved particularly difficult to cover.

Hans von Gersdorff used bandages as tourniquets above and below severed arteries. Ambroise Paré urged restraint in use of cautery and, harking back to works by Theodoric and even Hippocrates, emphasized clean water irrigation and clean cloth bandages.

In his 1827 *Lectures on Inflammation*, John Thomson made the controversial argument that hospital-acquired infections—an endemic problem in military medicine—came from dirty bandages. At about the same time, French surgeon Claude Pouteau proposed replacing cloth bandages that were regularly reused (without the benefit of an interim washing) with paper that could be used once and discarded. In 1832, William Henry of Manchester, England, demonstrated that the clothing of a patient with scarlet fever would not communicate the disease to another person if it was subjected to dry heat at 204°F.

In spite of that convincing demonstration, hospitals continued to solicit linen rags to use as dressing. Washed or partially boiled rags were still being used as dressings into the 19th century even though the United Kingdom and other European countries had passed laws banning the international rag trade as a danger to the public health. Even as late as World War I, it remained common practice to acquire dressings from the rag industry and to reuse them. Late in the war, sterilizable, disposable gauze finally became the standard for both hospital and battlefield use.

See also Gersdorff, Hans von; Hippocrates of Cos; Paré, Ambroise; Roman Military Medicine; Theodoric, Bishop of Cervia

(Teodorico Borgognoni); World War I Medicine

References

Bettman, Otto. *A Pictorial History of Medicine.* Springfield, IL: Charles C. Thomas, 1956.

Wangensteen, Owen, and Sarah D. Wangensteen. *The Rise of Surgery from Empiric Craft to Scientific Discipline.* Minneapolis: University of Minnesota Press, 1978.

Barber-Surgeons

Barber-surgeons were practitioners and competitors to master surgeons from the Middle Ages until the mid-18th century.

Throughout the Middle Ages, physicians were educated in universities, were fluent in Latin, held the status of educated professionals, and considered surgery beneath their dignity. As a consequence, most civilian and military surgery was carried out by a collection of itinerant lithotomists, bonesetters, and bloodletters who shaved and cut hair in their spare time. Because monastic rules required tonsure, barbers became a key part of the religious community and, after about A.D. 1000, were allowed to perform minor surgical procedures in religious facilities that often doubled as hospitals.

Thirteenth-century Parisian physicians-in-training were required to swear an oath that they would not perform surgery, so the field was left open to less educated practitioners. In 1210, the College of St. Côme was established under Jean Pitard as a protest against practice restrictions imposed by the physicians. Surgeons at St. Côme were divided into those of the long robe—master surgeons—and those of the short robe—barbers who could only operate after having been examined and certified. Although some didactic teaching took place at

St. Côme, most training was conducted by practical experience. Paradoxically, formal recognition of master surgeons led to expansion of French barber-surgery because physicians supported the barbers in an attempt to mitigate the increasing influence of the surgeons of the long robe. In 1361, the French king's first barber was made head of all barbers and surgeons in the realm, and, 10 years later, French barber-surgeons were afforded formal licensure.

Barbers also played a major role in British surgery. In 1308, they were granted guild status by King Edward II, and, in 1375, the guild was divided into those who shaved and those who did surgery. The same year, the king required that all surgical practitioners be licensed by the Crown. Women were allowed to be guild members and to be licensed as barber-surgeons but were not allowed to hold office in the organization. Both barber-surgeons and master surgeons accompanied King Henry V in his 1415 French campaign.

English barber-surgeons suffered a setback in 1421 when military surgeons and members of the College of Physicians worked together to obtain royal authority to conduct examinations for anyone seeking a license to practice either medicine or surgery. In 1435, the master surgeons separated from the barbers and were granted their own charter as the Guild of Surgeons. The barbers, however, continued to perform minor procedures, and, in 1462, the Guild of Barbers of London was chartered to oversee all "freemen surgeons" who also acted as barbers and was given control over the instruments they used and the medicines they prescribed. In spite of that, their status relative to the master surgeons continued to decline when the latter were granted a coat of arms and exempted from military service in 1492. The crushing

blow to barber-surgeons came when they were dropped from the order of procession in coronation ceremonies in 1534.

The status of surgery in Germany declined precipitously after the Thirty Years War and was, for the most part, left to executioners and barbers. German military surgeons were required to shave the officers, giving rise to the title *feldscherer*, which persisted into World War II in the abbreviated form *feldscher*. Most German surgery through the 14th century remained the province of barbers and bathhouse owners.

The division between surgery and medicine was never as great in southern Europe as in the northern countries. The medical school at Salerno recognized no division at all, although barbers were recognized as surgeons in Florence in 1349.

Barber-surgery died out as surgery evolved from craft into profession. Ironically, this change can perhaps be dated to the work of Ambroise Paré, who was himself a barber-surgeon and whose father and brother-in-law were barber-surgeons as well. Surgery as a profession in France received a great boost when Louis XIV had a fistula successfully repaired, and, in 1724, to the great distress of Parisian physicians, his grandson Louis XV established five academic chairs of surgery at St. Côme. Nineteen years later, all barbers and wig makers were banned from performing surgery. In 1745, surgeons and barbers were permanently separated in Great Britain as well.

See also Medieval Military Medicine; Paré, Ambroise

Reference
Fishbein, Morris. 1957. "The Barber Surgeons and the Liberation of Surgery." *Journal of the International College of Surgeons* 27: 766–779.

Baromedicine

Baromedicine is the study and treatment of physiologic effects of rapid decrease in ambient pressure on the human body. These effects have historically been of military importance in relation to operations conducted below the ocean's surface and have more recently been important in aviation medicine.

Several types of barotrauma have been documented, all of which are a result of gas expanding as the surrounding pressure decreases. The simplest and least life-threatening problems are those caused by expansion of air in closed spaces such as the middle ear, the paranasal sinuses, or the bowel. This expansion can cause pain and occasional bleeding from mucosal linings. Of more significance is expansion in isolated areas of the lung that can result in rupture of the organ and pneumothorax or collections of air under the skin, or subcutaneous emphysema. Gas (especially nitrogen) dissolved in the bloodstream can come out of solution to form bubbles that collect in joints and cause the extremity and back pain typical of the "bends" or obstruct blood vessels and cause ischemic infarction in tissues downstream from the occlusion. In the most severe form of this decompression sickness, the victim can suffer strokes in the brain or spinal cord resulting in paralysis, confusion, or death.

Decompression sickness was first completely described in 1843 in bridge builders who worked in sealed underwater caissons, but soldiers had been exposed to the danger of surfacing after prolonged periods of submersion for centuries. Alexander the Great used a diving bell in his 332 B.C. siege of Tyre, and Pliny referred to military use of swimmers and divers. More complicated diving equipment, including a device drawn by Leonardo da Vinci, has been in use or at least contemplated since the 14th century. Edmund Halley took a diving bell to a depth of 10 fathoms (60 feet) in the Thames in 1690. In 1819, Augustus Siebe invented the "open diving dress," which allowed a person to breathe air delivered by hose from the surface. The military significance was clear, but soldiers who attempted deep dives functioned so poorly that the British Army concluded, after studying the problem, that nitrogen narcosis and hypercarbia precluded adequate performance at depth. Those studies did, however, result in the first tables that related depth and time of submersion to risk of physiologic damage.

Military interest in diving physiology increased with the advent of submarines in the early 20th century. The difference between air embolism and the bends was clarified in 1932 by U.S. Navy physicians studying submarine escape trainees. The problem received more attention during World War II when British and Italian scientists developed the "human torpedo," a self-contained breathing apparatus that allowed divers to maneuver free of connection to the surface. With the addition of a demand regulator that delivered air only with inspiration, all the elements of a self-contained underwater breathing apparatus (SCUBA) were present.

The other mid-20th-century development with baromedical implications had to do with aviation rather than submarine medicine. The need for supplemental oxygen and external heating at altitudes above 10,000 feet led to development of pressurized aircraft cabins. When that pressurization fails, the physiologic effects are the same as those of a quick ascent from underwater. The fact that special forces might be required to fly, parachute, and dive on a single mission poses a unique set of physiologic problems, and the military remains actively involved in baromedical research.

See also Aviation Medicine

References

Polak, B., and H. Adams. 1932. "Traumatic Air Embolism in Submarine Escape Training." *United States Naval Medical Bulletin* 30: 165–177.

Sykes, J. J. W. 1994. "Fortnightly Review: Medical Aspects of Scuba Diving." *British Medical Journal* 308: 1483–1488.

Barton, Clara
(1821–1912)

Clara Barton was an American Civil War nurse and founder and first president of the American Red Cross.

Barton was born on Christmas day in Oxford, Massachusetts, the youngest of five children in a middle-class family. At the urging of a phrenologist, she became a teacher at age 15. As a young lady, Barton had her first experience with nursing when she cared for her older brother throughout a two-year illness. She returned to teaching and formed her own school in Bordentown, New Jersey, but resigned when a man was appointed principal over her. She then moved to Washington, D.C., where she became the first woman clerk in the U.S. Patent Office.

Barton organized relief efforts for the 6th Massachusetts Regiment when it came to the capital in the wake of the Baltimore riots of 1861. After the Battle of Bull Run, she organized efforts to collect medical supplies for the Union Army. By 1862, she had been given a pass to travel with the army, and her first effort at direct battlefield relief came that year when she brought Sanitary Commission supplies to physicians tending the wounded after the Battle of Antietam.

After the Civil War, Barton headed efforts to identify graves of those missing in action, including the more than 13,000 unmarked sites at the Confederate prison in Andersonville, Georgia. She traveled to Europe in 1870 intending to rest but instead became involved in the Franco-Prussian War.

While in Europe, Barton first encountered and was impressed by the International Red Cross. When she returned home, she led the effort to get the United States to sign the Geneva Treaty, and she organized the American Red Cross and became its first president in 1881. She expanded the Red Cross role from military relief to civilian projects and provided care during the 1882 and 1884 Mississippi River floods; the 1887 Florida yellow fever epidemic; and the 1889 Johnstown, Pennsylvania flood.

The American Red Cross's first military efforts were undertaken in 1898 when Barton and the Red Cross relief ship USS *Texas* helped care for 150 Spanish wounded from the Battle of San Juan Hill and furnished nurses and supplies to the makeshift American military hospital at Siboney, Cuba.

Clara Barton she was not a particularly talented administrator, and the American Red Cross was plagued by internal dissension until she was pressured to resign the presidency in 1904 at the age of 83. She retired to her home in Glen Echo, Maryland, and died of a viral infection on April 12, 1912.

See also Civil War in the United States; Nursing in the Military; Spanish-American War

References

Burton, David. *Clara Barton: In the Service of Humanity*. Westport, CT: Greenwood Press, 1995.

Oates, Stephen. *A Woman of Valor: Clara Barton and the Civil War*. New York: Manwell Macmillan International, 1994.

Pryor, Elizabeth. *Clara Barton: Professional Angel*. Philadelphia: University of Pennsylvania Press, 1987.

Beaumont, William
(1785–1853)

A military physician and clinical physiologist, William Beaumont was born into a farming family in Lebanon, Connecticut, on November 21, 1785. As a young man, he refused his father's offer of an adjoining farm and moved to upstate New York, where he worked briefly as a teacher before entering an apprenticeship with a physician in St. Albans, Vermont.

When the War of 1812 began, Beaumont, then 27 years of age, enlisted as a surgeon's mate. He participated in both the Battle of Niagara and the siege of Plattsburgh, where he took a particular interest in the pleurisy and other pulmonary infections that plagued the American force.

After the war, Beaumont entered private practice in Plattsburgh, but he found the practice of civilian medicine boring. In 1820, he convinced his friend Army Surgeon General Joseph Lovell to appoint him physician to the military base on Mackinac Island in the territory that later became Michigan.

In 1822 he was called on to treat 19-year-old French trapper Alexis St. Martin, who had suffered an accidentally self-inflicted shotgun wound to the stomach. Beaumont dressed the wound and waited for the trapper to die, but, over several months, the young man surprisingly recovered, although with a fistula that left his stomach lining visible through the skin of his upper abdomen. Beaumont took St. Martin into his home and began a series of experiments in which he introduced various substances directly into the trapper's stomach and documented the resulting gastric movements and secretions. He was able to show for the first time that gastric secretions only occurred after the stomach was presented with food and that hydrochloric acid and an unknown additional substance (later shown to be the enzyme pepsin) were responsible for food breaking down. When Beaumont was transferred to Fort Niagara in 1825, he took St. Martin with him, employed him as an orderly and personal servant, and continued his experiments. The relationship between the two men was less than cordial, and St. Martin repeatedly ran away to Canada, particularly when Beaumont insisted on displaying him during public lectures. Beaumont retrieved St. Martin several times, but the Frenchman disappeared for good shortly after Beaumont published his epochal *Experiments and Observations on the Gastric Juice and the Physiology of Digestion* in 1825.

Beaumont left the army soon after his book was published and practiced medicine in St. Louis until his death in 1853. St. Martin lived with his fistula to age 83 and died in 1881.

See also Abdominal Injuries in War

References

Edelson, Edward. *Healers in Uniform*. Garden City, NY: Doubleday & Company, Inc., 1971.

Epstein, Sam. *Dr. Beaumont and the Man with the Hole in His Stomach*. New York: Coward, McCann & Geoghegan, Inc., 1978.

Gillet, Mary. *The Army Medical Department, 1775–1818*. Washington, D.C.: Center of Military History, 1981.

Myer, Jesse. *Life and Letters of Dr. William Beaumont, including Hitherto Unpublished Data Concerning the Case of Alexis St. Martin*. St. Louis: C. V. Mosby Company, 1912.

Bell, Charles
(1774–1842)

Surgeon, artist, and professor of anatomy at the London College of Surgeons, Charles Bell was born in Edinburgh, Scotland, the youngest of six children of an Episcopal minister. In spite of the fact that the family was left impoverished when the elder Bell died in 1779, three of the children ultimately became famous: In addition to Charles, John was a noted surgeon and anatomist, and George Joseph achieved fame as a professor of law. Charles's mother saw to his early education and encouraged his obvious artistic talent. In spite of having been an indifferent student at the University of Edinburgh, Bell was a successful practitioner and was named to the Royal Society of Edinburgh in 1799.

In 1804 he moved to London, where he taught private lessons in anatomy and surgery, emphasizing the importance of cadaver dissection in learning both. He was convinced that all surgery was based on an understanding of human anatomy. Bell was especially interested in the nervous system, and it has been said that he did for neuronanatomy what William Harvey did for the study of the circulation.

In 1809, Bell published studies of gunshot wounds he had treated at the Battle of Coruna, including one magnificently disturbing drawing of a man grotesquely arched so that the back of his head nearly touches his feet in the *oposthotonus* typical of a tetanus-contaminated injury. In 1815, he went to Waterloo for Napoleon's last battle and operated alongside French surgeons for a week with almost no rest. At the end of that time Bell said his coat was rigid with dried blood and his arm—surely the one that wielded an amputation saw so many times—was so tired he could barely lift it.

After the Napoleonic Wars, Bell returned to London to a life of fame, fortune, and an eventual title. He lectured and operated at the hospital at Great Windmill Street for the next 24 years, where he was appointed professor of anatomy and named fellow of the Royal Society of London, both in 1824. In 1828, Bell accepted an appointment as professor of surgery at the University College. After retirement, he spent his final years fishing and traveling and produced a beautifully illustrated account of his tours of Italy before dying of heart disease at the age of 68.

See also British Military Medicine; Napoleonic Wars

References
Corson, Eugene R. 1910. "Sir Charles Bell: The Man and His Work." *Bulletin of the Johns Hopkins Hospital* 21 (June): 171–182.
Gordon-Taylor, G., and E. Walls. *Sir Charles Bell: His Life and Times*. Edinburgh, Scotland: Livingstone, 1958.

Bergmann, Ernst von
(1836–1907)

Ernst von Bergmann was a prominent German surgeon of the late 19th century, a volunteer military surgeon in three wars, and a champion of antiseptic surgery.

Bergmann was born in Riga, Latvia, a German-speaking Russian province, and received his medical degree from the Russo-German University of Dorpat, where he served as chief of surgery from 1871 to 1878 and conducted important experiments on fat embolism. From Dorpat, he went to the University of Würzburg as chief of surgery from 1878 to 1882, and then to the University of

Berlin, with which his name is usually linked and where he worked until his death.

Bergmann's career was punctuated by service in Prussia's wars with Austria (1866) and France (1871) and in the 1877–1878 Russo-Turkish War, where he served as a consultant to the Imperial Russian Army. He had a special interest in the surgery of battle injuries and, while serving in Bohemia, made the important observation that hemorrhage from gunshot wound often took place several days after the original injury. He also studied penetrating head wounds and became one of the first modern experts in that type of trauma.

In the 1866 war, Bergmann recognized the advantage of rail transport for the wounded and took advantage of hospital cars to transport injured soldiers back to Germany for treatment and convalescence. Although his cumulative experience as a military surgeon lasted only a few months, much of his international reputation and his own opinion of his ability derived from that time.

As a result of his military experience, Bergmann adopted Lord Joseph Lister's antiseptic techniques, in which bactericidal chemicals were used to decrease wound contamination during surgery, but was disappointed in the results and decided that prevention of bacterial contamination in the first place was better than letting organisms get into a wound and then trying to kill them. To that end, Bergmann introduced sterilization of skin edges and instruments, converting antiseptic to aseptic technique. He introduced sterile white gowns to the operating theater and was said to have claimed that his most important contribution to surgery was that, at Dorpat, they washed their hands *before* operating.

Bergmann died in Wiesbaden in 1907 and did not survive to see his theories ques-tioned in the face of World War I's grossly contaminated wounds.

See also Asepsis; Franco-Prussian War; Prussian and German Military Medicine

References
Blech, Gustavus. 1928–1935. "Ernst von Bergmann as a War Surgeon." *Bulletin of the Society of Medical History of Chicago* 4: 221–228.
Zimmerman, M. 2000. "Life and Work of the Surgeon Ernst von Bergmann." *Zentralblatt fur Chirurgie* 125: 552–560.

Biblical Military Medicine

Biblical military medicine covers the history of military medicine in the ancient kingdoms of Israel and Judah.

Study of Old Testament–era military medicine is problematic for several reasons. The only available written sources are the five books of the Torah, the Apocrypha, the Talmud, and the notoriously unreliable historian Josephus, and, if the number of references to physicians in those sources is a valid indicator, the Israelites had little regard for medicine in general and physicians in particular. Biblical Jews tended to see illness and injury as visitations from God and mistrusted anyone who interfered with the natural course of those misfortunes. The earliest biblical mention of a physician occurs when King Asa of Judah suffered from gangrene of the foot and was gently chastised for seeking the help of physicians rather than going first to God. The first mention of a battle injury is that of King Joram in a battle with the Syrians in 700 B.C.

Even at the height of their military power under Solomon and David, the Israelites never had large armies, and no evidence exists that they ever had dedicated military physicians. They were, however, exposed to Egyptian and Babylonian medicine and were the world's first documented experts in military sanitation and hygiene. When Moses led his people out of Egypt in approximately 1200 B.C., one of his primary functions was as hygienist for the group, and much of Mosaic law deals with problems of group sanitation.

Subsequently, Hebrew priests doubled as sanitary police with broad powers of quarantine over those with infectious illnesses, especially leprosy and venereal disease. They supervised rigid sanitation of water, food, and the utensils used in food preparation. Deuteronomy 23:9–14 describes policing a military camp, mandates that latrines should be located away from the camp, and orders that each soldier carry a flat blade for burying the latrines after they were used. Although sanitary regulation of military camps returned with the Romans, neither the Greeks nor the Macedonians had any such rules. The Talmud, mostly in relation to rules of ritual slaughter, contains the only detailed gross pathological descriptions of diseased organs before the work of Antonio Beniveni and Andreas Vesalius 17 centuries later.

The Bible says nothing of Hebrew military surgeons, although it is known that the Israelites adopted both splinting and circumcision from the Egyptians and knew how to suture wounds. Israelite physicians were also familiar with crutches and fashioned artificial limbs. A single skull from the Assyrian Sennacherib's defeat of Hezekiah's forces at Lachish in about 702 B.C. shows a healed trephine opening, proving both that Israelite physicians were capable of opening a wounded skull and having the patient survive.

See also Egyptian Military Medicine; Mesopotamian Military Medicine; Military Sanitation; Vesalius, Andreas

References

Garrison, Fielding. *Notes on the History of Military Medicine.* Washington, D.C.: Association of Military Surgeons, 1922.

Levin, Simon. *Adam's Rib: Essays on Biblical Medicine.* Los Altos, CA: Geron-X, Inc., 1970.

Majno, Guido. *The Healing Hand: Man and Wound in the Ancient World.* Cambridge, MA: Harvard University Press, 1975.

Ussishkin, David. *The Conquest of Lachish by Sennacherib.* Tel Aviv, Israel: University Institute of Archaeology, 1982.

Billings, John Shaw (1838–1913)

John Shaw Billings was a surgeon, statistician, hospital architect, historian, bibliographer, and military physician for more than three decades.

Billings was born on a frontier Indiana farm in 1838 and was noted early in his childhood to have an exceptional memory and facility for learning. He entered Miami University (Ohio) at age 14, graduated four years later, and enrolled in the Medical College of Ohio at Cincinnati in 1858. He graduated in two years and served briefly as a demonstrator in anatomy at the university before enlisting in the U.S. Army as a military surgeon in 1862.

Billings served in Washington and Philadelphia military hospitals until March 1863, when he was assigned to the Fifth Corps of the Army of the Potomac. He saw action at Chancellorsville, Gettysburg, the Wilderness, and Petersburg. His reputation for surgical skill brought him many of the most difficult cases during this period, but

John Shaw Billings, U.S. Army colonel and surgeon during the Civil War, founded the Surgeon General's Library, which later became the National Library of Medicine. (National Library of Medicine)

he tired from overwork and was forced to spend six months recuperating in hospital before rejoining the Army of the Potomac, now under Gen. Ulysses Grant, in March 1864. In August he was named medical director of the U.S. Army, and his reports formed a major part of the *Medical and Surgical History of the War of the Rebellion*.

In December 1864, Billings transferred to the Surgeon General's office, where he spent the next 30 years. In 1869, his review of the Marine Hospital Service resulted in its reorganization into the Public Health Service. His ability to design hospitals was widely recognized, and he was responsible for plans of the first inpatient facility at Johns Hopkins University. He also chose William Welch, William Osler, William Halsted, and Walter Kelly to be the first medical staff.

Billings has been called the father of American medical statistics and was responsible for medical information being included for the first time in the 1880 U.S. census. He also suggested using an as-yet-uninvented mechanical counting device to tabulate the 1890 census, an idea translated by Herman Hollerith into the first computerized data processing machine.

Billings created the Surgeon General's Library, which became the National Library of Medicine, and supervised the publication of the *Index Catalogue of the Library of the Office of the Surgeon General*, which has evolved into the *Index Medicus* and Medline.

He retired from the Army in 1895 to take the chair of hygiene at the University of Pennsylvania. In 1896 he left medicine to become director of the New York Public Library and designed that institution's current building. He served there and as chair of the Carnegie Institution until his death after a brief illness on March 11, 1913. He is buried at Arlington National Cemetery.

See also Civil War in the United States

References
Chapman, Carleton B. *Order out of Chaos: John Shaw Billings and America's Coming of Age*. Boston: Boston Medical Library, 1994.
Garrison, Fielding. *John Shaw Billings: A Memoir*. New York: G. P. Putnam's Sons, 1915.
Gillet, Mary. *The Army Medical Department, 1865–1917*. Washington, D.C.: Center of Military History, 1995.
Lydenburg, Harry Miller. *John Shaw Billings: Creator of the National Medical Library and its Catalogue. First Director of the New York Public Library*. Chicago: American Library Association, 1924.
United States Surgeon General's Office, Joseph K. Barnes, Janvier Woodward, Charles Smart, George A. Otis, and David

Lowe Huntington. *The Medical and Surgical History of the War of the Rebellion (1861–1865).* Washington, D.C.: Government Printing Office, 1870–1888.

Bilroth, Christian Albert Theodor (1829–1894)

Christian Albert Theodor Bilroth was considered the pioneer of surgery of the visceral organs and the leading German surgeon of the 19th century.

Bilroth was born in a fishing village on the Baltic island of Rügen, the oldest of five sons of a German Lutheran minister and a Swedish mother. His father died when Theodor was five, and financial considerations forced the young man into medicine rather than music, which he would have preferred.

Bilroth began studying medicine at the University of Göttingen and graduated from the medical school at Berlin in 1852, after which he became an assistant in Bernhard von Langenbeck's clinic. He served as professor of surgery at Zurich from 1860 to 1867 and at Vienna from 1867 to 1894. Bilroth was a dedicated teacher and a vigorous advocate of prolonged apprenticeships for aspiring surgeons augmented by frequent cadaver dissections and practice operations on laboratory animals.

Bilroth volunteered as a military surgeon in the Franco-Prussian War and served in military hospitals at Mannheim and Weissenberg. Prior to the war, he had written extensively on wound treatment and wound infections. He had sent two of his students to Edinburgh, Scotland, and to London to study with Lord Joseph Lister and had become a convert to Lister's antiseptic surgical practices (although not to his preference for carbolic acid). Bilroth's 1865 studies

of wound infection convinced him that granulating wounds were less susceptible to infection than fresh ones and led to his advocating delayed closure of war wounds rather than suturing them immediately. Bilroth was infuriated when he found nurses going from soldier to soldier bathing their wounds from a common basin until the water became a fetid mixture of blood and pus. The nurses' refusal to use clean water for each patient led him into an unsuccessful battle to make them directly responsible to the surgeons rather than the nursing administration.

After the Franco-Prussian War, Bilroth returned to his university position and became the first surgeon to perform a number of complex operations, including resection of the esophagus, resection of the distal stomach for cancer, complete removal of the larynx for cancer, and radical amputation of the lower extremity through the pelvis.

Bilroth remained vigorous and in active practice until shortly before his death. He also maintained a lively interest in music and was a close friend of Johannes Brahms, who dedicated two of his string quartets to the surgeon. Before his death in 1894, Bilroth frequently served as guest conductor of the Zurich Symphony Orchestra.

See also Antisepsis; Asepsis; Franco-Prussian War; Prussian and German Military Medicine

References
Lewis, J. M., and J. P. O'Leary. 2001. "Theodor Bilroth: Surgeon and Musician." *The American Surgeon* 67: 605–606.
Rutledge, R. H. 1979. "In Commemoration of Theodor Bilroth on the 150th Anniversary of His Birth. Bilroth I: His Surgical and Professional Accomplishments. Bilroth II: His Personal Life, Ideas, and Musical Friendships." *Surgery* 86: 672–693.

Zimmerman, Leo, and Ilza Veith. *Great Ideas in the History of Surgery*. Baltimore: Williams & Wilkins Co., 1961.

Blane, Sir Gilbert (1749–1834)

A British naval surgeon and administrator, Sir Gilbert Blane was responsible for instituting James Lind's preventive measures against scurvy.

Blane was born in the village of Blanefield in Ayrshire, Scotland, and graduated from the University of Edinburgh Medical School. He received additional training in London under William Hunter, who helped him get an appointment as personal physician to Lord Holdernesse and later to Admiral Lord Rodney.

As Rodney's physician, Blane accompanied a British fleet to the West Indies in 1779, where he served in six naval engagements during the American Revolution. In the first of these, because every deck officer was dead, wounded, or busy, Blane assumed the role of combatant and suffered a minor wound. His bravery in that action so impressed Rodney that the admiral promoted him to physician to the fleet.

Aware of James Lind's discoveries regarding prevention of scurvy with citrus juice, Blane was able to stop an outbreak of the disease in 28 ships of the line after his return to England in 1782. He further promoted the practice in his 1785 *Observations on the Diseases of Seamen*, in which he fully credited Lind. Blane was subsequently appointed commissioner to the Sick and Hurt Board and head of the Navy Medical Board.

In addition to his work with scurvy, Blane was responsible for introducing mandatory smallpox vaccination in the Royal Navy.

His *Memorial to the Admiralty* recommended clean, dry quarters for sailors; fresh soap; better naval hospitals; movement of ships' surgeries from the orlop deck deep in the ship's hold to the better ventilated, more accessible forecastle; and having drugs and medical supplies furnished by the Admiralty instead of by the ships' surgeons. Without Blane's reforms, the years-long British blockade of Napoleon's North Sea ports would not have been possible.

He was awarded a baronetcy and a life pension for his services in the ill-fated Walcheren expedition and ultimately returned to London, where he had a prosperous private practice and served as personal physician to King William IV, with whom he had served when the latter was a midshipman in Rodney's fleet.

See also American Revolutionary War; Lind, James; Napoleonic Wars; Naval Medicine; Scurvy; Smallpox

References
Brown, Stephen. *Scurvy: How a Surgeon, a Mariner, and a Gentleman Solved the Greatest Medical Mystery of the Age of Sail*. New York: St. Martin's Press, 2004.
Wharton, M. 1984. "Sir Gilbert Blane, Bt. (1749–1834)." *Annals of the Royal College of Surgeons (England)* 66 (September): 375–376.

Blast Injuries

Blast injuries are those caused by explosive devices. The study of blast injuries has become particularly important in light of recent attacks by terrorists and insurgents.

Weapons that cause blast injuries are of two general types: conventional bombs and enhanced blast explosive devices. The first generate a shock wave emanating from a point source that results in rapid increase and decrease of pressure followed by a blast of moving air and possibly by fragments from either the device itself or from surrounding structures. This effect can be multiplied if the primary blast is used as a trigger for a secondary explosion. The damage from either device is increased by reflected waves if the explosion occurs in a closed space.

Blast injuries are of four types. Injuries from direct pressure are principally the result of barotrauma and are most damaging to areas with an interface between air and fluid, especially air-containing organs, such as the ear, lung, or bowel, or fluid-filled organs exposed to the outside, such as the eye. Ear drum rupture occurs at the lowest pressure differential and is a sensitive indicator of potential damage to other organs. Eyes can bleed or rupture, as can the bowel. The most lethal injuries are those to the lung and include contusion, hemorrhage, and edema. Victims in close proximity to an explosion can also suffer traumatic amputation. Although body armor protects against flying fragments, it offers no protection from pressure injury.

The second effect is that from flying projectiles and has been the main cause of death from improvised explosive devices (IEDs) during the conflicts waged in Afghanistan and Iraq in the early 21st century. Secondary air movement from a blast can cause collapse of surrounding structures, resulting in crushing injury to those trapped within. Finally, burns, asphyxiation, or toxicity from inhaled gases or dust can also cause significant injury.

Prior to World War II, blast injury in war was relatively uncommon, but American and British air forces developed bombs designed to cause barotrauma. Incendiary bombs often contained secondary high explosives to deliver delayed blast specifically intended to hamper fire-fighting efforts. More recently, the Russian military has designed weapons to deliver combined thermal and blast injury and deployed them in both Afghanistan and Chechnya. The U.S. military tested the massive ordnance air blast bomb (MOAB, occasionally called the Mother of All Bombs) in 2003. The MOAB carries 18,700 pounds of high explosive and is expressly designed to deliver a massive blast wave.

Blast injuries from terrorist attacks have become increasingly common beginning in Israel after World War II and in Northern Ireland for the last four decades. In the October 1983 bombing of the Marine barracks in Beirut, Lebanon, 234 immediate blast-related deaths occurred and 122 more victims were injured, 59 percent suffering significant head trauma. The largest terrorist explosive attack in the United States was the 1995 detonation at the Alfred P. Murrah Federal Building in Oklahoma City that resulted in 518 injuries and 168 deaths. With that exception, blast injuries have been very uncommon in the United States, resulting in an average of fewer than 50 deaths a year. These injuries have, on the other hand, accounted for more than half the combat casualties in the Iraq War. Responsible weapons have included grenades, missiles, artillery shells, land mines, and especially IEDs. As in the Beirut experience, 59 percent of those wounded by blasts in Iraq have suffered traumatic brain injury.

See also Baromedicine; Iraq and Afghan Wars

References

DePalma, R. G., D. G. Burris, H. R. Champion, and M. J. Hodgson. 2005. "Blast Injuries." *New England Journal of Medicine* 352 (March 31): 1335–1342.

Mellor, S. G., and G. J. Cooper. 1989. "Analysis of 828 Servicemen Killed or Injured by Explosion in Northern Ireland 1970–1984:

The Hostile Action Casualty System."
British Journal of Surgery 76 (October):
1006–1010.

Stein, M., and A. Hirshberg. 1979. "Medical
Consequences of Terrorism: The Conventional Weapons Threat." *Surgical Clinics of
North America* 79 (December): 1537–1552.

Boer War

Fought between 1899 and 1902, at the dawn of modern understanding of sanitation and aseptic surgery, the Boer War was the last major war in which deaths from disease dwarfed those from trauma.

The United Kingdom's Royal Army Medical Corps was formed only 16 months before the war started and was hopelessly understaffed and underequipped in 1899. It included only 250 medical officers and was intended to care for two army corps and one cavalry regiment in a total of seven stationary and three general hospitals. The service tripled in size in the first months of the war with 700 new physicians, augmented by the British Red Cross Society, the St. Johns Ambulance, and Sir James Cantlie's Volunteer Forces, which provided both physicians and stretcher bearers. Those additions, however, did not prevent British army medical care from being dismally inadequate throughout the war.

Prior to the Boer War, typhoid and other enteric diseases had been relatively infrequent among British soldiers assigned to duty in the Cape Colony. Men stationed there had death rates equal to and often better than those of soldiers stationed in England. Unfortunately, the post of regimental sanitation officer had been abolished shortly before the war, and basic sanitary measures such as establishing adequate latrines and boiling drinking water were left to line officers, who had neither faith nor interest in the measures. As a result, dysentery was a major problem beginning with the first actions along the Modder River which was heavily contaminated with untreated sewage. At Bloemfontein in the spring of 1900, 5,000 men were hospitalized and an average of 40 died each day from bacterial diarrhea.

Triage and transport were rendered especially difficult by the fact that the contested area in South Africa stretched 1,100 miles north to south and more than 600 miles east to west. Wounded were usually transported in springless carts over impossibly rutted roads that made the trips painful at best and often lethal.

Development of high-velocity, jacketed bullets paradoxically rendered small-arms fire less damaging, because the projectiles tended to pass through the body without becoming deformed. As a result, the amount of tissue damage and contamination was less. In addition, the arid, infertile soil carried a lower bacterial load than was typical of cultivated areas where European battles were typically fought, so secondary tetanus and gangrene were less common than the British were accustomed to encountering.

British Army surgeons found that mortality and morbidity were lower if the wounds were not probed and were left open and if limbs remained attached rather than being amputated. Later attempts to extend those lessons to shrapnel wounds in the fields of Flanders in the early years of World War I, however, resulted in astronomical rates of both tetanus and gangrene.

X-ray, which had been introduced by American military physicians in the Spanish-American War, was widely applied in the Boer War. The Boer War also saw the first British use of standard field dressings, a gauze pad sewn to a bandage that could

Wounded British soldiers photographed in a filthy wagon during the Boer War. (Reinhold Thiele/Getty Images)

be safety-pinned around a wound. Early in the war, the dressings were covered with waterproof "jaconets," a procedure that was abandoned when surgeons decided that the occlusive dressing fostered infection. Shock was treated by placing patients in heated beds and giving intravenous saline; blood transfusions would not be available for another decade.

Wounded were typically carried by litter bearers (one of whom was the young Indian lawyer Mohandas Ghandi) to regimental aid posts for stabilization. From the aid posts, the injured were transferred to

100-bed field hospitals, where most surgery was done and, if necessary, on to 520-bed stationary hospitals for further treatment and convalescence. Ultimately, the British operated 21,000 hospital beds in 28 field hospitals, five stationary hospitals, and 16 general hospitals. In addition, the Royal Army Medical Corps had three hospital trains and two hospital ships staffed by 151 individuals as well as regimental medical units and 800 army nurses. The medical service received more decorations than any other part of the Army except the Royal Artillery.

Disease far outstripped accident and injury as a cause of both hospitalization and death in the Boer War. Among the 450,000 men who served in the British Army during the war, 440,000 were hospitalized for disease compared with just over 22,000 for injury. The general sickness rate was an appalling 958 per 1,000 men per year. Although Sir Almroth Wright had developed a typhoid vaccine in 1896, it was not mandatory and, because it regularly caused several days of malaise and fever, only 5 percent of the soldiers took it. Consequently, 10 percent of the Army was admitted with typhoid every year. While 5,774 men died from injury or accident, 14,000 died from disease—8,000 from dysentery alone.

The unacceptable medical record led to a variety of postwar reforms, including improvement and relocation of the Army Medical School, mandatory sanitation training for field officers, the establishment of a sanitary school at Aldershot, attachment of litter bearers to the medical service rather than individual regiments, and the establishment of the Home Hospital Reserve so the medical service could be more rapidly expanded in time of war.

See also Bandaging and Wound Dressing; Dysentery; Military Sanitation; World War I Medicine; Wright, Almroth

References
Curtin, Philip D. *Disease and Empire: The Health of European Troops in the Conquest of Africa.* Cambridge: Cambridge University Press, 1998.
Gabriel, Richard, and Karen Metz. *A History of Military Medicine from the Renaissance through Modern Times.* New York: Greenwood Press, 1992.
Lovegrove, Peter. *Not Least in the Crusade: A Short History of the Royal Army Medical Corps.* Aldershot, UK: Gale & Polden, Ltd., 1952.
Ogston, Alexander. *Reminiscences of Three Campaigns.* London: Hodder and Stoughton, n.d.

Botulism

Botulism is a disease resulting from the toxin produced by the soil-dwelling bacterium *Clostridium botulinum*.

This gram-negative, rod-shaped organism is a ubiquitous normal inhabitant of animal and human intestines. It has seven different antigenic types, four of which produce toxins that are extremely dangerous to humans. The organism is anaerobic and normally fragile but produces spores that are very hardy and can only be heat sterilized by temperatures in excess of 250ºF.

Clostridium botulinum produces a polypeptide chain that prevents release of acetylcholine from neuronal vesicles, causing failure of neural transmission and muscular paralysis. Botulism results in impaired brain stem–mediated functions, including swallowing, eye opening, facial movement, and speech within 12 to 72 hours of exposure, and progresses to generalized muscular weakness and respiratory failure shortly thereafter. The disease has a 65 percent fatality rate untreated and a 10 percent fatality rate with optimal management. By weight, botulinum toxin is the most poisonous substance known; it is estimated that one gram efficiently dispersed could kill 1 million people.

Because of its extreme lethality, botulinum toxin has been of interest as a biological weapon for more than 70 years. Japanese soldiers assigned to Unit 731 in China fed the toxin to prisoners in the 1930s, and U.S. military researchers produced botulinum at Fort Detrick in the early 1940s. Concern about possible German production led to stockpiling of more than 1 million doses of botulinum toxoid for injection if needed during the D-Day invasion in 1944.

During the Cold War, Soviet scientists produced large volumes of the toxin at Vozrozhdeniye Island and reportedly used genetic engineering techniques to create other bacteria able to produce botulinum. Terrorists in the Japanese Aum Shinrikyo cult attempted to release aerosolized botulinum in Tokyo three times between 1990 and 1995 but failed to produce disease either because of faulty microbiology or, possibly, internal sabotage. Iraqi officials told United Nations officials that they had produced 19,000 liters of botulinum (enough to kill every human being on the planet three times over) beginning in 1989 and had loaded 13 missiles with the bioweapon, although no evidence of the substance was found after the subsequent U.S. occupation of their country.

See also Chemical and Biological Warfare; Iraq and Afghan Wars; Japanese Military Medicine; Vozrozhdeniye Island; World War II Medicine

Reference

Arnon, S. S., R. Schechter, T. V. Inglesby, D. A. Henderson, J. G. Bartlett, M. S. Ascher, E. Eitzen, A. D. Fine, J. Hauer, M. Layton, S. Lillibridge, M. T. Osterholm, T. O'Toole, G. Parker, T. M. Perl, P. K. Russell, D. L. Swerdlow, K. Tonat, and the Working Group on Civilian Biodefense. 2001. "Botulinum Toxin as a Biological Weapon: Medical and Public Health Management." *Journal of the American Medical Association* 285 (February 28): 1059–1070.

British Military Medicine

The British armed forces have been a major influence in the development of military medicine from the beginning of the Christian era to the end of the 20th century.

The history of military medicine in Britain can be traced to A.D. 43, when the Roman emperor Claudius invaded the island with an army in which each cohort was accompanied by either a physician or a surgeon. Once settled, they established military hospitals, or *valetudinaria*, to care for their sick and wounded. When the Romans withdrew in the fifth century, all evidence of formal military medicine left with them save for sporadic mention of *medici* in the armies of the Welsh kings.

Military surgeons returned with the Normans in 1066, and King Richard the Lionheart included them in his retinue on his 1190 crusade in Palestine. The European physicians' therapeutic armamentarium was no match for the dysentery and typhus that ravaged King Richard's knights, and did not approach the sophistication of that available to Arab physicians. The crusade did, however, result in formation of the Knights of St. John of Jerusalem, the warrior monks whose order survives today as the St. John Ambulance Brigade.

Through the Middle Ages, England lacked a standing army. Wounded knights and soldiers were most often treated either by religious orders or by whatever civilian practitioners were locally available, although the very rich or the very powerful occasionally included a medical practitioner among their personal retainers. The first documented inclusion of medical practitioners as a paid part of an English army was in the 1298–1300 Scottish campaign in which King Edward I included surgeons who were also responsible for shaving the officers and whose salaries were paid out of daily deductions from soldiers' wages, a practice that persisted for the next two centuries.

Twenty surgeons and one physician accompanied Henry V at Agincourt and were equipped with a cart carrying panniers of medical stores. These men were ranked above washerwomen but below shoemakers; it would be another century and a half before English military surgeons surpassed drummers in status.

The first prominent British military surgeons were Thomas Gale, who served under Henry VIII, and John Woodall, who served under Elizabeth I and whose *Surgeon's Mate* anticipated James Lind by a hundred years in recommending citrus juice to prevent scurvy. In Elizabeth's army, each company was furnished a surgeon and had its own medical stores.

The English Civil War and Oliver Cromwell's Parliamentary Army saw organization of the English military into a regimental system that persisted largely unchanged until the reforms of 1873. Under this system, each regiment had its own surgeon and one or two surgeon's mates, all of whom were subordinate to the Army's surgeon general, physician general, and apothecary general. In addition, each regiment furnished its own hospital.

When the monarchy was reestablished in 1660, Charles II created a standing army, and military medicine became a career for the first time. Military surgeons were commissioned officers paid both for their medical services and as combatants, as they were also expected to fight. Their reimbursement and supplies continued to come from deductions from soldiers' wages, and the wounded were often required to pay for any care they received.

Poor sanitation among crowded armies led to rates of infectious disease so high that they assumed both humanitarian and tactical significance. John Pringle's *Observations on Diseases of the Army*, written while he was surgeon general of the English Army, stressed military hygiene, and the Duke of Marlborough made sanitation a major concern during his Flanders campaign. Hospitals located in whatever buildings were available, carts and barges for transportation of the wounded, and collecting posts and regimental aid stations, all predecessors of the World War I stepwise evacuation system, were featured in the Battle of Blenheim in 1704.

The main concerns of British military surgery through the latter half of the 18th century and the first half of the 19th century were sanitation, transportation, and organization. All three improved under the aegis of the Duke of Wellington and his two surgeons, Sir James McGrigor, who served as inspector general of hospitals, and George Guthrie, who was deputy inspector general during the Peninsular Campaign. Both men recognized the relation between filth and the typhus that was the scourge of British troops in Spain, and both struggled with the difficulties of transporting the sick and wounded in the Iberian mountains and the fact that Wellington refused to reserve any wagons or carts to the medical service.

McGrigor arranged for hospitals to be built in a chain from the front to the coast so men could be evacuated in stages and eventually shipped home. Although McGrigor's and Guthrie's efforts improved British effectiveness in Spain, those improvements were not universal in Britain's wars against Napoleon. More typical were the results of the Walcheren expedition to the Netherlands, in which 23,000 of a force of 39,000 died. Only 267 of those were injured in battle; the rest died of disease, which was the direct cause of the expedition's failure.

The first real change in British military medicine came as a result of the Crimean War. At the beginning of that war in 1854, the Army Medical Department had only 163 surgeons, and those few were scattered throughout the empire. The Army had no ambulance service, and the only stretcher bearers were men who had been assigned to the Hospital Conveyance Corps because they were physically, mentally, or morally unfit for combat. Abysmal sanitation, first in staging areas on the Black Sea and then on the Crimean peninsula itself, inevitably resulted in epidemic cholera, dysentery, and typhus. The only base hospital was 300 miles from the front at Scutari. Within seven months, 10,000 of the 28,000-man British invasion force had died of disease, leading to a series of scathing articles in *The Times* and the dispatch of Florence Nightingale who, with her female nurses and contentious reforms, was able to decrease mortality among those for whom she cared from 42 to 2 percent.

A royal commission organized in 1857 recommended sweeping changes, including formation of an army medical school, establishment of a statistical branch to track the results of military care, the opening of two general military hospitals, increased pay for military surgeons, and granting of commissions in the medical service by examination rather than purchase. Orderlies and stretcher bearers were put in the new Army Hospital Corps, where they were given regular army rank and, unlike other soldiers, were required to be literate. That reform, however, left the medical officers with little authority because nonphysicians involved in care and transport of the sick and wounded remained under line command.

The Army Medical School was opened at Fort Pitt in 1860 and moved to Netley and combined with the Royal Victoria Hospital in 1867, where it formed the basis of British military medical research and training for decades.

The regiments still had their own surgeons and hospitals until 1873, when war department leaders, appropriately impressed with the Prussian medical corps' performance in the war with France, placed all doctors and hospitals under the umbrella Medical Department and assigned a medical officer and a bearer company to each battalion. The system, first tried in the 1879 Zulu War and in the Egyptian Campaign of 1882, functioned so well that, in 1884, the support troops were placed under the Medical Department as well.

On June 23, 1898, a royal warrant was issued changing the Medical Department to the Royal Army Medical Corps and finally giving military surgeons the rank and status of army officers. The new corps was first tested in the Khartoum expedition, where British military surgeons had the opportunity to try chloroform anesthesia and their newly developed 200-bed mobile field hospitals.

A more severe test came in South Africa, where British commander General Sir Garnet Woolsey had derided the sanitation officer as the most useless man in the army. That sentiment undoubtedly contributed to the fact that 20 times as many British soldiers were hospitalized from disease as from wounds during the Boer War. Flooded with sick and wounded soldiers, the medical corps grew to manage 28 field hospitals, five stationary hospitals, and 16 general hospitals before the war's end. That war also witnessed the evolution of the Army Nursing Service into Queen Alexandra's Imperial Nursing Service and the provision of rank "equivalent to" that of an officer for nurses (although without an actual commission).

The Royal Army Medical Corps shrank after 1902, only to be forced into another dramatic expansion in 1914. By the end of World War I, the corps had cared for 2 million wounded and another 6 million sick. In 1914, there were only 18,000 hospital beds in the entire empire; by war's end, there were 637,000, with half in the British Isles. For almost five years, a constant stream of drugs and supplies went to the various fronts and a returning river of sick and wounded flowed back. World War I saw development of motor ambulance transport, virtually complete conquest of tetanus and typhoid by vaccines, and new methods of wound irrigation and early treatment in casualty clearing stations.

In the years between the world wars, the medical corps recognized the importance of transfusion and organized a service to collect and store blood. The development of sulfa and penicillin and new techniques of anesthesia made it possible to operate in body cavities where wounds had previously been almost uniformly fatal. Although air evacuation would come later, the Royal Army Medical Corps did develop airborne units that could parachute surgeons, aides, and supplies directly to remote areas during World War II.

See also Boer War; Crimean War; Crusades; Guthrie, George James; Hunter, John; McGrigor, James; Nursing in the Military; Roman Military Medicine; Royal Army Medical Corps; Sovereign Military Hospitaller Order of St. John of Jerusalem, of Rhodes, and of Malta; World War I Medicine; World War II Medicine

References
Blanco, Richard. 1974. "The Development of British Military Medicine, 1793–1814." *Military Affairs* 38 (February): 4–10.

Lovegrove, Peter. *Not Least in the Crusade: A Short History of the Royal Army Medical Corps.* Aldershot, UK: Gale & Polden, Ltd., 1952.

Brunschwig, Hieronymus (ca. 1450–1533)

Hieronymus Brunschwig was a German wound surgeon whose *Buch der Wundartzney*, or *Wound Surgery* (1497), gives the first detailed account of treatment of gunshot wounds (although a briefer account had been given in the lost 1460 *Buch der Bündth-Ertznei*, by Heinrich von Pfolspeundt).

Little is known of Brunschwig's life, although he probably spent most of his career practicing in Strasbourg, and it is not certain that he ever served as a military surgeon.

Brunschwig mistakenly believed that gunpowder was a poison that had to be cauterized out of wounds, an error that persisted for more than a century to the detriment of vast numbers of injured soldiers. Brunschwig described other penetrating wounds, fractures, amputations, and battlefield infections and wrote the first printed book on distilling. He used ligatures to tie off bleeding vessels and described a curved needle for pulling up severed arteries that is strikingly similar to that still in routine use. He irrigated wounds with lime water, which we now know releases a halogen compound that is an effective antiseptic, although he also used the much less effective turpentine irrigation later favored by Ambroise Paré and Guy de Chauliac. He recommended loosely suturing the skin over amputated extremities before taping the edges together. Because swelling wounds tended to tear out sutures, Brunschwig also recommended a tight bandage over the stump.

See also Bullet Wounds and Other Penetrating Injuries from Gunpowder Projectiles; Ligature; Pfolspeundt, Heinrich von; Prussian and German Military Medicine

References

Dealey, Carol. 2005. "German Wound Surgeons: 1450–1750." *European Wound Management Association Journal* 5: 48–52.

Sigerist, Henry. *The Book of Cirurgia by Hieronymus Brunschwig.* Milan: R. Lier & Co., 1923.

Bullet Wounds and Other Penetrating Injuries from Gunpowder Projectiles

Wounds from gunpowder-driven projectiles first appeared in European warfare in the late 15th century and became increasingly common over the subsequent hundred years.

Initially, these wounds were caused exclusively by metal or stone from large weapons or fragments created by them or, less commonly, by bits of hand-thrown grenades that were developed in the 16th century. Although these projectiles penetrated at low velocity, they were capable of imparting significantly more destructive energy than muscle-powered swords, pikes, and maces or even arrows.

Earlier weapons had been able to penetrate skin and soft tissue but rarely had enough force to break bones. Gunpowder weapons, even at low velocity, did have that power, and complex fractures open to the air became commonplace. Since the time of the ancient Greeks, physicians had known that open fractures regularly became infected and rarely healed, and Hippocrates had offered the sanguine opinion that they could be assumed to be fatal. The rash of compound fractures from gunpowder projectiles led to a proliferation of battlefield amputations. The high rate of infection in those wounds also led to the mistaken belief (especially fostered by Giovanni de Vigo and Hieronymus Brunschwig) that gunpowder itself was a poison and that the wounds should be irrigated with boiling elder oil to counteract the toxin. This practice persisted for half a century before French military surgeon Ambroise Paré accidentally found that simple irrigation yielded far better results.

Even with Paré's technique, wounds from gunpowder-driven projectiles continued to have a high rate of infection, no doubt complicated by the practice of probing such wounds with unsterile fingers and surgical instruments, which persisted until the end of the 19th century.

As personal firearms became more common, the instance of bullet wounds rose dramatically. During the Thirty Years War, Swedish king Gustavus Adolphus put muskets in the hands of 65 percent of his infantry and armed all his cavalry troops with pistols. Paper cartridges with standard powder loads and a complex but efficient manual of arms provided a constant hail of bullets and changed the nature of warfare. Wounds were more severe and, because effective range was greater, men had to be spread farther apart. Consequently, retrieval of the wounded became immensely more difficult.

Because military surgeons' ability to treat gunshot wounds failed to keep pace with improvement in the weapons, the 17th and 18th centuries saw a rash of bizarre therapies. The charlatan Sir Kenelm Digby successfully promoted his sympathetic powder supposedly compounded of moss from a cadaver's skull and powdered mummy flesh. "Transplantation treatment" involved soaking a piece of wood in pus

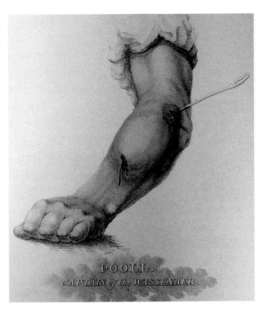

Probing an infected bullet wound. (John Bell. The Principles of Surgery, 1812)

and blood from a gunshot wound and sinking it into a living tree. If the graft took, the wound would presumably heal. Perhaps the strangest practice was applying healing salve not to the wound but to the weapon that inflicted it.

John Hunter's 1794 *Treatise of the Blood, Inflammation, and Gunshot Wounds* suggested more modern therapy, but it was not until the 1878 Russo-Turkish War that Russian surgeon Carl Reyher demonstrated that mortality from gunshot wounds could be cut by two-thirds with simple débridement and irrigation with sterile fluid.

Ten years later, the introduction of high-velocity rifles changed the nature of battlefield bullet wounds. A penetrating projectile causes damage in three ways: laceration and crushing, shock wave from the projectile, and cavitation. Bullets with a velocity of less than 400–500 feet per second—essentially all bullets prior to 1888—cause injury only

by the first of these methods. Introduction of high-muzzle-velocity weapons brought shock and especially cavitation to the fore as mechanisms of injury. Shock waves emanate from the surface of the bullet much as water radiates out from a pebble thrown into a pond. The shock waves generally do not have enough energy to damage bone, vessels, or nerves but can affect hollow organs such as the stomach or intestines. The real damage from high-velocity bullets, however, comes from their creation of a cavity that enlarges around them, collapses, and enlarges again in a pulsating fashion. When the energy is entirely expended, a residual track is left behind into which air and debris have been sucked behind the bullet. The size of the cavity is directly related to the velocity of the bullet, to its mass, and to how much it "wobbles" as it penetrates tissue. The last is a function of spin imparted by the rifling in the weapon's barrel. An unstable projectile loses its energy more quickly on penetration, and that energy is entirely transmitted to the surrounding tissue.

Mortality from rifle bullet–induced head injuries in the Viet Nam War was 22.73 percent, as opposed to 7.64 percent from low-velocity shell fragments. The energy imparted by a high-velocity bullet can be so great that surrounding tissues—such as the contents of the skull—can literally erupt, giving rise to occasional accusations that an enemy is using explosive bullets.

Infection is a common accompaniment of contaminated material being drawn into a cavitating wound. Although high-velocity rifles were used in the Boer War, infection was rare and the weapons were initially thought to be more humane than earlier weapons. In retrospect, the low infection rate was more likely due to dry conditions and the fact that battles were fought on ground not contaminated by fertilizer and domestic animals. Bullet wounds in the Boer War most often healed if simply bandaged and left alone. When those techniques were tried in the contaminated fields on the French-Belgian border in World War I, the incidence of tetanus and gangrene was astronomical and Reyher's lessons of débridement and irrigation had to be relearned.

Combinations of trinitrotoluene and ammonium nitrate brought grenades back into general use in World War I, and fragment wounds again became common and have remained so through subsequent wars.

See also Amputation; Antisepsis; Brunschwig, Hieronymus; Débridement; Hunter, John; Paré, Ambroise; Reyher, Carl

References

Gurdjian, E. Stephen. 1974. "The Treatment of Penetrating Wounds of the Brain Sustained in Warfare: A Historical Review." *Journal of Neurosurgery* 39 (February): 157–167.

Hopkinson, D. A. W., and T. K. Marshall. 1967. "Firearm Injuries." *British Journal of Surgery* 54 (May): 344–353.

C

Carrel, Alexis
(1873–1944)

A Nobel Prize winner, Alexis Carrel has been credited with being the father of vascular surgery and was an innovator in the treatment of war wounds.

Carrel was born in Sainte-Foy-les-Lyons, a suburb of Lyons, France, the son of a textile merchant. Both his undergraduate and medical education were completed at the University of Lyons, which he joined as a faculty member after serving as a military surgeon to the Alpine Chasseurs. Carrel's interest in mysticism and his calls for a scientific study of the miracles at Lourdes led to conflict with the French medical establishment and resulted in his emigration to Montreal and then to the United States, where he joined the faculty of the University of Chicago in 1904.

Carrel's father had died when Alexis was still a child, and his mother earned money doing embroidery. The young physician was fascinated with the delicate needlework and enlisted a professional embroiderer to teach him to sew. In 1902, he published a paper demonstrating that careful suturing made end-to-end anastamosis of severed blood vessels possible. Prior to that time, the only treatment for a wounded artery had been ligation and probable amputation.

He moved on to the Rockefeller Institute in New York in 1906, where his studies of vascular surgery and surgical physiology earned him the 1912 Nobel Prize for Physiology or Medicine. His ability to repair blood vessels and his meticulous aseptic technique made organ transplantation seem possible. In fact, Carrel was able to transplant a kidney from one cat to another, but the problems of immunity and rejection prevented his taking the technique to humans.

When World War I broke out, Carrel volunteered for the French Army, in which he became a major. He worked with chemist Henry Drysdale Dakin to develop an antiseptic wound irrigation technique that was credited with saving hundreds of thousands of wounded limbs that might otherwise have become infected and required amputation. He summarized his experience in *Treatment of Infected Wounds*, which he wrote with Georges Debelly.

After the war, Carrel returned to the United States, where he resumed his studies

Alexis Carrel was an experimental surgeon who perfected a method of vascular surgery. (Library of Congress)

of organ transplantation and tissue culture. He collaborated with aviator Charles Lindbergh to develop an extracorporeal perfusion pump that could be sterilized and used in open heart surgery. He and Lindbergh also shared an interest in eugenics and a conviction that Caucasians were innately superior to other races. When World War II started, Carrel returned to France and became director of the Carrel Foundation for the Study of Human Problems under Philippe Pétain's Vichy government. That association led to accusations of collaboration with France's Nazi occupiers, and it is likely that he would have been prosecuted after the war had he not died of heart disease in November 1944.

See also Carrel-Dakin Irrigation; World War I Medicine

Reference
Edwards, W. Sterling, and Peter D. Edwards. *Alexis Carrel: Visionary Surgeon*. Springfield, IL: Charles C. Thomas, 1974.

Carrel-Dakin Irrigation

The Carrel-Dakin irrigation method is a technique of combined débridement and antiseptic wound irrigation that, at the time of its introduction, was thought to be a revolutionary improvement in treatment of war wounds.

Battles on the Western Front were largely fought in French and Belgian fields that had been fertilized with manure for centuries and that, in consequence, carried an enormous bacterial load. Wounds contaminated by that soil had such a high rate of gas gangrene caused by soil-dwelling anaerobes that military surgeons began to suspect that the antiseptic surgical techniques developed by Lord Joseph Lister were a failure. French surgeons estimated that 60 percent of battlefield wounds sustained in the 1915 Battle of Champagne developed the almost uniformly fatal complication.

French surgeon Alexis Carrel and British chemist Henry Drysdale Dakin worked together to address the problem. Carrel left the Rockefeller Institute in New York when the war started to join the French Army as a major. Based partially on his prior research, he insisted on wide excision of all devitalized tissue in a wound. Dakin was convinced that chemical irrigation could be used to kill bacteria without damaging the surrounding tissues. To that end, he developed a buffered solution of sodium hypochlorite he called dichloramin-T that could be continuously washed into a wound and released significant quantities of chlorine, which was lethal to bacteria and mostly spared normal tissue.

Carrel would widely débride a wound and leave rubber catheters in its depths. After surgery the catheters would be hooked to bottles of Dakin's fluid, and the wound would be continuously washed until bacterial cultures were sterile, at which point the catheters were removed and the wound was allowed to heal. When New York surgeon C. L. Gibson visited the French Army hospital at La Panne in Belgium, he toured a ward in which 80 patients suffered open fractures, a type of wound that had previously had a near 100 percent infection rate, and saw not a single infection, a result he found almost impossible to believe. By the Battle of the Somme in 1916, the incidence of gas gangrene had dropped to a third that of a year earlier.

The method was introduced into civilian medical practice after World War I, but the results were not nearly as striking as they had been in French frontline hospitals. Later surgeons, and particularly bacteriologist Sir Alexander Fleming, argued that wounds that healed with Carrel-Dakin irrigation were simply well treated surgically and would have healed anyway. The argument became moot early in World War II when antibiotics brought a new standard to wound care.

See also Antisepsis; Asepsis; Carrel, Alexis; Débridement; World War I Medicine

References

Keen, W. W. *The Treatment of War Wounds.* Philadelphia: W. B. Saunders Co., 1918.
Wangensteen, Owen, and Sarah D. Wangensteen. *The Rise of Surgery from Empiric Craft to Scientific Discipline.* Minneapolis: University of Minnesota Press, 1978.

Casualty Clearing Stations and Staged Evacuation

Casualty clearing stations, introduced by the British Royal Army Medical Corps in World War I, were a major step in the evolution toward earlier care of those wounded in battle.

Baron Dominique-Jean Larrey, Napoleon Bonaparte's military surgeon, realized he could save more wounded men by operating on them close to the front line and as soon as possible after they were wounded. That lesson was evidently forgotten by the time of the Crimean War and had to be painfully relearned in the American Civil War. Following its disastrous performance in the Sino-Japanese War, the Japanese Imperial Army's military medical corps put forward-area dressing stations just 400 to 500 yards behind the line and field hospitals only two to three miles farther to the rear during the 1904–1905 conflict with Russia. The resulting improvements in survival contributed significantly to the Japanese victory in a war in which they were outnumbered and could little afford to lose soldiers who might be returned to combat.

The Royal Army Medical Corps introduced the field ambulance in 1906 to combine the functions of the bearer companies that retrieved the wounded from the field with the field hospital in which they received care. The Boer War convinced the British that treatment closer to the front was necessary, so they put a "clearing hospital" between the first aid and collection stations and the field hospital. In 1915, Colonel Arthur Lee coined the name "casualty clearing station" (CCS) for that facility.

Originally, the CCS was meant to be a movable facility where the wounded could be stabilized before transfer to a stationary field hospital. Early in the war, surgeons realized that the incidence of sepsis and gangrene decreased dramatically if dead tissue was débrided within 30 hours of injury, so, as the war progressed, the majority of surgery on the Western Front moved to casualty clearing stations.

The Royal Army Medical Corps' plan for evacuation and treatment of the wounded was specific, and, because the Western Front remained static through much of World War I, that plan worked well. Each battalion had a medical officer about 500 yards behind the line to collect the wounded and render first aid. About one-half mile behind the line were advanced dressing stations fed by four of the frontline stations. Treatment at the dressing stations was generally restricted to stopping hemorrhage, splinting, and the occasional unavoidable amputation. Men were typically moved by stretcher bearers or trench trolleys to the dressing stations and by motor cars from there to the CCS. From the CCS, which was usually placed next to a rail line, the men could be moved by train to fixed general hospitals and, if necessary, by ship back to the United Kingdom.

The CCS was typically about seven miles from the front. Although the intent was for these facilities to care for no more than 50 men in beds and another 150 in stretchers, the population could swell to as many as 500 during battles. Planned staffing was seven medical officers and 75 to 80 members of other ranks. The Royal Army Medical Corps recognized the importance of sisters of religious orders who served as nurses early in the war and included them as anesthetists, operating assistants, and ward nurses.

The CCS was the first facility behind the lines that could act as an actual hospital and was equipped with X-ray machines, laboratories, and operating rooms that could accommodate up to eight cases at once. In spite of their complexity, whole stations with their 35 tons of equipment could be dismantled and moved as much as 20 miles and be back in service in 24 hours.

The French arrangements were not nearly so well thought out. In 1910, the French medical corps had opted for a "hospital of evacuation" to serve as a temporary shelter for the wounded, who were to be taken to rear-area fixed hospitals for definitive treatment. The flood of patients into these temporary facilities early in the war forced development of the triage system to decide who should be treated first and who would have to wait. In general, the French had larger, more cumbersome hospitals than did the British; their most forward field hospitals required a minimum of 15 days to be torn down, moved, and reopened.

The French collected their wounded in first aid stations from which ambulance cars moved them to a surgical field hospital. The hospital and its vehicles comprised the "field ambulance." From the field ambulance, wounded were taken to an evacuation hospital that was typically located in a church, school, hotel, or other large building and was the first place real surgery could be done. Transport lines between these facilities, unlike the crisp, funnel-shaped British plan, resembled nothing as much as spider webs.

When the Americans entered World War I, they adopted a system similar to that of the British, with frontline first aid stations feeding dressing stations that, in turn, fed field hospitals, which acted much like casualty clearing stations. Behind these were fixed evacuation hospitals, base hospitals, and transport for movement to special and general hospitals in the United Kingdom or the United States.

The advent of casualty clearing stations represented a phase in the evolution from Larrey's *ambulances volantes* to the mobile army surgical hospitals used in Korea and the forward surgical teams in Iraq.

See also British Military Medicine; Iraq and Afghan Wars; Larrey, Baron Dominique-Jean; Mobile Army Surgical Hospitals in the Korean Conflict

References
Keen, William Williams. *The Treatment of War Wounds*. Philadelphia: W. B. Saunders Co., 1918.
Nichols, T. B. *Organization, Strategy and Tactics of the Army Medical Services in War*. London: Baillière, Tindall and Cox, 1937.

Cauterization

Cauterization is the application of heat or chemicals to a wound to stop bleeding.

Ancient and classical military surgeons relied on a variety of absorbents and styptics to control bleeding until Arab physicians—Albucasis in particular—recommended putting boiling oil or a red-hot iron into the wound to stop hemorrhage. The Islamic surgeons also used cautery to treat epilepsy, headache, toothache, depression, and hemorrhoids.

Metallic cauteries were usually made of iron, although other metals including gold were occasionally used, and the size and shape varied from a pea-sized ball on a handle to large, flat irons. European surgeons recognized that hot metal could be used to cut tissue bloodlessly as well as to control bleeding that had already started. Fabricius Hildanus used red-hot knives from the skin to the bone to perform relatively bloodless amputations in 1600.

Sixteenth-century military surgeons generally accepted the theory posited by Giovanni de Vigo in 1514 that gunpowder poisoned wounds and its toxic effect could only be reversed by application of boiling oil. Ambroise Paré empirically discovered in 1536 that wounds actually healed more readily without cauterization, and English surgeon Percival Pott condemned the practice, but it still remained commonplace for more than two centuries.

Cauterization was finally replaced by the combined use of tourniquets and ligatures in the 1800s, although most military surgeons continued to carry a small assortment of cauteries in their kits. Routine use of cauterization to decontaminate wounds vanished for good with Lord Joseph Lister's antisepsis method in the waning years of the 19th century.

Using heat to control bleeding and cut tissue resurfaced with the realization that electrical current applied to tissue produced heat in a more controllable fashion. Albrecht T. Middeldorpf described the galvanocautery process in 1854, and C. Pacquelin invented an electrical cautery in 1876. Two Americans, neurosurgeon Harvey Cushing and engineer W. T. Bovie, popularized this new form of cauterization with what they called electrical diathermy in 1928. Use of the "Bovie" to both cut and coagulate tissue has remained a surgical standard and has been refined to allow bipolar application of current, which is capable of restricting the applied current to the area between extremely fine forcep tips.

See also Albucasis; Amputation; Bullet Wounds and Other Penetrating Injuries from Gunpowder Projectiles; Cushing, Harvey Williams; Hemostasis; Islamic Military Medicine; Paré, Ambroise

References
Bennion, Elisabeth. *Antique Medical Instruments*. Berkeley: University of California Press, 1979.

Wangensteen, Owen, and Sarah D. Wangensteen. *The Rise of Surgery from Empiric Craft to Scientific Discipline.* Minneapolis: University of Minnesota Press, 1978.

Celsus, Aulus Cornelius (Early first century A.D.)

Aulus Cornelius Celsus was an encyclopedist, Latinist, and dilettante who lived during the reign of Tiberius Caesar (A.D. 14–37).

Celsus, a member of the wealthy Cornelii family, was probably not a physician—Pliny the Elder refers to him as *auctore*, or man of letters, rather than *medicus*—but was the author of an extensive encyclopedia covering agriculture, military tactics, rhetoric, and medicine. His *De Re Medicina* was not highly thought of by his contemporaries but, possibly because of its elegant use of Latin, became one of the most reproduced of all scientific books after the invention of movable type, the first edition having been printed in 1478.

The *De Re Medicina* is divided into eight books and is the oldest surviving medical text after that written by Hippocrates. Celsus refers to 72 other medical authors, none of whose works survive today. Most of the book refers to Greek sources and post-Hippocratic medical advances. Book Seven, "On the Extraction of Weapons from the Body," deals with surgery and includes instructions for removing barbed arrowheads, spearheads, and lead or stone bullets fired from slings or catapults. Celsus describes a complex arrow extractor, gives the technique for pulling a deep-seated projectile through the body's opposite side, and describes isolating and protecting vessels and nerves with a blunt hook.

Celsus recognized that knowledge of anatomy was essential to surgery and alleged that Herophilos and Erasistratos of Alexandria learned by dissection of live criminals. He did not personally engage in vivisection but did recommend examining open wounds in soldiers and gladiators whenever possible in order to see living organs. He described the ideal Roman *chirurgus* as youthful, steady of hand, ambidextrous, clear of vision, and strong of spirit. He also said a good surgeon should take pity on his patients but not to such an extent that his cries of pain distracted him or changed the way he conducted his operation.

See also Roman Military Medicine

References
Garrison, Fielding. *An Introduction to the History of Medicine.* Philadelphia: W. B. Saunders Co., 1929.
Majno, Guido. *The Healing Hand: Man and Wound in the Ancient World.* Cambridge, MA: Harvard University Press, 1975.
Salazar, Christine F. *The Treatment of War Wounds in Graeco-Roman Antiquity.* Leiden, the Netherlands: Brill, 2000.
Zimmerman, Leo, and Ilza Veith. *Great Ideas in the History of Surgery.* New York: Williams & Wilkins Co., 1961.

Chauliac, Guy de (ca. 1295–1368)

The second greatest medieval French surgeon after Henri de Mondeville and the most famous surgical author of the Middle Ages, Guy de Chauliac was born in the village for which he was named in the southern Auvergne region near the borders of Italy and Moorish Spain, a location that afforded him access to both Italian and Arabic learning. He probably came from a peasant family, and taking holy orders made it possible for him to obtain an education. Guy began his medical studies at Montpellier under Henri de Mondeville, a professor famous for his use of anatomical drawings and for his fine suturing technique. He continued his training at Toulouse, Paris, and Bologna before returning to Montpellier to practice.

Guy de Chauliac later moved to Lyons and then to Avignon, where he served as personal physician and commensal chaplain to Pope Clement VI, Pope Innocent VI, and Pope Urban V. While at Avignon, he wrote *Chirurgia Magna* (1363), which benefited from an increasing availability of ancient texts translated from Arabic or from the original Greek. The book went through more than 100 editions and was the standard surgical text until it was supplanted by that of Ambroise Paré almost 300 years later.

Chauliac's expertise in ophthalmology brought King John of Bohemia to Avignon. John had previously lost the vision in one eye to cataracts and had drowned the physician who failed to cure him. At Avignon, in spite of Chauliac's treatment, he lost the other eye and acquired the nickname John the Blind. He did not, however, drown the second surgeon.

Guy de Chauliac's contributions to military medicine were primarily in wound care. He recommended removing foreign bodies from fresh wounds and irrigating those wounds with brandy before taping the edges together. He also subscribed to the theory that profuse drainage of pus was a necessary part of healing, an error that persisted until the 19th century.

He described complicated arrangements of slings and pulleys to realign fractures and used ligatures and cauterization to stop bleeding. He required his students to attend dissections and used inhaled narcotics to lessen the pain of surgical procedures.

He was an astrologer in addition to being a physician and attributed the 14th-century plague epidemic that struck Avignon to a combination of the conjunction of Saturn, Jupiter, and Venus with inadequate sanitation and dietary deficiency common among the French poor. Chauliac arranged for Pope Clement VI to flee the city, although he remained to treat the ill and claimed to have survived the disease himself.

See also Medieval Military Medicine; Mondeville, Henri de

References

Forgue, F. 1956. "14th Century Origins of the Montpellier School of Surgery of Guy de Chauliac." *Montpellier Medicine* 50 (November): 333–339.

Thevenet, André. 1993. "Guy de Chauliac (1300–1370): The 'Father of Surgery.'" *Annals of Vascular Surgery* 7 (March): 208–212.

Chemical and Biological Warfare

Chemical and biological weapons are often combined with nuclear explosive devices under the rubric "weapons of mass destruction."

"Chemical" and "biological," when applied to weapons, are surprisingly difficult terms to define. The *U.S. Army Field Manual 3-100, NBC Defense, Chemical Warfare, Smoke, and Flame Operations* (1991) defines a biological agent as any microorganism that causes disease in man, plants, or animals, or deterioration of materiel. A chemical agent is defined as a substance intended for use in military operations to kill, seriously injure, or incapacitate humans through its physiological effects. This definition excludes riot control agents, herbicides, smoke, and flame and is a matter of diplomatic debate. Tear gas agents represent a special case now included under the heading of chemical agents, although they have been used by military forces in situations indistinguishable from civilian crowd control by police.

The history of chemical warfare goes back for millennia. More than 2,000 years ago, the Chinese used smoke pots and the Japanese used pepper spray as lachrymatory agents. During the sieges of Platea and Belium, the Spartans used burning pitch and sulfur in attempts to overcome the cities' inhabitants. Flaming chemicals ("Greek Fire") were used by Crusaders against the Saracens in A.D. 673, and the British used burning sulfur against the Russians in the 1855 siege of Sebastapol. Similar agents were used by both sides in the U.S. Civil War and remained available until, over U.S. Navy Ad. Alfred Thayer Mahan's objections, the 1907 Hague Conference declared chemical weapons inhumane.

Biological weapons have also been used for centuries. Ancient warriors poisoned wells with decomposing bodies of animals, and a possibly apocryphal story has it that Mongol soldiers catapulted infected corpses into Genoese trading settlements on the Black Sea in 1346. The return of those traders fleeing the subsequent outbreak of disease is credited as the origin of the first wave of European black plague. Francisco Pizarro was accused of giving smallpox-contaminated clothing to Mesoamerican natives, and Lord Jeffrey Amherst and the British Army were accused of giving similarly infected blankets to North American Indians in 1763. During World War I, the Germans attempted to ship animals infected with anthrax and glanders to the United States and were alleged to have tried to spread cholera in Italy and plague in St. Petersburg, Russia, although they denied these allegations after the war.

The French were actually the first to use chemical weapons during World War I when they launched grenades filled with the irritant xylyl bromide in August 1914. In October 1914 at Neuve Chapelle and again in January 1915 at Bolimov on the Eastern Front, the Germans fired artillery shells filled with chemical irritants. The first large-scale use of chemical weapons took place at the Second Battle of Ypres when Germany released a cloud of chlorine gas that drifted over British, Canadian, French, and Algerian forces. By September 1915, the British had begun using chlorine as well, although gas freely released at ground level was subject to the vagaries of shifting winds and was generally of limited effectiveness. This disadvantage led to repeat attempts to deliver the gas with artillery shells.

Besides being difficult to deliver, chlorine was of variable effectiveness and was eventually replaced by the more potent irritants phosgene and mustard gas. Phosgene (coded CX) caused less immediate coughing so more irritant was inhaled; in addition, it caused more severe delayed pulmonary damage than chlorine. Diphosgene (coded DG) and chloropicrin (coded PS) were subsequently developed pulmonary irritants. Mustard gas (both nitrogen and sulfur variants) was first used against the Russians at Riga in 1917 and was delivered in artillery shells from that time. Unlike the earlier agents, it blistered the skin as well as damaging the lungs and was more difficult to defend against because gas masks alone were insufficient protection. The final blistering agent developed was lewisite (coded L), a liquid arsenical agent for which dimercaprol (British antilewisite, or BAL) is an antidote.

French forces launch a gas attack on German trenches in Flanders during World War I. (National Archives)

Once combatants developed protection mechanisms, gas warfare became relatively ineffective. After May 1915, only about 9 percent of British casualties resulted from gas exposure, and only about 3 percent of those were fatal, although many victims had permanent disability from pulmonary damage.

The 1925 Geneva Protocol, signed by 108 nations (but not the United States), prohibited the use in war of "asphyxiating, poisonous, or other gases and of bacteriological methods of warfare" but contained no enforcement measures, and most European countries, the Soviet Union, Japan, and the United States continued and expanded research on both biological and chemical agents after World War I.

The greatest advances were made by Germany with its development of hydrogen cyanide (which interferes with cellular oxygen metabolism and one form of which, under the name Zyklon B, was used for genocide) and the nerve gases tabun (coded as GA by the U.S. military), sarin (GB), and Soman (GD). (Because "GC" was military medical shorthand for gonorrhea, those letters were not used as a gas designation.)

The nerve gases act by inhibiting breakdown of the neurotransmitter acetylcholine and cause runny nose, wheezing, drooling, involuntary defecation and urination followed by convulsions, coma, and death. After World War II, the Soviets developed a viscid version of Soman that could be deployed from spray tanks and made it the major part of their chemical arsenal. Sarin was used by Japanese terrorists in attacks on the Tokyo subway system in the 1990s.

Although Italy employed mustard gas in conquest of Ethiopia in 1935–1936 with devastating effect, the threat of retaliation kept most combatants in World War II from using poison gases. The sole exception was infrequent use by the Japanese in China.

In 1936 the Japanese Army established its infamous Unit 731 in Manchuria to test and refine biological weapons, including the agents that cause anthrax, bacterial meningitis, cholera, shigellosis, and plague. The Japanese also experimented with the fungal agent terodotoxin. Plague-bearing fleas were released over the Chinese city of Changteh in 1941 and may have been responsible for as many as 10,000 deaths. After the war the United States granted immunity from prosecution to the members of this unit in exchange for the information on the experiments, even though a number were conducted on prisoners of war. The U.S. government considered this work invaluable in its own biological warfare program. The Soviet government, on the other hand, prosecuted 12 members of Unit 731 in December 1949.

German researchers during World War II experimented with hepatitis, malaria, and rickettsial diseases, but Adolph Hitler personally banned their use. Both the United States and the United Kingdom experimented with biological agents during World War II, and some 5,000 anthrax-containing bombs were produced at the American biological warfare facility at Camp Detrick (later Fort Detrick).

VX gas, a neurotoxin, was developed at the Porton Down Chemical Research Centre in Wiltshire, United Kingdom, in 1952. The British subsequently traded the technology for VX production with the United States in return for data on production of thermonuclear weapons. Unlike sarin and tabun, VX is a liquid that adheres to surfaces, is difficult to remove, and persists for long periods. In the liquid form, it is absorbed through the skin and can cause death in one to two hours. In its gaseous form, it causes death almost instantly. It is usually fatal in doses of 10 milligrams, although the anticholinergic drug atropine is an effective antidote and is regularly supplied to troops at risk of chemical attack. Atropine can be applied subcutaneously to counteract liquid VX but must be given directly into the heart to counteract the gaseous form.

A final agent bridges the gap between chemical and biological warfare. Ricin is a protein toxin derived from castor beans, which causes respiratory failure 36 to 72 hours after being inhaled or clotting failure, shock, and multiple organ failure after being ingested or injected. Bulgarian exile Georgi Markov was said to have been assassinated in London in 1978 by a member of his country's secret service who stabbed him with a sharpened umbrella tip contaminated with ricin.

The fact that the Soviets considered chemicals viable weapons became evident during the Yom Kippur War of 1973, when the Israelis captured Soviet-manufactured Egyptian tanks found to be equipped with "overpressure systems" that protected against gas attacks and chemical agents by maintaining a constant pressure differential between the inside of the vehicle and the outside environment. This information reversed efforts within the U.S. Army to abolish the Chemical Corps, the agency charged with conducting chemical defensive and offensive operations. The corps was directed to enhance defensive procedures and develop new chemical "binary" weapons. These were designed to be safer to deploy for the troops using them; the lethal gases were not actually created until the projectiles were en route to a target, at which time two chemicals combined to produce the toxic agent.

After World War II, the United States continued both offensive and defensive biological warfare experiments—including experiments using humans—at the Fort Detrick and a second facility at Pine Bluff, Arkansas. Studies of bacterial spread using nonpathogenic organisms were secretly conducted in San Francisco and New York City between 1951 and 1954. The Soviet Union maintained a massive biowarfare research facility on Vozrozhdeniye Island in the Aral Sea.

Fort Detrick was decommissioned in 1970 when President Richard Nixon made a unilateral policy decision to abandon biological warfare in advance of the 1972 Geneva Convention which would prohibit development, production, or stockpiling of biological weapons. The convention had no enforcement provisions and was vague on inspection, so the Soviet facility remained open until 1992. In its final years, Vozrozhdeniye Island housed a small city of 1,500 scientists and support workers and sophisticated animal-testing facilities, although, according to Gennadi Lepyoshkin, who directed the facility until its closure, the majority of research was defensive and was concentrated on protection against bacterial agents such as plague, botulism, and anthrax. Those claims notwithstanding, a 1979 outbreak of anthrax in Sverdlovsk, a city of 1.2 million 1,400 kilometers east of Moscow, was almost certainly the result of an inadvertent release of weaponized bacteria.

Although smallpox was eradicated worldwide in 1977, both the United States and the Soviet Union retained samples of the organism, and suspicion persists that one or both might have altered the virus to make it a usable weapon.

In 2001, anthrax was included in mail sent to several U.S. government officials, although the source of the agent and the reasons for its use remain unknown.

Although neither the Soviet Union nor the United States overtly used chemical agents against humans during the Cold War, toxic chemicals were widely used against plants. Between 1962 and 1971, the United States sprayed about 11 million gallons of Agent Orange (a mixture of two phenoxy herbicides) over 6 million acres of Viet Namese forest. Claims have persisted that either the Agent Orange or dioxin with which it was contaminated caused birth defects, delayed neurological damage, or cancer, although these claims have been difficult to prove.

Since the close of the Cold War, there have been scattered rumored and verified uses of chemical weapons against enemy combatants or civilians, including use by Egypt against Yemen, by Iraq against Iran, and by Iraq against its own Kurdish population. The United States maintains an active educational and logistic chemical defense program at Fort Leonard Wood, Missouri.

See also Anthrax; Fort Detrick; Human Experimentation; Japanese Military Medicine; Nuremberg Code; Plague (Bubonic Plague, Black Death); Unit 731; Vozrozhdeniye Island; World War I Medicine; World War II Medicine

References
Adams, Valerie. *Chemical Warfare, Chemical Disarmament*. Bloomington: Indiana University Press, 1990.
Bailey, Kathleen C. *Doomsday Weapons in the Hands of Man*. Urbana: University of Illinois Press, 1991.

Gilchrist, H. L., ed. *Warfare Gases: Their History, Description, Medical Aspects, and After Effects*. Washington D.C.: War Department, 1925.

Harris, Robert, and Jeremy Paxman. *A Higher Form of Killing: The Secret Story of Chemical and Biological Warfare*. New York: Hill and Wang, 1982.

Heller, Charles E. *Leavenworth Papers: Chemical Warfare in World War I, the American Experience, 1917–1918*. Washington D.C.: U.S. Government Printing Office, 1943.

Koblentz, Gregory. 2003–2004. "Pathogens as Weapons: The International Security Implications of Biological Warfare." *International Security* 28 (3): 84–122.

Reidel, Stefan. 2004. "Biological Warfare and Bioterrorism: A Historical Review." *Baylor University Medical Center Proceedings* 17 (October): 400–406.

Williams, Peter, and David Wallace. *Unit 731: Japan's Secret Biological Warfare in World War II*. New York: Free Press, 1989.

Zatchuk, Russ, and Ronald Bellamy, eds. *Medical Aspects of Chemical and Biological Warfare*. Bethesda, MD: Office of the Surgeon General, 1997.

Chest Injuries and Surgery

Wounds that penetrate the chest wall have been among the most common and most lethal of war wounds for longer than men have written about combat.

Chest injury is described in *The Iliad*, in which King Idomeneus of Crete killed Aleathous by putting a spear through his heart. Lack of anatomical knowledge, lack of understanding of infection and antisepsis, lack of anesthesia, and lack of blood replacement made chest surgery all but impossible for millennia thereafter, and it was largely ignored by Roman and medieval Arab authors including Galen, Albucasis, and Avicenna. Classical and medieval military surgeons were restricted to removing spears and arrows, occasional probing for foreign bodies, and putting occlusive dressing over the wounds to stop air leaks from punctured lungs.

In the 13th century, Rolando of Parma resected part of a necrotic lung that had herniated through the chest wall from a wound inflicted six days earlier, and the young patient survived to accompany his master on a crusade. Theodoric later wrote that it was actually his father, Ugo de Lucca, who had performed the operation and that Rolando was merely an assistant who had tried to steal credit for the successful surgery. Theodoric also described the frothy blood and poor skin color that resulted from penetration of the lung and the subsequent hypoxia; he recommended that any surgeon bold enough to contend with such an injury say three Paternosters and one prayer to Nicodemus (who was said to have removed the nails from Christ's hands and feet) before pulling an arrow out of the chest. Considering the possibility that the arrow might have penetrated the heart or a major vessel and that the shaft may be all that plugged the hole, prayers might well have been appropriate. Theodoric also made the more practical recommendation that the skin be tightly sutured and covered with an occlusive dressing to stop the loss of air from a perforated lung. Here he took exception with his contemporaries William of Salicet and Lanfranc of Milan, who favored leaving the wounds open to drain under the theory that contained infection was a greater risk than asphyxiation. That controversy would not be settled for another 800 years.

In the 1300s, French surgeon Guy de Chauliac first wrote that chest wounds that had disrupted the lung could be identified by placing a candle over the wound, pinching off the patient's nose and mouth, and watching for the flame to flicker. He evidently understood that movement of air in and out of the chest is caused by expanding the chest wall and lowering the diaphragm, effectively increasing the volume inside the thorax and drawing air in through the trachea or, in this case, through the wound. Chauliac also knew that posterior wounds were more likely to involve the heart or a great vessel and were, consequently, more dangerous. He also noted that a patient not getting enough oxygen was peculiarly anxious. Rather than closing chest wounds, he recommended placing a tented drain and irrigating the wound with wine, water, and honey to encourage any fluid to come out rather than accumulate and press on the lungs. The wound was only to be closed when all drainage had stopped.

In the 1400s, Giovanni de Vigo posited that gunpowder from newly available firearms was, of itself, poisonous and that all gunshot wounds had to be cauterized with hot irons or boiling oil, a mistake that would persist for the next hundred years. De Vigo was a bold and aggressive surgeon and said all chest wounds except those involving the heart directly should be surgically explored and that bleeding vessels should be identified and suture ligated.

The next real advance in chest surgery came with Ambroise Paré in the mid-1500s. Paré did not think gunpowder was poisonous and recommended gentle irrigation of wounds and avoidance of the cautery wherever possible. He gave the first description of diaphragmatic injury with herniation of abdominal contents into the chest when he treated a soldier who had sustained an arquebus wound and subsequently died when his colon moved into his thoracic cavity through a finger-size hole. Paré's contemporaries Wilhelm Fabry and Nicholas

Tulp (subject of Rembrandt's *The Anatomy Lesson of Dr. Tulp*) both reprised Rolando's resection of herniated bits of lung from chest wall injuries. In the next century, Hermann Boerhaave offered the first description of ruptured esophagus, which had occurred in the Dutch grand admiral Baron de Wassenaer. He also suggested using anticoagulants and suction to liquefy and remove blood that had extravasated into the chest cavity.

Treatment of chest wounds took a great step forward with Leopold Auenbrugger's description of auscultation (tapping on the chest) in 1761 and René Laennec's stethoscope in 1861. Both furnished information about the lungs' state of inflation and the presence or absence of collections of blood in the thoracic cavity, and were all the physician had with which to make a diagnosis of intrathoracic injury until X-ray became available in the closing years of the 19th century.

At the same time X-ray made accurate diagnosis possible, surgical advances finally made the treatment of chest injuries feasible. In 1896, Stephen Paget published the first English text devoted entirely to thoracic surgery. Referring to data collected during the Franco-Prussian War, he noted that the mortality rate from gunshot wounds to the chest was 60 percent. The argument about whether those wounds should be closed or left open to drain was still not entirely settled; the suggestion that the wounds only be closed if a surgeon was readily available to reopen them as necessary was a compromise. The question of whether gunshot wounds should be probed or left alone was also unsettled, although Paget did note that, if one were to probe, the finger was the instrument of choice.

Modern chest surgery is the result of a series of late-19th- and early-20th-century discoveries. First, Lord Joseph Lister convinced surgeons of the need for antisepsis to prevent infection. Then, in 1909, Samuel Melzer and John Auer adapted a technique Andreas Vesalius had suggested 350 years earlier and used positive pressure through a tube in the trachea to make it possible to open a chest under anesthesia and still ventilate the patient. Those developments, together with Karl Landsteiner's blood typing and transfusion discoveries, finally made it possible to open a chest and repair even the serious injuries to the heart and great vessels and have the patient survive.

See also Antisepsis; Chauliac, Guy de; Fabry of
   Hilden, Wilhelm; Lanfranc of Milan; Lister,
   Lord Joseph; Salicetti, Guglielmo (William
   of Salicet); Theodoric, Bishop of Cervia
   (Teodorico Borgognoni); Transfusion;
   Vesalius, Andreas

References

Lindskog, Gustaf. 1961. "Some Historical
   Aspects of Thoracic Trauma." *Journal of
   Thoracic and Cardiovascular Surgery* 42 (July):
   1–11.
Melzer, Samuel J., and John Auer. 1909.
   "Continuous Respiration without Respira-
   tory Movements." *Journal of Experimental
   Medicine* 11: 622–625.

Chimborazo Hospital

Chimborazo Hospital was operated by the Confederate States of America during the American Civil War. It opened October 11, 1861, and operated until the fall of Richmond, Virginia, in 1865.

Chimborazo was America's largest military hospital, with more than 8,000 beds at its peak, and was established by order of Confederate surgeon general Samuel Preston Moore. It was made an independent post under the command of Dr. James B. McGaw, a Medical College of Virginia faculty member and Richmond practitioner who had begun the war as a cavalry officer before being called back to run the hospital. The Medical College of Virginia was the only Southern medical school that remained open through the war, and McGaw used Chimborazo to train more than 400 new physicians during the conflict.

The hospital occupied Chimborazo Heights above the James River outside Richmond on grounds that had originally been intended as winter quarters for the Army of Northern Virginia. It comprised 150 identical, one-story, wood-frame buildings measuring 100 feet long, 30 feet wide, and seven feet high with 10 windows in each structure. Each building housed from 40 to 60 patients, each of whom was intended to have 800 to 1,000 cubic feet of well-ventilated air space. In addition, eight to 10 convalescents occupied each of 100 Sibley tents pitched on the surrounding hillsides. The complex had five ice houses, Russian bathhouses, a bakery that produced 10,000 loaves of bread a day, a brewery that produced 400 kegs at a time of beer, and a farm with 200 cows and 3,500 goats. Careful attention was paid to sanitation and drainage from both hospital and farm facilities.

Chimborazo was divided into five administrative divisions of 30 buildings, each designated to care for men from specific states. Where possible, the men were housed with others from the same locality and cared for by physicians from as near their home counties as possible. Each division had a surgeon and a variable number of assistants with an average of 45 physicians assigned to the entire institution at any time. The divisions also had a matron and several assistants responsible for food preparation and laundry.

In spite of chronic shortages of medicine, supplies, and food, Chimborazo had an impressively low 9 percent mortality rate for the war. Beyond that, detailed statistics are lacking since virtually all the hospital's records were lost in the Richmond fires of 1865. The hospital was formally surrendered when the city fell in 1865, and McGaw returned to practice and teaching, eventually becoming dean of the Medical College of Virginia in Richmond. His son, Walter Drew McGaw, served as chief surgeon of the American Expeditionary Force and established a number of hospitals in France during World War I.

Richmond was the Confederacy's center of medical care during the Civil War. In addition to the Medical College of Virginia, Richmond boasted 19 other large hospitals, the next largest being Winder with just under 5,000 beds. Chimborazo remains the most famous of Civil War hospitals.

See also Civil War in the United States

References

Cunningham, H. H. *Doctors in Gray: The Confederate Medical Service*. Baton Rouge: Louisiana State University Press, 1958.

Hume, Edgar Erskine. 1934. "The Days Gone By: Chimborazo Hospital Confederate States Army; America's Largest Military Hospital." *Military Surgeon* 75 (September): 156–166.

Cholera

Cholera is an acute diarrheal disease caused by the gram-negative bacillus *Vibrio cholerae*.

The organism is transmitted when drinking water is contaminated with feces from an infected person. Cholera is manifested primarily as an extraordinarily copious diarrhea that typically results in the loss of as much as 30 liters of fluid a day. Shock follows, and, if untreated, cholera has a death rate of approximately 60 percent. Because the high-volume stools are contaminated with infectious organisms, the disease readily assumes epidemic or even pandemic proportions.

The first reports of "Asiatic" cholera came from British military authorities in India's Ganges River delta in 1770, and the first pandemic, which spread from Japan to the Mediterranean, occurred between 1817 and 1823. Eight subsequent worldwide outbreaks have occurred.

British physician John Snow (also known for delivering Queen Victoria's child using anesthesia and popularizing that practice in the United Kingdom) demonstrated that a London cholera outbreak in 1854 originated at a single community pump that drew contaminated water from the Thames River. By removing the pump handle, Snow was able to stop the epidemic. He subsequently performed a large-scale epidemiologic study that proved transmission of cholera by water containing sewage. Later in the 19th century, German bacteriologist Robert Koch isolated *Vibrio cholerae* and proved it to be the causative agent.

American military physicians have played a central role in understanding how cholera causes disease and in controlling it. In 1947, Commander Robert A. Phillips of the U.S. Naval Medical Research Unit 3 in Cairo, Egypt, showed that cholera stool was isotonic with blood and contained a high concentration of sodium bicarbonate. Those findings suggested that replacement of fluid and electrolytes might counteract the disease's direct effects, volume depletion and acidosis. Using high-volume intravenous fluids, Phillips was able to reduce the death

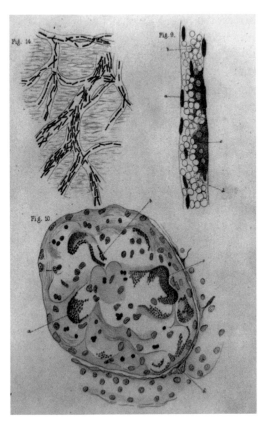

Illustration of the Vibrio cholerae *bacteria from Robert Koch's* Investigations into the Etiology of Traumatic Infective Diseases, *1880. (Library of Congress)*

rate from cholera to 7.5 percent, but his work was largely ignored until 1958 when he repeated it in a Bangkok epidemic.

He and his co-workers also cut a hole in the center of a standard army cot and attached it to a rubber funnel to drain off the "rice water" stools pouring from their patients. By combining fluid replacement and better nursing methods, Phillips and his Navy colleagues lowered the death rate in Bangkok to 0.6 percent.

During the 1960s, researchers at the National Institutes of Health and the Walter Reed Army Institute of Research showed that cholera does not destroy intestinal lining cells but merely changes those cells' ability to retain body fluids. That discovery led U.S. Army physician Norbert Hirschorn, working in Pakistan, to try giving replacement fluids by mouth rather than intravenously. He showed not only that fluids could be replaced orally but also that the treatment actually decreased the volume of diarrhea and shortened the disease. The American military developed packets of replacement salts that could be distributed to villagers who did not have access to medical care. The packets made it possible for people in rural areas to treat themselves and have proven highly effective in lowering the death rate not only from cholera but also from other diarrheal diseases.

Finally, in 1963, Richard Finkelstein, working at Walter Reed Army Medical Center, isolated the specific exotoxin responsible for cholera's effect on the intestinal lining.

See also Military Sanitation; Shock

Reference
Lim, M. L., G. S. Murphy, M. Calloway, and D. Tribble. 2005. "History of U.S. Military Contributions to the Study of Diarrheal Diseases." *Military Medicine* 170 (April Suppl.): 30–38.

Church, Benjamin (1734–1776)

Benjamin Church was the first director general and chief physician of the American army.

He was born in Newport, Rhode Island, and educated at Boston Latin School and Harvard College, from which he graduated in 1754. He received his medical degree from London Medical College and married an English woman while studying in London. After returning to the United States he practiced in Boston.

Church was named director general and chief physician of the Continental Army at a salary of $4 a day on July 27, 1775. Like his successors, he spent the bulk of his time struggling to get funding for personnel and supplies.

After serving for only three months, he was found to be communicating in code with a British officer. Although controversy exists over whether he was supplying legitimate information about American strength and positions or was deliberately misleading the British in an attempt to reach an early negotiated peace, he was tried successively by the Massachusetts Provincial Congress, a military court martial, and a council of the Continental Congress chaired by Gen. George Washington. Each found him guilty, and he was imprisoned at Norwich, Connecticut, for four months. His health failed, and he was released to Boston on parole but, in danger from irate citizens, was allowed to emigrate to the West Indies with his family. His ship was lost at sea, with no survivors found.

See also American Revolutionary War; Cochran, John; Morgan, John; Shippen, William, Jr.

References

Ashburn, P. M. *A History of the Medical Department of the United States Army*. Boston: Houghton Mifflin Co., 1929.

Gillet, Mary. *The Army Medical Department, 1775–1818*. Washington, D.C.: Center of Military History, 1981.

Packard, Francis. *History of Medicine in the United States*. New York: Paul B. Hoeber, Inc., 1931.

Reiss, Oscar. *Medicine and the American Revolution*. Jefferson, NC: McFarland & Co., Inc., 1998.

Civil War in the United States

Better weapons, better transport, and better surgery made the American Civil War (1861–1865) an inflection point in the history of military medicine.

Although anesthesia had been used sparingly in the Mexican-American War and more widely in the Crimean War, it became standard in the Civil War. The potential benefits were, however, tempered by the fact that Lord Joseph Lister would not apply emerging knowledge of bacterial infection and its control with antiseptics until the year after the war ended. More accurate rifles; rapid-fire, machine-operated guns; and better artillery released on masses of poorly defended troops resulted in unprecedented numbers of casualties. Even worse than the casualties resulting from improved firepower was the loss from infectious diseases precipitated by large numbers of men living in crowded, unsanitary conditions.

American medicine was just beginning to question "heroic" practices such as purging, bleeding, and liberal use of mercury and arsenic, but the majority of practitioners had yet to admit that their standard remedies seldom helped and almost always did harm. Most physicians thought sanitation important, although the conviction was based on empirical observation and the mistaken rationale that bad air (miasma) was responsible for most disease.

In the end, the most successful military medical advances of the war were in organizing transportation and care for masses of casualties.

When the war started, the U.S. Army had only 16,000 troops and 114 physicians, almost all of whom were attached to specific regiments. After secession, eight surgeons and 29 assistant surgeons resigned and joined the Confederacy. The Union Army grew to 109,000 in the first four months of the war, and the Confederacy experienced a similar expansion. Most of the new volunteers joined geographically based regiments of around 1,200 men, and the regimental commander was responsible for picking his own surgeon and assistant and assigning a steward (usually a noncommissioned officer) and 10 or 12 aides, who were most often either members of the regimental band or physically unfit for combat. The physicians were generally from the regiment's home area, had widely variable training and ability, and almost never had experience treating major injuries. Still, it was considered important for the new soldiers to be cared for by people they knew and trusted.

In the war's first few battles, each regimental surgeon set up his own aid station in whatever protected area he could find within a few hundred yards of the front line and raised a red flag so the wounded or those drafted to carry them could find him. Although there were often better protected and better supplied hospitals farther to the rear, the regimental surgeons were reluctant to release their wounded and the men were reluctant to leave their friends. As a result, some aid stations were overwhelmed with casualties while others were idle.

In the July 1861 Battle of Bull Run, the Union Army suffered 2,708 casualties. Appointed stretcher bearers fled, and the wounded lay on the field for days. Those who were able were forced to walk the 27 miles back to Washington before they could be treated. Men carried to an aid station were likely to have bullets removed, their skulls opened, or their limbs amputated by men who were doing the operations for the first time.

When the war started, Union surgeon general Thomas Lawton was more than 80 years old and had neither the energy nor the ability to manage the demands of the medical corps. He was replaced by Clement A. Finley shortly after Fort Sumter's surrender, but Finley was also well up in years and had no experience appropriate to his new job. Recognizing the seriousness of the situation, a minister, Henry Bellows, and three physicians, W. H. Van Buren, Elisha Harris, and Jacob Hansen, representing a variety of charitable and religious organizations, created the U.S. Sanitary Commission and modeled it after a similarly named British group. The commission successfully lobbied Congress for official status and, under Executive Secretary Frederick Law Olmsted, began furnishing food, clothing, and medical supplies to the Union troops. Over widespread objections from the medical corps, it also assumed supervision of camp sanitation. The latter was especially important as measles and dysentery had become rife among groups of previously unexposed young men thrown into close quarters with relatively immune former urban residents.

The commissioners also recognized Finley's shortcomings and pressed to have him replaced. In January 1862, 34-year-old William A. Hammond was named surgeon general. Hammond cooperated with the commission's efforts to sanitize camps, replaced the least qualified of his regimental surgeons, and removed some of the most dangerous drugs from the formulary. He went on to establish an army medical school, to build a general hospital in Washington using the new pavilion design, to create an army pathological museum that resulted in the monumental *Medical and Surgical History of the War of the Rebellion*, and to establish a central laboratory for the army.

Perhaps his greatest contribution was in improved transport of the wounded. Ham-

Newly organized ambulance corps conducts a drill during the Civil War. (Francis Trevelyan Miller and Robert Sampson Lanier. The Photographic History of the Civil War, *vol 7, 1911)*

mond insisted that ambulance transport be removed from line command and placed under the medical corps with designated bearers and drivers. Charles Tripler, who designed unwieldy 10-person ambulances, had been surgeon to the Army of the Potomac after August 1861, but was unable to cope with the flood of injured and the explosion of disease in the malarial swamps of the Peninsula Campaign. Hammond replaced him with Jonathan Letterman in July 1862. Letterman discarded Tripler's ambulances in favor of smaller, better-suspended wagons. He demanded and got one ambulance for every 150 soldiers and an additional two supply wagons for each regiment's medical supplies. He organized evacuation of the wounded so well that, at Antietam in September 1862, his stretcher bearers and ambulances had every one of the 9,420 Union wounded off the field before the day ended.

As a result of his challenges to the regimental medical system, his removal of treasured drugs from the formulary, his young age, and his frequent arguments with Secretary of War Simon Cameron, Hammond's career was in constant jeopardy. He was eventually court-martialed and relieved of his position, and Letterman resigned shortly thereafter.

The Confederacy had a similarly talented surgeon general in Samuel Preston Moore. In spite of the fact that his government only allocated $50,000 for hospital construction and supply and left the medical corps chronically short of drugs and supplies, Moore created a creditable hospital system, devised ingenious substitutes for missing materials, and maintained a generally high level of practice throughout the war.

From the beginning, field hospitals were most often housed in walled tents that could hold up to 20 patients or be strung to-gether to hold twice that many. The earliest general hospitals were set up in whatever large buildings could be commandeered—hotels, houses, and warehouses being common solutions—and were under regimental control. Their inefficiency and poor sanitation led to their being replaced by pavilion hospitals under the medical corps, especially after the numbers of sick and wounded went up in 1862. By 1863, the U.S. Army Medical Corps had 151 hospitals and 58,716 beds, mostly well ventilated and at least marginally clean. In 1864, Maj. Gen. Ulysses S. Grant authorized a 6,000-bed hospital at City Point, Virginia, that ultimately expanded to 10,000 beds and had 18 trains continuously running between it and the front near Petersburg, Virginia.

The Union also created specialized hospitals for particular injuries and illnesses, including Turner's Lane General Hospital in Philadelphia for nervous and neurologic problems, the DesMarres Hospital in Chicago for wounds and diseases of the eye, a hospital in Nashville for erysipelas, and another in New York City for treatment of the severely mutilated. The Confederates also built a number of hospitals, although, with the exception of a few large facilities such as Chimborazo and Winder in Richmond, Virginia, they tended to be dedicated to soldiers of particular states rather than to the army as a whole.

Throughout the war, most nursing care was done by men, but, particularly on the Union side, notable experiments were conducted using female nurses beginning with Dorothea Dix, who was appointed the first superintendent of female nurses for the army, and including such women as Louisa May Alcott and Clara Barton. By the war's end, 3,200 women had served as Union Army nurses. After 1862, Confederate hospitals were assigned matrons responsible for "the domestic economy" of the institutions and for supervising the male nurses and black staff assigned to ward duty, but the South never matched the Union in its use of women caregivers.

The major advance in surgical care was the general use of anesthesia. At the start of the war, chloroform was not universally accepted: Confederate John Chisolm's *Manual of Military Surgery* said, "We do not hesitate to say, that it should be given to every patient requiring a serious or painful operation" (Chisolm 1989, 381–382). On the other hand, Samuel Gross's similar volume for the Union surgeons recommended against its use in the severely wounded lest it exacerbate vascular collapse. Perhaps Southern surgeons had better luck because they routinely preceded anesthesia with a healthy dose of brandy.

Chloroform could be prepared by distilling chloride of lime with alcohol in a copper still and was usually administered by soaking a sponge and placing it over a folded cloth cone covering the face. The degree of anesthesia was gauged by the noise and depth of breathing. If anesthesia was too deep, the patient was revived with fresh air, cold water on the face, or cold water enemas. Ether was used occasionally and was generally safer but harder to initiate because of associated vomiting and a feeling of suffocation. In the end, about 80,000 operations were performed under anesthesia by each side.

About 94 percent of Civil War wounds were caused by bullets, as compared to World War I, in which 75 percent were caused by either shrapnel or artillery, and the Iraq War, in which the majority have thus far been blast injuries. The bullet most often used during the Civil War, the Minié ball, had a butt that expanded in the rifle's barrel, imparting a spin that gave the projectile a relatively long range considering its weight. The balls tended to wobble and create large tracks with a subsequent high risk of vascular injury. Injuries to the head, chest, and abdomen carried a universally high mortality rate. Wounds to the head requiring trephine had 61 percent death rate, those penetrating the chest 62 percent, and those penetrating the abdomen 87 percent. Although 70 percent of projectile wounds involved the arms or legs, extremity injuries that involved a joint, that caused a compound fracture, or that became infected usually resulted in field amputation, an operation Philadelphia surgeon William Williams Keen reckoned was seven times more dangerous than having fought at Gettysburg.

Even with those gruesome statistics, disease was a greater threat than battle injury on both sides. Early in the war, infections such as measles, tonsillar abscesses, and upper respiratory infections from putting nonimmune young men together were common. As conditions in camps deteriorated, sanitary shortcomings led to dysentery, typhoid, lice-borne typhus, erysipelas, and scabies. Venereal disease was common throughout the war, as was malaria.

Because of Hammond's insistence on meticulous record keeping, accurate mortality and morbidity numbers for the Union Army are available. Because the South had no such system and because most of what military medical records Confederate surgeons did collect were burned in Richmond near the war's end, numbers for that army are approximate. Of the 2,893,304 who served in the Union Army, 138,154 men died in bat-

tle and 224,586 succumbed to disease. The Confederacy lost about 94,000 in battle and 164,000 to disease of the approximately 1.3 million who served.

See also Ambulances and Transport; Amputation; Anesthesiology; Barton, Clara; Chimborazo Hospital; Hammond, William; Hospital Trains; Keen, William Williams; Letterman, Jonathan; Moore, Samuel Preston; Nursing in the Military

References

Ashburn, P. M. *A History of the Medical Department of the United States Army*. Boston: Houghton Mifflin Co., 1929.

Bayne-Jones, Stanhope. *The Evolution of Preventive Medicine in the United States Army, 1607–1939*. Washington, D.C.: Office of the Surgeon General, Department of the Army, 1968.

Chisolm, John Julian. *A Manual of Military Surgery for the Use of Surgeons in the Confederate Army: With an Appendix of the Rules and Regulations of the Medical Department of the Confederate Army*. San Francisco: Norman Publishing, 1989, 381–382 (originally published 1861).

Cunningham, H. H. *Doctors in Gray: The Confederate Medical Service*. Baton Rouge: Louisiana State University Press, 1960.

Freemon, Frank, *Gangrene and Glory: Medical Care during the American Civil War*. Urbana: University of Illinois Press, 2001.

Gillett, Mary. *Army Medical Department, 1818–1865*. Washington, D.C.: Government Printing Office, 1987.

Gross, Samuel. *A Manual of Military Surgery, or Hints on the Emergencies of Field, Camp, and Hospital Practice*. Philadelphia: Lippincott, 1861. Reprinted by Norman Publishing, 1988.

Moore, Samuel Preston, ed. *A Manual of Military Surgery Prepared for the Confederate States Army*. Richmond, VA: Ayres & Wade, 1863. Reprinted by Norman Publishing, 1989.

Packard, Francis R. *History of Medicine in the United States*. New York: Paul B. Hoeber, Inc., 1931.

Classical Greek Military Medicine

The classical period of Greek science is usually dated to Egyptian-trained Thales of Miletus (639–544 B.C.), who successfully predicted a solar eclipse based on reasoned analysis of prior events.

Early classical Greek physicians tended to be organizers and observers rather than experimenters, and most were seduced by the fallacies of Pythagorean numerology. Starting with the four elements of Empedocles (earth, air, fire, and water) and the four physical qualities (hot, cold, moist, and dry), they developed a humoral system in which hot and moist were equated with blood, which was, in turn, associated with air; hot and dry with yellow bile and fire; cold and moist with phlegm and water; and cold and dry with black bile and earth. Disease was thought to result from an imbalance in the humors, and later Galenic and Arabic pharmacologists went to great lengths to assign counterqualities (for instance, sugar was thought to have cold qualities to overcome fever's heat) to various herbs, chemicals, and concoctions that presumably allowed them to restore balance and health.

Greek physicians also attempted to restore humoral balance with a combination of blood letting, purging, and emetics. To their credit, they also emphasized massage, hydrotherapy, good diet, fresh air, and rest and, unlike their Egyptian and Mesopotamian predecessors, looked at illness as an abnormality of bodily function rather than invasion by an alien force.

Among the numerous classical schools of Greek medicine, the three most prominent were the above-mentioned Pythagoreans, the Cnidians from Asia Minor, and the Coans from the Ionian Islands. The Cnidian School stressed categorization of disease and espoused detailed treatments for each. Hippocrates, a scion of the rival Coans, ridiculed Cnidian practice as the medicine of library classifiers, although in retrospect, their chief physician, Euryphon, seems a direct precursor of the great Swedish taxonomist Carl Linné.

The Hippocratic school, based on the island of Cos, emphasized examination of the patient and prognosis in a framework of general rather than detailed categorization. It is likely that the two major schools of Greek medicine, both seated in or near Asia Minor, benefited from an infusion of Mesopotamian and Indian medical knowledge. Indeed, the humoral theories of Greek and Indian medicine are strikingly similar.

The classical Greek physician typically worked from a clean, well-lit clinic ($i\alpha\tau\rho\acute{e}i o\nu$) stocked with an assortment of surgical instruments, a pharmacy, and, often, its own library. Greeks knew how to use a tourniquet to stop bleeding and recognized that gangrene would result if circulation was cut off for too long. However, they did not know how to ligate vessels and were repeatedly faced with either leaving the tourniquet longer than they should or releasing it too soon and having hemorrhage resume. This may explain why the technique was lost until Ambroise Paré reintroduced it two millennia later.

Classical Greeks irrigated wounds with clean water, vinegar, and wine (demonstrated to have antibacterial properties unassociated with its alcohol content); sutured clean wounds with bronze needles; and dressed them with honey and oxides of copper, zinc, and mercury. They drained pus collections inside the chest with tin tubes, another technique lost until modern times. They located skull fractures by enlarging the wound and painting the bone with ink, which stained a subtle fracture line after being washed from the healthy bone. However, they then recommended opening the skull only if a fracture was not present, reasoning that evil humors that could escape a disrupted skull would be trapped if the bone was intact.

Greek physicians' ability to reason was both a blessing and a curse. The first documented use of the word "hypothesis" is in Hippocrates's *On Ancient Medicine* (also the first known treatise on medical history). Their reasoning, however, led them seriously astray in treating wounds. As virtually all wounds became infected, the Greeks made the false post hoc assumption that pus formation was a natural and necessary part of healing. They did recognize that white pus without an odor which resulted from liquefaction of dead tissue had a better prognosis than foul-smelling yellow exudates caused by infection, and they tried to encourage formation of the former by putting foreign objects such as lint and raw wool into the wound. The foreign bodies regularly led to wound sepsis and, unfortunately, the practice persisted to the mid-18th century and resulted in immeasurable suffering and uncounted deaths.

Greeks did not amputate injured limbs and treated most fresh wounds by cauterization, another unfortunate practice finally discredited by Paré. They accurately described the hydrophobia, trismus, and opisthotonic arching of tetanus and noted that it often followed seemingly minor wounds. Greek surgeons used metal probes rather than their fingers to examine wounds, although, because they did not sterilize the instruments, the technique was of doubtful benefit.

Greeks were the first to describe warfare's psychiatric effects; Ajax's massacring sheep under the delusion that they were enemy soldiers was a particularly graphic early example. They recognized mental problems in veterans in what was probably the first description of posttraumatic stress or battle fatigue.

With the exception of Sparta, the Greek city-states did not maintain standing armies and so did not have dedicated military surgeons. The Spartans did grant military surgeons the high status of noncombatant officials and housed them with nobles, soothsayers, and flute players. Lycurgus's law mandated that surgeons withdraw to the rear of the right flank during battle, presumably so the helots who carried wounded soldiers from the field would know where to find them. When Xenophon took his 10,000 soldiers on campaign into Mesopotamia, he included a small group of military surgeons and co-opted more from local cities. Besides wounds, his physicians were called on to treat snow blindness, frostbite, and gangrene on the retreat to Greece.

Xenophon's Persian opponents were served almost entirely by mercenary physicians—mostly from Egypt and Greece—who stressed the importance of clean campsites, good diet, and exercise for the troops' general health.

Estimates of casualty rates from surviving descriptions of classical battles were vastly different between winners and losers. On the victorious side, the death rate was 5.5 percent and another 5.8 percent were wounded. For the losers the death rate was 37.7 percent and the wounded 35.4 percent, for a total of 73.1 percent. The difference may reflect wounds inflicted on routed losers after the actual battle or, possibly, historical editing, as the numbers are generally drawn from texts written by the winners.

Alexander the Great maintained a large standing army and a regular medical corps. Seven named physicians accompanied him on his march to India, including his personal surgeon, who extracted arrows from the king's shoulder and eye during the campaign and was at his bedside when he died (probably of malaria) before returning to Macedonia. One of Alexander's physicians, Glaucus, was crucified for failing to cure Haephaestion when the warrior fell ill.

After the time of Hippocrates, Greek physicians divided medicine first into physiology, etiology, hygiene, semiology, and therapeutics. Later empiricists kept only semiology and therapeutics, which they subdivided into diet, pharmacology, surgery, and hygiene. Aristotle (384–322 B.C.) was a disciple of Aesculapius and a pupil of Plato credited with founding zoology, botany, embryology, comparative anatomy, and physiology. He used dissection to teach his students anatomy and was the preeminent authority in biology until Linné. Although Aristotle's works marked a signal advance in understanding of biology, they also gave rise to monumental and persistent errors such as the conviction that the heart was the seat of sensation and the brain was a gland that secreted cold humors to counteract the heart's heat.

The school at Alexandria was founded in 331 B.C. as a center of Greek medical education and research. The writings of Galen, Celsus, Soranus, Rufus of Ephesus, and Aretaeus of Cappadocia were based on works in the Alexandrine library, which was destroyed in the second century A.D. The greatest of the Alexandrian physicians were Herophilos, credited with bringing the scientific method to medicine and called the father of experimental anatomy, and Erisistratos, credited as the father of experimental physiology. According to Celsus in his *De Re Medicina*, these two did their research "in the best way by far, when they laid open men whilst alive—criminals retrieved from royal prisons—and whilst these were still breathing, observed parts which beforehand nature had concealed, their position, color, shape, size, arrangement, hardness, softness, smoothness, relation, processes, and depressions of each, and whether any part is inserted into or is received into another."

In Alexandria, Egyptian and Greek medicine merged and the result was exported to Mesopotamia, where it was augmented with Sumerian and Abyssinian knowledge and ultimately emerged in Arabic science. By the dawn of the Roman Empire, Greek, Egyptian, and Indian medicine had incorporated a broad range of skills and knowledge. Practitioners could stop hemorrhage with a tourniquet, clean wounds, establish sanitary surroundings for their soldiers, remove foreign bodies, treat fractures and dislocations, suture clean wounds, and use drugs for analgesia and limited anesthesia. However, the information was neither universal nor widely shared and was not organized into a single body of knowledge that could be generally disseminated. As a result, no single practitioner had access to all the available skills, and many useful techniques were lost for centuries.

See also Celsus, Aulus Cornelius; Galen of Pergamum; Hippocrates of Cos; Indian Military Medicine; Lister, Lord Joseph; Minoan and Ancient Greek Military Medicine; Paré, Ambroise

References
Daremberg, Charles. *État de la Medecine entry Homèr & Hippocrate*. Paris: Librairie Académique Didier et Cie., 1869.
Davis, Victor Hansen. *The Western Way of War: Infantry Battle in Classical Greece*. New York: Alfred A. Knopf, 1989.

Garrison, Fielding. *An Introduction to the History of Medicine.* Philadelphia: W. B. Saunders Co., 1929.

Grissinger, Jay. 1927. "The Development of Military Medicine." *Bulletin of the New York Academy of Medicine* 3 (May): 301–356.

Jones, W. H. S. *Philosophy and Medicine in Ancient Greece.* New York: Arno Press, 1979.

Majno, Guido. *The Healing Hand: Man and Wound in the Ancient World.* Cambridge, MA: Harvard University Press, 1975.

Salazar, Christine. *The Treatment of War Wounds in Graeco-Roman Antiquity.* Leiden, the Netherlands: Brill, 2000.

Clowes, William
(1540–1604)

William Clowes was the foremost Elizabethan-era military and naval surgeon and an expert on syphilis.

Clowes was born in Kingsbury, Warwickshire, England, the son of Thomas Clowes, who had high enough social stature to warrant his own coat of arms. William was apprenticed to London barber-surgeon George Keble at age 12. During his six-year apprenticeship, he personally witnessed Queen Elizabeth I's coronation. In the years to come, his fortune and career were closely associated with the new monarch.

Clowes completed his training at 19 years of age and joined the Earl of Warwick's unsuccessful venture to Normandy in support of the Protestant cause and its leader, the Prince of Condé. The English forces were pushed back into Le Havre and, crowded into the city and poorly supplied from across the English Channel, were devastated by a combination of plague and scurvy. Clowes, hampered by lack of adequate supplies, wrote that he found his fingers the best of surgical instruments and scabbards quite satisfactory splints.

When the defeated English forces came home, Clowes joined the Royal Navy and served as surgeon's mate for the next five years, during which time he acquired the experience treating syphilis that resulted in his work *De Morbo Gallico*, which he published in 1585. With Queen Elizabeth's support, Clowes was appointed assistant surgeon to St. Bartholomew's Hospital in 1576. He stayed there for eight years, rising to become the first in a line of distinguished surgeons associated with that institution.

At age 41, Clowes reentered the military and joined the Earl of Leicester in the Low Country wars. In 1588, he was named surgeon to the fleet that had gathered to meet the Armada that Philip II of Spain sent against England. After English forces defeated the Armada, Clowes returned to practice and trained his son in surgery. The younger Clowes later served as sergeant surgeon to King Charles I.

His 1581 *A Proved Practice for all Young Chirurgions Concerning Burnings with Gunpowder and Wounds Made With Gunshot* was the first book in English that dealt with gunshot wounds in a naval context. In 1596, Clowes published *A Profitable and Necessary Book of Observations*, a compendium of his extensive surgical and medical experience. Clowes spent his career as a wound surgeon, and neither these nor any of his several other books ever mention an elective operation.

Clowes died at 64 years of age in 1604.

See also British Military Medicine; Naval Medicine; 16th-Century Military Medicine; Syphilis

References
Roddis, Louis. *A Short History of Nautical Medicine.* New York: Paul B. Hoeber, Inc., 1941.

Zimmerman, Leo, and Ilza Veith. *Great Ideas in the History of Surgery*. Baltimore: Williams & Wilkins Co., 1961.

Cochran, John
(1730–1807)

John Cochran was the final director general of the Continental medical service during the Revolutionary War.

Cochran was born in Chester County, Pennsylvania. His medical training comprised only an apprenticeship under Dr. Robert Thompson, leaving him the only Revolutionary War medical director without formal education. He served as a surgeon's mate during the French and Indian War before practicing in Albany, New York, and then in New Brunswick, New Jersey. While in Albany he married the sister of Philip Schuyler, a wealthy landowner who was to become a general in the Continental Army.

Cochran specialized in variolation against smallpox and directed Gen. George Washington's compulsory inoculation program. He volunteered for the American army in December 1776 and was named physician and surgeon in chief to the Middle Department on Washington's recommendation in 1777. He helped William Shippen draft the medical service reorganization of 1777 and served as private physician to the Marquis de Lafayette when the latter contracted pneumonia.

He succeeded Shippen as director general of the medical service in 1781, a job he held until the end of the revolution. Cochran was mustered out in 1783 and returned to practice in New York City. Washington appointed him commissioner of loans for the state of New York, a job he held until his death from apoplexy in 1807.

In spite of his lack of formal education, Cochran was the most effective of the Revolutionary War medical directors.

See also American Revolutionary War; Church, Benjamin; Morgan, John; Shippen, William, Jr.; Smallpox

References
Ashburn, P. M. *A History of the Medical Department of the United States Army*. Boston: Houghton Mifflin Co., 1929.
Gillet, Mary. *The Army Medical Department, 1775–1818*. Washington, D.C.: Center of Military History, 1981.
Packard, Francis. *History of Medicine in the United States*. New York: Paul B. Hoeber, Inc., 1931.
Reiss, Oscar. *Medicine and the American Revolution: How Diseases and Their Treatments Affected the Colonial Army*. Jefferson, NC: McFarland & Co., Inc., 1998.

Cold Injury and Frostbite

Damage usually occurs when water molecules freeze and crystallize in biologic tissue, resulting in cellular and then tissue death. Frostbite and cold injury are complicated by vasospasm, which then leads to failure of circulation, infarction, and further tissue loss.

Cold injuries are divided into four degrees of clinical severity: blanching, clear blistering, hemorrhagic blistering, and frank necrosis. All are most common on body parts exposed to the cold and at the extreme reaches of the vascular tree, so 90 percent of frostbite occurs in either the hands or feet and most of the rest in the nose or ears. Fatigue, alcohol abuse, diabetes, and cigarette smoking all increase susceptibility to frostbite. Under similar conditions, females are twice as likely as males to suffer frostbite. A striking racial predilection has also been documented: African American troops in Korea had an incidence of the disease four times that of their Caucasian counterparts. It is also more common in younger than older adults. Two-thirds of the cases in the U.S. Army are in soldiers between 20 and 29 years of age.

Frostbite was primarily a military problem prior to the 1950s, at which time both an expanded interest in extreme outdoor sports and an increase in the urban homeless population brought the disease into the civilian population.

Frostbite was a major problem for Xenophon's army in Armenia in 400 B.C., and Hannibal lost half his army to cold injury while crossing the Alps from Spain in 153 B.C. That same year frostbite forced the Romans to give up the siege of Numentia. Cold injury nearly cost Gen. George Washington his army at Valley Forge, and most of the 250,000 men Napoleon Bonaparte lost on his retreat from Moscow were victims of the cold. French imperial surgeon Baron Dominique-Jean Larrey was the first to recognize that cold injury was aggravated when the extremity was warmed and then allowed to refreeze, a situation that virtually always resulted in necrosis and tissue loss.

During World War I, the British suffered 115,000 cold-related casualties on the Western Front and another 14,500 in the Dardanelles. This was also the first conflict in which frostbite became a common problem in pilots flying at altitudes where outside air temperature dropped significantly This problem became much worse in World War II, where airplanes reached altitudes at which it was impossible to retain a normal body temperature with clothing alone.

Cold weather injury was particularly severe among German troops on the Eastern Front, with 100,000 cases of frostbite in the Wehrmacht between December 1941 and January 1942, 1,500 of whom required amputation. The U.S. Army reported 46,000 cases of cold weather injury in the European Theater of Operations between the autumn of 1944 and the spring of 1945. Overall, 10 percent of American casualties in World War II were cold related.

During World War II, the Imperial Japanese Army operated Beijing Unit 1855 as a research facility in which Chinese prisoners were subjected to temperatures as low as –27°C to study cold weather injury. Similar experiments were conducted in German concentration camps in Europe with particular attention to limits of tolerance to immersion in cold water. German interest in this problem was stimulated by the frequent need to retrieve downed pilots from the North Sea during the Battle of Britain. During the postwar Nuremberg trials, defense attorneys attempted to justify those experiments as a necessary protection of national security in wartime.

Frostbite was again a severe problem during the Korean Conflict. At the Chosin Reservoir, temperatures approached –30°F, and 18,000 American troops suffered cold injury.

Even with current understanding of the mechanisms of cold injury and improved protective clothing, frostbite remains a significant military problem. In the Finnish Army, 44 percent of military recruits suffer cold injury at some time in their career, and 2.2 percent of the force will have that type of injury every year.

See also Korean Conflict; Napoleonic Wars; World War I Medicine; World War II Medicine

References
DeGroot, D. W., J. W. Castellani, J. O. Williams, and P. J. Amoroso. 2003. "Epidemiology

of U.S. Army Cold Weather Injuries, 1980–
1999." *Aviation Space and Environmental
Medicine* 74 (5): 564–570.
O'Sullivan, S. T., M. O'Shaughnessy, and
T. P. O'Connor. 1995. "Baron Larrey and
Cold Injury during the Campaigns of
Napoleon." *Annals of Plastic Surgery* 34
(April): 446–449.

Colonial Military and Naval Medicine

Because so many of the naval and military forces that operated in colonial North America were of Western European origin, their medical care closely mirrored practices in their home countries.

The 18th century was the first time that military medicine was generally accepted as a governmental responsibility. The origins of that change can be traced to 1660, when King Charles II of England created Europe's first standing peacetime army and with it the need for a professional corps of military surgeons. Like their counterparts in the regimental officer corps, the military surgeons purchased their commissions, and many functioned as both doctors and combatants and held rank and collected salaries in both capacities. A standing army also necessitated screening recruits and housing, feeding, and dressing them in a manner conducive to their health; and all of those responsibilities fell to a lesser or greater extent on the military surgeons.

Professional training in an era when surgeons were separate from and inferior to physicians was a problem. Through much of the 17th century, the Prussian Army drew almost all its medical corps from field barbers, or *feldscherers*, although Frederick the Great changed that practice during the Seven Years War when he solicited the help of French surgeons. In the first half of the 18th century, Paris was the only place in Europe where surgery was taught as a profession, and the Prussian king asked French military surgeon Louis Petit in 1744 to loan him trained operators to educate his military medical corps.

Once trained, Frederick's corps of Prussian physicians established field dressing stations near the front, intermediate-level field hospitals, and rear-area facilities for those with the most severe wounds, and generally improved transport and care of those wounded in battle. The Prussians and Austrians eventually established their own schools of military medicine and even began publishing German language journals of military medicine. They also promulgated printed regulations for camp sanitation and administration of military hospitals.

France had already done much the same under Louis XIV, who ordered that his army have a regular medical staff chosen by examination and built military hospitals in 51 French cities where his surgeons were annually required to take and pass courses in anatomy.

The British were slower to change, although, by the War of the Austrian Succession, the Duke of Marlborough had issued regulations dealing with health and sanitation for his armies and, by the Battle of Blenheim (1704), he had placed collecting stations for the wounded just out of musket range of the front lines. British articles of war mandated that one day's pay a year be withheld from a soldier's wages to pay for military hospitals and that any spoils taken after a battle be set aside for maintenance of the sick and wounded.

In 1752, Sir John Pringle published his *Observations on Diseases of the Army*, which contained rules for sanitation and ventilation of military hospitals and which took the radical point of view that cleanliness decreased the rate of hospital-acquired infection. Prior to Pringle's reforms, military hospitals were crowded, poorly ventilated, and filthy and were, of themselves, major sources of infection and death. Typhus, or "jail fever," had only just been recognized as identical to the "hospital fever" that plagued military facilities. Shortly after Pringle's book, James Lind's *Hygiene of the Sailors* (1757), Baron von Swieten's *Camp Diseases* (1758), and Richard Brocklesby's *Observations on Military Hospitals* (1764) offered major improvements in military medical care in a time when soldiers and sailors were fed diets almost entirely lacking fruits and vegetables, when water was often drawn from contaminated streams next to open latrines, and when wool uniforms sold to the troops by their officers regularly led to death from heat stroke during summer marches.

By the 18th century, the musket had become the primary weapon of set-piece battles, and Frederick the Great had perfected the use of close-range, coordinated volleys in which opposing forces lined up 200 yards apart and whichever side could load and fire the fastest was likely to win. As the bulk of training in military surgery was still obtained on the battlefield, treatment of gunshot wounds assumed primary importance during that century. John Hunter, the preeminent English surgeon of the 1700s, obtained much of his experience serving with British forces in the Belle Isle invasion and the Portuguese campaign and returned to write his landmark *Observations on Gunshot Wounds* (1794). There was still a general belief that gunpowder was, of itself, poisonous and that musket wounds should be cauterized with hot oil and dressed with a variety of salves. The ointments were of-

ten the surgeon's closely guarded secret and were never sterile. Wounds were usually probed with unsterile instruments in an effort to extract any foreign material and were then washed with antiseptics such as mercury-based corrosive sublimate, chalk, camphor, myrrh, or hot turpentine. They were then packed with charpie (unraveled linen cloth) soaked in wine or brandy. Infection was the rule rather than the exception, and the ubiquitous "laudable pus" was viewed as an essential phase of healing.

The most common operation performed by military surgeons in the 1700s was amputation, and removal of the limb was the routine treatment not only for gangrene but also for injuries to major vessels, for open fractures or penetration of a joint. and for any other trauma serious enough to defy easy repair,

Naval medicine in the colonial American era was, like its land-based counterpart, a combination of health maintenance—centered mostly around sanitary and dietary considerations—and wound surgery. Scurvy remained the plague of sailing ships because the Royal Navy did not mandate citrus supplements until 1793, even though James Lind had proven beyond question that the disease could be prevented by regular intake of citrus juice 46 years earlier. Diseases such as typhus, smallpox, yellow fever, and dysentery were fostered by close quarters, poor hygiene, unsanitary food and water, and visits to areas where infectious agents were endemic. Ships were notoriously dangerous places to work, with injuries caused by falls from rigging and blows from heavy tackle being common. Since a majority of seamen could not swim, drowning remained a frequent cause of death.

The sick and wounded were typically housed in the forward area of ships' gun

Physician James Lind recommended that fresh citrus fruit be included in the diet of seamen, resulting in the eradication of scurvy from the British Navy. (Bettmann/Corbis)

decks. Those decks were divided by the vessels' ribs into bays which, in the mid part of the hull, contained guns. Spaces in the bow, where hammocks were hung for the patients, came to be known as the "sick bays." During battles, the ship's surgeon set up shop below the water line, where he and his patients were less likely to be struck by cannonballs. Surgery was performed on sea chests laid side by side in the cable tier or orlop deck. Barrels for wash water and for collecting amputated body parts were arrayed around the makeshift operating tables. Young crew members, called loblolly boys after the porridge they delivered, were responsible for feeding and washing the sick and injured and for mopping the blood that accumulated around surgeries.

It was possible for ships' doctors to become relatively prosperous because they shared in prize money derived from sale of captured enemy vessels. Naval surgeons such as Carl Linné, Sir James Hooker, and later Charles Darwin were often the most educated men in the crew and frequently doubled as genteel amateur naturalists.

Physicians and surgeons were among the first colonists in both Massachusetts and Virginia. John Winthrop brought a barber-surgeon to the Massachusetts Bay Colony in 1645, but the man left after three years, complaining he was unable to make a living. Jamestown had a surgeon general (Dr. Thomas Wooten) in 1607, and Dr. Walter Russell and Dr. Anthony Bagnall served with John Smith in 1608. Wooten treated Smith for an injury and a local Indian for a gunshot wound that year, but the physicians, unhappy with the harsh conditions and lack of steady income, returned to

England in 1609. When Smith was injured by exploding gunpowder that year, there was no local physician to care for him and he was forced to make the long journey back to London for treatment.

Samuel Fuller came to Plymouth on the *Mayflower* as surgeon to the colony, although he probably lacked a medical degree. In one of the unusual instances in which Plymouth and the rival Massachusetts Bay Colony cooperated, Fuller helped treat an outbreak of scurvy in Charlestown. He remained in Plymouth Colony until dying of fever in 1633.

Care of wounded soldiers was recognized as a public responsibility relatively early in colonial history. In 1636, Plymouth Colony passed a law requiring that veterans injured in Indian wars be supported for life. Virginia and Rhode Island followed with provisions for lifetime half-pay for disabled soldiers.

In spite of those sporadic instances, for most of the 17th century and into the 18th century, American colonists were forced to rely on their own resources, on ministers doubling as medical practitioners, or on doctors from passing ships for their medical care. As late as 1775, there was still a dearth of trained physicians and surgeons in the colonies. On May 8 of that year, the Provincial Congress of the Massachusetts Bay Colony, anticipating the oncoming conflict with England, authorized a committee of physicians to examine the qualifications of the colony's potential military surgeons. What they found was primarily a collection of men trained by apprenticeship with little more knowledge than that gained on the job. Although the Continental Army medical corps was formalized after the Battle of Bunker Hill, medical care in the colonies remained well below European military medical standards throughout the war.

See also Disease and Mortality in Colonial America; Pringle, Sir John; Scurvy; 17th-Century Military Medicine

References

Bayne-Jones, Stanhope. *The Evolution of Preventive Medicine in the United States Army, 1607–1939*. Washington, D.C.: Office of the Surgeon General, Department of the Army, 1968.

Gillet, Mary. *The Army Medical Department, 1775–1818*. Washington, D.C.: Center of Military History, 1981.

Packard, Francis. *History of Medicine in the United States*. New York: Paul B. Hoeber, Inc., 1931.

Roddis, Louis. *A Short History of Nautical Medicine*. New York: Paul B. Hoeber, Inc., 1941.

Combat Fatigue

The term "combat fatigue" was coined during World War II; in other wars, the symptoms that comprise it have been variously referred to as battle fatigue, war neurosis, exhaustion, shell shock, and posttraumatic stress disorder.

Combat fatigue is a group of ill-defined symptoms including excessive fatigue, an exaggerated startle response, tremors, violence, nightmares, delusions, hallucinations, withdrawal, and catatonia.

Homer described delusional behavior by the warrior Ajax after a battle and Herodotus described combat-induced mental illness in the Athenian army during the Battle of Marathon, but diagnosing battle-related behavioral abnormalities as a disease was rare prior to the 20th century. The Russians established the first military psychiatric service during the Russo-Japanese War, and with the availability of trained psychiatrists, the diagnosis became common for the first time. In World War I, the problem was termed "shell shock" under the mistaken theory that explosive concussions caused small brain hemorrhages, leading to cerebral dysfunction. By World War II it was widely understood that the symptoms were psychiatric in nature, were similar to traumatic neuroses seen in the civilian population, and were not associated with identifiable anatomic brain damage.

In spite of an early British emphasis on battlefield psychiatry during World War II and an American attempt to exclude men with psychiatric illness from military service, mental illness remained a major cause of combat disability, with about 30 percent of Allied combat zone casualties being psychiatric in nature. Although physicians in World War I had shown that treatment close to the front lines made it possible to return a number of psychiatrically disabled soldiers to combat, the lesson had been forgotten. Early in World War II, patients with what was now called combat fatigue were routinely evacuated to rehabilitation hospitals, and most were discharged from the military. As manpower became scarce, more of these men were placed in pioneer or labor details in the rear area, but few returned to combat.

Captain Frederick R. Hanson, an American neurologist and neurosurgeon who had joined the Canadian Army early in the war and participated in the landing at Dieppe, transferred to the U.S. Army and developed what became a successful and widely employed treatment for combat fatigue, also euphemistically referred to as "exhaustion." The essential parts of the regimen included sedation, brief periods of rest, and treatment in a facility close to the front where the patients and staff continued to wear combat uniforms. Hanson realized that treating these patients as if they were mentally ill and physically separating them

from their units made it unlikely that they would return to duty. Using his treatment protocols, the British and American armies were able to return 70–80 percent of combat fatigue victims to their units, and only 15–20 percent of patients requiring evacuation to the zone of the interior were psychiatric.

Shortly after the Italian invasion, the U.S. Army established the post of division psychiatrist, and Hanson produced a manual for internists so nonpsychiatrists could use his methods. As the war went on, Allied military psychiatrists became convinced that no soldier was immune from combat fatigue. They hypothesized that any man subject to continuous combat for a long enough time would become nonfunctional and estimated that 200 days of constant action was about the maximum a soldier could be expected to tolerate. The British adopted a system of unit rotation to give their men regular periods of rest and were able to stretch the length of tolerance to nearly 400 days, but the Americans, except in the Army Air Corps, adopted a more haphazard approach of rotating individuals with the longest periods of service rather than rotating units as a whole. Individual rotation worked poorly and was finally replaced with the British system late in the war.

Military physicians, mindful of the heavy clinical and financial burden of long-term psychiatric illness after World War I, correctly predicted that the true cost of combat fatigue would not become evident until well after the soldiers returned to civilian life.

See also Posttraumatic Stress Disorder (PTSD); Shell Shock in World War I

References
Cowdrey, Albert E. *Fighting for Life: American Military Medicine in World War II*. New York: Free Press, 1994.

Slight, David. "Psychiatry and the War." In
William H. Taliaferro, *Medicine and the War*.
Chicago: University of Chicago Press, 1944.

Crile, George Washington (1864–1943)

An American surgeon famous for his studies on shock and surgical anesthesia and founder of the Cleveland Clinic, George Washington Crile was born on a small farm near Chili, Ohio, on November 11, 1864, the fifth of eight children of Scottish-Irish parents. He entered the Ohio Normal School at age 17, where he paid his expenses by teaching elementary school students. After graduation, he took a job as principal of the Plainfield, Ohio, School, where he was befriended by Dr. A. E. Walker, who allowed him to come along on patient visits and to perform simple procedures. Crile enrolled in the proprietary Wooster Medical School in Cleveland in the spring of 1886 and graduated with honors a year later. After graduation, Crile became a house officer at the University Hospital of Cleveland, where he was taught by Frank Weed. After graduation, he joined Weed and Frank Bunts, another Wooster graduate, in private practice.

Crile became interested in shock and spent three months at Columbia University's College of Physicians and Surgeons studying physiology, histology, and pathology. In 1892 and 1895, he traveled to Europe, where he studied with Theodor Billroth and Sir Victor Horsley. While in Horsley's laboratory, he met Charles Scott Sherington, Britain's preeminent physiologist, who was also studying shock. After returning to Cleveland, Crile won the Cartwright Prize for his essay "An Experimental Research into Shock," which became the first of his 24 books.

Crile joined the faculty of the Western Reserve Medical School in 1900. Three years later, he described an inflatable rubber suit for treatment of shock on which the pressurized flight suits of World War II were later based. That same year he joined Johns Hopkins University Medical School surgeon Harvey Cushing in a presentation to the Boston Medical Society urging routine monitoring of blood pressure during surgery. A committee of the society considered the recommendation and decided such monitoring was unnecessary.

In 1910, Wooster and Western Reserve merged, and Crile joined the faculty of the new institution as clinical professor of surgery. He continued with a busy private practice, performing as many as 20 operations a day, and developed a special interest in procedures on the thyroid. He described the first radical neck dissection and, in August 1906 at Cleveland's St. Alexis Hospital, performed the United States' first successful human-to-human blood transfusion.

Crile had a lifelong interest in improving the safety of surgical procedures. In order to prevent lethal endocrine storms in anxious patients about to have thyrotoxic goiters removed, he often performed "steal" procedures in which he would come into a hospital room without warning and remove the patient's tumor while he or she was still in bed to save them the psychological stress of being taken to an operating room. Crile supplemented gas anesthesia with morphine, scopolamine, and locally infiltrated cocaine—a combination still used with only minor modification.

Crile helped form the American College of Surgeons in 1912 and was named Honorary Fellow of the Royal College of Surgeons of England in 1913. When the United States entered World War I, he formed the Lakeside unit that became Base Hospital 4 and came to France with the first detachment of the American Expeditionary Force on March 25, 1917.

In 1921, Crile joined Bunts, William Lower, and John Phillips to form the Cleveland Clinic. In December 1942, Crile suffered a stroke related to an episode of endocarditis and died the following month.

See also Anesthesiology; Bilroth, Christian Albert Theodor; Cushing, Harvey Williams; Shock; Transfusion; World War I Medicine

References

Crile, Grace, ed. *George Crile: An Autobiography.* Philadelphia: J. B. Lippincott, 1947.
Herman, Robert. 1994. "George Washington Crile (1864–1943) *U2* (May): 28–83.

Crimean War

The Crimean War was fought from September 14, 1854, to July 12, 1856, between France, Great Britain, Sardinia, and the Ottoman Empire on one side and Russia on the other.

Medical historian Fielding Garrison said, "Of all recorded wars, the Crimean has perhaps the greatest teaching value for military medicine" (Garrison 1922). Actually, the war was more important as a caution against things done badly than as an example of things done well. Most of the Crimean War took place in the immediate vicinity of Sebastopol, the Black Sea port at which the Russian Navy was primarily based. The English and French were fighting far from home with generally inadequate medical, transport, and sanitary services.

The British came into the war especially unprepared. In 1854, the entire Army Medical Department comprised a director general, four inspectors general, 11 deputy inspectors, and 163 surgeons scattered throughout the empire. The whole ambulance service comprised two four-wheeled wagons, and these were delivered without horses or harness and so returned to Bulgaria. Each regiment had only a single pack pony and 10 canvas stretchers for moving the wounded. Stretcher bearers came from the Hospital Conveyance Corps, composed of men too old or too decrepit to be soldiers but also often incapable of carrying the wounded.

Dr. John Hall was given the task of readying the medical service for a 10,000-man force, but almost three times that many were actually sent to the Crimea. British soldiers were deployed without shelter tents, without winter uniforms, and without adequate food.

The French were modestly better off. Although they sent only about one surgeon for every 600 troops as compared to about one for every 200 in the British and Russian armies, the men they sent were better trained and equipped. The French brought spring-suspended ambulances and better shelter and clothing for their men and benefited immeasurably from nursing care by the Sisters of Charity. However, their supplies were gradually exhausted and not replaced, and the death rate among French soldiers steadily rose as the war progressed.

The Russian medical corps performed little better than that of their enemies, although Nikolai Pirogoff's use of female nurses was a notable exception.

Death from disease far outstripped that from injury in the Crimean War. The first epidemic of gastrointestinal disease broke out at Devna, near Constantinople, before the troops ever got to Russia because Sir George Brown insisted, over Hall's objections, on bivouacking his division on poorly drained ground because he found the site charmingly scenic.

In the end, the Crimean War had the highest combined mortality rate from injury and disease of any war in history. During the war, 4,354 French soldiers died of wounds, while 59,815 succumbed to disease. Comparable figures for the British and Russians were 1,847 to 17,225 and 14,671 to 37,454, respectively. Overall death rates from disease were 119.3 per 1,000 among the English, 253.5 per 1,000 among the French, and 161.3 per 1,000 among the Russians. The responsible illnesses were overwhelmingly the result of either poor nutrition or poor sanitation—scurvy, typhus, typhoid, and cholera being predominant. Within seven months of arrival in the Crimea, 10,000 of the 28,000 British soldiers sent there were dead of disease.

Calamita Bay, the main British base in the Crimea, was 300 miles by water from the hospital at Scutari near Constantinople. That facility was an abandoned Turkish barrack with almost four miles of beds in a chain of flea-infested buildings built beside filthy stables and above basements that conveniently housed several hundred working prostitutes. In the hospital's first three months of operation, 9,000 of its patients died of infections they did not have when they were admitted.

Because the Crimea was connected by cable to London and Paris, the war was the first in which newspaper correspondents furnished the public with daily reports, and *Times* reporter W. H. Russell described the horrors of Calamita Bay and Scutari in luridly effective detail. His articles got Queen Victoria's attention and, consequently, that of Secretary at War Sidney Herbert, who dispatched Florence Nightingale and a contingent of female nurses to alleviate the situation. Although she clashed with Hall, Nightingale was, through a combination of hard work and material support from England, able to significantly improve care at Scutari.

It is ironic that men suffered from scurvy, even though the Royal Navy had eradicated the disease in the 1790s with daily doses of lime juice ; men died from cholera, even though John Snow had demonstrated how to prevent it by avoiding fecally contaminated water in 1849; and men suffered surgery without anesthetics, even though chloroform had been available since 1831. Military surgeons had regularly failed to accept well-documented improvements in their science, and the men for whom they cared paid the price. As a result of its abysmal performance in the Crimean War, the British medical service was entirely reformed in the subsequent decade.

See also British Military Medicine; Cholera; Dysentery; Nightingale, Florence; Pirogoff, Nikolai Ivanovich; Russian Military Medicine; Scurvy

References
Baylen, Joseph O., and Alan Conway, eds. *Soldier-Surgeon: The Crimean War Letters of Dr. Douglas A. Reid, 1855–1856*. Knoxville: University of Tennessee Press, 1968.
Garrison, Fielding. *Notes on the History of Military Medicine*. Washington, D.C.: Association of Military Surgeons, 1922.
Laffin, John. *Surgeons in the Field*. London: J. M. Dent & Sons, Ltd., 1970.
McLaughlin, Redmond. *The Royal Army Medical Corps*. London: Leo Cooper, Ltd., 1972.

Crusades

Eight Crusades (1096–1272) in which European armies attempted to take ancient biblical lands from their Islamic rulers brought the West into contact with Arab culture, science, and medicine, although mostly without demonstrable benefit.

Military leaders and the nobility who participated in the Crusades occasionally took their personal physicians with them, but common soldiers were left almost entirely without medical care. That was not the misfortune it might seem, as Western medicine had not yet returned to the level attained a millennium earlier by the Romans and Greeks and offered little that would increase the chances of recovery from either illness or injury. That fact, together with a virtually complete failure to adopt more advanced Arab science when they encountered it, left the Crusades as an era that, as medical historian Fielding Garrison pointed out, contributed nothing of significance to the development of military medicine.

Baldwin, the first recorded casualty of the first crusade, suffered a spear wound to the thigh, and most subsequent wounds were either due to penetration by arrows or spears or were hacking wounds, particularly to the head. European surgeons found that, if penetrating projectiles were left in place, victims often bled internally, whereas, if they were removed, the patients had a distressing tendency to exsanguinate on the ground. It was a difficult choice, but, quite possibly, one's reputation was less damaged if the bleeding was not evident. Knights wounded in the Crusades received virtually no medical care beyond opium for pain. They were given a stimulant drink, hot oil for their wounds, and prayers for their souls before being left to die on the field.

Armor was both an advantage and a disadvantage. Wearing metal suits in the hot desert sun might result in heat stroke, but the long shield did serve admirably as a stretcher.

Crusaders were certainly wounded in battle, but were just as likely to die from diseases such as dysentery, typhus, and camp fever. Scurvy from poor diet was particularly common in the Fifth Crusade (1216–1220) and the Seventh Crusade (1249–1254). An estimated 25 to 40 percent of aristocrats who participated in the Crusades for as much as three years died, half from wounds and the other half from disease or malnutrition. In the Second Crusade, Louis VII's 100,000-man army dwindled to 5,000, with almost all the losses coming from starvation and disease. In 1218, during the Fifth Crusade, one-fifth of the European army occupied in the siege of Damietta died of plague in a single month.

Although camp followers were a characteristic of every crusade, syphilis, which would ravage Europe in the 15th century, was not a significant problem. Hygiene was a lost art and other infectious diseases were rampant, in spite of the fact that the Frankish physicians did learn a bit about sanitation from Muslim and Jewish physicians.

The Crusades gave rise to two great philanthropic orders—the Knights of St. John and the Teutonic Knights. When Jerusalem fell to the Crusaders on July 15, 1099, the Europeans took control of the hospital of St. John. The Hospitallers of Jerusalem became the Knights of St. John in 1211, the Knights of Rhodes in 1311, and the Knights of Malta in 1530, where they remained until dispersed by Napoleon I in 1798. The Teutonic Knights took over St. Mary's Hospital in Jerusalem and were headquartered at a second hospital in Acre from 1191 to 1291, after which they moved to Magdeburg (1309) and established several European hospitals. They also built forts and assumed control of Prussia and Lithuania, which passed to the Hohenzollern family in 1525. The Prussian hospitals were built around large, airy quadrangles with ex-cellent drainage and ventilation; they were by far the most sanitary structures of the Middle Ages.

See also Islamic Military Medicine; Medieval
Military Medicine; Sovereign Military
Hospitaller Order of St. John of Jerusalem,
of Rhodes, and of Malta

References
Mitchell, Piers D. *Medicine in the Crusades:
Warfare, Wounds and the Medieval Surgeon.*
Cambridge: Cambridge University Press,
2004.
Setton, Kenneth, ed. *A History of the Crusades.*
Madison: University of Wisconsin Press,
1977.

Cushing, Harvey Williams (1869–1939)

Harvey Williams Cushing is widely recog-nized as the father of neurological surgery and has also been credited with being the first endocrinologist.

Cushing was born April 8, 1869, in Cleve-land to a family descended from a long line of New England physicians. He finished secondary school in Ohio before going to Yale University with instructions from his Calvinist father that he avoid smoking, drinking, and college ball clubs.

After graduating from Yale, Cushing went to Harvard Medical School, from which he graduated in 1895. In the late 19th century, it was customary for medical students to ad-minister ether during surgery, and Cushing had the misfortune of losing a patient from an overdose of anesthetic gas. This incident led him to begin charting pulse and respira-tions—the first use of the graphic anesthetic record that remains standard practice. Cush-ing's interest in intraoperative monitoring

also led to his introduction of the Riva-Rocci blood pressure measuring apparatus to the operating room in 1901.

In 1897, Cushing went to the new Johns Hopkins Medical School to work with Wil-liam Halsted and to become the first Ameri-can surgeon to devote all his energies to brain surgery, although at the time, the mortality rate for intracranial surgery was so great that Halsted warned Cushing he would be unable to earn a living if that was all he did. In 1900, Cushing went to Europe, where he worked with Charles Sherrington, Sir Victor Horsley, and Theodor Kocher.

While in Kocher's laboratory, Cushing studied the elevation in blood pressure and decrease in pulse rate that accompany increased pressure on the brain. He pub-lished his findings without crediting Ko-cher, leading, on the one hand, to having the famous reflex named for him and, on the other hand, to being expelled from the Swiss laboratory.

On returning to Hopkins, Cushing helped form the Hunterian Laboratory, which be-came a world-renowned center of surgical and physiological research. Cushing's in-terest in pituitary tumors led to his devel-opment of techniques to reach the gland through the nose and to the development of endocrinology as a specialty. In 1912, Cushing moved to the Peter Bent Brigham Hospital in Boston as Harvard's Moseley Professor of Surgery.

Cushing was a committed Francophile and, in 1915, took the Harvard Ambulance Hospital to France to work with the Ameri-can Hospital of Paris in treating wounded French soldiers. When the United States entered World War I in 1917, Cushing re-turned to France as director of Base Hospi-tal 5 and senior consultant in neurosurgery to the American Expeditionary Force. His monograph on neurosurgery (which had been initially published as a section of W. W. Keen's *Surgery*) was reprinted by the surgeon general of the U.S. Army and was the standard neurosurgery reference for American military surgeons. Cushing's meticulous technique and concentration on hemostasis were credited with halving the mortality rate of intracranial surgery during the war. Cushing also introduced innovative methods of using X-ray to localize metallic foreign bodies and magnets to remove them from the brain.

Cushing was a notoriously slow surgeon who was fanatical about hemostasis. In 1911, he invented a silver clip that replaced the painstaking technique of individually tying off even very small severed blood vessels. In 1926, in cooperation with engineer Frank Bovie, he popularized the use of electrical currents to coagulate bleeding vessels, thus reintroducing heat cauterization to surgery.

Besides being a magnificent surgeon and teacher, Cushing was an accomplished artist who regularly augmented his written operative notes with elegant sketches. He was also an excellent writer and was awarded the Pulitzer Prize for his biography of Sir William Osler.

Cushing took a position as professor of medical history at Yale after his retirement from Harvard—an involuntary termination occasioned by Cushing's own rule that no surgeon could operate past age 62. Cushing finished his career at the New Haven, Connecticut, school and left one of the world's finest collections of antique medical books to the Sterling Library after his death on October 7, 1939.

See also Anesthesiology; Cauterization; Head Injury and Cranial Surgery; Hemostasis; World War I Medicine

References
Fulton, John. *Harvey Cushing: A Biography.* Springfield, IL: Charles C. Thomas, 1946.
Sweet, William. 1979. "Harvey Cushing: Author, Investigator, Neurologist, Neurosurgeon." *Journal of Neurosurgery* 50 (January): 5–12.
Thomson, Elizabeth. *Harvey Cushing: Surgeon, Author, Artist.* New York: Schuman's, 1950.
Walker, A. Earl. *A History of Neurological Surgery.* Baltimore: Williams & Wilkins Co., 1951.

Cutbush, Edward (1772–1843)

Edward Cutbush was a surgeon who has been called the father of American naval medicine.

Cutbush was born in Philadelphia, the son of a British immigrant. He entered Philadelphia College at the age of 12 and went on to study medicine at the Pennsylvania Hospital, where he worked under William Shippen. While still a student, he was honored by the city of Philadelphia for his services during the 1793 yellow fever epidemic. After graduation from medical school in 1794, Cutbush joined the Pennsylvania Militia in its campaign against the Whiskey Rebellion and became its surgeon general.

In 1799, he joined the U.S. Navy and was assigned to the USS *United States*. He made his first voyage to Europe when that ship carried an American delegation to negotiate the agreement ending America's "quasi war" with France. As surgeon on the USS *Constitution*, Cutbush participated in the 1802–1803 blockade of the Barbary ports in North Africa.

On his return to the United States, Cutbush served on the first board to examine candidates for the U.S. Navy's medical service. He was an early proponent of small-pox vaccine, giving it to the entire crew of the *United States* in 1799, just a year after Edward Jenner's pamphlet describing the procedure was published. His 1808 *Observations on the Means of Preserving the Health of Sailors and Soldiers, with Remarks on Hospitals and Their Internal Administration* was the first book dealing with naval medicine by an American.

Cutbush left the navy in 1828 after the election of President Andrew Jackson, whom he opposed, and joined the faculty of Geneva College in New York. He was eventually named dean of the medical faculty and remained in Geneva until his death in 1843.

See also American Revolutionary War; Naval Medicine

References
Luft, Eric. 2002. "Edward Cutbush, M.D. (1772–1843)." *Upstate Medical University Alumni Journal*, Spring.
Roddis, Louis. *A Short History of Nautical Medicine*. New York: Paul B. Hoeber, Inc., 1941.

D

DDT (Dichlorodiphenyltrichloroethane)

Dichlorodiphenyltrichloroethane (DDT) is an insecticide introduced in 1940 that was key to the control of insect-borne diseases in the later years of World War II.

Louse-borne typhus had killed 2.5 million soldiers and civilians on the Eastern Front during World War I and had broken out in Eastern Europe and North Africa when the United States entered the war in 1941. Insect-borne disease was not just a problem on the European fronts: American military surgeons estimated that up to half of all troops deployed in the Pacific Theater of Operations might be infected by malarial mosquitoes. With those risks in mind, the War Department enlisted civilian and governmental research agencies including the Rockefeller Institute and the Department of Agriculture's Orlando, Florida-based Bureau of Entomology and Plant Quarantine to develop an insecticide that could be effective at low concentrations, that would be easily spread, that would persist in the environment, and that did not harm humans.

The Rockefeller Louse Lab and the Bureau evaluated more than 8,000 chemicals using experiments that included infesting conscientious objectors with lice harvested from New York City homeless people. In 1942, pyrethrins derived from the heads of chrysanthemum flowers appeared to be the most effective way to kill lice, and the chemical was distributed to military units beginning in August of that year. However, most chrysanthemum supplies came from Japan or from Dalmatia, which was under German control, so an alternative source for the chemical was necessary.

In August 1942, Geigy Colour Company, Ltd., of Basel, Switzerland, offered use of its insecticide Gesarol. The agent was based on DDT, had been patented in 1940, and had already been proven effective against potato beetles. Because Switzerland maintained neutrality in the war, the chemical was made available to both the Allies and to Germany, but German scientists showed little interest. American investigators, on the other hand, quickly demonstrated that DDT powder admirably satisfied all their requirements. It did, however, have distressing side effects at high concentrations in some animals, particularly when used as a solution rather than as a powder. Army physicians ultimately decided that the risk of insect-borne disease outweighed the risk of side effects and started general distribution of the insecticide in May 1943.

During the remainder of that year, American laboratories produced 193,000 pounds of the chemical, and, by June 1945, production had reached 3 million pounds a month. DDT was hailed as the war's greatest contribution to human welfare and as equivalent in importance to penicillin and sulfa. Geigy's Paul Müller received the Nobel Prize for Physiology or Medicine in 1948 for his work with DDT.

When the insecticide was widely used after the war, a variety of undesirable effects, particularly on wildlife and the environment, became evident, and use of DDT in the United States was almost entirely banned in 1972.

See also Malaria; Typhus; World War II Medicine

References
Perkins, John. *Insects, Experts and the Insecticide Crisis: The Quest for New Pest Management Strategies.* New York: Plenum Publishing Corp., 1982.

Russell, Edmund. *War and Nature: Fighting Humans and Insects with Chemicals from World War I to Silent Spring.* Cambridge: Cambridge University Press, 2001.

Stapleton, Darwin H. 2005. "A Lost Chapter in the Early History of DDT: The Development of Anti-Typhus Technologies by the Rockefeller Foundation's Louse Laboratory, 1942–1944." *Technology and Culture* 46 (3): 513–540.

Débridement

Débridement is the practice of removing foreign bodies and devitalized tissue from wounds. The term derives from the French for "unbridling."

The practice of removing weapons or other foreign material that have penetrated the body is as old as recorded surgery. In fact, the Greek word for physician, ἰάτροσ, is derived from a root that means "remover of arrows." For the first millennium of the Common Era, débridement was primarily accomplished by retrieving bits of stone, metal, or bone and using boiling oil to liquefy the damaged tissue at the margins of those penetrating wounds. Cauterization, in addition to stopping bleeding, was an unselective form of débridement. Guy de Chauliac recommended the less traumatic method of opening wounds widely and allowing any dead or foreign material to drain out—in effect a passive débridement. This practice was augmented by packing the wound so it could not spontaneously close, a technique that remains in use. By the 1500s, military surgeons' kits included a variety of probes and forceps specifically designed to locate and retrieve foreign bodies.

Actual surgical removal of devitalized tissue was proposed by Pierre-Joseph Desault, who worked at the Hôtel Dieu in Paris in the late 18th century, with the recommendation that wound edges be freshened with a scalpel prior to suture. It remained for Russian military surgeon Carl Reyher to suggest wide débridement of war wounds in 1881, although the practice did not become general until World War I.

See also Chauliac, Guy de; Reyher, Carl

Reference
Wangensteen, Owen, and Sarah Wangensteen. *The Rise of Surgery from Empiric Cult to Scientific Discipline.* Minneapolis: University of Minnesota Press, 1978.

Dengue Fever

Dengue fever is a systemic disease caused by one of four sero-types of a virus from the genus Flavivirus, which also includes the pathogens responsible for yellow fever and Japanese encephalitis.

The first known cases of dengue fever occurred in Batavia in 1779, and Benjamin Rush, a prominent American Revolutionary War physician and a signer of the Declaration of Independence, gave the first detailed description of the disease when it caused an epidemic in Philadelphia in 1780.

Dengue most often manifests itself with the sudden onset of fever five to eight days after a bite from one of several species of Aedes mosquito, including *A. aegyptii, A. albopictus*, and *A. scutellaris*. After two to four days of headache, fever, and muscle aches, the disease eases for 12 to 48 hours before returning with a skin rash, chills, swollen and reddened eyes, and the severe joint pains that caused Rush to name it "breakbone fever," an eponym that remains in use. Dengue fever is usually benign and self-limited, but a small number of cases will progress to the hemorrhagic form, in which bleeding from multiple organs and mucosal surfaces occurs and for which the mortality is about 5 percent. No vaccine is available for dengue, and there is no effective treatment. Because the mosquitoes that transmit the disease are day-biting, mosquito netting is of limited usefulness, and the only effective means of control has been to eliminate the Aedes vectors.

Dengue fever was sporadic until the middle of the 20th century, but it has become pandemic in recent decades. In terms of prevalence and morbidity, it is currently the most important mosquito-borne disease in the world, with an endemic presence in more than 100 countries and with about 2.5 billion of the world's population exposed. An estimated 90 million to 100 million cases a year occur, with 500,000 progressing to the hemorrhagic form that is responsible for at least 25,000 deaths a year.

Dengue became an important military consideration in the Pacific Theater during World War II. Epidemics struck American troops in Queensland, Australia, and Hawaii in 1943, and an outbreak in Espiritu Santo in the New Hebrides took 5,000 men (25 percent of the active force) out of service. In 1944, there was an epidemic among American troops on Saipan. More than 84,000 cases of dengue fever among Americans in the South Pacific were documented, although it is likely that the disease was underdiagnosed and that the actual numbers were considerably higher.

The disease spread from the South Pacific and Southeast Asia in the late 1940s and 1950s to become a pandemic affecting Sri Lanka, India, Pakistan, the Maldive Islands, the People's Republic of China, Taiwan, and East Africa. American troops fighting in the Korean Conflict contracted 21 cases of dengue fever, but no fatalities resulted. Although geography and environmental conditions made dengue a concern during the Viet Nam War, only sporadic cases were diagnosed.

In recent decades, dengue fever has become endemic in Central and South America, and sporadic cases have appeared in the southern United States. Dengue in American military forces has most recently been reported among troops stationed in Haiti and Somalia in the 1990s.

See also Korean Conflict; Viet Nam War; World War II Medicine; Yellow Fever

References
Diasio, J. S., and F. M. Richardson. 1944. "Clinical Observations on Dengue Fever:

Report of 100 Cases." *Military Surgeon* 94
(June): 365–369.
Gibler, D. J. 1998. "Dengue and Dengue
Hemorrhagic Fever." *Clinical Microbiological
Reviews* 11 (July): 480–496.

Dioscorides, Pedacius (First Century A.D.)

Pedacius Dioscorides was a Greek surgeon
who served in Emperor Nero's (A.D. 54–68)
Roman Army and who, in the course of his
military travels, compiled what some consider to be the best description of medical
botany to his time.

Except for the fact that he was born in
Cilicia (modern-day Turkey) and served
with the Roman legions, little is known of
Dioscorides's personal history. His *De Materia Medica* described more than 600 plants
with medical uses, 90 of which are still in
use. He was the first to treat medical botany
as a science, and, although he sorted plants
according to their uses rather than their
structure, he preceded Carl Linné as a bo-
tanical classifier by 1,700 years. *De Materia
Medica* remained a standard reference for
centuries, and, until the early 1600s, books
on medical botany were little more than
commentaries on Dioscorides's work. He
recommended mandragora wine as a sedative and analgesic for surgical procedures
and cauterization and suggested hanging
copper over vinegar until a blue film (copper sulfate) formed that could be scraped
and put on wounds as an antiseptic. He also
suggested using lanolin from sheep wool
on wounds, a practice in keeping with recent research demonstrating better healing
if wounds are kept moist.

The earliest surviving version of Dioscorides's book is the Vienna Codex dating to A.D. 512. A stone box found in the
garden of the Prussian consulate in Alexandria in 1847 and labeled *Three Tomes of Dioscorides* may be the only surviving artifact
from that city's famous ancient library.

See also Anesthesiology; Roman Military
Medicine

Reference
Majno, Guido. *The Healing Hand: Man and
Wound in the Ancient World.* Cambridge,
MA: Harvard University Press, 1975.

Disease and Mortality in Colonial America

Because North America's original European
settlers arrived over long distances in small,
underprovisioned vessels, disease was the
primary cause of mortality from the earliest
immigration to the New World.

Under the best of circumstances, the
voyage from England in the early 1600s
took more than six weeks; rations consisted mostly of meat, bread, and dried le-
gumes, and passengers were crowded into
small, poorly ventilated spaces. Seasickness,
scurvy, smallpox, dysentery, and various
febrile diseases were the rule rather than
the exception. Of John Blackwell's 150 Puri-
tans who sailed in 1618, 130 died in transit.
Of 100 Pilgrims who landed at Plymouth in
1620, only 50 were still alive three months
later, most having died of scurvy or infections acquired onboard the ship. Of the
initial 4,170 settlers who came to Jamestown in 1621, more than 2,000 succumbed
to disease, and survivors complained that
moaning from the sick and dying made it
impossible to sleep at night.

Ironically, disease itself was not altogether
detrimental to the colonists. It is likely that
the Pilgrims were saved from annihilation
by local Indian tribes because the native

The British prison ship Jersey *moored in New York Harbor, housed American prisoners during the Revolutionary War. Thousands of captives in British hands died of disease and poor diet aboard overcrowded and filthy hulks like this. (North Wind Picture Archives)*

population had been cut by 90 percent in the previous four years by epidemic disease.

Scurvy had been the primary killer of sailors and nautical passengers since improvements in navigation made long voyages out of sight of land possible. The disease results from lack of vitamin C (ascorbic acid), which is normally acquired from citrus fruits and to a lesser extent from leafy vegetables such as cabbage or from onions and potatoes. In the absence of an ongoing supply of dietary vitamin C, symptoms of scurvy appear within two weeks and include weakness, swelling of the legs, softening of the gums culminating in loss of teeth, bleeding from mucous membranes, and, ultimately, death from heart failure. British naval surgeon James Lind had proven the disease could be prevented by prophylactic ingestion of

lemon juice in 1747, but the practice did not become routine in the Royal Navy until 1793, and scurvy was a plague to both military and civilian sailors through the 18th century. In British ships posted to the West Indies during that time, about one man in seven died of scurvy while on post.

Close quarters aboard ship made transmission of infections likely. Typhus, which was transmitted by omnipresent lice, was pervasive and infected nearly every prisoner held by the British in hulks anchored in New York Harbor during the American Revolution. Epidemics of measles, scarlet fever, influenza, and diphtheria also recurred regularly. Seasickness was significant both because of the direct misery it caused and because it weakened passengers and left them susceptible to more lethal diseases.

Smallpox was a particular problem, with cyclical epidemics beginning in 1663 in New Netherlands and recurring every few years thereafter. William Penn's ship alone lost 30 settlers to the disease in 1682. Soldiers often carried the disease, and Pennsylvania suffered a disastrous outbreak when British troops brought it to Philadelphia in 1756. A smallpox epidemic in Boston after the British Army retreated from the city affected local citizens far more than the revolution.

In 1721, Lady Mary Wortley Montague brought the Turkish practice of inoculating people who had not had smallpox with matter acquired from the sores of people with relatively mild cases. Inoculation (also known as variolation) caused real cases of the disease and, although not without risk, carried a lower mortality than naturally acquired smallpox. John Adams commented that the only reason he was picked for the Continental Congress was that he had been inoculated against smallpox and was, therefore, immune. After smallpox forced troops under Gen. Benedict Arnold to withdraw from their Canadian invasion, Gen. George Washington mandated that all Continental Army soldiers be inoculated. Smallpox remained a significant problem until 1798, when Edward Jenner demonstrated that inoculation with the almost entirely safe cowpox virus conveyed lasting immunity against the disease.

Dysentery was a problem both on shipboard and on land. George Percy, the Earl of Northumberland's brother, complained in 1607 that the Jamestown settlement was being destroyed by "swellings, fluxes, and burning fevers" as much as by wars with the Indians. Ships might bring contaminated water aboard and repeatedly distribute it through a voyage. Settlements were often built with little concern for drainage and with latrines close to water used for washing and drinking. The more concentrated the population became, the higher was the likelihood of water supplies becoming contaminated. Wherever a military expedition went, dysentery followed the troops. A 1709 British expedition against French Canada had to be abandoned when dysentery broke out near Wood Creek, New York. The disease was widespread in the earliest Continental Army encampments in 1775 and 1776.

Yellow fever, although less common than other febrile diseases, was uniquely terrifying because it carried a mortality rate approaching 30 percent. The disease came from West Africa with the slave trade and was especially well adapted to transmission over the sea-lanes. The disease is carried by the *Aedes aegyptii* mosquito that reproduces only in standing fresh water such as that found in ships' water barrels. It first appeared in Barbados in 1647 and, beginning with 1699 epidemics in Philadelphia and Charleston, repeatedly struck port cities from Boston to New Orleans throughout the colonial period. A single episode in New York in 1702 cost the city 10 percent of its population.

See also Colonial Military and Naval Medicine; Dysentery; Scurvy; 17th-Century Military Medicine; Smallpox; Typhus; Yellow Fever

References
Garrison, Fielding. *Notes on the History of Military Medicine*. Washington, D.C.: Association of Military Surgeons, 1922.
Packard, Francis. *History of Medicine in the United States*. New York: Paul B. Hoeber, Inc., 1931.
Reiss, Oscar. *Medicine and the American Revolution: How Diseases and Their Treatment Affected the Colonial Army*. Jefferson, NC: McFarland & Co., Inc., 1998.

Roddis, Louis. *A Short History of Nautical Medicine*. New York: Paul B. Hoeber, Inc., 1941.

Dix, Dorothea Lynde (1802–1887)

A reformer and superintendent of nurses for the U.S. Army during the Civil War, Dorothea Dix was born in Hampton, Maine, the first of three children of a lethargic mother and a maniacal father who divided his time between selling books and proselytizing for the Methodist Church. Her father's harsh religiosity drove Dix to leave home at age 12 and spend her adolescence with relatives. She was educated in a private school in Worcester, Massachusetts, and opened her own school in Boston in 1821 where she also began writing books of advice for children and their parents and became an active Unitarian.

Through her church, she became involved in attempts to reform jails and asylums, first in Massachusetts and then in other states and in Europe. In 1861, she offered her services to the Union Army and was named the first superintendent of U.S. Army nurses with responsibility for organizing first aid stations, recruiting nurses, and supplying field hospitals. She related poorly to others and was unpopular both with army physicians, whom she criticized for their personal and professional shortcomings, and with nurses, who found her rigid and overbearing.

After the Civil War, Dix returned to her reform efforts, concentrating on improving conditions in insane asylums. She retired in 1879 and died in Cambridge, Massachusetts, in 1887.

See also Civil War in the United States; Nursing in the Military

References

Brown, Thomas J. *Dorothea Dix: New England Reformer*. Cambridge, MA: Harvard University Press, 1998.

Gollaher, David. *Voice for the Mad: The Life of Dorothea Dix*. New York: Free Press, 1995.

Dodge Commission and the Typhoid Board

The Dodge Commission and the Typhoid Board were representative of the attempts made to reform military medicine in the United States in the early 20th century.

In the wake of the extraordinary personnel losses from disease in military camps in the United States during the Spanish-American War, public outcry ensued, and demands were made for assignment of responsibility. Surgeon General George Sternberg's first response was to appoint Army Medical School professor of bacteriology Walter Reed to head a commission to look into losses from infectious disease during the war. The resulting Typhoid Board also included two volunteer members of the army medical service: Maj. Victor C. Vaughan, a professor of medicine at the University of Michigan, and Maj. Edwin Shakespeare, an internationally recognized authority on epidemic and tropical disease. Together, they inspected all major U.S. military campsites and reviewed records of 107,973 officers and men who had been hospitalized for illness during the war.

They concluded that at least 82 percent of febrile illnesses in the camps had been typhoid, and not malaria or "typho-malaria" as originally diagnosed, and that the disease had, in almost all cases, originated with asymptomatic carriers among the volunteers and had been spread by abysmal sanitary conditions in the camps, highlighting contaminated water, poor hand washing, and the presence of flies as particular culprits. They also concluded that sanitation in a rapidly expanded army was impossible and that the best chance of avoiding typhoid in the future was vaccination. Their advice would be widely accepted and incorporated into general practice from the earliest days of United States involvement in World War I.

As a further response to public indignation, President William McKinley appointed the War Investigating Commission, headed by Maj. Gen. Grenville Dodge, on September 24, 1898. The Dodge Commission was charged with explaining why the death rate among soldiers during the war was five times that in peacetime, a fact the public and press attributed to either incompetence or intentional neglect on the part of Washington bureaucrats and senior military officials. The commission amassed 3,180 pages of testimony from 495 witnesses and compiled it into an eight-volume report that was especially critical of Congress for not providing sufficient funds to support the army and the medical corps. The majority of the commission did not directly blame Secretary of War Russell Alger, but the public did, and the resulting storm of criticism forced his resignation.

The Dodge Commission recommended expansion of the medical corps, establishment of a reserve of trained nurses and of a standing hospital corps, stockpiling of a year's worth of supplies for an army four times the size of that maintained in peacetime, and authorization for military physicians to requisition whatever supplies and food they needed to care for sick soldiers.

An ancillary issue to medical care during the Spanish-American War was the "embalmed beef scandal" precipitated by Commanding General Nelson Miles. Although canned beef had been a standard since 1878 and meatpackers had recently become skilled at refrigerating fresh beef, the general had demanded delivery of live cattle to his troops in the Caribbean. After the war, Miles, who was unable to get his demands for meat on the hoof satisfied, insisted that much of the illness during the conflict had resulted directly from tainted canned meat. A special Beef Court was convened in 1899 and failed to find any evidence that the canned meat played any role in causing disease. A general feeling that Miles had acted out of self-promotion permanently damaged his reputation and played a role in thwarting his presidential ambitions.

See also Reed, Walter; Spanish-American War; Sternberg, George Miller; Typhoid Fever

References

Cirillo, Vincent J. *Bullets and Bacilli: The Spanish-American War and Military Medicine.* New Brunswick, NJ: Rutgers University Press, 1999.

Gillett, Mary C. *The Army Medical Department, 1865–1917.* Washington, D.C.: Center of Military History, U.S. Army, 1995.

Dooley, Thomas Anthony (1927–1961)

Thomas Anthony Dooley was a Viet Nam War–era U.S. Navy physician also known as Dr. America.

Dooley was born the first of three sons of Thomas A. Dooley, Jr., a prominent St. Louis businessman and a pillar of the local Catholic Church. The younger Dooley was initially educated in St. Louis Catholic schools, was a pianist and organist, and was encouraged by his family to become a professional musician. He enrolled in the University of

Notre Dame in 1944, but abandoned college to enlist in the navy the same year. While in the Navy, he trained first as a pharmacist's mate and then as a corpsman.

After World War II, Dooley returned to Notre Dame where he spent three years as an undergraduate before entering St. Louis University's medical school. He was a poor medical student, finishing near the bottom of his class and was forced to repeat his senior year. He subsequently had his internship extended six months for "immaturity" but, with the help of influential friends, was accepted into the Navy Medical Corps in 1953.

In 1954, he was assigned to the USS *Montague*, which was detailed to assist in transferring refugees from northern to southern Viet Nam after the French defeat at Dien Bien Phu led to the country's division. During his participation in what was called Operation Passage to Freedom, Dooley wrote numerous letters home, many of which were printed in the *St. Louis Globe-Democrat*. Most of the letters overstated his personal role in the evacuation. In 1955, Dooley wrote *Deliver Us from Evil*, which, with promotion from *Reader's Digest*, became a best seller and was, for many Americans, the first introduction to Viet Nam.

The U.S. Chamber of Commerce named Dooley one of the Outstanding Young Men in America, and he was the youngest member of the Naval Medical Corps to receive the Legion of Merit. In 1956, Dooley abruptly resigned his commission on the verge of being prosecuted for violating the Navy's prohibition of homosexuality. Dooley had made little effort to conceal his sexual orientation and was rumored to have seduced an admiral's son just before being detailed to Viet Nam.

After leaving the navy, Dooley organized the Medical International Cooperation Organization and donated the royalties from his book to the organization. He also embarked on an extensive speaking and fundraising effort and got financial support from the International Rescue Commission that enabled him to start a hospital at Muong Sing in Laos. His efforts there earned him the nickname Than Mo America (Dr. America).

Dooley was diagnosed with malignant melanoma in 1959 and died of the disease at Memorial Hospital in New York City on January 18, 1961. Investigations incident to an attempt to have him canonized led to discovery that he had used his position in Laos to furnish information on local sentiment and troop movements to the Central Intelligence Agency on several hundred occasions.

See also Naval Medicine; Viet Nam War

References

Dooley, Thomas A. *Deliver Us from Evil: The Story of Viet Nam's Flight to Freedom.* New York: Farrar, Straus & Cudahy, 1956.

Fisher, James T. *Dr. America: The Lives of Thomas A. Dooley.* Amherst: University of Massachusetts Press, 1997.

Drug Addiction

Although narcotic drugs have been used medicinally for 6,000 years, addiction in military forces is a relatively recent problem.

Opium smoking had been a widespread addictive behavior in China since the 1600s, but it was the introduction of the hypodermic syringe during the American Civil War that made high doses of the narcotic easy to deliver. The drug and syringes were distributed for self-administration to Union soldiers suffering from chronic pain. In addition, a wide variety of oral morphine preparations were used to treat pain, diarrhea, and fevers.

Estimates of the number of men who returned to civilian life addicted vary from a low of 80,000 to a high in excess of 400,000. So many came home from the Civil War as "opium eaters" and "morphinists" that "soldier's disease" became the second name for addiction. Although narcotic use was not illegal, veterans who were known to be addicted were automatically denied pensions, so many kept their habit a secret. It is likely that narcotics addiction was also a significant problem among veterans of the Franco-Prussian War, although, as in the earlier conflict, reliable numbers are not available.

Concern that addiction would recur as a major problem after World War I contributed to President Woodrow Wilson's recommending legislation to limit narcotics distribution to that prescribed for a medical reason in 1915. In 1922, the Narcotic Drug Import and Export Act limited importation and purification of narcotics to licensed pharmaceutical companies. The Federal Bureau of Narcotics, convinced that drug use would soar after World War II, convinced Congress to enact draconian minimum penalties for illicit drug distribution, including the death penalty for trafficking.

Drug addiction was not as great a problem after World War II as it had been after the earlier wars, but it again became a major concern during the Korean Conflict since a dose of heroin could be bought in Korea for as little as 80 or 90 cents. Military physicians and epidemiologists in Korea, however, noted that, although intermittent use of marijuana and heroin was common, addiction was rare. That experience was repeated in Viet Nam, where heroin, barbiturates, amphetamines, and opium were widely available and cheap and where up to half of enlisted men used illicit drugs. Drug use in Southeast Asia was so common that the U.S. Army instituted an amnesty program in which any soldier who voluntarily presented himself for treatment would not be punished. Post–Viet Nam studies confirmed that fewer than 1 percent of those who had used drugs during the war remained addicted on return to civilian life.

See also Civil War in the United States; Korean Conflict; Morphine; Viet Nam War; World War I Medicine; World War II Medicine

References

Cowdrey, Albert. *United States Army in the Korean War: The Medics' War.* Washington, D.C.: Center of Military History, U.S. Army, 1987.

Neel, Spurgeon. *Medical Support of the U.S. Army in Viet Nam: 1965–1970.* Washington, D.C.: Department of the Army, 1973.

Robins, Lee, Darlene Davis, and Donald Goodwin. 1974. "Drug Use by U.S. Army Enlisted Men in Viet Nam: A Follow-Up on Their Return Home." *American Journal of Epidemiology* 99: 235–249.

Dysentery

Dysentery is an inflammatory disease of the bowel characterized by fever, abdominal pain, and bloody or purulent diarrhea and most often caused by *Escherichia coli*, *Shigella*, *Salmonella*, or *Campylobacter* species.

Because these organisms are usually transmitted by water or food contaminated with human feces as a result of poor sanitation, dysentery regularly marches with armies. Diarrheal disease among soldiers was described in considerable detail by the Hebrews, the ancient Greeks, and the Romans. Both Hippocrates and Roman military surgeons recognized the relationship between dysentery and unclean water, and Gen. George Washington cited Deuteronomy in his order that latrines be located as far as possible from camps.

Perhaps the earliest well-documented instance in which sanitation determined a military outcome was Charles V's 1552 siege of Metz. The Holy Roman Emperor had 220,000 men around the city, which was defended by the Duke of Guise and 6,000 supporters. The duke, however, took great pains to ensure a clean food supply, to throw human waste and animal carcasses over the walls, and to isolate the sick, especially those with diarrhea. As a result, while Charles V lost 20,000 of his troops to dysentery, typhus, and scurvy, the citizens of Metz survived the 65-day siege with no serious outbreaks of disease, and the city did not fall.

Dysentery remained a constant accompaniment to wars for the next four centuries and was especially troublesome as the numbers of combatants increased. England's King Henry V died of it, and diarrheal disease spread throughout Europe with the armies of the Thirty Years War. In the 1845 U.S. war with Mexico, diseases—of which dysentery was by far the most common—killed seven times as many combatants as did battle injuries. During the American Civil War, dysentery and other diarrheal diseases were again the most common causes of hospitalization, accounting for 1,585,236 admissions and 44,448 deaths in the Union Army alone. By comparison, the North lost 110,070 to battle injuries, a situation that led directly to formation of the U.S. Sanitary Commission.

Dysentery was once again a prominent factor in the Spanish-American War, where the death rate in training camps in the United States significantly exceeded the death rate on Cuban battlefields. The situation was even worse in the Boer War, where the British lost 6,000 men to battlefield injury but 16,000 to typhoid and dysentery. Among the Boers, 4,000 died from trauma while 9,000, mostly women and children confined to concentration camps, died of dysentery.

In the 1894 Sino-Japanese War, Japan suffered 12,052 cases of dysentery and almost 50,000 other cases of infectious disease in an army of 200,000. The impact on military effectiveness precipitated drastic reform of the Imperial Army Medical Corps so that, in the Russo-Japanese War a decade later, out of a total force of 600,000 only 10,565 infectious illnesses occurred, and the death rate was only 1.2 percent. This was the first time a major military force had so effectively lowered disease rate with an organized sanitary program, and it served as a model for armies for the balance of the 20th century.

In 1910, U.S. Army Maj. Carl Rogers Darnall showed that water could be purified by anhydrous chlorine, and, five years later, Maj. William Lyster developed the "Lyster bag," which effectively chlorinated water with sodium hypochlorite contained in cloth. In World War I, Sir Almroth Wright's typhoid vaccine finally controlled that disease but did nothing to prevent the other forms of dysentery. During World War II, the German Afrika Korps under Gen. Erwin Rommel was severely hampered by dysentery. Dysentery became easier to control after the war with the development of broad-spectrum antibiotics generally effective against diarrhea-causing bacteria.

Recently, antibiotic-resistant strains of *E. coli*, Shigella, nontyphoid Salmonella, and Campylobacter have emerged among U.S. troops in Southeast Asia. During Operation Desert Shield, 57 percent of American troops stationed in Saudi Arabia had suffered at least one bout of diarrhea within two months of deployment, and the majority of organisms isolated from those patients were *E. coli* and Shigella resistant to available antibiotics. It appears that dysentery will continue to be a problem for military physicians and that sanitation and prevention will continue to be the principal means of control.

See also American Revolutionary War; Boer War; Civil War in the United States; Mexican-American War; Typhoid Fever; World War I Medicine; World War II Medicine

References

Bayne-Jones, S. *The Evolution of Preventive Medicine in the Unites States Army: 1607–1939.* Washington, D.C.: Office of the Surgeon General, Department of the Army, 1968.

Hyams, K. C., A. L. Bargeris, and B. R. Merrill. 1991. "Diarrheal Diseases during Operation Desert Storm." *New England Journal of Medicine* 325 (May 16): 1423–1428.

Lim, M. L., G. S. Murphy, M. Calloway, and D. Tribble. 2005. "History of U.S. Military Contributions to the Study of Diarrheal Diseases." *Military Medicine* 170: 30–38.

Lim, Matthew, and M. R. Wallace. 2004. "Infectious Diarrhea in History." *Infectious Disease Clinics of North America* 18: 261–274.

E

Egyptian Military Medicine

The Nile River valley provided the first congenial location for the aggregation of large populations and the large armies they could support.

The area is fertile enough to sustain up to 450 people per square mile. Farmers in the Nile valley were able to produce more than they required for personal consumption, and the excess could be used to support administrative and military establishments and those organizations made it possible to fight large battles. Mass graves dating to 2000 B.C. in which the bones are fractured and arrows are wedged into skeletal remains are graphic residua of those developments.

Egyptian physicians served as both priests of the goddess Sekhmet and as empirical practitioners. In the empire's later years, the two tended to separate, with the priests holding a higher social position but the practitioners being more technically skilled. Military physicians were most often of the latter class, known as *swnw* (possibly pronounced soo-noo). Each Egyptian district (*nomo*) had its own military unit and barracks, and each unit had its own physicians. When Egyptian armies went on campaign, they were accompanied by physicians paid by the state, and medical care for soldiers was free.

Anyone who practiced medicine in ancient Egypt was required to follow a strictly defined formulary and employ standardized treatment regimens. Physicians bore no responsibility for bad results if they followed those rules but could be put to death if they did not and the patient failed to survive. The idea that few physicians were better than the time-tested system compiled by the best of their predecessors anticipates the modern "best practice" doctrine. This is the earliest example of medicine as a science ruled by observation and analysis rather than by art and magic. That said, Egyptian physicians were also priests and magicians and tended to restrict tested techniques of scientific medicine and surgery to lesser injuries and to fall back on magic for more difficult problems.

Since the Bronze Age dawned in Egypt about 2000 B.C., the earliest war-related injuries were probably inflicted by flint. Only pictures of Egyptian surgical instruments from that era are available as no actual examples survive. Also available are pictographs of splints made from palm fiber and crutches from a slightly later time.

The Egyptians and Greeks were able, using a process that has been lost, to harden bronze and put a razor-sharp edge on instruments made of the metal. It is also possible that a few instruments were made of iron, although, because techniques for refining iron ore were not known until about 1300 B.C., the metal had to be recovered from meteorites and was of utmost rarity and value.

The advent of iron smelting made weapons widely available and allowed for conscription and arming of large fighting forces. Just after the dawn of the Iron Age, Ramses II's army numbered 100,000, and, in the Battle of Kadesh (1304 B.C.), the Egyptians pitted 20,000 men against the Hittites' 17,000.

Egyptian military physicians demonstrated a surprising empirical command of battlefield surgery. They opened the skull by trephining and anticipated Galen by two millennia in describing the brain's folds, which they likened to slag from molten metal. They knew brain injury resulted in paralysis, but some confusion exists as to whether they understood that injuries on one side of the brain affected the body's opposite side. These ancient physicians recognized and counted the pulse and knew that the rate correlated with the severity of injury, but they did not understand that blood circulated and did not differentiate among vessels, tendons, and nerves. They apparently refrained from violating the chest or abdominal cavity. Egyptians were, however, adept at embalming and (possibly employing chemicals similar to those that preserved corpses) used drugs for some infectious diseases.

The oldest extant medical treatise is a rolled papyrus bought from an Egyptian antiquities dealer by Edwin Smith in 1862. The papyrus, quite possibly a manual of military medicine, was transcribed from an original written before the wheel was invented between 2600 and 2200 B.C. and was translated between A.D. 1920 and 1930 by James Breasted. The book divides various wounds and ailments by body part from the head down and by severity within sections, for example, simple linear skull fracture, comminuted or shattered skull fracture, and comminuted fracture beneath an open scalp wound. In keeping with the rules of practice, for each illness or wound the physician is advised to treat, try to treat, or not to treat. The scribe who transcribed the book in about 1650 B.C. apparently tired and quit his job in the middle of a word in the middle of a sentence, having written about 48 cases but having only reached the thorax. We are left to wonder what was in the remainder of the text. Four other Egyptian medical papyri survive (in London, in Berlin, in Leipzig, and at the University of California) along with a few fragments elsewhere, but they are almost entirely recipes for various medicines and potions and shed little light on military medical practice.

The Smith papyrus contains the first description of closing a wound with suture but also speaks of using gum adhesive from the acacia tree to glue the wound edges and of leaving contaminated wounds open to heal later, all techniques still in use. Padded boards were used to pry open the mouths of patients afflicted with tetanus ("lockjaw") so they could be fed. Wounds were often bound with fresh meat under the theory (later adopted by homeopathy) that injuries and illnesses could be treated by substances similar to themselves. Egyptian use of honey on wounds was reasonable as we now know that it contains several substances that inhibit bacterial growth. In fact, honey has been used to treat wounds as recently as the Boer War and World War I. Willow leaves, which contain salicylates similar to aspirin, were also applied to wounds and may have served as an analgesic. Egyptians also used the extract of the opium poppy and, by 1500 B.C., were importing distilled opium from Cyprus for use as an analgesic and possibly as an anesthetic. Copper containing malachite was used cosmetically for eye shadow, but Egyptian military physicians also knew it aided wound healing, although they did not know that the effect probably derived from the bacteriostatic properties of copper in the paste. Mercury containing cinnabar was used similarly. Wounds were cauterized by "fire drills"—sticks rapidly rotated with a leather strap similar to modern Boy Scout campfire starters that generated enough heat to sterilize their edges or by hot knives fresh from the fire. Egyptian

physicians as early as 2750 B.C. knew how to make moldable splints from linen or papyrus impregnated with resin that would harden in place and allow accurate fixation of long bone fractures.

Egyptians had the first organized armies, the first military physicians, and the oldest known medical text, and they were the first to systematically apply empirical science to medicine.

See also Imhotep; Scalpel; Trephine, Trepan, and Trephining

References
Breasted, James Henry. *The Edwin Smith Surgical Papyrus Published in Facsimile and Hieroglyphic Transliteration with Translation and Commentary in Two Volumes*. Chicago: University of Chicago Press, 1930.
Wilson, John. 1962. "Medicine in Ancient Egypt" *Bulletin of the History of Medicine* 36 (2): 114–123.
Zimmerman, Leo, and Ilza Veith. *Great Ideas in the History of Surgery*. Baltimore: Williams & Wilkins Co., 1961.

F

Fabrizio d'Aquapendente, Geronimo (1537–1619)

A pioneering anatomist considered the premier Italian surgeon of the Renaissance, Geronimo Fabrizio d'Aquapendente was also known as Hieronymus Fabricius and Fabricius ab Aquapendente.

Fabrizio was born in the village of Aquapendente, between Rome and Sienna, to a modest family and was sent to study at the university in Padua at age 17. He went on to study at the city's medical school, where he was taught by Gabriele Fallopio, who had studied under Andreas Vesalius. He graduated and started in practice in 1559 but continued to study anatomy.

Fabrizio succeeded Fallopio as professor of anatomy at Padua in 1565, taught there for more than 50 years, and established the first permanent anatomical amphitheater, a facility still used by Giovanni Morgagni more than a century later and copied by John Monro, father of Alexander Monro primus, in Edinburgh.

Fabrizio taught William Harvey and was a close friend of Galileo Galilei. His studies of the veins inspired Harvey, and the latter's plates in *De motu cordis* were drawn from those of his teacher, although Fabrizio incorrectly believed that the valves only served to slow blood flow through the body.

He was a successful practicing surgeon who received a generous stipend and a knighthood from the Venetian government, and his 1617 *Opera Chirurgica* described a number of new techniques and remained a standard for more than a century. Fabrizio was one of the first to use the term "trachea" and wrote detailed descriptions of the operation, although he evidently never performed the procedure himself.

He died at age 82, honored and mourned by his students, friends, and fellow citizens.

See also Amputation; Harvey, William; Vesalius, Andreas

Reference

Zimmerman, Leo, and Ilza Veith. *Great Ideas in the History of Surgery.* Baltimore: Williams & Wilkins Co., 1961.

Fabry of Hilden, Wilhelm (1560–1634)

Known as the father of German surgery, Wilhelm Fabry was also known by the Latin name Fabricius Hildanus.

Fabry was born near Düsseldorf, the son of a clerk in the local court of justice. He lost his father when he was 10 and his stepfather shortly thereafter. He then caught plague, and the disease rendered him bedridden and unable to go to university. As a substitute, Fabry was apprenticed for 12 years as a surgeon, during which time he married Marie Colinet, who was an accomplished surgeon and obstetrician in her own right. Fabry lost both his wife and two daughters to plague.

Fabry was a skilled surgeon and inventor of a number of surgical instruments; he was the contemporary of the Italian Fabrizio d'Aquapendente. Fabry's monograph on gangrene, published in Cologne in 1593, was the first to recommend amputation for gangrene in healthy tissue above the diseased area. He was the first to successfully perform above-the-knee amputations with a reasonable survival rate because he used ligatures and a twistable tourniquet to control the inevitable hemorrhage. His observations on wound surgery, collected in groups of 100 cases and spanning four decades, was perhaps the most comprehensive collection of surgical experiences of his time. He anticipated Harvey Cushing's World War I experiments by 350 years in removing iron splinters from the eye with a magnet. He also showed that head injuries could cause abnormalities in behavior and described a field medicine chest for military surgeons that was adapted in Janus Abraham a Gehema's 1689 medical manual for field officers.

Fabry's practice was an odd mixture of science and superstition. He favored the cautery over a cold knife in amputation and recommended applying healing salves to weapons, believing their use would lessen complications of wounds they had inflicted. He preferred taping wounds closed to suturing and alleviated the pain of battlefield surgery by having the patient breathe from a sponge soaked in opium, hyoscyamus, and belladonna. Fabry's 1614 *De Combustionibus* was the first text devoted solely to the treatment of burns for which he prescribed a dressing of onion, soaps, rose oil, and almond oil mixed with raw eggs. Although the last ingredient seems odd, the albumin from the eggs would have formed an occlusive dressing similar to modern ones using collodion. He divided burns into three types depending on severity in a way not unlike current practice and may have been the first to describe removing the eschar in cases of third-degree burn. His treatment of scars included various salves, local resection, and use of splints to prevent contractures.

See also Amputation; Cauterization; Fabrizio d'Aquapendente, Geronimo; 17th-Century Military Medicine

References
Dealey, Carol. 2005. "German Wound Surgeons: 1450–1750." *European Wound Management Association Journal* 5: 48–51.
Kirkpatrick, J. J. R., B. Curtis, A. M. Fitzgerald, and I. L. Naylor. 1995. "A Modern Translation and Interpretation of the Treatise on Burns of Fabricius Hildanus (1560–1634)." *British Journal of Plastic Surgery* 48: 460–470.
Thomsen, M. 1977. "Historical Landmarks in the Treatment of Burns." *British Journal of Plastic Surgery* 30: 212–217.
Zimmerman, Leo, and Ilza Veith. *Great Ideas in the History of Surgery.* Baltimore: Williams & Wilkins Co., 1961.

Fergusson, Sir William (1808–1877)

William Fergusson was known as the founder of "conservative surgery," in which whatever body parts that could be saved were left in place.

Fergusson was born in Prestonpans, Scotland, and served as student and assistant to Scottish anatomist Robert Knox. Fergusson's mentor was controversial, having been mobbed and nearly hanged for buying bodies for dissection from a supplier who had murdered the victims specifically to supply the anatomist. Fergusson was himself a remarkably skilled dissector especially famous for his blood vessel preparations. He was said to have practiced playing the violin to improve his surgical dexterity and was described as having the eye of an eagle, the heart of a lion, and the hand of a lady.

Fergusson was appointed surgeon to the Royal Infirmary in 1839 and to the chair of surgery at King's College the following year, where he worked for the next 30 years until resigning and being succeeded by Joseph Lister. His *System of Practical Surgery* was a standard that went through five editions and numerous translations. Fergusson was also a skilled carpenter and metalworker who designed and built a number of his own surgical instruments. He was an adept operator who insisted on absolute silence while he worked. He said any competent surgeon should be able to amputate a leg in between 30 seconds and three minutes, including applying the dressing, a feat he regularly performed, admittedly with the help of four assistants.

Fergusson was a Fellow of the Royal College of Surgeons; Fellow of the Royal Society; Surgeon in Ordinary to Albert, Prince Consort of Queen Victoria; Surgeon Extraordinary to Queen Victoria; Sergeant Surgeon; and Hunterian Orator before his death on February 10, 1877.

See also Amputation

Reference
Comrie, John. *History of Scottish Medicine.* London: Ballière, Tindall & Cox, 1932.

Field Hospitals

Field hospitals are mobile treatment facilities that began as rudimentary shelters near the front lines and have evolved into containerized modules with beds, laboratories, X-ray facilities, and operating suites.

The oldest forerunners of field hospitals were the facilities provided by Queen Isabella for her troops in the 15th century wars to expel the Moors from Iberia. Her grandson Charles V perpetuated the practice when he became Holy Roman Emperor.

At the siege of Amiens in 1597, the Duc de Sully arranged for traveling hospitals to accompany his troops and paid for them with a special tax on tavern keepers, haberdashers, tailors, and shoemakers. Thirty years later, Cardinal Richelieu's forces during the siege of La Rochelle also had well-organized and well-equipped field hospitals. In 1638, Richelieu issued an ordinance providing for Jesuits to serve as cooks, nurses, and purveyors of food for the sick and wounded on campaign. Surgeons for these facilities were largely drawn from the new training program at St. Côme in Paris, and service in a field hospital became something close to a requisite step in French surgical careers.

The British were slower than the French to provide mobile hospitals for their troops.

At Fontenoy in 1745, they provided for the first "flying" hospitals, in which tents with surgeons were arrayed behind the line of battle to await the wounded. Moving casualties unable to drag themselves from the field to these facilities, however, became the responsibility of other soldiers lucky enough to be given permission to leave the battle to carry their compatriots. Eighteenth-century field hospitals still served as dressing stations and places to stabilize wounds. Large operations and amputations remained the province of fixed, rear-area hospitals.

The principal change in field hospitals through the middle of the 19th century was their increased use for performance of larger surgical procedures. French surgeons Baron Dominique-Jean Larrey and Pierre François Percy recognized that wounds, especially those inflicted by artillery or bullets, healed best if treated early. They introduced organized retrieval of the wounded by designated litter bearers and designed ingenious self-contained wagons with the equipment necessary to perform major surgical procedures that could follow armies and be deployed close to the front lines.

Although the development of anesthesia, antisepsis, and X-ray in the latter half of the 19th century brought new opportunities for field surgery, mobile hospitals were less important in the static trench warfare of World War I than in the more mobile conflicts that had preceded it.

Field hospitals again became important in World War II. By the 1940s it was possible to load laboratories, blood banks, X-ray machines, and fully equipped operating rooms onto trucks, so field hospitals could follow the troops and were typically set up a few miles behind the front. The wounded were taken directly from forward-area dressing stations and all but the largest surgical procedures could be done in them. Convalescents could even be held for several days of postoperative observation. By the Korean Conflict, the field hospitals had grown into mobile army surgical hospitals (M.A.S.H. units) of up to 60 beds and were nearing the size and status of evacuation hospitals.

In the Viet Nam War, helicopter transport and improved management of shock and multiple trauma resulted in a death rate for soldiers who arrived at a field hospital of only 2.6 percent. Current U.S. Army practice is to staff field hospitals with forward surgical teams typically composed of three general surgeons, one orthopedist, two nurse anesthetists, three nurses, and various medics and other support personnel. These teams travel with the troops and can set up a fully functioning hospital with four ventilator-equipped beds and two operating suites in 60 minutes. The entire facility, including three deployable rapid-assembly shelter units that can be joined to form a 900-square-foot facility, is carried in six Humvees. Surgical and laboratory facilities are sufficient to perform surgery on up to 30 wounded soldiers.

Modern field hospitals have also become a major element in planning for nonmilitary disasters, and civil authorities around the world have stockpiled these units.

See also Casualty Clearing Stations and Staged Evacuation; Larrey, Baron Dominique-Jean; Mobile Army Surgical Hospitals in the Korean Conflict; Percy, Baron Pierre François

References
Gawande, Atul. 2004. "Casualties of War—Military Care for the Wounded from Iraq and Afghanistan." *New England Journal of Medicine* 351 (December): 2471–2475.
Heizmann, Charles. 1917–1918. "Military Sanitation in the Sixteenth, Seventeenth

and Eighteenth Centuries." *Annals of Medical History* 1: 281–300.

Stewart, John, and Frank Warner. 1945. "Observations on the Severely Wounded in Forward Field Hospitals: With Special Reference to Wound Shock." *Annals of Surgery* 122 (August): 129–146.

Fleming, Sir Alexander (1881–1955)

A noted researcher and lecturer and the discoverer of penicillin, Alexander Fleming was born on a farm at Lochfield in Ayrshire, Scotland, the third of seven children. He went to school at Louden Moor, Carvel, and Kilmarnoch Academy before attending the Polytechnic Institute in London. He then worked in a shipping office for four years before enrolling in St. Mary's Medical School of London University, from which he graduated with a gold medal and an M.B.B.S. in 1908. After graduation, Fleming worked as a lecturer at St. Mary's and joined Sir Almroth Wright's Inoculation Division at the hospital, researching immunization solutions to infectious disease.

Fleming remained at St. Mary's until the beginning of World War I; in 1914 he joined the Royal Army Medical Corps as a captain. During the war, he continued to work under Wright. Their research convinced Fleming that, contrary to Alexis Carrel's recommendation, antiseptics applied directly to wounds impeded healing and did little or nothing to control contaminating bacteria.

After the war, Fleming returned to St. Mary's, where he continued to look for

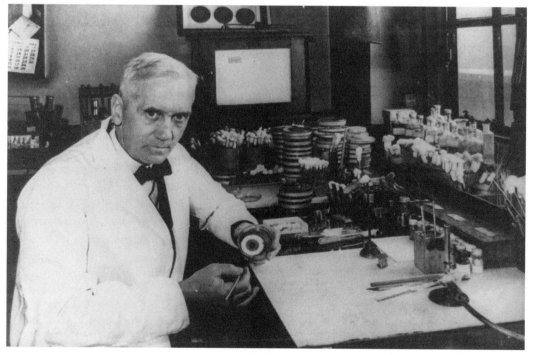

Alexander Fleming in his laboratory holding a petri dish. Fleming was awarded the Nobel Prize in Medicine in 1945 for his discovery of penicillin. (Library of Congress)

substances that would kill microorganisms without harming animal tissues. In 1921 he isolated a naturally occurring bactericidal enzyme, which he named lysozyme. In late August or early September 1928, while working on the influenza virus, he noticed that a petri dish with staphylococcus had a ring of killed bacteria around a contaminated mold that a co-worker identified as *Penicillium rubrum*. (In fact, the organism had been misidentified and was actually *Penicillium notatum*.) Although Fleming described the substance and its activity against gram-positive bacteria, the chemical (which he named penicillin) was unstable and difficult to isolate, and he doubted it would be useful in treating humans. Fleming did not report his findings at the time, but he also found it impossible to repeat his original experiment. It remained for Howard W. Florey and Ernst Chain to extract and purify penicillin and render it clinically useful 12 years later.

Fleming was named a Fellow of the Royal Society in 1943, knighted in 1944, and shared the Nobel Prize for Physiology or Medicine with Florey and Chain in 1945. He died March 11, 1955, and is buried in St. Paul's Cathedral in London.

See also Penicillin; World War II Medicine

References
Maurois, Andre. *The Life of Sir Alexander Fleming*. New York: E. P. Dutton and Co., 1959.
McFarlane, Gwyn. *Alexander Fleming: The Man and the Myth*. Oxford: Oxford University Press, 1984.

Forceps and Extractors

Among the oldest tools in the military surgeon's armamentarium, forceps and extractors probably were first modeled after the prehensile human thumb and forefinger and intended as an extension of the operator's hand.

Pictures of metal forceps, with a sliding slot construction and rings around the arms to hold the instrument closed, date at least to 800 B.C., and actual working examples of the instrument were unearthed from the ruins at Pompeii. Forceps remain key surgical instruments, with more than 1,000 variations in current production and use.

Forceps have two primary uses. They can act as extensions of the surgeon's fingers in extracting foreign bodies and can also be used to grasp and temporarily close a bleeding vessel, leaving the operative field dry and freeing the surgeon's hands for other tasks.

As an instrument of extraction, forceps became especially important after the introduction of firearms in the 13th century. The oldest surviving bullet extractor is a 1532 instrument consisting of a hollow tube through which a sharp-tipped screw could be introduced into the depths of the wound and drilled into a soft-lead projectile, which could then be pulled out of the wound.

Ambroise Paré devised an entire set of forceps with jaws of different sizes, shapes, and curvatures for drawing out bullets and named his various instruments after birds and reptiles he thought they resembled—crane's bill, drake's bill, parrot's bill, swan's bill, crow's bill, and snake's head. In the aggregate, he referred to them as *tires-fonds*, or deep pullers. The French surgeon said the first thing to do in caring for a gunshot wound was to probe so one could locate bits of cloth, paper, and leather carried into the body with a projectile. Next one used the appropriate forceps to remove the detritus along with the bullet and any accompanying bone fragments. Paré's contemporaries designed instruments with cup-shaped jaws, blades with files, or tips shaped like alligator jaws for better grasping. By the late 1600s, a creative assortment of bullet-extracting forceps was part of every military surgeon's kit, but the instruments were not without problems of their own. Reacting to a growing number of injuries caused by overly aggressive forceps use, Johannes Scultetus cautioned against opening the instrument's jaws before the tip touched the bone or bullet it was meant to remove lest the surgeon rip out an artery, a vein, or a nerve.

In addition to using forceps as extractors, Paré also employed the instrument to stop bleeding. He recommended his *bec de Corbin ou de Perroquet* as a replacement for irrigation with boiling oil in stopping arterial hemorrhage. Scultetus described 15 different types of forceps, including one that could be spread rather than closed and could open a wound so the surgeon could find a foreign body or a bleeding artery.

In 1840, Joseph Frederic Charrière introduced the first truly effective arterial clamp, a cross-legged, spring-closing instrument that could be applied with one hand and would tightly grasp a vessel. This ingenious tool replaced two flat pieces of wood tied together with a string and was succeeded by J. F. Dieffenbach's spring-loaded "bulldog" clamp, which could be applied and released, entirely freeing the surgeon's hands to do other things while the forceps controlled bleeding. With this advance, forceps design was substantially complete, and modern instruments offer little more than refinements on that basic design.

See also Classical Greek Military Medicine; Medieval Military Medicine; Paré, Ambroise; Roman Military Medicine

References

Bennion, Elisabeth. *Antique Medical Instruments.* Berkeley: University of California Press, 1979.

Crooke, Helkiah. *An Explanation of the Fashion and Use of Three and Fifty Instruments of Chirurgery Gathered out of Ambrosius Pareus, the Famous French Chirurgien, and Done into English, for the Behoose of Young Practitioners in Chirurgery.* London: Michael Sparke, 1634 (reprinted in facsimile, Edinburgh: West Port Books, 1982).

Thompson, C. J. S. *The History and Evolution of Surgical Instruments.* New York: Schuman's, 1942.

Wangensteen, Owen, and Sarah D. Wangensteen. *The Rise of Surgery from Empiric Craft to Scientific Discipline.* Minneapolis: University of Minnesota Press, 1978.

Fort Detrick

Fort Detrick was home of the U.S. biological warfare program originally known as the U.S. Biological Laboratories and more recently as the U.S. Army Medical Research Institute of Infectious Diseases (USAMRIID).

First named Camp Detrick, the facility occupies a 1,200-acre farm in Frederick County, Maryland, about 40 miles north of Washington, D.C.

After World War II, scientists from Camp Detrick were given the opportunity to interrogate Japanese physicians who had been involved in the biological warfare experiments at Unit 731 in Manchuria. The first American biowarfare experiments were directed against food crops and, by 1951, Army scientists had developed antiagricultural agents intended to attack Russian wheat and Chinese crops. Experiments were also conducted on organisms with potential antipersonnel applications including tularemia, Venezuelan equine encephalitis, and staphylococcus enterotoxins. Weaponized biological materials were stored at the nearby Edgewood Arsenal in Maryland and at the Rocky Mountain Arsenal near Denver. In the 1960s, scientists from Fort Detrick conducted experiments in which nonpathogenic microorganisms were released over Washington, D.C.; New York; Boston; and Los Angeles to study their distribution in concentrated populations.

In November 1969, President Richard Nixon signed an executive order renouncing biowarfare and ordered all biological weapons destroyed. Fort Detrick was officially turned over to the National Cancer Institute, although USAMRIID has remained at the facility.

See also Chemical and Biological Warfare

Reference
Covert, Norman. *Cutting Edge: A History of Fort Detrick, Maryland—1943–1993*. Fort Detrick, MD: Public Affairs Office, 1997.

Fracastro, Girolamo (1484–1553)

Girolamo Fracastro was an Italian humanist, scientist, and physician who practiced in the Lake Garda region of northern Italy.

Fracastro was a large, hirsute man known for his jovial demeanor and penetrating curiosity. Along with Leonardo da Vinci, he was the first to recognize the significance of fossils, and he was the first to describe the earth's magnetic poles. He was most famous for his long medical poem *Syphilis sive Morbus Gallicus,* published in Venice in 1530, in which he recognized the contagious nature of the venereal disease and questioned the common belief that it had been brought by the Spanish from America.

His most important work was *De Contagione,* in which he laid out a theory of infectious disease that anticipated Joseph Lister's work by 350 years. Fracastro hypothesized that infectious diseases could be transmitted three ways: (1) by simple contact; (2) by indirect contact with small particles he called "fomites" that were not, of themselves, harmful but that could harbor tiny disease-causing organisms; and (3) by transmission through the air. He also recognized that smallpox, measles, tuberculosis, rabies, leprosy, and scabies were infectious diseases.

See also Lister, Lord Joseph; Scabies; Syphilis

Reference
Martin, John. *Heirs of Hippocrates: The Development of Medicine in a Catalogue of Historic Books in the Health Sciences Library of the University of Iowa.* Iowa City: Friends of the University of Iowa Libraries, 1980.

Fractures

Broken bones are generally classified as either simple fractures, in which the fragments do not penetrate skin, or compound fractures, in which the fragments are in contact with the outside world.

Because bones, especially skulls, are available for archaeological study, fractures are the oldest documented battle injuries. A depressed fracture apparently caused by a blow from an antelope bone has been documented in an *Australopithecus afarensis* skull found in East Africa.

The oldest documented treatment of a simple fracture was in a mummy from Egypt's Fifth Dynasty (ca. 2450 B.C.), which was interred with a bark splint still in place on a broken forearm. Fractures seem to have been relatively frequent in ancient Egypt; one study of 6,000 mummies included 32 with broken bones.

Although simple fractures often healed, compound fractures have resulted in a historically high mortality rate. The force necessary to break a bone and drive its fragments through the skin is great enough to also inflict significant damage on the surrounding soft tissues. The combination of devitalized tissue and an open wound led to a high incidence of infection and frequently lethal sepsis. Hippocrates recommended dressing open fractures with goat skin after sawing off protruding bone fragments, but the generally poor outcome led Greek physicians to avoid treating compound fractures when possible.

Plaster was probably introduced by Arab physicians as early as the 10th century, and Turkish surgeons used plaster of paris in the early 19th century, but Artemius Mathijsen of the Netherlands is credited with modern methods of stabilization for having put plaster into bandages that could be wrapped into a splint that hardened in the shape of the injured extremity in 1852. His bandages hardened in a couple of hours as opposed to previous preparations that had taken hours to days to set.

The role of compound fracture in military medicine fundamentally changed in the 16th century with the introduction of gunpowder weapons. Metal projectiles striking extremities at high velocity have a great propensity to smash bone, and compound fracture became the leading cause of amputation and one of the leading causes of death in battle. Because of the high incidence of infection and the likelihood of death from sepsis, amputation was the primary treatment for compound fractures between 1600 and the end of the 19th century. A few military sur-

geons—most notably John Hunter and Felix Würtz—argued for more conservative therapy, but they remained a distinct minority. Both Ambroise Paré (in 1561) and Percival Pott (in 1756) argued for amputation in spite of the fact that each had sustained an open fracture himself, both declined amputation, and both healed. When Johannes Bilguer, surgeon general under Frederick the Great of Prussia, boasted that he had saved 1,800 soldiers from amputation by treating their injuries conservatively, Pott vilified him.

Amputation for compound fractures caused by gunshot wounds was anything but universally successful. George Guthrie, the premier British military surgeon during the Napoleonic Wars, noted that two-thirds of patients with a gunshot wound to the thigh died with or without amputation, although he argued that all such injuries should be treated with immediate removal of the limb. Oddly, he thought fractured upper extremities could be saved. French results were even more dismal. At Salpetriére, Jean Nicolas Marjolin said in 1814 that he had seen only one patient survive amputation for a thigh fracture. Baron Dominique-Jean Larrey claimed a 75 percent recovery rate in amputations after the Battle of Borodino, but in Paris after the 1830 revolution, nearly half of his patients with similar operations died. Mortality from amputation for fracture in Paris during the 1870 siege approached 100 percent and was 92 percent in the Crimean War. Confederate surgeons experienced patient mortality from thigh-level amputations between June 1862 and February 1864 of 49 percent. Union surgeons fared slightly better, with mortality from gunshot wounds to the femur being 31.7 percent, of the lower leg 14.4 percent, of the humerus 30.7 percent, and of the forearm 21.9 percent.

The high rate of infection and death may account for the fact that most orthopedic treatises written in the first half of the 19th century were silent on the subject of compound fracture. The first real change came with the introduction of antiseptics. Larrey began using resin from the styrax tree (later purified as tincture of benzoin) in the bandages he used to stabilize fractures in his post-Napoleonic role as honorary surgeon in chief to the Old Guard.

In 1867, Joseph Lister recommended irrigating open fractures with carbolic acid after hearing about Louis Pasteur's isolation of disease-causing microorganisms. His report in the New Sydenham Society's *Biennial Retrospect* was the first public statement of the antiseptic technique for which he became famous. An expansion of the paper appeared later the same year in the journal *Lancet.* Military surgeon Carl Reyher conducted controlled studies of Lister's technique in gunshot wounds to the extremities suffered during the Russo-Turkish wars of 1878 and 1881.

By World War I, débridement and open wound irrigation with antiseptics had become standard treatment for compound fractures of the extremities, but those techniques were largely superseded by the appearance of antibiotics and the general acceptance of aseptic surgical technique between the world wars.

Although Arbuthnot Lane had introduced metal plates and screws to stabilize fractures in 1903, those techniques could not become standard until antibiotics and asepsis decreased infection rates to an acceptable level. During World War I, Harvard Medical School surgeons used plaster casts above and below open wounds with the two connected by heavy wire for stabilization, leaving the actual wound open for drainage and dressing. By the early 1940s, it was possible not only to reunite fracture fragments but also to insert metal rods the length of long bones, and studies had begun that would reveal techniques to replace entire joints.

See also Antisepsis; Civil War in the United States; Classical Greek Military Medicine; Egyptian Military Medicine; Guthrie, George James; Islamic Military Medicine; Larrey, Baron Dominique-Jean; Lister, Lord Joseph; Napoleonic Wars; World War I Medicine

References

Fauntleroy, A. M. *Report on the Medico-Military Aspects of the European War from Observations Taken behind the Allied Armies in France.* Washington, D.C.: Government Printing Office, 1915.

Majno, Guido *The Healing Hand: Man and Wound in the Ancient World.* Cambridge, MA: Harvard University Press, 1975.

Wangensteen, Owen, and Sara Wangensteen. *Rise of Surgery from Empiric Craft to Scientific Discipline.* Minneapolis: University of Minnesota Press, 1978.

Franco-Prussian War

The war between France and the German confederation led by Prussia lasted only five months in 1870–1871 but resulted in a surprisingly high rate of casualty and mortality from illness as well as from injury.

The Prussians mobilized over just eight days (July 16–24, 1870), and the French accepted a draconian peace on January 28, 1871. The war's brevity belies the losses on both sides occasioned by the size of the opposing armies and the use of high-velocity firearms. France started the war with 244,828 men under arms and increased its army to a maximum of 584,000. The Prussians and their allies started with 384,000 men and increased that number to 788,213 as the war progressed. Rail transport made it possible to move large numbers of men rapidly and led to the war's atypically large set-piece battles, with correspondingly high numbers of casualties. Prussia had introduced the Dreyse needle gun, a breechloader with a sharp-pointed striker that ignited the bullet's powder, in its wars with Denmark and Austria. The needle gun had a high firing rate and a high muzzle velocity, which combined to make the rifle effective at longer ranges than had previously been possible. The French had the chassepot, a breechloader with twice the range of the Dreyse, and the mitrailleuse, a 25-barrel machine gun that could fire 125 rounds a minute and that was effective at 1,200 yards.

Military surgeons learned early that wounds from these high-velocity weapons, if they did not strike a vital organ, tended to perforate the body with less overall damage than that caused by the slow, heavy, wobbling projectiles from older muzzle loaders.

The French railroads' topography virtually forced France to mass its troops at the Metz and Strasbourg railheads, which were separated by the Vosges Mountains. General Helmuth von Moltke recognized this fact and entered the war determined to accept large losses (50 percent at Mars-la-Tour) in order to take advantage of the concentration and separation of the French forces to bring the war to an early conclusion. Von Moltke's strategy led to a quick series of large battles with exceptionally high casualty rates on both sides.

The Prussians had fought wars with the Danes and the Austrians in the decade prior to their war with France, and their military physicians had learned from those conflicts. The Prussians entered the war with 3,853

physicians, later increased to 5,548 through civilian draft. In addition, the Prussians had 5,858 hospital attendants, 2,921 nurses, and 468 apothecaries. Each 30,000-man corps had twelve 200-bed field hospitals, which followed the army as it advanced. Under Surgeon General H. G. Grimm, the Prussian military medical service had a progressive hierarchy with chief surgeons at the army, corps, division, battalion, and unit levels. Significantly, each corps had 124 designated litter bearers equipped with hand-wheeled stretchers that had been developed during the Danish war. The litter bearers were assisted by volunteers from the Johanniter Order (Order of St. John). The armies of the North German confederacy, Wurttemberg, Baden, and Bavaria had similar organizations.

The French, not having learned the lessons of their abysmal experience in the Crimea, were not nearly so well prepared. They entered the war with only 1,020 military surgeons, a number unchanged since 1854. Each French division had an "ambulance" (field hospital) with four or five physicians, 20 nurses, and an assortment of wagons but with no litter bearers. Men were left to be retrieved from the field by soldiers taken from the ranks. The French had no organized system of rail evacuation for the wounded.

The Germans had a well-organized sequential evacuation program beginning with forward collection stations just behind the front lines and progressing through dressing stations to rear-area field hospitals located near rail lines and finally to major evacuation hospitals in large German cities such as Hamburg and Berlin. The Germans also had a series of specially designed trains dedicated to evacuation of the wounded to hospitals in the interior. The French had

Nuns tend the wounded inside the Church of Saint Roch during its time as a military hospital for the Prussian Army in the Franco-Prussian War. (Hulton-Deutsch Collection/Corbis)

forward first aid stations as well, but their main dressing stations, where the first doctors worked, were four kilometers behind the lines.

Both the French and Germans were assisted by volunteer medical units. The Anglo-American Ambulance was manned by a collection of British volunteers and American physicians, many of whom, like chief physician James Marion Sims and physician Charles C. Mayo, had served in the American Civil War. Mayo's unit served with the Prussians throughout the war, while Sims's Anglo-American unit served with the French until the surrender at Sedan, after which they switched sides and worked with the Prussians.

The Franco-Prussian War was the first major conflict in which the number of men who died from battlefield injuries outnumbered those who succumbed to disease. Although that trend was partially due to lethal high-velocity weapons, the brevity of the war was probably more important. The likelihood of infectious disease outbreaks was markedly decreased by the war's short duration and the fact that armies did not spend long periods of time in camp. One signal exception came during the siege of Metz, when 35,000 French died, mostly from typhus and dysentery.

During the war, German forward hospitals treated 468,487 sick and 92,164 wounded. Counting those who died without coming to hospital, the Germans lost 116,826 from battle injuries and only 14,904 from disease. They evacuated 250,000 men to hospitals in the interior. The French hospitals treated 339,421 sick and 131,010 wounded and lost a total of 136,540 during the war.

Lord Joseph Lister's theories of aseptic wound management were so new that they were only sporadically applied during the war. Lister developed an eight-layer bandage in which impervious silk was placed over the wound, followed by a layer of silk soaked in carbolic acid, followed by a layer of waterproof mackintosh, followed by seven more layers of carbolic-soaked silk. The first layer protected the wound from the acid; the mackintosh kept the wound dry; the rest of the layers were meant to keep the wound free of bacterial contamination. The dressing was complicated and time consuming to apply, and battlefield surgeons, especially on the French side, often fell back on the traditional practice of packing the wound with unsterile lint fibers laboriously picked from old linen cloth by wives and sisters on the home front. As a result, sepsis was more common in French hospitals, where 25 percent of the wounded and 40–50 percent of amputees died. Late in the war, the French took to soaking the lint in carbolic acid and putting that preparation directly on the wound. During the siege of Paris, the British supplied mackintosh and carbolic acid to both sides.

The Germans had more faith in Lister's theories and, in fact, received the British surgeon as a hero after the war. The Germans used Lister's carbolic acid as a spray to sterilize their operating areas and instruments. The French never did, and one volunteer from the Anglo-American unit said if they had never done a single secondary operation at Sedan, their results would

have been far better. The French hospitals were plagued by a high incidence of secondary hemorrhage, dysentery, sepsis, and hospital gangrene, all of which can be attributed to the fact that no attempt was made to sterilize either the surroundings or the instruments.

The Prussians attempted the first battlefield transfusions during this conflict, but their results were unsatisfactory due to the inability to stop blood clotting and ignorance of blood typing. The war was also the occasion of an inadvertent experiment proving the effectiveness of smallpox vaccination. The French Army, inconsistently vaccinated, lost 1,963 men to smallpox, while the Germans, all of whom were presumably vaccinated, lost only 278.

The Franco-Prussian War was medically significant for several reasons. It was the first European war in which large armies were armed with high-velocity, rapid-firing weapons and were quickly mobilized and moved by rail in large numbers. Both armies had established medical corps and organized, hierarchical provisions for evacuation and hospitalization. Although inconsistently applied, Lister's aseptic technique was employed and proven effective.

See also Amputation; Lister, Lord Joseph; Smallpox; Transfusion

References

Garrison, Fielding. *Notes on the History of Military Medicine.* Washington D.C.: Association of Military Physicians, 1922.

Haller, John S. *Farmcarts to Fords: A History of the Military Ambulance, 1790–1925.* Carbondale: Southern Illinois University Press, 1992.

Laffin, John. *Surgeons in the Field.* London: J. M. Dent & Sons, Ltd., 1970.

Ryan, Charles. *With an Ambulance during the Franco-German War: Personal Experiences and Adventures with Both Armies.* New York: Charles Scribner's Sons, 1896.

G

Galen of Pergamum
(A.D. 131–201 or A.D. 129–199)

Galen was considered the most influential Greco-Roman physician, a prolific author, and the most cited ancient experimental physiologist.

Galen was born in the Anatolian city of Pergamum, which had only come under Roman rule three years earlier and which boasted the finest library in the world after Alexandria's. It is said that parchment (*charta pergamena*) was invented in the city as a substitute for papyrus when a jealous Egyptian king forbade its export to his competitor. Galen's father was a successful architect who paid for his son's extensive education and left him with enough money to lead a comfortable life of study and writing.

In addition to its library, Pergamum had one of the world's finest Asclepiad medical schools, and Galen began studying and dissecting at an early age. He had written three books by age 13 and finished his first medical studies by 20. He then went to Alexandria, where he trained for an additional 12 years, concentrating on anatomy. After additional travels to Smyrna and Corinth, Galen returned to Pergamum, where he practiced and was surgeon to the gladiatorial school for several years. He moved to Rome in A.D. 164 and remained for 24 years, earning a reputation as the most successful practitioner of his time.

Galen published as many as 500 books, only a portion of which survive. He wrote nine books on anatomy, 17 on physiology, six on pathology, 14 on therapeutics, and 30 on pharmacy. All were written in Greek. Galen spoke Latin only occasionally and did so poorly.

He was an avid experimentalist, and dissected thousands of animals, concentrating on apes for postmortem studies and pigs and dogs for live dissections but applying himself to whatever species came his way, even camels and elephants. His study of animals rather than humans led him to a number of anatomic errors, which persisted in the medical literature for 15 centuries after his death.

Unlike Hippocrates, who was primarily an observer, Galen was an active experimenter. He cut the spinal cord in a variety of ways to produce different forms of paralysis, he stopped vocalization by cutting the recurrent laryngeal nerve (although Suśruta of India had done the same experiment with the same result three hundred years earlier), he proved that blood moved from the heart into the arteries, and he demonstrated that an excised heart would continue to beat and an excised muscle would contract. He proved that, if one severed an optic nerve, blindness resulted. He combined his experimental findings with the philosophy of Hippocrates and Pythagoras into a fanciful physiological system that, although incorrect, went essentially unchallenged for 1,400 years.

Galen served as a military surgeon with Marcus Aurelius and, although he seems never to have written a book solely on surgery, he was a talented operator. He identified and differentiated degenerative and traumatic aneurysms. He controlled bleeding by finding the end of the severed vessel and twisting or tying it on itself or by suturing it with silk. This was the first surgical use of the rare material that had been imported from the Orient to make the wardrobes of Roman women.

Galen was the first to describe the four cardinal signs of inflammation (*rubor et tumor cum calore et dolore*, or redness, swelling, heat, and pain). While with the military, Galen also wrote the first differentiation of malingering from real illness.

Galen's pharmacology was much like that of his Roman contemporaries—odd. The most famous Galenic drug was his theriac concocted from a litany of more than 70 ingredients but primarily based on meat from a live viper and opium. The drug's name derives from the Greek *theria*, or wild animal, and refers to the fact that all bites were assumed to be poisonous and to re-

quire an effective antidote. The viper meat was chosen because snake bites were particularly feared, but the opium's euphoric and addictive properties likely accounted for the drug's popularity. Theriacs, although therapeutically useless, remained an essential part of pharmacy for centuries and were still present in the official German pharmacopoeia of 1872.

Late in life, Galen returned to Pergamum, where he died, leaving no heirs.

See also Morphine; Roman Military Medicine

References
Garrison, Fielding. *An Introduction to the History of Medicine*. Philadelphia: W. B. Saunders Co., 1929.
Salazar, Christine. *The Treatment of War Wounds in Graeco-Roman Antiquity*. Leiden, the Netherlands: Brill, 2000.
Zimmerman, Leo, and Ilza Veith. *Great Ideas in the History of Surgery*. Baltimore: Williams & Wilkins Co., 1961.

Gas Gangrene

Gas gangrene is an infection with one of several anaerobic bacteria that, if untreated, results in death in about half of those affected.

More than 80 percent of gas gangrene cases are caused by the rod-shaped bacterium *Clostridium perfringens*, although other bacilli of the Clostridia family and group *A. Streptococcus, Staphylococcus aureus*, and *Vibrio vulnificus* can also cause the disease. The bacteria are typically carried into the body by contaminated material such as cloth or dirt and are most likely to arise in a wound with a small entrance and widespread destruction of tissue below the skin such as typically occurs from artillery shells, shrapnel, or cavitating high-velocity bullets.

Gas gangrene's clinical signs can appear as early as five hours after the initial infection and can progress to death in less than 16 hours. The skin turns blue or orange-red around the wound. Vesicles then form along the lines of superficial veins and coalesce into blisters that break and weep a foul-smelling brown fluid. Small subcutaneous gas bubbles may cause a crackling sound when the skin is pressed, while larger collections can give a drum-like tympanitic sound when the overlying area is tapped. Pockets of gas beneath the skin release a characteristic hiss and distinctive foul odor when punctured. The gas is produced as a harmless by-product of bacterial metabolism and can be found not only in the tissues but also in the vessels and even the heart. The bacteria also produce a variety of toxins, at least four of which can cause death. The toxins can dissolve surrounding muscle tissue (myonecrosis); they can break down red blood cells leading to jaundice and shock; they can cause vascular collapse from direct effect on the vessels; and they can damage the brain stem, leading to shock and respiratory arrest.

Although Clostridium was first cultured in 1892 by William Welch (after whom it was originally called *Bacterium welchii*) and Eugen Fraenkel (hence, the Welch-Fraenkel bacillus in Germany), clinical cases of gas gangrene were rare. William Williams Keen noted in his text for World War I military surgeons that he had seen only one case during all of the American Civil War. It was similarly unusual in the Sino-Japanese War, the Spanish-American War, and the colonial and Balkan wars at the end of the 19th century, and military surgeons went into World War I believing that either antiseptic surgical techniques favored by French surgeons or the aseptic procedures developed by

Ernst von Bergmann combined with recent advances in bacteriology would prevent future occurrences. They were mistaken. The war on the Western Front was fought in muddy fields that had been fertilized for centuries with bacteria-laden animal manure. After antitoxin brought tetanus under control in 1915, gas gangrene became the main cause of death from wound infection. Although only about 0.5 percent of wounds resulted in gas gangrene, those that did carried a 50 percent mortality rate.

Attempts to create a vaccine or an antitoxin against gas gangrene started early in the war, and, although several were tried, none proved effective. Military surgeons realized early that opening the wounds (débridement) and removing all dead tissue (épluchage) were effective, but only if done very early. Once the infection was established, the only treatment was amputation well above the wound. Injections of hydrogen peroxide were tried but too frequently resulted in death from gas that entered disrupted vessels and migrated to the lungs. German physicians tried using poultices of steam-heated linseeds to blister the skin and cause a local increase of blood flow (cataplasm) or rhythmic compression of the wounded area by air-filled bands to accomplish the same effect. The former was of questionable benefit and the latter was too expensive to be widely applied. By the end of World War I, death rates from gas gangrene were not significantly lower than they had been at the beginning.

Development of penicillin in the interwar years made gas gangrene a rarity by 1941. Its main significance in World War II was in human experiments done by Japanese military surgeons of Unit 731 attempting to develop Clostridial toxins as a biological weapon. As recently as the months leading up to the Iraq invasion by the United States in 2003, it was rumored that Iraq had accumulated the toxin for the same purpose.

See also Amputation; Bergmann, Ernst von; Débridement; Unit 731; World War I Medicine

References

Fauntleroy, A. M. *Report on the Medico-Military Aspects of the European War from Observations Taken behind the Allied Armies in France.* Washington, D.C.: Government Printing Office, 1915.

Keen, William Williams. *Treatment of War Injuries.* Philadelphia: W. B. Saunders Co., 1918.

Linton, Derek S. 2000. "The Obscure Object of Knowledge: German Military Medicine Confronts Gas Gangrene during World War I." *Bulletin of the History of Medicine* 74 (2): 291–316.

Geneva Conventions

The Geneva Conventions are a series of four international agreements that, together with ancillary conventions, form a body of law governing war.

As early as the sixth century B.C., Chinese military writer Sun Tzu suggested limiting the conduct of war, and, in 200 B.C., the Hindu Code of Manu introduced the idea of a war crime. The judicial treatment of war crimes began in 1305 when Scottish patriot Sir William Wallace was tried for killing civilians during his country's war with England. In 1865 in the United States, Henry Wirz was executed for murdering Union prisoners of war at the Confederacy's Andersonville prison.

On June 24, 1859, the Austrian Army fought a combined French and Sardinian force near the northern Italian city of Solferino. Swiss businessman Henry Dunant, on his way to visit French emperor Napoleon III, found more than 9,000 wounded without adequate care in various buildings in the nearby village of Castiglione. His impassioned description of the carnage, *A Memory of Solferino*, became a best seller and led to formation of the International Red Cross and to a conference held from August 8 to August 28, 1864, to consider regulating treatment of war casualties. Representatives from 16 nations attending that conference signed the Geneva Convention for the Amelioration of the Condition of the Wounded in Armies in the Field, the first international humanitarian law. By the end of 1864, France, Switzerland, Belgium, the Netherlands, Italy, Spain, Sweden, Norway, Denmark, and the Grand Duchy of Baden had ratified the agreement. The United States, although a conference participant, did not ratify the agreement until 1882 after a lengthy campaign led by Clara Barton.

Several subsequent conferences have aimed at amending the original convention. In 1899, restrictions on use of asphyxiating gases and expanding bullets were added. The Hague Conventions of 1907 extended protection to maritime combatants. In 1925, poisonous gases and bacteriologic warfare were banned. In 1929, additional clauses dealing with treatment of the wounded and prisoners of war were added. In 1949, protections were added for the shipwrecked, and, in 1977, protections were extended to medical personnel and civilians and attacks on the environment were banned. The conventions' protections were also extended to participants in civil wars. Finally, in 2005, a third emblem (a red square on edge on a white background) was added to the Red Cross and the Red Crescent for use by nations not following either Christianity or Islam. The four existing conventions are:

1. Convention for the Amelioration of the Condition of the Wounded and Sick in Armed Forces in the Field
2. Convention for the Amelioration of the Condition of the Wounded, Sick and Shipwrecked Members of Armed Forces at Sea
3. Convention Relative to the Treatment of Prisoners of War
4. Convention Relative to the Protection of Civilian Persons in Time of War

See also Barton, Clara; Chemical and Biological Warfare; Red Cross and Red Crescent

References

Bennett, Angela. *The Geneva Convention: The Hidden Origins of the Red Cross.* Phoenix Mill, Gloucestershire, UK: Sutton Publishing, 2005.
International Committee of the Red Cross. 2006. "The Geneva Conventions: The Core of International Humanitarian Law." January 9. www.icrc.org/WEB/Eng/siteeng0.nsf/html/genevaconventions (accessed May 22, 2006).
Moorehead, Caroline. *Dunant's Dream: Switzerland and the History of the Red Cross.* New York: HarperCollins, 1998.

Wound Man *by Hans von Gersdorff, from his* Feldbuch de Wundartzney (Wound Surgery). *(National Library of Medicine)*

Gersdorff, Hans von (16th Century)

Along with Heinrich von Pfolspeundt and Hieronymus Brunschwig, Hans von Gersdorff was a founder of Prussian military medicine.

Gersdorff was born in Strasbourg, although the dates of his birth and death are uncertain. He trained as a surgeon by apprenticeship and by serving with the military. Gersdorff was the town surgeon of Strasbourg and followed its army when it joined the Swiss Confederacy in wars against Téméraire.

He was the author of the important 16th-century German military medical text *Feldbuch de Wundartzney,* or *Wound Surgery,* published in vernacular German in 1517. The *Feldbuch* contains one of the most famous illustrations in the early printed medical literature—the *Wound Man*—showing the various weapons with which someone could be injured in combat. His text expanded on that of Hieronymus Brunschwig and contained the first illustration of an amputation as well as a striking depiction of St. Anthony's fire, the neuropathic pain suffered by soldiers who ate grain contaminated with ergot fungus.

Unlike his contemporaries, Gersdorff did not believe gunpowder poisoned wounds, although he still recommended irrigating those wounds with hot oil after probing to find the projectile. He did not rely solely on cauterization to stop bleeding, but rather used a tourniquet combined with a styptic powder composed of lime, aloe, nutgalls, alum, and vitriol to chemically burn and close vessel ends. He invented an ingenious tripod-mounted screw that could be inserted into fragments of depressed skull bone to extract them from within the brain.

See also Amputation; Hemostasis; Prussian and German Military Medicine; 16th-Century Military Medicine; Tourniquet

References

Dealey, Carol. 2005. "German Wound Surgeons: 1450–1750." *European Wound Management Association Journal* 5: 48–51.

Zimmerman, Leo, and Ilza Veith. *Great Ideas in the History of Surgery.* Baltimore: Williams & Wilkins Co., 1961.

Glanders

Glanders is a systemic disease caused by the gram-negative bacillus *Burkholderia* (formerly *Pseudomonas*) *mallei*.

Glanders is primarily a disease of animals and is resident in horses and other domestic mammals but can be transmitted to humans either through skin penetration or by inhalation. It causes skin ulcers or pneumonia, depending on the route of entry and can progress to septicemia with fever, lymphadenopathy, and myalgias. The mortality rate in glanders can be as high as 50 percent.

Germany used glanders against Allied cavalry mounts during World War I, and the Soviet Union began experimenting with glanders as a weapon against humans at the Solovetsky Island prison camp in the mid-1930s. Although no vaccine has been developed to protect against glanders, interest in the organism as a weapon waned with the advent of effective antibiotic therapy. Interest in both the Soviet Union and the United States returned with the possibility of a genetically engineered resistant strain. The organism was probably used against Afghan forces by the Soviets between 1982 and 1984 as an aerosol released from airplanes, and United States intelligence agencies estimated in 1999 that the research facility at Vozrozhdeniye Island had produced up to 2,000 metric tons of *Burkholderia mallei* a year.

See also Chemical and Biological Warfare; Fort Detrick; Vozrozhdeniye Island; World War I Medicine

References

Alibek, Ken, with Stephen Handelman. *Biohazard.* London: Arrow Books, 2000.

Centers for Disease Control and Prevention. 2005. "Glanders." October 11. http://www.cdc.gov/ncidod/dbmd/diseaseinfo/glanders_g.htm#whatis (accessed August 1, 2007).

Gonorrhea

Gonorrhea is an infection of the mucous membranes of the male or female urogenital tracts caused by *Neisseria gonorrhoeae.*

The gonococcus and its close relative the meningococcus are responsible for virtually all human disease from gram-negative cocci. The disease is characterized by burning and pain on urination and may be accompanied by a genital ulcer. In rare cases, gonorrhea may progress to septicemia with involvement of joints and widespread, pustular skin rash. Although penicillin was, at one time, the main treatment, most gonorrheal organisms are now resistant and must be treated with third-generation cephalosporins.

Until the late 17th century, medical writers failed to distinguish between syphilis and gonorrhea, a situation made more confusing when English military surgeon John Hunter deliberately injected himself with material from the pustule of a patient with gonorrhea. The man had syphilis as well and, when Hunter acquired both diseases, he incorrectly concluded that the two were one illness.

With control of syphilis, gonorrhea became the predominant venereal infection among soldiers. During World War II, venereal disease accounted for as many admissions as all other infections combined, with the majority being from gonorrhea. Among American troops, 1,250,846 soldiers were treated for sexually transmitted diseases. Because penicillin was still effective in the 1940s, it was used widely among both troops and German prostitutes. When antibiotic supplies were limited, a tactical decision was made to use available penicillin for gonorrhea rather than for wounds on the theory that treating soldiers suffering from the former was more likely to result in an effective combatant than treating the latter. After the war, prostitutes received penicillin preferentially rather than making it available for more serious illnesses in other civilians.

Venereal disease during the Korean Conflict came, in large part, as a result of infection acquired from Japanese prostitutes, 75 percent of whom had gonorrhea. Incidence of venereal disease in Viet Nam varied from 196 to 281 per 1,000 troops between 1965 and 1970 and was mostly gonorrhea, making it by far the most common infectious disease during that war.

See also Hunter, John; Korean Conflict; Syphilis; Viet Nam War; World War I Medicine; World War II Medicine

References

Cowdrey, Albert. *United States Army in the Korean War*. Washington, D.C.: Center of Military History, 1987.
Lada, John. *Medical Statistics in World War II*. Washington, D.C.: Office of the Surgeon General, 1975.
Neel, Spurgeon. *Medical Support of the U.S. Army in Vietnam: 1965–1970*. Washington, D.C.: Department of the Army, 1973.

Görcke, Johann
(1750–1822)

Johann Görcke was the reorganizer of Prussian military medicine.

When Görcke began his career, German surgeons had little prestige, so he left his home to devote two years to studying medicine in Europe's best universities. The backwardness of German medicine had become obvious in the revolutionary wars from 1792 to 1795, and the Pépinière—a model military hospital—was founded in Berlin at Görcke's insistence in 1795. Frederick the Great, who had a level of interest in the well-being of his troops that was unusual for the time, appointed Görcke chief of military sanitation and general staff surgeon in 1797, an office he occupied until his resignation six weeks before his death in 1822.

Under Görcke's supervision, military surgeons were subject to periodic review, and the hospitals he organized to care for the wounded after the Battle of Eylau in 1807 emphasized sanitation and ventilation. Baron Pierre François Percy, Napoleon's surgeon in chief, thought so highly of Görcke that he convinced the emperor to make a donation to the Pépinière in 1805. That hospital, which changed its name to Friedrich Wilhelm Institut in 1818, trained 1,359 medical officers between 1795 and 1821.

In addition to the Pépinière, Görcke organized a series of field hospitals after 1809 and, by 1813, his service had nine facilities comprising 8,400 beds. Conditions in the hospitals, a new corps of voluntary nurses, and advanced land and river transportation of the wounded made Prussian medical care the best of any country involved in the Napoleonic Wars.

See also Napoleonic Wars; Prussian and
    German Military Medicine

Reference
Garrison, Fielding. *Notes on the History of
    Military Medicine.* Washington, D.C.:
    Association of Military Medicine, 1922.

Gorgas, William Crawford (1854–1920)

William Gorgas was a sanitarian and the surgeon general of the United States during World War I.

Gorgas's maternal grandfather had been governor of Alabama, and his father, although born in Pennsylvania, had served as chief of ordnance to the Confederacy and had risen to the rank of brigadier general. Gorgas was raised on the family plantation near Mobile, Alabama, and had a lifelong desire to serve in the U.S. Army. He graduated from the University of the South in 1875 but was unable to obtain an appointment to West Point. He decided to enter the Army as a physician and graduated from Bellevue Medical College in 1879. Gorgas took a commission as assistant surgeon in the medical corps in June 1880, and he spent the next 20 years as a post physician.

William Gorgas served as a medical doctor in the U.S. Army. While stationed in Cuba he implemented sanitation programs designed to stem the transmission of yellow fever and malaria by mosquitos. (United States Army)

In 1882, Gorgas contracted yellow fever and, while recuperating at Fort Brown, Texas, met and married fellow patient Marie Cook Doughty. Because he was thereafter immune, he was frequently placed in charge of yellow fever camps including 10 years at Fort Barrancas, Florida, a post notorious for harboring the disease. In 1898, he was posted to Havana and became the city's chief sanitary officer after Gen. Leonard Wood (also a physician) was named the island's military governor.

Gorgas was aware of Cuban Dr. Carlos Finlay's hypothesis that mosquitoes carried yellow fever, but he did not believe the theory until Walter Reed's experiments proved it beyond question. With Wood's support, Gorgas used Reed's findings to institute an extensive mosquito control program that virtually eliminated yellow fever and markedly curtailed malaria in Cuba.

Gorgas left Cuba with the rank of colonel and was charged with extending his control of mosquito-borne disease to the proposed Panama Canal project. He traveled to Suez and Panama to study France's successful and unsuccessful canal efforts and, in June 1904, took a group to Central America to begin mosquito control efforts. The project proved more difficult than that in Havana, and a significant incidence of both yellow fever and malaria still prevailed in Panama in 1905. The Panama Canal commission and Col. George Goethals viewed Gorgas's efforts as wasteful and ineffective and would have removed him except for the support of Gorgas by President Theodore Roosevelt. Gorgas was eventually successful, and his control of these tropical diseases was generally recognized as key to the American success in digging the canal.

In 1913, Gorgas traveled to South Africa to help control epidemic pneumonia among black mine workers in the Rand. In January 1914, he was promoted to brigadier general and named surgeon general of the Army. A planned world tour sponsored by the Rockefeller Institute and intended to help combat yellow fever in the tropics was forestalled by American entry into World War I. Gorgas served as surgeon general through the war and was retired on account of age on October 3, 1918. He resumed his yellow fever work but suffered a stroke while visiting London. He died on July 4, 1920, and, after a funeral service in St. Paul's Cathedral, was buried in Arlington National Cemetery.

Gorgas was the recipient of numerous honorary degrees and foreign honors, including being knighted by Britain's King George V just prior to his death. He also served as the president of the American Medical Association and the American Society of Tropical Medicine.

See also Reed, Walter; Spanish-American War; World War I Medicine; Yellow Fever

References

Gibson, John M. *Physician to the World: The Life of General William C. Gorgas.* Durham, NC: Duke University Press, 1950.

Gillet, Mary. *The Army Medical Department, 1865–1917.* Washington, D.C.: Center of Military History, 1995.

Phalen, James M. 1940. "Chiefs of the Medical Department, U.S. Army 1775–1894, Biographical Sketches." *Army Medical Bulletin* 52 (April): 88–93.

Guillemeau, Jacques (1550–1612)

Ambroise Paré's son-in-law and favorite pupil, Jacques Guillemeau served as private physician to French King Charles IX.

Guillemeau was one of France's most prominent 16th-century surgeons and described ligating an artery above an aneurysm 250 years before Hassler, who is commonly credited for first performing that operation. He was also author of the important medieval ophthalmology text, *Traité des Maladies de l'Oeil* (1585) and wrote extensively on obstetrics and pediatrics.

His primary contribution to military medicine was his *Les Oeuvres de Chirurgie*, which was not published until 1649. The book described his experiences as an army surgeon following the armies of Charles IX and his successors through their European campaigns. He abandoned hemostasis by ligating specific vessels and returned to more traumatic cauterization, arguing that his "crow's bill" forceps were too likely to tear the vessel when an unanesthetized patient thrashed about during surgery.

See also Ligature; Paré, Ambroise; 16th-Century
Military Medicine

References
Dumaitre, P. 1996. "Around Ambroise Paré: His
Pupils and Friends." *History of Science and
Medicine* 30: 351–357.
Wangensteen, Owen, and Sarah Wangensteen.
*The Rise of Surgery from Empiric Craft to
Scientific Discipline*. Minneapolis: University
of Minnesota Press, 1978.

Gulf War

The 1990–1991 Gulf War was notable from
a medical point of view for its paucity of
deaths, injuries, and illness.

A total of 2,225,000 active-duty personnel
from the U.S. Army, Navy, Air Force, and
Marines served, with a total of 147 combat-
related deaths, 235 other deaths, and 467
battle-related injuries. During the war,
33,000 medical personnel, including 3,100
physicians, were deployed to the Gulf Theater of Operations.

Many of the changes in provision of military medical care prior to the Gulf War were
derived from the 1973 Israeli experience in
the Sinai War and the British experience in
the 1982 Falklands War. Both the Israelis
and the British had emphasized the need
for highly mobile medical units that could
provide care very close to the front lines and
could keep up with rapidly moving combat
units. The British Army Parachute Clearing Troop, in which 36 officers and enlisted
men could provide forward-area care with
supplies carried entirely in their backpacks,
took account of recent research suggesting
that control of bleeding and management of
traumatic shock within the "golden hour"
right after wounding significantly improved
survival. The Israeli experience also suggested that 80–85 percent of injuries would
involve an extremity, and most of these
would be soft tissue wounds with a high
likelihood of return to duty. The other 15–20
percent were expected to involve the head,
chest, or abdomen and have a low probabil-
ity of return to duty.

The American forces in the Persian Gulf
planned for a battalion aid station (BAS)
to be the first site of organized care and
to be located within one-half kilometer of
the front line, staffed with two physicians
and a physician's assistant to stabilize the
wounded within 30 minutes of injury. The
availability of fixed-wing transport was expected to move most major surgery to rear-
area central hospitals. In fact, only 3 percent
of major surgery had been done in forward
areas during the Sinai War, and a "bed to
bed" goal of four hours for major trauma
seemed an achievable goal.

Each BAS had two Humvee ambulances
equipped to carry two stretchers for transport from the front line, although these vehicles proved to have a number of deficiencies.
They were completely unarmored and vulnerable to both small-arms fire and roadside
explosives and mines. The stretchers were
stacked, and the medics were unable to access any area below the patients' waists without stopping and unloading the stretchers.

Moving the BAS required two five-ton
trucks, each equipped with a trailer. These
vehicles were also expected to resupply
the station and to move some wounded
to rear areas. Because the front moved so
rapidly, there were never enough trucks to
do either job. In addition, the trucks could
only move through heavily mined territory
on designated cleared paths. The stations
were reliant on radio communications and
global positioning satellites (GPS) to find
the front. Available radio frequencies were

often saturated and unreliable and the positioning systems went "off the net" when the satellites passed below the horizon.

After the war, a number of veterans complained of a variety of symptoms, including chronic fatigue, headaches, muscle aches, sleep disturbance, and various cardiovascular and gastrointestinal disorders. A smaller number developed malignancies (particularly of the brain), were diagnosed with amyotrophic lateral sclerosis, or had children with birth defects. It has been suggested but not proven that these problems might be related to the use of depleted uranium projectiles, organophosphate chemical weapons, or anthrax vaccine during the war, known as Operation Desert Storm.

See also Ambulances and Transport; Anthrax; Chemical and Biological Warfare; Field Hospitals

References

Gray, G. C., B. D. Coate, C. M. Anderson, H. K. Kang, S. W. Berg, F. S. Wignall, J. D. Knoke, and E. Barrett-Connor. 1996. "The Postwar Hospitalization Experience of U.S. Veterans of the Persian Gulf War." *New England Journal of Medicine* 335 (November 14): 1505–1513.

Kang, Han, and Tim Bullman. 1996. "Mortality among U.S. Veterans of the Persian Gulf War." *New England Journal of Medicine* 335 (November 14): 1498–1504.

Smith, Arthur M., and Craig Llewellyn. 1991. "Caring for Our Casualties." *Proceedings of the Naval Institute* 117 (December): 72–78.

Guthrie, George James (1785–1856)

With James McGrigor, George Guthrie was one of two Scots who revolutionized British military medicine during the Peninsular Campaign.

Guthrie was apprenticed to a practicing surgeon at age 13 and sat the exams to become a member of the Royal College of Surgeons at 15. He began his military career as regimental surgeon to the 29th Foot and served on the Iberian Peninsula from 1808 to 1814, finishing his army career as deputy inspector general.

At the battle of Talavera (1809), Guthrie, acting as principal medical officer, was personally responsible for tending to more than 3,000 wounded. He advocated a conservative approach to amputation that was out of keeping with the practice of the time and undoubtedly saved many limbs that would otherwise have been sacrificed by more aggressive surgeons. He pioneered the military use of the long leg splint, the ligation of both the proximal and distal ends of a severed artery, and irrigation of gangrenous wounds with dilute mineral acid.

Guthrie was in private practice in Brussels when the Battle of Waterloo was fought and he returned to service as a volunteer to help care for the flood of British wounded. When he returned to England, he founded the Royal Westminster Ophthalmic Hospital, where he served as visiting surgeon and professor of anatomy and surgery. He wrote the *Treatise on Gunshot Wounds of the Extremities Requiring Amputation* (1815), a book that went through six editions and set the standard for its time. Guthrie also wrote *Commentaries on the Surgery of the War, 1808–1815*, which he published in 1853 with a supplement dealing with the military medical experience in the Crimea. For 30 years after his retirement from the army, Guthrie continued to give lectures without charge to young military surgeons. He served as president of the Royal College of Surgeons on three separate occasions and refused an offer of knighthood.

See also Amputation; British Military Medicine; McGrigor, James; Napoleonic Wars

References
Blanco, Richard. 1974. "The Development of British Military Medicine, 1793–1814." *Military Affairs* 38 (February): 4–10.

Lovegrove, Peter. *Not in the Least Crusade: A Short History of the Royal Army Medical Corps.* Aldershot, UK: Gale & Polden, Ltd., 1952.

McGlaughlin, Redmond. *The Royal Army Medical Corps.* London: Leo Cooper, Ltd., 1972.

H

Haitian Campaign (1801–1802)

The Haitian campaign was Napoleon Bonaparte's attempt to reclaim French hegemony over the colony of Saint-Domingue, in which yellow fever changed the future of the United States.

The French colony in western Hispaniola had been the most profitable in the Caribbean, accounting for more than half of Europe's tropical imports, but had been in a state of unrest since the early 1790s when the island's mulatto population, demanding civil rights similar to those of the white plantation owners, had revolted under the leadership of Toussaint-Louverture. In the wake of the Spanish cession of the eastern part of the island to France in 1801, Louverture had taken control of all Hispaniola.

Eyeing creation of an American empire in which Saint-Domingue controlled the entrances to the Caribbean and resumed profitable sugar and coffee exports while Louisiana controlled the Mississippi River and fed the Caribbean colonies, Napoleon dispatched his brother-in-law Gen. Charles Victor Emmanuel Leclerc and 30,000 troops from France, Poland, and the Army of the Rhine in 1802 to reestablish French control of the island and probably to reinstitute slavery, which had been abolished in 1793.

The fact that there were 500,000 blacks, 30,000 mixed-race mulattoes, and only 30,000 whites on the island posed a formidable challenge, but it was disease rather than military resistance that doomed Leclerc's forces. The Haitians opted to burn the cities and withdraw into the countryside, forcing the French to remain on the island through the winter. By February of 1802, 1,200 of Leclerc's troops were hospitalized with tropical illnesses, and that number increased fourfold by April. When the rainy season brought mosquitoes and yellow fever, the French forces collapsed. In the end, more than 25,000 French troops died of disease, mostly yellow fever. Only about 2,000 died from wounds received in battle.

When Napoleon's war with England resumed in 1803, it was no longer possible to send either men or supplies to the Caribbean, and the emperor elected to abandon Saint-Domingue to the black insurrectionists. Disgusted with his losses, he also responded to American ambassador Robert Livingston's request for rights to use the port of New Orleans with an offer to sell the entire Louisiana territory for $15 million.

See also Yellow Fever

Reference
Girard, Philippe. 2005. "French Revolutionary Ideals and the Failure of the Leclerc Expedition to Saint-Domingue." *French Colonial History* 6: 55–77.

Hammond, William (1828–1900)

Responsible for the reorganization of the U.S. Army medical service during the Civil War before being court-martialed and dismissed as surgeon general of the Army, William Hammond was also a founder of American neurology.

Hammond was born in Annapolis, Maryland, on August 28, 1828, the son of a physician. Both of Hammond's parents were descendants of prominent Maryland families. Hammond received his doctorate in medicine from the University of the City of New York in 1848 and enlisted as an assistant surgeon in the Army. He served in a variety of frontier posts during the Indian Wars before resigning in 1860 on account of ill health.

When the Civil War began he reenlisted as an assistant surgeon, having lost both his rank and seniority. His superiors recognized his ability and experience and assigned him to inspect camps and hospitals in Gen. William Rosecrans's army in West Virginia. The Union Army medical service was hopelessly inadequate at the beginning of the Civil War, and the civilian Sanitary Commission was appointed to evaluate and improve care, one result of which was the resignation of Surgeon General Clement Finley. The commission recommended that Hammond assume the post in spite of his youth and lack of rank, and he was appointed surgeon general on April 28, 1862, over a number of senior medical officers and over the man preferred by Secretary of War Edwin Stanton.

Almost all of the improvements in the Union Army's medical care came during Hammond's brief tenure. He started the Army Medical Museum, which became the Armed Forces Institute of Pathology; he adopted Jonathan Letterman's methods of patient transfer and his use of well-ventilated pavilion hospitals; and he instituted the data collection that resulted in the monumental *Medical and Surgical History of the War of the Rebellion*. In addition, he proposed formation of a permanent ambulance corps, an army medical school, a military medical laboratory, a permanent military research hospital in Washington, D.C., and a national library of medicine, all of which subsequently came to pass.

Hammond was an imposing 6'2" and weighed more than 250 pounds with a booming voice and an unhealthy measure of self-importance and arrogance. He got along poorly with Stanton, who finally removed him from Washington and stripped him of virtually all his powers, at which point Hammond demanded a formal investigation or a court-martial to clear his name. He got the latter. The court found him innocent of charges that included fraud and corruption, but Stanton reversed that decision and directed a guilty verdict. Hammond was cashiered on

August 18, 1864. In fairness to Stanton, Hammond had spent freely for drugs and supplies and had bought mostly from Philadelphia purveyors with whom he had a personal relationship, most notably the Wyeth brothers. Although his behavior was so careless as to border on impropriety, no evidence exists that Hammond personally profited from his dealings. In fact, he was forced to borrow money to move his family to New York and restart his life after his dismissal.

In New York Hammond achieved both fame and fortune as a neurologist and "alienist" (psychiatrist), published a number of professional books and articles including the first American textbook of neurology, held a series of academic appointments, and (like his friend and colleague Dr. Silas Weir Mitchell) wrote several plays and novels. He was a founding member of both the New York and American neurological associations. Hammond's dogged efforts to clear his reputation culminated in 1878 in a congressional investigation that vindicated him and restored his rank of brigadier general.

Hammond retired from his New York practice in 1888 and moved to Washington, D.C., where he operated a private sanitarium for neurological disease until his death from cardiac failure on January 5, 1900.

See also Civil War in the United States; Mitchell, Silas Weir

References

Gillet, Mary. *The Army Medical Department, 1818–1865*. Washington, D.C.: Center of Military History, 1987.

Klawans, Harold. "The Court Martial of William A. Hammond." In *The Medicine of History from Paracelsus to Freud*. New York: Raven Press, 1982.

McHenry, L. C., Jr. 1963. "Surgeon General William Alexander Hammond." *Military Medicine* 128: 1199–1201.

Harvey, William (1578–1657)

William Harvey was to physiology what Andreas Vesalius was to anatomy, and often regarded as the finest medical intellect of the 17th century.

Harvey was born the oldest of seven children in Kent, England, during the reign of Elizabeth I. He graduated from Cambridge at age 20 and studied under Fabrizo d'Aquapendente and Caserius at Padua from 1599 to 1603, after which he returned to London and lectured and cared for patients at St. Bartholomew's Hospital for the next 30 years. He married the daughter of the queen's personal physician and, in 1615, was named professor of anatomy and surgery at the College of Physicians in London. He subsequently became physician to the court of King James I and personal physician to King Charles I, who served as his sponsor. In 1643, he retired to Oxford, where he became warden of Merton College. He endowed an Oxford lectureship and a boys' school in his hometown of Folkestone, both of which remain in operation.

Harvey was short, black haired, and given to fidgeting with the handle of the dagger he habitually wore and was said by his contemporaries to bear a striking resemblance to William Shakespeare.

It had long been recognized that blood moved within vessels, and Harvey's teacher Fabricius had described valves in the walls of veins. The true nature of circulation, however, had been obfuscated by Galen's insistence that blood merely moved to and fro rather than around a closed circuit. Harvey used dissection and experimentation to prove the unidirectional nature of blood flow, although he never understood the structure of capillaries that allowed the

William Harvey revolutionized the understanding of how blood circulates through the body and, in the process, laid the groundwork for the discipline of physiology and later, modern embryology. (Library of Congress)

liquid to move from the arterial to the venous circulation. He did understand that the heart was the pump and that there were separate systemic and pulmonary circuits. He began his investigations in 1616 and published his findings in 1628 in *De Motu Cordis*, which might well be the most important book in the history of medicine. His application of physical principles to a biological problem was the beginning of modern scientific medicine.

Harvey's last years were plagued by gout and kidney stones. He failed in an attempt to commit suicide with an overdose of opium-containing laudanum but died of a stroke at age 79.

See also Fabrizio d'Aquapendente, Geronimo; 17th-Century Military Medicine

Reference
Harrison, W. C. *Dr. William Harvey and the Discovery of Circulation*. New York: MacMillan Co., 1967.

Head Injury and Cranial Surgery

Head injury remains one of the major causes of death from war wounds.

Head injuries can be divided into those caused by acceleration-deceleration (such as falls or vehicular injuries, from chariots to motorized personnel transports), low-velocity impact injuries (rocks, clubs, maces, and swords), and high-velocity impact injuries (bullets, shrapnel, and blast injuries). The first two have been present since before recorded history, while the last is unique to more modern times.

Although no written record exists of skull injuries prior to 3200 B.C., ample archaeological evidence has been found of traumatic head injuries and their treatment. Trephined skulls—many of which show evidence of healing that prove the patient survived having his skull opened—have been found in Europe, the Americas, Africa, and the South Pacific. Many of the wounds were clearly inflicted with weapons, and some even demonstrate removal of fracture fragments and replacement of the missing bone with beaten metal prostheses.

The first written record of traumatic brain injury (as opposed to simple bony trauma) is in the Edwin Smith papyrus, a 1500 B.C. copy of a text that may well be more than 1,000 years older and parts of which have been attributed to the pharaonic physician and architect Imhotep. The papyrus clearly delineates head injuries that penetrate the brain's lining (dural membrane) as those that were universally fatal and should not be treated.

Egyptian warriors from 20 centuries before Christ wore quilted head protectors and, in 1500 B.C., Pharaoh Thutmose III wore a golden helmet into battle. Two hundred years later, Egyptian mercenaries routinely used brass head protection, as did warriors described in the Old Testament of the Bible. Assyrians, Babylonians, and ancient Greeks beat helmets from bronze and added extensions to protect the sides of their heads and their faces. By 500 B.C., the entire head and face were covered, leaving only small holes for vision and ventilation.

The Greeks and, later, the Romans surgically treated a limited range of wartime head injuries. They sutured scalp lacerations and removed nonimpacted bone fragments but, like their Egyptian predecessors, did not pursue wounds that penetrated the dura.

Greek and Roman understanding of cerebral anatomy and physiology was limited and often incorrect, and many of their mistakes persisted well after the Renaissance. Herophilus believed the brain's ventricular cavities to be the site of the soul; Galen thought the brain substance contained the soul but believed that vital spirit was converted to animal spirit in the ventricles. In the 17th century, René Descartes pronounced the pineal gland the seat of the soul but continued to believe the animal spirit resided in the ventricles. Those misconceptions notwithstanding, the brain's importance was uncontested and, prior to the late 19th century, surgeons rarely violated it voluntarily.

The range of head injuries changed dramatically in the 15th century with the adaptation of gunpowder to warfare. High-velocity wounds penetrated the brain with a violence previously unimagined. Besides recognizing the direct tissue trauma from projectiles, early military surgeons were convinced that gunpowder itself was toxic.

In the 18th century, Percival Pott and Lorenz Heister independently suggested exploratory trephine in cases of paralysis. With the emerging understanding of cerebral localization, the idea that specific parts of the brain had specific functions, they recognized that relieving pressure from the side of the brain opposite the paralyzed parts might be of benefit, and they recommended drilling exploratory holes looking for blood clots that might cause that pressure. Still, they were only looking for blood between the dura and the skull and, although Pott suggested opening a tense, blue dura to look for deeper blood collections, he held out little hope that the patient with such a problem would survive. No one had the temerity to hunt for clots in the brain substance.

Realistic opportunities for survival from penetrating head injuries came as the result of a flurry of technical advances that began in the mid-19th century and included (roughly in order of development) anesthesia, antiseptic and then aseptic surgery, better diagnostic techniques including localization by physical examination and X-ray, antibiotics, and rapid transport and resuscitation.

Mortality from penetrating head wounds in the Crimean and American Civil wars was 73.9 percent and 71.6 percent, respectively. After 1865, Lord Joseph Lister's antiseptic and Ernst von Bergmann's aseptic surgical techniques and X-ray localization became available. Mortality from penetrating head wounds in World War I dropped to 35 percent. After development of sulfa and penicillin antibiotics, that mortality rate dropped to 14 percent in World War II. Emergency life support with artificial ventilation, better treatment of shock, and helicopter transport from the battlefield to well-equipped surgical facilities became standard during and after the Korean Conflict. Mortality from penetrating head injuries in Korea was 9.6 percent and that in Viet Nam was 9.7 percent.

See also Aeromedical Evacuation; Antisepsis; Asepsis; Bergmann, Ernst von; Brunschwig, Hieronymus; Civil War in the United States; Cushing, Harvey Williams; Egyptian Military Medicine; Gersdorff, Hans von; Imhotep; Korean Conflict; Pott, Percival; Prehistoric Military Medicine; Roman Military Medicine; Shock; Transfusion; Trephine, Trepan, and Trephining; Viet Nam War; World War I Medicine; World War II Medicine

References

Coats, J. B., and A. M. Meirowsky. *Neurological Surgery of Trauma*. Washington, D.C.: Office of the Surgeon General, Department of the Army, 1965.

Cushing, Harvey. 1918. "Notes on Penetrating Injuries of the Brain." *British Medical Journal* 1: 221–226.

Gurdjian, E. S. *Head Injury from Antiquity to the Present with Special Reference to Penetrating Head Wounds*. Springfield, IL: Charles C. Thomas, 1973.

Hamman, W. H. 1971. "Analysis of 2187 Consecutive Penetrating Wounds of the Brain from Vietnam." *Journal of Neurosurgery* 34: 127–131.

Heister, Lorenz
(1683–1758)

Lorenz Heister was a military surgeon whose 1718 *General System of Surgery* remained a standard for more than a hundred years.

Heister was born in Frankfurt, Germany, the son of a lumber merchant and innkeeper and studied at the Frankfurt gymnasium before going to the University of Geissen where he performed his first human dissection. He later went to Leiden and studied under Dutch anatomists Frederik Ruysch and Johannes Rau. During the War of the Spanish Succession he worked as an assistant surgeon and obtained considerable operative experience in field hospitals at Brussels and Ghent before returning to the University of Hardewijk, where he finally received his medical degree in 1708. He then rejoined the Dutch Army as a surgeon and participated in several battles, during one of which he was wounded. He returned to Amsterdam in late 1709 and was appointed professor of surgery at the University of Altdorf in 1711. He joined the faculty of the University of Helmstädt in 1720, where he spent the rest of his career and trained numerous physicians and surgeons.

Heister understood that gunpowder was not, as had been believed for more than a century, a poison, and he recognized the importance of removing not only the bullet but all other fragments of cloth and foreign material from a wound. He recommended packing the cleaned wound with lint for three days, after which the cloth was to be removed and the wound filled with honey (now known to have antibacterial properties) and covered with a plaster bandage. Heister also irrigated wounds with turpentine and lime water, a mixture that releases microorganism-killing halogens. He coined the term "tracheotomy" and provided detailed pictures of battlefield bandaging.

See also Bullet Wounds and Other Penetrating Injuries from Gunpowder Projectiles; Prussian and German Military Medicine

References

N.a. 1967. "Lorenz Heister (1683–1758). Eighteenth Century Surgeon." *Journal of the American Medical Association* 202: 1048–1049.

Reisinger, M. M. 2002. "Lorenz Heister and the Challenge of Trepination: Neurosurgical Case Study from the 18th Century." *Journal of the History of the Neurosciences* 11 (3): 286–300.

Hemostasis

Hemostatis is the control of bleeding, the perennial nemesis of military surgeons.

For millennia hemorrhage was the principal cause of battlefield death, and its control was the primary job of the military surgeon. Blood loss was recognized as a serious problem by the Egyptians, who warned surgeons to be particularly careful of violating large vessels while probing wounds. The earliest known mention of using the cautery to stop bleeding is in the Ebers papyrus and is repeated in the Smith papyrus. Egyptian surgeons also bound fresh meat on wounds, a technique which may have created a mechanical plug and probably triggered the natural clotting sequence. When those measures failed, they fell back on prayer and incantation.

The ancient Greeks were even less skilled than their Egyptian predecessors in managing hemorrhage. Homer viewed bleeding as essentially hopeless, and the only treatment mentioned in the *Iliad* is to wrap the wound and pray. If the *Iliad* is to be believed, blood loss was by far the most common cause of death from wounds during the Trojan campaign.

Management of hemorrhage in India in Homeric times was slightly better. Suśruta recommended sewing up the bleeding wound as quickly as possible. If that failed, the wound was to be washed with hot clarified butter or packed with a poultice. If the bleeding persisted, a sandbag was to be placed on the extremity; it is likely that the weight of the bag served as a compression dressing to slow the bleeding. If that failed, and hypotension did not ameliorate the hemorrhage, the patient died.

With time, the Greeks got better at controlling blood loss. Hippocrates describes using cold compresses around the wound, a technique that causes the vessels to constrict and is somewhat effective in controlling hemorrhage. The major Hippocratic advance, however, was use of the tourniquet. Hippocrates knew that bleeding could be stopped by applying a tight bandage above the wound, but the dilemma of how long to leave a tourniquet in place was one the Greeks never solved. Their physicians repeatedly either removed the pressure too soon in which case the bleeding resumed or left it too long in which case the extremity was lost to gangrene.

The Romans finally came up with the answer. Celsus recommended first packing the wound with lint and applying pressure. If that failed, he suggested irrigating the wound with vinegar or a caustic substance to cause the blood to clot. Failing that, he suggested the correct solution, although with a slight anatomic misconception. Celsus believed that only veins carried blood and that the arteries carried air, so his recommendations for controlling hemorrhage directly spoke only of the former. Nonetheless, the Roman said that, if the first two methods failed, one should grasp the ends of the bleeding vein in forceps and tie them off. This was the first accurate description of ligating vessels for hemostasis.

Not only did the Romans understand what to do, but they also created ingenious instruments to help them do it. Roman forceps have been discovered with slip rings around the arms that allow them to be held closed and even with locking handles so the vessel could be caught and held by the instrument, leaving the surgeon's hands free to apply the ligature. If even that failed, Celsus resorted to the cautery. Finally, the surgical armamentarium was complete, although modern tweaks such as collagen dressings instead of lint and electricity instead of hot coals would refine the techniques.

See also Amputation; Bandaging and Wound Dressing; Classical Greek Military Medicine; Hippocrates of Cos; Indian Military Medicine; Minoan and Ancient Greek Military Medicine; Paré, Ambroise; Roman Military Medicine; Tourniquet

Reference
Majno, Guido. *The Healing Hand: Man and Wound in the Ancient World.* Cambridge, MA: Harvard University Press, 1975.

Hippocrates of Cos
(ca. 460–370 B.C.)

Hippocrates was the father of both Greek and scientific medicine.

Little is actually known of Hippocrates, although multiple admiring references from his Athenian contemporaries survive and leave no doubt that he played a key role in the development of Greek medicine. He was said to have been the son of Heraclides, a Coan physician who legend said was descended in a direct line of 18 generations from Aesculapius. Hippocrates's mother was Phenarete (sometimes Praxithea), who was said to be descended through 19 generations from Hercules. Hippocrates was educated by his father, his uncle Gorgias the Sophist, and the philosopher Democritus.

After completing his education, Hippocrates traveled widely before coming to Athens, where he was a contemporary and acquaintance of Sophocles, Socrates, Plato, Euripides, Aristophanes (who satirized him), Herodotus, and Thucydides. He treated patients during the Great Plague of Athens. He later served as court physician to Persian emperor Artaxerxes (although he remained a loyal Greek) before returning to Thessaly, where he died between 85 and 104 years of age.

Hippocrates is credited with separating physicians and the practice of medicine from priests and religion. The collected works of Hippocrates are almost certainly a compilation from the library at Cos, only a small portion of which were actually written by him. Even those attributed to him were likely the product of three Coan physicians with Hippocrates, exerting the right of seniority that remains characteristic of medical publications, putting his name first on the authors list.

The oath bearing his name is the oldest and most durable statement of medical ethics but probably originated in the Pythagorean School of southern Italy. The Hippocratic corpus was later collected by Greco-Roman and Arabic physicians including Galen and Avicenna and serves to organize Greek medical knowledge, which had previously been largely aphoristic, and provides vivid case descriptions and detailed instructions in caring for specific illnesses and injuries. Later scholars' enthusiasm for Greek civilization of the fifth century B.C. served to enhance Hippocrates's reputation, probably to an inordinate degree.

Still, Hippocrates's descriptions of surgery, particularly of wounds and orthopedic injuries, were the best available before those of Aulus Cornelius Celsus in the first century A.D. He recommended trephine to relieve pressure from head injury (albeit for the wrong reasons), knew how to align clavicle fractures, and provided excellent descriptions of reducing dislocations and fixing long bone fractures. The descriptions are of particular interest to the history of military medicine because many of the wounds were inflicted in battle. In fact, Hippocrates said the only appropriate training for a surgeon was to find an army and follow it.

He described opposite-side paralysis from a brain injury, knew that epilepsy would disappear with a malarial infection, associated the wasting of syphilitic tabes with sexual activity, and provided the first descriptions of human anthrax. Hippocrates recommended irrigating wounds with wine and clean water and insisted that physicians wash their hands with hot water and work only with the best available natural or artificial light, preferably with trained assistants in a room dedicated to surgical procedures. These descriptions and treatments continued to be referred to until well into the 17th century and are valuable as primary examples of observation and clinical diagnosis rather than as works in experimental medicine. Hippocrates was an unusually honest observer (60 percent of his 42 cases expired) who considered the ability to predict an outcome at least as important as effecting a cure.

Unlike the descriptive and surgical works, the theoretical portions of the Hippocratic corpus were based on error and persisted to the detriment of Western medicine for centuries. Illness and response to trauma were assumed to be a function of imbalance among the four humors: black bile, yellow bile, blood, and phlegm based upon the four essential Pythagorean elements (earth, air, fire, and water). Treatments designed to restore balance such as bleeding and purging continued to do harm well into the 19th century.

See also Anthrax; Antisepsis; Classical Greek Military Medicine; Malaria

References
Adams, Francis. *The Genuine Works of Hippocrates Translated from the Greek.* London: Baillière, Tindall & Cox, 1939.
Garrison, Fielding. *An Introduction to the History of Medicine.* Philadelphia: W. B. Saunders Co., 1929.
LeClerc, Daniel. *Histoire de la Médecine.* Amsterdam: Depens de la Compagnie, 1723.

Holtzendorff, Ernst Conrad (1688–1751)

Ernst Holtzendorff was appointed the first surgeon general of the Prussian Army in 1716.

Holtzendorff won Frederick Wilhelm I's confidence when he successfully treated the monarch's personal illness in 1719. He had begun his career as a *feldscherer*, or field barber, and his subsequent insistence that these military wound surgeons be trained in anatomy and perform their own dissections helped raise the status of surgeons to bring them closer to the better-educated physicians. Frederick Wilhelm appointed Holtzendorff surgeon general of the Prussian Army and director of surgery in Prussia with direct supervision of all surgeons, *feldschers*, barbers, and midwives in the kingdom.

As a result of Holtzendorff's influence with the king, Prussian military surgeons were sent abroad to study at government expense. This practice evolved into the Collegium Medico-Chirurgicum, where prospective military surgeons were given basic science training followed by clinical training in the *Charité*, Berlin's former pesthouse. The building, located adjacent to Spandau Gate, was converted in 1714 to a civilian and military hospital by royal decree and was funded by the government. Holtzendorff's graduates of the *Charité* had to take courses in anatomy and medical theory and serve apprenticeships under qualified doctors before graduating as *Artzen* with credentials in both medicine and surgery.

See also Prussian and German Military Medicine

References

Blair, J. S. 2006. "Ernst Conrad Holtzendorff." *Journal of the Royal Army Medical Corps* 152 (March): 66–67.

Ruster, D. 1988. "The Surgeon to the Soldier King: On the 300th Anniversary of the Birth of Ernst Conrad Holtzendorff." *Arzt Fortbild (Jena)* 82: 913–916.

Hospital Ships

Vessels dedicated for use as floating hospitals date at least to the Spanish Armada, which sailed with 15 such ships.

The *Goodwill* (1608) was the first hospital ship in the English Royal Navy and, by the middle of the 17th century, hospital ships had become a regular part of the French and Spanish navies as well. Seventeenth-century hospital ships were, in general, converted sixth-rate warships with operating facilities and curtained-off sections for cases deemed infectious.

Besides ships detailed to accompany the fleet, hospital vessels were also designated for treatment and transport of land-based units. In 1683, a British expedition to evacuate Tangier was accompanied by two ships (the *Welcome* and the *Unity*) with that specific charge. In 1800, Surgeon General Thomas Keate recommended that hospital ships be made permanently available to the British Army for transport of the ill from stations in the West Indies. The vessels were a boon to the patients with their natural ventilation and general cleanliness, both a significant improvement over the dismal conditions in shore hospitals. The Royal Navy experimented with using sailors' wives as nurses on the hospital ships but abandoned the practice in favor of male nurses as a result of repeated complaints about the women's morals and affection for alcohol.

Hospital ships were particularly important in the Crimean War when casualties had to be transported 300 miles from Russia's Black Sea coast to the British Army's only military hospital at Scutari near Constantinople. In the last three months of 1854, a total of 41 converted vessels carried 8,106 sick and wounded to Scutari. In all, 14,500 British soldiers and 202 Russian prisoners of war started the journey although 516 failed to survive the voyage.

The first ships actually equipped as floating hospitals rather than as floating ambulances were the 2,000-ton steam and sail ships *Melbourne* and *Mauritius*, manned by the newly created Medical Staff Corps that accompanied the British Army to China in 1860. The ships had 230 cubic feet of space for each patient between eight-foot-high decks, and each had an operating room lit by a skylight.

In the spring of 1862, the U.S. Sanitary Commission and Frederick Law Olmsted oversaw conversion of several freighters including the *Daniel Webster* for transport of sick and wounded from the Chesapeake Bay during the Peninsula Campaign. At the same time, Union forces at Fort Henry converted the river steamer *City of Memphis* and four other commandeered vessels for the same purpose. In April 1862, General Ulysses S. Grant captured four Confederate steamers and converted one, the *Red Rover*, into the first real American hospital ship. It was equipped with a kitchen and bakery, an elevator, and a fully furnished operating theater.

During the 1877–1878 Russo-Turkish War, the British Red Cross Society furnished and dispatched a steel-hulled hospital ship with five surgeons and the carbolic acid and chloroform necessary to perform surgery under anesthesia and with antiseptic technique. Similarly equipped steam launches went up and down the Nile River during the 1885 British campaign in Egypt. The U.S. Navy deployed six hospital ships during the Spanish-American War including the USS *Missouri*, the sister ship to the USS *Maine*, whose sinking had precipitated the conflict. Both the Russian and Japanese navies used hospital ships during their 1904–1905 war, with those of the latter nation being especially well designed and well equipped.

During World War I, most hospital ships were converted ocean liners, painted white with red crosses, and registered with and presumably protected by the Geneva Convention as adapted to maritime warfare in 1864 and revised in 1907. The Royal Navy commissioned five such vessels in the first month of the war and had a total of 77 hospital ships and transports in service by war's end. Although hospital ships saw service in the Atlantic, in the English Channel, in the rivers of Mesopotamia, and in Southwest and East Africa, they were especially important in Gallipoli, where 42 hospital ships and transports evacuated more than 110,000 sick and wounded to Egypt between April and December 1915.

In World War II, hospital ships participated in the evacuation of Dunkirk and were back in service at Tobruk in December 1941 and in the Mediterranean over the next three years. The first 18,000 casualties at

Normandy during the D-Day invasion had to be evacuated in landing craft because the necessary docking facilities for ships had not been secured. One such landing ship tank (LST) made three channel crossings, the longest of which took 32 hours, during which time surgeons performed a total of 45 operations.

The greatest challenges for American hospital ships came in the Pacific, where the island war presented unique problems in medical evacuation; the distances were inordinately long and there was almost never an accessible general hospital to augment basic field hospital care. At the beginning of the war, the U.S. Navy had only two hospital ships (the USS *Relief* and the USS *Solace*), and only one of these was in the Pacific. Over the next three-and-a-half years, the United States commissioned an additional eight hospital ships and developed an entire class of troop transports equipped to provide limited hospital services. The Navy also deployed a series of adapted landing craft—LST (H)s—manned with four surgeons and 27 corpsmen and capable of serving as field hospitals for up to 350 wounded. Hospital ships, required by the Navy to be held well back from areas of direct combat, served essentially the same role as land-based general hospitals.

A total of seven ships formally served as floating hospitals or patient transports during the Korean Conflict. Their role changed dramatically from that originally envisioned as the war progressed. The *New Haven* class were dedicated 500-foot hospital ships first built during World War II. The USS *Consolation* was in commission in 1950 and made a rapid trip from the eastern United States to Korea when hostilities broke out. The rest of the class was in the reserve fleet in San Francisco. The USS *Benevolence* and the

USS *Repose* were activated, but *Benevolence* sank in the Golden Gate channel on her way to Korea. The *New Haven* was activated in her place and joined the *Consolation* and the *Repose* in Korean waters by mid-October. Almost from the outset, the decision was made to use the ships as stationary floating hospitals. They were initially berthed at Pusan but moved north along both the east and west coasts of Korea after the United Nations forces broke out into the peninsula. In the frantic early days of the war (before organized air evacuation from Korea to Japan was in place) the troop ships USNS *Sgt. George D. Keathley* and USNS *Sgt. Andrew Miller* were pressed into service to move the wounded to rear-area hospitals. Early on, even these resources were overwhelmed and local ferries were used as well. The Royal Navy furnished the HMHS *Maine*, a captured World War II–era Italian liner that was present in Far Eastern waters in June 1950. The ship was ill suited for medical duties; she was overcrowded and had only a single air-conditioning unit, allowing temperatures in the lower decks to exceed 100°F. The Danish ship *Jutlandia* also served in the early part of the war. She was a converted passenger and cargo vessel staffed with volunteers and made two trips from the Pacific to Europe to return wounded United Nations troops to their home countries.

As helicopter and fixed-wing transport became available, the role of the hospital ships changed dramatically. The C-47 Dakotas and C-54 Skymasters assumed essentially all transport duties, so the ships were moored close to combat areas to serve as fixed base hospitals. At first flat-topped barges were moored next to the ships to allow helicopter access. Later, formal "helo" decks were added so patients could be brought directly on board. At various times, the ships were also moored directly to piers and served as both floating hospitals and outpatient clinics. The upper three decks housed up to 800 inpatients while the lower three decks were administrative and clinic spaces. By September 1952, the U.S. Navy hospital ships had admitted 40,662 patients; about 35 percent were battle casualties and the rest were diseases and nonbattle injuries.

See also Civil War in the United States; Crimean War; Geneva Conventions; Japanese Military Medicine; Korean Conflict; Russo-Japanese War; World War I Medicine; World War II Medicine

References
Cowdrey, Alfred E. *United States Army in the Korean War: The Medic's War*. Washington, D.C.: Center for Military History, 1987.
Coyl, E. B. 1953. "Hospital Ships in Korea." *Military Surgeon* 112: 342–344.
Kimura, S. *The Surgical & Medical History of the Naval War between Japan & Russia*. Tokyo: Toyo Printing Co., Ltd., 1911.
Olmsted, Frederick Law. *Hospital Transports: A Memoir of the Embarkation of the Sick and Wounded from the Peninsula of Virginia in the Summer of 1862*. Boston: Ticknor and Fields, 1863.
Plumridge, John H. *Hospital Ships and Ambulance Trains*. London: Seeley, Service & Co., 1975.
Wilbur, C. Keith. *Civil War Medicine*. Guilford, CT: Globe Pequot Press, 1998.

Hospital Trains

Initially used to evacuate the wounded the seven miles between Balaklava and Sebastapol in the Crimea, hospital trains remained a major means of medical transportation through World War I.

In the 1854 Crimean War, British and French forces had taken advantage of the fact that freight cars moving food and supplies from the docks to the front could, once emptied, be used to carry the wounded in the opposite direction. Only eight such cars were available, and American military observers did not consider them important enough to mention in their official reports. The first dedicated ambulance car was used by the French at Châlons in 1857 and, in the 1859 Italian-Austrian War, trains moved more than 89,000 wounded from field hospitals to general hospitals in Milan, Turin, Brescia, and Pavia.

When the American Civil War started, the United States had 31,000 miles of railroads (21,000 of which were in Union states), and President Abraham Lincoln put them under federal management and appointed Col. Daniel McCallum superintendent of the U.S. Military Railroad in January 1862. The intent was primarily to use railcars to move food, forage, ammunition, and some medical supplies with no real thought of using railroads to move the wounded.

The first time railroads were used for that purpose in the United States was in August 1861 when Assistant Surgeon S. H. Melcher used boxcars to move Union wounded from Rolla, Missouri, to the general hospital at St. Louis after the Union defeat at the Battle of Wilson's Creek. As in the Crimea, empty cars returning from the front became a preferred method of evacuating the wounded for both the Union and the Confederacy in spite of the fact that the men often had to lie on straw, leaves, or bare boards in cars that were either open entirely or closed boxes without ventilation. When stretchers were available, they were usually either hung by ropes from the ceiling or rested on stanchions bolted to the walls of the car. In either case, they left the men subject to the rocking and jerking of a moving train.

As part of Jonathan Letterman's reform of medical transport beginning in 1862, evacu-

ation trains from the front to rear-area hospitals became standard in the Army of the Potomac. In October 1862, Dr. Elisha Harris of the U.S. Sanitary Commission designed a car in which stretchers were suspended by their handles with rubber-ring shock absorbers to ease suffering during evacuation of the wounded. The Philadelphia, Wilmington, and Baltimore Railroad subsequently built 15 of the Harris cars.

After the Battle of Antietam, Letterman was able to move more than 9,000 wounded to the general hospital in Frederick, Maryland, in less than three days. After the Battle of Gettysburg, 11,425 men were transported by rail to hospitals in Baltimore; York, Virginia; and New York City. The wounded at Gettysburg were initially taken to a field hospital, and those able to be moved were then transferred to Sanitary Commission tents that had been erected at the railhead. The large numbers of wounded led to a bottleneck at the railhead, but, as trains became available, movement farther to the rear was generally smooth.

By 1864 J. McCricket, assistant superintendent of Union military railroads, had designed hospital cars that could hold up to 60 wounded on permanently mounted stretchers. Eighteen trains a day ran the 20 miles from the front at Petersburg to the 6,000-bed Union hospital at City Point, Virginia, in June of that year. Although these were primarily boxcars in the beginning, by January 1865 they had all been replaced by dedicated hospital cars.

The Confederates never got beyond using back-loaded freight cars and commandeered passenger cars and never had an organized program of rail evacuation.

Similar informal rail evacuation persisted in the 1864 Prussian war in Schleswig-Holstein and in Prussia's war with the

Wounded soldiers loaded onto a hospital train in France during World War I. (National Library of Medicine)

Austrians in 1866. By the 1871 Franco-Prussian War, the Germans had adopted the Harris cars and used hospital trains to move 90,000 wounded from France to Berlin. The British also used hospital cars in the 1879 Zulu Wars, in the 1884–1885 Egyptian Campaign, and in the 1896 Rhodesian rebellion. In the 1899–1902 Boer War, the English used both converted passenger cars and dedicated hospital trains extensively to evacuate their wounded.

During the 1904–1905 Russo-Japanese War, the Russians used 78 trains (many donated by the imperial family or Russian aristocrats), each of which could carry up to 600 wounded in 28 cars the 5,000 miles from Siberia to Moscow. These trains were equipped with baths, a pharmacy, and an operating room.

Combined Franco-British "ambulance trains" not only transported wounded from the front during World War I but also acted as mobile medical and surgical wards and kitchen and supply cars. In spite of those advances, men continued to be transported on straw palettes in empty boxcars on return journeys from the line. In a single month in 1914, trains evacuated 138,000 British casualties from Flanders. In addition, men were frequently transferred from the trenches on hand-powered, narrow-gauge Barnton Tramways capable of carrying up to four men each or on horse-drawn railcars. The Royal Army Medical Corps also used trains in Italy, in the Balkans, in Egypt, in Mesopotamia, in East Africa, and within Britain.

Trains were again used to move casualties within France after D-Day in World War II and during the Burma Campaign as well as within Britain after evacuation from France. Various sorts of rail transport were also used during the Korean Conflict. More recently, rail transport has largely been supplanted by road or air evacuation.

See also Boer War; Civil War in the United
States; Crimean War; Franco-Prussian War;
Italian Campaign of 1859; Korean Conflict;
Letterman, Jonathan; Russo-Japanese War;
World War I Medicine

References

Haller, John S. *Farmcarts to Fords: A History of the
Military Ambulance, 1790–1925*. Carbondale:
Southern Illinois University Press, 1992.
Hawk, Alan. 2002. "An Ambulating Hospital:
Or, How the Hospital Train Transformed
Army Medicine." *Civil War History* 48:
197–219.
Plumridge, John H. *Hospital Ships and Ambulance
Trains*. London: Seeley, Service & Co., 1975.

Human Experimentation

Human experimentation is the use of human subjects, usually with, but sometimes without, their consent to gain information about the effects of chemical, physical, or biological agents on the body.

Although British Royal Navy sailors used in James Lind's mid-18th-century experiments on scurvy were a prominent exception, human experimentation was rarely employed prior to the end of the 19th century when scientific medicine and the control of some infections raised the possibility of elimination of broad disease categories and gave impetus to experiments that might contribute to those advances.

The military was involved in those experiments almost from the beginning for two widely disparate reasons. First, scientific medical experiments are best done in tightly controlled environments with relatively large numbers of experimental subjects. Asylums, prisons, and military facilities fill both of those requirements. Second, many of the physical, chemical, and biological agents that can damage a human body are potential weapons.

The first well-controlled medical experiment was probably Lind's use of various possible remedies for scurvy and the recording of their effectiveness. Walter Reed's use of Spanish immigrants and American soldiers to prove that mosquitoes were the vector of yellow fever was a model of experimental design. The ethics of the study were, however, questionable in spite of the fact that the researchers used themselves as experimental subjects and then incorporated the first attempt to obtain written consent from later participants.

Both the Japanese and the German military medical corps used captured combatants and civilian prisoners during World War II to test the effects of physiological stress such as extremes of atmospheric pressure, cold, and immersion in hopes of improving survival of their own personnel in harsh conditions. Both also used prisoners to test potential chemical and biological weapons. Experimenters justified the studies on the basis that sacrifice of human subjects was warranted in time of national emergency. These experiments directly resulted in the Nuremberg Code and the Helsinki Declaration, both of which emphasized the necessity for subjects to be fully informed of the risks of their participation in experiments and for that participation to be voluntary. In spite of the fact that both codes were broadly accepted, violations have been common.

As early as October 1942, the Committee on Medical Research of the U.S. Office of Scientific Research and Development recommended tests of the effect of ionizing radiation on humans. Beginning in 1946, both U.S. Army and Navy personnel were intentionally exposed to fallout from nuclear weapons tests. In the July 1946 Project Able, 150 ships carrying 37,000 military personnel were stationed near a 23-kiloton low-altitude atmospheric nuclear explosion and taken directly into the target area the following day. Later that month, the experiment was repeated with an underwater explosion. In both cases, radiation levels at various parts of the observer ships were carefully measured. In subsequent tests, pilots flew through clouds from nuclear explosions and ground observers were carefully monitored for their physiologic response to those explosions. More than 100 chemical, biological, and nuclear tests involved U.S. military personnel and carried such colorful names as Copperhead, Flower Drum, Eager Belle, Fearless Johnny, Half Note, Purple Sage, Scarlet Sage, and Autumn Gold.

Ethical questions raised at the time did not stop the studies. The Department of Defense, citing Reed's yellow fever studies as justification for experimental use of military personnel, sought a waiver of the Nuremberg Code restrictions. The Wilson Memorandum (named for Secretary of Defense Charles E. Wilson) defined how each service would experiment on human subjects and effectively superseded the Nuremberg restrictions.

In the early 1950s, Seventh-Day Adventist conscientious objectors were recruited into Operation Whitecoat in which they were exposed to Q fever at Utah's Dugway Proving Grounds and then returned to Fort Detrick for observation. The Q fever studies were terminated in 1958, but other studies of tularemia and yellow fever continued until the program was terminated in 1975.

The British also used military personnel in human experimentation between 1939 and 1989 under the supervision of their chemical and biological warfare unit at Porton Down. Soldiers at the facility who were told they were part of experiments on the common cold were actually exposed to chemical warfare agents. In a 1970 test of aerosolized delivery of biowarfare agents, the HMS *Andromeda* was sailed through a cloud of *Escherichia coli* and *Bacillus globigii* and the inhaled dose and clothing contamination of the crews measured. Both bacteria were thought at the time to be innocuous; however *Bacillus globigii* (subsequently renamed *Bacillus subtilis*) is now known to cause sepsis, endocarditis, pulmonary infections, and meningitis. Similar studies were done with the HMS *Achilles* in 1973 and on basic training recruits at Portsmouth in 1976.

At a Nevada test site, American soldiers were exposed to nuclear flashes with and without protective eyewear to measure how long it took them to be able to read instruments after the explosion. In another experiment, officers were placed 2,000 yards from a 40-kiloton nuclear explosion to measure the physiological effects of exposure in spite of medical recommendations that they be no closer than seven miles from the blast. The British used soldiers from their own army as well as from Australian and New Zealand forces to evaluate physiologic effects of radiation and as training for men intended to teach their fellow soldiers about nuclear warfare. In that program, more than 35,000 troops were used between 1953 and 1963 in what was euphemistically called the Indoctrination Force.

Perhaps the most notorious use of American military personnel was in Project MKULTRA, authorized by Central Intelligence Agency director Allen Dulles in 1953, in which both civilians and soldiers were exposed, without their knowledge or consent, to drugs such as lysergic acid diethylamide (LSD) thought to have a behavior-altering potential. The program was terminated in 1964 amid concerns about its public relations ramifications.

See also Chemical and Biological Warfare; Fort Detrick; Lind, James; Nuclear Warfare and Radiation Injury; Nuremberg Code; Q Fever; Reed, Walter; Tularemia; Yellow Fever

References

Goliszek, Andrew. *In the Name of Science: A History of Secret Programs, Medical Research, and Human Experimentation*. New York: St. Martin's Press, 2003.
Goodman, Jordan, Anthony McElligott, and Lara Marks. *Useful Bodies: Humans in the Service of Medical Science in the Twentieth Century*. Baltimore: Johns Hopkins University Press, 2003.
Marks, John. *The Search for the Manchurian Candidate: The CIA and Mind Control; The Secret History of the Behavioral Sciences*. New York: W. W. Norton & Co., 1979.

Hunter, John
(1728–1793)

John Hunter is credited with having taken surgery from a technical exercise to a science.

Hunter was probably born near midnight on February 13, 1728, in the village of East Kilbride near Glasgow, Scotland, although the date has been variously cited as February 7, February 9, and July 14. His father was a moderately successful farmer, and John was the youngest of 10 Hunter children including William—10 years John's senior—who became London's premier anatomist and was the father of obstetrics as a medical specialty.

Unlike his older brother, John Hunter did not attend university. He came to London and took a job helping his brother prepare anatomical specimens in 1748, a job he kept for the next 11 years. He first studied surgery in the summer of 1749 under William Cheselden, a prominent surgeon famous for the speed of his procedures. Hunter also studied for short periods at Chelsea Hospital, St. Bartholomew's Hospital, and St. George's Hospital, where he became house surgeon in 1756. Throughout that time, he continued to teach anatomy with his brother.

Hunter served as a staff surgeon in the British Army from 1760 to 1763 and participated in the invasion and occupation of Belle Isle in 1761. The amphibious invasion of the small rocky island off Brittany ultimately required 17,800 British soldiers and more than 100 ships to dislodge fewer than 3,000 French defenders. The British suffered a large number of casualties and, since Hunter was one of only three surgeons in the force, he acquired a unique experience in treating gunshot wounds. Ambroise Paré's recommendation that such wounds be widely opened and the projectile removed seemed to Hunter to cause more harm than benefit, and he recommended that no gunshot wound be enlarged except as needed to manage an associated injury. To the horror of his colleagues and the ultimate benefit of his patients, he left most wounds unexplored, later publishing his experience in the monumental *Treatise on the Blood, Inflammation, and Gunshot Wounds*.

He accompanied the British Army to Portugal, but his ability to advance in the military was hopelessly impeded by his lack of a formal medical degree, and he returned to London and private practice in 1763.

Hunter was an avid naturalist, and his extensive publications resulted in his being elected Fellow of the Royal Society in 1767. In 1768 he became a member of the Corporation of Surgeons and attending surgeon to St. George's Hospital. He wrote extensively on medical problems including tendon repair (a subject that got his interest after he ruptured his own Achilles tendon while dancing), the pathology of shock, artificial feeding through a flexible tube, forced respiration, and treatment of arterial aneurysm by high ligation of the feeding vessel.

He continued to teach surgery, and his pupils included Edward Jenner, John Abernethy, William Shippen, and John Morgan. In 1776 he was named surgeon extraordinary to King George III. In 1785 he became deputy surgeon general of the Army, and, in 1790, he was named inspector of hospitals and surgeon general of the British Army with a much-needed salary of £1,200 a year.

Hunter had, for years, been an avid collector of anatomical curiosities, both animal and human, and the cost of acquiring and storing what eventually numbered 13,000 specimens weighed heavily on his finances. The collection survives as the basis of London's Hunterian Museum and secured Hunter's reputation as the founder of experimental and surgical pathology.

Hunter inadvertently infected himself with syphilis and, from the age of 45, he suffered from bouts of severe chest and back pain, often accompanied by loss of pulses in his arms. The episodes were particularly aggravated by loss of his famously uncontrolled temper and, during a board meeting in which he was vigorously advocating admission of two questionably qualified students to St. George's, he abruptly died. Although it has been widely stated that his chest pains were angina pectoris from coronary artery disease, his autopsy and symptoms were most compatible with a syphilitic aortic aneurysm.

After Hunter's death, his brother-in-law, Sir Everard Home, assumed the role of successor and plagiarized a number of his unpublished papers. Home ultimately burned all of Hunter's surviving manuscripts in an evident attempt to hide the theft. Virtually all that was left of Hunter's legacy were his published works and his museum.

See also British Military Medicine

References

Home, Everard. "A Short Account of the Author's Life." In John Hunter, *A Treatise on the Blood, Inflammation, and Gun-Shot Wounds.* London: George Nicol, 1794.

Kobler, John. *The Reluctant Surgeon: A Biography of John Hunter, Medical Genius and Great Inquirer of Johnson's England.* Garden City, NY: Doubleday & Co., Inc., 1960.

I

Imhotep
(ca. 26th Century B.C.)

Imhotep is the earliest named physician; he also served as grand vizier, priest, astrologer, poet, sage, and pyramid builder during the reign of Pharaoh Djoser of Egypt (2630–2611 B.C.)

The name "Imhotep" translates from the ancient Egyptian as "the one who comes in peace." He may have been born either in Ankhtowë, a suburb of Memphis, or in Gebelein, south of Thebes, and his father was probably an architect. Although born a commoner, Imhotep, largely by virtue of his intellectual talents, became second only to the pharaoh in power and reputation in Egypt.

Imhotep founded a medical school at Memphis 2,000 years before Hippocrates, and it is possible that he authored parts of the Edwin Smith papyrus, which is the oldest known manual of military medicine. Even if he was not the actual author, it is very likely he knew and employed the text's contents.

Imhotep lived to an old age, and his already considerable reputation increased after his death. He was considered a demigod within 100 years and became a full member of the Egyptian pantheon in 525 B.C., joining Pharaoh Amenhotep as the only two mortals to be considered complete deities. Temples were built in his honor at Karnak and on the island of Philae; his identity merged into that of the Greek god Asclepios, the Roman deity Aesculapius; and, for early Christians, he was conflated with Christ.

See also Aesculapius; Egyptian Military Medicine

References
Clayton, Peter A. *Chronicle of the Pharaohs: The Reign by Reign Record of the Rulers and Dynasties of Ancient Egypt.* London: Thames and Hudson, Ltd., 1994.
Hurry, J. B. *Imhotep: The Vizier and Physician of King Zoser and Afterwards the Egyptian God of Medicine.* London: Oxford University Press, 1926.
Shaw, Ian. *The Oxford History of Ancient Egypt.* New York: Oxford University Press, 2000.

Indian Military Medicine

Medicine occupied a special status in ancient Indian learning.

Veda, the name for the four divinely inspired books of Sanskrit wisdom, shares its origin with *vaidya*, which means one who knows and was the common term for "physician." *Ayurveda*, which means knowledge of life, also comes from that root and refers to the Indian system of medicine.

Indian medicine went through three distinct phases between 1500 B.C. and A.D. 100. The first was the Vedic, in which Iranian medical tradition was translated into Sanskrit. The *Brahmanas* were commentaries on the *Vedas*; they were written between 1000 B.C. and 400 B.C. and include the *Charaka Samhita* (collection of Charaka) and the *Suśruta Samhita* (collection of Suśruta), which dealt respectively with medical and surgical treatments, although each has a bit of both. In their earliest forms, the written works, which were produced by the Brahmin upper class, did not mention surgery as contact with wounds, injuries, and corpses was considered unclean and surgery was done entirely by the lower castes. Later, surgery and medicine came together. Most of early Indian history is oral and undated, so placing an exact time of this change is difficult. Charaka probably worked in the first century A.D. and Suśruta around 750 B.C.

The Indian physician approached a sick or wounded patient with four questions: Was the disease real or psychosomatic? If the disease was real, what was its cause? Could the disease be treated? If it could, what was the best method? The third question and the implication that physicians should avoid problems they could not effectively treat are also found in Mesopotamian and ancient Egyptian medicine. Like the Greeks, the Indians thought disease might result from an imbalance of humors, although they only recognized three: breath, bile, and phlegm corresponding to the physical principles wind, fire, and water. Both the categorization and assumption

of humoral cause of disease are suspiciously similar to Greek theory and have led to unproven suggestions that the two cultures shared information.

Indian physicians believed many diseases were caused by ingested poisons and were especially interested in their patients' diets. In that same vein, they advocated frequent purges and enemas to remove toxins, and Charaka listed more than 600 purgatives in his text. Fever was considered the root of many other diseases and was depicted as a deformed, three-headed, six-handed, nine-eyed monster.

On a more scientific level, Indian physicians recognized the relationship between mosquitoes and fever in general and probably with malaria in particular. They recognized that intestinal worms were disease-causing parasites but thought they arose spontaneously from the patient's body. Anticipating Albert Camus by two millennia, Indian physicians warned that when rats began to die and fall out of the rafters, plague was not far behind.

Indian surgeons were indispensable to the military. In fact, just as in Greek, the Sanskrit name for surgeon (*shalyahara*) means arrow remover. Indian surgeons used bamboo splints that were copied by the British military as late as the 20th century. They used opium and cannabis as analgesics and operated on patients under the influence of cannabis, hyocyamine, and hypnosis. Suśruta said, "A physician fully equipped with a supply of medicine should live in camp not remote from the royal pavilion, and there the persons wounded by shafts of arrows or any other war projectiles or suffering from the effects of any imbibed poison should resort to him." In fact, it was one of the military physician's jobs to test camp food and water to ensure it had not been poisoned by an enemy.

As an introduction to their rigorous training, aspiring Indian physicians were required to memorize the entire *Suśruta Samhita* even before they learned the Sanskrit in which it was written. They practiced incisions on melons, gourds, and cucumbers and sutured shaved animal skins. They learned to drain abscesses by cutting into leather bags filled with water or mud and became adept at opening hollow organs by incising lotus stalks. They learned to extract foreign bodies by picking seeds out of fruit or extracting teeth from the jaws of dead animals, and learned venipuncture by threading needles into the veins of cabbage leaves.

Indian military surgeons had an impressive array of surgical instruments, usually of high-quality steel. A typical kit might include 20 different kinds of knives and needles, 20 sorts of tubes, 30 varieties of probes, 26 dressing implements, and various hooks and tongs. Among the two dozen or so forceps and pincers were instruments whose jaws were made to resemble those of a crocodile, a lion, a heron, and a jackal.

The Indians controlled bleeding with pressure, poultices, hot oil, and sutures, but they never learned to ligate vessels. They closed delicate wounds, including open bowel wounds, by placing the two lips of the opening between the jaws of large ants. When the ants bit down and pulled the edges together, the head was twisted off and left in place until the wound healed. Indian surgeons were particularly adept at plastic surgical repair of missing noses and ears both because they were common battle wounds and because they were also the result of civil punishment.

For all their cleverness, Indian surgeons were dismally ignorant of anatomy. Their religion viewed touching a corpse as un-clean, so dissection was virtually unheard of. To get around the prohibition, it was suggested that a dead body be placed in a cage and submerged in a river for a week, after which the softened tissues could be picked apart with a stick without directly coming in contact with the corpse. The information thus gained, even if the dissector got past the smell, was of only marginal use and caused strange conclusions such as the belief that all blood vessels arose in the navel.

Indian military surgeons usually estimated a wound's prognosis based on its site of entry, and they acquired an extensive empirical knowledge of the results of wounds in more than 100 specific locations. They knew that penetrations of areas that we now know lie over nerves often caused lameness, and that wounds over other areas were associated with hemorrhage (arteries), paralysis (spinal cord), or death (the skull's temporal bone).

Indian surgeons devised a number of ingenious ways of extracting arrows, including tying the end to a horse's bridle and making the animal toss its head and tying the end to a bent tree branch, which could then be released like a spring. Indian military surgeons probably carried their art as far as ingenuity without knowledge of anatomy allowed.

See also Forceps and Extractors; Malaria; Minoan and Ancient Greek Military Medicine

References
Geissinger, Jay. 1927. "The Development of Military Medicine." *Bulletin of the New York Academy of Medicine* 3 (May): 301–356.
Sigerist, Henry. *A History of Medicine: Early Greek, Hindu, and Persian Medicine.* New York: Oxford University Press, 1961.
Zimmer, Henry R. *Hindu Medicine.* Baltimore: Johns Hopkins University Press, 1948.

Influenza

Influenza is a viral disease that recurs in epidemics and pandemics and has repeatedly affected the outcomes of both military campaigns and entire wars.

The first description of what was probably an influenza pandemic came from Hippocrates in 412 B.C. Since then, influenza epidemics have recurred almost annually and, prior to modern transportation, sometimes remained within a restricted geographic area. Although exposure to a specific variant of the virus confers lifelong immunity, the pathogen has the ability to subtly alter its protein structure, making it less recognizable to the host's immune system so exposure to last year's virus is unlikely to provide complete protection from the current strain. Occasionally the virus will develop a whole new gene, allowing it to look like an entirely unique organism to which the body has no immunity whatsoever. These drastic changes, known as antigenic shifts, lead to pandemics, or worldwide disease outbreaks.

The most devastating influenza pandemic, and the most lethal outbreak of any infection prior to AIDS, occurred early in the 20th century. More deaths resulted from influenza between 1918 and 1921 than from all other war-related causes between 1914 and 1919; estimates of total mortality from the pandemic range from a conservative 20 million to nearly 100 million compared to 9.2 million combat fatalities and 15 million deaths from other causes during World War I. Influenza was the predominant cause of a decrease in life expectancy in the United States from 51 years in 1917 to 39 years in 1918.

The disease had a predilection for young adults and was particularly devastating in the military. The U.S. armed forces alone experienced 729,381 cases of flu with a 7.2 percent mortality rate; 40 percent of the U.S. Navy and 36 percent of the Army were infected in 1918 alone.

The 1918 pandemic was caused by a variant of the influenza A virus, which could stick to the surface of alveolar cells in the lung, penetrate those cells, co-opt the intracellular machinery, and cause the cell to manufacture new virus particles that could be coughed up to infect a new host.

The first recorded cases of the 1918 pandemic were in the Spanish town of San Sebastian in February of that year, accounting for the disease's most common eponyms—the Spanish flu or the Spanish Lady. The first military case occurred on March 4 at Camp Funston (currently Fort Riley), Kansas, and cases were reported in British and French troops on the Western Front in early April. A curious aspect of the disease was its ability to move over long distances faster than could be accounted for by existing ground or sea transportation. It is not certain how the disease moved from Spain to Kansas or from Kansas to northeastern France, although the virus is now known to be carried by migratory birds.

In May 1918, more than 10,000 British sailors confined to port with the Grand Fleet became ill. German general Erich von Ludendorff initially thought the flu might be the serendipitous natural intervention that would save Germany's failing war effort, but his hopes were dashed when the disease broke out among his own troops and effectively halted his July offensive. By midsummer, the disease, which had swept through Europe and North America, mysteriously disappeared without striking Asia or the Southern Hemisphere. In the first wave of the pandemic, although the virus often caused a debilitating illness, it typically abated after about three days and was rarely fatal.

The disease came back with a vengeance in the fall. It started in central Asia, swept through India (where fatalities, though poorly recorded, may have reached 20 million), Southeast Asia, China, Japan, the Pacific Islands, and South America. By September the disease reached Boston and, shortly thereafter, the western Massachusetts military facility at Fort Devens. The second wave was an entirely different disease. Unlike the usual influenza, which shows a predilection for the very young and the very old, this pandemic had three peaks of age preference: birth to five years; 70 to 74 years; and, atypically and of special importance to the military, 20 to 40 years. In fact, young adults were the primary target.

The new disease was of remarkably rapid onset; people were found dead sitting in chairs, died on the subway going home from work, or were healthy on arising and dead before sundown. The illness started with an abrupt onset of flushing, chills, and fever followed by a cough productive of thick, bloody sputum. Within hours the patients, unable to move air, turned blue and suffocated. Many of those lucky enough to survive the early stages developed bacterial pneumonia a few days later and died from that complication. Death was frequent and ugly, and public panic was widespread. Cities mandated stiff fines for citizens who ventured out in public without a mask; theaters and churches—but rarely saloons, as alcohol was mistakenly thought to convey some protection—were closed, and the U.S. Army canceled its 142,000-man September draft.

Rumors circulated that the disease had been released by a combination of poison gas and rotting bodies from the battlefield, that the Germans had contaminated the American East Coast from submarines, and that Germany's Bayer chemical company had contaminated aspirin with a new germ. No treatment was available, but, just as it had earlier in the year, the disease spontaneously disappeared. It reemerged in an attenuated form in 1920 before again disappearing, this time for good.

A curious aspect of the epidemic is its relative historical obscurity. In the mid-1980s, the *Encyclopaedia Britannica* accorded it only three sentences, and the *Encyclopedia Americana* only one. Fielding Garrison's monograph on military medicine, while noting that there were three-quarters of a million cases in the American military in World War I, gave the disease only a single sentence. The recent concern about emerging viral diseases has reexcited interest in influenza, and a plethora of recent popular and technical publications have been seen dealing with pandemic influenza.

An illness equivalent to the 1918 pandemic has not reappeared, although fear of its recurrence led directly to the swine flu panic and vaccination effort of 1976, and concerns have arisen that avian influenza might be caused by a similar virus.

See also World War I Medicine

References

Collier, Richard. *America's Forgotten Pandemic.* London: Allison & Busby, 1996.

Crosby, Alfred W. *The Plague of the Spanish Lady.* Cambridge: Cambridge University Press, 1989.

Kolata, Gina. *Flu: The Story of the Great Influenza Pandemic of 1918 and the Search for the Virus that Caused It.* New York: Farrar, Straus & Giroux, 1999.

Levine, Arnold. *Viruses.* New York: Scientific American Library, 1992.

Iraq and Afghan Wars

Waged by the U.S. military and coalition forces, the Iraq and Afghan wars are also called Operation Iraqi Freedom and Operation Enduring Freedom, respectively.

Through October 13, 2007, 383 American troops died in and around Afghanistan, with 256 of those killed in action. In the initial combat phase of Operation Iraqi Freedom, which extended from March 19, 2003, through April 30 of that year, 139 American troops died, with 109 of those killed in action. From the end of the combat phase to October 19, 2007, 3,678 troops died, with 3,005 listed as killed in action. An additional 15,488 were wounded in action but returned to duty within 72 hours, and 12,243 were wounded in action and did not return to duty. That number of casualties is greater than in the American Revolution, the War of 1812, or the Spanish-American War, but, because of a much lower death rate from injury, the number of soldiers killed was significantly less. The death rate from injury in the Revolutionary War was 42 percent, in World War II it was 30 percent, and in Viet Nam and the first Gulf War it was 24 percent.

In the current conflict, the death rate for soldiers wounded in action has been only 10 percent. Much of that improvement is probably due to decreased mortality from gunshot wounds resulting from better resuscitative and surgical technique, an assumption supported by the fact that, in the civilian arena, the mortality from gunshot wounds in the United States dropped from 16 percent in 1964 to only 5 percent in 2003.

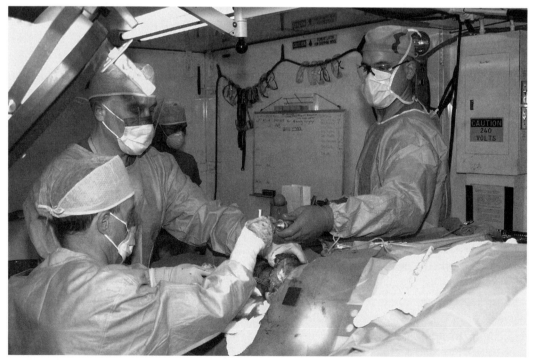

U.S. Army Colonel Richard Gonzalez (right), leads a team of surgeons and technicians from the 325th Field Surgical Team, at the Kandahar Airfield Hospital in Afghanistan, 2004. (Department of Defense)

Providing personnel to deliver medical care has been one of the military's greatest challenges in the Iraq conflict. The regular Army had only about 120 general surgeons on active duty in 2003, and the Army Reserves, which have assumed much of the war's burden, had a similar number; further, unlike other recent wars, there was no physician draft. As a result, the Department of Defense decided to deploy only from 30 to 50 general surgeons and 10 to 15 orthopedists in Iraq. Most of these were assigned to forward surgical teams (FSTs), which comprised about 20 people: three general surgeons, one orthopedist, two nurse anesthetists, three nurses, and a variety of medics and support personnel. These FSTs were deployed in six Humvees that traveled directly behind forward-area troops. They carried two tents that could be set up as a 900-square-foot mobile hospital in about 60 minutes. The unit carried two operating suites with ventilators and a rudimentary laboratory capable of measuring hematocrit and arterial blood gases. They lacked X-ray facilities, under the interesting assumption that trained orthopedists could generally diagnose and reduce fractures by feel.

Iraq has seen a major shift in military surgical practice. Rather than attempt to definitively treat complex injuries, the decision was made to have the FSTs merely stabilize the patients for transport to a more fully equipped facility. Consequently, body cavity injuries were packed and irrigated and lacerated bowels were stapled, and the open wounds were covered with sterile plastic sheeting, leaving surgical clamps in place. Every attempt was made to limit surgery in FSTs to under two hours. The patients were transferred sedated and ventilated for completion of the operation elsewhere.

The second level facilities were the combat support hospitals (CSHs), portable 248-bed units that could be set up in 24 to 48 hours but that were converted to permanent hospitals as the conflict progressed. These units typically had six operating rooms, were staffed with specialty surgeons, and were intended for lengths of stay under four days. Beyond the CSHs were Level IV hospitals in Kuwait; Rota, Spain; and Landstuhl, Germany. If hospitalization was anticipated to exceed 30 days, the wounded were transferred to Brooke Army Medical Center in San Antonio, Texas. Whereas the average time to transfer to the United States during the Viet Nam War was 45 days, soldiers were moved to the United States in as little as 36 hours in the Iraq War.

As the Iraq conflict evolved into an insurgency, the nature of injuries changed from gunshot wounds to blast injuries primarily from improvised explosive devices. These injuries often combined multiple lacerations with penetration by foreign bodies such as bolts, nails, bits of clothing, and fragments of bone from the suicide bomber with burns and blast injuries. Kevlar vests limited the number of torso injuries, although they proved vulnerable to fragments entering under the armor or through arm holes. Protection from body armor combined with more effective emergency medical care have allowed more soldiers to live but many of the survivors have had severe disabilities including multiple amputations, disfiguring facial injuries, and blindness. Of particular concern is the fact that, of those referred to Walter Reed Army Medical Center for rehabilitation, 59 percent were found to have traumatic brain injury.

See also Anesthesiology; Débridement; Field Hospitals; Triage

References

Gawande, Atul. 2004. "Casualties of War—Military Care for the Wounded from Iraq and Afghanistan." *New England Journal of Medicine* 351 (December 9): 2471–2480.

Peake, James B. 2005. "Beyond the Purple Heart—Continuity of Care for the Wounded in Iraq." *New England Journal of Medicine* 352 (January 20): 219–222.

U.S. Department of Defense. "U.S. Casualty Status." http://www.defenselink.mil/news/casualty.pdf (accessed October 19, 2007).

Ireland, Major General Merritte Weber (1867–1952)

Maj. Gen. Meritte Ireland was chief surgeon of the American Expeditionary Force (April–October 1918) and surgeon general of the U.S. Army (1918–1931).

Ireland was born in Columbia City, Indiana, the son of a physician. He received his medical degree from Detroit College of Medicine in 1890 and received a second doctorate in medicine from Jefferson Medical College in Philadelphia in 1891, after which he entered the Army as an assistant surgeon.

Ireland served in a series of western forts until the Spanish-American War broke out, at which time he was assigned to the camp at Chickamauga Park, Georgia, then Port Tampa, and finally the Reserve Divisional Hospital at Siboney, Cuba. From Cuba, he was transferred to Camp Wickoff at Montauk Point, Long Island, New York, as executive officer of the camp hospital. He served as a medical officer with the Division of the Philippines from 1899 to 1902.

From 1902 to 1912 he served in the office of the surgeon general in several administrative capacities. Ireland returned to the Philippines as post surgeon for Fort McKinley from 1912 to 1915. After returning to the United States, he served as medical officer

to Fort Sam Houston, where he supervised medical care for Brig. Gen. John J. Pershing's Mexican expedition.

When the United States entered World War I, Pershing asked for Ireland to be his chief surgeon, but the post was given to Col. Alfred E. Bradley. Ireland accompanied Pershing to France as Bradley's first assistant and served in that role until Bradley retired in April 1918. He had been promoted to colonel in May 1917, brigadier general in May 1918, and major general in August 1918. When William Gorgas retired as surgeon general, Ireland succeeded him.

As surgeon general, Ireland oversaw army demobilization and the reconstruction of Walter Reed and Letterman general hospitals. He arranged new buildings for the Army medical, dental, and veterinary schools and started the Medical Field Service School at Carlisle Barracks, Pennsylvania. The multivolume medical history of the American forces in World War I was completed during his tenure. Ireland retired May 31, 1931, on reaching the statutory age limit of service.

Ireland was decorated by the American, British, French, and Polish governments; served as president of the American College of Surgeons; and was a fellow of the American College of Physicians and the Royal College of Surgeons of Edinburgh. After retirement he served as an adviser to his successors as surgeon general and was an active adviser to Gen. George C. Marshall during World War II. In an obituary in the *Annals of Internal Medicine*, Maj. Gen. George E. Armstrong credited him with being largely responsible for the development of modern concepts of field medicine during World War I and paving the way for many of the medical achievements of World War II and the Korean Conflict.

See also Gorgas, William Crawford; World
War I Medicine

References
Armstrong, G. E. 1952. "Major General Merritte
W. Ireland." *Annals of Internal Medicine* 37
(October): 836.
Phalen, J. M. 1952. "Major General Merritte W.
Ireland, U.S. Army, Ret." *Military Surgeon*
111 (September): 2221–2222.

Ishii, Shiro
(1892–1959)

Shiro Ishii was the Japanese military physician in charge of Unit 731 programs in biological and chemical warfare during World War II.

Ishii was born in the village of Chiyoda about two hours from Tokyo to a relatively wealthy family. He entered the Imperial University at Kyoto in 1916. On graduation in 1920, Ishii joined the Imperial Army and was commissioned lieutenant in 1922.

From early in his career, he concentrated on infectious diseases. At the same time he was developing a portable water purification system, Ishii pressed for development of bacteria as a weapon. In 1928, he toured Europe, devoting special interest to the Allied and German experience with gas warfare in World War I. In 1932, the same year Japan withdrew from the League of Nations, he was placed in command of the Epidemic Prevention Research Laboratory at Tokyo, an organization which, in spite of its name, had the primary task of creating chemical and biological weapons.

Ishii moved his main research facilities to Manchuria after the Japanese assumed control there and was responsible for an infamous series of human experiments that continued until the end of World War II.

After the war, he negotiated immunity from war crimes prosecution but was unable to find consistent employment and died of throat cancer in 1959.

See also Chemical and Biological Warfare;
Japanese Military Medicine; Unit 731;
World War II Medicine

References
Gold, Hal. *Unit 731 Testimony*. Boston: Tuttle
Publishing, 1966.
Harris, Sheldon. *Factories of Death: Japanese
Biological Warfare 1932–45 and the American
Cover-up*. New York: Routledge, 1994.
Williams, Peter, and David Wallace. *Unit 731:
Japan's Secret Biological Warfare in World War
II*. London: Hodder and Stoughton, 1989.

Islamic Military Medicine

Islamic military medicine is a combination of preservation of classical Greek science with that of India and China.

When Bishop Nestorius was expelled from Constantinople for heresy in A.D. 431, the history of military medicine took a fortunate turn. The bishop and his followers relocated to the Mesopotamian city of Edessa and set about translating the existing body of Greek and Latin medical literature into Syriac. When the Nestorians were expelled from Edessa in A.D. 489 and resettled in the Persian town of Jundi-Shapur, they took their entire library of translated texts and founded a university with an adjacent hospital, creating the clinical-research-educational model of medical training that persists to the present. Benefiting from its geography, the school at Jundi-Shapur was able to merge Greek and Roman knowledge with that from Persia, India, and China.

In just 80 years, the new religion of the prophet Muhammad (A.D. 570–632) spread from the Arabian Peninsula across the Middle East and west to Iberia. Persia fell to the Arabs in A.D. 642, and the Muslim conquerors not only preserved the university and hospital but also reproduced its model throughout their empire, spreading medical knowledge from the Indus to the Pyrenees.

Under the direction of Abbasid caliph Al Mansur, who founded the city of Baghdad and the Eastern Caliphate, translation of the Jundi-Shapur library from Syriac to Arabic was begun in A.D. 765. Following Koranic mandates to care for the sick and weak, the Baghdad caliphs undertook an ambitious program of hospital construction; by A.D. 1160, there were 60 hospitals in the capital alone. The hospital at Damascus continued to furnish charity care for more than 300 years.

The Koran, however, prohibited dissection. Consequently, little innovation took place in either Arabic medicine or surgery, and Galen's anatomic errors were perpetuated virtually in their entirety. Surgery was denigrated and separated from medicine under the caliphate. Even medicine held a low status, and practitioners were frequently Christians, Jews, or Persians rather than Arabs. In fact, the three greatest Islamic physicians (Rhazes, Avicenna, and Abul Kassem) were all Persian.

Islamic medicine emphasized drug treatment with extensive pharmacopoeias that included such medicines as cannabis, opium, and bhang (hemp or hyoscyamus.) Ibn Batar's text included 1,400 substances, more than 300 of which, having come from India, Persia, or China, were unknown to Dioscorides and Western medicine.

A formal program of physician training and licensure was instituted in Baghdad in A.D. 931, in which candidates were trained at universities and their attached hospitals and then served apprenticeships with established practitioners. The model was later copied by the Italian school at Salerno and persists in modern medical education.

The Eastern Caliphate developed camel-borne tent hospitals for their armies. Each had its own instruments and a full staff and could follow the troops, but surgical techniques remained crude. Amputation was done with a mallet and cleaver, followed by cauterization with hot oil to stop bleeding. Splinting of fractures was inexpert and regularly resulted in limbs that ranged from crooked to grotesque. Muslim military physicians did follow Roman sanitary advice and insisted on proper camp location and field hygiene, and the best of their physicians, including Rhazes, Albucasis, and Avicenna, honed their craft while serving in the military.

See also Albucasis; Avicenna (Ibn Sena); Rhazes (Abu Bakr Mohammed ben Zakariah)

Reference
Garrison, Fielding. *Notes on the History of Military Medicine*. Washington, D.C.: Association of Military Surgeons, 1922.

Italian Campaign of 1859

The Italian campaign of 1859 was a brief war between France, the Kingdom of Sardinia, and the Austrian Empire that furnished the impetus for both the International Red Cross and the Geneva Conventions.

The war was fought between armies personally led by King Victor Emmanuel II of Sardinia (about 70,000 men), Emperor Napoleon III of France (about 128,000 men), and young Emperor Franz Josef of Austria (about 230,000 men) in five battles culminating in the June 24, 1859, Battle of Solferino in an area south of Lake Garda between the Italian cities of Milan and Verona.

The battle began at 3:00 a.m. and continued until nightfall the following day, at which time the Austrians withdrew, leaving the French and Sardinians victorious but too exhausted to pursue them. Casualty figures vary, but, if one totals losses on both sides, roughly 35,000 men were wounded and another 6,000 were killed or missing. The Austrian Army had brought ambulances, field hospitals, and sanitary companies, but the medical corps was overwhelmed even though a number of Austrian military surgeons stayed behind to care for wounded in the field, allowing themselves to be made prisoners of war. French military medical preparations were uniformly dismal. French chief surgeon Baron Francis Xavier Larrey was forced to wait for instructions from his *intendant* in Paris rather than respond to conditions as he found them. Bandage wagons had been left behind, there were more veterinarians than surgeons, and there were no provisions for removing wounded from the field.

About 9,000 of the wounded who could do so walked to the nearby village of Castiglione, where they flooded into houses, barns, and the local church, the Chiesa Maggiore. Those too ill to walk were left on the field for up to three days, long enough for maggots to infest open wounds and convince the soldiers that the vermin were coming from within their own bodies.

Henry Dunant (1828–1910), a 30-year-old Swiss businessman on his way to meet Napoleon III to request his help in an Algerian business project, volunteered to help with the casualties at the Chiesa. He subsequently met with Napoleon III, but, rather than discussing business, he convinced the French leader to release captured Austrian physicians and to allow enemy wounded to return home.

As a result of his experience, Dunant wrote "Un Souvenir de Solferino" in 1862. The pamphlet was widely circulated and resulted in the 1863 International Conference of the Red Cross Societies and the 1864 Geneva Convention.

After his early successes, Dunant drifted into bankruptcy and obscurity until he was rediscovered in a German nursing home by a British correspondent. He shared the first Nobel Peace Prize with Frédéric Passy in 1901.

See also Red Cross and Red Crescent

References
Dunant, Henry. *A Memory of Solferino.* New York: American Red Cross, 1939.
Rothkopf, Carol Zeman. *Jean Henri Dunant.* New York: Franklin Watts, Inc., 1971.
N.a. 1859. "The Battle of Solferino," *Harper's Weekly,* July 23, 470–471.

J

Jackson, Robert
(1750–1827)

Robert Jackson was responsible for major reform of the administration and sanitary policies of the British Army.

Jackson served as inspector general of Army hospitals and assistant surgeon in Jamaica from 1774 to 1780. He went on to serve as surgeon to the 71st Regiment and to study medicine in Paris; he received his doctorate from the University of Leiden in 1786. He returned as a military surgeon and served in Holland and the West Indies, where he became medical director, the first who was not a member of the College of Physicians.

Jackson's difficult temperament impeded the acceptance of what were generally good ideas, although his *Scheme of Medical Arrangement for Armies* (1798) eventually became a standard for Napoleonic-era British military surgeons. His campaign for improvement in status and pay of medical officers was largely motivated by his own desire to rise to the rank of gentleman.

Jackson saw operating as the least important part of a military surgeon's duty and pressed for dedicated sanitary officers, recognizing that disease killed far more of his soldiers than battle wounds. With that in mind, Jackson recommended two medical officers for every 1,000 soldiers in peacetime and an increase to only three for every 1,000 during war.

Physician Gen. John Hunter had promised Jackson promotion from warrant officer to subaltern status. Hunter, however, died in 1793 and his successor, Sir Lucas Pepys, refused to grant the commission on the basis that a surgeon who did not hold a license from the Royal College of Physicians or a degree from the university either at Oxford or Cambridge could never be a physician in His Majesty's army. Pepys was overruled by the Duke of York, an action that resulted in a campaign against Jackson by the military medical establishment. Although an investigatory board vindicated him, Jackson chose to retire to private practice in Stockton-on-Tees and to devote his energies to writing books on reform of military medical practice and administration.

See also British Military Medicine; Napoleonic Wars

References

Crowe, Kate Elizabeth. 1973. "The Walcheren Expedition and the New Army Medical Board: A Reconsideration." *The English Historical Review* 88 (October): 770–785.

Kopperman, P. E. 1979. "Medical Services in the British Army, 1742–1783." *Journal of the History of Medicine and the Allied Sciences* 34 (October): 428–455.

Japanese Military Medicine

The emergence of scientific medicine in Japan between 1860 and 1910, one of the most remarkable achievements in the history of science, was largely the result of input from military physicians and surgeons.

The feudal Tokugawa shogunate kept Japan almost entirely isolated from the rest of the world between 1638 and 1853, and medicine under that regime was largely practiced by upper-class samurai using techniques memorized from ancient Chinese texts. The heavy concentration on herbal medicine and an almost absolute proscription against dissection that persisted to the mid-19th century precluded understanding or development of physiology, diagnosis, or surgery. What anatomic knowledge there was came mostly from guesses, tradition, or the rare study of the corpse of an executed criminal. The typical physician memorized classical texts and served a clinical apprenticeship, usually under a relative as the profession was hereditary and its secrets were carefully guarded. Treatment centered on biologicals, acupuncture, and moxibustion, application of smoking balls of leaves from the artemesia tree.

The Portuguese came to Japan in 1542 and were followed by the Spanish 50 years later. The latter brought proselytizing monks but neither brought medical advances beyond a few small hospitals. When the Iberians were expelled by the shoguns in 1638, the only remnant of Western contact was the Dutch trading post on the tiny island of Dejima in Nagasaki Harbor. The island, only 760 feet by 190 feet and surrounded by stockade walls, was a virtual prison in which the Europeans were confined save for an annual trek to the capital at Edo (modern Tokyo). The Dutch, however, stationed a series of physicians on the island, many of whom were trained at the best new universities in Holland, Belgium, or Germany. These men brought texts, anatomic atlases, and surgical instruments, all of which leaked into Japan. By the early 1800s, several medical schools teaching Western medicine had opened.

Otto Mohnike (1814–1887), trained at the university in Bonn before joining the Military Medical Corps of the Dutch East India Company, came to Dejima in 1848 and found that scabies was epidemic, syphilis—which had come with the Portuguese—was widespread, and lepers were allowed to wander freely in the general population. Mohnike trained a number of Japanese physicians to perform surgery and found them both skillful operators and excellent instrument makers. He recognized that wounds under their disposable paper dressings healed more readily than those covered with European linen ones that were almost always filthy from repeated use.

Smallpox had come to Japan from Korea in the seventh century and, although the Japanese had practiced inoculation with live virus since about A.D. 1000, the disease remained a scourge until the Dutch introduced Edward Jenner's vaccination in 1849.

Mohnike was succeeded in 1853 by Jan Karl van den Broek, who had joined the corps of Royal Rifles prior to being sent to Dejima. In his four years in Japan, van den

Broek instituted formal training in medicine for Japanese students who came to the island. In addition, he taught telegraphy, shipbuilding, and engineering. The program evolved into a formal medical school under his successor, Pompe van Meedervoort, who got official permission to teach anatomy by dissection and who opened Japan's first teaching hospital. One of van Meedervoort's students, Hashimoto Tsunatsune, founded the Japanese Red Cross. Van Meedervoort was followed by Antonius Baudouin, who started the first Japanese school of military medicine after the fall of the shogunate in 1869.

With the establishment of the Meiji regime, both Dutch influence and Japanese isolation faded. Although U.S. Naval commodore Matthew Perry had forced the Japanese to admit foreigners in 1853, the American Civil War precluded American involvement in the subsequent decade. The British, however, had active interests in China and wanted a post from which they could monitor Russian activities in East Asia. The vice consul in Britain's first legation to Japan was military surgeon William Willis, who was also the first Westerner to enter the imperial compound in Kyoto when he was summoned to care for the wounded after a battle at the village of Fushima between imperial forces and those of the shoguns in 1868. His amputations were the first real Japanese military surgery.

Willis was succeeded by Joseph Bower Siddall, who served as surgeon to the imperial forces during the 1868–1869 civil war and who taught Japanese surgeons techniques of bandaging and splinting by having them practice on amputated limbs. The Imperial Division of Military Medicine was formed in 1871 under Ryojun Matsumoto, who had been trained by van Meedervoort

and who had actually served as chief physician to the shogun rebels before being taken prisoner in 1868.

After the civil war, the new imperial government dispatched delegations to Europe to choose a model for Japanese modernization. The Japanese had planned to pattern their army after the French, but France's loss to Prussia in 1871 redirected Japanese interest. The University of Berlin, which had absorbed the Pépinière (the former military medical faculty), was chosen as the archetype. In 1870, Kensai Ikeda was sent to Berlin to study military medicine and surgery. Simultaneously, the Japanese government asked Germany to send medical consultants to Tokyo. The Germans opted to send a group of military surgeons, arguing that these men were the best of their profession and commanded the most respect, and they chose Karl Leopold Mueller to head the delegation. Under the Germans, the Japanese became avid students of the new science of bacteriology and adopted anesthesia and Listerian antisepsis.

In spite of those advances, Japanese military sanitation remained abysmal, and, in the 1894–1895 war with China, imperial troops suffered far greater losses to beriberi, typhus, and dysentery than to battle injuries. That experience led to radical reorganization of the Japanese military medical and sanitary services. When the war with Russia started in 1904, Japan had decided that 10 percent of the manpower in any field command would be devoted to medical care. Japanese senior officers took the point of view that, although the Russians had more men, the deficit could be overcome if they could return more of the sick and wounded to combat. They incorporated evacuation hospitals equipped with bacteriology laboratories and X-ray facilities in their Manchurian invasion force. Their ability to keep their own men fighting contributed significantly to their success on the battlefield, and their willingness to care for sick and wounded left behind by retreating Russians was generally admired by both their enemy and the rest of the Western world. The success of both the Japanese army and naval medical services stood in sharp contrast to American failures in the Spanish war and to the British experience in South Africa.

Unfortunately, the reputation of Japanese military physicians was severely tarnished during World War II by their participation in barbaric human experiments performed on Chinese civilians and prisoners of war at the notorious Unit 731.

See also Dysentery; Russo-Japanese War; World War II Medicine

References

Bowers, John Z. *When the Twain Meet: The Rise of Western Medicine in Japan.* Baltimore: Johns Hopkins University Press, 1980.

Gold, Hal. *Unit 731 Testimony.* Boston: Tuttle Publishing, 1966.

Seaman, Louis. *The Real Triumph of Japan: The Conquest of the Silent Foe.* New York: D. Appleton and Co., 1908.

John of Arderne
(ca. 1306–1390)

John of Arderne was the first famous English surgeon.

Nothing is known of John's early life, although he must have had a certain amount of formal education because he wrote his own manuscripts in Latin. His surgical experience came during the Hundred Years War, where he served under the Duke of Lancaster and John of Gaunt. He fought at the siege of Algeciras, where gunpowder weapons were used for the first time in Europe, an experience he continued to cite in writings three decades later.

He left the military in 1349 and opened a practice in the town of Newark, where he continued to perform surgery and took a special interest in disorders of the rectum, achieving fame for his ability to successfully close anal fistulae.

After 20 years in Newark, John moved to London, where he was admitted to the Surgeon's Guild and continued to practice until his death.

See also British Military Medicine; Medieval Military Medicine

References

Weiss, G. N. 1956. "John Arderne, Father of English Surgery." *Journal of the International College of Surgeons* 25 (February): 247–261.

Zimmerman, Leo, and Ilza Veith. *Great Ideas in the History of Surgery.* Baltimore: Williams and Wilkins Co., 1961.

Jones, John
(1729–1791)

Author of *Plain, Concise, Practical Remarks on the Treatment of Wounds and Fractures*, the only American medical text prior to the start of the Revolutionary War, John Jones was born in Jamaica, Long Island. He was the grandson of Welsh physician Edward Jones, who came to Pennsylvania with William Penn, and the son of physician Evan Jones, who brought the family to New York. John Jones began his studies under Thomas Cadwalader in Philadelphia before traveling to Europe, where he studied under William Hunter and Percival Pott in London, Jean-Louis Petit and Henri-François LeDran in Paris, and the elder Alexander Monro in

Edinburgh before taking his degree at the University of Rheims in 1751.

He returned to the United States to practice in New York and served as military surgeon to the British troops in the 1755 war against France. After the war, he served as professor of surgery at the Medical School of New York before moving to Philadelphia and the Pennsylvania Hospital in 1780, where he was one of the founders of the College of Physicians of that city. Jones was a severe chronic asthmatic and, although he helped organize the American medical corps in the Revolutionary War, he was unable to serve himself. After the revolution, he remained a respected physician and attended both George Washington and Benjamin Franklin in their final illnesses. He was particularly close to the latter and was remembered in his will. Jones died in his sleep in Philadelphia at the age of 62.

See also American Revolutionary War

References

Kelly, Howard, and Walter Burrage. *Dictionary of American Medical Biography*. Boston: Milford House, 1971.

Packard, Francis. *History of Medicine in the United States*. New York: Paul B. Hoeber, Inc., 1931.

Keen, William Williams
(1837–1932)

William Williams Keen was one of the most famous late-19th-century American surgeons and arguably the founder of American neurosurgery. He was born the third son of merchant William W. Keen and Sarah Budd Keen, graduated from Brown University in 1859, and enrolled in Jefferson Medical College in 1860. He took time off to serve as a surgeon in the Union Army in 1861 before returning to his studies and graduating from Jefferson in 1862.

After graduation, Keen rejoined the Army and was assigned to Turner's Lane Hospital in Philadelphia, where he assisted neurologist Silas Weir Mitchell and participated in studies of gunshot wounds, especially those involving the nervous system.

He returned to Jefferson to teach surgical anatomy in 1866 and remained there until 1875, when he formed the Philadelphia School of Anatomy, where he taught for the next 14 years. In 1889 he was appointed professor of surgery at Jefferson and remained there until his retirement in 1907. During that time he also taught artistic anatomy at the Pennsylvania Academy of Fine Arts and was professor of surgery at the Women's Medical College of Pennsylvania.

Keen's *Surgery: Its Principles and Practice* was the standard textbook of that specialty for decades. In 1893, Keen assisted at the operation to remove a cancer from President Grover Cleveland's lower jaw. The procedure was performed on the president's yacht anchored in Long Island Sound and was kept secret for fear of disturbing already unsettled American financial markets. In 1917, Keen rejoined the Army as a consultant in surgery and was, with William Halsted, a major advocate of sterile technique in military surgery and wound care.

After retirement, he became an outspoken advocate for the theory of evolution and animal experimentation and died in Philadelphia at the age of 95.

See also Civil War in the United States; Cushing, Harvey Williams; Mitchell, Silas Weir; World War I Medicine

Reference

N.a. 1932. "William Williams Keen." *Canadian Medical Association Journal* 27 (August): 181–182.

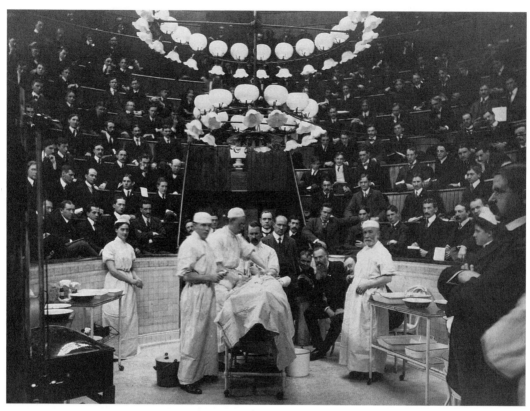

Surgeons assist Professor William Keen as he performs surgery in an auditorium full of medical students, Jefferson Medical College Hospital in 1902. (Corbis)

Koch, Robert
(1843–1910)

Robert Koch was, with Louis Pasteur, a founder of the scientific study of infectious disease.

Koch was born in Klausthal in the Harz Mountains of Hannover, the son of a mining engineer. He graduated from the university at Göttingen in 1866 after studying with Joseph Henle, who was an early proponent of microorganisms as causes of disease and who interested Koch in problems of infection. After graduation, Koch studied under famous pathologist Rudolf Virchow. He served as a military surgeon in the Franco-Prussian War before returning to Wollstein, where he became a district physician.

While practicing, Koch continued experimenting with microorganisms. He worked out the life cycle and sporification of the anthrax bacillus by growing it in the aqueous humor of ox eyes and then reproduced the disease by injecting the cultured organisms into animals using slivers of wood as needles. With these experiments, Koch demonstrated that it was possible to grow pure cultures of a disease-causing organism outside a host's body and reproduce the illness by reinjecting the organisms. Koch's findings were ridiculed by prominent French physician Paul Bert but were ultimately reproduced and confirmed by Louis Pasteur. Koch eventually replaced the ox eyes with a solution of meat in gelatin layered onto flat dishes designed by his colleague Julius Richard Petri and put laboratory bacteriology within the reach of scientists worldwide.

Prior to Koch's studies, most diseases were generally believed to be caused by either nutritional or constitutional deficiencies. In his 1878 *Study of the Etiology of Wound Infection*, Koch described six different microorganisms that could cause specific types of infection. He was appointed to the Imperial Health Department in 1880 and, in 1882, published his paper on the tubercle bacilli in which he delineated the four steps necessary to prove that a specific organism causes a disease, a construct that took his name as Koch's Postulates.

In 1883, Koch was named head of the German Cholera Commission, in which capacity he traveled to Egypt and India, where he discovered *Vibrio cholera*, the organism that caused the disease, and demonstrated its transmission in contaminated water. In 1885, he was named professor of hygiene and bacteriology at the University of Berlin, where he discovered the protein tuberculin, which he mistakenly thought would be an effective treatment for tuberculosis. It was not, but it does remain useful as the diagnostic test for the disease. In 1891, he helped found the Institute for Infectious Disease in Berlin and remained its head until his retirement in 1904. In 1905, Koch received the Nobel Prize in physiology or medicine for his work with tuberculosis. Koch's later years were spent largely alone and unhappy, and he died of heart failure in 1910.

See also Franco-Prussian War; Pasteur, Louis; Prussian and German Military Medicine

Reference

Brock, Thomas D. *Robert Koch: A Life in Medicine and Biology*. Madison, WI: Science Tech Publishers, 1988.

Korean Conflict

Although it began only a half-decade after the end of World War II, the Korean Conflict engendered signal advances in military medicine, including the refinement of the mobile army surgical hospital (M.A.S.H. units); helicopter transport of the sick and wounded; and improvements in the treatment of vascular injuries, head injuries, and shock, many of which became standards of civilian medical care.

U.S. military medicine was in an even more tenuous state than the Army's combat arm when the North Korean Army crossed the 38th parallel on Sunday, June 25, 1950. After World War II, largely in response to civilian demand for return of their doctors, U.S. military physicians and ancillary members of the medical services had been rapidly demobilized; between June 1945 and June 1950, the Army Medical Corps lost 86 percent of its officers and 91 percent of its enlisted personnel. To alleviate the inevitable shortfall, residency training programs had been opened at Army hospitals. In return for being paid during postgraduate training, the new specialist physicians agreed to serve for a time in the military, typically one extra year of service for each year of training. However, the program was new when the Korean Conflict started, the first groups of residents were still in training, and physician supply reached a nadir in June 1950. The problem was compounded by the fact that there was still a shortage of civilian physicians caused by a dip in medical school enrollment during

World War II, and doctors in domestic practice were busy, prosperous, and generally unwilling to volunteer for service in Korea. A draft specifically for physicians was instituted in August 1950 but produced no direct help in Korea through the balance of 1950. Within a year, however, the draft took effect, and, by 1952, 90 percent of the physicians serving in Korea were draftees.

The Advance Command and Liaison Group of 15 officers and two enlisted men dispatched by the Far Eastern Command on June 27, 1950, was the first Army medical contingent to reach Korea. Its mission was to care for American refugees fleeing the North Koreans and to begin replenishing the supplies abandoned in the fall of Seoul.

For medical purposes, one can divide the war into three phases: offensive operations, defense against invading forces and withdrawal, and static defensive operations. This distinction is important because the rate and type of injury were unique to each phase.

For the first time in the history of military medicine, data on each battle casualty and nonbattle casualty (divided into disease and nonbattle injuries) were collected on punch cards and returned to Washington for computer analysis by the Medical Department and the surgeon general. An entirely separate set of data was collected by the adjutant general, and the two sets do not always agree. The surgeon general's records report 18,769 killed in action, 77,788 wounded in action and admitted to treatment facilities, and 14,575 with wounds not requiring admission. The adjutant general's records report 19,658 killed in action and 79,526 wounded in action. Only the surgeon general collected data on disease and nonbattle injury. A total of 443,163 patients were admitted to treatment facilities during the war, of which 365,375 admissions

(82.4 percent) were not directly related to battle. Of these, 290,210 were for disease and 75,165 were for trauma not sustained in battle. Over the course of the war, 30 of each 1,000 active-duty personnel were killed in action, 121 of each 1,000 were admitted for battle injury, and 570 of each 1,000 were admitted for disease or nonbattle injury. In general all of these incidences declined as the war progressed.

The most common battle injuries were penetrating wounds (57 percent) and fractures (23 percent), although the specific mechanism of injury varied with the type of combat. Counter to what one might expect, average casualties per division per day were 119 in withdrawal, 77 in defense against a main force, and 67 in offense against a main force. In addition, the death rate among casualties was 25.2 percent in defense and only 14.6 percent in offense. Death rates also varied according to the weapon with which the casualty was inflicted: 28.4 percent for small arms, 23.8 percent for mines and booby traps, 18.4 percent for artillery, and 10.8 percent for hand grenades.

A total of 89,974 surgical procedures were performed at Army hospitals in Korea; 59 percent of those admitted with battle wounds required an operative procedure, with a case fatality rate of 2.5 percent (compared to 4.5 percent for World War II). Many patients required more than one operation, with the average being 1.2 procedures per wounded patient admitted. Surgery in Korea tended to be quick and of the salvage variety, with definitive treatment assigned to rear-area hospitals.

One of the most important technical advances during the war was the increased use of whole blood transfusions to resuscitate patients in shock. A wounded soldier received an average of 3.3 pints of whole blood, although transfusions of 15 to 30 units were not unusual. This rate of use placed a predictable strain on the donation system, with 21,188 pints collected in the United States and 22,099 pints collected in Japan in 1950 alone. Caucasian and native Japanese blood was segregated, although it is not clear whether this was for medical or racial reasons.

Neurosurgery posed a particularly difficult problem both because of the complexity of the injuries and the extreme shortage of trained personnel. By 1952 a special evacuation path through the 8209th (and later the 8063rd) M.A.S.H. units under the command of Lt. Col. Arnold Meirowsky was established to care for wounds of the head and spinal cord.

Vascular injuries posed another technical challenge. Use of vein grafts to repair arterial injuries was a significant advance, and, by 1951, these repairs resulted in salvage of 85 percent of limbs with major vascular disruptions.

Cold injuries were an especially common cause of nonbattle traumatic admissions. During 1950 there were 1,791 cases of cold injury for an incidence of 34 per 1,000. Medics were particularly hampered in the actions around the Changjin and Pujon reservoirs when it became so cold that medicine, intravenous fluids, and plasma froze and could not be used.

Infectious disease was a persistent problem. Of those treated for nonbattle-related causes and not requiring admission, 90 percent had infectious or parasitic disease. The most common were respiratory disease (20 percent), ill-defined febrile illnesses, and diarrheal disease. The latter was especially severe early in the war when hygienic facilities were lacking. Gastrointestinal disease (especially shigellosis) occurred at a rate of

120 cases per 1,000 actives a year in August 1950. Other common infectious problems were encephalitis, polio, hemorrhagic fever, hepatitis, and venereal disease. Malaria and plague were locally endemic but never became a serious problem for United Nations troops.

The third most common disease problem was neuropsychiatric illness. The frequency of disability from psychiatric illness varied greatly with the stage of the war. Early in the war, young psychiatrists were stationed at the rear. Because they were not close to battle and were inexperienced, they tended to be liberal in sending soldiers with psychiatric complaints home. As the war progressed, the physicians were moved closer to the front and became less sympathetic, and the rate of psychiatric disability dropped. A second factor was the kind of fighting going on at the time. The rate of "NPs" dropped from 249 per 1,000 before the Pusan breakout to 18.4 per 1,000 during the advance, though it rose again when the winter weather set in.

Deployment of medical facilities proceeded rapidly in the fall of 1950. By November four M.A.S.H. units (with bed capacity increased from a planned 60 to 150), three 400-bed semi-mobile evacuation hospitals, four 400-bed field hospitals, one station hospital, and three hospital ships had been built or deployed in Korea. Two additional M.A.S.H. units were deployed in 1951, and one of the evacuation hospitals was moved to Japan in December 1950. After the Chinese entered the war, three additional evacuation hospitals were committed, but they functioned as stationary hospitals while the field hospitals were converted to treat prisoners of war.

The evacuation sequence from facility to facility was as follows: battalion aid station

⇒ regimental collecting station ⇒ division clearing station ⇒ evacuation hospital at Pusan ⇒ Korean airfields ⇒ 118th Station Hospital at Fukuoka (Kyushu, Japan) ⇒ other Army hospitals in Japan (Osaka and Tokyo) ⇒ Tripler Army Hospital (Hawaii) ⇒ Travis Air Force Base (California) or Lackland Air Force Base (Texas) ⇒ zone-of-the-interior hospitals. Patients requiring emergency stabilization or surgery could be sent from either the regimental collecting stations or the division clearing stations to the M.A.S.H. units. From there, the stabilized patients were sent on to either the evacuation hospital at Pusan or directly to Fukuoka. Of admissions for battle injury, 10 percent received final disposition at a forward unit (aid, clearing, or collecting station), 57 percent at Army hospitals in the Far Eastern Command, 6 percent at non-Army hospitals (Navy or Air Force), and 26 percent at hospitals in the United States. These figures include both discharge and death, although 96 percent of all deaths occurred in one of the Far Eastern Command hospitals. Of division wounded, 80 percent eventually returned to duty.

Transport changed as the war progressed. Because the terrain was difficult, the initial stages were by hand-carried litter, especially when the combat units were moving either in advance or retreat. From the aid and clearing stations, transport was primarily by rail. Early in the war, gasoline-powered railcars ("Doodlebugs") carried patients from the front at Chochiwon to Taejon. They held 17 litters or 50 ambulatory patients and traversed the 30 miles in about 45 minutes. As the front stabilized later in the war, formal rail transport was more frequent. Rail facilities were brought to within 8,000 yards of the front line; evacuation trains typically comprised eight ward cars, two orderly cars,

a kitchen, a dining car, a pharmacy car, an officer personnel car, and a utility car.

Because of both improved transport (rail and air) and treatment facilities relatively close to the front line, a remarkable 58 percent of soldiers wounded in battle received medical care within two hours of injury and 85 percent were treated within six hours. The median time from wound to first care was 90 minutes, and 55 percent of casualties were hospitalized the same day they were wounded—a number that rose to nearly 100 percent by 1953.

Early in the war, evacuation from Pusan to Fukuoka was principally by ship, with hospital ships, troop transports, and even ferries pressed into service. This relatively slow and expensive method of transport was, however, replaced by air evacuation within a few months. In the first year of the war, C-47s were used, though, as the war progressed, they were replaced by larger C-54s with a longer range that allowed direct transfer to Honshu. Transports were divided 40-40-20 between Itazuki Air Base (Fukuoka), Itami Air Base (Osaka), and Tachikawa Air Base (Tokyo).

Because there was an initial shortage of all physicians and a persistent lack of some specialists, triage and transport were used as a substitute for personnel. The Army realized that scarce personnel could be most efficiently used by concentrating them in hospitals in rear areas. Patients who were predicted to recover in less than 30 days were kept at Pusan, those expected to recover in 30 to 120 days were kept in Japan, and those anticipated to have prolonged recovery were returned to the United States. A complex of evacuation units grew around the 8054th Evacuation Hospital at Pusan. The 8054th was initially housed in the Pusan Middle School but grew to several buildings with 1,200 beds that handled up to 12,000 admissions a month. It was assisted by the Swedish Red Cross Hospital, the 1st Prisoner-of-War Hospital, and several hospital ships and specialized units.

The overall record of Army medicine in Korea compares favorably to that of World War II. The case fatality rate for those wounded in battle in the earlier war was 4.5 percent, dropping to about 2.5 percent in the latter. Even that rate improved as the war progressed—that for 1950 is not known, for 1951 it was 2.1 percent, and by 1952 it was down to 1.8 percent. Of those wounded but not killed in Korea, 87.9 percent returned to duty, 8.5 percent were separated as disabled, and 1.4 percent were separated for administrative reasons. Overall, medical care in Korea was characterized by rapid transport, effective early resuscitation and surgery, advances in surgical technique, and overall decline in mortality rates from battle injury.

See also Aeromedical Evacuation; Ambulances and Transport; Cold Injury and Frostbite; Field Hospitals; Head Injury and Cranial Surgery; Shell Shock in World War I; Shock; Transfusion; Triage

References

Cleaver, Frederick *U.S. Army Battle Casualties in Korea.* Chevy Chase, MD: Operations Research Office, 1956.

Cowdrey, Albert E. *United States Army in the Korean War: The Medic's War.* Washington, D.C.: Center of Military History, United States Army, 1987.

Smith, Allen D. 1953. "Air Evacuation—Medical Obligation and Military Necessity." *Air University Quarterly* 6: 98–111.

L

Laennec, René-Théophile Hyacinthe (1781–1826)

René-Théophile Hyacinthe Laennec was the inventor of the stethoscope, the most important diagnostic tool prior to Wilhelm Conrad Röntgen's X-ray.

Laennec was born in Quimper in Brittany, the son of a lawyer-poet. His mother died when he was six, and he was sent to live first with his granduncle, the Abbé Laennec, and then, at age 12, with his uncle. He began his medical training with his uncle, who was professor of medicine at Nantes before going on to the medical school at Paris, where he won a first prize in medicine and surgery at age 19 while studying under Lucien Corvisart, who was later Napoleon Bonaparte's personal physician.

Laennec served as a regimental surgeon during the French Revolution before becoming physician to the Hôpital Beaujon in 1806 and the Hôpital Necker in 1816. Although only 5'2" tall, he was fine featured, with a strong cleft jaw, thick brown hair, and luxuriant sideburns. Even though he was the most prominent French internist of his time, Laennec was more proud of his ability as a horseman than of his skill as a physician.

He invented the stethoscope in 1809, first as a wooden tube that would allow him to listen to a woman's chest without violating her modesty by placing his ear directly on her skin. The instrument opened a new world of sounds that led to diagnoses, and he published extensive studies of his clinical findings supported by his own pathological studies in 1819. In a subsequent work in 1826, Laennec added a section on treatment and his compendium became the most important single work on diseases of the chest ever written.

Ironically, Laennec died in 1826 of a chronic lung disease that may well have been tuberculosis.

See also Napoleonic Wars

References

Block, H. 1993. "The Inventor of the Stethoscope: Réné Laennec." *Journal of Family Practice* 37 (August): 191.

O'Shea, J. G. 1989. "Réné Laennec: His Brilliant Life and Tragic Death." *Scottish Medical Journal* 34 (June): 474–477.

Lanfranc of Milan
(d. 1315)

With Henri de Mondeville, Lanfranc of Milan was a founder of the 14th-century French school of surgery.

Lanfranc was born in Milan at an unknown date and was trained in surgery at Bologna by Guglielmo Salicetti. As a result of becoming involved in the feud between the Guelphs and the Ghibellines, he was forced to move to Paris. Because he was married, he was unable to join the faculty of the University of Paris, which was restricted to members of the Catholic clergy. Instead, Lanfranc lectured at the Collège de St. Côme, which had been established under Louis IX specifically to train surgeons and elevate their status. He later became personal physician to French king Philip the Fair, to whom he dedicated his *Chirurgia Magna* in 1296.

Lanfranc campaigned for a higher status for surgeons and, arguing against the separation between surgeons and physicians, said, "All practice is theory. All surgery is practice. Therefore, all surgery is theory." Lanfranc gave the first detailed description of cerebral concussion, and his descriptions of skull fracture and the circumstances in which they required surgery are close to current practice. He attempted to sew back severed nerves and experimented with animal tracheas as stents to hold open sutured bowel. He used the cautery to stop bleeding but also recommended a paste made of egg whites, aloe, and rabbit fur. He preferred to close wounds primarily after irrigation with wine.

See also Hemostasis; Medieval Military Medicine; Mondeville, Henri de

Reference
Bullough, V. L. 1959. "Training of the Nonuniverstity Educated Medical Practitioners in the Later Middle Ages." *Journal of the History of Medicine and the Allied Sciences* 14: 446–458.

Larrey, Baron Dominique-Jean
(1766–1842)

The preeminent French military surgeon of his time and called by Napoleon Bonaparte the most virtuous man he had ever known, Baron Dominique-Jean Larrey served as surgeon in chief to the Grande Armée, participated in 60 battles and more than 400 engagements, and was wounded three times. His technical skill and his dedication to French soldiers earned him an unparalleled respect among veterans of the Napoleonic Wars, who were generally more likely to fear than to love their surgeons.

Larrey was born in a small village in the Pyrenees to a family with several surgeons. He was trained by his uncle Alexis Larrey and served briefly in the French Navy before continuing his surgical education at Paris's Hôtel Dieu under Pierre-Joseph Desault, who taught him the importance of wide excision of nonviable traumatized tissue. While a student, he led a group of 1,500 radical medical students in attacks on the Bastille and the Hôtel des Invalides on July 13–14, 1789. In March 1792 he was drafted as surgeon major into the Army of the Rhine.

Between the time of the Roman Empire and the late 18th century, military medicine hardly existed in Europe. The wounded had been viewed as of little use, and those who were not lucky enough to find and pay for their own care were likely to be left to die on the field. Larrey recognized both the cruelty and the waste implicit in abandoning the wounded and created a revolutionary system of evacuation. He took the flying

Praised by Napoleon as the most virtuous man he had ever met, Dominique-Jean Larrey personified military surgery during the Napoleonic Wars. (The Art Archive/Musée du Louvre Paris/Dagli Orti)

artillery units attached to French advanced guards as his model, reasoning that the same sort of horse-drawn vehicles could accompany the units and both treat and retrieve wounded during and immediately after battles. He contrived a four-wheeled, spring-mounted carriage (the *fourgon*) to be drawn by either two or four horses and capable of carrying four supine patients. These wagons became the famous flying ambulances or *ambulances volantes* that were an integral part of the Napoleonic Wars. He went on to create medical units comprising 340 men in three divisions under a chief surgeon. These units, in place by the Italian campaign of 1796–1797, were also confusingly referred to as ambulances.

Besides being a creative administrator, Larrey was also a gifted surgeon and revolutionized the battlefield treatment of wounds. Most wounds during the Napoleonic era were either from musket balls or cannons. Unrifled muskets were effective at only 30 to 40 yards and caused mostly localized injuries. Cannons, canisters, and bombs, however, were effective at up to 1,000 yards and led to extensive shattering wounds associated with a high rate of amputation. The standard technique, especially among Russian and German surgeons, had been to delay treatment for several days and then to cut the limb circumferentially and to stretch the skin over the raw stump. This led inevitably to infected wounds, breakdown of the closure, and, with grim frequency, death from gangrene. Larrey adopted Henri-François LeDran's technique of cutting the muscle and bone well above the wound and leaving a cuff of skin for a tension-free closure. He also operated as early as possible—frequently in the field—correctly reasoning that the wounds could be kept cleaner if closed early. In addition, Larrey was the first to successfully perform a hip disarticulation (amputation at the hip joint), the first to describe trench foot, and the first to recognize the infectious nature of Egyptian ophthalmia. He invented the curved surgical needles, which passed more efficiently through tissue than the straight ones in common use, and he anticipated the Carrel-Dakin technique of World War I by irrigating wounds with antiseptic solutions.

Larrey was named chief surgeon to Napoleon's Imperial Guard and participated in the campaigns in Italy, Egypt, Prussia, and Russia. At Wagram, 1,200 of the Imperial Guards were wounded, and virtually all passed through his dressing station. A remarkable 600 of the wounded returned to duty and only 45 died. After the battle, Larrey was named a baron and given lands in Swedish Pomerania that for the first time afforded his family an adequate living. Between campaigns, he served on the faculty at the École de Médicine Militaire at Val-de-Grâce.

In 1812, Napoleon named Larrey surgeon in chief to the Grande Armée in preparation for the Russian invasion. At Borodino, Larrey's dressing station cared for two-thirds of the 9,000 French wounded, and Larrey personally saw to the most serious operations, performing an astounding 200 amputations in a single 24-hour period. Even the francophone Russian prisoners, having heard of the French surgeon's skill, demanded to be taken to Larrey's station. Although 20,000 of Napoleon's 110,000 troops who finally entered Moscow were either sick or wounded, care was good enough that 100,000 were able to leave the city and only 1,200 sick and wounded were left behind.

When Napoleon reconstituted his army after the 1815 escape from Elba, Pierre François Percy was restored as surgeon in chief. Larrey returned to his surgical duties and was severely wounded and captured at Waterloo. He was initially ordered shot but was rescued from the firing squad by a British soldier who had attended his prewar lectures in Berlin. Larrey was taken to Field Marshal Blücher, whose son he had treated. The grateful field marshal freed the surgeon and sent him home with a generous reward.

Larrey, whose dedication to Napoleon was well known (the emperor had left his surgeon 100,000 livres and high praise in his will), remained out of favor during the Restoration, but, after the 1830 Revolution, he was named surgeon in chief to the Hôtel des Invalides, where he was able to teach and to care for 4,000 of his old Grande Armée comrades. He was also appointed consultant surgeon to the new monarch, Louis-Philippe, but his perennially prickly personality and inability to submit to authority led to his being sacked in 1836. He maintained a position as inspector general for medical affairs in the Army and, on July 25, 1842, died of pneumonia while returning from an inspection of facilities in Algeria.

See also Ambulances and Transport; Amputation; Casualty Clearing Stations and Staged Evacuation; Field Hospitals; Napoleonic Wars; Percy, Baron Pierre François; Trench Foot

References
Dible, J. H. *Napoleon's Surgeon*. London: Heinemann, 1970.
Richardson, Robert G. *Larrey: Surgeon to Napoleon's Imperial Guard*. John Murray Publishers Ltd., 1974.

Laveran, Charles Louis Alphonse (1845–1922)

Alphonse Laveran was a French military surgeon who identified plasmodium as the cause of malaria and suggested that it might be transmitted by mosquitoes.

Laveran was born in Paris on June 18, 1845, the son of a military surgeon and professor at the École de Val-de-Grâce and a mother who came from a long line of military officers. Although his father continued to teach in France, Alphonse and his mother moved to Algeria when Laveran was a boy and remained there until he returned to Paris to attend medical school. In 1863, Laveran enrolled in the Public Health School at Strasbourg. He served briefly as an officer in a field ambulance (hospital) at Metz during the Franco-Prussian War and, in 1874, took the chair in military diseases and epidemics at Val-de-Grâce that had previously been held by his father. He remained in the military and, in 1878, was assigned to the Algerian military hospital at Bône and then at Constantine, where he acquired an old microscope and began studying parasites. On November 6, 1880, he wrote that he had seen, "on the edges of a pigmented spherical body, filamentous elements that move with great vivacity." He had seen plasmodium in one of its motile forms.

The marshes at Campagna were infamous hotbeds of malaria, and, in 1882, Laveran made a protracted visit to Rome's San Spirito hospital to collect specimens from malaria patients and to isolate the organisms he had seen on slides in Algeria. Although he was widely ridiculed, his work was ultimately verified by laboratories around the world, and, in 1889, Laveran received the prestigious Bréant Prize and general recognition as discoverer of the parasite responsible for malaria. In 1884, he was appointed professor of military hygiene at Val-de-Grâce and, in 1894, was promoted to director of health services for the 11th Army Corps based at Nantes. In 1896, he resigned his commission and joined the Pasteur Institute in Paris. He was awarded the Nobel Prize in 1907 and used half the money to found the Laboratory for Tropical Disease at the institute.

Laveran suggested that the mosquito might be responsible for transmitting malaria, a hypothesis repeated by Patrick Manson and ultimately proven by Ronald Ross. He was named commander of the Legion of Honor in 1912 and died at the Pasteur Institute on May 18, 1922, after a protracted illness.

See also Franco-Prussian War; Malaria; Ross, Sir Ronald

References
Centers for Disease Control and Prevention. 2004. "Laveran and the Discovery of the Malaria Parasite." www.cdc.gov/malaria/ history/Laveran (accessed July 26, 2005).
Ouvrage Collectif. *Les initiateurs français en pathologie infectieuse, Pasteur, Widal, Roux, Calmette, Nicolle, Laveran.* Paris: Flammarion, 1942.

Leishman, Sir William Boog (1865–1926)

A British military physician and expert in tropical medicine, Leishman was born in Glasgow, Scotland, the son of the professor of midwifery at Anderson College. He was educated at Westminster School in London before returning to Glasgow for his medical training. After qualifying as a physician at age 20, Leishman joined the Royal Army Medical Corps and was posted to India, where he took a special interest in the slum city of Dum Dum, 10 miles outside Calcutta.

The disease now known as kala azar was so common in that city that it was locally known as Dum Dum fever. Leishman had taken a microscope to India and his fascination with the fever persisted after he transferred back to England as assistant professor of pathology to the military hospital at Netley. When a soldier from Dum Dum died after being transferred back to Netley for care, Leishman performed an autopsy and stained organisms from the man's spleen. The microbes were first thought to be identical to the trypanosomes that cause sleeping sickness but were later recognized to be a previously unrecognized protozoan that was named *Leishmania donovani* in his honor. The latter part of the name honors Charles Donovan, who independently discovered the organism and published his findings within weeks of Leishman's article. Soon after its discovery, the parasite was shown to be transmitted by the sand fly.

In 1903, Leishman succeeded Sir Almroth Wright as holder of the Millbert chair at the Royal Army Medical College. He and Wright worked together to develop the typhoid vaccine that saved thousands of lives during World War I. After the war, he supervised the contentious cuts in the British Army Medical Service. Leishman also developed a stain specifically for the malarial organism, which bears his name and is still in use.

See also British Military Medicine; Typhoid Fever; Wright, Almroth

Reference
N.a. "Sir William Leishman: 1866–1926." *Lancet* (February 5): 310–311.

Letterman, Jonathan (1824–1872)

Jonathan Letterman was the reorganizer of the Union Army medical service during the Civil War.

Letterman was born in Cannonsburg, Pennsylvania, on December 11, 1824, the son of a surgeon. He graduated from Jefferson Medical College in 1849 and enlisted in the Army as an assistant surgeon. For the next 12 years, Letterman served in a variety of Army posts and in a number of Indian campaigns. On July 1, 1862, Surgeon General William Hammond appointed him to succeed Maj. Charles Tripler as chief surgeon in Maj. Gen. George McClellan's Army of the Potomac.

From that position, Letterman instituted the changes that became standard practice in Army medical services through World War I. Realizing that wounded men were being left in the field for as much as a week, Letterman first instituted an organized system of evacuation. He arranged for rapid construction of carts and two- and four-wheeled horse-drawn vehicles to evacuate the wounded. He also combined Larrey's *ambulance volante* with Percy's *brancardiers* into a permanent group of stretcher bearers and ambulance drivers. The litter bearers were taken from line regiments but were organized by division and placed under the corps medical officer. The ambulance vehicles were restricted to transporting the sick and wounded rather than doubling as carriers of ammunition and supplies. By the Battle of Antietam on September 7, 1862, Letterman had 200 new ambulances (roughly one for every 175 combat soldiers) and was able to remove all wounded from the field in less than 48 hours.

Letterman adapted lessons learned in the Crimean War to completely reorganize the Union hospital system. He replaced converted public buildings and warehouses that had previously served as fixed hospitals with well-ventilated, modular pavilions organized on a divisional rather than a regimental level that became the model for Type A and B hospitals of the American Expeditionary Force in France. He established a sequential evacuation that started with tented hospitals near the front from which patients were moved to field hospitals and then to general hospitals in rear-area cities. This step-wise evacuation was subsequently adopted by all the powers in World War I.

Letterman resigned from the Army in 1864 after Hammond's court-martial. He unsuccessfully tried business in Southern California before moving to San Francisco, where he went into private practice and briefly served as city coroner. He died at age 47 on March 15, 1872.

See also Ambulances and Transport; Civil War in the United States; Hammond, William

References

Ashburn, P. M. *A History of the Medical Department of the United States Army.* Boston: Houghton Mifflin Co., 1929.

Gillet, Mary. *The Army Medical Department, 1818–1865.* Washington, D.C.: Center of Military History, 1987.

Haller, John S. *Farmcarts to Fords: A History of the Military Ambulance, 1790–1925.* Carbondale: Southern Illinois University Press, 1992.

Packard, Francis. *History of Medicine in the United States.* New York: Paul B. Hoeber, Inc., 1931.

Ligature

The term ligature refers to either tying a blood vessel to prevent hemorrhage or the suture used to perform the procedure.

Control of bleeding from vessels—particularly arteries—transected by a penetrating wound or intentionally cut by the surgeon in the course of an operation (usually amputation) has plagued surgeons for as long as they have accompanied armies to battle. Tying off the open vessel with suture or twine was mentioned by the first-century Roman writer Aulus Cornelius Celsus and subsequently by Avicenna, Guy de Chauliac, Giovanni de Vigo (who was paradoxically famous for his insistence on cauterization as a way to stop hemorrhage from gunshot wounds), Andreas Vesalius, Jean Tagault, and Giovanni della Croce, but it was generally felt that finding the open vessel and controlling it with suture was too difficult and too time consuming in a battlefield situation. As a consequence, military surgeons generally fell back on pressure, styptics, the cautery, or simply the dropping intra-arterial pressure resulting from blood loss to control hemorrhage. It remained for young French surgeon Ambroise Paré, who, in his 1564 *Dix Livres de Chirurgie*, argued for abandonment of hot oil in favor of irrigation and ligating vessels in battlefield amputation to challenge that practice.

Ligation is technically much more difficult than simple application of a red hot iron to a bleeding wound. In the absence of anesthesia, the patient was unlikely to hold still, a situation made more challenging when the wound filled with spurting blood. Paré at least partially solved both problems by applying tourniquets above and below the wound. The tight bands furnished both a measure of pain relief and temporary control of hemorrhage. The vessel could then be identified and tied above and below the intended site of transection. In open wounds, the cut vessel could be extracted with a "crow's beak" forceps and tied. Failing that, a curved needle could be passed around the vessel and its surrounding tissue and tied.

For the first three centuries after Paré, vessels were tied with silk or twine, and the loose ends of the ligature were brought out through the closed wound. After several days, the wound suppurated and the ligatures loosened and were gently pulled free. If the surgeon pulled too soon, there was great risk of resumed hemorrhage and death of the patient was not unlikely. If they were left too long, they became a source of persistent drainage and infection. Joseph Lister, who is best known for his work in antiseptic surgery, addressed that problem as part of his overall technique. In an effort to find suture that would reabsorb, he first tried catgut—a misnamed fiber made from cured sheep intestines that was used primarily as strings for musical instruments. Although the gut did dissolve, it required prolonged curing and, if improperly prepared, softened and came loose before the vessel had healed. After painstakingly trying a number of chemicals to improve catgut's performance, Lister came upon chromic acid, which adequately stabilized the suture while allowing it to dissolve in two to three weeks—just the right period of time for vessel scarring. His technique, presented to the Clinical Society of London in 1881, remains in use with only minor modification.

See also Amputation; Cauterization; Celsus, Aulus Cornelius; Lister, Lord Joseph; Paré, Ambroise

References

Gibson, T. 1990. "Evolution of Catgut Sutures: The Endeavour and Success of Joseph Lister and William MacEwen." *British Journal of Surgery* 77 (July): 824–825.
Zimmerman, Leo, and Ilza Veith. *Great Ideas in the History of Surgery*. Baltimore: Williams and Wilkins Co., 1961.

Lind, James
(1716–1794)

James Lind is considered the father of nautical medicine.

Lind was born in Edinburgh and began training as an apprentice in the College of Surgeons of that city in 1731. He was a physician in the British Royal Navy from 1739 to 1748, serving in Minorca, the West Indies, the Mediterranean, and the Channel Fleet. While on the last post, he treated 350 cases of scurvy during one 10-week period and acquired the interest in the disease which led to his epochal experiments.

Lind was aware that the Dutch had used oranges and lemons to treat scurvy as early as 1593 and that John Woodall had recommended lemon juice to treat the disease in his 1636 *Surgeon's Mate*. While stationed on the HMS *Salisbury*, Lind devised an experiment in which he took 12 sailors suffering from scurvy and divided them into six groups who received either cider; dilute sulphuric acid; a quart of sea water; vinegar; a pill made of garlic, mustard seed, radish, balsam of Peru, and gum myrhh; or one lemon and two oranges a day. Within six days, the last group was back at work while the other five groups remained ill. It still took Sir Gilbert Blane's influence and another 41 years before daily lemon juice was required in the British Navy and scurvy disappeared from the fleet.

After his service in Channel Fleet during the War of the Austrian Succession (1740–1748), Lind returned to Edinburgh University, obtained his medical degree in 1748, and published his findings in *A Treatise of the Scurvy* in 1753. Lind also recognized that typhus or "ship fever," a disease that had cost the Royal Navy 25,000 men in the 1739–1740 epidemic alone, was related to the fact that sailors seldom (or never) bathed. In his *Treatise on Naval Hygiene* (1757) he recommended delousing the men by quarantining new recruits in receiving ships until they had been thoroughly washed and reclothed and suggested regularly bathing the men and baking their clothes to remove lice. He recommended regular uniforms in place of the random "slops" that had been traditionally used, devised a method of distilling seawater, and introduced powdered foods and "portable soups" to the shipboard diet.

In his *Essay on Diseases Incidental to Europeans in Hot Climates* (1768), Lind addressed the problems of tropical diseases and introduced the idea of hospital ships in which men with contagious diseases could be quarantined from the rest of the fleet.

Lind left the navy in 1758 and became physician to the Royal Naval Hospital at

Haslar, an appointment probably made possible by the intercession of Lord Aston, to whom he had dedicated the book on scurvy. He worked there until 1783, during which time he perfected the technique of supplying ships with fresh water through salt water distillation and published *An Essay on the Most Effectual Means of Preserving the Health of Seamen.*

Better hygiene and control of scurvy and typhus—all of which were the direct result of Lind's work—resulted in a halving of the death rate from disease in the British fleet between 1780 and 1813. Lind's son succeeded him as chief physician at Haslar in 1783. Lind died in Gosport (where the hospital is located) in 1794 and was buried at Portchester Church.

See also Blane, Sir Gilbert; Scurvy; Typhus

References

Brown, Stephen. *Scurvy: How a Surgeon, a Mariner, and a Gentleman Solved the Greatest Medical Mystery of the Age of Sail.* New York: Thomas Dunne Books, 2004.

Hill, J. R. *The Oxford Illustrated History of the Royal Navy.* Oxford: Oxford University Press, 1995.

N.a. 1966. "James Lind (1716–1794). Physician to the Fleet." *Journal of the American Medical Association* 195: 309–310.

Roddis, Louis H. 1950. *James Lind, Founder of Nautical Medicine.* New York: Schumann, 1950.

Lister, Lord Joseph (1827–1912)

Joseph Lister popularized antisepsis, and in doing so, revolutionized surgery.

Lister was born in the town of Upton in Essex to a family of Quaker physicians, although his father was a wine merchant and amateur lens grinder. Because of his nonconformist religious beliefs, Lister was not eligible for admission to either Oxford or Cambridge universities (both of which required membership in the Anglican Church), so he completed his medical studies at the University of London in 1852. While still a student, he acquired an interest in histology, probably due at least in part to his father's interest in microscopes. Lister took a position in Edinburgh as house surgeon under James Syme in 1854, eventually marrying his professor's daughter. By 1857 he had already published important papers on inflammation and blood coagulation.

In 1860, Lister was named professor of surgery at the University of Glasgow. He had a busy surgical practice and was deeply depressed by the mortality rate from hospital infections such as tetanus, erysipelas, and gangrene. The mortality rate from amputations in his own patients exceeded 45 percent in spite of using Syme's silver sutures, wound drainage, frequent dressing changes, and general cleanliness. Undoubtedly, his poor results were due at least in part to his persistent belief in the efficacy of "laudable pus."

Looking for a solution, Lister immediately recognized the significance of Louis Pasteur's proof that microorganisms could cause disease. The French scientist's use of heat to prevent bacterial growth was of little practical use in surgery, so Lister sought other ways to keep bacteria out of wounds. He tried covering wounds with zinc chloride and various sulphites before stumbling on carbolic acid, which was in common use as a disinfectant for sewage. He described his use of carbolic acid–soaked dressings in his application for the chair of systematic surgery at the University College of London in 1866 and in his 1867 *On the Antiseptic Principle in the Practice of Surgery*, which was widely criticized.

Lister worked for decades on various antiseptic dressings and was the first to use dissolvable catgut sutures in vascular surgery. By 1871 he had moved on to more direct methods of surgical antisepsis. He dipped his hands in phenol and then dilute mercuric chloride, but he continued to operate in a blood-caked black coat with the collar turned up to avoid its being drenched by the carbolic-soaked towel pinned to his chest. He also recommended a continuous spray of aerosolized carbolic acid in the operating room to kill ambient bacteria. Lister differed significantly from Ignaz Semmelweis in that he thought antisepsis (killing bacteria that had contaminated a wound) preferable to asepsis (not introducing contamination into the wound in the first place).

In 1869, Lister succeeded his father-in-law in the chair of surgery at Edinburgh, and, in 1877, he was named to the chair of surgery at King's College in London. His antiseptic techniques remained controversial, and, in his new job, he frequently found himself lecturing to empty rooms. His ideas were more readily accepted on the Continent than in England and were adopted as standard practice by the Prussian military medical service during that country's war with France. After the Franco-Prussian War, Lister toured Germany as a hero.

He was named baronet in 1883 and was president of the Royal Society from 1895 to 1900. Lister retired in 1896 and, in 1897, became the first physician to be named a peer of the realm. He died in 1912, too soon to see his antiseptic technique, which had been supplanted by surgical asepsis, return on the battlefields of World War I as the Carrel-Dakin method of wound management.

See also Antisepsis; Franco-Prussian War; Pasteur, Louis

References
Fisher, Richard B. *Joseph Lister, 1827–1912.* New York: Stein & Day, 1977.
Lister, Joseph. *The Collected Papers of Joseph, Baron Lister.* Oxford, UK: Clarendon Press, 1909.
Rains, Harding. *Joseph Lister and Antisepsis.* London: Priority Press, 1977.

Madagascar Campaign

The French invasion of Madagascar in 1895 had the highest death rate from malaria of any military campaign in history.

Although the French had maintained coastal settlements for the Indian Ocean trade since the 1600s, Malagasy natives under Andrianampoinimerina had consolidated power in the central highlands in the 1780s and armed themselves with European guns and artillery. The Franco-Imerino War of 1883–1884 had ended with a treaty allowing the French to control Imerino foreign affairs, and Great Britain had recognized the island as a French protectorate. In 1894, the French, envisioning a new agricultural colony similar to Algeria, decided to invade the interior and take actual control of the entire island.

As recently as 1875, famed military surgeon and malariologist Alphonse Laveran had called Madagascar the most dangerous of France's overseas posts. There are no statistics regarding 19th-century malaria outbreaks on the island, but the death rate from an epidemic on nearby Réunion Island in 1870 was 510 per 1,000 inhabitants, and a 1988 epidemic in Madascar killed 100,000

people. The especially fulminant falciparum strain carried by *Anopheles funestus*, *Anopheles gambiae*, and *Anopheles arabiensis* mosquitoes was the most common cause of disease on the island.

In 1895, the French formed the 200th line of infantry and the 40th battalion of *chasseurs á pied* from a variety of existing units so the entire army could share in the invasion's glory. They also included troops from the West African colonies and Foreign Legionnaires from Algeria who, possessing some immunity, proved to be the only functional soldiers. The French landed 12,000 soldiers on Madagascar's northwest coast, intending to use roads and rivers to transit the 380 miles to the Merino capital at Antinanarivo. They sent only 20 physicians and enough field hospital beds to accommodate 2,500, or 17 percent of the invasion force. The French progression to Antinanarivo was relatively uneventful, and only 25 men had been lost to hostile action when the capital surrendered. The French established a protectorate under Gen. Joseph Galliéni and exiled the Merina queen.

Unfortunately for Galliéni, his occupation started an eight-year insurrection and was the beginning of a medical disaster. By the end of 1895, one-third of the French occupying force had died of disease—72 percent from malaria, 12 percent from typhoid, 8 percent from dysentery, and the rest from tuberculosis, tetanus, and heat stroke. The troops were given 200 to 300 milligrams a week of quinine, a dose French tropical medicine specialists had pointed out was far too low to be effective. Ultimately, the French invasion force had to withdraw to the coast to wage a desultory campaign against native insurrectionists for most of the subsequent decade.

See also Laveran, Charles Louis Alphonse; Malaria

Reference
Curtin, Philip D. *Disease and Empire: The Health of European Troops in the Conquest of Africa.* Cambridge: Cambridge University Press, 1998.

Magati, Cesare (1596–1647)

An Italian expert in the treatment of wounds, Cesare Magati was born in Scandiano and studied medicine at Bologna and the Hospital of the Conzolazione in Rome. He subsequently became a Capuchin monk and professor of surgery at Ferrara. Magati believed wounds should be covered with simple, clean dressings and that keeping air out of open wounds allowed them to heal more easily. His method was largely ignored until adopted and popularized 80 years later by Agostino Belloste (1654–1730). Magati authored a famous two-volume text, *De Rara Medicinae.*

See also 16th-Century Military Medicine

Reference
Romanini, Luigi. 2000. "About Cesare Magati, His Method of 'Cover' Dressing of Wounds, and the Full Discussion with Agostino Belloste." *European Journal of Orthopedics* 13 (November): 13–14.

Malaria

Malaria is a protozoal disease caused by one of five subspecies of plasmodium.

Although 80 percent of the world's cases of malaria occur in tropical Africa, the disease has also been seen throughout Asia, Europe, and the Americas and has been endemic in both Europe and North America. Ancient writings in both Sanskrit and Chinese clearly describe malaria.

The organism is transmitted by the female of one of several species of Anopheles mosquito that bite humans and ingest malarial gametocytes, one of the stages of the organism's complex developmental cycle. The protozoan multiplies in the mosquito's abdominal cavity before migrating to the insect's salivary glands, from which it is injected into a new victim. Once in the human bloodstream, the organism migrates to the liver, where it multiplies before returning to the bloodstream to enter red cells and feed on hemoglobin. When the victim is bitten by another mosquito, the malaria organism is ingested and the cycle begins again.

The genus *Plasmodium* has four species of which *falciparum* is the most lethal. An inoculation with the *falciparum* parasite can lead to cerebral malaria and death within a few days of infection. The three other species, sometimes popularly referred to as "baby" malaria, can lead to decades of recurring fever but are rarely fatal.

French military surgeon Alphonse Laveran first saw the malarial parasite in a blood smear from a patient with "ague" while stationed in North Africa. Seventeen years later, while stationed in India, British Army physician Ronald Ross proved the mosquito was the vector and worked out its life cycle. Both men received the Nobel Prize for their discoveries.

Malaria (from the Italian *mal aria*, or bad air) was endemic in Athens as early as the fifth century B.C. and was ubiquitous in ancient Rome, where it almost certainly contributed to the empire's decline. Malaria was brought to the Western Hemisphere by Spanish conquistadors and their slaves and was a factor in the demographic collapse of Mesoamerican civilizations. Ironically, its presence in West Africa limited European incursions and slowed colonization; one West African children's song praises the mosquito for protecting the local inhabitants from white people. The death rate among soldiers in Senegal in the 1830s reached 200 per 1,000 soldiers, and the high death rate among Royal Navy sailors on antislavery patrol off the "fever coast" led to mandatory use of quinine in that service. However, quinine was combined with purging, which aggravated the disease's dehydration and bleeding, worsening anemia and, taken together, actually aggravated the problem.

Malaria has been a recurrent problem for military forces. Oliver Cromwell refused to take quinine containing cinchona bark because it came from Catholic sources and was known as "Jesuit's powder," and, as a result, died of malaria. George Washington, Andrew Jackson, and Napoleon Bonaparte all suffered from the disease. In 1800, Napoleon ordered a half-ton of quinine-containing powdered bark from the South American cinchona tree for French cities where malaria was endemic. The Union Army in the American Civil War reported 1,315,000 cases of malaria with 10,000 deaths, and Union rations often included doses of whiskey spiked with quinine sulfate.

Malaria was endemic in Central and South America throughout the 19th century. Of the 26,000 men employed in the French effort to dig the Panama Canal, 21,000 were hospitalized with "fever," a nonspecific diagnosis that included malaria, yellow fever, and a variety of gastrointestinal infections. The French failure to dig a canal and the U.S. success two decades later were largely a result of endemic malaria in the isthmus and the subsequent proof by American military surgeons of the importance of mosquito eradication programs.

In the 1860s cinchona seedlings were smuggled from Peru to Java, which, by the beginning of World War II, produced 95 percent of the world's quinine. When that island fell under Japanese control, the Allied forces were left without a reliable source of the drug. In the early stages of the Pacific campaign malaria disabled five times as many troops as did the Japanese, although subsequent development of the synthetic antimalarial drug Atabrine alleviated the problem. Because malaria was endemic in the southern United States where many troops were being trained, local wetlands were drained and hundreds of thousands of acres were treated with insecticides.

It has been estimated that 70 percent of hospital admissions in the Viet Nam War were for arthropod-borne diseases including malaria. Officers of the Republic of South Africa reported being infected as many as 20 times in the African Bush War. Beginning with the U.S. invasion of Panama in the early 1990s, American military forces deployed to endemic malaria areas have been issued uniforms, tents, and bedding impregnated with permethrin, a synthetic form of the natural insect repellent produced by chrysanthemums. Still, of the 725 members of the U.S. Army Ranger task force deployed to eastern Afghanistan between June and September 2002, 38 were infected with *Plasmodium vivax*.

There is no vaccine to prevent malaria, and, although there is chemoprophylaxis to prevent the disease and chemotherapy to treat it, resistance to those drugs is increasingly common. Malaria remains the world's most common cause of death from infectious disease.

See also Civil War in the United States; Laveran, Charles Louis Alphonse; Madagascar Campaign; Quinine; Ross, Sir Ronald

References
Cartwright, Frederick, and Michael Biddis. *Disease and History*. New York: Dorset Press, 1972.
Karlen, Arno. *Man and Microbes: Disease and Plagues in History and Modern Times*. New York: Simon & Schuster, 1996.
McNeil, William H. *Plagues and Peoples*. Garden City, NY: Anchor Press, 1976.

McGrigor, James
(1771–1858)

James McGrigor was one of two Scots (the other being James Guthrie) who organized and improved care by the medical service of the British Army in the Peninsular Campaign.

McGrigor studied medicine at Edinburgh and Aberdeen, where he received his degree in 1788. He served as surgeon to the Connaught Rangers in 1793 and saw duty in India, Flanders, the West Indies, and Egypt. He was named inspector general of hospitals in 1809 and participated in the disastrous Walcheren expedition in which British forces were virtually wiped out by febrile illness.

McGrigor went to Spain as chief of Wellington's medical service in 1812, where his outspokenness and vigorous advocacy for the sick and wounded led to frequent clashes with the Iron Duke. He set up a chain of evacuation hospitals across Spain and Portugal and moved the injured in wagons commandeered from the commissary department over Wellington's objections. McGrigor imported prefabricated buildings to house the convalescents in Portugal and placed responsibility for determining who was to be invalided out with medical boards. He anticipated Ignaz Semmelweis's work on hospital contagion by separating men with wounds from those with febrile illnesses. He also instituted a system of medical reports and statistics that became the famed Blue Book.

Although McGrigor tried Wellington's patience, he earned the latter's respect, convincing him to commend surgeons for the first time in official dispatches. The general later called McGrigor one of the most industrious, able, and successful public servants he had ever met. After the British victory at Toulouse (1814), the Royal Army medical service was in the best condition in its history, although that situation proved temporary as interest and investment in the service rapidly declined after the war. Even as early as the Battle of Waterloo (1815), most of McGrigor's improvements had lapsed and care was at the disastrous level, where it would remain until the Crimean War.

McGrigor served as director general of hospitals from 1815 to 1851. He founded the pathological museum and library at the Fort Pitt facility that became Netley Hospital and was named a Fellow of the Royal Society in 1816. He was knighted in 1814, was created baronet in 1830, and received an honorary LLD from his Edinburgh alma mater in 1850.

See also British Military Medicine; Guthrie,
George James; Napoleonic Wars

References
Blanco, Richard. 1974. "The Development of
British Military Medicine, 1793–1814."
Military Affairs 38 (February): 4–10.
Lovegrove, Peter. *Not in the Least Crusade: A
Short History of the Royal Army Medical
Corps.* Aldershot, UK: Gale & Polden, Ltd.,
1952.
McGlaughlin, Redmond. *The Royal Army
Medical Corps.* London: Leo Cooper, Ltd.,
1972.

Medieval Military Medicine

For purposes of military and social history,
the Middle Ages can be thought of as beginning with the fall of the Western Roman
Empire in A.D. 476 and ending with the fall
of the Eastern Empire to the Turks in 1453.
However, for purposes of scientific and
medical history, the Middle Ages probably
ended with Copernicus's use of observation
to challenge Aristotelian authority and Andreas Vesalius's use of dissection to challenge Galenic anatomy.

The foundation of medicine's scientific
emergence from medieval magic and superstition was built on Greco-Roman knowledge preserved in libraries at Constantinople
and the Western Caliphate and by copyist
monks sequestered in Europe's monaster-
ies. In the West, military medicine vanished
with the Roman army's dissolution into
tribal units. Formal medical care for soldiers
disappeared, and medical science regressed
to the Bronze Age, from which it would not
emerge for a millennium and a half.

Between A.D. 200 and 400, the Roman legions had evolved to being almost entirely
composed of non-Italians garrisoned on
the empire's periphery in the ultimately fu-

tile attempt to stem the influx of Germanic
tribes. Scattered around the boundaries of
Europe, the legions and their medical services lost central organization, and the Roman hospital system withered and died. The
trained Roman *medici* were entirely replaced
by uneducated civilian wound dressers, or
curantes. Skills such as arrow extraction, use
of the tourniquet, and suturing arteries were
lost, and the wounded were most often left
to bleed and die where they fell or, if they
had the misfortune to be on the losing side,
to be slaughtered by the victors.

By the late fourth or early fifth century, not
only had Roman military medicine ceased
to exist but Roman civilian medicine had
atrophied as well and had largely been replaced by Germanic shamanism and magic
such as monastic prayer and fasting. Instead
of cleaning wounds as the Romans had, medieval physicians packed them open with a
variety of foul substances (including human
and animal feces) in order to promote suppuration under the theory that pus formation
was a necessary step in healing. The tourniquet disappeared and did not return until
described by Ambroise Paré in the 1500s.

The Visigothic Code of the fifth to ninth
centuries actively discouraged professional
surgery by mandating draconian penalties
(including death) for surgeons whose patients did not survive, and the practice of
civilian and military surgery passed almost
entirely to barbers who were not subject to
that standard. Church-sponsored hospitals
did begin to appear after A.D. 350, but they
primarily furnished bed and board and seldom ventured into actual treatment. Over
the next seven centuries, the hospitals gradually passed from Church to monastic control, but their role changed little. Disease
was attributed to demons, and therapy involved invoking saints to drive them away.

Medicine in general and military medicine in particular fared better in the Eastern Empire. The Western Roman Empire lasted 500 years, but the Eastern Empire survived twice that long and maintained a 150,000-man Roman-style standing army for four centuries. The Byzantine army after Justinian (A.D. 527–565) was a well-organized force with a formal medical service. Under Emperor Mauritius (A.D. 582–602), one physician and up to 18 medics (*deputati*) were assigned to every *cataphract* of 200–400 cavalry. The latter were charged with carrying water for the wounded and retrieving them from the field if they could not manage for themselves. The *deputati* were paid a piece of gold for every man rescued and were awarded a share of the spoils in the event of victory. In his *Tactics*, Emperor Leo (A.D. 886–912) wrote, "Give all the care you possibly can to your wounded, for if you neglect them, you will make your soldiers timorous and cowardly before a battle, and, not only that, but your personnel, whom you might preserve and retain by proper consideration for their health and welfare, will be otherwise lost to you through your own negligence."

The Byzantine military cared not only for its wounded but also for its sick, and long-term facilities were provided to care for injured veterans. Hospitals built by Justin II (A.D. 565–578) and Alexius Comnenus I (A.D. 1048–1118) for their veterans were the first such institutions in history.

In contrast, little improved in Western European military medicine for a thousand years. Charlemagne was crowned Holy Roman Emperor in A.D. 800 and his empire was divided at Verdun in A.D. 814, but what few military physicians the empire possessed served kings, popes, and other princes of the Church and state and rarely stooped to caring for commoners. Surgery had separated almost entirely from medicine, and most wound care and operations were done by barbers whose primary purpose and income derived from shaving tonsured monks. No organized care existed for wounded soldiers. Surgery was so barbaric and the results were so bad that the Church hesitated to have its monks and priests participate, and, at the Fourth Lateran Council in A.D. 1215, religious officials banned it altogether for the higher orders of clergy, stipulating that using the knife or cautery precluded one from participating in the mass.

General medical care often fell to women who nursed the disabled and collected medicinal herbs for their treatment.

In Iberia, medical care began to slowly improve toward the end of the millennium. In 1085, Toledo, along with its library and a population of Jewish scholars capable of translating the Arabic texts into Greek and Latin, fell to the Spanish Christians, one of whom, Gerard of Cremona (1114–1187), came to Toledo intent on learning Arabic and spent his entire life translating the library.

The rediscovered knowledge gave a reason for new institutions of medical treatment and education. Hospitals had been a major part of Byzantine medicine, where facilities (*nosokomeiae* and *xenones*) such as St. Sampson's in Constantinople often exceeded 200 beds and included facilities for surgery and for medical education. After 1198, the Benedictines built a network of hospitals, initially to provide general care to the sick and wounded and then for treatment of syphilis and isolation of patients with communicable disease. The hospital movement spread through Europe in the subsequent century, with a 225-bed hospital being built at York in 1287 and even larger facilities established at Paris, Milan, and Siena.

Northern Italy saw a renaissance of medical writing beginning in 1063 when Alphanus, the bishop of Salerno, visited Constantinople and was exposed to that city's ancient Greek texts. His *Premnon Physicon* reintroduced Galen to Western Europe. Constantinus Africanus, a monk at nearby Monte Cassino, brought Arab and Greek texts from Iberia to the city, and the combination resulted in the *Regimen Sanitatus Salernitatum*, the first of the modern European medical texts. In 1224, Emperor Frederick required physicians to be licensed by an examination in medicine and surgery and required candidates to demonstrate knowledge of anatomy. In 1231 he chartered a medical school at Salerno and made the faculty responsible for administering the licensure examinations. Schools modeled on Salerno were founded at Montpellier, Paris, Bologna, and Oxford. In 1201, Jean Pitard started a formal surgical training program at the College of St. Côme in Paris.

By the 14th century, Western European physicians (looking back to Rhazes's 10th-century doctrine of the eight diseases) believed that plague, phthisis, epilepsy, syphilis, erysipelas, anthrax, trachoma, and leprosy could be passed from person to person. That belief gave rise to ideas of sanitation and isolation and, ultimately, to legal quarantine. The spread of plague from the Asian steppes resulted in mandatory maritime quarantine in Venice in 1374, in Ragusa in 1377, and in Marseilles in 1383, where the 40-day holding period for ships arriving from infected areas (the *quaranta*) gave the practice its name.

Military medicine also underwent a gradual reawakening beginning in the 13th century when the Spanish monarchs sent mobile hospitals with their forces in the Moorish wars. Jean Froissart, chronicler of the Hundred Years War, rarely mentioned treatment of the wounded and, although John of Arderne is mentioned as physician to John of Gaunt, it is likely that few surgeons or physicians accompanied those armies. Wounded soldiers were carried from the field by their comrades, and nobles relied on their retinues for battlefield aid. The armies were subject to jaundice, typhus, dysentery, malaria, and plague, and their treatment was limited to what dressings and herbals were included in supply wagons. Prince Edward of England did take surgeons with him to the Holy Land when he went on crusade, and he took seven doctors when he invaded Scotland. His personal physician and surgeon were paid on a level with knights while their assistants were paid half as much—a rate equivalent to that of a squire. The Welsh troops took their own surgeon to Crécy, and Henry V had both a personal physician and a surgeon at Agincourt.

In England, master surgeons were elevated to guild status in 1368 and were united with physicians in 1421, while barber-surgeons were given a separate charter in 1462. Surgery had achieved a professional status in Germany in 1406.

Aseptic theories of wound treatment were advocated by Hugh of Lucca and his student Theodoric in 13th-century Italy and by Henri de Mondeville in France. In his *Chirurgia Magna* (1363), Guy de Chauliac cited more than 3,000 former experts and began the elevation of surgery to a learned art. The introduction of gunpowder weapons in the late 15th century led to wounds never contemplated by Galen and to new methods of treatment described by Heinrich von Pfolspeundt, Hieronymus Brunschwig, and Hans von Gersdorff. By the end of the 15th century, Isabella of Castile and Aragon funded camp hospitals and ambulance wagons for her troops and, in the siege of Alora (1484), she sent six furnished hospital tents along with a contingent of physicians and surgeons.

See also Barber-Surgeons; Brunschwig, Hieronymus; Chauliac, Guy de; Crusades; Gersdorff, Hans von; Islamic Military Medicine; Pfolspeundt, Heinrich von; Rhazes (Abu Bakr Mohammed ben Zakariah); Theodoric, Bishop of Cervia (Teodorico Borgognoni)

References
Forest, R. D. 1982. "Development of Wound Therapy from the Dark Ages to the Present." *Journal of the Royal Society of Medicine* 75 (April): 268–273.
MacKinney, Loren. *Early Medieval Medicine with Special Reference to France and Chartres.* Baltimore: Johns Hopkins University Press, 1937.
Mitchell, Piers. *Medicine in the Crusades: Warfare, Wounds and the Medieval Surgeon.* Cambridge: Cambridge University Press, 2004.
Popp, A. J. 1995. "Crossroads at Salerno: Eldridge Campbell and the Writings of Theodorico Borgognoni on Wound Healing." *Journal of Neurosurgery* 83 (July): 174–179.

Melioidosis (Whitmore's Disease)

Melioidosis is a systemic disease caused by *Burkholderia* (formerly *Pseudomonas*) *pseudomallei*, a gram-negative, rod-shaped bacterium endemic in sheep, goats, cattle, horses, pigs, dogs, and cats. Humans contract melioidosis through skin penetration, inhalation, or ingestion, and the disease can cause rash, pneumonia, or sepsis.

Melioidosis is endemic in Southeast Asia, where it is a common soil and water con-

taminant and was frequent in troops stationed in that area. Tetracycline, the usual treatment during the Viet Nam War, has more recently been supplanted by broader spectrum antibiotics.

The Soviet Union experimented with melioidosis as a biological weapon at its Vozrozhodeniye Island facility, where the organism was weaponized in parallel with glanders and anthrax.

See also Chemical and Biological Warfare; Vozrozhdeniye Island

References
Alibek, Ken, with Stephen Handelman. *Biohazard.* London: Arrow Books, 2000.
U.S. Centers for Disease Control and Prevention. "Melioidosis." www.cdc.gov/ncidod/dbmd/diseaseinfo/melioidosis_g.htm (accessed May 8, 2006).

Mesopotamian Military Medicine

Mesopotamia, a name derived from the Greek for "between the rivers," refers to the area between the Tigris and the Euphrates rivers and is encompassed in modern Iraq.

With the other great river valleys along the Tropic of Cancer (the Nile, the Indus, and the Yellow and Yangtze), Mesopotamia shares the distinction of being a cradle of civilization. The area's fertility, especially the valley's ability to produce large amounts of wheat, made concentrations of people possible, and cities appeared between the rivers by 4000 B.C. It was not uncommon for these cities to reach populations of 30,000–35,000 and to spread over as much as 1,800 square miles if one includes the surrounding farms and fields. Concentrated populations brought specialization that had been impossible for nomadic hunter-gatherers. With cities came leaders who could precipitate wars, soldiers who could fight them, and farmers and workers who could generate the wealth that made them worthwhile. The various empires that ruled Mesopotamia lasted almost 5,000 years beginning with the ancient Sumerians, who created the mathematics from which our decimal system is derived, the time divisions still in use, and writing.

In 2750 B.C., Sargon I of Akkad in the northern part of Mesopotamia invaded Sumer and united the entire valley for the first time. Six hundred years later, the Amorites under Hammurabi conquered the valley and, as is often true of conquerors, were absorbed into the Akkadian-Sumerian culture. Mesopotamia and its capital, Babylon, were conquered by the Assyrians in 1100 B.C. and again in 745 B.C. After the latter conquest, the Assyrians stayed and built a second capital city at Nineveh. The Medes and Persians under Cyrus displaced the Assyrians in 539 B.C. and were themselves conquered by Alexander the Great in 331 B.C. In spite of repeated, albeit infrequent, conquests, the Mesopotamian civilization remained remarkably coherent with the conquerors generally being absorbed into the local culture rather than replacing it.

The Mesopotamians were, for most of their ascendancy, aggressively militaristic. Early on, the various city-states in the valley fought constantly among themselves. After the valley united, the various governments directed their energies against their neighbors. The oldest known fortified city, Uruck, was built in 2900 B.C., and battering rams and siege towers to destroy city walls soon followed.

Sumerians erected the Stele of Vultures, the world's oldest known military monument, in 2525 B.C. The great stone shows a king in his chariot (the oldest known mili-

This Sumerian tablet inscribed with cuneiform writing from around 2300 B.C. is the world's oldest-known medical manual. A translation of a portion of the right column reads: "White pear tree, the flower of the 'moon' plant, grind into a powder, dissolve in beer, let the man drink." (Bettmann/Corbis)

tary use of the wheel) leading troops in phalanx formation wearing helmets and body armor and carrying metal-tipped weapons. Within 500 years, Sumerians had added the compound bow to their armamentarium.

In some areas, the Sumerians were accomplished empirical scientists. They understood the relation between poor sanitation and disease and built sophisticated water supply and sewer systems. They knew a surprising amount about parasites and insects and their relation to disease. Sumerian priests had specific prayers against mosquitoes, and the fly was the symbol of Nergal, the god of death.

Only two incomplete clay tablets survive that deal directly with Sumerian medicine, although these writings, which date to 2300 B.C., are the oldest known medical documents. The tablets deal almost exclusively with prescriptions and herbal remedies, but it is possible to infer a good deal about Sumerian medicine from later tablets as the transfer of knowledge in Mesopotamia seems to have been smooth and well maintained from century to century. The eight-foot-tall black stone inscribed with the Code of Hammurabi includes, in laws 215–233, several statutes dealing with fees and with penalties for malpractice but little else of medical interest. However, Assurbanipal (668–626 B.C.), the last of the great Assyrian kings, was a compulsive book collector. When his library at Nineveh was destroyed, some 30,000 clay tablets, including 800 that deal specifically with medicine, were buried in a trench, from which they were unearthed in 1853. Most are prescriptions, but 40 tablets comprise the *Treatise of Medical Diagnosis and Prognosis* and form the backbone of what we know about Mesopotamian medicine.

Sumerian medical practitioners were, like their Egyptian counterparts, divided into priests and sorcerers (the *ashipu*) and empirical practitioners (the *asu*). The *asu* were technicians rather than magicians and were of the educated middle class. In 2400 B.C. they were formally separated from the priests and placed under the secular government. This separation, besides improving their level of practice, made the *asu* available to the king and to his armies as military surgeons. A plaintive letter from a field commander lamenting his lack of masons to build walls and physicians to treat his soldiers implies that medical care was a routine and necessary part of Mesopotamian military service.

Mesopotamian medicine recognized three ways of healing: incantations and prayers by the *ashipu*; drugs, most of which were botanicals; and a limited repertoire of surgical procedures. No text survives that deals specifically with military medicine, so we are forced to guess about the treatment of war wounds and diseases based on what we can glean from knowledge of Mesopotamian medicine in general. The *asu* recognized fever and local heat and swelling as the general and local signs of inflammation and, unlike the Greeks and all other practitioners to modern times, had no illusions about pus being a laudable development. They used metal tubes to drain pus and incised abscesses and other wounds with tempered brass knives identical to those used by barbers for shaving. Wounds were treated in three phases: washing, application of poultices, and bandaging. The washes were most often a mixture of beer and hot water, although with an alcohol concentration too low to be antiseptic. Unlike the Egyptians, Mesopotamians seem never to have learned to suture wounds or splint fractures.

Although the various Mesopotamian civilizations lasted for millennia, their medical skill seems to have increased little over time, and, even though they fought almost constantly, we have only scant indirect evidence of how they cared for their armies.

See also Débridement; Egyptian Military Medicine; Prehistoric Military Medicine; Scalpel

References
Garrison, Fielding. *Notes on the History of Military Medicine.* Washington, D.C.: Association of Military Surgeons, 1922.
Majno, Guido. *The Healing Hand: Man and Wound in the Ancient World.* Cambridge, MA: Harvard University Press, 1975.

Oppenheim, A. Leo. 1962. "Mesopotamian Medicine." *Bulletin of the History of Medicine* 36 (March–April): 97–107.

Mexican-American War

Except for brief expeditions into Canada during the American Revolution and the War of 1812, the Mexican-American War represents the first time the U.S. Army and its medical corps had ventured outside the United States.

From the point of view of improvement in military medicine, the Mexican-American War was nearly a complete failure. Of 78,718 who served in the U.S. Army, 13,283 died, but only 1,733 of those succumbed to battle-related wounds. The rest died of disease, primarily dysentery augmented by malaria and yellow fever. A total of 4,152 men suffered nonfatal wounds.

The Army medical corps entered the war abysmally underprepared with only one surgeon general, 20 surgeons, and 50 assistant surgeons, to which were later added two more surgeons, 12 assistants, and 48 volunteer medical officers. There were no cooks, nurses, or stewards; these jobs were later filled primarily by men recovering from dysentery and still quite capable of spreading the disease to those for whom they cooked and cared.

The Army established a general hospital at Corpus Christi in the weeks leading up to the war and a second at Veracruz after the landing there. Additional facilities were set up on the road between Veracruz and Mexico City, but they all lacked even the most basic supplies. The U.S. Army went to Mexico with no ambulance service, no hospital tents or shelters, and no hospital equipment. The soldiers came with only a single suit of clothes and one pair of boots, and Maj. Gen. Winfield Scott complained that almost one-fifth of his men who were fit for duty were occupied sewing pants and making shoes.

Scott felt compelled to leave Veracruz for Mexico City on April 7, 1846, before he was fully prepared to get his men away from the low-lying coast before the onset of yellow fever season, but he did not capture the capital until September 14, by which time more than a third of his force was too ill to fight. The disease rate in Mexico was 110 per 1,000 soldiers, as compared with 65 per 1,000 in the Civil War and only 16 per 1,000 in World War I.

Military surgery saw little in the way of advancement during the Mexican-American War. Ether anesthesia was tried but generally dismissed as deleterious to wound healing and poisonous to the blood. Army surgeons were aware of débridement of wounds but chose not to use it. The one advantage for military surgeons, although of little use to the men for whom they cared, was that they were finally accorded formal rank in the regular army.

See also Anesthesiology; Dysentery; Malaria; Yellow Fever

References

Aldrete, J. A., G. M. Marron, and A. J. Wright. 1984. "The First Administration of Anesthesia in Military Surgery: On Occasion of the Mexican-American War." *Anesthesiology* 61 (November): 585–588.

Ashburn, P. M. *A History of the Medical Department of the United States Army.* Boston: Houghton Mifflin Co., 1929.

Gillet, Mary. *The Army Medical Department, 1818–1865.* Washington, D.C.: Center of Military History, 1987.

Packard, Francis R. *History of Medicine in the United States.* New York: Paul B. Hoeber, 1931.

Porter, John B. 1852. "Medical and Surgical Notes of Campaigns in the War with Mexico." *American Journal of Medical Science* 23: 33.

War Casualty Lists and Statistics: http://www .history.navy.mil/library/online/american %20war%20casualty.htm#t1 (accessed October 19, 2007).

Military Sanitation

Military sanitation is the application of hygiene to individual environments in an attempt to decrease the incidence of disease.

Although British admiral Lord Nelson warned a superior in the very early years of the 19th century that it was easier for a ship's captain to keep his men healthy than for a physician to cure them, it was not until the end of that century that scientific sanitation was generally accepted as a keystone of military success. The years between Lord Joseph Lister's 1866 application of Louis Pasteur's bacteriologic discoveries to clinical medicine and Sir Alexander Fleming's 1928 discovery of penicillin were the highwater mark of clinical sanitation.

Infectious disease can be managed by four basic techniques. Quarantine is the oldest of these, but it is antithetical to the needs of a military campaign. Vaccination is effective, but, in the years between Lister and Fleming, the only effective vaccines were those against smallpox and typhoid fever. Prior to Prontosil, sulfa drugs, and penicillin—all products of the 20th century—direct treatment of infectious disease was limited to a few biologicals like quinine and the Chinese antimalarial artemisinin. That left manipulation of the environment as the only effective way to apply bacteriology to disease prevention.

Military sanitation aims to prevent disease by decreasing individual susceptibility—principally by picking healthier people to be soldiers and providing them with an adequate diet, protection against the elements, and physical training—and by decreasing exposure to potentially harmful microorganisms. The second addresses issues of clean water, clean food, clean bodies, and waste disposal.

The general categories of infectious diseases promoted by crowding or difficult living conditions are, not coincidentally, those that have historically plagued armies and navies. The enteric illnesses such as dysentery, cholera, and typhoid fever are usually transmitted by ingestion of food or water contaminated with the feces of an infected individual. Since a 1,000-man battalion produces more than 600 pounds of feces a day that must be either burned or buried and that must be kept out of contact with water used for drinking or cooking, a large army—particularly a stationary one—is faced with an immense logistical problem.

Plague and typhus are transmitted by vermin that bite an infected individual and then an uninfected one. Because infected fleas lay their eggs in the seams of unwashed clothing, typhus is particularly fostered by the poor hygiene necessitated by battle conditions, of which World War I trench warfare was perhaps the worst example. Between 1880 and 1910, almost five times as many British soldiers died of disease—predominantly typhus and dysentery—as were killed in battle.

By the late 19th century, partially for reasons of comfort, but mostly for reasons of sanitation, cotton had replaced wool in the German and British armies. The French, chauvinistically fond of their red and horizon blue wools, were slower to change. With that exception, khaki uniforms had come into vogue in the Spanish-American War and were in general use by the Boer War. The cotton could be washed repeatedly and, on the World War I Western Front, both armies regularly brought men out of the trenches for delousing showers and to have their uniforms steam sterilized.

Robert Koch isolated the bacterium responsible for cholera in 1884, 30 years too late to save the 10,000 British and French troops who had died of the disease in the Crimean War. In 1872, the death rate from cholera in the British Army had been 5 per 1,000 men serving. By 1905, as a result of rigorous sanitation, that rate had dropped to 0.5 per 1,000. A combination of relocating and covering latrines and keeping them well separated from food preparation areas and an effective vaccine virtually eliminated typhoid fever from the British, French, and German armies by early 1915.

Although infections—especially malaria and venereal disease—occasionally plague armies fighting in remote equatorial parts of the planet, effective treatments, vaccines, and general acceptance of sanitary principles have markedly reduced the danger from infectious diseases. That situation may change if new pathogenic microorganisms or drug-resistant organisms emerge, if vaccine and drug supplies are depleted, or if microbes are weaponized.

See also Antisepsis; Boer War; Cholera; Fleming, Sir Alexander; Lister, Lord Joseph; Pasteur, Louis; Penicillin; Quinine; Spanish-American War; Sulfonamides; Typhoid Fever; Typhus; World War I Medicine

References
Ashburn, P. M. *The Elements of Military Hygiene.* Boston: Houghton Mifflin Co., 1909.
Lelean, P. S. *Sanitation in War.* Philadelphia: P. Blakiston's Son & Co., n.d.

Minoan and Ancient Greek Military Medicine

The origins of Greek culture can be traced to 2500 B.C. when the Pelasgian inhabitants of the Greek peninsula adopted the Minoan civilization that had emerged on the Mediterranean island of Crete.

The Minoans had developed a cultural complexity on a par with that of the Indians by 3000 B.C., exemplified by the bizarre labyrinthine palace at Knossos, a structure that showed a remarkable concern for and knowledge of sanitation. The terra-cotta pipes carrying fresh water in and sewage out of the palace's living quarters were designed with a level of sophistication that made outhouses and chamber pots still common in Europe 4,000 years later appear primitive.

Around 2000 B.C., Aryan Doric invaders from the north moved into Greece and intermarried with the Mediterranean residents. The Homeric war epics of around 1200 B.C., in which the Achaeans under Agamemnon besieged Troy, may reflect that original clash. Homer's epics, together with a smattering of archaeological evidence and references from later Greek history and literature, are our only sources of knowledge about military medicine in this era.

Judging from those epics, it is evident that medicine at the time was a jumble of magic, religion, observation, and empiricism. When the Greek army at Troy suffered an epidemic of diarrhea that decimated both men and livestock, it was assumed to be a manifestation of Apollo's wrath and was managed with chants and prayers with no attention whatever to sanitation. Drugs in ancient Greece were most often herbs and potions and were, with few exceptions, worthless. Wine was occasionally used as an antiseptic, and, although Homer does not mention opium, the Egyptians bought the substance from the Greeks so it is likely that they used it as well. Greek models and jewelry contain accurate representations of the poppy capsule from which the drug-containing sap is extracted, and it is reasonable to assume they were aware of its analgesic properties. Indeed, a statue of a Minoan goddess dating to around 1300 B.C. was found in a secret chamber in Knossos wearing poppy capsules in her hair and a distant stare suggestive of pharmacologic bliss.

Chemicals may have been used for harm as well as solace. In the *Odyssey*, Homer's hero goes in search of arrow poison; in fact, the word "toxic" derives from *tóxon*, or bow. Poisoning was so common that wound suckers charged with using their mouths to draw out those toxins were a frequent part of the Achaean army.

Ancient Greek surgery comprised almost entirely the treatment of war wounds. With that in mind, Hippocrates advised that anyone who would learn surgery should find himself an army and follow it. Just as in Hindu, the ancient Ionian word for "doctor" (ἰατρός) means "extractor of arrows." Wounds were cared for not only by physicians but also by warrior chieftains such as Patroclus and Achilles. The military leaders Machaon and Podalirius were said to be Aesculapius's sons and to have learned medicine from their father. Besides being the first physicians mentioned in connection with a Greek army, they each captained 30 ships, making them both the earliest Greek military and naval surgeons.

A bit can be inferred about ancient Greek military medicine from the catalogue of wounds mentioned in the *Iliad*. The epic describes 147 wounds: 106 by spear with 80 percent mortality; 17 by sword with 100 per-

cent mortality; 12 by arrow with 42 percent mortality; and 12 by sling stones with 67 percent mortality. The overall mortality rate from wounds was 77.6 percent with 31 head injuries, 13 neck injuries, 67 chest injuries, and 21 extremity injuries. The dominance of chest injuries no doubt reflects the fact that there was no effective treatment for wounds of the lungs, heart, or great vessels combined with the fact that the trunk affords a prominent target and body armor was only partially effective. The relatively low overall number of wounds was characteristic of phalanx warfare, which was less lethal than later forms of battle. In general, only the first two rows of the phalanx actually fought while the rest, protected by their comrades in front, served mainly as pushers. In addition, the close quarters limited the range of arm movement and impaired use of both stabbing weapons and projectiles.

A brief passage from the *Iliad* in which a warrior treats a fellow soldier's arrow wound gives a good deal of information about Homeric wound management:

> Patroclus cut the forky steel away
> While in his hand a bitter root he pressed
> The wound he washed and styptic juice infused
> The closing flesh that instant ceased to glow
> The wound to torture, and the blood to flow.

First we have extraction of the barbed arrowhead. These projectiles were made of iron or bronze, had two or three barbs, and their removal posed a formidable surgical challenge. Because ancient Greeks had no instrument for arrow extraction, they either had to enlarge the wound or push the projectile all the way through the body to be pulled out from the other side. The wound was washed—probably with wine—and dressed with an herbal mixture the contents of which are lost to us. Wine has been shown to be a modestly effective antiseptic both from its alcohol content and from esters left by fermentation of grapes and their skins. If styptic herbs and dressings failed to stop bleeding, ancient Greek physicians fell back on chants and prayers. They had no knowledge of ligating vessels, and hemorrhage was probably the most common cause of death from battlefield injury.

Soldiers invading Troy who suffered severe wounds were left to die on the field, while those amenable to treatment were carried by their companions to *klisiai*—timbered, thatched huts built on the beach in the shadow of their black ships. There the wounded were given an analgesic draught of wine and herbs while their wounds were cleaned and dressed. Anticipating Florence Nightingale by three millennia, treatment in the *klisiai* was provided not just by other soldiers but also by women (said by the poet to be unvaryingly beautiful) brought to Asia Minor for that purpose.

Good evidence exists that Greek medicine after the seventh century B.C. was influenced by that of Egypt. The first contacts between Greeks and Egyptians appear to have been between 663 and 609 B.C., when 26th Dynasty pharaoh Psammetichos I hired Greek mercenaries to fight in his wars against invading Assyrians. Pythagoras, author of the oldest known Greek medical texts, was said to have been trained by the Egyptian Unnefer in Heliopolis a generation later.

In the pre-classical period, medicine other than the treatment of wounds remained mostly magic; empiricism off the battlefield would have to await the birth of Greek observational science with Thales of Miletus (639–544 B.C.). Ancient Greek military surgeons, however, laid the first stones of the foundation of scientific surgery in the West.

See also Aesculapius; Anesthesiology; Antisepsis; Classical Greek Military Medicine; Field Hospitals; Forceps and Extractors; Hemostasis; Military Sanitation

References

Majno, Guido. *The Healing Hand: Man and Wound in the Ancient World.* Cambridge, MA: Harvard University Press, 1975.

Saunders, J. B. de C. M. *The Transitions from Ancient Egyptian to Greek Medicine.* Lawrence: University of Kansas Press, 1963.

Sigerist, Henry. *A History of Medicine: Early Greek, Hindu, and Persian Medicine.* New York: Oxford University Press, 1961.

Mitchell, Silas Weir (1829–1914)

Silas Mitchell was the foremost practitioner of both clinical and experimental neurology during the American Civil War.

Mitchell was born February 15, 1829, in Philadelphia, the son of a well-to-do physician and professor at the Jefferson Medical College, from which Mitchell himself graduated in 1850. He went on to study with Claude Bernard in Paris before returning to Philadelphia and entering private practice. While in practice he became friends with William Hammond, who later became surgeon general of the Union Army, and the two coauthored several papers.

Mitchell enlisted in the U.S. Army in October 1862 as a contract surgeon and was assigned to the hospital at the old Armory building at 16th and Fulton streets in Philadelphia where he began his studies of nerve injury. On May 5, 1863, Hammond ordered the establishment of the U.S. Army Hospital for Diseases of the Nervous

System at Christian Street, also in Philadelphia. That facility was overwhelmed with casualties from the Battle of Gettysburg and moved to a larger building at Turner Lane, where Mitchell joined with George R. Morehouse and William Williams Keen in directing what had become America's first large hospital devoted to injuries of the nervous system. The three collaborated on the groundbreaking *Gunshot Wounds and Other Injuries of Nerves* (1864), which Mitchell expanded to *Injuries of Nerves*, published in 1872. That volume became a standard that, in its English and French versions, remained in use through World War I. Mitchell also wrote *Reflex Paralysis* (1864), in which he coined the term "causalgia" (intractable pain and skin changes caused by partial nerve injury) and described shock caused by the brain's reaction to bodily injury.

After the war Mitchell became America's foremost clinical neurologist. He was elected the first president of the American Neurological Association by acclamation but declined to serve. He published 19 novels after the age of 50 and gained as much fame among his contemporaries for his literary ability as for his medical skills, although the latter has withstood the test of time while the former did not. He also published a controversial biography of George Washington, seven books of poetry, and a number of professional books and articles.

Mitchell died January 4, 1914.

See also Civil War in the United States;
    Hammond, William; Keen, William Williams

References

Burr, A. R. *Weir Mitchell, His Life and Letters.* New York: Duffield and Co., 1929.
Earnest, E. S. *Weir Mitchell, Novelist and Physician.* Philadelphia: University of Pennsylvania Press, 1950.
Walter, R. D. S. *Weir Mitchell, M.D., Neurologist.* Springfield, IL: Charles C. Thomas, 1970.

Mobile Army Surgical Hospitals in the Korean Conflict

Mobile army surgical hospitals (M.A.S.H. units) are fully equipped mobile hospitals complete with tentage, supplies, and personnel with portability that allows them to accompany military units in either advance or retreat.

Semi-mobile medical units that could be placed close to the front and still function as surgical hospitals had been pioneered by the British in World War I as casualty clearing stations. The American Expeditionary Force in World War I had adopted the model, and Gen. Douglas MacArthur deployed mobile surgical units in the Pacific during World War II, although with limited success. Between 1948 and 1949, five M.A.S.H. units were created, although none were based in the Pacific.

When the Korean Conflict broke out, the necessity for such units was evident, and three M.A.S.H. units were activated—the 8055th on July 1, 1950, the 8063rd on July 17, and the 8076th on July 19. The 8055th left Sasebo for Pusan on July 6 and proceeded by train directly to Taejon. The 8063rd left July 18 for Pohang-dong to support the 1st Cavalry. The 8076th arrived in Pusan July 25 and moved up the Taejon-Taegu corridor to support the Eighth Army. All three would later follow their combat units after the breakout and invasion of North Korea.

In 1951 the 8225th M.A.S.H. unit was deployed, and an additional unit was organized by the Norwegians and sent to Ujongbu the same year. Two additional M.A.S.H. units, one of which (the 8209th) specialized in caring for neurosurgical cases, were deployed in 1952.

The M.A.S.H. was initially intended to be a 60-bed unit to provide triage and early stabilization prior to transfer to an evacuation

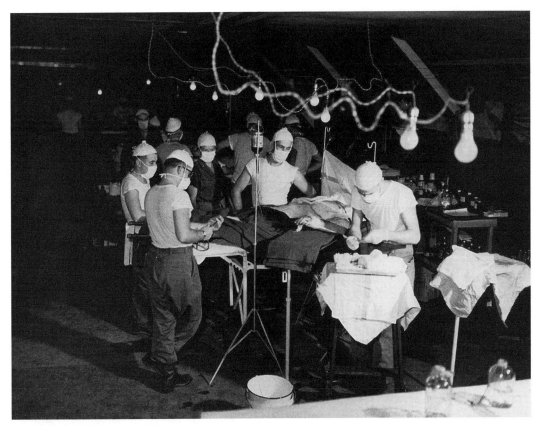

Surgeons at the 8209th Mobile Army Surgical Hospital (M.A.S.H.) perform an operation on a wounded soldier during the Korean Conflict, 1952. (National Archives)

hospital farther from the front. Each was to have a headquarters detachment, a preoperative and shock treatment area, an operating section, a postoperative area, a pharmacy, an X-ray section, and a holding ward. It was to be staffed by 14 medical officers, 12 nurses, two Medical Service Corps officers, one warrant officer, and 97 enlisted men. One of the medical officers was assigned as commander, and there were two anesthesiologists, one internist, four general medical officers, and five surgeons. The number of beds, mission, and staffing never exactly fit that plan. Because of the excess of wounded over treaters—especially in the early part of the war—the M.A.S.H. units actually served as small evac-

uation hospitals. At one point, just the holding area of the 8076th had 200 beds.

The chain of evacuation had the M.A.S.H. units receiving patients (usually by rail or helicopter) from aid or collecting stations. After initial treatment, the wounded requiring additional care were transferred to either the evacuation hospitals at Pusan or directly to one of the Far East Command's facilities in Japan.

Early in the war, there was a severe shortage of personnel to staff the M.A.S.H. units. The residency programs in the Army hospital system were tapped to provide partially trained specialists on temporary duty. These young physicians and dentists were often asked to perform jobs for which they had little or no training; it was not uncommon for dentists to give anesthesia, psychiatric residents to perform surgery, or radiologists to set fractures.

The combination of inadequate training and high patient volume led to less than fastidious surgical technique. Open wounds were often cleaned but not closed, leaving the definitive surgery to hospitals farther down the chain. A typical abdominal operation involved making a large incision for control of any obvious bleeding. Then the gut was examined for visible perforations, which were clamped and repaired. The abdominal cavity was then rinsed to clean out loose food and parasites (including worms up to a foot long). The viscera were then replaced and the skin closed with the expectation that further surgery would be necessary to manage unaddressed details.

The doctor shortage was eased by the draft of 1950, but a new set of problems arose. Ninety percent of the military physicians who ultimately served in Korea were drafted, and many had previously served in World War II as enlisted men. They had only recently completed their medical training and begun busy civilian practices, and they had little enthusiasm for their new predicament and little inclination to cooperate with military rules and discipline. Disciplinary and morale challenges worsened as the war progressed and the lines stabilized. The M.A.S.H. units evolved into fixed hospitals relatively remote from the front lines staffed with female nurses and with access to a variety of recreational facilities and temptations.

Although quirky and often confused, the pattern of care—early stabilization followed by more orderly completion of care in specialized facilities—that began in Korea's M.A.S.H. units joined the helicopter transport model (also developed in Korea) to form the template for the shock-trauma services now present in virtually every large city in the United States.

See also Aeromedical Evacuation; Casualty Clearing Stations and Staged Evacuation; Field Hospitals

References
Cleaver, Frederick. *U.S. Army Battle Casualties in Korea.* Chevy Chase, MD: Operations Research Office, 1956.
Cowdrey, Albert E. *United States Army in the Korean War: The Medic's War.* Washington, D.C.: Center of Military History, 1987.
Reister, Frank. *Battle Casualties and Medical Statistics: U.S. Army Experience in the Korean War.* Washington, D.C.: Office of the Surgeon General, 1973.

Mondeville, Henri de (1260–1320)

A cleric and physician, Henri de Mondeville joined Lanfranc of Milan to found the medieval French school of surgery.

De Mondeville was born in Normandy and studied at Montpellier and Paris. He was trained by Theodoric before returning first to Montpellier and then to Paris, where he taught surgery and anatomy. De Mondeville served as personal physician to two French kings (Philip the Fair and Louis X), both of whom he accompanied into battle. That experience led to his being the first to describe treating battle injuries in soldiers wounded while wearing armor.

De Mondeville's copiously illustrated *Chirurgie* was written between 1306 and 1320 but remained an unpublished manuscript until copies were independently discovered in Berlin, Erfurt, and Paris in the late 19th century. The manuscript, which draws heavily on Avicenna, Theodoric, and Lanfranc, was never completed and was never as influential as Guy de Chauliac's surgical treatise. De Mondeville emphasized anatomy as the basis for surgery. Among his technical innovations were trephines modeled on carpenters' drill featuring a complicated two-part bit that was meant to first perforate the skull and then elevate depressed bone fragments. He favored primary closure of clean wounds only and recommended packing contaminated wounds open with cloth and salves until infection had time to subside. This was much the same as the practice that finally became general in World War I. Like Theodoric, de Mondeville argued that suppuration was not necessary to healing, an attitude that, although correct, won him the enmity and criticism of his surgical contemporaries.

De Mondeville suffered from both asthma and tuberculosis, a combination that took his life before he could complete his magnum opus.

See also Lanfranc of Milan; Medieval Military Medicine; Salicetti, Guglielmo (William of Salicet); Theodoric, Bishop of Cervia (Teodorico Borgognoni)

References
Cohen, S. G. 1995. "Henri de Mondeville (1260–1320): French Pioneer Surgeon." *Allergy Proceedings* 16 (July–August): 216–217.
Zimmerman, Leo, and Ilza Veith. *Great Ideas in the History of Surgery*. Baltimore: Williams & Wilkins Co., 1961.

Monro, Alexander primus
(1697–1767)

Alexander Monro was a military surgeon and founder of the Edinburgh school of anatomy.

Alexander's father, John Monro, was an army surgeon who started the medical school at Edinburgh with the specific intention of creating an institution where he could train his son. Although Alexander began his education in Edinburgh, he went on to study in London, Paris, and in the Tuscan city of Livorno. In the course of his travels, he studied with William Cheselden and Hermann Boerhaave, both of whom became his close friends. Monro returned to Edinburgh in 1719, was certified by the city's surgeons' guild, and was named professor of anatomy at his father's medical school in 1720. He went on to train his son and grandson (known respectively as Alexander Monro secundus and tertius) and a second son, Donald. Between them, the first two Alexanders taught anatomy to more than 12,800 students and made their city an international center of medical and surgical education.

Monro lectured in the Edinburgh Hall of Surgeons from 1719 to 1725, when he was threatened by public riots against the practice of stealing fresh bodies from either the gibbet or the grave. Although politically a supporter of the Hanoverian kings, Monro treated wounded from both sides after the 1745 Battle of Prestonpans.

See also British Military Medicine

Reference
Comrie, John. *History of Scottish Medicine.* London: Baillière, Tindall & Cox, 1932.

Monro, Donald
(1727–1802)

Donald Monro was physician general to the British Army and author of books on military hygiene.

Donald was the son of Alexander Monro primus and brother of Alexander Monro secundus. He received his doctorate from the University of Edinburgh in 1753. His thesis, "An Essay on the Dropsy and its Different Species," included the first documented suggestion that systemic fluid accumulation could be caused by cardiac valvular disease.

Monro went to London after completing his education and was named to the Royal College of Physicians in 1756. He then became physician to St. George's Hospital, a position he held until his death. He was commissioned physician to the British military hospital in Germany in 1760 during the Seven Years War and was promoted to physician general before returning home in 1763. He returned to active duty in 1778 during the American Revolution but remained in England, where he was a colleague and neighbor of John Hunter.

Monro wrote *An Account of the Diseases which were most Frequent in the British Military Hospitals in Germany from January 1761 till the return of the Troops to England in March 1763: to which is added An Essay on the Means of Preserving the Health of Soldiers and Conducting Military Hospitals* in 1764 and *Observations on the Means of Preserving the Health of Soldiers and of Conducting Military Hospitals; on the Diseases Incident to Soldiers in the time of Service and of the Same Diseases as they have Appeared in London* in 1780. Both were standards of military medical practice in the latter half of the 18th century.

See also British Military Medicine; Monro, Alexander primus

References

Comrie, John. *History of Scottish Medicine.* London: Baillière, Tindall & Cox, 1932.
Wright–St. Clair, R. E. 1971. "Donald Monro." *Medical History* 15 (January): 95–96.

Moore, Samuel Preston (1813–1889)

Samuel Moore was surgeon general of the Confederate Army.

Moore was born in South Carolina and was a descendant of Mordecai Moore, who had come to Maryland as Lord Baltimore's personal physician. He received his medical degree from the Medical College of South Carolina in 1834, and entered the U.S. Army as an assistant surgeon the following year. Over the next 17 years, he served at a variety of posts including West Point and fought in the Mexican-American War, reaching the rank of major.

When South Carolina seceded, Moore resigned his commission and moved to Arkansas with the intention of entering private practice, but President Jefferson Davis, with whom he had served in Mexico, prevailed upon him to become the Confederacy's surgeon general in June 1861. He went on to hold that position for the remainder of the war.

From the beginning, Moore established a system of professional standards and educational requirements that defined the Confederate medical corps. When the Union blockade made it nearly impossible for the South to get drugs, Moore promoted Francis Peyre Porcher's *Resources of the Southern Fields and Forests: Medical, Economical, and Agricultural* and encouraged his surgeons to replace the missing medicines with locally gathered botanicals. He introduced the well-ventilated, single-story pavilion hospital that was later adopted by the Union and became the model for postwar facilities. He organized and was president of the Association of Army and Navy Surgeons of the Confederate States, supervised publication of the *Confederate States Medical and Surgical Journal*, and prepared and published *A Manual for Military Surgery*, the standard reference for Southern military surgeons.

After the war, Moore retired to Richmond but never resumed the practice of medicine. He participated in education and politics and was elected president of the Association of Medical Officers of the Confederate States and vice president of the Section of Military and Naval Surgery at the Ninth International Medical Congress. He died at home on May 31, 1889.

See also Civil War in the United States

References

Pilcher, James Evelyn. "Samuel Preston Moore." In Howard A. Kelly and Walter L. Burrage, *Dictionary of American Medical Biography.* Boston: Milford House, 1928.

Rutkow, Ira. "Samuel Preston Moore." In *A Manual of Military Surgery Prepared for the Use of the Confederate States Army.* San Francisco: Norman Publishing, 1989.

Morgan, John
(1735–1789)

John Morgan was founder of the first American medical school and second director of the American army medical service.

Morgan was born in Philadelphia in 1735, the son of a Quaker Welsh immigrant. He was educated with Benjamin Rush and William Shippen, Jr., at the Academy of Nottingham and apprenticed as an apothecary.

Morgan spent the first four years of the French and Indian War as a regimental surgeon. In 1760 he went to London, where he studied anatomy with John and William Hunter before taking a medical degree at the University of Edinburgh in 1763. He then studied in Paris and was elected to the Royal Academy of Surgery before returning to Edinburgh, where he was elected to the Royal Society and the Royal College of Physicians.

He returned to America in 1765, founded the medical school at the College of Philadelphia, and became its professor of theory and practice of medicine. In October 1775 he succeeded Benjamin Church as medical director of the Continental Army after the former was dismissed for treason. Morgan introduced a program of examinations for military physicians and attempted to supervise medical care in the American army. His reforms angered the previously independent regimental surgeons and, when his disagreements with Shippen and Dr. Samuel Stringer of the Northern Department became public, Congress instituted a formal investigation which culminated in the dismissal of both Stringer and Morgan in January 1777. Morgan published a strident pamphlet defending his role and condemning Shippen, and, although Congress ultimately exonerated him, he remained bitter and retired from public life.

Morgan's unhappiness was made worse by the destruction of his valuable library and art collection by the British during the revolution. He remained on the staff of Pennsylvania Hospital until 1783. After that, he retired from the practice of medicine and died childless and alone on October 15, 1789.

See also American Revolutionary War; Church, Benjamin; Hunter, John; Rush, Benjamin; Shippen, William, Jr.

References

Ashburn, P. M. *A History of the Medical Department of the United States Army.* Boston: Houghton Mifflin Co., 1929.

Gillet, Mary. *The Army Medical Department, 1775–1818.* Washington, D.C.: Center of Military History, 1981.

Packard, Francis. *History of Medicine in the United States.* New York: Paul B. Hoeber, Inc., 1931.

Reiss, Oscar. *Medicine and the American Revolution: How Diseases and Their Treatments Affected the Colonial Army.* Jefferson, NC: McFarland & Co., Inc., 1998.

Morphine

Morphine is an alkaloid and is the chief active ingredient in opium. It is extracted from immature seed capsules of the *Papaver somniferum* plant.

The opium poppy is native to southeastern Europe and western Asia but is currently cultivated in Europe, India, Canada, South and Central America, and much of central Asia. Heroin, codeine, meperidine (Demerol), oxycodone, and fentanyl are all semi-synthetic derivatives of morphine. Morphine's pain-relieving properties were known to the Sumerians as early as 4000 B.C. and to the Egyptians two millennia later. In his 1517 *Fieldbook of Wound Surgery*, Hans von Gersdorff described performing battlefield amputations after having the patient inhale from a "sleeping sponge" soaked in opium, mandrake root, henbane, hemlock, and lettuce. By the late seventeenth century, a typical military surgeon's field chest contained his instruments; a variety of folk remedies such as sandalwood, dog fat, and mummy dust; and a handful of useful drugs such as aloe and, especially, opium.

Rosengarten and Company of Philadelphia (the predecessor to modern pharmaceutical company Merck, Sharpe and Dohme) began manufacturing morphine salts in 1832, and, by the beginning of the American Civil War in 1861, a variety of opioid preparations were available, including Laudanum (tincture of opium), paregoric (tincture of camphorated opium), powdered opium (which contained 9–12 percent morphine), opium gum, Dover's powders (10 percent opium and 10 percent ipecac), and an assortment of narcotic-containing patent medicines and elixirs.

Medicinal use of morphine underwent a dramatic change during the Civil War with the introduction of the hypodermic syringe. Injected morphine proved such an effective pain reliever that it went from prescribed use in field and general hospitals to self-administration by soldiers with chronic pain who were supplied with both the drug and syringes for self-administration. Paregoric was also routinely used to manage diarrhea from the ubiquitous dysentery, and various morphine powders were standard therapy for malarial fevers.

During World War I, the U.S. Army had the Mulford Company of Baltimore devise "hypo units" containing morphine that a soldier could administer to himself with one hand, and several hundred thousand of the syringes were produced. In 1938, the Army and the Navy asked Squibb to improve on the Mulford unit, and, ultimately, 75 million of the improved syrettes were produced during World War II.

See also World War II Medicine

Reference
Albin, Maurice. "'Opium Eaters' and 'Morphinists'—Narcotic Addiction and the Civil War: Did It All Start There?" *Anesthesiology* 2002: A1162.

N

Napoleonic Wars
(1792–1815)

Although 18th-century military medicine was consistent primarily for its ineffectiveness, some administrative and scientific advances, such as Louis XIV's institutionalization of military medicine and the scientific discoveries of James Lind and Edward Jenner, set the stage for later improvements in care of combatants.

Publication of the *Journal de Médicines Militaires*, the first periodical devoted solely to military medicine, and a series of lectures on the subject in Lille, Metz, and Strasbourg helped create a pool of practitioners with at least rudimentary knowledge when hostilities broke out. Given their prolonged engagements, large numbers of combatants, more lethal weapons, and the brutal climatic and geographic conditions, the revolutionary and Napoleonic wars presented a range of entirely new challenges to military surgeons.

The Wars of the Revolution began in 1792 when the French National Convention declared that émigrés massing on French borders placed the republic in danger and declared war on Austria and Prussia (later joined by Great Britain, Holland, Spain, Naples, and several smaller Italian states). The performance of the French medical establishment was inconsistent in the early years. At first, 1,400 physicians and surgeons volunteered to participate in Lazare Carnot's *levée en masse*, and, on August 1, 1793, the Convention put all of France's physicians, surgeons, and apothecaries between the ages of 18 and 40 at the disposal of the minister of war. By 1794, 8,000 of them were in the military.

In 1792, the Convention closed France's 15 medical schools and abolished the Royal Society of Medicine and the Academy of Surgery. In 1794, the schools were replaced by *Écoles de Santé*, institutions notorious for burdening the French Army with poorly qualified, dismally trained, generally incompetent *officiers de santé*. That sad situation persisted until Napoleon (who complained that his surgeons cost him more men than the Russian artillery) restored the medical faculties in 1804.

After 1794, the situation was aggravated when military hospitals, which had previously been commanded by medical officers, were transferred to local administrators and the Committee of Public Safety. Thereafter, the facilities were plagued by inefficiency and corruption, and hospital-based physicians and surgeons abandoned them for regimental positions in the field where they might be less useful but were at least safer from political pressures and were better appreciated.

Muskets, cannonballs, and masses of soldiers collided and the failings of European military medicine became brutally obvious. Gen. Adam Custine's surgeon Dominique-Jean Larrey found himself expected to salvage thousands of men whose limbs had been shattered and shredded by musket and cannonballs. Tradition dictated that the wounded be left in the field until a battle ended before being collected and transported to the rear for dressings and amputation, often after days of agonizing delay. Larrey correctly reasoned that the astronomical mortality from such wounds might be decreased by earlier treatment, so he conceived the brilliant idea of bringing the "hospital" to the battlefield. His flying ambulances (*ambulances volantes*), complete with surgical instruments and supplies, brought treatment in hours instead of days and earned Larrey the adoration of his soldier-patients.

As would be true throughout the Napoleonic Wars, disease was at least as important as injury in determining the outcome of battle. Dysentery may well have been a more important military asset to the Convention than its ill-trained army. Friedrich Wilhelm II brought 42,000 troops against the French, and the Austrians and Prussians would probably have taken Paris had not 30,000 of the invaders been rendered *hors de combat* by epidemic diarrhea and vomiting.

Larrey met the young Napoleon Bonaparte during the 1793 siege of Toulon and accompanied him on the ill-fated Egyptian expedition in 1798. Medical historian Fielding Garrison called sanitation in Napoleon's armies almost the worst in recorded history, and the French troops paid a high price for their shoddy personal habits along the banks of the Nile. They suffered from granular conjunctivitis, dysentery, typhus, and parasitic liver disease; of 30,000 French troops who went to Egypt, 4,157 died of disease. Among the dead were 1,689 who died from bubonic plague outside Jaffa during the attempted escape through Syria.

After his return to France in 1800, Napoleon took steps to reorganize his hapless medical service. The *Service de Santé* comprised physicians, surgeons, and apothecaries outfitted in blue uniforms with facing colors indicative of their degrees, each decorated with swords, but none with an officer's epaulettes. The medical officers were divided into *medicines-chirurgiens-apothécaires major*, *aides-major*, and *sous aides-major* as well as two more junior ranks-in-training. The two senior levels were accorded the courtesy of officers, even though they did not actually have military rank. The *sous-aides* were mostly draftees from medical schools or promoted noncommissioned officers. The medical men were typically armed with carbines and frequently armed and organized their patients and led them into battle. In fact, unlike their British counterparts, who tended to stay as far behind the lines as possible, French physicians regularly served as combatants and suffered a consequently high casualty rate.

Early in the wars, French hospital attendants were primarily contract employees. For the most part, they were indolent, unwashed, and notoriously willing to steal from both the government and their patients. In 1808, Pierre Percy reorganized the hospital service into soldier-attendants whom he outfitted in captured Spanish uniforms and charged with collecting the wounded from the battlefield and providing basic nursing care—duties they performed only marginally better than their civilian predecessors.

The situation was, however, not entirely bleak; French military surgeons created a brilliant tiered system of care in which the regimental surgeon set up an aid station similar to Larrey's flying ambulance as near the front as possible and was often able to treat the wounded within hours of injury. Corps headquarters assigned one *division d'ambulance* (note that "ambulance" refers to the unit supplying care as well as the vehicle providing transport) to each infantry and cavalry division, and the former set up a field hospital, usually in a nearby château, church, or other large building to receive the patients from the aid stations. From the field hospital, the most severely wounded could be evacuated by wagon or hospital barge to large receiving hospitals in the French interior. This system of progressive care and evacuation persisted virtually unchanged through World War I.

As the wars progressed, other countries—notably Great Britain and Prussia—improved care for their soldiers and sailors as well. Much of the Prussian improvement came under Johann Görcke, who served as surgeon general from 1797 to 1822. In response to the disastrous care during the 1792–1795 wars, the Pépinière was founded in Berlin in August 1798 specifically to train military surgeons. The school, which changed its name to the Friedrich Wilhelm Institut in 1818, graduated 1,359 medical officers between 1798 and 1821. Görcke opened Prussia's first military field hospital in 1793 and, while surgeon general, standardized evaluation of military surgeons. Although there was

initially a severe shortage of Prussian military hospital beds, the situation improved after the 1807 Battle of Eylau, and, by 1813, Prussia's army had three general hospitals of 1,200 beds each, one 3,000-bed reserve hospital, nine 200-bed field hospitals, and 124 less formal "provisional hospitals" scattered in cities and towns throughout the kingdom. A voluntary nursing service anticipating Florence Nightingale's Crimean War effort was formed under the patronage of Princess Marianne of Prussia.

The Peninsular War (1808–1814) cast a harsh light on the inadequacies of British military medicine. When the British forces first landed in Portugal, their entire stock of medical supplies filled only two wagons. During that campaign, the average sick rate (principally from dysentery, respiratory infections, various fevers, tetanus, and hospital-acquired gangrene) was more than one in five combatants per year, with a mortality rate in the early years of nearly 60 percent. Of 61,511 British soldiers who fought in Spain, 24,930 died of disease while only 8,889 were lost to wounds. The French fared little better; at any given time, one out of four French soldiers was incapacitated due to illness.

Dr. James McGrigor joined Wellington's army in 1812, having just served in the Walcheren expedition in which Britain lost 217 men in battle and 4,175 from disease. McGrigor was determined not to repeat that experience, and, although his incessant demands for supplies and transportation taxed the Duke's patience, he proved remarkably effective. A total of 93,348 sick and wound were hospitalized during McGrigor's first nine months in Spain, but improved sanitation; better housing for the sick and wounded; and new hospitals, including a village of prefabricated structures sufficient to house 4,000 along the River

Duoro, allowed him to reduce the sick list to only 5,000 by the end of the campaign.

Beyond housing, nutrition, and sanitation, Napoleonic-era military physicians had a thin armamentarium with which to fight ubiquitous disease. It had been known since the early 16th century that quinine was effective against malaria, and the drug was liberally used against that and every other fever. Opium was available for pain, and irrigation with antiseptics (although the physicians had no concept of infection) such as wine, brandy, and vinegar gradually replaced cauterization in cleansing wounds. Quicklime was used to clean latrines and hospital trash, including gangrene-infested dressings. When men's jaws clamped shut from tetanus, their front teeth were extracted so they could be fed with a straw. Camphor, gunpowder, and a plethora of herbs found their way into military medicine chests. The botanicals were of little help but were seldom harmful. The same cannot be said for the emetics, purgatives, cupping, scarifying, blistering, and bleeding which were widely inflicted on the sick, the wounded, and the well alike.

Military surgeons, although ignorant of the relation between malaria and mosquitoes, were well aware that the fever was associated with low-lying, moist campsites and exposure to night air—especially in the hours around dusk and dawn when the arthropods are most prone to feed. It was empirically decided to camp at higher elevations, avoid nighttime marches, and keep the men in bed until an hour after sunrise.

Syphilis, which was an especially serious problem in the Egyptian campaign and in Berlin in 1806, was managed by isolating the sufferers in special venereal hospitals. Attempts were made to keep the men away from local women, and those infected were penalized by having their pay stopped and often being forced to pay for their own care.

Typhus was rampant in the French and Russian armies, both of which were justifiably famous for their poor hygiene. The disease was ubiquitous during the 1812 Russian campaign, at the end of which the French were so cold they refused to remove their lice-infested clothes even to defecate. At Tourgeau in 1813–1814, out of a garrison of 24,600, almost 20,000 died of disease, mostly of typhus and dysentery. Napoleon's military surgeons recognized the relation between filth and typhus and, although unable to enforce cleanliness in their own men, took pains to isolate them from Russian prisoners whom they considered even dirtier.

Napoleon did recognize the significance of Edward Jenner's 1798 description of smallpox vaccine and, after 1805, vaccination of French troops remained mandatory until the order was rescinded with the 1815 Bourbon Restoration.

Perhaps the most impressive achievement in early 19th-century military medicine was the Royal Navy's control of shipboard disease; the eradication of scurvy has been called the most important single factor in Napoleon's defeat. That dietary deficiency of vitamin C causes weakness, swelling in the extremities, erosion of the gums, and diffuse hemorrhage from mucous membranes before progressing to pneumonia, heart failure, sepsis, and death. In the Channel Fleet, charged with spending months or years at sea blockading France, the disease was particularly widespread and debilitating. In 1747 naval surgeon James Lind had proven that scurvy could be eradicated with daily doses of lemon juice, but his discovery had not percolated up through the Royal Navy's hierarchy until 1793, when Dr. John

Harness persuaded Admiral Lord Hood to use citrus juice in his blockading fleet. Scurvy disappeared from Hood's ships, and Sir Gilbert Blane repeated the experiment in Admiral Rodney's flagship HMS *Formidable* on the West Indian station. The incidence of scurvy dropped from one man in seven to zero, and, in 1795, Blane convinced First Lord of the Admiralty Lord Spencer to require lemon juice throughout the fleet. The success of that treatment no doubt made it easier for Blane to convince their lordships to require smallpox vaccination as well; that disease too vanished from the fleet.

Lind's device for distillation of seawater eased the need for shore water that was often contaminated and dramatically reduced the incidence of cholera and other dysenteries. He, Blane, and Thomas Trotter instituted shipboard sanitary measures including use of standard-issue uniforms that nearly eliminated typhus. To that time, the disease had been so common in the Navy that it carried the eponym "shipboard fever." Between 1779 and 1794, one Royal Navy man in four was hospitalized for sickness every year. Between 1794 and 1806, that number dropped to one in six, and, between 1806 and 1810, it was one in 16.5.

Although the great advances in scientific medicine and surgery were still several decades in the future, important discoveries in nutrition and communicable disease and compassionate, skillful care of the sick and wounded significantly improved a soldier's or sailor's chance of survival in the opening years of the 19th century.

See also Blane, Sir Gilbert; British Military Medicine; Dysentery; Görcke, Johann; Holtzendorff, Ernst Conrad; Larrey, Baron Dominique-Jean; Lind, James; Malaria; McGrigor, James; Percy, Baron Pierre François; Prussian and German Military Medicine; Russian Military Medicine; Scurvy; Smallpox; Syphilis; Trotter, Thomas; Typhus

References
Elting, John. *Swords around the Throne: Napoleon's Grand Armée*. New York: Free Press, 1988.
Garrison, Fielding. *Notes on the History of Military Medicine*. Washington, D.C.: Association of Military Surgeons, 1922.
Roddis, Louis. *A Short History of Nautical Medicine*. New York: Paul B. Hoeber, Inc., 1941.

National Naval Medical Center

The National Naval Medical Center is a U.S. Navy hospital located on the site of a 247-acre farm in Bethesda, Maryland.

The first American naval facility was established in a rented building adjacent to the Washington Navy Yard during the War of 1812. The hospital was enlarged and moved to the Marine Barracks at 8th and I streets in Washington, D.C., in 1843. During the American Civil War, that facility was not able to accommodate the number of wounded needing care, and the hospital moved to the Government Hospital for the Insane (currently St. Elizabeth's Hospital). In 1866, Congress authorized $115,000 to build a 50-bed facility on Pennsylvania Avenue. In 1906, the hospital was moved to 23rd and E streets, a building that currently houses the Navy's Bureau of Medicine and Surgery. In 1935, a medical school was added and the facility's name was changed to the Naval Medical Center.

When Congress allocated funds for a new hospital in 1938, President Franklin D. Roosevelt personally chose the Bethesda site. Bethesda's bed capacity has been tailored to meet the needs of various conflicts. During World War II, temporary buildings were used to expand the hospital to 2,464 beds. During the Korean Conflict, the hospital had 1,167 permanent beds, and, during the Viet Nam War, 1,122. The new hospital opened in February 1942. The naval medical school has become the Uniformed Services University Medical School.

See also Naval Medicine

Reference

"NNMC History." http://www.bethesda.med
.navy.mil/visitor%5Cpride_of_place%5C
pop_committee%5Chistory.html (accessed
October 20, 2007).

Naval Medicine

Long periods away from land in closely confined quarters and the possibility of violent conflict with powerful weapons make medical care a primary component of naval effectiveness.

Mention of surgeons in association with naval operations dates to the Homeric description of the reputed sons of the god Aeschylus, who accompanied the Greeks on their Trojan expedition. The first reference to naval sanitation is also included in Homer's work in which the Greeks note the advantages of their ships' cleanliness. The Romans were the first to record use of officially designated naval surgeons, and, by the second century A.D., the emperor Hadrian's navy assigned a medical officer to every trireme—about one surgeon for every 200 men, a ratio similar to that still in use. Based on ship names such as *Therapia*, it is likely the Romans also had designated hospital ships.

Little information is available concerning naval medicine in the subsequent millennium. In Europe, only the city-states of Venice and Genoa and military orders such as the Knights of St. John and the Knights of Rhodes maintained formal navies, and, although some of their ships did carry barbers or barber-surgeons, there is no record of an organized system of naval medicine. One signal advance was the introduction of quarantine of arriving vessels which originated in Venice in 1348 in response to the spread of plague from Asia and was adopted throughout the Mediterranean over the next decade.

Nautical medicine changed dramatically in the 15th century when sails replaced oars and the magnetic compass and charts of currents and winds made protracted journeys out of sight of land feasible. Sustaining large numbers of men confined together for weeks at a time required attention to sanitation, ventilation, and diet, while voyages to new parts of the world brought exposure to new diseases for which the ships often proved ideal tools of dissemination. Long voyages exposed men to diseases fostered by small spaces such as typhus, to diseases of close human contact such as tuberculosis and venereal disease, to diseases spread by poor sanitation such as dysentery, and to diseases of dietary deficiency such as scurvy. The ships were also uniquely suited as platforms for large gunpowder weapons, and seagoing surgeons were faced with treating a broad range of wounds in less than ideal conditions.

Along with its unique challenges, naval medicine saw several unique advances, especially among the British seagoing forces. The first official surgeon and surgeon's mate were appointed to the Royal Navy under King Henry VIII in 1512. These men were assisted by ship's boys, or "loblolly boys," responsible for nursing the sick and for cleaning the blood and amputated body parts from the deck during combat surgery and were named for the stew they fed the sick and injured.

Beginning with William Clowes's *A Proved Practice for all Young Chirurgions Concerning Burnings With Gunpowder and Wounds Made With Gunshot*, published in 1581, British naval surgeons regularly contributed to improvement in health and medical care of men serving their countries at sea. James Lind conducted his landmark experiments on scurvy in 1747 while serving as ship's surgeon to HMS *Salisbury*, although his demonstration that citrus juice could prevent scurvy was not incorporated as routine practice until 1795. Ultimately, the success in preventing that disease made it possible for mandatory vaccination against smallpox to be adopted much more quickly (within less than two years after Edward Jenner's 1798 publication) and made the Royal Navy one of the first populations to be freed from the latter disease.

Provision of clean, fresh water was also a major concern, and, in addition to his contribution to smallpox prevention, Lind deserves credit for introducing distillation procedures to the British Navy. Actually, the Phoenicians had tried distillation to convert salt water to fresh water, and the Elizabethan navy had used the process as well, but its usefulness was limited by the fact that it takes about eight men and three hours to distill just a pint of fresh water from seawater. Because a man requires about two quarts of fresh water a day for drinking and cooking (up to a gallon a day in the heat of the tropics) and up to seven-and-a-half gallons a day if fresh water is used for laundry and bathing, distillation was impractical until ships were powered by steam boilers that produced potable water in addition to motive power.

Diet and sanitation remain key concerns for the naval surgeon. A major sanitary advance came in 1800 when British ships replaced gravel, which was virtually impossible to sanitize, with pig iron as ships' ballast. Foul ballast had been a particularly severe sanitary problem in the French and Spanish navies, because the bodies of deceased sailors were typically stored in the rocks to rot during transport home. The British and American navies had avoided that problem with their customary burial at sea. At about the same time, wind scoops connected to canvas duct work were introduced to bring fresh, cool air to previously unventilated spaces below decks.

The British were also in the forefront of treatment of naval combat injuries. The term "sick bay" for the ship's infirmary originated in the Royal Navy practice of treating ill sailors in the forward part of the gun deck. Timber ribs supporting the ship's hull divided the man-of-war's gun deck into sections, or bays, most of which housed one cannon. In the ship's forward areas, where the hull slanted inward, the bays were inappropriate for guns and were reserved for the sick and injured, thus, "sick bays." The areas were chosen both because they were not needed for ordnance and because the sick could be curtained off and separated from the rest of the crew.

In battle, it was important to protect the surgeons and their patients from enemy cannon shot, so surgery was typically performed below the water line in the cable tier or orlop deck. Combat surgeries were also located in the ward room reserved to junior officers where procedures were typically done on planks laid across those officers' chests. There were usually two buckets beside the makeshift, sail-covered operating tables—one full of water for washing the surgeon's hands and a second for collecting amputated extremities for removal by the loblolly boys.

As long as ships were made of wood, splinters were a more frequent cause of injury than direct hit by a cannonball. On the other hand, wood was a good insulator, so problems of heat in the summer or in the tropics and cold in the winter and the high latitudes were relatively manageable. That changed in the last part of the 19th century with the evolution to iron and steel hulls. Steel hulls combined with coal- or oil-fired boilers made ambient heat an especially serious problem, with temperatures in the engine spaces often rising above 120ºF. On the positive side, it was possible to clean steel deck and hull surfaces in a way never achievable in wooden ships, and splinters ceased to be a problem.

The 20th century brought a new series of problems. Penetrating injuries from wooden splinters were replaced by blast and burn injuries from explosive projectiles, and naval medicine had to cope with challenging new environments with the evolution of submarine warfare and naval aviation. Provisions also had to be made for attack by nuclear, biological, and chemical agents.

See also Blane, Sir Gilbert; Cutbush, Edward; Hospital Ships; Scurvy; Sovereign Military Hospitaller Order of St. John of Jerusalem, of Rhodes, and of Malta

References

Herman, Jan. *Battle Station Sick Bay: Navy Medicine in World War II*. Annapolis, MD: Naval Institute Press, 1997.

Oman, Charles M. *Doctors Aweigh: The Story of the United States Navy Medical Corps in Action*. Garden City, NY: Doubleday, Doran and Co., Inc., 1943.

Roddis, Louis. *A Short History of Nautical Medicine*. New York: Paul B. Hoeber, Inc., 1941.

Nightingale, Florence (1820–1910)

Widely credited with founding nursing as a profession, and specifically as a profession for women, Florence Nightingale was born in 1820 in the Italian city for which she was named. The first of two daughters of wealthy parents, she was delivered during their two-year European honeymoon. Her father was a Cambridge University–trained Unitarian and a Whig active in the British antislavery movement who personally saw to his daughter's early education. To her parents' distress, Nightingale took an interest in caring for the sick living around the family's summer home in Derbyshire, England, from a young age. During a European tour in 1850, she visited Theodore Fliedner's Kaiserwerth Institute near Dusseldorf in Westphalia to which she returned the following year for three months' training as a nurse.

In 1853, Nightingale became superintendent at the Establishment for Gentlewomen during Illnesses on Harley Street in London. Soon after the Crimean War began in 1854, press reports began appearing in the British press of abysmal conditions for the sick and wounded at the front. Minister at War Sidney Herbert had met Nightingale socially and appointed her to recruit female nurses to serve in the Crimea. She and her first contingent of 38 ladies arrived at the barracks hospital in Scutari near Constantinople on November 4, 1854. They were not well received by regular military medical personnel but proved invaluable 10 days later when a flood of casualties arrived from the front. The soldiers loved Nightingale and her ladies and she became a national hero. A subscription fund was raised to enable her to extend her efforts to civilian hospitals after the war.

Known the world over as the "The Lady with the Lamp," Florence Nightingale rose to fame during the Crimean War for introducing the first female nurses to military medical facilities. (Library of Congress)

In 1856, Nightingale returned to England, but, painfully shy, she went into seclusion and confined herself to working behind the scenes with Herbert, who had been appointed chairman of a commission to investigate the health of the British Army. As part of that role, she used mathematical skills learned from her father to develop the field of medical statistics, as a result of which she was named the first woman fellow of the Statistical Society in 1860. Nightingale went on to publish more than 200 books, pamphlets, and reports.

In 1865 she settled in Mayfair in London's West End, where she used the money from her public subscription to found the Nightingale School for Nurses at St. Thomas Hospital. She remained closely involved with the school for the remainder of her life in spite of the fact that she went blind in 1895 and was an invalid for her last 15 years.

See also Crimean War; Nursing in the Military; Queen Alexandra's Imperial Military Nursing Service

References

Piggott, Juliet. *Queen Alexandra's Royal Army Nursing Corps*. London: Lee Cooper, Ltd., 1975.

Strachey, Lytton. *Eminent Victorians*. London: Penguin Books, 1971.

Woodham-Smith, Cecil. *Florence Nightingale, 1820–1910*. New York: McGraw-Hill, 1951.

Nuclear Warfare and Radiation Injury

Although there has been very little direct experience with injury from nuclear weapons, the numbers of such devices in various nations' stockpiles and their potential lethality made them the 20th century's most dreaded weapons.

The first nuclear weapon to be used in warfare was dropped on Hiroshima, Japan, on August 6, 1945. The uranium-235 bomb was detonated at an altitude of 570 meters above ground level, had the destructive force of 12.5 kilotons of TNT, destroyed every structure within a five-square-mile area, and killed approximately 64,000 people during the subsequent 30 days. Three days after the first explosiion, a second bomb was dropped on Nagasaki. This was a 29-kiloton plutonium-239 bomb that killed 40,000 people within 30 days. By comparison, the total number of fatalities was less than those in the Allied firebombing of either Dresden or Tokyo in 1945, and the United States dropped bombs with three times the explosive force of the two Japanese bombs combined on Viet Nam in 1972 alone. Nevertheless, the atomic weapons came in single packages, were relatively cheap to produce and deliver, and provided no opportunity for flight or protection.

Immediate damage to the human body from atomic weapons is of three kinds: blast injury, burns, and radiation damage. The temperature in the 15-meter radius of the Hiroshima fireball was 300,000 °C, so the primary injuries close to detonation were from blast effect and burns. Bare skin was burned as far as 3.5 kilometers from the blast site. About 70 percent of those who died had blast injury, 65 percent had burns, and 30 percent had radiation injury—many, of course, having more than one kind of injury.

The type of injury varies with the size of the weapon. A 1-kiloton device (typical for a tactical battlefield weapon) would produce lethal blast effect to an average radius of 0.55 kilometers from detonation, lethal burns to 0.35 kilometers, and lethal radiation to 0.7 kilometers, making the last the most deadly. On the other hand, a 1-megaton device would have lethal thermal effect to a radius of 2.6 kilometers, while the blast would be lethal to 5.5 kilometers and radiation death would occur as far away as 9 kilometers.

While radiation would be irrelevant as a cause of death immediately after detonation, its residual effects would be devastating. A fissile explosion produces multiple unstable isotopes that emit primarily beta particles and gamma rays as they decay to stability. The radioactive half-lives of these isotopes vary from as little as a few seconds to as much as 10 million years. Ultimately,

most of those within an area of 450 square miles around a 1-megaton detonation would become ill.

In an air burst, about half of the radioactive particles produced will fall to earth within 24 hours, but smaller amounts will continue to be carried in the wind and will fall on virtually every part of the planet over the subsequent six months. Radiation dose can be acquired externally from either the air or ground or internally by ingestion or inhalation and can damage a number of organs including the skin, eyes, bone marrow, thyroid, lungs, liver, and sexual organs.

Acute radiation sickness affects primarily the gastrointestinal and neuromuscular systems. It begins with anorexia, nausea, vomiting, diarrhea, abdominal cramps, and dehydration. At high doses, radiation causes apathy, fatigue, fever, sweating, hypotension, shock, and death from cardiovascular collapse. About 90 percent of people with an exposure greater than 390 rads will get radiation sickness, and virtually all those with a dose of 500 rads will die. Delayed effects include asphyxia from pulmonary edema and widespread bleeding and inability to fight infection related to bone marrow failure and loss of platelets and white blood cells.

Much of our knowledge of the long-term effects of radiation comes from following survivors of the Japanese bombs and from sporadic inadvertent human exposures. Information on local effects of radiation fallout was gleaned from an episode in which a 15-megaton device was detonated over Bikini Atoll in the Pacific Ocean. Wind carried a radiation plume over inhabited parts of Micronesia, including the island of Rongelap, 105 miles away, where the inhabitants absorbed doses in excess of 175 rem in the 48 hours after the explosion. They suffered skin and corneal burns, had abnormal blood counts for

15 years, and had a high incidence of hypothyroidism and neoplastic thyroid nodules.

The Atomic Bomb Casualty Commission began collecting information on Japanese atomic bomb survivors in 1947 and continued to do so until it was replaced by the binational Japanese-American Radiation Effects Research Foundation in 1975. These groups studied life span and disease in survivors and in people who were in utero at the time of the explosions and compared them with matched controls. Nearly 80 percent of survivors came for annual checkups and almost 45 percent of those who subsequently died came to autopsy. The most striking late effect was leukemia, which peaked in incidence in 1952 and 1953. Those less than 10 years old at the time of exposure were most likely to develop one of the acute leukemias, while those over 50 in 1945 were susceptible to one of the chronic forms. Incidence of both increased with exposures as low as 20 to 30 rads. Multiple myeloma and cancers of the thyroid, breast, lung, and stomach developed for up to 20 years. Those exposed in utero were subject to microcephaly, mental retardation, and growth failure.

See also Blast Injuries; World War II Medicine

Reference

Adams, Ruth, and Susan Cullen, eds. *The Final Epidemic: Physicians and Scientists on Nuclear War.* Chicago: University of Chicago Press, 1981.

Nuremberg Code

The Nuremberg Code defines standards for human medical experimentation and originated with the war crimes trials of German physicians following World War II.

In 1946, the United States conducted 12 trials of Germans key to various parts of the Third Reich including finance, law, ministry, manufacturing, and medicine. The first of these, the Doctors Trial, convened on October 25, 1946, and lasted to August 20 the following year, with U.S. Army lawyer Telford Taylor as the chief prosecutor. Of the 23 defendants accused of murder and torture while performing medical experiments on concentration camp inmates, 20 were physicians. Seven of the defendants were sentenced to be hanged at Landsberg Prison (ironically, the place Adolf Hitler had been imprisoned before the war and where he had written *Mein Kampf*), five were sentenced to life in prison, two were sentenced to serve 25 years, one to 15 years, one to 10 years, and seven were acquitted.

Prior to December 1946, written ethical standards of human experimentation were rare, although the Prussian government had mandated that participation of human subjects in medical experiments be voluntary as early as 1899 and, in 1900, had banned all medical research on minors whether voluntary or not. Agreement about what restrictions on human experimentation were appropriate was central to Taylor's prosecution; to that end, he solicited the opinion of American neuropsychiatrist Leo Alexander, who proposed three broad principles. With attention to the biomedical ethical principle of autonomy, Alexander proposed that no human experiment should be conducted unless the subject participated of his own free will. Taking the Hippocratic proscription that a physician should never willingly harm a patient (*primum non nocere*) as a Kantian categorical imperative, he said no experiment should be done if there was an a priori reason to expect that the subject would be harmed. Finally, he argued that no experiment involving human subjects should be done if its design did not conform to the practices of good science. Alexander's three basic principles were the foundation upon which the subsequent Nuremberg Code was built. The code says:

The voluntary consent of the human subject is absolutely essential. This means that the person involved should have legal capacity to give consent; should be so situated as to be able to exercise free power of choice, without the intervention of any element of force, fraud, deceit, duress, overreaching, or other ulterior form of constraint or coercion; and should have sufficient knowledge and comprehension of the elements of the subject matter involved as to enable him to make an understanding and enlightened decision. This latter element requires that before the acceptance of an affirmative decision by the experimental subject there should be made known to him the nature, duration, and purpose of the experiment; the method and means by which it is to be conducted; all inconveniences and hazards reasonably to be expected; and the effects upon his health or person which may possibly come from his participation in the experiment. The duty and responsibility for ascertaining the quality of the consent rests upon each individual who initiates, directs or engages in the experiment. It is a personal duty and responsibility which may not be delegated to another with impunity.

The experiment should be such as to yield fruitful results for the good of society, unprocurable by other methods or means of study, and not random and unnecessary in nature.

The experiment should be so designed and based on the results of animal experimentation and a knowledge of the natural history of the disease or other problem under study that the anticipated results will justify the performance of the experiment.

The experiment should be so conducted as to avoid all unnecessary physical and mental suffering and injury.

No experiment should be conducted where there is an a priori reason to believe that death or disabling injury will occur; except, perhaps, in those experiments where the experimental physicians also serve as subjects.

The degree of risk to be taken should never exceed that determined by the humanitarian importance of the problem to be solved by the experiment.

Proper preparations should be made and adequate facilities provided to protect the experimental subject against even remote possibilities of injury, disability, or death.

The experiment should be conducted only by scientifically qualified persons. The highest degree of skill and care should be required through all stages of the experiment of those who conduct or engage in the experiment.

During the course of the experiment the human subject should be at liberty to bring the experiment to an end if he has reached the physical or mental state where continuation of the experiment seems to him to be impossible.

During the course of the experiment the scientist in charge must be prepared to terminate the experiment at any stage, if he has probable cause to believe, in the exercise of good faith, superior skill, and careful judgment required of him, that a continuation of the experiment is likely to result in injury, disability, or death to the experimental subject.

The Nuremberg Code has never been adopted as law by any nation or even as an ethical standard by any major medical organization, although it has been central to the judgments by institutional review boards that have become the sine qua non of modern medical research. The informed consent provisions are incorporated in Article 7 of the United Nations International Covenant on Civil and Political Rights of 1966 and are part of the International Ethical Guidelines for Biomedical Research Involving Human Subjects issued by the World Health Organization.

Recent attempts have been made to modify the Nuremberg Code, particularly in substituting peer review of proposed experiments for some parts of informed consent as exemplified in the Declaration of Helsinki issued by the World Medical Association in 1964. Current practice in the United States is a combination of the Helsinki Declaration and the Nuremberg Code.

See also Prussian and German Military Medicine; World War II Medicine

References

Annas, G. J., and M. A. Grodin, eds. *The Nazi Doctors and the Nuremberg Code: Human Rights in Human Experimentation.* New York: Oxford University Press, 1992.

Shuster, Evelyne. 1997. "Fifty Years Later: The Significance of the Nuremberg Code." *New England Journal of Medicine* 237 (November 13): 1436–1440.

Nursing in the Military

The care of the sick, wounded, and convalescing members of the military was generally afforded little interest and limited resources prior to the second half of the 19th century.

Military nursing can be dated to at least the first century A.D., when the Romans established a series of hospitals to care for their army's sick and wounded. Little is known of the details of care in those institutions, although they persisted until A.D. 335, when the emperor Constantine, having converted to Christianity, closed them as remnants of paganism. Churchmen of that era felt that care of the sick should be a vocation ordained by God. During the Crusades, most military nursing was done by men, usually members of religious orders including the Templars and the Knights of St. John of Jerusalem, who operated hospitals to care for the combatants.

With those exceptions, most hospital care for the next several centuries fell to women in holy orders such as the Augustinian sisters, who founded the Hôtel Dieu in Paris in 1443. During the English Civil War in 1642, the Hospital of St. John the Baptist was converted to military use, as were St. Thomas's, St. Bartholomew's, and Bethlem, and all retained women to work as professional nurses. However, when standing armies went on campaign after the Restoration, nursing was left to female camp followers, who often outnumbered the soldiers they accompanied.

Seventeenth century nursing care was much more custodial than medical; the nurse's main jobs being bathing, laundering, cleaning, and cooking. The fact that the camp followers also saw to more intimate domestic needs played a considerable role in giving female nurses an unsavory reputation.

Until well into the 19th century, informal care provided by available females was augmented by soldiers who were themselves recovering from disease or injury or who were otherwise physically, mentally, or morally unfit for combat. Donald Monro, who campaigned with King George III in Germany from 1761 to 1763, recommended that each military hospital have a matron who would report to a physician, surgeon, or apothecary and who would be responsible for seeing that the rest of the male and female nurses were clean and sober. He further suggested that nurses who did not meet those standards be either confined or whipped.

Military nursing changed profoundly in 1854 when Florence Nightingale, a politically well-connected upper-class English lady who had spent time as an observer at the model German hospital in Kaiserwerth, used her influence with the secretary at war to organize a contingent of nurses to be dispatched to the scandalous military hospital in Scutari during the Crimean War. Of her 38 volunteers, 24 were from either Catholic or Anglican religious orders. Nightingale's choice of volunteers, combined with her insistence on modest, standardized uniforms and rigid discipline, brought a new air of professionalism that was perpetuated with the founding of a school to train nurses at St. Thomas Hospital after the war.

The British Army nursing service was established in 1881, by which time the role of nurses had expanded to include changing surgical dressings, giving medication (including injections), and administering enemas in addition to cooking and cleaning, although each nurse still had her own small stove to prepare tea for her charges. The workload was heavy, each nurse at the Netley Army hospital being responsible for 60 to 70 patients.

In the United States prior to the Civil War, nursing had generally been the province of available female relatives, although, in the years just preceding the war, increasing numbers of women had begun to do the job for pay. Early in the war, Clara Barton arranged to bring supplies to Union wounded and participated in the foundation of the Sanitary Commission, which played a major role in improving military medical care during that conflict. Women, particularly from religious orders such as the Sisters of Charity, provided care for both the Union and the Confederacy, but military surgeons generally preferred that care be provided by men, and the women were frequently relegated to menial housekeeping tasks.

After the war, nursing became an increasingly popular employment for women, and, by 1870, 10,000 women were working as nurses in the United States (a number that would grow to 100,000 by 1940), and the country's first nursing school opened in 1873.

Although American military physicians continued to prefer male nurses, personnel shortages during the training camp typhoid outbreaks early in the Spanish-American War forced them to accept females. When the war started, the Army's Hospital Corps had only 791 privates and noncommissioned officers to care for an anticipated army of 250,000. Recruitment and organization of female volunteers was delegated to the Daughters of the American Revolution, who enlisted 1,158 volunteers by September 1898. As the typhoid epidemics in training camps came under control, most of the women were dismissed, although a few remained under contract to care for soldiers as they returned to the United States. Nursing in Cuba remained the province of men.

The British sent women to South Africa during the Boer War, where the main challenges were contamination from generally poor sanitation and pervasive dysentery. Although the British nurses served as civilian auxiliaries to the military, their Canadian counterparts came with the rank, pay,

Nurses tend to injured soldiers at Scutari Hospital in Constantinople during the Crimean War, the first time female nurses were admitted to military medical facilities. (Library of Congress)

and allowances of a lieutenant, marking the first time female nurses had been accorded officer status.

Female nurses were finally made part of the U.S. Army Medical Department in 1901, although the Army Nurse Corps was not formalized until 1918. After 1908, the Red Cross had collected a pool of volunteer nurses that would be available when the United States entered World War I. By November 1918, 21,480 nurses had served with the military, 10,660 of whom had gone to Europe with the American Expeditionary Force. Racial as well as gender prejudices persisted. Only 18 black nurses served, and even they were assigned only to segregated hospitals in the United States to care for influenza victims and were dismissed as soon as the epidemic ended.

Most nurses served in rear-area hospitals, and many were included as part of base hospitals, recruited to serve as a unit from the existing staff of a specific American hospital. Those nurses went with the same status and job descriptions they had held at home and worked with the same people. Very few female nurses ventured as far forward as field hospitals.

Even more than their American counterparts, British nurses played a major role in their army's medical care. Queen Alexandra's Imperial Military Nursing Service fielded 10,404 nurses and an additional 9,000 women in volunteer aid detachments (VADs) during World War I.

Julia Stimson, the cousin of Secretary of War Henry Stimson, had been placed in charge of the Army Nurse Corps during the war and continued in that role after the armistice, although the corps shrank to only 672 women by 1939. In June 1920, American nurses were finally given the "relative rank" and pay of officers ranging from second lieutenant to major, although they were still not formally commissioned. In 1941, nurses were the only women in the American military, although they still had only relative rank and were in reality an auxiliary, not receiving status as officers until 1943 and not formally becoming part of the Army until 1948. The fact that only registered nurses were commissioned served to separate them from licensed nurses with less training and played a major part in the postwar professionalization of nursing.

American women were not subject to the draft during World War II, and the Red Cross assumed responsibility for soliciting volunteers. By 1945, 51,000 women were serving in the Army Nurse Corps, and a total of 75,000 had served at some point during the war. In fact, there was a surplus of Army nurses, many of whom were bored and underutilized. No men were allowed in either the Army or Navy nurse corps, although women rarely served in forward combat areas where most care was still done by male orderlies and medics. British and American nurses were, however, among prisoners of war taken at Singapore, at Guam, and in the Philippines.

When the Korean Conflict started, the American military nurse corps was still entirely female, and it had shrunk to just 500 members. The shortage led to hiring contract nurses and abolishing the eight-hour workday. It was suggested that men be incorporated into the nurse corps, but the idea was rejected in 1951 and again in 1953. A new role for military nursing came when "flight nurses" were detailed to care for wounded during aeromedical evacuations from Korea to rear-area hospitals in Japan during the conflict.

The Viet Nam War saw military nursing evolve to its modern status. The first 13 Army nurses came to Nha Trang in March 1962, and their numbers peaked at 9,000 in January 1969. Men had finally been allowed in the corps in 1955. Army nurses, like the combatants, served one-year tours, and most worked at either fixed hospitals or at the 6th Convalescent Center at Cam Ranh Bay. The lack of a defined front during that conflict meant that military nurses worked closer to actual combat than in previous wars. Although nurses continued to serve on wards, they were increasingly assigned to specialty teams in areas such as orthopedics, neurosurgery, psychiatry, and thoracic surgery. Army nurses, especially the men, worked with surgical teams or as nurse anesthetists, and many took that role back to civilian life.

See also Aeromedical Evacuation; Barton, Clara; Crimean War; Korean Conflict; Nightingale, Florence; Roman Military Medicine; Sovereign Military Hospitaller Order of St. John of Jerusalem, of Rhodes, and of Malta; Spanish-American War; Viet Nam War; World War I Medicine; World War II Medicine

References

Ashburn, P. M. *A History of the Medical Department of the United States Army.* Boston: Houghton Mifflin Co., 1929.

Campbell, D'Ann. 1987. "Women in Uniform: The World War II Experiment." *Military Affairs* 51 (July): 137–139.

Cowdrey, Albert. *United States Army in the Korean War: The Medic's War.* Washington, D.C.: Center of Military History of the United States Army, 1987.

Cowdrey, Albert. *Fighting for Life: American Military Medicine in World War II.* New York: Free Press, 1994.

Jensen, Kimberly. 2005. "A Base Hospital Is Not a Coney Island Dance Hall: American Women Nurses, Hostile Work Environment, and Military Rank in the First World War." *Frontiers: A Journal of Women's Studies* 26 (2): 206–235.

Neel, Spurgeon. *Medical Support of the U.S. Army in Vietnam, 1965–1970.* Washington, D.C.: Department of the Army, 1973.

Piggot, Juliet. *Queen Alexandra's Royal Army Nursing Corps.* London: Leo Cooper, Ltd., 1975.

Reverby, Susan. *Ordered to Care: The Dilemma of American Nursing, 1850–1945.* Cambridge: Cambridge University Press, 1987.

Omdurman Campaign (1896–1898)

More lives were lost to typhoid during the Omdurman Campaign than in any other war in British military history.

The campaign was a response to Gen. Charles Gordon's attempt to reestablish Anglo-Egyptian control over the Sudan and to imperial concerns about French incursions from the West African Congo River basin. The British invasion force comprised 17,200 Egyptian and 8,200 British troops transported up the Nile River in 140-foot steam-powered boats that could be disassembled and carried around falls and rapids. British forces fought three campaigns—1896, 1897, and 1898—and the effort culminated in the British defeat of the Mahdi's army at Omdurman in September 1898.

It had been known that typhoid was caused by a water-borne bacillus since the early 1800s, and the British Army recognized that quarantining the sick and boiling all drinking water were effective measures against both typhoid and cholera. Nonetheless, the men found it irresistibly convenient to simply dip drinking water from the river and generally refused to take the trouble to boil it or to use porcelain filters that were both effective and available but that had an annoying tendency to clog with Nile sediment. As a result, disease death rates on the campaign were six times those of troops in barracks in Lower Egypt and the death rate from typhoid in 1898 reached 5.5 per 1,000 combatants—11 times that of other troops stationed nearer the Mediterranean.

See also British Military Medicine; Typhoid Fever

Reference

Curtin, Philip D. *Disease and Empire: The Health of European Troops in the Conquest of Africa.* Cambridge: Cambridge University Press, 1998.

P

Paracelsus (Aureolus Theophrastus Bombastus von Hohenheim) (1493–1541)

Paracelsus was perhaps the most original thinker and certainly one of the oddest characters of the 16th century.

It is unclear why von Hohenheim took the name Paracelsus, although it has been suggested that he meant to imply that he was greater than the first-century Roman writer Aulus Cornelius Celsus. Given his bent for self-promotion and outré behavior, it is tempting to conclude that the adjective "bombastic" came from his middle name; the word is actually derived from "bombaste," another name for cotton fluff.

Paracelsus was born in Einsiedeln near Zurich, the son of a physician and member of the Teutonic Order. He began training in medicine with his father and entered the University at Balse at the age of 16. Along the way, he attended a school of mines and studied under the famous alchemist Trithemus. He traveled to Vienna, Cologne, Paris, and Montpellier, visiting medical schools in each city before completing his training in the Italian city-state of Ferrara under the renowned syphilologist Nicolai Leoniceni in 1515. In the course of his travels, Paracelsus had studied astrology, alchemy, and magic, all of which he incorporated into his medical practice.

After leaving Ferrara, Paracelsus joined the Dutch army and participated in the Danish siege of Stockholm in 1518. After that war, he traveled widely and generally gravitated to society's lower echelons, learning much of practical value from barbers, tavern owners, midwives, bath keepers, and executioners. Paracelsus, chronically attracted to the military, joined the Venetian army only to be captured by the Tartars and taken to the court at Constantinople, where he became one of the sultan's favorites and was allowed to travel as far as China.

Eventually, Paracelsus returned to Germany and became surgeon to a variety of European armies before settling down to teach at Freiburg, Strasbourg, and Balse. In the latter job, he championed Aristotle's methods of observation and rejected Galen's generally accepted authority. He went so far as to publicly burn the Roman physician's books, earning the sobriquet "Luther of the physicians." His career at Balse was shortened by both his truculence and accusations that he overcharged his patients, and he was forced to resume his wanderings.

Paracelsus believed disease was caused by the influence of the stars, but he also recognized the hereditary tendency to some afflictions and saw maladies characterized by concretions and calcifications as disorders of body chemistry. He believed some illnesses were psychogenic and some were from external poisons. He referred to the latter as contagia, anticipating his student Severinus's contribution to the theory of infectious disease. Paracelsus made opium a regular part of his pharmacopoeia, but he also recommended less beneficial remedies including mercury, arsenic, and lead. He taught that all life originated in primordial ooze and anticipated Charles Darwin by theorizing that life forms gradually improved as the stronger ones defeated and removed the weaker.

Paracelsus's *Treatise on Open Wounds* (1528) and *Chirurgica Magna* (1536) were widely circulated. In the latter, he anticipated Ambroise Paré's recommendation that wound treatment be kept as simple as possible: "Warily must the surgeon take heed not to remove or interfere with Nature's balsam, but protect and defend it in its working virtue. It is in the nature of flesh to possess, in itself, an innate balsam which healeth wounds." Paracelsus was admired and respected in his own lifetime and was mentioned by William Shakespeare in the same sentence as Galen.

He died at age 48, the victim of a Salzburg barroom brawl.

See also Medieval Military Medicine

References

Hall, Manly. *Paracelsus: His Mystical and Magical Philosophy*. Los Angeles: Philosophical Research Society, 1990.

Hartmann, Franz. *Paracelsus: Life and Prophecies*. Whitefish, MT: Kessinger Publishing, 1993.

Klawans, Harold. *The Medicine of History from Paracelsus to Freud*. New York: Raven Press, 1982.

Temkin, Oswei. 1952. "The Elusiveness of Paracelsus." *Bulletin of the History of Medicine* 26: 210–217.

Paré, Ambroise (1510–1590)

Ambroise Paré was considered the foremost military surgeon of the 16th century.

Paré was born in the village of Bourgon Hersent near Laval and came to Paris at the age of 19 as a barber-surgeon's apprentice. He served as a dresser at the Parisian hospital the Hôtel Dieu before becoming an army surgeon in 1536, a role in which he went on to serve under five kings.

Paré was ridiculed by his colleagues for writing in vernacular French rather than Latin, including having the temerity to translate Andreas Vesalius's iconic work on anatomy. He was, however, adored by French soldiers for his skill in treating battlefield injuries and was the only Protestant spared at the infamous St. Bartholomew's massacre of the Huguenots.

Citing the Hippocratic doctrine that diseases caused by iron are best cured by fire, compounded by the belief that gunpowder was, itself, a poison, 16th-century military surgeons treated gunshot wounds with a combination of red-hot cauteries and boiling elder oil. After a battle during the French campaign in the Piedmont, Paré ran out of oil and was forced to substitute a mixture of egg yolks, oil of roses, and turpentine to irrigate wounds. Unable to use the entire standard treatment, he also elected to forgo the cautery. The following morning he found wounds treated with the new mixture lacked the typical inflammation and, in subsequent days, went on to heal better than those given the usual treatment. With this evidence, Paré had the audacity to question papal physician Giovanni de Vigo's assertion that gunshot wounds contained an innate poison that had to be burned out.

Paré also reintroduced Aulus Cornelius Celsus's use of ligature to control bleeding during amputation. Ligatures made it possible to control vessels too large to cauterize, which, in turn, made it possible to amputate well above the necrotic areas of a gangrenous limb and thereby significantly improve the patient's chances of survival.

He created a series of artfully designed surgical instruments adorned with such decorations as the carving of a beautiful woman who languished on the handle of his amputation knife. Paré was probably the first clinician in the modern era to recognize that flies carry infectious disease as well as being one of the first to successfully reimplant avulsed teeth.

In 1552, he became surgeon in ordinary to French king Henry II and continued in that capacity through the reigns of three more monarchs. He became particularly close to Charles IX, for whom he held the rank of principal surgeon. His works include a treatise on gunshot wounds (1545) and his great 10-volume treatise on surgery (1564).

Paré died in 1590 and was buried at Saint-André-des-Arcs in Paris.

See also Amputation; Barber-Surgeons; Cauterization; Ligature; 16th-Century Military Medicine

References

Malgaigne, J. F. *Surgery and Ambroise Paré.* Norman: University of Oklahoma Press, 1965.

Packard, Francis P. *The Life and Times of Ambroise Paré.* New York: Paul B. Hoeber, 1921.

Pasteur, Louis (1822–1895)

Along with Robert Koch, Louis Pasteur founded experimental bacteriology.

Pasteur was born in the village of Dôle in the French Jura, the son of a tanner who had fought as a private soldier under Napoleon Bonaparte. He studied at Besançon and graduated from the École Normale in Paris in 1847. From childhood, Pasteur was a talented artist. In 1848, he moved to Dijon, where he served as professor of physics at the city's lyceum. In 1852, he was appointed professor of chemistry at the University of Strasbourg, where he served until 1854, at which time he was named professor of chemistry and dean of the faculty of sciences at Lille. In 1857, Pasteur moved to Paris as director of scientific studies at the École Normale. In 1863, he was named professor of geology and chemistry at the École des Beaux Arts on Paris's Left Bank, where he taught until moving to the Sorbonne as professor of chemistry. In 1869, he assumed directorship at the Institut Pasteur, where he spent his final 26 years.

Pasteur's first great discovery was the racemic structure of tartaric acid, which led him to a study of fermentation and the discovery of the lactic acid bacilli so important to the French wine industry. In 1861, he demonstrated that bacteria could be either aerobic or anaerobic and that they could

Louis Pasteur, the French inventor of the pasteuriza-tion process, is also known for developing the rabies vaccine. (Library of Congress)

convert atmospheric oxygen into carbon dioxide. He subsequently showed that wine could be kept from spoiling by gentle heating that sterilized but did not change the flavor of the beverage, a process that was subsequently applied to dairy products and that carries his name. He received an honorary doctorate in medicine from the university at Bonn for his work—a degree he returned during the Franco-Prussian War. The fact that the degree was honorary did not prevent his morphing from laboratory scientist to physician.

After the French defeat in 1871, he returned to the laboratory, where he confirmed Robert Koch's demonstration that a bacillus caused anthrax. He also cultured both staphylococci and streptococci from infected wounds. English surgeon Joseph Lister adapted Pasteur's work to the operating room and credited the French scientist as being directly responsible for the development of antiseptic surgery. Pasteur accidentally discovered that cultures of chicken cholera that had been allowed to die could be injected into test animals and would prevent the disease, thus developing the first successful vaccine since Edward Jenner's use of cowpox against smallpox. He went on to develop a vaccine against anthrax and, in 1885, to use his rabies vaccine on Joseph Meister, an Alsatian child who had been bitten by a rabid dog.

Pasteur died in his apartment at the Institut Pasteur in 1895.

See also Antisepsis; Cholera; Franco-Prussian War; Koch, Robert; Lister, Lord Joseph

References
Debré, Patrice, and Elbeg Forster. *Louis Pasteur.* Baltimore: Johns Hopkins University Press, 2000.
Vallery-Radof, René, *The Life of Pasteur.* Garden City, NY: Garden City Publishing Co., 1926.

Paul of Aegina
(625–690)

Paul of Aegina was a Greek eclectic and the last of the great Byzantine physicians.

Paul of Aegina was trained in Alexandria and may have been in the city when it fell to the Arabs in 642. He was the author of *De Re Medica*, which remained influential well into the Renaissance, although he modestly called himself only a scribe for the ancients. The *De Re Medica* was translated by English scholar and medical historian Francis Adams between 1844 and 1847 and published as *The Seven Books of Paul of Aegina*. The sixth book deals entirely with surgery and is by far the most complete account of Byzantine military medicine and surgery. It remained a standard until Albucasis's 11th-century work, which was largely derived from it.

Book six of the *De Re Medica* contains an extensive discussion of removal of spears and arrow points, which Paul called the most important aspect of surgery. He recommended pulling the arrow back if close to the entry point and pushing it through if closer to the body's opposite side while warning the surgeon to avoid transecting tendons, vessels, or nerves as he pressed the point forward. He discussed techniques appropriate to the various types of arrow tip and described tubes and extractors to ease removal of barbed weapons. Paul also mentioned débridement of tissue surrounding the poisoned arrows favored by Dalmatians and Dacians. He offered the first complete description of removing arrows from delicate organs such as the liver, lung, heart, and brain and recommended using a tooth extractor to remove stones or lead pellets fired from slings.

Paul described cutting to clean tissue and resuturing maimed lips and ears and gave a detailed description of cutting down to the third or fourth tracheal ring (still the standard technique for tracheotomy) to open an obstructed airway. He also described reclosing the opening when the normal airway was again patent. He described survival from wounds and infections involving the liver and the peritoneal cavity and gave detailed instructions for multilayer closure of openings into the abdomen. He described the hissing noise from open injuries into the chest cavity and the throbbing of an arrow shaft sticking out of a penetrated heart, advised tying a severed carotid artery above and below the injury before removing a penetrating arrow, and gave instructions for removing bone fragments and debris from a depressed skull fracture.

Paul described an iron lever for realigning long bone fractures and a pulley system for straightening broken backs, although he pointed out that any injury to the spinal cord itself led to rapid death. His amputation technique—cutting quickly to the bone, which was then rapidly sawn through, followed by ligating large vessels and cauterizing the stump with hot iron—remained essentially unchanged for the next thousand years.

See also Abdominal Injuries in War; Albucasis; Amputation; Cauterization; Celsus, Aulus Cornelius; Chest Injuries and Surgery; Forceps and Extractors; Fractures; Head Injury and Cranial Surgery; Ligature; Rehabilitation and Reconstructive Surgery; Tracheotomy

References

Adams, Francis. *The Seven Books of Paulus Aegineta translated from the Greek with a Commentary embracing a Complete View of the Knowledge Possessed by the Greeks, Romans, and Arabians on All Subjects Connected with Medicine and Surgery*. London: Sydenham Society, 1846.

Salazar, Christine. *The Treatment of War Wounds in Graeco-Roman Antiquity*. Leiden, the Netherlands: Brill, 2000.

Penicillin

Penicillin was the first biologically derived antibiotic, and its application marked the beginning of a new era in battlefield surgery.

Molds had been recommended for wound treatment for more than 1500 years, but never in a systematic or generally effective way. In an 1897 dissertation, French medical student Ernest Duchesne, whose primary interest was the interaction between fungi and bacteria, had shown that extract from the mold *Penicillium glaucum* protected laboratory animals subsequently inoculated with the bacterium that produces typhoid fever. Duchesne enlisted in the army, where he contracted and died of tuberculosis before he could complete his research.

In late August or early September 1928, bacteriologist and stereotypically absent-minded professor Alexander Fleming returned to his laboratory at St. Mary's Hospital in London's Paddington suburb to find that cultures of staphylococcus that he had left scattered about had become spoiled by airborne molds. On the verge of dipping them in Lysol, he noticed that some had a ring of killed bacteria around the clumps of cultured mold. Fleming incorrectly identified the mold as *Penicillium rubrum* (it was really *Penicillium notatum*) and reported his findings in the *British Journal of Experimental Pathology*, in which he named the active agent penicillin. Penicillin, however, proved to be extraordinarily difficult to extract and almost impossible to stabilize, and his mold cultures completely stopped producing the substance after about eight days. Unable to produce usable quantities of penicillin—and, in fact, unable to reproduce his original accidental experiment—Fleming moved on to other areas of research.

In 1938, Oxford University's Howard W. Florey had assembled a research team that included immigrant bacteriologist Ernst Chain and Norman C. H. Heatley to look for effective antibacterial agents. Florey had been taught by Cecil Paine, who had been one of Fleming's students and had been an editor of the journal that published Fleming's original paper, so it is likely he already had some knowledge of penicillin when he adopted it as one of his areas of interest. By 1940, with the assistance of a grant from the Rockefeller Foundation, Florey and his co-workers—it is likely that much of the work was in fact done by Chain—were able to

extract enough penicillin to test it on four laboratory mice with four more animals serving as controls. All the controls died while half of the treated mice survived, and the Oxford group was convinced it had a success. The first human—a healthy volunteer—was injected with 100 milligrams of penicillin on January 27, 1941, but she suffered a severe febrile reaction from a contaminant in the preparation. The first actual clinical use of penicillin was February 1, 1941, when it was administered to London policeman Albert Alexander, who had cut himself shaving and gotten staphylococcal sepsis with osteomyelitis, pneumonia, and a necrotizing infection of his eye. Alexander initially improved, but Florey did not have enough penicillin to continue treatment in spite of recovering and reusing crystallized drug from the patient's urine. When the drug was stopped, Alexander relapsed and died. With the thought that children, being smaller, would need less drug, Florey next treated five children with sepsis that would have previously proven fatal. Four survived, and the fifth died of a brain hemorrhage without autopsy evidence of remaining infection.

By this time, the Battle of Britain was occupying the country's attention and all of its industrial capacity, leaving no resources for production of penicillin, so the Rockefeller Foundation paid for Florey and Heatley to come to the United States in July 1941, where Department of Agriculture officials put them in touch with the Northern Regional Research Laboratory at Peoria, Illinois. That laboratory was a national center of research on fermentation. At Peoria, three signal developments occurred. First, it was shown that addition of corn steep liquor (a by-product of corn syrup production) to Penicillium cultures could increase penicillin output by a factor of 10. Then, a strain of Penicillium retrieved from a moldy cantaloupe found in a Peoria market was shown to increase penicillin production by a factor of 200. Mutations of that organism induced by X-ray and ultraviolet radiation increased that rate to a factor of more than 1,000. Finally, cultures that had previously only grown on the surface of milk bottle–sized flasks were induced to grow throughout aerated 25,000-gallon tanks. That application made commercial production possible, and Alfred N. Richardson of the Office of Scientific Research and Development's Medical Research Committee enlisted Merck and Company, Charles Pfizer Company, and E. R. Squibb and Sons to the effort. It is likely that Richardson and the U.S. government were already considering the possible military uses of penicillin should the U.S. enter World War II.

In early 1943, only enough penicillin was produced to treat 100 people, even with urine recovery and reuse of the drug. By summer of that year, more drug was available, but it still cost more than $20 a dose. By 1944, American pharmaceutical companies were producing 300 billion units a month, and, by D-Day, enough penicillin was available to treat every British and American casualty from the invasion. In May 1945, when the drug was released to the civilian population, the price had dropped to $0.55 a dose.

By the end of the war, a previously unimaginable 95 percent of battlefield injuries that came to treatment were surviving, the death rate from pneumonia had dropped from 18 percent to less than 1 percent, and syphilis could be reliably treated. Fleming, Florey, and Chain were awarded the 1945 Nobel Prize for physiology or medicine. As Fleming had predicted, however, resistant strains of staphylococci began emerging almost as soon as penicillin became available.

The bacteria acquired the ability to produce an enzyme—penicillinase—that broke the drug down and passed that trait from generation to generation. The first penicillin-resistant staphylococcus was identified in 1942, and, by 1952, 60 percent of staphylococci were resistant to even massive doses of the drug. In addition, widespread use of the drug led to allergic reactions; the first fatal case of penicillin-induced anaphylaxis was reported in 1949. Resistance and allergies triggered a search for variants of penicillin and entirely new drugs that is ongoing.

See also Fleming, Sir Alexander; Gonorrhea; Syphilis; World War II Medicine

References
Boetcher, Helmuth M. *Wonder Drugs: A History of Antibiotics.* Philadelphia: J. B. Lippincott, 1963.
Maurois, André. *The Life of Sir Alexander Fleming, Discoverer of Penicillin.* New York: E. P. Dutton and Co., 1959.
Sheehan, John C. *The Enchanted Ring: The Untold Story of Penicillin.* Cambridge, MA: MIT Press, 1984.

Percy, Baron Pierre François (1754–1825)

Baron Pierre Percy was surgeon in chief of Napoleon Bonaparte's army.

Percy was the son of a physician and a brilliant student who entered the French Army in 1776. Like his contemporary, Baron Dominique-Jean Larrey, he recognized the need for forward treatment of battle casualties. To that end he devised a sausage-shaped casket drawn by six horses containing enough bandages and supplies to treat 1,200 wounded. Eight surgeons rode astride the wagon while orderlies rode the horses pulling it. The wagons were originally named for the Würtz carriage works, where they were manufactured, although their unique shape led to the more playful and more descriptive name "Percy's *wursts.*"

Initially Percy concentrated on early treatment of the wounded in the field and neglected their transport to the rear. In fact, he became famous for being able to perform a field amputation in under 20 seconds. By the time of the 1808 Spanish campaign, he realized both the need for continuing care of those wounded in combat and the drain placed on fighting forces when men left the field to carry their injured comrades to safety. To answer the latter problem, Percy created corps of stretcher bearers. His bearers carried lances that, when paired, doubled as litter poles and wore sashes that could be laced to the poles to form a litter or *brancard.*

The *brancardiers* carried the wounded to forward-area dressing stations manned by five physicians, an apothecary, and several attendants. The dressing stations were equipped with hospital wagons that could evacuate the wounded to nearby villages for more definitive treatment and from which the men could be moved to rear-area fixed hospitals if more protracted care was needed. This tiered system became standard for Europe's armies and presaged that used by all the participants in World War I's Western Front. Although the evacuation system was widely adopted, Percy's pleas for a permanent French corps of military surgeons fell on deaf ears, and the evolution of military surgery as a separate branch of the army had to wait for later wars.

Percy was named baron after the Battle of Wagram in June 1809. That same year, hampered by age and failing vision, he left the field army to assume supervision of the military hospital at the Hôtel de Villeroy

and to join the faculty of medicine at the university in Paris. He was later elected to the chamber of deputies, but continued to practice and, late in life, was credited with inventing wire suture.

Percy died in Paris on February 10, 1825.

See also Ambulances and Transport; Casualty Clearing Stations and Staged Evacuation

References
Haller, John W. *Farmcarts to Fords: A History of the Military Ambulance, 1790–1925.* Carbondale: Southern Illinois University Press, 1992.
Richardson, Robert G. *Larrey: Surgeon to Napoleon's Imperial Guard.* London: John Murray Publishers Ltd., 1974.

Pfolspeundt, Heinrich von (15th century)

Heinrich von Pfolspeundt was a Bavarian army surgeon credited with being the first German military medical practitioner.

Little is known of Pfolspeundt's life except that he was a brother of the German Order who had little formal education and probably learned what he knew of surgery from practical experience. His *Buch der Bündt-Ertznei,* written in 1460, was in manuscript only and was lost until rediscovered and printed in 1868. It contains the first known description of treating wounds from firearms in the surgical literature. He saw no difference between gunshot wounds and other types of battlefield wounds save for the fact that he thought the powder had to be removed from the former.

When operating on gunshot wounds, Pfolspeundt first gave the patient a narcotic drink, the formula of which he adapted from Nicholas of Salerno, and then probed the wound to locate the projectile and then removed it. He gave the first description of powder burns and created artificial noses to replace those destroyed in battle using techniques learned from Hindu medicine, a skill for which he has been called a founder of cosmetic surgery.

See also Bullet Wounds and Other Penetrating Injuries from Gunpowder Projectiles; Larrey, Baron Dominique-Jean; Napoleonic Wars; Stretchers and Litters

Reference
Dealey, Carol. 2005. "German Wound Surgeons: 1450–1750." *European Wound Management Association Journal* 5: 48–52.

Phlebotomy and Venesection

Phlebotomy and venesection comprise the practice of removing blood, usually from a vein in the forearm, as therapy for presumed imbalances in body function.

Phlebotomy is mentioned in Egyptian medical papyri and was recommended by Hippocrates to restore balance of the four humors—blood, phlegm, yellow bile, and black bile. Although the practice was questioned by Alexandrian Greek physicians, it was recommended and extensively discussed by Roman writers Aulus Cornelius Celsus and Galen of Pergamum and remained common for nearly two millennia. During the Middle Ages, venesection was usually performed by barber-surgeons who often also operated bathhouses. Their dual role as bandagers and letters of blood inspired the red-and-white-striped poles that remain the barber's hallmark.

After a brief decline in popularity, bleeding underwent a striking resurgence beginning in the later half of the 18th century. Under the influence of American physician Benjamin Rush (who resorted to the drastic therapies often called "heroic"), Washington had 80 ounces of blood removed to treat what was probably a bacterial sore throat, a treatment that almost certainly played a major role in his demise. Physicians at that time reasoned that, as febrile diseases were usually accompanied by hot, flushed skin, they must also be associated with an excess of blood and that excess would best be removed.

François-Joseph-Victor Broussais (1772–1838), who began as a sergeant in the French Republican Army and went on to serve three years as a military surgeon in Napoleon Bonaparte's imperial forces, put forward the thesis that nature alone could not heal wounds or illnesses without man's active assistance. He considered bleeding a major part of that assistance and combined blood removal with food deprivation to the point of near starvation in his "antiphlogistic" regimen. Broussais found leeches a more convenient means of bloodletting than opening a vein, and the popularity of his ideas led to importation of a purported 41,500,000 leeches into France in 1833 alone.

Bleeding (either by venesection or leech application) remained an accepted means of treatment well into the 19th century in spite of statistical studies by Pierre-Charles-Alexandre Louis unequivocally proving its uselessness in treating pneumonia. The practice was not fully discredited until the majority of inflammatory diseases were proven to be the result of infection with microorganisms. Even with that proof, Sir William Osler's 1892 *The Principles and Practice of Medicine*, the standard textbook of internal medicine of the first half of the 20th century, continued to recommend its judicious use in treating inflammation and especially in pneumonia. That recommendation was still present in the book's 16th edition in 1947.

See also Barber-Surgeons; Celsus, Aulus
Cornelius; Galen of Pergamum;
Hippocrates of Cos

References
Ackerknecht, Erwin. 1953. "Broussais: Or a
Forgotten Medical Revolution." *Bulletin
of the History of Medicine* 27 (July–August):
320–343.
Hackett, Earle. *Blood: The Paramount Humour.*
London: Jonathan Cape, 1973.

Pirogoff, Nikolai Ivanovich (1810–1881)

Nikolai Pirogoff was the most influential
19th-century Russian military surgeon.

Pirogoff was born the son of a major
in the commissary service. He learned to
read at a young age and was said to have
been fluent in several languages while still
a child. His father died in 1814, leaving
the family destitute, but the family's physician arranged for the young Pirogoff to
enter the University of Moscow at age 14
even though the minimum age for admission to that institution was 16. Pirogoff obtained his degree in only three years but,
convinced his training was inadequate,
went on to Dorpat (now Tartu), for further
training. He then traveled to Germany and
studied at Berlin and Göttingen before returning to take the chair of surgery at Dorpat while still only 26.

Pirogoff, a remarkably quick and deft
surgeon, was named professor of surgery
at the Medico-Chirurgical Academy (also
known as the Military Medical Academy)
at St. Petersburg in 1841.

Pirogoff emphasized the importance
of basing surgical technique on a sound
knowledge of anatomy and personally conducted more than 11,000 autopsies, includ-

ing 800 from the 1848 cholera epidemic.
He saw military service in the Caucasus in
1847 and in the Crimea in 1854. During the
latter campaign, he spent 14 months at Sebastopol, during which time he helped the
Grand Princess Helena Pavlovna bring female nurses to the front much as Florence
Nightingale was doing for the British.

Pirogoff had begun animal experiments
with ether anesthesia administered rectally
as early as 1847 and had even experimented
on himself. He brought that technique and
the use of intravenous ether to battlefield
surgery while in the Crimea. After watching a sculptor work with plaster of paris
models, he devised the quick-setting plaster cast for immobilizing fractures. In spite
of his successes in the Crimea, Pirogoff was
so critical of the government and military
administration during that war that he was
forced to resign his professorship and retire
to his estates in the southern Ukraine.

While touring Italy with a group of
young Russians being trained to educate
future teachers, Pirogoff helped treat Giuseppe Garibaldi, who had sustained a
severe leg wound in the Battle of Aspro-
monte. After he returned to Russia, he confined himself almost entirely to his estate
but continued to write. In his treatise on
military medicine published in 1864, Pirogoff contended that large hospitals were, by
their very nature, responsible for much of
the contamination that led to wound infections. In 1870, he ventured out as a representative of the Red Cross to inspect both
Prussian and French medical facilities during the Franco-Prussian War, and, in spite
of his age, he served as a surgeon in the
1877 Russo-Turkish War.

He last appeared in public in May 1881 at
a celebration of his 50 years of service to the
state and died in December of that year. The

current Russian museum of the history of military medicine carries Pirogoff's name.

See also Anesthesiology; Crimean War

References
Fried, B. M. 1955. "Pirogoff in the Crimean Campaign." *Bulletin of the New York Academy of Medicine* 7 (July): 519–536.
Secher, O. 1986. "Nikolai Ivanovich Pirogoff." *Anaesthesia* 41 (August): 829–837.

Plague (Bubonic Plague, Black Death)

Bubonic plague is a systemic disease caused by *Yersinia* (formerly *Pasturella*) *pestis*, a gram-negative, rod-shaped bacillus of the enterobacter family.

The organism appears pink in standard bacterial gram stain and has rounded ends, giving it a microscopic appearance similar to a safety pin. The plague bacillus ordinarily lives in the intestine of any one of 1,500 varieties of flea or in the bodies of mammals, usually ground-dwelling rodents such as rats, mice, squirrels, and occasionally domestic cats and dogs. Humans acquire the disease either by direct contact with an infected animal or, more commonly, by being bitten by an infected flea. Droplets expelled from infected lungs can also transmit the organism, and this aerosol transmission leads to a more rapidly lethal illness than that carried by fleas.

Once within a human host, the organism is consumed (phagocytized) by monocytic

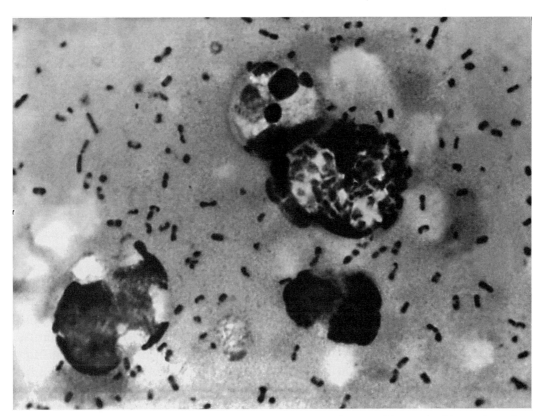

Bubonic plague smear demonstrating the presence of Yersinia pestis *bacteria. (Centers for Disease Control)*

blood cells but, because of its protective capsule, is not destroyed. The monocytes collect in lymph nodes, which swell and necrose, causing the characteristic swellings, or buboes. The organism can also spread in the blood stream and involve the liver, spleen, and lungs. Toxins from Yersinia can impair blood coagulation, leading to subcutaneous hemorrhage. This bleeding, together with the cyanosis caused by pulmonary failure, results in the black skin that led to the disease being called the black death.

Plague typically starts within two days of exposure as fever, malaise, and headache. Shortly thereafter, lymph node swelling causes tenderness and rigidity in the limbs with painful buboes typically located near the joints. Antibiotics such as tetracycline are highly effective if administered within 24 hours of exposure. The disease can usually be prevented with either of two vaccines. Without treatment, approximately 60 percent of patients with bubonic plague and 90 percent of those with the airborne pneumonic variety will die.

Epidemics have been vividly described throughout recorded history. The Philistine epidemic described in Samuel I:3–4 was very likely plague, as was the rat-related disease described in the *Iliad*. Rufus of Ephesus described a first-century plague epidemic that affected what is now Libya, Syria, and Egypt and referred to earlier episodes dating as far back as 300 B.C., although it is impossible to be certain these were all bubonic plague.

There have been four well-documented pandemics: the Plague of Justinian of A.D. 542–543, in which as many as 10,000 people a day died in Constantinople; the Black Death of the 14th century, which decreased the population of China by half and of Eu-

rope by one-third; the Great Plague of 1665–1666, which cut the population of London nearly in half; and the plague of 1890, which started in Burma and spread through Asia and to the United States and which established a worldwide reservoir of the disease in feral rodents. The last plague outbreak was in Surat, India, in 1994, with approximately 5,000 cases but, because of antibiotic treatment, only about 100 deaths.

The first mention of plague as a biological weapon was in 1346. In what may have been an apocryphal incident, a contemporary historian accused besieging Tatars of catapulting plague-infected corpses over the walls of a Genoese trading post at Caffa in the Crimea. What is certain is that the Genoese returned home that year carrying the disease that spread through the rest of Europe as the Black Death and the Tatars went on to spread the disease in Russia and the rest of West Asia. The Japanese dropped plague-infested fleas over Manchurian cities during World War II, causing several thousand deaths. Soviet scientists developed an antibiotic-resistant, readily aerosolized form of the plague organism that could be dropped from pilotless drones or delivered in warheads or artillery shells and produced up to 1,500 tons a year of weaponized Yersinia at the height of their country's biological weapons program. It is believed that, along with anthrax and botulinum toxin, plague was central to the Iraqi bioweapons program of the 1980s and early 1990s.

A vaccine against plague, made with killed Yersinia organisms, was developed, but it is no longer produced. There are no adequate controlled studies of antibiotic treatment of plague, but it is assumed that drugs of the tetracycline and aminoglycoside families remain somewhat effective. In spite of treatment, of the seven victims of pneumonic plague in the United States in the last 50 years, four have died.

See also Chemical and Biological Warfare; Unit 731; Vozrozhdeniye Island; World War II Medicine

References
Cartwright, Frederick, in collaboration with Michael Biddiss. *Disease and History.* New York: Dorset Press, 1972.
Inglesby, T. V., D. T. Dennis, D. A. Henderson, J. G. Bartlett, M. S. Ascher, E. Eitzen, A. D. Fine, A. M. Friedlander, J. Hauer, J. F. Koerner, M. Layton, J. McDade, M. T. Osterholm, T. O'Toole, G. Parker, T. M. Perl, P. K. Russell, M. Schoch-Spana, K. Tonat, and the Working Group on Civilian Biodefense. 2000. "Plague as a Biologic Weapon: Medical and Public Health Management." *Journal of the American Medical Association* 283 (May 3): 2281–2290.
Miller, Judith, Stephen Engelberg, and William Broad. *Germs: Biological Weapons and America's Secret War.* New York: Simon & Schuster, 2001.
Reidel, Stefan. 2005. "Plague: From Natural Disease to Bioterrorism." *Baylor University Medical Center Proceedings* 18: 116–124.

Posttraumatic Stress Disorder (PTSD)

Fear, hopelessness, or horror in the face of threat of injury of death occurring for longer than a month and usually within three months after physical or psychological trauma, posttraumatic stress disorder (PTSD) can also be associated with elevated blood pressure, asthma, or chronic pain. Other symptoms necessary to the diagnosis include tendency to reexperience the triggering event, such as in nightmares or flashbacks; avoidance of reminders of the event; and hyperarousal, often manifested as insomnia, irritability, impaired concentration, hypervigilance, or an increased startle response.

Recent studies have demonstrated a number of physiologic abnormalities in people suffering from PTSD. Circulating levels of norepinephrine and increased activity of receptors to that hormone are present, as is increased thyroid hormone. Brain activity in the amygdala and hypothalamus in response to trauma have also been demonstrated. Because these are brain areas involved in both memory and fear response, they may represent the disease's anatomic substrate.

Posttraumatic stress disorder is more common after episodes involving interpersonal violence than other types of trauma, and it has been particularly common in wartime and in terrorist attacks. About 35 percent of those directly involved in the 1995 bombing of Oklahoma City's Murrah Federal Building were subsequently diagnosed with PTSD. The diagnosis is probably closely related to, if not identical with, World War I's shell shock and World War II's combat fatigue.

About 5 percent of males and 10–14 percent of females in the civilian population suffer from PTSD at some time in their lives. By comparison, the incidence of the disease is 15 percent in Viet Nam veterans and between 2 and 10 percent in veterans of the Gulf War. Prior to the Afghanistan and Iraq deployment, 6 percent of active-duty members of the American military sought treatment for PTSD. Since that deployment, the incidence of PTSD has been linearly related to combat exposure. It has been less common in Afghanistan, where the number of firefights has been relatively low. In Iraq, the incidence has been 4.5 percent in those never involved in a firefight and as high as 19.3 percent in those involved in five or more engagements.

See also Combat Fatigue; Shell Shock in World
War I

References
Hoge, C. W., C. A. Castro, S. C. Messer,
D. McGurk, D. I. Cotting, and R. L.
Koffman. 2004. "Combat Duty in Iraq and
Afghanistan, Mental Health Problems, and
Barriers to Care." *New England Journal of
Medicine* 351 (July 1): 13–22.
Yehuda, Rachel. 2002. "Post Traumatic Stress
Disorder." *New England Journal of Medicine*
346 (January 10): 108–114.

Pott, Percival
(1714–1788)

Percival Pott was a prominent English surgeon who described the type of fracture, the inflammatory disease of the spine, and the frontal sinus abscess that bear his name.

Pott was born in a house on Threadneedle Street in London where the Bank of England now stands. His family was prominent, but his father died when Pott was only three, leaving his wife and children in dire financial straits. He was apprenticed to Edward Nourse, assistant surgeon to St. Bartholomew's Hospital, at age 15 and passed the examination to be admitted to the Company of Barber Surgeons in 1736. He then opened what was to become one of London's most successful surgical practices.

In 1745, Pott was appointed assistant surgeon to St. Bartholomew's and, four years later, succeeded Nourse as surgeon to the hospital and ultimately became the institution's most renowned 18th-century physician. The year Pott joined St. Bartholomew's, the Company of Surgeons separated from the barbers, and Pott's clinical expertise, elegant demeanor, and social prominence played a major role in enhancing the status of surgery as a profession. In 1751, he joined William Hunter as master of anatomy at Surgeon's Hall and, at Hunter's recommendation, taught his brother John. In 1765, Pott became a fellow of the Royal Society.

Pott sustained a compound fracture of the tibia in the winter of 1756 and, although amputation was the standard treatment for that injury at the time, he elected conservative therapy (with Nourse's consultation and encouragement) and recovered without consequence. In spite of his own recovery, he continued to recommend removal of the limb when he treated patients with a similar injury. Four diseases bear his name: Pott's Puffy tumor, a swelling of the forehead over an infected frontal sinus; Pott's disease of the spine, the deformity due to tuberculous infection of the vertebrae; Pott's fracture, a fracture of the fibula above the ankle (not the injury he had sustained himself); and Pott's gangrene, which occurs due to loss of circulation in the extremities. He also described the testicular cancer that was an endemic occupational hazard among London chimney sweeps. Pott was especially adept at cranial surgery. His *Observation on the Natural Consequences of Those Injuries to Which the Head is Liable from External Violence*, published in 1768, set the standard for management of cranial injuries for almost a century.

Pott received the first honorary diploma ever granted by the Royal College of Surgeons of Edinburgh in 1786. He died of a chill in 1788.

See also Barber-Surgeons; Trephine, Trepan,
and Trephining

References
Dobson, Jessie. 1972. "Percival Pott." *Annals of
the Royal College of Surgeons* 50: 54–65.
Zimmerman, Leo, and Ilza Veith. *Great Ideas in
the History of Surgery.* Baltimore: Williams
& Wilkins Co., 1961.

Prehistoric Military Medicine

Because no written record exists of care for sick or injured combatants in the prehistoric period, military historians are forced to rely on information gained indirectly, such as the study of artifacts for information about types of weapons, bones for evidence of injury or attempts to treat it, or surviving primitive cultures for clues to how ancient people with similar technology and lifestyles might have behaved.

Archaeological evidence confirms the use of rocks, clubs, slings, spears, and arrows as weapons, so we can assume that prehistoric fighters suffered both crushing and penetrating injuries. In one of the earliest written descriptions of transport of casualties by barbarian warriors, first-century Roman historian Gaius Cornelius Tacitus noted approvingly that the primitive Germanic tribes were careful to remove their dead and wounded from the battlefield.

By far the most common direct evidence of injury from combat and its treatment is in surviving skulls. Trephined skulls have been found in Europe, the Americas (primarily Peru and the United States), Africa, and the Pacific Islands. Many of these remains suggest intentional efforts to repair depressed fractures—likely the result of a blow from a blunt object—and 63 percent of those in one collection show signs of healing that suggest that the wounded individual survived the surgery. Some South American skulls have even been fitted with silver plates to cover bony defects. Although they lacked writing, Incas recorded trephine on both vases and statues. The prehistoric technique for repairing skull fractures is suggested by that of early 20th-century Berbers, who rotated pointed iron rods against the head to penetrate bone.

However, we know next to nothing about prehistoric treatment of soft tissue injuries as those wounds leave no evidence in skeletal remains.

See also Head Injury and Cranial Surgery

References

Gurdjian, E. S. *Head Injury from Antiquity to the Present with Special Reference to Penetrating Head Wounds.* Springfield, IL: Charles C. Thomas, 1973.

Mooche, R. L. 1927. "Studies in Paleopathology XXI. Injuries of the Head among the Pre-Columbian Peruvians." *Annals of Medical History* 9: 277–307.

Pringle, Sir John
(1707–1782)

Sir John Pringle may be considered the founder of modern military medicine.

Born the youngest son of Sir John Pringle of Stitchel, Roxburghshire, Scotland, Pringle was educated at home prior to matriculating at St. Andrews University where he lived with a cousin who was a professor of Greek. He began his study of medicine at Edinburgh before moving to the Continent where he received his medical degree from the University of Leiden in the Netherlands. During that time, he studied under Hermann Boerhaave and became friends with Albrecht Haller and Gerard von Swietan. He returned to Edinburgh, where he taught moral philosophy at that city's university and became personal physician to the Earl of Stair, who commanded the British forces in Flanders during the War of the Austrian Succession.

Pringle was named physician to the military hospital in Flanders in 1742 and physician general to the army in the Low Countries in 1745. After the Battle of Dettingen, he suggested to the Earl of Stair that

French and English commanders agree to make military hospitals immune from attack. The earl reached an agreement with the Duc de Noailles to that effect, and that accord formed the totality of military medical protection until Henry Dunant inspired the Geneva Convention in 1854. In 1746, he accompanied the Duke of Cumberland to Scotland and participated in the Battle of Culloden. In 1747 and 1748, he again joined the army in Europe.

After the peace of Aix-la-Chapelle in 1749, Pringle returned to London, where he served as personal physician to the Duke of Cumberland. In 1750, he published his 52-page essay "The Hospital and Jayl-Fevers," based on his experience at Culloden in which he was the first to claim that hospital and jail fevers—now known to both be louse-borne typhus—were one and the same. He also recommended that all prisoners should be given clean clothes prior to release and their jail garments be burned. In 1752, the same year he married Charlotte Oliver, he published *Observations on the Diseases of the Army*, the most important military medical text of the time.

Pringle was a pioneer of antisepsis (a term he may well have coined) and described 48 experiments conducted over three years in which he used various chemicals to stop decomposition in freshly killed animals and for which he received the Copley Gold Medal. Although he identified mineral salts with antibacterial properties and described them as antiseptics, he failed to recommend applying them to wounds. He encouraged sanitation in military facilities and improved ventilation in barracks, ships, and jails and claimed that hospitals themselves were a major cause of illness and disease in the army. He also recognized that scabies, previously thought to be due to poor air or

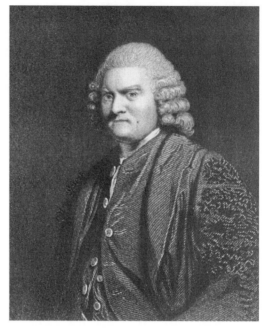

Sir John Pringle, British physician sometimes called the founder of modern military medicine. (National Library of Medicine)

bad diets, was due to the microscopic insects visible in material from pustules examined under Anton von Leeuwenhoek's recently described microscope. He recommended sulfur ointment as a treatment for the rash.

In 1761, Pringle was appointed physician to the household of Queen Charlotte and, shortly thereafter, her physician in ordinary. Pringle received his baronetcy in 1766 and was appointed physician-in-ordinary to the king's mother as well. He was elected president of the Royal Society in 1772 and named physician extraordinary to the king in 1774. Pringle was quite wealthy and, upon retiring at age 70, moved back to Edinburgh where he planned to live out his years in comfort. His age and the northern climate proved incompatible, so he returned to London, where he died at age 75. His grave at Piccadilly was destroyed in a World War

II bombing raid, although a monument to him remains in the Poets' Corner in Westminster Abbey.

See also Antisepsis; British Military Medicine

Reference
Selwyn, Sydney. 1966. "Sir John Pringle: Hospital Reformer, Moral Philosopher and Pioneer of Antiseptics." *Medical History* 10 (July): 266–274.

Prussian and German Military Medicine

Together with France, Prussia and its successor German empire were the founders and principal innovators in European military medicine.

Modern military medicine began when Holy Roman Emperor Maximilian V and King Charles VII of France restored standing armies to Europe for the first time since the Roman Empire. Each placed troops under direct royal control and, by implication, became responsible for their care and well-being.

Maximilian's innovation was carried on by his successor, Charles V, whose grandmother, Isabella of Castille, had introduced field hospitals for her troops. In 1555, Georg von Frundsberg introduced sanitary measures to Charles's armies that have been credited as the foundation of subsequent German military medicine. Each company of infantry and each squadron of cavalry had its own *feldscherer* or *feldscher* (field shaver or barber-surgeon), the field marshal of cavalry had a physician, and the commander of artillery had a surgeon. A physician in chief was in charge of the lower-rank surgeons and *feldschers* and was responsible for seeing that they had

the necessary instruments and supplies. He was also responsible for approving any proposed amputation, for transport of the wounded, for placing dressing stations, and for settling disputes over fees between the barbers and the soldiers they treated. The physician in chief was required to remain "on call" and readily findable next to the field commander's tent. The sick and wounded in Charles's army convalesced in the baggage train, where they were cared for by female camp followers. Those too sick to travel were left behind in makeshift hospitals in the most convenient town.

By the 16th century, gunpowder was in common military use. In the early years, German military surgeons had not yet been convinced that those wounds were poisoned and did not regularly treat them with amputation as would be done by their successors. Through the Thirty Years War and the wars of Louis XIV, weapons and tactics outstripped the ability of military surgeons to treat the wounds they inflicted.

Through the 17th century, the Electorate of Brandenburg (which did not unite with the Duchy of Prussia until 1705) maintained a standing army. *Feldschers* continued to serve as regimental surgeons, officers' barbers, standard bearers, and combatants. The first medical college in Brandenburg opened in 1685, established by the Great Elector of the Holy Roman Empire. The same year, Friedrich I of Prussia began requiring his *feldschers* to pass examinations before being accepted into the army. Matthias Purmann, who served in the Brandenburg army, was widely viewed as the most accomplished surgeon of his era. Wilhelm Fabry of Hilden was the father of German surgery, and Johannes Schultes (Scultetus) published the standard German atlas of surgical operations in 1653.

In 1620, disabled soldiers who had served in the Prussian army were given the "privilege" of begging for a living after discharge. Citizens who refused to donate a penny were liable to being beaten with a cudgel. That same year, Maximilian I of Bavaria organized Germany's first military hospitals for his soldiers fighting with the Catholic League. The hospitals had large, well-ventilated wards segregated by type of disease and with special care taken to limit contact between patients with dysentery and the rest of the population.

In the 18th century, military medicine finally became a function of and the responsibility of the government. Prussia got its first military hospital near Berlin's Spandau Gate in 1710, and the institution was chartered by royal warrant as the *Charité* in 1725. In 1713, Friedrich Wilhelm I made regimental barbers junior officers, a considerable elevation in status. He also dispatched some of his military physicians to study in Paris and appointed Ernst Conrad von Holtzendorff the first surgeon general of the Prussian Army in 1716. In 1724 he created the *Collegium Medico-Chirurgicum* to train military medical officers and, following his own successful treatment for gout, endowed the *Charité*. Among the supervisory rules in his army was the requirement that every patient who died in the care of a *feldscher* be the subject of an autopsy observed by an independent officer.

When Frederick the Great found himself fighting on four fronts during the Seven Years War, he recognized that he could not afford to lose any combatants and, consequently, took a personal interest in his sick and wounded, including personally picking sites for dressing stations and rear-area hospitals. Frederick abandoned the Prussian tradition of tending to the wounded only after bugles signaled the end of a battle and authorized removing the injured from the field while fighting was still in progress. He also saw to the removal and treatment of his wounded enemies after his own men were cared for.

Through the 1700s, German surgeons steadily rose in status, and, in 1797, surgeon Johann Görcke became chief of military sanitation and general staff surgeon to the Prussian Army, the first time positions of that importance had been given to a surgeon rather than a physician. He held those offices and was in charge of training military surgeons in Berlin for 55 years. The *Collegium Medico-Chirurgicum*, which Görcke directed, was renamed the Pépinière in 1795 (it would become the Friedrich Wilhelms Institut in 1821 and the Kaiser Wilhelms Akademie in 1895), and training for military surgeons progressively improved through the century. The Prussians built clean, well-ventilated rear-area hospitals and designed field hospitals capable of holding 1,000 patients, and, by 1813, the Prussian military medical service was managing more than 10,000 beds.

The Prussians entered their mid-19th-century wars with Austria and France with a well-manned, well-supplied medical service. By 1848, surgery in Germany had become a respected academic discipline with greater status than elsewhere in Europe. By 1870, the army was able to draw on a large, well-trained civilian reserve to augment its full-time medical service. Prussia went to war with France with five times as many medical officers as its opponent. Prussia had sanitary companies, stratified care facilities from dressing stations to rear-area general hospitals, dedicated companies of litter bearers, ambulances modeled after those designed by Jonathan Letterman for the

American Union Army, and 200 specially designed hospital railcars. The French, on the other hand, relied on volunteer charity hospitals, volunteer nurses, and litter bearers drawn from combat units.

The Prussians also adopted Joseph Lister's antiseptic surgical technique. The stunning success in decreasing surgical mortality and morbidity led to Lister's being treated as a German national hero on his postwar tour through the new empire. The French did not adopt antisepsis, did not vaccinate their soldiers, and suffered disastrous rates of operative infection and a smallpox rate four times that of their adversaries. The Franco-Prussian War was the first time a modern military force had lost fewer men to disease than to trauma, and that success led to Prussia being the model for the reform of the British medical service and the creation of the imperial Japanese service.

Germany incorporated the best aspects of the Prussian system into its medical services in World War I. In 1914, Germany mobilized virtually its entire medical establishment. German military physicians pioneered steam sterilization of surgical instruments, use of sterile gowns and masks for the surgical team, general use of rubber gloves (although credit for their invention belongs to American surgeons), and the replacement of open surgical amphitheaters with closed, clean operating suites. German soldiers were trained to use first aid kits, benefited from forward-area surgery, and used a sophisticated network of water and rail transport to move the wounded to rear-area hospitals. The German Imperial Army even experimented with evacuation by airplane.

World War II German military medicine saw a significant decline in quality, partially due to removal of some the country's most talented practitioners who were Jewish and partially because physicians were often promoted for political rather than scientific reasons. In 1939, the German Army had no blood-banking capability, no access to penicillin, and had only limited supplies of sulfa drugs. What had once been indisputably the best military medical establishment in the world had, under the Nazi regime, become decidedly second rate. To complicate the problem further, German military physicians were actively involved in horrific human experiments that led to a number of them being tried for crimes against humanity after the war.

See also Barber-Surgeons; Fabry of Hilden, Wilhelm; Franco-Prussian War; Gersdorff, Hans von; Görcke, Johann; Holtzendorff, Ernst Conrad; Nuremburg Code; Purmann, Matthias; Scultetus, Johannes (also Johannes Schultes); 17th-Century Military Medicine; 16th-Century Military Medicine; Torture; World War I Medicine; World War II Medicine

References

Dealey, Carol. 2005. "German Wound Surgeons: 1450–1750." *European Wound Management Association Journal* 5: 48–52.

Sigerist, Henry. *The Book of Cirurgia by Hieronymus Brunschwig*. Milan, Italy: R. Lier & Co., 1923.

Swain, Valentine A. J. 1970. "Franco-Prussian War, 1870–1871: Voluntary Aid for the Wounded and Sick." *British Medical Journal* 29 (August): 514–517.

Purmann, Matthias (1648–1721 or 1649–1711)

Matthias Purmann was surgeon to the Brandenburg army; his main contribution was improvement in the treatment of gunshot wounds.

Born in Lüben, the son of that city's mayor, Purmann's *Fifty Unusual and Wonderful Cases of Gunshot Wounds* (1694) and *Twenty-five Remarkable Gunshot Wounds* (1697) questioned the use of cauteries, plasters, hot oil, and ointments on fresh gunshot wounds. Instead, he recommended cleaning the wounds thoroughly, loosely closing the edges, and bandaging them to prevent further contamination. He insisted that all good surgery must be based in a solid knowledge of anatomy. Purmann performed more than 40 trephines for head injury, attempted blood transfusions from lambs to humans, and successfully sewed torn intestines, but, for all the skill and good sense he showed in directly treating battlefield injuries, he succumbed to Paracelsus's odd recommendation that healing ointments be applied to the weapon that had administered a wound in the hope that the patient would be mysteriously healed at a distance.

Purmann served as physician to the city of Breslau until his death.

See also Bullet Wounds and Other Penetrating Injuries from Gunpowder Projectiles; Cauterization; Prussian and German Military Medicine; 17th-Century Military Medicine

References

Garrison, Fielding. *An Introduction to the History of Medicine*. Philadelphia: W. B. Saunders Co., 1929.

Sachs, Michael, Jörg Bohunga, and Albrecht Encke. 1999. "Historical Evolution of Limb Amputation." *World Journal of Surgery* 23 (October): 1088–1093.

Q Fever

Q fever is a rickettsial disease caused by *Coxiella burnetii* and is primarily of military interest for its potential as a biological weapon.

Q fever got its name from "query," a reflection of the fact that its cause was originally a mystery. The disease is, in fact, caused by a small, rod-shaped or coccobacillary gram-negative bacterium that is endemic in sheep, goats, and cattle and can spread through the air in fomites originating from animal feces. In humans, Q fever causes an initial flu-like illness followed by chills, fever, headache, and face pain. If it involves the central nervous system, it can cause speech abnormalities and delirium; if inhaled, it can cause pneumonia. The infection can also cause inflammation of the heart lining (endocardium) or valves and can result in cardiac failure and death. Although mortality from Q fever is unusual, it is incapacitating and is a good candidate for weaponization because disease can be caused by as little as a single organism, and the bacterium can be easily aerosolized and survives well outside its hosts.

The Soviet Union began experiments with Q fever as a weapon at the Solovetsky Island Gulag in the 1930s. Although naturally occurring Q fever is virtually nonexistent in the Soviet Union, a suspicious outbreak was documented in German troops on leave in the Crimea in 1943, suggesting that it may have been caused deliberately. The disease also occurred—probably naturally—among German troops in southeastern Europe, where it was called Balkan grippe, and among British troops in Greece, where the attack rate may have reached 30 percent. It was also seen in American troops serving in Corsica and Italy.

After World War II, the U.S. Army experimented with Q fever at biowarfare research facilities at Fort Detrick, Maryland, and at the Dugway Proving Ground in Utah, where the organism was tested on Seventh-Day Adventist conscientious objectors. *Coxiella burnetii* was produced in bulk at the Pine Bluff Arsenal in Arkansas after 1951. It was also one of the agents tested by the Japanese Aum Shinrikyo cult prior to their releasing sarin gas in a Tokyo subway. The World Health Organization estimates that 50 kilograms of *Coxiella burnetii* released as an aerosol over a 20-kilometer urban area would incapacitate 125,000 people and kill about 500.

See also Chemical and Biological Warfare; Vozrozhdeniye Island

References

Alibek, Ken, with Stephen Handelman. *Biohazard*. London: Arrow Books, 2000.

Kelly, Daryl J., Allen L. Richards, Joseph Temenak, Daniel Strickman, and Gregory A. Dasch. 2002. "The Past and Present Threat of Rickettsial Diseases to Military Medicine and International Public Health." *Clinical Infectious Diseases* 34: S145–S169.

Queen Alexandra's Imperial Military Nursing Service

The nursing service of the British Army was formed by royal warrant on March 27, 1902.

Military nursing in Britain dates to Roman army hospitals established in A.D. 43. Between A.D. 335, when Emperor Constantine closed all military hospitals, and the formation of a standing army in Britain in 1660, military nursing was almost entirely the province of various religious orders. Through the 17th, 18th, and most of the 19th centuries, soldiers had been nursed either by their comrades or by wives and other women who followed the various campaigns.

This situation changed in 1854 when Florence Nightingale, an educated upper-class British woman with extensive social and political connections, took it upon herself to improve care for the sick and injured in the Crimean War. She recruited 38 ladies (the majority from religious orders) to work at the notoriously filthy military hospital at Scutari near Constantinople. Her nurses proved singularly effective and above

moral reproach and set nursing on the road to becoming a profession.

In February 1880, the National Society to Aid the Sick and Wounded in War established a fund to pay for training nurses to serve at British military medical facilities. In June of that year, Mrs. Jane C. Deeble became the first superintendent of nurses at the Royal Victoria Hospital at Netley as well as that hospital's training program. In 1881, the Army Nursing Service was formed and headquartered at Netley. Deeble's nurses gave medicines, changed dressings, gave enemas, washed patients, made beds, and prepared special diets and teas. They were chosen from the middle class with the thought that adherence to the British caste system would lead to their being obeyed by orderlies and attendants who generally came from the lower social ranks. Their numbers were augmented in 1897 when Princess Christina, Queen Victoria's third daughter, chartered the Army Nursing Service Reserve under her warrant. The enlarged service came just in time for the Boer War, and the new reserve ultimately sent 1,400 women to South Africa.

Medical failures in that war led to formation of the Royal Commission on the Care and Treatment of the Sick and Wounded during the South African campaign in 1902 charged with reorganization of both the army medical and nursing services. As a result, Queen Alexandra's Imperial Military Nursing Service (QAIMNS) was formed from a combination of the Army Nursing Service and the Indian Nursing Service on March 27, 1902. Nursing "sisters"—a term harking back to the time when hospital care was the province of nuns—were to be paid £30 a year to start, with progressive raises to a maximum of £50; were to have rank equivalent to officers but not commissions;

and were to be in charge of hospital wards and personnel. From that time, "QAs" served anywhere in the world where there was a British Army hospital.

The QAIMNS entered World War I in August 1914 with fewer than 300 members. By 1919, there were 10,404 Army nurses augmented by 9,000 members of volunteer aid detachments (VADs) who served under them. The QAs went to France with the British Expeditionary Force commanded by Dame Maud McCarthy, a formidable Australian-born matron in chief. They ultimately saw service in Lemnos, Salonika, Egypt, and Mesopotamia in addition to France and accompanied the British expedition to Archangel after the war. Although they were subject to a certain amount of teasing at the hands of the regular soldiers (including having their acronym reconfigured to Queer and Impossible, Mostly Not Sane or Queer Assortment of Individuals, Mainly Non-Sexed), they were generally respected and appreciated for their service.

The status of nursing in Britain changed dramatically in 1919 with passage of laws regulating the profession and its educational requirements. In 1926, members of the QAIMNS were officially allotted officer's rank, although that status was not recognized by the Japanese when a number of the nurses became prisoners in World War II.

In addition to being captured in Hong Kong and Singapore, QAs served with the British Expeditionary Force and in North Africa. Even in the desert heat, the nurses were required to wear the ankle-length gray wool dresses and white aprons that were virtually unchanged from their original 19th-century uniforms. Finally, in 1944, they were allowed to change to khaki and to wear pants on duty. On February 6, 1949, the unit was changed to the Queen Alexandra's Royal Army Nursing Corps by warrant of King George VI, and, for the first time, the nurses were made full members of the British Army. In 1950, the corps, with admission of its first noncommissioned officers, had all the accoutrements of a regular military unit.

See also Boer War; Crimean War; Nightingale, Florence; World War I Medicine; World War II Medicine

Reference
Piggott, Juliet. *Queen Alexandra's Royal Army Nursing Corps.* London: Leo Cooper, Ltd., 1975.

Quesnay, François (1694–1774)

A surgeon and an economist who played a central role in the development of surgery for brain injuries, François Quesnay was born in Metz in northeastern France to a well-to-do rural family and worked on that family's farms until the age of 16. It is said he was illiterate until apprenticed to a local barber-surgeon, under whose tutelage he learned to read French, Latin, and Greek and in whose library he read voraciously. Quesnay moved to Paris, where he lived with famous engraver Charles Nicolas Cochin, from whom he learned artistic techniques he would later use to illustrate his own work and where he was admitted to the Collège de St. Côme, from which he graduated in 1718.

After graduating from St. Côme, Quesnay opened a practice in Paris and, when François de la Peyronie founded the Royal Academy of Surgeons, he was appointed secretary of that organization. Quesnay was responsible for publication of the society's *Memoires*, to which he regularly contributed.

While only 34, he lost his wife and was left to raise two children and suffer recurrent episodes of gout alone. He was appointed *Chirurgien Royal* in 1723 and became close to both Louis XV and the king's mistress, Madame de Pompadour, who was also Quesnay's patient. It was rumored that, in addition to being the lady's doctor, Quesnay helped the couple conceal their liaison and gave them advice to overcome her bothersome distaste for sex. He took an apartment at Versailles and treated the dauphin for smallpox, for which the king elevated him to the nobility.

Quesnay contributed to Denis Diderot's encyclopedia and became close friends with economist Adam Smith. His interest in economics led him to become the most famous specialist in that area among the Enlightenment physiocrats, and Quesnay is perhaps better remembered as an economist than as a physician.

In the first volume of the Academy of Surgeons' *Memoires*, Quesnay wrote essays on using multiple trephines to control skull infections, recommended surgery for elevation of all depressed skull fractures, and suggested that surgery on the head only be performed outside the hospital to avoid infection. He recognized that aggressive use of exploratory surgery in head injuries would result in many negative explorations but thought the risk worth the possible benefit of relieving masses pressing on the brain that would otherwise be missed. He was one of the few surgeons of his time who was convinced that, with proper treatment and removal of all foreign bodies, the injured brain could recover as well as any other organ.

Although he had previously been on good terms with his British colleagues (and had even been named a fellow of the British Royal Society) in the mid-17th century,

Quesnay's reputation outside France plummeted during the Napoleonic Wars. His work was bitterly denounced by John Bell, who accused him of having been far too cavalier about opening the head.

Quesnay's finances also declined late in life, and he died poor at the age of 80 in 1774.

See also Head Injury and Cranial Surgery

Reference
Bakay, Louis. 1985. "François Quesnay and the Birth of Brain Surgery." *Neurosurgery* 17: 518–521.

Quinine

Quinine is an alkaloid derived from the chinchona (or cinchona) tree used to both treat and prevent fevers, especially malaria.

Peruvian natives knew that tree bark, which they called cinchona (or bark of bark), was effective against malaria long before Francisco Pizarro and his Spanish *conquistadores* conquered the Incan empire. The powdered bark came to Europe in the early 1640s with the name chinchona after Anna Del Chinchon, wife of the Spanish viceroy of Peru who was said to have recovered from a near-fatal bout of fever with the drug's help. In gratitude, she made the powder available to the poor in Peru and, with the help of Jesuit priests, exported it to Spain.

Spanish attempts to maintain a monopoly on chinchona production were foiled by British and Dutch adventurers who, in the 1860s, stole seeds from Peru and started the plantations in Java that subsequently supplied 95 percent of the world's needs prior to World War II. French chemists Pierre Pelletier and Joseph Cavertou extracted quinine, the active alkaloid, from the bark in the 1820s, and the drug was synthesized from coal tar in 1944, although it remains more economical to produce from natural sources. The chinchona tree or bush belongs to the family Rubiaceae, which includes the gardenia and coffee plants. Only a few varieties of chinchona actually produce significant amounts of quinine.

National rivalries delayed universal use of chinchona, but its efficacy and the prevalence of malaria in the colonies eventually overcame objections to taking "Jesuit powder," and it became a mainstay of tropical life. Perhaps its greatest disadvantage is an unpleasantly bitter taste that led the Spanish to put it in sherry wine, which they labeled *quiñada*, and the British to combine it with lime and spirits as gin and tonic.

Quinine became a staple of the Royal Navy in the early 19th century and was a major factor in Britain's ability to maintain a blockade of the West African slave coast through the 1830s. After 1814, ships' surgeons were ordered to dispense the drug prophylactically, although the dose was not well defined and the sailors often refused to take it. During an expedition up the Niger River, T. R. H. Thompson experimented with quinine dosage and proved that eliminating malarial episodes required 380–650 milligrams a day, about three times the previously recommended dose. Even at that, the disease often recurred after the men returned home and stopped taking the drug.

The drug has a number of unpleasant side effects, including vomiting; disturbances of vision; ringing in the ears, which can progress to deafness; headache; and rash. These side effects and concerns about access to chinchona bark led to the development of mepacrine hydrochloride (Atebrin or Atabrine) just before World War II. Although Atabrine turned the skin yellow and often caused vomiting and anxiety, it proved remarkably effective in preventing malaria during the Burma and New Guinea campaigns. Atabrine was later replaced by mefloquine and, in Viet Nam, by single doses of pyrimethamine and sulphormetoxine. Drug-resistant strains of malaria have brought quinine back into more common use in recent years and have also stirred renewed interest in Atabrine.

See also Malaria; Viet Nam War; World War II
Medicine

Reference
Hobhouse, Henry. *Seeds of Change: Five Plants that Transformed Mankind*. New York: Harper & Row, 1957.

R

Red Cross and Red Crescent

A humanitarian movement comprising three components—the National Societies, the International Federation of Red Cross and Red Crescent Societies, and the International Committee of the Red Cross (ICRC)—is collectively known as the Red Cross and the Red Crescent.

The Red Cross movement began in June 1859 when Swiss businessman Henry Dunant happened on the Italian town of Castiglione della Stiviere after the Battle of Solferino, in which 6,000 men were killed and another 42,000 were wounded. Many of the latter had found their way to Castiglione, and about 500 had taken refuge in the Chiesa Maggiore, the town's church, where Dunant collected volunteers to render aid. He was appalled at the French military's lack of supplies and personnel and later described his experience in his 1862 *Un Souvenir de Solferino*.

In 1863, Genevan Gustave Moynier helped Dunant organize the International Committee for the Relief of Wounded Soldiers, composed of other prominent citizens of Geneva, including Commander of the Swiss Army General Guillaume-Henri Dufour, with the goal of establishing a series of national relief committees. The group called an international conference in Geneva in October 1863 which included 36 attendees and 18 official delegates from 14 countries. Among the proposals from that group was the suggestion that volunteer medical personnel from all countries should wear a white arm band with a red cross (a reverse of the Swiss national flag) which had been designed by Dufour. Within a year, nine national societies had been formed.

Dunant also thought that all medical personnel on the battlefield should be treated as neutrals, and, to that end, a second conference was convened in the Swiss capital, which drafted the Geneva Convention of August 22, 1864, for the Amelioration of the Condition of the Wounded in Armies in the Field. The conventions' 10 articles called for, among other changes, universal use of the red cross emblem and protection of medical personnel, hospitals, and wounded or sick combatants.

Swiss businessman Henry Dunant wrote A Memoir of Solferino *in which he chronicled the devastation and suffering after a battle in Italy. His efforts led to the creation of the International Committee of the Red Cross and earned him the first Nobel Peace Prize. (Library of Congress)*

Although the red cross was never intended as a religious symbol, Islamic countries found it objectionable. During the 1876 Russo-Turkish War, the Ottoman Society for Relief to the Wounded chose a red crescent on a white background, and that emblem was subsequently adopted by the majority of Muslim nations.

The Geneva Convention elevated rules regarding care and protection of the sick and wounded from ad hoc agreements to the status of international law. The conventions were expanded in 1899, 1906, 1907, 1929, 1949, and 1977 and currently comprise four

conventions and a collection of additional protocols. Dunant's committee, renamed the International Committee of the Red Cross, is the protector of the conventions and is also responsible for admitting new national societies to the movement.

In 1919, Henry Davison, the head of the American Red Cross, called an international conference to associate the various national societies. That conference resulted in the League of Red Cross Societies, subsequently renamed the International Federation of Red Cross and Red Crescent Societies in 1991. In 1928, the League, the International Committee of the Red Cross, and the various national societies joined as the International Red Cross which was renamed the International Red Cross and Red Crescent Movement in 1986.

The ICRC maintains a permanent administrative and medical staff and acts to both protect the rights of wounded combatants, prisoners, and civilians during wars and to provide medical care, sanitary services, and general assistance in time of war.

See also Geneva Conventions

Reference

Vassallo, D. J. 1994. "The International Red Cross and Red Crescent Movement and Lessons from the Experience of War Surgery." *Journal of the Royal Army Medical Corps* 140: 146–154.

Reed, Walter
(1851–1902)

Walter Reed was an Army surgeon and chairman of the U.S. Army Yellow Fever Commission following the Spanish-American War.

Reed was born in Gloucester County, Virginia, on September 13, 1851, the son of a Methodist minister. He entered the University of Virginia at age 16 and graduated from the university's medical division a year later, the youngest man ever to do so. He then went to New York for an additional year at Bellevue Medical College, from which he received a second medical degree in 1870. After additional clinical training at several New York hospitals, he accepted a commission as assistant surgeon and first lieutenant in the Army medical corps in 1875. The following year he was posted to Arizona and spent the next 13 years at a series of western forts.

In 1889, Reed arranged to be posted as examiner of recruits in Baltimore, a position from which he was able to take courses in pathology and bacteriology at the new Johns Hopkins Medical School laboratories. In 1893, he was appointed curator of the Army Medical Museum and was named professor of bacteriology at the Army Medical School.

Shortly after the Spanish-American War broke out in 1898, typhoid fever emerged as a serious problem in army training camps, and Reed was named to a commission to investigate the disease. This appointment led to a subsequent assignment from Surgeon General George Sternberg to study infectious diseases in Cuba. That commission, composed of Reed, Aristides Agramonte, James Carroll, and Jesse Lazear, narrowed their studies to yellow fever at the suggestion of Surgeon Major Jefferson Keen. The commission devised a series of ingenious experiments using human volunteers to prove Cuban physician Carlos Finlay's hypothesis that the disease was transmitted by the *Stegomya fasciata* (*Aedes aegyptii*) mosquito. The commission performed the first experiments on themselves, although Reed declined to participate on the grounds that

he was too old and too important to risk his own life. Lazear died from his self-inflicted infection, and Carroll nearly did as well. In the end, almost all the credit for demonstrating that mosquitoes transmitted yellow fever and that the disease was caused by a "filterable virus" went to Reed, even though the original hypothesis was not his, he did not participate in the self-experimentation, and he did not design some of the most important experiments.

When the commission's work ended in 1901, Reed returned to the Army Medical School as professor of bacteriology and microscopy. He died of peritonitis in 1902 following surgery for appendicitis and was buried at Arlington National Cemetery.

See also Spanish-American War; Yellow Fever

References
Altman, Lawrence K. *Who Goes First? The Story of Self-Experimentation in Medicine.* New York: Random House, 1986.
Bean, William. *Walter Reed: A Biography.* Charlottesville: University of Virginia Press, 1982.
Truby, Albert E. *Memoir of Walter Reed: The Yellow Fever Episode.* New York: Paul B. Hoeber, Inc., 1943.

Rehabilitation and Reconstructive Surgery

Although a certain number of soldiers and sailors have survived their wounds for as long as wars have been fought, the percentage of those who live and the severity of survivable wounds have dramatically increased since anesthesia, antisepsis, and antibiotics entered the surgical armamentarium. The number of survivors with serious disabilities has increased as well. Rehabilitation and reconstruction are most often necessary in four general categories of trauma: amputations, burns, neurological injury, and wounds to the face and skin.

Amputations became particularly common after gunpowder weapons emerged as the primary means of warfare. These weapons were the first capable of producing enough power to regularly shatter bones and leave the fractures exposed to the outside world. Because of the high incidence of contamination in these "compound" fractures and the lack of effective treatment for the resulting infections, amputation became the standard method of treatment for gunshot wounds to the bone. Although some amputees survived 19th-century battlefield surgery, enough died to limit the demand for long-term care. By World War I, that trend had changed, and more than 8 million men came home from battles in Europe needing help to return to productive lives. That demand fueled rapid advances in prosthetic technology led by military hospitals, especially the Walter Reed Army Medical Center in Washington, D.C.

Coincidentally, rehabilitation and physiotherapy as professions had begun in the 1890s with the development of treatments based on massage, heat, and electrotherapy. These measures were outside the medical mainstream until the therapists convinced the military to use them, and electrotherapists became physiotherapists and acquired legitimacy and a professional status. Rehabilitation was co-opted as a medical specialty during the 1930s and was virtually entirely done either by physicians or therapists under their direct control by the beginning of World War II.

As in the United States, the government in Germany took an active responsibility for rehabilitation and support of its World War I veterans; the British and French governments generally did not. American government aid declined after the 1920 Vocational Rehabilitation Law, which allowed for occupational support but did not fund ongoing medical care for veterans. The situation again changed after the 1943 Vocational Rehabilitation Law, which funded medical care—both physical and psychological—and led to dramatic expansion in rehabilitation programs, notably in Veterans Administration hospitals.

Spinal cord injuries present a special rehabilitation challenge. Lord Horatio Nelson's death from such an injury was quite typical of his era. The admiral was carried below decks and allowed to die with his fellow officers circled around his bedside. Even though 45 percent of the 642 Union soldiers with spinal cord injuries documented in the *Medical and Surgical History of the War of the Rebellion* survived their initial trauma, those who were paralyzed were given supportive care only with the expectation that they would eventually die from complications such as pneumonia, urinary tract infection, or decubiti. Better wound and bladder care resulted in a few survivors during World War I and a few more during World War II, although Gen. George S. Patton's cervical spinal cord injury was still beyond his surgeon's ability to treat. The provision of continuing medical care for disabled veterans after World War II led for the first time to several thousand long-term cord injury survivors, and the average length of survival increased from several weeks to a decade or more.

Faster, more adept surgery and better neurosurgical intensive care has also resulted in an increasing number of survivors of traumatic brain injury. The long-term sequelae of these injuries range from mood swings, anxiety, and depression to severe

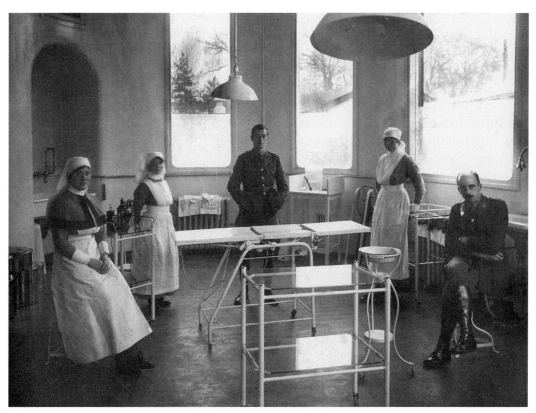

Harold Gillies (right) and staff in the cosmetic surgery theater, Queen Mary's Hospital, Kent, England, in 1917. Designed as the first plastic surgery center, doctors at the hospital performed more than 11,500 facial reconstruction procedures during World War I. (The Gillies Archives)

cognitive and motor deficits and are too often complicated by other disabilities such as loss of hearing or vision. Many of these wounds leave irreversible deficits and require multiple operations and permanent financial and social support.

Attempts at plastic surgical repair of battle injuries have been documented for centuries. Ambroise Paré attempted to replace severed facial parts with *papière maché*, silver, gold, and copper prostheses. During World War I, the British military enlisted artists to design and paint porcelain and metal substitutes for destroyed faces, and Harold Gillies established a dedicated plas-

tic reconstructive surgical unit at Aldershot, where he treated more than 2,000 facial injuries from the 1916 Battle of the Somme alone. That work was carried on during World War II by his cousin Archibald Hector McIndoe at the Queen Victoria Hospital. McIndoe specialized in facial burns and treated about 4,000 airmen, most injured by ignited airplane fuel, during which time he coined the term "reconstructive surgery."

Explosives are also particularly likely to cause burns, and the most severe of those from recent American wars have been referred to Brooke Army Medical Center in San Antonio, where both the prosthetic and the plastic surgical requirements of severely burned patients are addressed before a transition to local Veterans Administration care. These patients and their families are also afforded occupational and psychiatric support.

Modern battlefield surgical techniques have dramatically lowered the percentage of men and women who die from their initial injury and have consequently increased the numbers with persistent disabilities. By January 2005, the U.S. military had issued more than 5,000 Purple Hearts to those serving in Iraq and had evacuated 14,700 people to the United States for long-term care. Although small-arms fire accounted for most of the injuries early in that conflict, improvised explosive devices subsequently assumed dominance; these most often result in blast and burn injuries. Body armor, although relatively effective in protecting the torso, leaves the victims susceptible to extremity injuries, and there have been a large number of amputations. The American military has been active in prosthetic research, particularly at Walter Reed Army Medical Center, and has been in the forefront of research into devices such as computerized limbs and specialized artificial joints.

See also Blast Injuries; Iraq and Afghan Wars; World War I Medicine; World War II Medicine

References
Arluke, Arnold, and Glenn Gritzer. *The Making of Rehabilitation.* Berkeley: University of California Press, 1985.
Dillingham, J. R. 2002. "Physiatry, Physical Medicine, and Rehabilitation: Historical Development and Military Roles." *Physical Medicine and Rehabilitation Clinics of North America* 13 (February): 1–16.
Fauntleroy, A. M. *Report on the Medico-Military Aspects of the European War from Observations Taken Behind the Allied Armies in France.* Washington, D.C.: Government Printing Office, 1915.
Min, S. K. 2000. "A History of Maxillofacial Prostheses." *Journal of the Korean Association of Plastic and Reconstructive Surgery* 22 (July): 383–396.
Okie, Susan. 2005. "Traumatic Brain Injury in the War Zone." *New England Journal of Medicine* 352 (May 19): 2043–2048.
Peake, James. 2005. "Beyond the Purple Heart—Continuity of Care for the Wounded in Iraq." *New England Journal of Medicine* 352 (January 20): 219–222.

Reyher, Carl (1846–1890)

Carl Reyher was a Russian military surgeon best known for his work in débridement of gunshot wounds.

Reyher graduated from the medical school at Dorpat in 1870 and enlisted as a surgeon in the Prussian Army during the Franco-Prussian War. After the war, he worked with K. W. Heine treating the wounded at the hospital in Nancy. In 1872, he returned to Dorpat, where he worked with Ernst von Bergmann until 1877. In 1878, Reyher returned to the military as a surgeon in the Russian Army during the Russo-Turkish War.

After visiting Lord Joseph Lister in London, he returned to Germany, and, in 1881, he presented his landmark "Primary Débridement for Gunshot Wounds" to the International Medical Conference in London. In that paper, he recommended wide removal of devitalized tissue followed by antiseptic irrigation in gunshot wounds. The irrigation was remembered, but his contemporaries ignored the recommendation for débridement in spite of the fact that Reyher managed to decrease the mortality in these wounds from 66 percent to 23 percent. His technique lay dormant for more than three decades before being rediscovered and becoming standard practice in World War I.

See also Bullet Wounds and Other Penetrating Injuries from Gunpowder Projectiles; Franco-Prussian War; Russian Military Medicine; World War I Medicine

Reference

Wangensteen, O. H., and S. D. Wangensteen. 1973. "Carl Reyher (1846–1890), Great Russian Military Surgeon: His Demonstration of the Role of Débridement in Gunshot Wounds and Fractures." *Surgery* 74 (November): 641–649.

Rhazes (Abu Bakr Mohammed ben Zakariah) (ca. 860–932)

Rhazes was the most influential of the medieval Arab-Islamic physicians.

Rhazes was born in the village of Ray (near modern Tehran) in the Eastern, or Baghdad, Caliphate and took his name from his place of birth. He spent his early years studying first music, poetry, and philosophy and then alchemy, astrology, and mathematics. He did not take up medicine until he was almost 30 years old after being inspired by a visit to a Baghdad hospital. As a junior physician, he helped choose the site for Baghdad's new hospital by hanging bits of raw meat around the city and seeing in which location it lasted the longest without rotting, reasoning that this would be the site least prone to corruption and disease. Rhazes subsequently became chief physician at that hospital and divided his time between the capital, a second institution in his home village, and travels in Syria, Egypt, and Spain.

Rhazes joined Avicenna in the Eastern Caliphate and Albucasis of Cordova in the Western Caliphate as the great triumvirate of medieval Arabic physicians. Like the other two, he was principally a medical encyclopedist and organizer of both Greek and Eastern science. Although Persian was his first language, he wrote in Arabic and adopted Arab culture. His *Almansour* dealt with many of the problems of military medicine. Rhazes recommended placing tents in summer camps at the top of hills facing north with wide spaces between them. In the winter, he recommended camping at the base of hills facing south and joining tents in groups of two to preserve heat. He also recommended keeping animals, especially those with diseases, well away from the camps. The book contained a chapter on extraction of arrows which mirrored the recommendations of Aulus Cornelius Celsus and Paul of Aegina. *The Almansour* also discussed fractures, various operations, alchemy, astrology, snakes, and angels. A second Rhazes book, the *Mansoury*, contained sections on surgery, poisons, hygiene, and travel, all subjects appropriate to military medicine. The *Mansoury's* ninth book was frequently reprinted in Latin translation and remained a standard in therapeutics well into the European Renaissance.

Rhazes wrote the encyclopedic *El Hawi*, or *Continens*, in which he attempted to coalesce all known medical knowledge from Greek, Islamic, and Hindu sources and combine it with descriptions from his personal experience. The *Continens* included the first detailed, accurate descriptions of both smallpox and measles and was first translated into Latin in 1279 by Jewish scholar Farj ibn Salim for Charles of Anjou, the king of Sicily. During a remarkably productive career, Rhazes wrote as many as 230 books and articles, 61 of which dealt with medicine. The rest were dedicated to a wide range of subjects including mathematics, music, and chess.

Rhazes served as court physician to Prince Abu Salih al-Mansur and continued to practice in Baghdad until his sight failed. He is said to have died in his home village in around 932.

See also Albucasis; Avicenna (Ibn Sena); Islamic Military Medicine

Reference

LeClerc, Lucien. *Histoire de la Médecine Arabe.* New York: Franklin Burt, 1971 (originally published 1876).

Roman Military Medicine

The Roman military provided the only organized military medical services in the classical age and the best in Europe prior to the 19th century.

The original Roman army was a citizen militia established shortly after 753 B.C., the legendary founding date of the republic. Early Roman soldiers were responsible for providing their own arms and armor and served without pay as part of every property holder's responsibility of citizenship under the Servian Constitution (Servius Tullius, 578–534 B.C.). That constitution mandated liability for service in the field from age 17 to 46 and within the city walls from age 47 to 60. These armies were divided into *centuriae* of cavalry comprising 1,800 men and horses and legions composed of 3,000 heavy and 1,200 light infantry. Foot soldiers carried man-sized shields that conveniently doubled as stretchers for their wounded comrades.

Although soldiers of the early republic had no shortage of opportunity for combat as Rome was in almost constant combat with other Italian states, Romans seem to have had little expertise and less interest in medicine. For the most part, medical science was confined to herbalism, people were expected to be their own doctors, and what professional physicians there were generally found themselves distrusted and denigrated. Those few physicians came almost entirely from Greece and were often slaves. Those who were free were despised for charging for their services, and those who were not were suspected (with some justification) of poisoning their masters' enemies for money. The first Greco-Roman physician whose name we know was Archagathus, who emigrated to the city in 219 B.C. and established his *taberna* (clinic) with state help. He showed such a proclivity for the knife and cautery that he acquired the nickname *carnifex* (butcher) and a general opprobrium.

That attitude changed after the fall of Corinth in 146 B.C. and the absorption of Greece into the Roman state. The subsequent flood of Greek physicians to Rome led Pliny the Elder to complain that the city had done perfectly well for 600 years without doctors and he failed to see the need for them now. The standing of Greco-Roman physicians improved dramatically in 91 B.C. when Asclepiades of Prusa came to the city. His use of diet, baths, exercise, and massage and his avoidance of surgery and poisonous medicines enhanced both his personal reputation and that of his profession.

The republican Roman army had no formal medical corps, and wounded soldiers were bandaged by their comrades and cared for in the homes of local citizens. Soldiers on campaign were at high risk of epidemic disease. Livy (Titus Livius) described an epidemic during the siege of Syracuse in which so many soldiers died that the overwhelmed survivors stopped burying the dead and left them to rot where they fell. Legionnaires became so despondent that they flung themselves unprotected on the enemy lines, preferring to die by the sword rather than from disease. Disease was not the only problem. Livy also noted that a Roman soldier was more likely to die from his wounds after a battle than be killed directly during the fray.

As the Roman army moved beyond the peninsula and began to extend the city's power across Europe, the inefficiencies attendant to lack of medical care became glaringly obvious. Beginning in 105 B.C., the citizen army was replaced by a tough, professional corps whose training mirrored that of the city's gladiators. Julius Caesar (54–44 B.C.) was able to use that army to conquer Gaul and then to conquer the republic itself. One of his earliest acts as emperor was to improve the state of medicine in Rome and in its army. In order to encourage more Greek doctors to come to Rome, Caesar made physicians citizens with a consequent elevation of their social standing. He made physicians a regular part of his army and provided wheeled ambulances to move the wounded from the field to a place where his surgeons could treat them. His successor, Augustus, created the first professional military medical corps in the wake of the disastrous casualty rate from the 15-year civil war that brought him to power. He bestowed the *dignities equestris* (a status similar to that of a knight), land grants, retirement benefits, and exemption from some taxes and civic duties on military physicians. Access to physicians was so popular among soldiers that Tiberius Caesar (A.D. 14–37) seduced his troops into serving in the hinterlands by promising warm baths, litters for the wounded, and guaranteed medical care.

By the first century A.D., the army included legionary physicians (*medici legionis*), camp physicians (*medici castrorum*), and the less-well-trained *medici ordinarii*. The Roman general Germanicus paid for his soldiers' care from his own purse while on the northern campaigns, and his wife, Agrippina, personally nursed the sick and wounded. Trajan (98–117), Hadrian (117–138), and Alexander Severus (222–235) all furnished care to their army's sick and injured, and Aurelian (270–275) mandated that medical care be free for all soldiers. The fact that the life span of the Roman soldier averaged five years longer than that of his civilian counterpart is evidence of the effectiveness of those measures.

By the time of Trajan and Hadrian, every army unit and every navy vessel of any size had physicians. Under Trajan, the Roman army comprised 25 to 30 legions, each of which had 10 cohorts of 6,500–7,000 men and a physician. Each of the nine Praetorian cohorts, the four urban cohorts, and the *vigilii* who served as the city's police and firemen had four physicians. The increased number may reflect the 24-hours-a-day, seven-days-a-week responsibilities of these units. These physicians' status had, however, declined since the time of Julius Caesar. They were ranked as *principales*, or noncommissioned officers roughly equivalent to accountants, clerks, and other noncombatants attached to field units. Romans were generally not fond of the sea, and it was difficult to recruit physicians for the ships, which may account for the fact that naval surgeons were paid at twice the rate of their army counterparts.

The decline in status was at least partially due to the poor state of medical training in imperial Rome, which had no medical schools. A license to practice was not required until the reign of Septimus Severus

(A.D. 193–211), and the first medical lecture halls were established by Alexander Severus (A.D. 222–235). Later imperial physicians were mostly trained by apprenticeship.

The military surgeon in Trajan's army wore a standard, distinctive uniform consisting of a woolen undershirt, a doublet, leather pants to the knees, knee-high boots, and a pot-like round helmet. He wore the *gladius*, or short sword, and carried a surgical kit containing an assortment of scalpels and knives, hooks, probes, and forceps along with a potpourri of medicines and ointments. The army did have standardized manuals of medical care and a program for training its own doctors, a paradigm not repeated until 1865. The *medici* were assisted by *capsarii*, or bandagers, who, much like modern medics, furnished emergency frontline care and assisted in rear-area hospitals.

The imperial Romans had an organized ambulance corps and sophisticated field hospitals. On the Italian peninsula, wounded soldiers were cared for in civilian homes, but in the far reaches of the empire, a different solution was required. Ruins of a string of 25 military hospitals built in the first and second centuries A.D. are scattered around the empire's periphery from the British Isles across Eastern Europe to Arabia. They are of remarkably standard design with a square of five- to six-bed wards lined around an open courtyard and with great care taken to adequately ventilate each patient room. The buildings had piped-in water, piped-out sewage, and central heat. A typical hospital could accommodate about 200 patients, or 5 to 10 percent of its unit's total manpower. Wounded soldiers were triaged at the battlefield, and emphasis was placed on early return to duty whenever possible. Interestingly, there was never a civilian Roman equivalent of those hospitals.

In spite of the fact that medical science in imperial Rome was based largely on empirical observation, Roman military surgeons achieved a surprising degree of sophistication. They combined henbane (hyoscyamus niger), which has atropine-like activity, with poppy extract (opium) to make a sedative quite similar to that used in modern surgery. A variety of chemicals and potions were used to augment wound healing. A bas relief from Herculaneum shows Achilles scraping rust from his lance tip into a comrade's wound; oxides of iron (rust), copper (verdigris), and mercury (cinnabar) all have a degree of antibacterial activity. Their marginal benefit is, however, outweighed by their toxicity, and their use probably was of more harm than benefit. Wounds were also cauterized with quicklime, cantharides, and salt and cleaned with vinegar, wine, honey, and cobwebs, the last two of which have recently been shown to promote healing. They also stuffed egg whites, macerated snails, and animal dung into the wounds before applying "poppy tears" (opium) to alleviate the pain that surely followed.

Roman surgery was more impressive. The empire's physicians had an extensive array of instruments, more than 200 of which have been recovered from the ruins of Pompeii. They used scalpels with replaceable (and cleanable) blades, retractors that opened with screws, self-locking clamps, complicated arrow extractors, straight metal fasteners for closing wounds, and pins almost identical to modern safety pins to hold bandages. They cleaned their instruments with hot water, tied bleeding vessels in knots, and knew to ligate arteries before amputating an extremity. They recognized that it was best to amputate above diseased tissue, to remove dead tissue when changing wound dressings (débridement), and to let infected wounds drain. Virtually all Roman medical advances came from the military rather than from civilian physicians, and the best of Roman physicians, including Dioscorides and Galen, served with the army. Roman medical educators advised those who would be surgeons to find themselves an army and follow it in battle because they would never see enough wounds in the civilian practice to become competent in their craft.

In sum, Rome brought the organization of military medicine to a level never before achieved. Its military hospitals surpassed anything again seen until the late 19th century, and the technique of its surgeons was probably as good as it could have been with neither anesthesia nor antisepsis.

See also Asclepiades of Bithynia; Celsus, Aulus Cornelius; Débridement; Dioscorides, Pedacius; Field Hospitals; Galen of Pergamum; Hemostasis; Ligature; Tourniquet

References
Drabkin, I. E. 1944. "On Medical Education in Greece and Rome." *Bulletin of the History of Medicine* 15 (April): 333–351.
Nutton, Vivian. 1969. "Medicine and the Roman Army: A Further Reconsideration." *Medical History* 13 (July): 260–270.
Salazar, Christine. *The Treatment of War Wounds in Graeco-Roman Antiquity*. Leiden, the Netherlands: Brill, 2000.
Scarborough, John. 1968. "Roman Medicine and the Legions: A Reconsideration." *Medical History* 12 (July): 254–261.

Ross, Sir Ronald
(1857–1932)

Ronald Ross was a British military surgeon who identified the Anopheles mosquito as the vector of malaria and delineated the parasite's complex life cycle.

Ross was born May 13, 1857, in Almora, India, three days before the outbreak of the Great Mutiny. He was the son of a British captain who would eventually end his career as a general and descended from a family that had been in India for three generations. As was customary in the Indian service, Ross was sent back to England for his education at the age of eight. At his father's urging, he entered medical school at St. Bartholomew's Hospital in London in 1875 and joined the Indian Medical Service in 1881 after taking additional course work at Netley. He then returned to Asia, where he served in the third Anglo-Burmese War in 1885.

After that war, Ross returned to London to study bacteriology and received a diploma in public health in 1889. He went back to India for five years before returning again to London, where he met Patrick Manson, who had recently won recognition for demonstrating that filarial parasites responsible for causing elephantiasis were transmitted by the Culex mosquito. Manson showed Ross parasites in red blood cells retrieved from malaria patients and suggested that they might represent a stage in the life cycle of a mosquito-borne parasite. The same suggestion had previously been made by Alphonse Laveran, who was ultimately credited with proving the disease's parasitic origin.

In 1895, Ross returned to India and embarked on four years of study in a primitive laboratory equipped only with an outdated microscope. His research was repeatedly interrupted by military assignments to remote posts lacking even rudimentary laboratories. During that time, Manson was a constant source of support, writing Ross 110 letters, showing his work to Lord Lister, interceding with the secretary of state for India to allow him time to do experiments, and convincing the Royal Society to fund Ross's work and even to send him an assistant.

Ross induced malaria in caged sparrows and larks and ultimately found the disease-causing parasite in the abdominal cavity and the salivary glands of the Anopheles (spotted wing) mosquito. That discovery, made in 1897, was the first step toward unraveling the organism's complicated life cycle. In 1898, Ross demonstrated that he could use the mosquito to infect healthy birds. Meanwhile, Manson retrieved infected mosquitoes from Rome's chronically malarial marshes and induced the disease in two Londoners, one of whom was his own son. He then arranged for two healthy London physicians to spend the summer season in screened houses in the Roman marshes, and neither man contracted malaria. The experiment was widely seen as definitive, and Ross's and Manson's work on the mosquito's role in malarial transmission finally achieved general acceptance.

Ross returned to England in 1899 to join the faculty of the Liverpool School of Tropical Medicine. He was named a fellow of the Royal College of Surgeons of England in 1901 and held the Sir Alfred Jones Chair of Tropical Medicine at the University of Liverpool from 1902 to 1912. He then served five years as physician for tropical diseases at Kings College Hospital in London, during which time he led expeditions to Sierra Leone, West Africa, Mauritius, Spain, Cyprus, and Greece to study ways to control malaria.

Ross was awarded the Nobel Prize for physiology or medicine for his work on malaria in 1902 and was knighted in 1911. During World War I, having been commissioned in the Royal Army Medical Corps, he went to Alexandria, Egypt, to study dysentery in troops in Gallipoli. He went on to serve as director in chief of the Ross Institute and Hospital of Tropical Diseases and as president of the Society of Tropical Medicine. He continued to investigate tropical diseases, created innovative mathematical models of the epidemiology of malaria, and published the landmark *The Prevention of Malaria* in 1910.

Ross was an accomplished painter and a published author of poems and plays. He was also a difficult man who feuded with his students, his colleagues, and at least one biographer. He died after a long illness at the hospital named for him on September 16, 1932.

See also British Military Medicine; Laveran, Charles Louis Alphonse; Malaria

References
Ross, Ronald. *Memoirs.* London: John Murray, 1923.
"Sir Ronald Ross. 1857–1932." *Obituary Notices of Fellows of the Royal Society* 1 (December) 1933: 108–115.

Royal Army Medical Corps

The Royal Army Medical Corps (RAMC) was established by royal warrant on June 25, 1898, as the medical arm of the British Army.

Medical care of English soldiers can be traced to at least 1253, when King Henry III took Master Thomas Weseman, who was reputed to be skilled in curing wounds, on his campaign in France. Edward I took a small contingent of paid surgeons on his Scottish expeditions (1298–1300), and his successor Edward II's armies had "chirurgeons" charged with both treating and shaving his soldiers. There were 20 surgeons and one physician with the English at the Battle of

Agincourt (1415), although under the military code of Henry V, surgeons ranked below shoemakers and tailors and just above washerwomen.

The status of military surgeons improved slightly over the next century, and, under Elizabeth I, every company had a surgeon, although he held equivalent rank to and received the same pay as a drummer. In the Parliamentary army during the 17th-century English Civil War, every regiment had its own surgeon and either one or two assistants. In addition, the army as a whole had a physician general, a surgeon general, and an apothecary general. When Charles II restored the Stuart monarchy, he established Britain's first standing army and, with it, the country's first formal medical corps. For the first time, military surgeons had officer's rank. Medical commissions, like those of line officers, were purchased. Medical officers also frequently bought second commissions in the regular army. They both treated the wounded and fought, and were paid separately for each role.

Under the Duke of Marlborough in the mid-1700s campaigns in Iberia and the Low Countries, British military physicians led by Sir John Pringle and surgeons influenced by John Hunter instituted policies intended to improve camp sanitation and practices directed toward better surgical treatment of casualties. Further advances came during the Napoleonic Wars, especially in the armies led by the Duke of Wellington in Spain, where George Guthrie and Sir James McGrigor introduced dedicated ambulance wagons to transport the wounded and built chains of hospitals for progressive evacuation of the wounded from the battlefield to rear areas. Many of these hospitals were collections of ingeniously engineered prefabricated huts shipped from England. Brit-

ish military medicine's record in those wars was, however, not unblemished. During the Walcheren campaign in Holland, 23,000 of the 39,000-man invasion force died of disease during four months in which only 217 died of battle-related wounds.

The real catalyst for change came in 1854 with the Crimean War. The Royal Army entered that conflict with a medical department composed of a director general, four inspectors general, 11 deputy inspectors, and only 163 surgeons. The entire army had only two four-wheeled ambulance wagons, and even those were left in Bulgaria to make room for officers' horses on ships transporting the force to the Crimea. The only stretcher bearers were the hopelessly antiquated members of the Hospital Conveyance Corps drafted almost entirely from pensioners deemed either too old or too infirm to fight. As a result, most wounded were carried from the battlefield by either their comrades, orderlies, or the surgeons themselves.

As bad as care of the wounded was, cholera, dysentery, and typhus were far more lethal than sabers or bullets. It only took a few weeks for more than half the British army to be incapacitated by disease. There were only two base hospitals, and both were in Scutari, across the Bosporus from Constantinople and more than 300 miles from the front. Within seven months, 10,000 of the 28,000-man British force were dead from disease. The subsequent scandal led first to Florence Nightingale being sent to Scutari and eventually to reorganization of the entire medical corps.

The Medical Staff Corps was formed in June 1855 and comprised nine companies recruited from civilians, disabled noncommissioned officers, and the best of the old Hospital Conveyance Corps, which had been combined with the Land Transportation Corps. The new corps was headquartered at Fort Pitt in Chatham and had a quasi-military structure with its own peculiar ranks, including stewards, wardmasters, orderlies, washermen, cooks, and barbers more or less equivalent to regular ranks from sergeant to private. These support personnel had only one officer and were, for the most part, poorly disciplined and inefficient.

A royal commission was appointed in 1857 to investigate the notoriously poor sanitation in military camps. It recommended establishment of an army medical school, organization of a statistical branch, construction of two general hospitals, and commissioning of regimental surgeons based on examination rather than by appointment. The commission also recommended that military surgeons have a voice in any decision related to the health of soldiers, including choice of uniforms, diet, and placement of camps. The first British Army medical school was founded at Fort Pitt in 1860 and moved to Netley in 1863, where it was combined with the newly built Royal Victoria Hospital.

The royal commission also reorganized the Medical Staff Corps. Renamed the Army Hospital Corps, it was charged with providing orderlies and stretcher bearers. The corps started with its odd assortment of ranks that were, after 1875, changed to coincide with those of the regular army. Still, it had only a single officer, and discipline and organization remained poor. It was said that the Hospital Corps' problem was that it had all men and no officers and the Army Medical Department's problem was that it had all officers and no men.

When the Prussian Army crushed the Austrians in 1866 and the French four years later, the British Army took note of its military and especially of its medical effectiveness. In the

subsequent reorganization, the system of attaching surgeons to specific regiments that had begun with Oliver Cromwell's army in the 1600s was abandoned in favor of well-equipped garrison hospitals with surgeons answering only to the Medical Department. Under the new arrangement, every battalion had a surgeon and 16 stretcher bearers whose only responsibility was moving the wounded. The new system was first tried in the 1879 Zulu Wars and again in the Egyptian campaign of 1882 and met most of the demands of those short engagements.

In 1884, the doctors of the Army Medical Department and the quartermasters who supplied them were put in the new Army Medical Staff and were given command of the Army Hospital Corps, which went back to being called the Medical Staff Corps. Pay and status of military physicians remained scandalously low, causing the British medical establishment to boycott the military and to refuse to recommend enlistment of any medical school graduates for the next 12 years. The British Medical Association finally intervened, and the Royal Army Medical Corps was chartered by the queen in 1898 to include the Medical Department and all the warrant officers, noncommissioned officers, and men of the Medical Staff Corps with ranks equivalent to those of the regular army.

The RAMC got its first test at Khartoum in 1898 where it won the praise of Maj. Gen. Sir Herbert Kitchener, although the campaign, like the previous two, was short. The Boer War proved a greater challenge. As in the Crimea, disease was a much greater threat than injury with contaminated water causing the worst problems. Only 22,000 British soldiers were treated for wounds in the Boer War, while 74,000 were hospitalized for dysentery, 8,000 of whom died. The medical corps was chronically overextended, and its officers were regularly overruled by commanders in matters related to sanitation, even though recent discoveries in infectious disease had finally given such recommendations actual scientific validity.

Failures in southern Africa led to yet another general reorganization between 1904 and 1914, largely under the leadership of Gen. Sir Alfred Keogh, who directed the RAMC from 1905 to 1910. In 1902, the Army Nursing Service was replaced by Queen Alexandra's Imperial Military Nursing Service. The *Journal of the Royal Army Medical Corps* was founded in 1903. The School of Sanitation, intended to teach sanitary principles to line officers, was established in 1906, and sanitary knowledge became a prerequisite for promotion. That same year field ambulances, which combined the functions of the bearer company and the field hospital, were formed. The new system allowed bearers who were chronically overworked during a battle and underemployed shortly after and orderlies whose workload was the reverse to share duties. Next, the clearing hospital was introduced as an intermediary between the frontline collecting station and the rear-area general hospital. The army medical school was moved to London and renamed the Royal Army Medical College in 1907.

The RAMC's greatest test came in World War I. In 1914, the entire Royal Army comprised only about 100,000 men. By 1918, the army had swollen to 4 million and the RAMC alone had 13,000 officers and 154,000 other ranks. Two million British soldiers were injured in the war and another 6 million were hospitalized for disease. In 1914 there had been only 18,000 hospital beds in the whole empire; in 1918 there were 637,000. The first three years of the war virtually exhausted Britain's medical establishment, and, when the United States entered the war, the Crown's first request was not for American soldiers but rather for doctors. By war's end, 1,400 U.S. Army medical officers, 1,200 enlisted men, and 1,000 nurses had been seconded to the Royal Army. Unlike virtually every other protracted conflict in history, the volume of wounded and the complexity of their treatment proved a greater challenge than managing disease in World War I. Wounds contaminated by the bacteria-ridden farm soils of Belgium and northern France were a particular problem. The only instances in which diseases were more important than injuries were in Serbia, East Africa, and Mesopotamia where dysentery and malaria were endemic.

Although the RAMC did not have to deal with the volume of wounded in World War II that it had in the previous conflict, it was forced to function in Europe, North Africa, Italy, Norway, Greece, Crete, Syria, Lebanon, Iraq, Persia, East Africa, Madagascar, Burma, Malaya, Borneo, and Hong Kong. Unlike World War I, this war was fought on highly mobile fronts, especially in North Africa where, at one point, a regimental aid post was more than 500 miles from its general hospital and where one mobile surgical facility was captured, liberated, and recaptured four times. By 1942, the RAMC was parachuting entire field hospitals with their equipment and staff to areas just behind the front lines.

At the Normandy invasion, every battalion landed with its own field hospital and a staff carrying its equipment in waterproof packs. A field ambulance accompanied every brigade and set up dressing stations and surgical facilities on the beach within an hour of the first landing. Fifteen RAMC surgical units were functional before the D-Day invasion was over. In a week, the RAMC had two 200-bed hospitals in France.

For the balance of the conflict in Europe, the disease rate in the Royal Army was less than half that of World War I. Surgical survivals were significantly better due to a combination of antibiotics and better surgical and anesthetic techniques. In the war's final days, the corps was particularly challenged with the flood of seriously ill patients released from prisoner of war camps, from concentration camps, and from German civilian and military hospitals. Overall, the RAMC treated more than 5 million sick and wounded before the war was over.

See also Boer War; Crimean War; Dysentery; Guthrie, George James; Hunter, John; Malaria; McGrigor, James; Nightingale, Florence; Nursing in the Military; Pringle, Sir John; Queen Alexandra's Imperial Military Nursing Service; Royal Victoria Hospital (Netley); World War I Medicine; World War II Medicine

References

Lovegrove, Peter. *Not Least in the Crusade: A Short History of the Royal Army Medical Corps*. Aldershot, UK: Gale & Polden, Ltd., 1952.
McLaughlin, Redmond. *The Royal Army Medical Corps*. London: Leo Cooper, Ltd., 1972.

Royal Victoria Hospital (Netley)

The Royal Victoria Hospital (or Netley Hospital) was founded in 1856 to care for wounded in the British Army.

Queen Victoria had met Florence Nightingale at Balmoral Castle September 21, 1856, and was deeply affected by both the lady and her stories of hardships among British soldiers in the Crimea. As a consequence, the queen made laying the foundation stone of Netley Hospital at the edge of Southampton Water her first official act after the Crimean War ended. Although

that day began auspiciously with Victoria's ceremonial arrival in the royal yacht, it was marred by the premature detonation of a salute cannon, which killed two soldiers and injured another.

The hospital was an elegant structure on 227 acres of waterfront. It stretched over 1,424 feet with a three-story Portland stone facade divided into two wings separated by a grand dome, but its architectural grandeur was, in many ways, in conflict with its mission. Nightingale objected to its north-facing windows, poor ventilation, and proximity to outhouses and coal piles, but was unsuccessful in altering the plans. The largest military hospital in the world, Netley had its own water and electrical power supplies and a 170-meter-long dock onto which the injured could be unloaded. However, the dock proved inadequate for the deep draft ships bringing patients from South Africa during the Boer War, and the hospital was forced to build a direct railroad connection to Southampton Central Station in 1900.

The facility, subsequently renamed the Royal Victoria Hospital, received its first patient on May 19, 1863. The Army Medical School was sited at Netley from 1863 until 1903, when it was relocated to London to be nearer the other major British medical facilities. The Army Nursing Service was also headquartered there.

During World War I, the hospital handled more than 50,000 sick and injured. The United States took over the Royal Victoria in 1944 and treated more than 68,000 patients there in the subsequent 18 months in spite of the fact that American physicians found the hospital's corridors so long that they brought Jeeps indoors to navigate them. The old structure became too expensive to maintain after the war and it was finally

Royal Victoria Hospital at Netley, Southampton, 1859. Netley Hospital was the headquarters of the Army Medical School and many distinguished pathologists worked there. (Science Museum/SSPL/The Image Works)

abandoned in 1958. In 1963, the building suffered major damage when water pipes froze and broke, and, later that year, the hospital was gutted by a fire probably set by vandals. It was razed in 1966.

See also Boer War; Queen Alexandra's Imperial Military Nursing Service; Royal Army Medical Corps; World War II Medicine

References

Hoare, Philip. *Spike Island: The Memory of a Military Hospital.* London: Fourth Estate, 2001.
Piggot, Juliet. *Queen Alexandra's Royal Army Nursing Corps.* London: Leo Cooper, Ltd., 1975.

Rush, Benjamin
(1745–1813)

Benjamin Rush was a signer of the Declaration of Independence and known variously as "the American Sydenham" and "the American Hippocrates."

Rush was born in Byberry Township near Philadelphia on December 24, 1745. He was educated at Nottingham Academy, entered New Jersey College at Princeton at age 15, and graduated the following year. Rush then spent five years apprenticed to Dr. John Redmond, during which time he translated the *Aphorisms* of Hippocrates into English and wrote a classic account of the 1762 Philadelphia yellow fever epidemic.

After finishing his apprenticeship, Rush went to England, where he studied in London and received his medical degree from the University of Edinburgh in 1768. He returned to Philadelphia the following year to become professor of chemistry at John Morgan's new College of Philadelphia medical school where he, along with Morgan, William Shippen, Jr., and Adam Kuhn comprised the faculty. Rush was active in

Philadelphia society and politics, was a member of the Continental Congress, and signed the Declaration of Independence. He chaired the Congress's medical committee and served as physician and surgeon general of the middle department of the Continental Army from April 1777.

Rush became involved in Gen. Thomas Conway's attempt to have George Washington relieved of his command and Morgan's failed attempt to discredit Shippen. He resigned under pressure in 1778, but not before publishing the *Directions for Preserving the Health of Soldiers*, a useful compendium of recommendations on military hygiene and camp sanitation.

Rush returned to a prosperous, genteel life of teaching and practice. He fathered 13 children and is said to have educated 2,872 physicians in his career. However, he taught vigorous purging with calomel and bleeding as the mainstays of therapy and is accused of having cost the lives of tens of thousands through a combination of personal influence and misguided ideas. During his life, though, his reputation remained unchallenged and he died in April 1813, the subject of general adoration and respect.

See also American Revolutionary War; Morgan, John; Shippen, William, Jr.

References
Gillet, Mary. *The Army Medical Department, 1775–1818*. Washington, D.C.: Center of Military History, 1981.
Packard, Francis. "[Benjamin Rush]." In Howard Kelly and Walter Burrage, *Dictionary of American Medical Biography: Lives of Eminent Physicians of the United States and Canada, from the Earliest Times*. Boston: Milford House, 1928.
Packard, Francis. *History of Medicine in the United States*. New York: Paul B. Hoeber, Inc., 1931.
Reiss, Oscar. *Medicine and the American Revolution*. Jefferson, NC: McFarland & Co., Inc., 1998.

Russian Military Medicine

Russian military medicine has historically and persistently been the most backward military medical establishment among the major Western powers.

Czar Ivan III (1468–1505) was the first Russian ruler to import foreign physicians in an attempt to remedy the virtually total absence of medical training in Russia. The practice of bringing physicians from outside Russia was expanded by his successors Peter the Great and Catherine the Great and persisted to the end of the monarchy in 1917. Peter did, however, plant the seeds of a native Russian medical profession when he sent Peter Postnikoff to study in Padua in 1694.

The first physician attached to the Russian Army was brought from Brandenburg in 1615. Between importation of physicians and local training of lesser practitioners, by 1707 the Russian Army had a physician, a barber-surgeon, and an apothecary for each division, a proportion comparable to that in contemporary Eastern European armies. Medical expenses were covered by monthly deductions from each soldier's pay.

To remedy the persistent lack of Russian-trained physicians, Peter established the *Gofshopital*, a military hospital principally meant to be a training facility, and brought Dutch physician, surgeon, and anatomist Nicola Bidloo as director. Because medicine in general and surgery in particular had little status in Russia, Bidloo's students were almost entirely drawn from the lower social classes. Between 1712 and 1727, every graduate was drafted into military service—

typically for 25 years. The lack of prestige and the prospect of long service kept the number of graduates down to an average of 10 a year during that time and forced the military to fall back on apothecaries, barbers, and field dressers to fill the deficit in spite of additional training facilities opening in St. Petersburg, Raval, Kronstadt, Astrakhan, Tarvov, and Archangel, all of which were intended to produce military physicians.

By the time Russia entered the Crimean War, there were still three *feldschers* (field shearers or barbers) for every physician in the military, although Russia's total number of medical personnel per combatant was actually higher than either England or France. The general lack of professional training coupled with poor hospitals and virtually nonexistent transportation for the sick and wounded, however, made the Russian situation even worse than that which would precipitate a complete overhaul of the British medical corps after 1855. The nearest Russian aid station to Sebastopol was 16 miles away and took more than seven hours to reach on foot.

Russian military medicine's one bright spot in the Crimea was Nikolai Pirogoff. Among his accomplishments, Pirogoff may well have been the first to use plaster of paris to stabilize fractures sustained in combat. He also helped bring female nurses to the front.

Pirogoff notwithstanding, the czarist military medical situation had seen little improvement when Russia went to war with Japan in 1904. Trench and siege warfare in northeast China was particularly bloody, resulting in 146,000 Russian wounded and a wound-related death rate of about 4.2 percent. Even that rate might have been tolerable had the death rate from disease not

been so catastrophic. The Russian practice of disposing of fecal waste by throwing it over the edges of trenches led not only to an unbearable stink but also to repeated outbreaks of typhoid, dysentery, and cholera. Poor diet made scurvy and beriberi endemic. Physicians and surgeons were still in short supply, and much of the care was supplied by *feldschers* and volunteer nurses, many of whom were recruited from among the soldiers' own family members. As in the Crimea, there were no dedicated stretcher bearers, and there was no organized transportation service for the wounded.

Russian battlefield psychiatry stood in surprising contrast to the otherwise bleak medical picture. Battle-related stress had cost Russia significant numbers of men in the Crimean War, and Russian physicians had remained interested in the problem after that war. In the Russo-Japanese War, they were the first to formally recognize and treat mental symptoms, although they incorrectly attributed them to invisible brain injury. The military psychiatric hospital at Harbin treated more than 2,000 men during the war, a number that increased after men learned they could be removed from combat with the right set of psychiatric complaints. The Russian classification and treatment of these problems was the paradigm for World War I's diagnosis of shell shock.

Russia remained the worst of the great powers at treating its military sick and wounded into World War I. They had the war's highest incidence of typhus, typhoid, dysentery, and cholera. Long after scurvy and smallpox had ceased being a significant problem for other European forces, they remained a significant cause of death for the Russians. Transport was so poor that thousands of soldiers who initially survived their wounds died without ever reaching medical care.

See also Crimean War; Pirogoff, Nikolai Ivanovich; Russo-Japanese War; World War I Medicine

References
Alexander, John. 1974. "Medical Developments in Petrine Russia." *Canadian-American Slavic Studies* 8 (Summer): 198–221.
Halperin, George. 1956. "Nikolai Ivanovich Pirigov: Surgeon, Anatomist, Educator." *Bulletin of the History of Medicine* 30 (July–August): 347–355.

Russo-Japanese War

Fought between February 6, 1904, and October 15, 1905, the Russo-Japanese War is of medical interest primarily for the performance of Japanese military surgeons, which was the best organized and most effective of any such corps in history to that point.

Much of the information about medical care during the Russo-Japanese War relates to the Japanese performance because the Imperial Army medical corps kept meticulous records, whereas the Russians did not. Japanese military medicine performed abysmally in the 1894 conflict with China, leading imperial authorities to undertake sweeping reforms that included sending a number of physicians to Europe—particularly to Germany—for additional training. By 1904, the medical corps of both the Japanese Imperial Army and Navy was commanded in large part by surgeons who had trained in Europe.

The Japanese Army medical officers were divided into three classes: graduates of imperial universities, graduates of other universities, and license holders who were allowed to practice after passing an examination. Surgeons trained in foreign universities were accorded the same rank as those

from imperial universities but were generally considered to be of higher status.

Physicians were initially commissioned as second lieutenants and could rise to a rank as high as lieutenant general. Medicine as a profession was held in high esteem in turn-of-the-century Japan, and preference for appointment to the medical corps was given to members of samurai families. In addition to physicians, the medical corps had apothecaries who held rank from sergeant to colonel and who were responsible for maintaining instruments, supervising nurses, and dispensing medications. Besides these practitioners, the Japanese Imperial Army had sanitary soldiers responsible for camp cleanliness, a service developed as a direct result of the devastating loss of life to infectious disease during the Sino-Japanese War.

The Japanese Army entered the Russo-Japanese conflict with 1,076 active surgeons and 2,317 reserves and 33,753 sanitary soldiers. Nurses were enlisted, and noncommissioned males and line soldiers were trained to be litter bearers. Additional bearers were commandeered from the Chinese population. The Chinese were widely admired for their ability to run with a stretcher with virtually no bouncing.

The sanitary system performed so well that European observers entertained the theory that Japanese soldiers were racially resistant to infectious disease. There were no cases of either cholera or malaria (both of which were endemic in China) among Japanese troops during the war. The rate of typhus and dysentery was one-sixth that of the Russians. All drinking water was sterilized, and even canteen water on the march had to be boiled. Japanese troops took creosote pills intended to sterilize the intestine and thought to prevent typhoid. There was virtually no hospital gangrene among the Japanese forces.

One disease that plagued the Japanese—and that military surgeons incorrectly believed to be contagious—was beriberi, a deficiency of vitamin B1 resulting from a diet primarily composed of milled rice. The Russian Army had no problem with that disease, while it accounted for half of all illness among the Japanese and 16 percent of the Imperial Army suffered from it. The other significant problem for both armies was frostbite during the bitter winter of 1904–1905.

Battle injuries accounted for a higher percentage of personnel loss in the Russo-Japanese War than in the American Civil War or the Boer War, with the ratio of death from wounds to death from sickness being 1:0.47 among the Japanese. Of battle wounds, 85 percent were from rifle shot, 14 percent were from shrapnel or artillery, and only 1 percent were caused by bayonets. Japanese surgeons, who were better trained, more likely to adhere to aseptic technique, and more conservative in their procedures, had consistently better outcomes than did the Russians.

In battle, the Japanese established dressing stations within 400 to 500 yards of the front line. Wounded were carried to these stations by a company's bearers and had dressings and splints applied before being carried to better-equipped facilities about a mile behind the lines. After stabilization, the wounded were transferred to field hospitals in existing buildings two to three miles farther to the rear. There were intended to be six such field hospitals for each division, but there were never enough personnel to meet that goal. Each field hospital was staffed with six surgeons, one apothecary, 49 nurses, and 45 support personnel.

From the field hospitals, casualties could be moved by rail to one of the 24,000 beds in a "line of communication" hospital in Manchuria. There were no formal hospital cars, and the wounded often had to be moved in boxcars on straw mats or even in open flat cars. The Japanese Army had 18 ships dedicated to moving wounded to the home islands, and the Imperial Red Cross (a special project of the empress) had two more. During the war, 329,000 Japanese casualties and an additional 18,000 wounded Russian prisoners of war were transported to the home islands for treatment. The Russians used the newly constructed 5,000-mile Trans-Siberian railway to move casualties back west of the Ural Mountains.

Accurate Russian casualty figures for the war are unavailable, although the Russians suffered an estimated 89,000 casualties at the Battle of Mukden alone. During the entire war, the Japanese forces had 47,387 men killed in action and another 11,500 who subsequently died of wounds. A remarkable 161,925 were wounded and recovered. Only 27,185 died of illness.

See also Cold Injury and Frostbite; Hospital Ships; Japanese Military Medicine

References

Kimura, S. *The Surgical & Medical History of the Naval War between Japan & Russia*. Tokyo: Bureau of Medical Affairs, Navy Department, 1911.

Lynch, Charles. *Reports of Military Observers Attached to the Armies in Manchuria during the Russo-Japanese War*. Washington, D.C.: Government Printing Office, 1907.

Seaman, Louis. *The Real Triumph of Japan: The Conquest of the Silent Foe*. New York: D. Appleton and Co., 1908.

Salicetti, Guglielmo (William of Salicet) (1210–1277)

One of the most famous surgical teachers of the 13th century and author of the first textbook of anatomy written specifically for surgeons, Guglielmo Salicetti was among the original Italian Renaissance surgeons. He was born in the village of Saliceto in Lombardy and was university trained in both medicine and surgery. He was, however, especially proud of the practical surgical experience he had gained on the battlefield.

He started the medical school at Bologna before moving on to Verona, where he worked as the city's physician. In 1275, he wrote the *Chirurgia*, which was intended to teach his son medicine and surgery. Rather than relying solely on Galen as did most of his contemporaries, Salicetti included a number of his own case histories as illustrations and devoted one of the book's six sections to regional anatomy.

As a surgeon, Salicetti favored cleaning wounds with a scalpel rather than the cautery recommended by Islamic physicians. He questioned the prevailing doctrine that pus formation was necessary to wound healing and recommended early closure of clean wounds. He recognized crepitus—the crackling sound of gas in tissue—as a sign of infected fracture and pioneered wiring the maxilla to the mandible in cases of fractured jaw.

Salicetti trained Lanfranc of Milan, who subsequently moved to Paris and helped start the medieval French school of surgery.

See also Lanfranc of Milan; Medieval Military Medicine

References
Wangensteen, Owen, and Sarah Wangensteen. *The Rise of Surgery*. Minneapolis: University of Minnesota Press, 1975.
Zimmerman, Leo, and Ilza Veith. *Great Ideas in the History of Surgery*. Baltimore: Williams & Wilkins Co., 1961.

Saw

In all likelihood the saw was the earliest surgical instrument, dating to the Neolithic era.

The earliest surgical saws were probably derived from serrated sharks' teeth used to cut bone for other reasons. More fancifully, Pliny credits the mythical Daedalus with having invented the saw after noticing that he could cut wood with the teeth and jaw of a snake skeleton. Pieces of serrated flaked flint have been found in Swiss lake settlements and in Egyptian sites dating to 2700 B.C. Greek surgeons used bronze saws, and Romans had similar instruments made of steel.

Trepan (opening the skull) and amputation are the two oldest operations, and both require saws. Aulus Cornelius Celsus gives the first detailed description of the use of a saw in amputation, and Paul of Aegina (seventh century A.D.) describes a small saw used to open skulls. By the 12th or 13th century, both bow saws, in which the replaceable blade is held by an arch of metal, and the tenon saw, with a fixed blade resembling a modern carpenter's saw, were in common use, although the latter eventually became predominant.

Around 1590, Fabrizio d'Aquapendente described using a red-hot saw in amputation to combine cutting with the hemostatic effect of cauterization. Modern surgical saws are often powered by compressed gas or electricity, but tenon saws almost exactly like those of 900 years ago remain a mainstay of the orthopedic armamentarium.

See also Amputation; Celsus, Aulus Cornelius; Fabrizio d'Aquapendente, Geronimo; Paul of Aegina; Trephine, Trepan, and Trephining

References

Bennion, Elisabeth. *Antique Medical Instruments.* Berkeley: University of California Press, 1979.
Kirkup, J. R. 1981. "The History and Evolution of Surgical Instruments." *Annals of the Royal College of Surgeons of England* 63: 279–285.
Thompson, C. J. S. *The History and Evolution of Surgical Instruments.* New York: Schuman's, 1942.

Scabies

Scabies is a skin disease caused by the mite *Sarcoptes scabei var humanis* that has plagued armies throughout recorded history.

Egyptian mummies from 1500 B.C. have been found with skin lesions typical of scabies, and the *zaraath* mentioned in the Hebrew scriptures may well have also been scabies. Aristotle referred to "lice in the flesh," and scabies was probably one of several diseases described by the Greeks as *psora*. Quintus Curtius in his *Wars of Alexander* described scabies in the Macedonian troops, and Aulus Cornelius Celsus recommended sulfur dissolved in liquid pitch to treat it. In 1687, Giovan Cosimo Bonomo attributed the disease to barely visible mites that he drew after observing them with a microscope. This was the first attribution of a specific disease to a parasite, an insight that was ignored for the next century and a half.

The mite that causes scabies spends its entire life on people and is an obligate human parasite, unable to reproduce on other mammals. Humans can be infected with horse, dog, cat, pig, or ferret scabies, but those parasites cannot reproduce on humans and cause only transient disease. The mite, which is a 0.3–0.4 millimeter white dot barely visible to the human eye, crawls onto the skin. It is unable to hop or fly and is usually transmitted by direct skin-to-skin contact, although it can live outside the body—usually in clothing—for up to 48 hours. The female burrows into the epidermis where it lives for one to two months and deposits its eggs. Because the organism is an air breather, it must stay close enough to the surface for its trachea to be exposed to the outside. The scabies rash is caused by hypersensitivity to the mite, its eggs, or its packets of deposited feces and is typically a red, s-shaped track. Intense itching leads to excoriation and frequent super-infection with streptococcus, staphylococcus, or pseudomonas organisms. Secondary involvement of the kidneys or generalized sepsis can, in unusual cases, lead to death. The disease can be treated with lotions containing pemethrim, lindane, or crotamiton, and sulfur-based salves remain in use.

Worldwide scabies pandemics still occur and coincide temporally with major wars, two of the most recent having occurred in 1919–1925 and 1936–1949. The disease was common during the American Revolutionary War and particularly plagued George Washington's soldiers at Valley Forge in the winter of 1777–1778. Sulfur was in short supply that winter, and the physicians had to compete with artillery forces (who needed the mineral to combine with saltpeter and charcoal to make gunpowder) for it. Besides the salves, American troops were treated with Ethiop's mineral, a compound of mercury sulfide and hog's lard, and were purged with antimony every eight days. Some self-medicated with rum, and at least one soldier died of alcohol overdose from that remedy.

Civil War soldiers referred to scabies variously as "army itch," "prairie dig," and "Missouri mange" and thought it was caused by a combination of poor internal constitution and exposure to rough wool uniforms. The disease was particularly common in the trenches on the Western Front in World War I, and, as recently as 1946, 65 percent of visits to an American army skin clinic were for scabies. The disease remains endemic in Africa, in aboriginal people in Australia, in South American tribes, and in Bangladesh.

See also Trench Fever (Volhynian Fever); Typhus

Reference
Chosidow, Olivier. 2006. "Scabies." *New England Journal of Medicine* 354 (April 20): 1718–1727.

Scalpel

The scalpel is among the earliest surgical instruments, with the most primitive forms probably being pieces of flaked flint or obsidian.

The term derives from the Latin *scalpellus*, meaning a surgical knife but which is the diminutive of *scalprum*, or chisel. A carving of a case of surgical knives on a votive recovered from the temple of Aesculapius dates to about 300 B.C. and is the earliest known image of a scalpel. The oldest surviving actual instrument is Roman, and its sharp point and curved cutting edge bear a remarkable resemblance to knives still in use. Ancient scalpels were often double ended with the handle in the middle, a scalpel at one end and another instrument such as a spatula on the other. Roman surgical knives frequently included elaborately carved ivory or tortoise-shell handles inlaid with gold, silver, and pictures of gods or animals and were designed with blades that could be removed for cleaning and sharpening. The bistoury was a variant of the scalpel with a long, straight cutting edge used for incising internal organs.

In 600 B.C., Suśruta, the father of Hindu medicine, described scalpels among the 121 instruments a surgeon should take into battle and cautioned that blades should be sharp enough to bisect a hair. Aulus Cornelius Celsus provided detailed descriptions of using a scalpel to enlarge an entry wound to remove a barbed weapon or to allow a surgeon to probe with forceps to remove a projectile.

See also Celsus, Aulus Cornelius; Indian
Military Medicine; Minoan and Ancient
Greek Military Medicine; Roman Military
Medicine

References
Bennion, Elisabeth. *Antique Medical Instruments.*
Berkeley: University of California Press,
1979.
Kirkup, J. R. 1981. "The History and Evolution
of Surgical Instruments." *Annals of the Royal
College of Surgeons of England* 63: 279–285.
Thompson, C. J. S. *The History and Evolution of
Surgical Instruments.* New York: Schuman's,
1942.
Zimmer, Henry R. *Hindu Medicine.* Baltimore:
Johns Hopkins University Press, 1948.

Scrub Typhus

Scrub typhus (Tsutsugamushi fever, or
chigger-borne rickettsiosis) is a systemic
disease caused by the small, rod-shaped,
gram-negative *Orientia tsutsugamushi.*

The disease is transmitted to humans
by the Leptotrombidium mite that acts as
both reservoir and vector. Scrub typhus
is endemic to East and South Asia and to
the western South Pacific and is found at
altitudes from sea level to the high mountains and in climates varying from tropical
to near Arctic cold. The illness begins with
a rash and eschar at the bite location and
progresses to fever, chills, headache, and
delirium. In untreated cases, diffuse intravascular coagulation with uncontrollable
bleeding can lead to death. The disease lasts
10 to 28 days and may enter a chronic phase
in which recovery takes up to four months.

Scrub typhus was probably described by
the Chinese as early as A.D. 313 and, under
the name Tsutsugamushi fever, by the Japanese in 1810. Although military authorities,
remembering the Eastern Front experience
during World War I, feared a typhus (Rickettsia prowazekii) outbreak during World
War II, scrub typhus proved to be the latter
conflict's most important rickettsial disease.
Allied forces suffered 16,000 casualties and
the Japanese another 20,000 from scrub typhus in their Pacific forces. Overall mortality varied from 7 to 9 percent, second only
to malaria among infectious diseases. It was
especially common in New Guinea and in
the China-Burma-India Theater.

Chloromycetin, the first antibiotic effective against scrub typhus, was available
after 1948. Because DDT effectively controlled the insect vector, scrub typhus was
rare during the Korean Conflict; however,
the mites became resistant to the insecticide,
and the disease reemerged in Viet Nam,
where it was probably the most common
cause of fevers of unknown origin, which
were, in turn, the most common diagnoses
after venereal disease among infections. Although scrub typhus could be effectively
treated with a variety of antibiotics by the
late 1960s and there were no deaths in Viet
Nam from the disease, it was a major cause
of lost man-days during that war.

See also Viet Nam War; World War II Medicine

Reference
Kelly, Daryl J., Allen L. Richards, Joseph
Temenak, Daniel Strickman, and
Gregory A. Dasch. 2002. "The Past and
Present Threat of Rickettsial Diseases to
Military Medicine and International Public
Health." *Clinical Infectious Diseases* 34:
S145–S169.

Scultetus, Johannes (also Johannes Schultes) (1595–1645)

Johannes Scultetus was official physician to
the town of Ülm, a skillful operator, and the

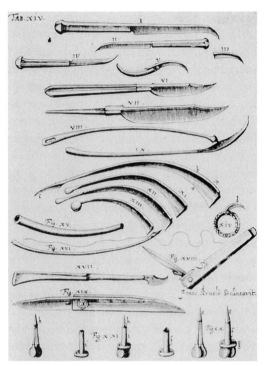

Variety of instruments including several types of lancets used for bloodletting, from Scultetus's Armamentarium Chirurgicum. *(National Library of Medicine)*

best educated of the early German military surgeons.

Scultetus was born in Ülm in 1595. Unlike his contemporaries, who were mostly self-taught barber-surgeons, he went to the university at Padua at age 15, where he studied under Fabrizio d'Aquapendente and Adriaan van den Spieghel (Spigellius) and earned doctorates in medicine, surgery, and philosophy in 1621. He practiced briefly in Padua and then in Vienna before returning to Ülm at age 30.

His *Armamentarium Chirurgicum* (published posthumously in 1653) was the best illustrated of the 17th-century surgical texts, containing detailed drawings of the curved

amputation knife and screw tourniquet that became standard parts of the military surgeon's kit as well as illustrations of bandaging and splinting.

Scultetus wrote extensively on head injuries, recommending that the injured head be shaved and packed with hemp and egg white. Collodion, a clear, colorless protein-based glue similar to the albumin in egg white, is still used to stop minor bleeding and hold skin edges together. He also recommended washing wounds with cool oil and wine (a modestly effective antiseptic) and one dram of dragon's blood until the patient passed out. If the patient survived, he packed the wound with hemp or flax until "laudable pus" appeared and could be drained.

Scultetus died in Stuttgart in 1645 while tending to a patient.

See also Head Injury and Cranial Surgery; Prussian and German Military Medicine; 17th-Century Military Medicine

References

Bakay, Louis. *The Treatment of Head Injuries in the Thirty Years War, 1618–1648: Joannis Scultetus and His Age.* Springfield, IL: Charles C. Thomas, 1971.
Zimmerman, Leo, and Ilza Veith. *Great Ideas in the History of Surgery.* Baltimore: Williams & Wilkins Co., 1961.

Scurvy

Scurvy is both the greatest scourge and the greatest triumph of naval medicine.

Although the disease is best known for causing soft, bleeding gums and loss of teeth, its effects are protean and, if untreated, fatal. Scurvy does cause ulceration and bleeding from mucous membranes such as the gums and an associated foul breath, but it also leads to bleeding elsewhere, including under the skin (bruises); in joints and muscles; and from the bladder, bowels, and lungs. Bleeding between the bones and surrounding periosteum causes knots and swelling in the arms and legs. Blood loss can be enough to result in anemia and lethargy. Headache, delirium, and coma characterize scurvy's final stages.

Scurvy is now known to be caused by lack of dietary vitamin C, an essential nutrient humans are incapable of manufacturing that, consequently, must come from food. An appropriate supply of vitamin C will completely prevent the disease, and supplying the vitamin to a patient with scurvy will reverse its effects.

Scurvy became a maritime concern when sailing ships and navigation techniques allowed protracted voyages away from land. Meats and carbohydrates were less perishable than fruits and vegetables and comprised almost the entire seagoing diet in the first three centuries of transoceanic voyages. During Sir Francis Drake's circumnavigation in 1585, 300 of his original 2,300-man crews died of scurvy within three months of leaving England. Commodore George Anson, who sailed around the world from 1740 to 1744, lost 1,050 of his 1,955 men to scurvy. Ironically, Anson's logs noted that the men transiently improved after eating Tahitian oranges, but the observation was ignored.

That was not the only time the observation was made and ignored. East India Company physicians, at the time of the company's 1600 expedition to India, suspected that citrus fruits might prevent scurvy. One of their four ships was supplied with lemons and oranges, and, although only the crew given the fruit remained free of scurvy, the practice still did not become general for nearly 200 years.

In May 1747, British naval surgeon James Lind (1716–1794) designed what may have been scientific medicine's first controlled experiments: He divided 12 sailors with scurvy into six groups, each assigned one of the commonly accepted treatments for the disease. Only the group given lemons and oranges benefited—and they were cured.

In spite of the strength of Lind's experiment, general acceptance of citrus juice to prevent and treat scurvy was slow. Even Lind continued to believe that "good air" was at least as important as lemons in treating the disease. Largely due to the encouragement of Sir Gilbert Blane, the Royal Navy finally introduced lemon juice as a treatment for scurvy in the early 1790s. First Lord of the Admiralty Earl Spencer ordered that it be a mandatory part of the British sailor's diet in 1795. Lemons and oranges were replaced by cheaper—but less effective—West Indian limes shortly thereafter, leading to the sobriquet "limey." The timing of Spencer's mandate was fortuitous as it is unlikely the British blockade of Napoleonic France would have been possible in a fleet subject to scurvy.

As late as 1900, Sir William Osler still believed overcrowding, damp quarters, prolonged fatigue, and depression contributed to scurvy, especially in a military setting. It was not until well into the 20th century that the exact nature of the vitamin deficiency leading to scurvy was delineated, by which time Lind's empiric treatment had long since eliminated the disease as a factor in naval medicine.

See also Blane, Sir Gilbert; Lind, James; Naval Medicine

References
Gordon, Maurice Bell. *Naval and Maritime Medicine during the American Revolution.* Ventnor, NJ: Ventnor Publishing, 1978.

Hudson, Robert P. *Disease and Its Control: The Shaping of Modern Thought.* Westport, CT: Greenwood Press, 1983.

Osler, William. *Practice of Medicine.* New York: D. Appleton & Co., 1899.

17th-Century Military Medicine

The 17th century was the first time that European scientists demonstrably relied more on knowledge gained from their own experience and experiments than on information culled from classical Greek and Roman texts.

Isaac Newton's successful use of experiments and observations to understand the relationships between astral and terrestrial objects precipitated a headlong and often unsuccessful rush to apply those same tools to living creatures. Early attempts to apply the new tools of mathematics, physics, microscopy, and Vesalian anatomy to clinical medicine—especially in the treatment of diseases and injuries of war—proved too often futile and occasionally counterproductive. These failings were compounded by lethal advances in military technology and the rise of large, state-supported standing armies, which subjected the individual soldier to a previously unimagined level of risk from both disease and injury.

The 17th century saw a series of prolonged, destructive wars including the Thirty Years War (1618–1648), the English Civil War (1642–1653), the Anglo-Dutch Wars (1652–1654, 1665–1667, 1672–1674, 1680–1684), and the wars of Louis XIV of France (1672–1697), all of which were characterized by large battles between ground and sea forces that, because they were funded by the state, were of previously unimagined size and lethality.

France, Austria, Sweden, Russia, and the Electorate of Brandenburg all maintained standing armies. Sweden's King Gustavus Adolphus introduced an effective military organization with his 600–800-man battalions in common uniforms and armed principally with muskets rather than pikes, which they used in a complex but effective manual of arms. The French introduced flint muskets in 1635 and the bayonet, which made the gun the equivalent of the pike at close range, in 1640. Some bullets were round lead balls, but others might be bits of stone, glass, iron, or copper, and the velocity (and consequent destructiveness to tissue) increased as the century progressed. Artillery units fired canisters filled with pellets and bombs or lofted hand grenades.

Massing large groups of men inevitably resulted in propagation of infectious diseases. Typhus, typhoid fever, smallpox, syphilis, influenza, and dysentery followed the armies across Europe. Bubonic plague was particularly severe, with London losing 69,000 in 1665, Vienna 70,000 in 1679, Prague 80,000 in 1681, and the Venetian states a combined 500,000 during the century.

Military medicine was unable to keep up with either military organization or technology. Andreas Vesalius and his fellow Italians had aroused great interest in dissection, but, although anatomy was widely taught across the Continent, it had scarcely any beneficial effect in clinical surgery. Military surgeons suffered from a number of disabilities, perhaps the greatest of which was their organizational separation from physicians, who, by virtue of their university education and presumptively superior classical knowledge, remained a caste above surgeons and barbers, who merely operated. For their part, the physicians respected only academic knowledge and disdained learning derived from experience. The surgeons, on the other hand, respected only that which they had personally seen or learned from the observations of others. The barbers often ignored all education in favor of hucksterism and quackery. Surgeons and barbers, although they usually belonged to the same guild, were professional rivals, the former most often caring for nobles and officers, and the common soldier left in the uncertain hands of the latter. Both, however, were under the jurisdiction of the physicians.

The ancient authorities had nothing to offer regarding treatment of gunshot wounds, and, as those injuries became increasingly common, military surgeons were forced to improvise. Their mistakes, beginning with Giovanni de Vigo's 15th-century contention that the gunpowder was itself a poison, were frequent and often deadly. The routine practice of probing wounds with unsterile instruments or fingers, the widening of wounds to release supposed toxins, packing with unsterile lint (charpie), and dressing with a variety of noxious salves and ointments led to an infection rate in battlefield wounds that approached 100 percent. To make the situation worse, military surgeons almost unanimously viewed the development of "laudable pus" as necessary to healing, so they favored dressings and poultices (even including various types of animal and human feces) known to cause inflammation.

The high death rate from battlefield wounds led to a variety of creative suggestions for their treatment. Among the more curious was Sir Kenelm Digby's "sympathetic powder" compounded of such fanciful ingredients as moss from a dead man's skull and powdered mummies, which remained in common use through much of the century. The idea that wounds could be "cured at a distance" led to coating blades that had inflicted injury with salve in the hope that they would heal as well as they

had injured. The "transplantation cure" involved dipping a stick in the pus or blood from a wound and driving it into a tree. If the graft took, the wound would presumably heal. It is likely that none of these was as harmful as the general practice of cauterizing a wound with hot oil or red hot iron in an attempt to reverse gunpowder's presumed toxicity. Amputation, despite its abysmal survival rate, remained the most common battlefield operation and was used regularly for wounds that entered a joint or for open fractures.

In the absence of formal training, the best way for a surgeon to learn his craft was to follow the army, and the best known of the century's operators all served in either the Thirty Years War or the English Civil War.

Perhaps the most influential 17th-century German surgeon was Wilhelm Fabry, also known as Fabricius of Hilden, who invented a number of useful instruments, including a tourniquet that could be tightened with a stick, and who was the first to advocate amputating proximally enough to leave healthy tissue in the healing stump. Another German, Matthias Purmann, in his *Fifty Strange and Wonderful Cures for Gunshot Wounds* (1693), suggested all surgeons should have an intimate knowledge of anatomy and performed an impressive array of operations including suturing torn intestines. He also was an advocate of Digby's sympathetic powder and believed in cures at a distance. The most famous of the English surgeons was Richard Wiseman, whose *Several Chirurgical Treatises* was the century's most complete and accurate English-language surgical text.

The 17th century saw a number of scientific advances that should have formed the basis for significant improvement in medical care but that, in general, did not. William Harvey's 1616 proof (not published until 1628) that blood circulated rather than simply being pulsed back and forth by the pumping heart formed the basis of clinical physiology and was the first application of Newtonian physics to living humans. René Descartes described the physiology of reflexes, Robert Boyle's gas laws made it possible to understand respiration, and the astronomers' discoveries in optics led to an understanding of human vision. Athanasius Kircher, Robert Hooke, Anton von Leeuwenhoek, and Marcelo Malpighi all used the microscope to see animal and human anatomy in previously unimagined detail.

None of these had any significant impact on military medicine. The artificial division between physicians and surgeons and the former's lack of respect for empirical knowledge led to persistence of a plethora of useless and often harmful practices. The typical field medical chest weighed more than 300 pounds and was burdened with such nostrums as mummy dust, scorpion oil, plaster of frog spawn, and dog's fat. Only quinine-containing Peruvian bark, mercury (which, though toxic, was of some use in syphilis), and opium were of actual benefit. Still, the best of the English internists—William Harvey, Thomas Sydenham, and Thomas Willis—all served as military physicians. One particularly bright spot was Tobias Cober's 1606 recognition of the relationship between body lice and typhus in army camps.

In spite of the explosion of vernacular scientific publications in the 1600s, relatively few books on military medicine were published. Between 1600 and 1650, only eight original volumes dealing with surgery appeared, compared with 45 in the previous century. There were 30 new works on infectious disease affecting armies in the century, and the first periodicals devoted solely to medicine appeared in France (*The French Journal of Medicine* and *French Progress in Medicine*) and England (*Medicina Curiosa*).

Although clinical military medicine and surgery saw little advance in the 17th century, strides were made in organization of care for sick and wounded soldiers. During the 1597 siege of Amiens, the duc de Sully had established government-funded "ambulance" hospitals for wounded soldiers, and his king, Henri IV, had opened the Maison de la Charité Chrétienne in Paris to care for disabled and destitute veterans and their families. In January 1629, Cardinal Richelieu issued an ordinance establishing a home for disabled soldiers at the Maison des Invalides, although the facility was not completed until 1676. France's King Louis XIV and Cardinal Mazarin built several military hospitals and placed their administration under a royal *intendant*, thus removing care of wounded soldiers from its traditional reliance on the Church. Louis XIV also established the Hôtel des Invalides, although probably with the cynical aim of getting maimed soldiers off the streets of Paris and out of the public eye. All of these were beneficial steps in the direction of making care of sick and wounded soldiers a responsibility of government, although field care of those men remained dreadful.

Elsewhere, Gustavus Adolphus mandated four barber-surgeons for every regiment of 400–500 men and for every ship of his navy. Peter the Great and Catherine the Great of Russia imported numbers of foreign (primarily English and Dutch) physicians to care for their armies, and, by the end of Peter's reign in 1707, every Russian division had at least one barber-surgeon, one apothecary, and one physician.

Perhaps the apex of the century's military medicine can be found in the works of Polish horse soldier and physician Janus Abraham á Gehema, whose pleas for better care for the sick and wounded fell almost entirely on deaf ears.

See also Barber-Surgeons; Bullet Wounds and Other Penetrating Injuries from Gunpowder Projectiles; Dysentery; Fabry of Hilden, Wilhelm; Harvey, William; Purmann, Matthias; Sydenham, Thomas; Typhoid Fever; Typhus; Wiseman, Richard

References
Forrest, Richard D. 1982. "Development of Wound Therapy from the Dark Ages to the Present." *Journal of the Royal Society of Medicine* 75 (April): 268–273.
Garrison, Fielding. *Notes on the History of Military Medicine.* Washington, D.C.: Association of Military Surgeons, 1922.
Garrison, Fielding. *An Introduction to the History of Medicine.* Philadelphia: W. B. Saunders Co., 1929.

Sharp, Samuel (ca. 1700–1778)

An English founder of anatomically based surgery, Samuel Sharp was born in Jamaica about 1700 and was apprenticed to William Cheselden at St. Thomas's Hospital in London from 1724 to 1731. He spent part of his training in France, where he became fluent in the French language, met Voltaire, and learned French surgical technique. He was admitted to the Company of Barber-Surgeons in London in 1731 and served as surgeon to Guy's Hospital from 1733 to 1757. He helped Cheselden with his famous *Osteographia*, published in 1733, and was a well-known teacher of anatomy until he turned his classes over to William Hunter in 1746.

His landmark *Treatise on the Operations of Surgery* was published in 1739 and included detailed descriptions of technique and instrumentation that remained standard for nearly a century. Sharp was named a fellow of the Royal Society of London in 1749. In his mid-sixties, Sharp traveled in Europe and published *Letters from Italy, describing the customs and manners of that country, in the years 1765, and 1766. To which is annexed, an Admonition to gentlemen who pass the Alps, in their tour through Italy.*

See also British Military Medicine

References
Kirkup, J. 1996. "Samuel Sharp and the Operations of Surgery, 1739." *Journal of Medical Biography* 4 (February): 1–7.
Stevenson, Lloyd. 1956. "A Portrait of Samuel Sharp." *Journal of the History of Medicine and Allied Sciences* 11: 101–102.

Shell Shock in World War I

Also known as neurasthenia and war neurosis, "shell shock" was the name applied in World War I to an assortment of symptoms including anxiety, an exaggerated startle response, tremors, nightmares, hallucinations, delusions, withdrawal, and catatonia.

There were a few cases of battlefield psychosis during the Boer and Spanish-American wars, and the Russians were the first army to establish an independent psychiatric service during their 1905 war with Japan. Psychiatric casualties were, however, common among British, French, and German soldiers from the outset of trench warfare on the Western Front.

Throughout the war, 20–30 percent of battlefield casualties were psychiatric. Although few articles were written about this problem prior to World War I, a 1924

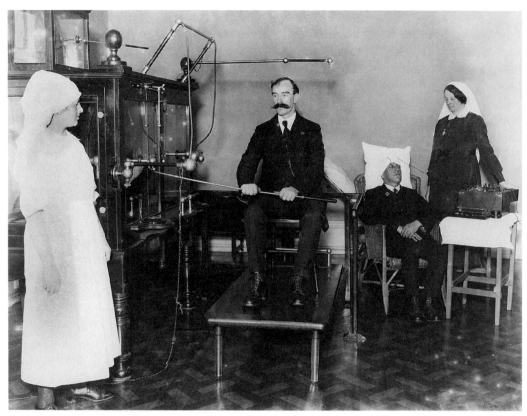

Nurses at the Sir William Hospital using experimental electrotherapy to treat soldiers suffering from shell shock, 1917. (Hulton-Deutsch Collection/Corbis)

review of the medical literature uncovered 3,000 articles and books written about psychiatric illness in soldiers after 1914. The combination of a relatively static front, agonizingly long battles, atrocious living conditions, and high incidence of injury and death contributed to the new prevalence of mental breakdown.

Early in the war the British diagnosed psychiatric casualties as "shellshock," with a "W" (wounded) appended to the diagnosis, possibly under the mistaken idea originally suggested by Russian neuropsychiatrists that the symptoms resulted from small brain hemorrhages caused by explosive concussions. The "W" entitled

men to a wound stripe and disability with a pension. The alternative diagnosis, neurasthenia, was a sickness with an "S" designation which carried no honors and no pension. The British established neurasthenia centers in the home islands and, prior to 1917, medical officers were liberal with the diagnosis of shell shock and transfer home for rest and hypnotherapy.

By 1917, the drain on frontline manpower from psychiatric illness became serious, and medical officers were encouraged to use the "S" designation. The Royal Army Medical Corps established designated casualty clearing stations near the front, where psychiatric casualties were treated for up to a month with sedatives, rest, and reassurance. Using this scheme, 55 percent of men returned to their units, 29 percent were reassigned to labor brigades (mostly working on French farms), and only 16 percent were evacuated to base hospitals. Just before the Third Battle of Ypres, the British General Staff issued General Routine Order Number 2384 forbidding the diagnosis of shell shock and ordering that all psychiatric casualties be sent to a single designated hospital with a diagnosis of "NYDN" (Not Yet Diagnosed, Nervous), with the dual intent of returning as many men as possible to the front and of discouraging malingering.

The Germans were more punitive and inclined to view shell shock as a character defect, which they managed with a variety of painful treatments including electroshock therapy. The Americans adopted the British scheme and, in spite of the fact that the number of psychiatric casualties distressed Gen. John J. Pershing, 85 percent of his men with shell shock returned to their units and only 1 percent were evacuated to the United States.

Postwar treatment of the psychiatrically injured was a difficult and expensive problem. In 1921, 65,000 British veterans were on a pension for psychiatric disability, and there were still 30,000 on pension in 1938. In the United States as late as 1940, 27 of 90 veterans hospitals were designated as psychiatric facilities and treatment of shell shock victims had cost in excess of $1 billion.

See also Combat Fatigue; World War I Medicine

References

Ecksteins, Modris. *Rites of Spring: The Great War and the Birth of the Modern Age*. Boston: Houghton Mifflin, 1989.
Fenton, Norman. *Shell Shock and Its Aftermath*. St. Louis: C. V. Mosby Co., 1926.
MacDonald, Lyn. *The Roses of No Man's Land*. New York: Atheneum, 1989.

Shippen, William, Jr. (1736–1808)

William Shippen was physician in chief and surgeon general of the American army from 1777 to 1781.

Shippen was born in Philadelphia in 1736, the son of a prominent physician of the same name. He studied in a private academy at which John Morgan and Benjamin Rush were fellow students and then at the College of New Jersey at Princeton, where he lived with the university president, Aaron Burr. After graduating as valedictorian of his class, he went to London, where he studied anatomy, surgery, and obstetrics with John Hunter, William Hunter, and William McKenzie. He received a medical degree from the University of Edinburgh, where he was taught by Alexander Monro primus and became friends with Sir John Pringle. The latter even arranged for him to visit Paris in spite of the fact that England and France were at war at the time.

Shippen returned to Philadelphia in 1762, where he taught private lessons in anatomy, obstetrics, and surgery. In 1765, he was appointed professor of surgery at the newly organized College of Philadelphia Medical School, where Morgan was professor of medicine. Shippen remained on the faculty when the school was reorganized as part of the new University of Pennsylvania in 1779.

Shippen was named medical director of the Flying Camp of the Jerseys under Morgan's command when the American Revolution began and, in October 1777, was named director of hospitals west of the Hudson. In April 1777, Morgan was relieved and Shippen was ordered to reorganize the hospital system. Following the reorganization, he assumed overall command of medical services as director general of the Military Hospital and physician in chief of the army.

Morgan and Rush resented Shippen's ascendancy and both publicly attacked him. Rush formally accused Shippen of malpractice and financial misconduct, including speculation in medical supplies. Shippen was tried and acquitted but censured, and he resigned his post in 1781. He returned to private practice and prospered until 1798, when a favorite son unexpectedly died, after which he entered a profound depression and saw his practice dwindle until his death 10 years later.

See also American Revolutionary War; Hunter, John; Morgan, John; Pringle, Sir John; Rush, Benjamin

References

Ashburn, P.M. *A History of the Medical Department of the United States Army*. Boston: Houghton Mifflin, 1929.

Gillet, Mary. *The Army Medical Department, 1775–1818*. Washington, D.C.: Center of Military History, 1981.

Packard, Francis. "William Shippen, Jr." In Howard Kelly and Walter Burrage, *Dictionary of American Medical Biography: Lives of Eminent Physicians of the United States and Canada, from the Earliest Times*. Boston: Milford House, 1928.

Shock

Shock is generally defined as a peak or systolic blood pressure of less than 100 torr (millimeters of mercury), although it is actually a constellation of clinical symptoms including compensatory increase in heart rate; peripheral vascular constriction with cold, blue extremities; and decrease in blood flow to the kidneys resulting in decreased urine output. In extreme cases, shock results in inadequate blood flow to other organs, particularly the brain, with anxiety progressing to decreased consciousness and, ultimately, death.

The clinical signs of shock have been recognized for centuries; for example, Napoleonic surgeon Baron Dominique-Jean Larrey noted that amputation was actually made easier by the vasoconstriction and the decreased sensitivity to pain in a patient in shock. But lack of understanding of its cause and lack of effective treatment left the problem largely unstudied until the years just before World War I. Between 1910 and 1914, British physicians and pharmacologists Henry Dale and George Berger found that histamine isolated from the ergot fungus caused vasodilatation. Dale and his co-workers ultimately demonstrated that acetylcholine was the chemical responsible for that reaction and that it acted as a transmitter for nerve impulses in the parasympathetic nervous system, discoveries for which he shared the 1936 Nobel Prize for Physiology or Medicine with Otto Loewi. Physiologist Edward Mellanby (who became famous for his studies of vitamin D, vitamin A, and nutrition) noted that large doses of histamine caused a fall in body temperature, slowed respiration, drowsiness, and a fall in blood pressure very similar to what was seen in patients during complicated surgery.

Harvard physiologist Walter Cannon, studying traumatic shock in World War I soldiers, published *Bodily Changes in Pain, Hunger, Fear, and Rage* in 1915 and *Traumatic Shock* in 1923, in which he demonstrated that administration of an adrenaline-like hormone that stimulated the sympathetic nervous system, which he called sympathin, led to increased heart rate and vasoconstriction, temporarily reversing hypotension from shock.

Although the vascular basis of shock was fairly well understood by the early years of

World War I, there was considerable debate about the best way to treat the problem. Initial efforts focused on treating the most obvious external symptoms. Soldiers evacuated to casualty clearing stations on the Western Front were warmed—occasionally in electric cribs—and given hot liquids because their cold, blue skin was the most obvious finding. The peripheral vasodilatation from warming the gut and extremities, however, often paradoxically made the patient worse as vessels in the skin and gastrointestinal tract lining filled with blood at the expense of more important organs. Cardiac stimulants similar to the one discovered by Cannon were, however, shown to be of temporary use in reversing shock.

Attempts to replace blood or its equivalent with some other fluid had begun prior to World War I with intravenous administration of saline or glucose and occasional transfusions of whole blood, but the absence of effective storage and the tendency for blood to clot when removed from the body limited its usefulness. In a few cases—most often those involving delayed hemorrhage after an injury—direct transfusion from a donor to a recipient by a cannula sutured into the artery or vein of the first and the vein of the second were used. Occasionally, waxed glass or oiled syringes were tried in an attempt to circumvent coagulation when blood was removed from a donor's body. Late in the war, it was discovered that addition of citrate to the blood stopped clotting, but transfusions seldom exceeded one pint and were rarely enough to reverse the effects of severe blood loss.

There continued to be an argument about whether surgical and traumatic shock resulted from blood loss or from the toxic effect of neurotransmitters until Alfred Blalock, working at Vanderbilt University

in the late 1920s, conclusively demonstrated that the shock was from hypovolemia. He also showed that the fluid loss could be either from bleeding to the outside or from internal leakage of fluid from the vessels into the tissues as was typically seen in burns and crushing injuries.

During the interwar years, military surgeons turned their attention to the problem of blood typing and storage, and, by the beginning of World War II, Great Britain had a formal transfusion service in place at Bristol. Blood banking became more feasible with the demonstration that addition of glucose to citrate allowed blood to be stored for up to 14 days. The British also learned to separate and store plasma and studied fluid replacement with whole blood, components, and various crystalloids. The combination of banking and an armamentarium of fluids made it possible to replace large volumes for the first time. By the end of World War II, fluid replacement was begun early in transport and continued until bleeding could be controlled and the patient stabilized. Through the Korean Conflict and the Viet Nam War, surgeons debated whether whole blood, plasma, or crystalloid was the most effective replacement. Current practice favors the first of these. Techniques of fluid resuscitation learned on the battlefield have become standards of management for civilian trauma.

See also World War I Medicine; World War II
  Medicine

References
Blalock, Alfred. 1930. "Experimental Shock: The Cause of Low Blood Pressure Caused by Muscle Injury." *Archives of Surgery* 20: 959–996.
Brunschwig, Alexander. "Shock and Blood Substitutes." In William Taliaferro, *Medicine and the War*. Chicago: University of Chicago Press, 1944.

Sims, James Marion (1813–1883)

Marion Sims was the first surgeon to successfully operate within the peritoneal cavity and is generally considered the father of surgical gynecology.

Sims was born in the Lancaster district of South Carolina, the son of the county sheriff and grandson of an American Revolutionary War soldier who narrowly escaped execution at the hands of notorious Loyalist Col. Banastre Tarleton. Sims graduated from the South Carolina College at Charleston in 1832 and enrolled in the Charleston Medical School the following year. His performance at both institutions was, by his own admission, singularly undistinguished. He received his doctorate in 1835 from Jefferson Medical College of Philadelphia.

Sims began his career in his home county, but, extending the lack of success he had begun in college, his practice faltered and he moved to Alabama. In his new home, his luck changed and his skill at surgery and especially at repairing birth-related tears between the bladder and vagina brought him local notoriety and considerable professional prosperity. That success was largely due to his use of wire sutures, which he first created from the wire springs used to give suspenders elasticity before India rubber became available. The wires were easier to clean and less prone to infection than either the fiber or gut material in general use. Sims was an inveterate innovator; he was the first to successfully operate on an abscess of the liver, managed to remove a lower jaw from an incision inside the mouth to avoid an external scar, and devised an operation to drain an obstructed gall bladder (although he had been preceded in that by a few months by a surgeon in Indiana).

In 1853, he moved to New York City and founded the Women's Hospital of the State of New York and is credited with having started the specialty of gynecology in the United States. In 1861, he moved to Europe for health reasons, where he visited Napoleon III at St. Cloud and treated the Empress Eugénie. While in Paris, he demonstrated his surgical technique to the greatest of French surgeons, including Baron Dominique-Jean Larrey, and started a phenomenally successful referral practice with patients from across the continent seeking his help. He briefly returned to the United States in 1865 but returned to France when the war with Prussia started in 1870.

During the Franco-Prussian War, Sims accepted a position as surgeon in chief to the Anglo-American Ambulance Corps, a volunteer medical unit that initially served with the French and then with the Prussian army. His experience in France led to his landmark paper "The Careful Aseptic Invasion of the Peritoneal Cavity for the Arrest of Hemorrhage, the Suture of Intestinal Wounds, and the Cleansing of the Peritoneal Cavity, and for all Intraperitoneal Conditions," which he presented to the New York Academy of Medicine on October 6, 1881, and which is credited with initiating surgery of the abdominal cavity. Sims was later named commander of the Legion of Honor for his services at Sedan.

After the war, Sims divided his time between Europe and New York City and continued an active surgical practice in both. He died in New York City in 1883 and was honored with a statue in Bryant Park in that city.

See also Abdominal Injuries in War; Franco-Prussian War

References

Packard, Francis. *History of Medicine in the United States*. New York: Paul B. Hoeber, 1931.

Wyeth, John Allan. "James Marion Sims." In
    Howard Kelly and Walter Burrage, *Diction-*
    ary of American Medical Biography: Lives of
    Eminent Physicians of the United States and
    Canada, from the Earliest Times. Boston:
    Milford House, 1928.
Zimmerman, Leo, and Ilza Veith. *Great Ideas in*
    the History of Surgery. Baltimore: Williams
    & Wilkins Co., 1961.

16th-Century Military Medicine

The 16th century was a time of religious
wars, gradual coalescence of the European
nation-state, the first tentative ventures
from the safety of scholasticism into empiricism, and very limited change in the practice of military medicine.

The Protestant Reformation led to a prolonged revolt by the people of the Netherlands against their Habsburg monarchs
(1572–1609), even longer wars between the
French kings and their Huguenot subjects
(1562–1609), and Spain's disastrous sea-
borne attempt to return England to Catholi-
cism (the 1588 Armada). The descendants
of Ferdinand and Isabella added the Holy
Roman Empire to their domains, the Tudors
cemented their rule in England, and civil
war brought the Bourbons to the French
throne. Nicholas Copernicus challenged
Ptolemaic astronomy and threatened the
Church, while Leonardo da Vinci and Andreas Vesalius (who served as a military
surgeon in the army of Holy Roman Emperor Charles V) used dissection and their
own powers of observation to upend Galen
and the mistranslations of his work that had
been perpetrated by Arab scholars.

Europe was flooded with scholars fleeing
Constantinople after the Eastern Empire fell
in 1453, and the printing press spread knowledge that had previously been confined to a
handful of collections to libraries across the
continent. As the century progressed, works
in the vernacular made learning available
to those curious but deficient in Latin and
Greek. Cumbersome volumes were reduced
to pocket-sized duodecimos, so wound
surgeons had, for the first time, anatomical drawings based on actual dissection to
guide them through the vagaries of combat
surgery, but, because the texts were almost
all in Latin, that information was mostly
available to the physicians who did not operate and the few educated wound surgeons
who treated royalty and officers. The common soldier remained in the hands of illiterate barbers, "cutters," and assorted quacks.

Militarily, the century saw increasing use
of gunpowder weapons and the emergence
of professional soldiery. Bowmen, who had
displaced armored knights as the most effective tools of war at Crécy (1346), Poitiers
(1356), and Agincourt (1415), were, along
with their supporting pike men, being replaced by arquebusiers. Mercenary armies
such as the Italian condottieri and the Swiss
guards provided trained fighters organized
into a regimental system that would evolve
into standing national armies later in the
century. Already, Charles VII of France
(1422–1461) had his *compagnies d'ordonnance*
and Holy Roman Emperor Maximilian I
(1459–1519) the *Landesknechte*, a professional army drawn from his citizenry that
would be greatly expanded by his successor, Charles V.

The wheel lock arquebus made personal
gunpowder weapons feasible in 1515 and
evolved into the matchlock weapon ignited
by smoldering fire carried in a tin box. Powder was poured in a flat igniting pan and
the match touched to it as the arquebusier
raised the weapon against his cheek and just
below his eye; the prevalence of premature

explosion and severe facial burns from those weapons gave the phrase "flash in the pan" a particularly grim connotation.

Switzerland's rugged, mountainous cantons provided an excellent incubator for fighters, and, after proving their mettle in internecine battles, the Swiss rented themselves out across Europe. These mercenary units were also the first since the Romans to treat medical care for their sick and wounded as a government responsibility. The cantons hired barber-surgeons from public funds and continued to pay the wounded and even to cover the living expenses of their families until the soldiers recovered. The term *feldscherer* (or, more commonly, its shortened form *feldscher*), or field barber, first appeared on Basel's city rolls in 1542 and would persist as a description for a lesser trained wound dresser and field surgeon until well into the 20th century, when the Russian Army finally retired it. Swiss barber-surgeons doubled as combat personnel and were expected to fight as well as treat.

Even though they made provisions for their wounded after a battle, the rigid Swiss rules of engagement made the lot of an injured man during combat less than admirable. Wounded Swiss soldiers were required to remain where they lay, and those well enough to move themselves were treated as deserters if they left the field of battle. This was a particularly onerous requirement as it was common practice for victors to collect and massacre all prisoners and wounded men after a battle ended. Ironically for the country that gave birth to the International Red Cross and the Geneva Convention, Swiss soldiers took an oath to spare no enemy and to allow none of their own to be captured. This dour practice showed some signs of abatement late in the century with the first postcombat prisoner exchanges.

Under Henry VIII (1509–1547), the English army had regular physicians and surgeons, although their pay was generally drawn from "hospital funds" withheld from soldiers' wages. Spain retained the mobile "ambulance" hospitals—tented facilities for soldiers in the field first supplied by Charles V's grandmother Isabella—where the wounded were mostly cared for by barber-surgeons and female camp followers. The Armada was the first naval force since the Romans that we know to have been accompanied by a dedicated hospital ship.

During the 16th century, sieges were twice as common as battles, a situation that ensured that disease and famine would be more important than battles and wounds in determining wars' outcomes. Diseases that we now associate with childhood but that are in fact the result of concentrating masses of people without prior immunity—measles, diphtheria, whooping cough, influenza—were common and commonly fatal. Smallpox was repeatedly epidemic across Europe. Typhus, not yet known to be spread by lice, was a regular accompaniment to prolonged deployment and the attendant lack of sanitation, as were dysentery and cholera. Dietary deficiencies and toxins such as scurvy (vitamin C deficiency), ergotism (a disease of blood vessels and the nervous system caused by a fungus that most often grows on rye), and lead poisoning were also common. Perhaps the most feared disease was the Great Pox or syphilis, which, although it may have been endemic for centuries, first became epidemic in the 16th century and seems to have had a profoundly different and more disastrous clinical course than its modern version.

Greek and Roman authorities were of no help in treating gunshot wounds, and 16th-century military surgeons were unable to arrive at a consensus on their management. Giovanni de Vigo, personal physician to Pope Julius II, held that gunpowder and the projectiles it propelled were, of themselves, poisonous, and he used his considerable authority to propagate the practice of probing for bullets, widely opening the wounds, and cauterizing the cavity with hot oil or hot iron. The practice, in spite of frequent objections based on patently dismal results, remained common, and the argument about whether to explore the wounds or leave nature to heal them persisted into the 20th century. Although Hans von Gersdorff in his landmark *Field Book of Wound Surgery* (1571) held that the wounds were not poisoned, he still recommended cauterization. To their credit, 16th-century wound surgeons generally used "sleeping sponges" soaked in opium, henbane, mandragora root, lettuce, and hemlock to lessen pain, but their probing and cauterizing were unquestionably the major factor in the near universal lethality of gunshot wounds.

Although the practice of military medicine remained benighted and largely ineffective through the 16th century and aggressive wound surgeons most often made things worse instead of better, there were a few bright spots in military surgery. In his *Grosse Wund Artzney* (1536), Paracelsus vainly argued against cauteries, probes, and salves: "What do wounds need? Nothing. Inasmuch as the flesh grows from within outwards, and not from without inwards, so the surgery of a wound is a mere defensive, to prevent Nature from suffering any accident from without, so that she may proceed unchecked in her operations" (Garrison 1922). He also advocated removing the artificial distinction between physicians and surgeons and was the inspiration for the preeminent military surgeon of the century, Ambroise Paré.

Paré, who abandoned cauterizing gunshot wounds when he ran out of hot oil after a battle, revolutionized both wound care and battlefield medicine in general. Only marginally educated, he was unpolluted by scholastics and Arab physicians and their misapplication and mistranslation of the ancients. He advocated minimal manipulation of wounds beyond irrigation and substituted the ligature for the cautery in managing hemorrhage. His willingness to treat all wounded and not just the upper class made him a favorite of French soldiers. But, in the absence of understanding of infection and of adequate anesthesia, battlefield surgery, even with the greatness of Paré, would not come of age for more than three centuries.

See also Barber-Surgeons; Bullet Wounds and Other Penetrating Injuries from Gunpowder Projectiles; Cauterization; Dysentery; Gersdorff, Hans von; Paracelsus (Aureolus Theophrastus Bombastus von Hohenheim); Paré, Ambroise; Scurvy; Smallpox; Syphilis; Typhus; Vesalius, Andreas

References
Forrest, Richard D. 1982. "The Development of Wound Therapy from the Dark Ages to the Present." *Journal of the Royal Society of Medicine* 75 (April): 268–273.
Garrison, Fielding. *Notes on the History of Military Medicine.* Washington, D.C.: Association of Military Surgeons, 1922.
Malgaigne, J. F. *Surgery and Ambroise Paré.* Norman: University of Oklahoma Press, 1965.
Packard, Francis P. *The Life and Times of Ambroise Paré.* New York: Paul B. Hoeber, 1921.

Smallpox

Smallpox, a systemic viral disease, occurs in two forms: variola major, which carries 25 percent mortality rate, and variola minor, with a 1 percent mortality rate.

The disease is caused by an orthopoxvirus, a DNA-based organism and the largest virus that infects animals. The agent initially multiplies in the bloodstream before infecting internal organs, especially the lungs, liver, and spleen. About 12 days after exposure there is a secondary viremia, at which time the organism infects the skin, causing a rash that develops into vesicles after two to three more days. Fluid from either infected lungs or from weeping vesicles carries viral particles and can cause infection. The virus is passed directly from human to human, usually by inhalation of infected fluids, although it can also be passed by skin contact. Smallpox is relatively contagious, with one drop of pulmonary secretion typically carrying 1,000 more viral particles than are needed to cause an infection. A carrier is usually infectious for only three to four days.

There is no treatment for an established infection; however, smallpox was the first disease successfully prevented by creating artificial immunity in potential hosts. For centuries the Chinese and later the Turks intentionally exposed susceptible people to infectious material from patients suffering from mild forms of smallpox. This "variolation" or "buying the pox" carried a mortality of 1–10 percent but conferred permanent immunity. In 1796 English physician Edward Jenner proved that exposure to cowpox (vaccinia) was almost universally safe and, in 99 percent of cases, conferred lasting immunity to the related smallpox virus.

In 1958, smallpox was still killing 2 million people a year, and the Soviet Union asked the World Health Organization to sponsor a worldwide program to eradicate the disease. The program was started in 1967, and the last naturally occurring case of smallpox was documented in Somalia in 1977, making smallpox the first infectious

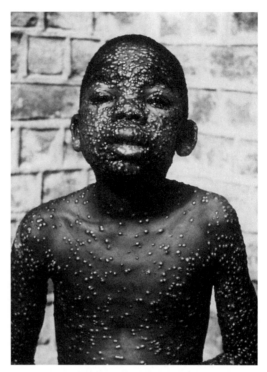

African child displaying the rash typical of smallpox on his face, chest, and arms, 1970. (Centers for Disease Control)

disease intentionally eradicated. Samples of the virus were maintained at the Center for Communicable Disease in Atlanta and at the Soviet State Research Center of Virology and Biotechnology (Vector) in Siberia, presumably for scientific research.

Smallpox has played an intentional and an unintentional military role over the centuries. A probable smallpox epidemic in Rome in A.D. 165 cost the city one-third of its population. Crusaders brought the disease to Western Europe on their return from the Levant. A combination of smallpox, influenza, and measles reduced the population of Mexico by 90 percent over less than five generations and made the military and cultural conquest of the Aztec and Incan empires by the Spanish possible. Lord Jeffrey Amherst attempted to use smallpox as a weapon by giving infected blankets to hostile North American Indians in 1763.

The American Central Intelligence Agency was found to have a small supply of the virus, presumably for use as a weapon, in 1975. The Soviet Vector lab is thought to have produced about 100 metric tons of weaponized smallpox a year in the 1970s, much of which is not accounted for and may have been sold to other countries. The risk that smallpox will reappear as a biological weapon has resulted in vaccination programs for the military and for health care providers and to discussions of widespread civilian vaccination.

See also American Revolutionary War; Chemical and Biological Warfare

References
Alibek, Ken, with Stephen Handelman. *Biohazard*. New York: Random House, 1999.
Henderson, D. A., T. V. Inglesby, J. G. Bartlett, M. S. Ascher, E. Eitzen, P. B. Jahrling, J. Hauer, M. Layton, J. McDade, M. T. Osterholm, T. O'Toole, G. Perker, T. Perl, P. K. Russell, K. Tonat, and the Working Group on Civilian Biodefense. "Smallpox as a Biological Weapon: Medical and Public Health Management." *Journal of the American Medical Association* 281 (June 9): 2127–2137.
Levine, Arnold. *Viruses*. New York: Scientific American Library, 1992.
McNeill, William. *Plagues and Peoples*. Garden City, NY: Anchor Press, 1976.
Miller, Judith, Stephen Engelberg, and William Broad. *Germs: Biological Weapons and America's Secret War*. New York: Simon & Schuster, 2001.

Smollet, Tobias
(1721–1771)

A naval surgeon and author, Tobias Smollet was born in the Scottish village of Dalquhum in Dumbartonshire, the son of a prominent Whig politician. His father died while Smol-

let was still young, leaving him and his eight siblings destitute. He was educated at Dumbarton and apprenticed to surgeon John Gordon of the University of Glasgow at age 14. Smollet joined the Royal Navy as a surgeon in 1739, and his service over the next five years furnished the material for his novel *Roderick Random*, a brutal satire of his naval experience and medicine in general. He was particularly critical of the low status of ships' surgeons and of corruption in the examinations for surgeon's mate.

Although he continued as a novelist, Smollet also rewrote his friend William Smellie's books on midwifery and on anatomy after the latter's death.

Smollet died at 50 years of age in the Italian city of Leghorn.

See also Naval Medicine

Reference
Comrie, John. *History of Scottish Medicine.* London: Baillière, Tindall & Cox, 1932.

Sovereign Military Hospitaller Order of St. John of Jerusalem, of Rhodes, and of Malta

This charitable order was originally formed to maintain a hospital in Jerusalem but survived to fill a number of medical, military, and political roles.

Construction of a "hospital," or house to receive pilgrims, next to the Church of the Holy Sepulchre was originally authorized in A.D. 600 by Pope Gregory the Great. The hospital was restored in 800 on order of Charlemagne, and, in 1070, a group of merchants from the Italian city of Amalfi built a grand new structure dedicated to St. John the Almsgiver and intended to deliver medical care to pilgrims on that same site. The Hospital of St. John was given formal Church recognition by a papal bull in 1113 and became a military facility in which French was the primary language. The knights who managed that hospital also maintained hospices in Syria and were granted special privileges and properties throughout Christendom to support their charitable work.

The brothers of the Order of St. John fell into three grades—knight, sergeant, and chaplain—and took vows of poverty, chastity, and obedience. The order was governed from a chapter house in Syria, and, after Jerusalem fell to the Saracens in 1187, the hospital was relocated to Acre. That city, too, was lost in 1291, although the Hospitallers fought grimly to hold it. The few survivors relocated to Cyprus and established yet another hospital at Limassol.

In 1306, the Hospitallers invaded the small, scenic island of Rhodes and, after four years of bitter fighting, expelled the Greeks and Turks who had been its inhabitants. In 1307, Avignon pope Clement V declared the hospital the owner of Rhodes, largely because he favored the French-speaking order to the Venetians, who were supported by Rome and who also claimed the Greek islands. The hospital was moved to Rhodes and, between fighting with the Genoese, Venetians, Greeks, and Turks, they found time to also care for the sick and aged travelers. By the mid-14th century, the order was so wealthy that much of its energy was diverted to managing its extensive European estates and recruiting new members.

In 1403, under a treaty with Mameluke Sultan Faraj, the order was allowed to once again maintain a hospital in Jerusalem, and its members were allowed to travel freely in the sultan's lands. The hospital, however, remained subordinate to the order's large standing army and navy. In 1437, the order built a second hospital on Rhodes that survives as an archaeological museum.

Constantinople fell to the Muslims in 1453 and, in 1523, the Hospitallers were forced to abandon Rhodes. Holy Roman Emperor Charles V gave them the island of Malta in 1530, where they remained headquartered until they were expelled by Napoleon Bonaparte in 1798. In 1834, the order moved to Rome, where they abandoned all their military activities and reverted entirely to providing medical care. Although there are few Knights of St. John now, there are more than 10,000 lay members of the order around the world.

After the Reformation, four primarily Protestant Orders of St. John were formed, including surviving chapters in Germany, the Netherlands, and Sweden. In addition, the Grand Priory of the Most Venerable Order of the Hospital of St. John of Jerusalem was chartered in Great Britain in 1827 to attempt reclamation of Greece from the Ottoman Empire and was converted by order of Queen Victoria in 1888 to the St. John Ambulance Service.

See also Ambulances and Transport; Medieval Military Medicine

References
Bedford, W. K. R., and Richard Holbeche. *The Order of the Hospital of St. John of Jerusalem: Being a History of the English Hospitallers of St. John, and Their Rise.* London: F. E. Robinson & Co., 1902.
Riley-Smith, Jonathan. *The Knights of St. John in Jerusalem and Cyprus C. 1050–1310.* New York: Palgrave Macmillan, 1967.

Spanish-American War

A brief war at the close of the 19th century, the Spanish-American War was, in many ways, the first triumph of modern military surgery and the last great failure of military medicine.

After the USS *Maine* exploded in Havana Harbor on February 15, 1898, it was only a matter of time until sensationalist American journalists were able to prod President William McKinley into declaring war on Spain. At 27,000 men, the entire U.S. Army had only one-third as many troops as Spain had stationed in Cuba alone, so there was an immediate need for rapid expansion. Congress authorized increasing the regular army to 65,000 and calling for 125,000 volunteers. With additional calls, a total of 306,760 men served between April 21 and the end of hostilities with Spain on August 13, 1898.

Congress initially refused to allow Surgeon General George Sternberg to stockpile supplies, and the Army Medical Corps entered the war desperately short of doctors, hospital attendants, equipment, and experience. The Army was authorized to enlist 123 new surgeons and assistant surgeons and to contract with additional civilian surgeons to serve for the duration, and the service increased to 650 by war's end. The Army Medical School was closed so its professors could assume clinical duties.

The various state volunteer regiments usually came with their own doctors, but these, unlike the carefully selected, well-trained professional military surgeons, had inconsistent qualifications and no experience dealing with either battle casualties or large groups of men in small spaces. In the end, the medical record for the Spanish-American War was a sorry one. Of 2,446 deaths between May 1 and August 31, 1898, only 385 were from battle-related wounds; almost all of the rest were from disease, usually acquired in training camps in the United States. The overall ratio of death from disease to that in battle was 7.4:1 as compared with 2:1 in the Civil War.

Besides poorly trained, inexperienced physicians, a variety of systemic and environmental disabilities contributed to this death rate. First, volunteers arrived in large numbers at hastily constructed training facilities. The men were often from urban areas and were accustomed to living at close quarters but were also accustomed to a sanitation infrastructure. In camps, they resorted to defecating on open ground and, within weeks, the grounds were hopelessly contaminated.

Camp locations were chosen more for political than environmental reasons and, almost without exception, were poorly drained and short of potable water. To make matters worse, the few latrines that were dug were often placed adjacent to kitchens and water supplies. Most regimental surgeons lacked training in basic sanitation, and those who understood had little influence because military doctors answered directly to line officers rather than to other physicians and the regular army officers had little knowledge of and virtually no interest in sanitation.

Initially, most hospital attendants were transferred from the line and were untrained and often undisciplined. One of the few bright spots came in April 1898 when Sternberg was authorized to hire 1,700 contract female nurses who ultimately formed the Army Nurse Corps Division of the Surgeon General's Office under Dr. Anita Newcomb McGee, who was granted the rank of acting assistant surgeon.

The Army had planned to establish three 200-bed divisional hospitals manned by six officers and 99 enlisted men for each corps. These were to be fed by collecting stations one or two miles behind the line, from which men were to be moved to field hospitals two to three miles farther back. These plans became moot because of both the war's brevity and the fact that only V

Corps was deployed in Cuba and actions in Puerto Rico and the Philippines, at least during the war, were almost bloodless.

General William Shafter's V Corps landed without resistance at Daquírí on Cuba's southeast coast on June 22, 1898. They fought a small battle at Las Guasamás shortly thereafter. Wounded from that battle had to be cared for on the SS *Olivette*, one of the transports that had brought the force from Tampa, because the unit's portable field hospital and its supplies were temporarily lost in various ships' holds. By the Battle of Kettle Hill and San Juan Hill, in which 1,200 men were wounded, the Army finally had collecting stations and a field hospital in place at Siboney on the coast. After a brief siege of Santiago, the Spanish Navy, which had sought refuge in the city's harbor, came out and was sunk in its entirety, effectively ending the hostilities.

Almost all battlefield injuries in Cuba were from either rifles (primarily high-velocity Mausers) or pistols, with virtually no artillery or blast injuries. Survival rates from surgery in Cuba were much better than those in the Civil War; 4.1 percent of those wounded in battle died in 1898, compared with 17.5 percent in the earlier conflict. About 40 percent of the operative procedures in Cuba were amputations, with a mortality rate of 20.7 percent. After it was recognized that nonoperatively treated extremity injuries had only 0.4 percent mortality, 90 percent of those wounds were treated without surgery. Besides the nature of the injuries and better surgical judgment, use of antiseptic hand washing before operations and sterilization of instruments contributed to better clinical results.

The Spanish-American War saw two signal innovations in the treatment of battlefield injury. The Army placed 17 X-ray machines in hospital ships off the coast, so manual probing for lost bullets became unnecessary. Also, the repeated problem of arrival of unidentifiable bodies of those killed in action led an Army surgeon to suggest that, in the future, each soldier be supplied with a metal identification tag to be worn around his neck, the first dog tags.

The Army's record with disease in 1898 was not nearly as good as that with trauma. Three large camps were opened in the spring and summer of 1898: Camp George Thomas at Chickamauga, Georgia, just south of Chattanooga; Camp Cuba Libre outside Jacksonville, Florida; and Camp Alger at Falls Church, Virginia, seven miles outside Washington, D.C. Camp Thomas housed 58,000 men of I and III Corps and was in the grip of a typhoid outbreak by early summer. Camp Cuba Libre had 5,000 of the 19,000 members of VII Corps hospitalized by August. In both cases, camp physicians blamed the illness on either malaria or the Civil War–era pseudodiagnosis typho-malaria and adamantly denied that the problem was fecally transmitted typhoid fever. At Camp Alger, Col. Alfred C. Girard understood that typhoid was the problem and, aided by a staff of Red Cross nurses and the fact that he could isolate the ill in the general hospital at Fort Myer, that camp seldom had more than 600 men in the hospital at any one time.

Within weeks, it was obvious that the grounds in and around all the camps were contaminated beyond recovery, and the decision was made to abandon the facilities and move the men to new camps with better drainage.

Within 40 days of V Corps' arrival in Cuba, illness had rendered the army virtually useless, but, instead of typhoid, the problem there was a combination of malaria, dysentery, and yellow fever. Fear that soldiers would bring yellow fever home with them led to the establishment of a quarantine facility at Camp Wikoff on Montauk Point, Long Island. Although 80 percent of the soldiers who returned to New York from Cuba were sick and more than half required hospitalization, none ever died of yellow fever. There was a relatively mild typhoid outbreak, although of 21,870 men who passed through Camp Wikoff, only 357 died of illness.

Public outrage at the death rate from disease led to formation of the Typhoid Board and the Dodge Commission and, eventually, to significant reforms in the Army Medical Corps.

See also Reed, Walter; Sternberg, George Miller; Typhoid Fever; X-Ray; Yellow Fever

References

Bayne-Jones, Stanhope. *The Evolution of Preventive Medicine in the United States Army, 1607–1939.* Washington, D.C.: Office of the Surgeon General, Department of the Army, 1968.

Cirillo, Vincent J. *Bullets and Bacilli: The Spanish-American War and Military Medicine.* New Brunswick, NJ: Rutgers University Press, 1999.

Gillett, Mary. *The Army Medical Department, 1865–1917.* Washington, D.C.: Center of Military History, United States Army, 1995.

Sternberg, George Miller (1838–1915)

A bacteriologist, epidemiologist, paleontologist, and surgeon general of the U.S. Army, George Sternberg was born in upstate New York, the son and grandson of Lutheran ministers. He was largely self-educated and took a teaching job at age 16 to help with the family's finances. After two years, he decided to try medicine and started as apprentice to a Cooperstown, New York, physician. After a year, he enrolled in the College of Physicians and Surgeons in New York City, graduating in 1860. He practiced briefly before joining the Army as an assistant surgeon at the beginning of the Civil War.

Sternberg was captured at the Battle of Bull Run but escaped after a few days and rejoined the army, where he served in several battles before nearly dying of typhoid fever in 1862. Thereafter, he served in hospitals behind the lines until the war ended. He remained in the Army Medical Corps after the war, serving in a variety of western forts and Indian campaigns. While in the west, he avidly collected fossils and, although he did not publish in that area, corresponded widely with other paleontologists and eventually divided his large collection among several museums, including the Smithsonian in Washington. He lost his first wife to a cholera epidemic at Fort Harker, Kansas, in 1867; witnessed yellow fever epidemics in 1873 and 1875 at Fort Barrancas, Florida; and was himself a victim in the latter outbreak.

Perhaps because of his personal experiences with infectious diseases, he made them his special interest. Sternberg first worked on chemical disinfectants in 1878. He subsequently became an accomplished microbiologist and published one of the first books on photomicrography in 1884. In 1892 he published what became a standard text in microbiology.

He was named surgeon general of the Army in May 1893, a position he held until retired on account of age in June 1902. During that tenure, Sternberg was responsible for founding the Army Medical School and establishing the contract dental service and the Army nurse corps.

Sternberg served on international commissions to study yellow fever in 1879, 1885, and 1887 and published 143 articles dealing with the disease. At one time he erroneously thought he had discovered a bacterium that caused yellow fever but was proven wrong by the Walter Reed Commission on infectious diseases, which he had organized and sent to Cuba.

Sternberg served as president of the American Public Health Association, the American Medical Association, and the Association of Military Surgeons of the United States.

He died at his home in Washington, D.C., at age 77 on November 3, 1915.

See also Reed, Walter; Spanish-American War; Yellow Fever

References
Gibson, John M. *Soldier in White: The Life of General George Miller Sternberg.* Durham, NC: Duke University Press, 1958.
Sternberg, Martha. *George Miller Sternberg: A Biography.* Chicago: American Medical Association, 1920.

Stretchers and Litters

Stretchers and litters are used to carry wounded men off the field of battle.

Getting men unable to move themselves from the battlefield to a place they can receive care is a problem as old as warfare itself, and solutions have ranged from having a comrade carry the wounded soldier on his back to the most sophisticated forms of aeromedical evacuation. The word "litter" derives from the Latin *lectica*, or bed, and bearers in the Roman army were called *lecticarii*, or bed carriers. Among the earliest litters were the Greek soldiers' own long shields, and that method of transporting the

wounded persisted through the Crusades. With cavalry came the option of suspending the shield between two horses.

It was mostly left to either fellow soldiers or drafted civilians to physically remove the wounded until the early 19th century. During Napoleon Bonaparte's Spanish War, Baron Pierre François Percy organized a corps of *brancardiers* (after the French *brancard*, or stretcher) charged with collecting the wounded. Each *brancardier* carried a lance that doubled as a stretcher pole and wore a sash that formed half the stretcher's bed. Two men equaled one litter and there were 32 bearers attached to each company of hospital attendants. Percy's *brancardiers*, together with Baron Dominique-Jean Larrey's ambulance wagons and mobile hospitals, formed the pattern for delivery of medical care at the front.

A variety of animal-borne stretchers, including those carried by oxen, horses, mules, elephants, camels, and llamas, were deployed through the 19th century. Among the most popular were the French paired chairs suspended across a mule's back known as *cacolets* that were favored during the Crimean War and persisted into the American Civil War. Although the Union Army started the war with 300 mule-borne litters, the devices fell out of favor when trained mules proved scarce and were often commandeered for other purposes in the heat of battle. Ultimately, armies in the Civil War fell back on manpower to move the wounded, although the bearers were occasionally equipped with wheelbarrow-like carts.

The Union Army deployed 52,489 stretchers (one for every 25 soldiers) during the conflict. They were primarily the bulky Satterlee or Halstead types that were more than two feet wide, eight feet long, and weighed in excess of 25 pounds. Neither would fit in

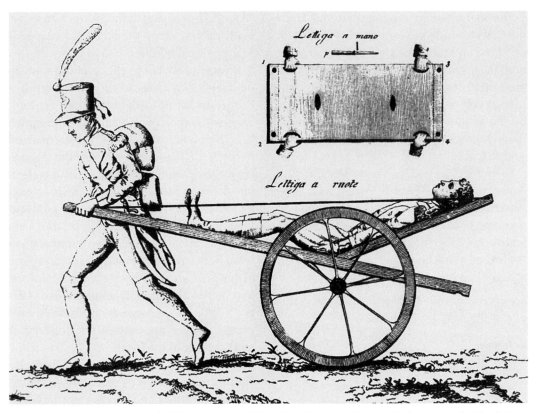

Stretcher cart designed to be pulled by one man and hinged so that the patient can be kept somewhat level, from an Italian medical manual, 1812. (National Library of Medicine)

an ambulance, necessitating often painful transfer of the patient, but both persisted in use until 1895, when they were supplanted by a 9-pound folding litter that could be loaded directly into an ambulance wagon. The Prussian Army developed stretchers on skids that could slide into railcars, and the British put wooden wheels on their litters to make loading into an ambulance easier.

After the Geneva Convention following the Austro-Prussian War, stretcher bearers wore red crosses that gave them immunity from capture although they were afforded no protection from enemy fire. Evacuating the wounded remained one of the most physically demanding and dangerous jobs in the army.

As battlefield medicine and surgery became more effective with introduction first of anesthesia and then asepsis, it became more important to stabilize patients until they could be treated, and the litter bearer's role was expanded to provision of first aid. The first battlefield dressing kits were issued during the Crimean War. In the Sudan War of 1894, the Royal Army Medical Corps issued carbolic acid–soaked cloth covered with tin foil and parchment to stretcher bearers so wounds could be disinfected on the spot.

World War I trench warfare placed a new set of demands on the bearers. The numbers of wounded were unprecedented. Royal Army Medical Corps bearers alone moved more than 9 million wounded during the war. A variety of carts on wooden rails and overhead trench monorails were devised to move stretchers across the French and Belgian mud. Germany entered the war with 2,000 ambulance dogs, some of which were trained to carry ropes into no man's land so the wounded could grab on and be dragged to the safety of their own trenches.

Although late-20th-century helicopter evacuation has brought mechanized transport very close to the front lines, it still falls to medics to administer first aid and often hand-carry the wounded to a mechanized means of transport.

See also Aeromedical Evacuation; Ambulances and Transport; Civil War in the United States; Crimean War; Franco-Prussian War; Larrey, Baron Dominique-Jean; Napoleonic Wars; Percy, Baron Pierre François

Reference
Haller, John S. *Farmcarts to Fords: A History of the Military Ambulance, 1790–1925.* Carbondale: Southern Illinois University Press, 1992.

Sulfonamides

Sulfonamides were the first class of chemical agents with wide applicability as specific antibiotics.

The story of synthetic antibiotics begins with German chemist Paul Ehrlich, who reasoned that, if histological dyes would selectively attach themselves to parts of bacteria, there might be other chemicals that would behave in a similar fashion and be toxic to the organisms instead of simply changing their color. His experiments with organic arsenicals led to discovery in 1909 of arsphenamine (or Compound 606, as it was the 606th compound his laboratory had tested), which had some activity against syphilis. Ehrlich's

success encouraged I. G. Farbenindustrie to investigate possible antibacterial activity of the aniline dyes they manufactured. Farben chemist Gerhard Domagk found Prontosil in 1934 after empirically testing thousands of compounds. Domagk was awarded the Nobel Prize for Physiology or Medicine in 1939, but Germany's Nazi government would not allow him to accept it. (He finally received the award in 1947.) In 1935, French chemist Ernest Fournou of the Pasteur Institute showed that Prontosil was hydrolyzed to sulfanilamide, the actual antibacterial chemical, after administration. Sulfanilamide had been isolated and patented in 1908 by Austrian Paul Gelmo, but he thought its only use was as a dye, and the patent had been allowed to expire.

After Fournou's discovery, sulfanilamide's importance was almost immediately recognized by researchers and clinicians, and a rush ensued to develop variants that eventually included sulfapyridine, sulfathiazole, and sulfaguanidine.

Sulfa drugs were used by both sides in the Spanish Civil War, and they were a regular part of every modern army's supplies when World War II started in 1939. Sulfa powder was widely distributed and used to dust fresh wounds early in the war. American production of sulfa drugs started at 350,000 pounds in 1937 and rose to more than 10 million pounds by 1942. The indiscriminate use of the antibiotic led to early development of bacterial resistance and, by the end of the war, parenteral penicillin had largely replaced it. Nonetheless, sulfa drugs were used to treat President Franklin Roosevelt's skin infection and Prime Minister Winston Churchill's pneumonia during the war, and they played a major role in lowering the death rate from penetrating wounds, especially those involving the head. Sulfa drugs were also widely used against gonorrhea, and their effectiveness against dysentery gave Americans a significant advantage over their Japanese opponents in the Pacific who had only limited access to the drug. On a more sinister note, the Japanese did test sulfa drugs against deliberately administered plague in the Unit 731 human experiments during the war.

By the end of World War II, bacterial resistance had rendered sulfa drugs largely ineffective in treating penetrating wounds, although they continued to have a role in treatment of burns, venereal disease, and urinary tract infections.

See also Unit 731; World War II Medicine

References

Miller, C. P., and M. Bornhoff. 1950. "The Development of Bacterial Resistance to Chemotherapeutic Agents." *Annual Review of Microbiology* 4 (October): 201–222.

Mohler, Henry K. 1941. "The Therapeutic Use of Sulfanilamide and Related Compounds." *The Military Surgeon* 88 (January): 473–486.

Surgical Gloves

Use of gloves during surgical procedures had been suggested as early as 1834 by Richard F. Cooke, and rubber gloves were patented by British surgeon Thomas Foster in 1878, but they were intended to protect the surgeon rather than the patient and did not achieve even limited acceptance.

Widespread use of thin rubber gloves began in 1899 when William Halsted of Johns Hopkins University asked his friend Charles Goodyear to make a pair for his scrub nurse. Caroline Hampton (daughter of Confederate Gen. Wade Hampton and Halsted's future wife) had developed an allergy to the corrosive sublimate used to cleanse the operating team's hands and would have had to retire without skin protection. The gloves proved effective and were adopted by Halsted's surgical residents and assistants. Halsted, claiming that the gloves reduced his tactile sensitivity, was the last member of the team to begin using the gloves, although they became generally accepted by the rest of the Hopkins surgeons sometime between 1897 and 1899.

The original gloves came nearly to the elbow and were worn under sterile arm bands that covered the skin between the gloves' cuffs and the short sleeves of the standard operating gowns. The usual procedure was for the surgical team to wash their hands in tincture of green soap, rinse with potassium permanganate, rinse again with oxalic acid until the permanganate stain was removed, then rinse with bichloride of mercury, and, finally, rinse the last of the chemicals off with saline.

In 1899, the gloves cost $1.75 a pair and were reused up to 12 times. They were usually steam sterilized between cases, but some surgeons wore the same gloves all day, merely rinsing them in carbolic acid between operations.

Acceptance of the gloves elsewhere was gradual. After 1905, when Herbert Fox and E. A. Schumann proved that the rubber was impermeable to bacteria, full-length gowns and gloves became standard in the United States (masks were widely used after 1906). Surgeons commented that the gloves had the serendipitous advantage of preventing the smell of the operating room accompanying them to evening social events. Adoption of surgical gloves was slower in Europe. The Germans used them almost from the turn of the century, but there were still prominent European surgeons operating with their bare hands well into the 1920s.

See also Antisepsis; Asepsis

Reference
Wangensteen, Owen, and Sarah D. Wangensteen. *The Rise of Surgery from Empirical Craft to Scientific Discipline*. Minneapolis: University of Minnesota Press, 1978.

Suture

Suture is a material used to close a wound or to join tissues.

Documented use of suture dates to 1600 B.C., when the Egyptians described using linen, cotton, flax, or hemp lubricated with wine or oil to repair lacerated tissue; the technique undoubtedly predates the written record. The Indian surgeon Suśruta (ca. 750 B.C.) described using black ants to bite the edges of torn intestine: After the two jaws closed on the open margins, the head was cut off and left in place as the biological equivalent of modern staples used for the same type of repair. Indian physicians also used suture made of human hair to close external wounds. Aulus Cornelius Celsus described both fiber suture and metal clips, to which Galen added silk and catgut (which, its name notwithstanding, is actually made from sheep's intestine). In another example of an early, biologically derived monofilament suture, the Arabic physician Avicenna recommended sewing with pig's bristles.

Although it was not until the end of the 19th century that bacteriologists proved suture material to be a major source of infection, its adverse effects on healing had been recognized long before that. In an attempt to decrease inflammation, French surgeon Ambroise Paré limited himself to four stitches supplemented by adhesive plaster in closing wounds after battlefield amputation. Glue, tape, and metal staples have been substituted for thread with the same intent. It was not just the material but also the way in which it was used that made suture such an integral part of wound infection. Into the early years of the 19th century, surgeons draped suture from the buttonholes of their generally filthy coats in order to have it conveniently available. Their assistants often licked the ends of the material to make it easier to thread into small-eyed needles. Ironically, Confederate surgeons in the American Civil War probably benefited from their government's inability to find adequate supplies of suture material. They substituted horse hair, which they boiled to soften it and make it easier to tie. This inadvertent sterilization undoubtedly contributed to the fact that they had a lower wound infection rate than their Northern colleagues.

In the years before World War I, Johns Hopkins pathologist William Welch demonstrated that suture passing through the skin carried bacteria with it into the subcutaneous tissues and recommended closing skin with stitches buried in deeper tissues and then taping the skin edges together, a practice that remains in common use. Although based in well-documented science, that subcuticular technique is seldom used by battlefield surgeons because antibiotics have decreased the need for meticulous antisepsis and subdermal suturing is time consuming.

Besides, even buried suture can be a source of infection. It takes approximately 10,000 staphylococcal organisms to cause clinical infection in a clean wound, but that number drops to 100 in the presence of retained suture material.

Modern military surgeons use a wide variety of suture material including cotton, silk, nylon, wire, catgut (both plain and treated with chromic acid), and various artificial polymers. The size of suture varies from #3, which is approximately the size of kitchen twine, to 12–0, which is a fraction of the diameter of a hair and can be seen only with magnification.

See also Amputation; Antisepsis; Egyptian Military Medicine; Indian Military Medicine

Reference
Snyder, C. C. 1976. "On the History of Suture." *Plastic and Reconstructive Surgery* 58 (October): 401–406.

Sydenham, Thomas (1624–1689)

One of the greatest figures in internal medicine, Thomas Sydenham is sometimes referred to as the "English Hippocrates" because of his insistence on careful observation and documentation of his clinical experience.

Sydenham was born in the village of Winford Eagle, the son of an English squire. He entered Oxford University in 1642 but left after two months to join his four brothers in Oliver Cromwell's Puritan army where he served with the rank of captain. Two of Sydenham's brothers and his mother died in the revolution, and he was left among the dead during one battle and was almost killed during another. In the course of the revolution, he became a close personal friend of the future Lord Protector. After the revolution, Sydenham returned to Oxford, receiving his medical degree in 1648 and going on to Montpellier in France for further study in 1659. In spite of his medical training, Sydenham always thought of himself as a soldier first and a physician second.

Sydenham left the army for a private practice in London in 1655, but, when Charles II was restored to the throne, he fell from favor

and was never granted a university chair or named a fellow of the Royal Society.

Sydenham ignored the Galenic theory popular among his colleagues and relied almost entirely on what he could learn at the bedside. He believed each disease was an individual entity and could be categorized in much the same way Carl Linné was categorizing the natural world. He observed epidemics of bubonic plague and smallpox firsthand and became a founder of epidemiology as a specialty. He believed that the course of infectious diseases could be altered by the position of the stars and that contagion arose from "miasms" in the earth. More correctly, he presaged Louis Pasteur in believing that epidemics died out because of evolutionary changes in the organisms that caused them.

Sydenham left excellent clinical descriptions of cholera, malaria, measles, pneumonia, dysentery, and gout (from which he personally suffered). He popularized the use of Peruvian bark (cinchona) and insisted on adequate ventilation of sick rooms. He also popularized the use of liquid opium, which remained one of the most useful drugs in the pharmacopoeia for the next two centuries. He was a close friend of English scientist Robert Boyle and philosopher John Locke.

Sydenham died in Pall Mall in 1689.

See also Morphine; 17th-Century Military Medicine

References
Dewhurst, Kenneth. *Dr. Thomas Sydenham (1624–1689): His Life and Original Writings.* Berkeley: University of California Press, 1966.
Fielding, H. Garrison. 1933. "On Sydenham's View of Causation in the Light of Seventeenth Century Thought." *Bulletin of the New York Academy of Sciences* 9: 53–58.

Syphilis

Syphilis is a venereal disease caused by *Treponema pallidum* and has accompanied armies at least since the 15th century.

Syphilis is transmitted by human sexual contact and begins as a painless genital ulcer that typically arises within a few weeks of exposure and resolves spontaneously. If untreated, syphilis can progress to a secondary stage characterized by skin rash and fever. The organism can again become dormant to reemerge years later in its tertiary form with infection of the meninges, brain, spinal cord, and nerves; with masses in various organs known as gummas; and with damage to the heart and blood vessels—all potentially lethal complications. Syphilis is sensitive to penicillin, which remains the primary means of treatment.

Although prostitutes (*hetaerae*) frequently accompanied Greek armies, "housekeepers" were accepted in Roman camps by Septimus Severus (A.D. 193–211), and camp followers were so common during the Crusades and Middle Ages that they were a burden on chains of supply, there is no ancient or medieval reference to any disease resembling syphilis until writers from the School of Salerno and William of Salicet in the 13th century. It has been hypothesized that syphilis came to Europe in the 12th century as a variant of African yaws, another skin disease caused by treponemes. Although this theoretical etiology remains unproven, Arab physicians in North Africa were using mercury-based ointments to treat a strange new skin disease at that time, and mercury is known to have antisyphilitic properties. The exact history of syphilis is clouded by its confusion with leprosy and scabies, although, of the three, only syphilis is sensitive to mercurials.

For unexplained reasons, the clinical nature of syphilis underwent a fundamental change in the late 15th century. In 1495, physicians described what they thought was a new disease characterized by pain so severe that patients drowned themselves attempting to decrease the burning in their limbs accompanied by a red rash that progressed to foul-smelling, black pustules. The first epidemic of the "new" disease came during the Italian Wars (1494–1559) and spread across Northern Europe as either the *Mal Francese* or the Great Pox. The French understandably attributed the disease either to the Italians or the Spanish. By 1505, the pox had accompanied the Portuguese to India, China, and Japan. The virulence and easy transmissibility suggest that the disease, if not altogether new, was at least a significant bacterial mutation.

Because it coincided temporally with Christopher Columbus's return from the New World, medical authorities after 1539 credited his sailors with having imported the illness. The 1490s had also seen expulsion of Jews and Arabs from Spain and, as a number of both had gone to Naples where syphilis seemed to have arisen, they were also blamed for the epidemic. Both were undoubtedly incorrect.

Regardless of where the disease originated, syphilis remained a major European problem for the next two centuries, especially in areas frequented by migrating armies. It affected all levels of society, and infection in ruling families may have led to the decline of Valois France between 1559 and 1589 and the Ottoman Empire in 1566. In 1575, Ambroise Paré dubbed syphilis *Lues Venera*, or the lovers' plague. In his 1585 *A Brief and Necessarie Treatise*, British naval and military surgeon William Clowes said that fully half of all admissions to London's St. Bartholomew's Hospital were for syphilis.

Syphilis remained a serious problem through the Thirty Years War, aggravated by the large numbers of prostitutes that followed armies from both sides. During the siege of Nuremberg, there were 15,000 camp followers with Albrecht von Wallenstein's army, and it was common for prostitutes and their children to outnumber soldiers on campaign. The disease seems to have moderated by the late 1600s, although French Gen. Lazare Carnot said in 1793 that syphilis killed 10 times more of his men than did enemy fire.

With general acceptance of the bacterial nature of infectious disease in the second half of the 19th century, control of venereal disease among soldiers became largely a matter of policing and controlling prostitutes. The British Contagious Diseases Act of 1866 required that all prostitutes around naval or military stations be periodically examined in a government dispensary and be hospitalized for treatment if found to be infected. This law was singularly effective although it was repealed in 1883 in favor of the self-control advocated by Victorian morality.

Although prophylactics were issued to soldiers during World War I, American officials, like their English predecessors, preferred to emphasize "education" and self-restraint. Syphilis was the seventh most common disease in the American Expeditionary Force, and, between April 1917 and December 1919, the incidence of venereal disease in the U.S. Army was 87 per 1,000 with a total of 259,621 cases treated or hospitalized. Many of these cases were, however, present at the time of enlistment, since 5 percent of all draftees were found to have a venereal disease.

During World War II, the incidence of syphilis among American troops was 16 per 1,000, and venereal disease overall accounted for 1,250,846 admissions during the conflict.

See also Gonorrhea; Medieval Military Medicine; Paré, Ambroise; Salicetti, Guglielmo (William of Salicet); World War I Medicine; World War II Medicine

References
Arrizabalaga, Jon, John Henderson, and Roger French. *The Great Pox: The French Disease in Renaissance Europe.* New Haven, CT: Yale University Press, 1997.
Lada, John, ed. *Medical Statistics in World War II.* Washington, D.C.: Office of the Surgeon General, 1975.
McNeill, William H. *Plagues and Peoples.* Garden City, NY: Anchor Press, 1976.
Sun, Sue. 2004. "Where the Girls Are: The Management of Venereal Disease by United States Military Forces in Vietnam." *Literature and Medicine* 23 (1): 66–87.

T

Tagliacozzi, Gaspare
(1546–1599)

The father of modern reconstructive surgery, Gaspare Tagliacozzi studied under Girolamo Cardano at Bologna and went on to become professor of anatomy and surgery at that university. He lived in a time of almost constant violence on the Italian peninsula and turned his attention to treating facial wounds largely because they were so common. Among the more common battlefield injuries were loss of pieces of a nose or an ear that had been either sliced or bitten off in the heat of battle.

Reconstructing facial wounds with skin flaps rotated from the forehead had been practiced for centuries by the hereditary caste of Indian potters and had been learned by the itinerant Sicilian Brancas clan, who kept details of the technique a family secret. When Tagliacozzi brought the practice to Bologna, he was widely reviled by his contemporaries—especially Ambroise Paré—and was satirized by English author Samuel Butler in his poem "Hudibras." Repair of facial injuries was barred entirely

Gaspare Tagliacozzi's innovative technique for transplanting skin from an arm to a nose, illustrated in De Curtorum Chirurgia per Instionem. *(National Library of Medicine)*

from academic surgical programs in Paris as late as 1788 and remained in disrepute until revived by Johann Diefenbach in the 19th century.

Tagliacozzi's two-volume *De Curtorum Chirurgia per Instionem* (1597) described plastic repair of the nose, lip, and ear in detail with beautiful drawings, including a precise depiction of the brace necessary for immobilizing a patient while skin was transferred from the arm to the nose.

Catholic priests criticized Tagliacozzi's efforts as interference with the will of God, and, even though he had been widely honored in life, they had his body exhumed after his death in 1599 and buried in unconsecrated ground.

See also Paré, Ambroise; Rehabilitation and Reconstructive Surgery; 16th-Century Military Medicine

References
Gaudi, M. T., and J. T. Webster. *The Life and Times of Gaspare Tagliacozzi, Surgeon of Bologna, 1545–1599. With a Documented Study of the Scientific and Cultural Life of Bologna in the Sixteenth Century.* New York: Herbert Reichner, 1950.
Monasterio, Fernando. *Pain and Beauty: Gaspare Tagliacozzi, Surgeon of the Renaissance.* Mexico City: Landucci Editores, 2000.

Tetanus

Tetanus is a frequently fatal disease caused by contamination of a wound with the bacterium *Clostridium tetani*.

The organism is pervasive in soil worldwide, but, because it is resident in animal intestine, it is most common in soil that has been fertilized with manure. Clostridium produces a toxin that migrates through nerve cells to the motor neurons in the spinal cord or brain stem, where it causes spasms and paralysis both of skeletal muscles and of the muscles responsible for swallowing and facial movement. The result is the rigors and *risus sardonicus*, or fixed smile, characteristic of the disease. Although intensive care and artificial ventilation have decreased mortality from clinical tetanus, it remains highly lethal.

Because battles are often fought on cultivated land, tetanus has been of concern to military physicians through all of recorded history. In his *Aphorisms*, Hippocrates notes that spasms occurring after a wound are a sign of impending death, and that prognosis did not materially change until late in the 19th century. Mortality from tetanus in the American Civil War was 89.3 percent and was 90 percent in the Franco-Prussian War.

The situation finally changed after 1884, when the organism causing the disease was first identified. In 1889, *Clostridium tetani* was grown in the laboratory, and clinical tetanus was produced in laboratory animals infected with the organism. Japanese bacteriologist Shibasaburo Kitasato, working in Robert Koch's Berlin laboratory, demonstrated that the clinical signs of tetanus were the result of a toxin produced by the bacterium. He and Emil von Behring produced an antitoxin that, although it could not treat the disease once it started, could prevent its development if given soon after a wound occurred.

Tetanus antitoxin was in short supply in the first months of World War I, and the fields of northern France were particularly contaminated with Clostridia. Consequently, the incidence of tetanus among wounded British soldiers in 1914 was 32 percent, with a mortality approaching 50 percent. The Royal Army Medical Corps saw to a rapid increase in production and administration of the antitoxin as soon as possible after wounding—usually at the frontline dressing station—with a subsequent decrease in tetanus incidence to less than 0.1 percent of those injured by 1917. Of the American forces deployed to the Western Front between April 1917 and the end of 1919, there were only 21 cases and four deaths. The initial dose of antitoxin was followed by three more doses at seven-day intervals. The antitoxin was also given prophylactically prior to all surgery. Interestingly, Royal Army instructions recommended not sterilizing the syringes between uses as the serum was (incorrectly) assumed to have antibacterial properties.

Although the antitoxin was generally effective if given early, it did nothing to prevent future infection and did not treat the disease once it occurred. In 1927, Gaston Ramon and Christian Zoeller, working at Paris's Pasteur Institute, found that tetanus toxin could be treated with formaldehyde or alum. The treated poison was no longer toxic but did cause an immune response that lasted for several years after the injection. By 1938, tetanus toxoid immunization was standard in the British Army, and the American and French armies followed shortly thereafter. There were only 11 known cases of tetanus in the U.S. Army in World War II, all in men who had refused immunization. Although the responsible organism remains pervasive and clinical tetanus still has a mortality rate in excess of 20 percent, the toxoid and antitoxin have rendered the disease inconsequential for modern armies.

See also Civil War in the United States; Franco-Prussian War; World War I Medicine

References

Dowling, Harry F. *Fighting Infection: Conquests of the Twentieth Century.* Cambridge, MA: Harvard University Press, 1977.

Keen, W. W. *The Treatment of War Wounds.* Philadelphia: W. B. Saunders Co., 1918.

Parish, J. H. *A History of Immunization.* Edinburgh: E & S Livingstone, 1965.

Theodoric, Bishop of Cervia (Teodorico Borgognoni) (ca. 1205–1296)

Theodoric was a medieval Italian surgeon who anticipated Henri de Mondeville, Paracelsus, and Lord Joseph Lister in suggesting that cleanliness was of major importance in wound healing.

Theodoric was either the son or the disciple of Hugh of Lucca (Ugo Borgognoni), who had trained at the School of Salerno and founded the medical school at Bologna. Theodoric joined the Dominican Order and served, successively, as bishop of Bitonto and Cervia, although he also continued to practice and teach surgery. A compendium of Theodoric's work, the *Cyrurgia*, published in 1498 and 1499, was reviled by Guy de Chauliac for recommending primary closure (which had also been taught by Hugh) and rejecting the doctrine of laudable pus. Theodoric wrote, "For it is not necessary, as Roger and Roland [two famous surgeons of the Salerno School] have written, as many of their disciples teach, and as all modern surgeons profess, that pus should be generated in wounds. No error can be greater than this. Such practice is indeed to hinder nature, to prolong the disease and to prevent the conglutination and consolidation of the wound."

Theodoric was loath to use the cautery, preferring hemostasis with a mercurial styptic salve. He dressed his wounds with wine and emphasized the importance of realigning broken spines. He operated with the "surgical sponge" soaked in a mixture of opium, hyoscyamus, lettuce seed, hemlock, mandragora, ivy, and mulberry juice that could either be inhaled or swallowed and was thought to be reversible with fennel juice. The concoction's efficacy was not known only to physicians. Thomas Marlowe's Jew of Malta said, "I drank of poppy and cold mandrake juice, and being asleep, belike they thought me dead." Shakespeare's Othello said, "Not poppy, nor mandragora, nor all the drowsy syrups of the world shall ever medicine thee to that sweet sleep which thou ow'dst yesterday."

Theodoric was unique in that he actively practiced surgery even while serving as a bishop of the Catholic Church. He amassed a considerable fortune from his medical practice which he left to charity on his death.

See also Anesthesiology; Antisepsis; Chauliac, Guy de; Lister, Lord Joseph; Paracelsus (Aureolus Theophrastus Bombastus von Hohenheim)

References

Campbell, E. C., and J. B. Colton. 1954. "Theodoric: Master Surgeon of the Thirteenth Century." *New York State Medical Journal* 54: 191–194.
Deshaies, Eric, Arryl DiRisio, and A. John Popp. 2004. "Medieval Management of Spinal Injuries: Parallels between Theodoric of Bologna and Contemporary Spine Surgeons." *Neurosurgical Focus* 16 (January): 1–3.
Edwards, H. 1976. "Theodoric of Cervia: A Medieval Antiseptic Surgeon." *Proceedings of the Royal Society of Medicine* 69: 553–555.

Tilton, James
(1745–1822)

A surgeon general of the U.S. Army and one of the first graduates of the Philadelphia School of Medicine, James Tilton was

James Tilton was a military surgeon during the American Revolutionary War and the War of 1812. He later served as surgeon general of the U.S. Army. (Library of Congress)

born in the town of Kent, which was at the time part of Pennsylvania Colony and is now in Delaware. He joined the Continental Army as surgeon to the Delaware regiment in 1776 and was promoted to hospital surgeon in 1778. Tilton was present at the Yorktown surrender, after which he stayed behind to care for the sick and wounded. After the Revolutionary War, he served as state legislator and representative to Congress from Delaware while continuing to practice medicine.

He published his experience as a military surgeon in the *Economical Observations on Military Hospitals, and the Prevention and Cure of Diseases Incident to an Army*, which led to his appointment as physician and surgeon general of the Army in 1812, an office that had been created specifically for him. During the War of 1812, Tilton dedicated his efforts to reforming administration of the Army's medical system and improving military sanitation. Among his recommendations was the curious suggestion that the sick be kept in wood huts without chimneys so fireplace smoke would accumulate and presumably disinfect the surroundings. He also recommended that beds be placed around the hut's circumference with the patients' feet directed toward a fire at the center of the room.

Tilton was an abstemious 6'6" bachelor who never drank coffee and took pride in the fact that his house contained not a single cup. He remained in the Army until cancer cost him a leg and forced his retirement. He died on his Delaware farm at the age of 76 in 1822.

See also American Revolutionary War

References

Gillet, Mary. *The Army Medical Department, 1775–1818*. Washington, D.C.: Center of Military History, 1981.

Kelly, Howard, and Walter Burrage. *Dictionary of American Medical Biography: Lives of Eminent Physicians of the United States and Canada, from the Earliest Times*. Boston: Milford House, 1971.

Packard, Francis. *History of Medicine in the United States*. New York: Paul B. Hoeber, 1932.

Torture

The International Convention against Torture or Other Cruel, Inhuman, or Degrading Treatment or Punishment (ratified by the United States in 1994) defines torture as "any act directed against an individual in the offender's custody or physical control by which severe pain or suffering . . . whether physical or mental, is intentionally inflicted on that individual."

Three professions are necessarily involved in the military use of torture: military officers, lawyers, and physicians. Military physicians are in a complicated position with regard to torture because they are governed by medical ethics, by the Uniform Code of Military Justice (if members of the U.S. military), by the chain of command, and by the Geneva Conventions. Physicians are of use in torture in four ways: (1) they may be asked to keep a subject alive and conscious; (2) they may be asked to reduce subsequent scarring or disability; (3) they may be asked to alter medical records or death certificates to hide torture; (4) they may be asked for advice in extracting information from a subject using either environmental or pharmacologic manipulations.

The word "torture" derives from the Latin verb for "twist" and was initially used in the 16th century in reference to procedures used by either the state or the Church to extract information and confessions. Its first documented use as a verb in English was in William Shakespeare's *Henry VI*, but it was probably in common use before that. Physicians were an integral part of state-sponsored torture in the 16th and 17th centuries and were regularly required to certify that subjects were physically able to withstand the ordeal. Torture was legally abolished in the 18th century beginning with the Habsburg empire's 1769 *Nemesis Theresiana*, which placed limits on judicial torture. By the end of the century, the practice was banned across Europe. One paradoxical aspect of that abolition was Dr. Joseph-Ignace Guillotin's 1789 invention of the decapitation instrument that bears his name and that was specifically devised to allow execution without physical suffering. In practice, the guillotine was most often used on the rich, while the poor were relegated to more traditional and less humane deaths.

Medical torture reemerged in the 20th century, most notoriously in Nazi Germany. A major focus of the postwar Nuremberg trials was the role of physicians in designing and conducting procedures that inflicted pain, physical damage, or death on the subjects. Defense attorneys at the trial argued that torture was justified in pursuit of medical research necessary to the German national well-being. American prosecutor Gen. Telford Taylor categorically rejected that argument: "To kill, to maim, and to torture is criminal under all modern systems of law . . . yet these defendants, all of whom were fully able to comprehend the nature of their acts . . . are responsible for wholesale murder and unspeakably cruel tortures" (Annas 2005). After the Nuremberg trials, both the Geneva Conventions and the World Medical Association have taken the unequivocal position that torture is a crime against humanity and is not justified for any reason. In spite of that, Amnesty International estimates that 150 countries currently practice state-sponsored torture.

After the American invasions of Afghanistan and Iraq, the question of state-sponsored torture has excited considerable discussion. The International Red Cross has accused American medical personnel of monitoring and designing interrogations at the Guantánamo Bay prison in Cuba and of falsifying medical records and death certificates to conceal torture at the facility. The U.S. government argued that the Geneva Conventions do not apply to Guantánamo detainees, and former secretary of defense Donald Rumsfeld authorized interrogation techniques stringent enough to require medical clearance for their application. The U.S. Department of Justice has argued that the president has the authority to order interrogation techniques that could be considered torture in the national interest. Justice Department attorney Jay S. Bybee sent a memo to President George W. Bush's then legal adviser, Alberto Gonzales, saying torture "may be justified" and limiting the definition of torture to only those acts that cause pain equal to that which would cause serious injury, organ failure, or death. The memo was withdrawn after being made public in June 2004.

See also Geneva Conventions; Nuremberg Code

References
Annas, George. 2005. "Unspeakably Cruel: Torture, Medical Ethics, and the Law." *New England Journal of Medicine* 352 (May 19): 2127–2132.
Bernadac, Christian. *Les Médecins Maudit: Les Expériences Médicales Humaines dans les Camps de Concentration.* Geneva: Éditions Farnot, 1984.
Bybee, Jay S., "Memorandum for Alberto R. Gonzales, Counsel to the President, re Standards of Conduct for Interrogation under 18 U.S.C. §§ 2340-2340A. http://www.washingtonpost.com/wp-srv/nation/documents/dojinterrogation memo20020801.pdf (accessed October 25, 2007).
Klawans, Harold L. "Torture in Vienna." In *The Medicine of History from Paracelsus to Freud.* New York: Raven Press, 1982.
Miles, Steven H. *Oath Betrayed: Torture, Medical Complicity, and the War on Terror.* New York: Random House, 2006.
Okie, Susan. 2005. "Glimpse of Guantánamo: Medical Ethics and the War on Terror." *New England Journal of Medicine* 353 (December 15): 2529–2537.

Tourniquet

A tourniquet is a device used to create pressure on an artery and thereby stop blood flow and hemorrhage distal to its application. It derives its name from the French *tourner*, meaning "to turn."

Roman surgeons, not yet having discovered tourniquets, were forced to rely on chemical styptics to enhance blood clotting and retard hemorrhage. Arabic physicians of the Middle Ages resorted first to boiling oil and then to red-hot iron cauteries to accomplish the same end, but neither was adequate to control bleeding from larger arterial vessels. Because amputation was thought necessary for any open fracture and for any fracture caused by a gunshot wound, control of large-vessel hemorrhage was of vital importance to the military surgeon, but, prior to the 17th century, the operation could not be performed safely except in the distal parts of limbs where the arteries were of relatively small caliber.

In the 14th century, Guy de Chauliac described wrapping a tight band above and below the site of amputation to decrease both pain and bleeding. Two centuries later, Fabrizio d'Aquapendente improved the tourniquet by adding a stick that could twist the band tighter, and Leonardo Botallo resorted to three separate tourniquets for amputation, with the incision coming between the distal two. In the 1600s, Johannes Scultetus devised a screw device that left at least one of the operator's hands free while compressing a limb. A surgeon named Morell used a field garrote to stop bleeding in a soldier during the 1674 siege of Besançon, and a naval surgeon from Plymouth named Young used a similar device to perform a high amputation four years later.

Early tourniquets were made of a wooden compressing block and leather bands, later replaced by brass and linen, respectively. In 1718, Jean Louis Petit described a screw tourniquet that was fixed by straps to the pa-

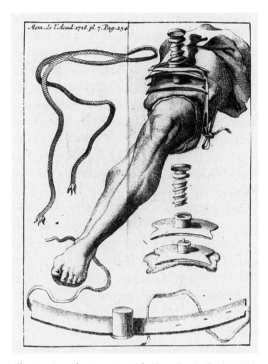

Illustration of a tourniquet by Jean Louis Petit, 1718. (National Library of Medicine)

tient's abdomen so both the surgeon's hands were free and enough steady pressure could be applied to stop bleeding even from the largest arteries in an extremity. This device remained in common use until the mid-1800s when, during the Crimean War, British surgeons reverted to the strap and buckle for its simplicity and ease of application.

Lord Joseph Lister devoted much of his early career in the fruitless search for an effective abdominal tourniquet that could stop flow in the aorta. He invented a series of variations on the idea of a half-circle of steel with a compressing pad driven by a screw on the front and a plate in the lower back, but none of his inventions was effective enough to warrant general acceptance. He did, however, make the useful suggestion that a limb about to be incised be elevated for four minutes before applying a standard tourniquet in order to empty it of venous blood. This technique was improved by German military surgeon Johannes Friedrich August von Esmarch in 1873 with his flat rubber bandage that could be sequentially wrapped from the fingers or toes to the level of the incision to squeeze out venous blood. The tourniquet could then be applied above the bandage, leaving the operative field almost entirely bloodless.

In 1904, American surgeon Harvey Cushing adapted the Riva-Rocci blood pressure measuring device into a pneumatic tourniquet that he inflated with a bicycle pump. Cushing even tourniquets around the head to control scalp bleeding in cranial operations. Esmarch's bandage and the pneumatic tourniquet remain in routine use.

Although Ambroise Paré's technique of directly ligating disrupted vessels proved the most effective way to control bleeding until techniques of actual vascular repair were developed in the 20th century, countless lives were no doubt saved by tourniquets used to temporarily stop hemorrhage until it could be definitively managed. This was especially true in military situations where a surgeon might be faced with a line of bleeding men awaiting his attention.

See also Chauliac, Guy de; Fabrizio
    d'Aquapendente, Geronimo; Hemostasis;
    Lister, Lord Joseph; Paré, Ambroise; Sculte-
    tus, Johannes (also Johannes Schultes)

References
Bennion, Elisabeth. *Antique Medical Instruments.*
    Berkeley, CA: Southeby Parke Bernet
    Publications, 1979.
Kleinerman, L. 1962. "The Tourniquet in
    Surgery." *Journal of Bone and Joint Surgery.*
    44B: 937–943.
Thompson, C. J. S. *The History and Evolution of
    Surgical Instruments.* New York: Schuman's,
    1942.

Tracheotomy

Tracheotomy is an operation in which one creates an external opening in the trachea to bypass obstruction of the upper airway or to provide a means of artificial respiratory support.

Galen, who mistakenly believed the trachea to be an artery, said tracheotomy had been done by the Greek physician Asclepiades, who lived from 124 to 40 B.C. Aretaeius of Cappodocia also mentioned tracheotomy but opposed its use, arguing that it made coughs worse and that the wound would not heal. Geronimo Fabrizio d'Aquapendente was the first to actually use the term "tracheotomy" but thought the operation should only be done as a last resort. In 1620, Nicolas Habicot performed a tracheotomy to remove blood from the airway of a man who had suffered multiple stab wounds to the neck and left behind a metal cannula to keep the wound open. The procedure, although effective, was not widely adopted, and, over the next 200 years, only 23 more such operations were documented.

When George Washington was dying of upper airway obstruction as a result of a throat and upper airway infection, Elisha Dick, the youngest of his three attending physicians, recommended tracheotomy but was overruled by his senior colleagues. The procedure became commonplace after Pierre Bretonneau demonstrated its lifesaving effectiveness in diphtheritic pharyngitis. In 1887, the new German emperor Frederick, British queen Victoria's son-in-law, was found to have laryngeal cancer. Tracheotomy and surgical removal of the growth were recommended by German surgeon Ernst von Bergmann. Queen Victoria sent British surgeon Sir Morell MacKenzie to Germany to offer a second opinion. MacKenzie, supported by renowned pathologist Rudolf Virchow, convinced Frederick to forgo the operation. In February 1888, Frederick, who had been king for only three months, worsened, requiring an emergency tracheotomy. The operation was done by von Bergmann but was complicated by intra-operative hemorrhage and postoperative infection from which the emperor never recovered. He died four months later.

See also Bergmann, Ernst von; Prussian and German Military Medicine

References

Goodall, E. W. 1934. "The Story of Tracheotomy." *British Journal of Children's Diseases* 31: 167–176, 253–272.

Stevenson, R. Scott, and Douglas Guthrie. *A History of Otolaryngology*. Edinburgh: E. and S. Livingstone, 1949.

Transfusion

Transfusion is the administration of blood or blood products obtained from one person into another.

The earliest historical reference to transfusion was in 1492, when three young clerics volunteered to have blood removed and given to Pope Innocent VIII, who was comatose from a recent stroke. It is likely that the pope actually drank the blood rather than receiving it intravenously, and neither he nor his donors survived the experiment.

William Harvey's demonstration in 1628 that blood circulated from the heart to the arteries and then back through the veins was the crucial piece of information that made transfusion in the modern sense possible. In 1665, English surgeon John Wilkins and, shortly thereafter, Richard Lower of Oxford successfully transfused blood collected from one dog into the vein of another. The success

of that experiment led Lower to attempt administration of dog blood into a human, and, in 1667, French surgeon Jean Baptiste Dénis described transfusion of sheep blood into humans. The practice was tried by a number of other Parisian practitioners, but the complication rate was so high that the city's Society of Physicians outlawed the practice 11 years later, effectively stopping experiments in animal to human transfusion.

In 1795, Philadelphia physician Philip Syng Physick successfully transfused blood from one person to another, but he did not publish the results of his experiment, and the practice did not become general. The next documented transfusion was in 1818, when English obstetrician James Blundell saved an exsanguinating patient by giving her blood collected from her husband. Twenty-two years later, he and an assistant, Samuel Armstrong Lane, repeated the experiment on a patient bleeding to death from hemophilia.

Difficulties with clotting and deterioration of collected blood as well as lack of knowledge of blood typing continued to make transfusion impractical throughout the 19th century. Milk (obtained from cows, goats, and humans) was tried as a substitute for blood but had a high rate of unacceptable complications, and that practice was replaced with the first saline transfusion in 1884.

The modern era of transfusion began in 1901 when Karl Landsteiner discovered the three major blood groups—A, B, and O—for which he was awarded the 1930 Nobel Prize for Physiology or Medicine. In 1907, Reuben Ottenberg successfully typed and cross-matched blood between donor and recipient and recognized that people with type O blood were universal donors, able to give blood to those with all other types. In

1908, Alexis Carrel successfully transfused blood directly from the artery of a donor to the recipient's vein, thus avoiding the problem of clotting.

The clotting problem was partially solved in 1915 when Dr. Richard Lewisohn of New York's Mount Sinai Hospital discovered that addition of sodium citrate to whole blood kept it from clotting. The following year, Francis Rous and J. R. Turner developed a citrate-glucose combination that allowed blood to be stored for several days. American Army officer Oswald Robertson, recognizing the importance of that discovery for the British war effort, organized "blood depots" to supply military hospitals.

Interest in transfusion continued after the war, and, in 1926, the British Red Cross started the world's first formal transfusion service. The first blood bank opened in Leningrad in 1932, and the first hospital blood bank was organized by Bernard Fontus at Chicago's Cook County Hospital five years later.

In 1939, Landsteiner, Alex Weiner, Philip Levine, and R. E. Stetson discovered the Rh blood groups (named for the Rhesus monkey) and removed what had been the major cause of transfusion reactions after Landsteiner's original discovery. Edwin Cohn's demonstration that blood plasma could be broken into albumin, gamma globulin, and fibrinogen using cold ethanol fractionation gave military surgeons a new way to resuscitate the severely injured.

University of Pennsylvania surgeon Isidor Ravdin successfully resuscitated severely wounded soldiers and sailors after the Pearl Harbor attack in 1941, using albumin rather than whole blood. In response to the need for whole blood during World War II, J. F. Loutit and Patrick Mollison developed acid citrate dextrose solution, which anticoagulated blood without sig-

nificantly adding to its volume and which significantly extended its shelf life. The replacement of glass bottles with plastic bags for storage in 1950 and the discovery of CDPDA-1 anticoagulant, which allows refrigerated blood to be safely stored for 35 days, bring the technology to date.

See also Carrel, Alexis; Shock; World War I Medicine; World War II Medicine

References
Schmidt, P. J. 1968. "Transfusion in America in the Eighteenth and Nineteenth centuries." *New England Journal of Medicine* 279: 1319–1320.
Starr, Douglas. *An Epic History of Medicine and Commerce.* New York: Alfred A. Knopf, 1998.

Trench Fever (Volhynian Fever)

Trench fever, also known as Volhynian fever, is a disease caused by *Rochalimaia quintana* (named for its discoverer, H. da Rocha Lima, and the disease's typical five-day course).

Rochalimaia is a rickettsial organism related to that which causes typhus and Rocky Mountain spotted fever. Humans are the only reservoir for the disease, which is transmitted when the louse bites a carrier and defecates on the skin of another host. When the new host scratches and breaks skin contaminated by the feces, the microorganism enters the bloodstream.

Trench fever is typically manifested as a rash, fever, and bone and joint pain. The bone pain lasts for several weeks after the illness has subsided and is often incapacitating. True typhus, although common and lethal on the Eastern Front during World War I, was virtually nonexistent in France during the war. Trench fever, on the other hand, accounted for one-fifth of the illness in the German and Austrian armies and as much as one-third of that in the British army between 1915 and 1918.

By 1916 experiments on human volunteers had confirmed the role of the body louse in transmission of trench fever, and delousing became a priority. Men were rotated to rear areas as often as possible, where they were bathed, shaved, and chemically deloused. Clothing was also rotated, with uniforms traded for those left by the preceding group, which had been steam cleaned for reuse.

After World War I, trench fever largely disappeared until the 1990s, when it re-emerged among homeless alcoholics in France and the United States; in impoverished populations in Russia, Mexico, and Poland; and in patients with AIDS.

See also Typhus; World War I Medicine

References
Biddle, Wayne. *A Field Guide to Germs*. New York: Anchor Books, 1995.
Schaechter, Moselio, Gerald Medhoff, and Barry I. Wisenstein. *Mechanisms of Microbial Disease*. Baltimore: Williams & Wilkins Co., 1993.

Trench Foot

Trench foot is an incapacitating deterioration in the skin of the foot that was particularly common in the trenches of the Western Front during World War I.

Trench foot became a serious problem on the Western Front as soon as the battle lines became fixed and the weather turned cold. Men in the trenches stood for hours in cramped spaces, often up to their ankles in nearly freezing mud. Their tightly wrapped puttees further hampered blood circulation, and the men went for weeks without removing wet, filthy socks and shoes. When they did leave the trenches and took off their socks, soldiers often found white, swollen,

insensate feet and, in the worst cases, rotting toes were left behind in their shoes.

By the winter of 1916, up to one-fifth of some units were incapacitated by trench foot. Senior officers initially viewed the problem as self-inflicted, and it became the responsibility of every junior officer to ensure that his men carried dry socks at all times and removed their shoes and socks and rubbed their feet with whale oil daily. When the English recognized that Belgian soldiers—who did not wear tight leg wraps—rarely got trench foot, they abandoned puttees. Still, the problem was severe enough that many men, when they were rotated to the rear, found it impossible to walk and had to be carried out on their comrades' backs. Nurses in rear-area hospitals massaged the dead feet with warm oil, and military surgeons removed necrotic toes as necessary while waiting for the extremities to turn from white to pink. By 1917, military surgeons recognized that trench foot carried an exceptional risk of associated tetanus, and sufferers were routinely vaccinated.

See also World War I Medicine

References
Fauntleroy, A. M. *Report on the Medico-Military Aspects of the European War*. Washington, D.C.: Government Printing Office, 1915.
Keen, W. W. *The Treatment of War Wounds*. Philadelphia: W. B. Saunders Co., 1918.
MacDonald, Lyn. *1914–1918: Voices and Images of the Great War*. London: Michael Joseph, Ltd., 1988.

Trephine, Trepan, and Trephining

These terms refer to instruments used to penetrate the skull and procedures used to enter the cranium surgically.

Trephining is one of the few surgical procedures that can be unequivocally traced to prehistory. There is ample evidence in skeletal remains, and it is still practiced by pretechnological societies. It is, of course, not possible to know the precise motivation for trephining in prehistorical societies, but recent studies of surviving Stone Age–like societies in Africa and Oceania suggest that it was a magical or religious ritual intended to rid the body of evil spirits.

The Egyptians were adept at opening the skull to treat trauma, but, recognizing the high likelihood of death when the underlying brain was injured, they recommended that the surgeon decline to treat a patient with spinal fluid draining from the wound. When the Spanish came to South America, they found trephining common among the Incas, where as many as one in 20 recovered skulls show evidence of having been surgically opened.

Because the greatest risk in opening the skull was inadvertent damage to the brain, tools for the operation have historically been designed to prevent uncontrolled plunging as the bone is penetrated. Prehistoric flint and copper instruments were typically blades with a thickened area behind the edge that were used to cut four sets of straight lines that could be joined to extract a square of bone. The Greeks developed a cone-shaped drill bit mounted on a shaft that could be rotated between the palms or by a bow with the string looped around the shaft. This instrument, variously called the *tenebra serrata* or *prion charatos*, was the model from which all subsequent cranial drills and saws derived and was frequently referred to by classic Greek and Roman physicians, from Hippocrates to Aulus Cornelius Celsus and Galen of Pergamum. Celsus described opening the skull with what he call a *modiolus*, a circular saw from the center of which extended a pin that went into

the bone before the saw and served to hold the drill steady. The pin was withdrawn after the saw had safely cut grooves in the bony outer table. The Roman writer also recognized that, given time, bone that had been removed tended to re-form. Instruments identical to the *modiolus* remained in use well into the 14th century.

In the 16th century, Andrea della Croce suggested replacing the flat handle or bow for rotating the trephine's shaft with a triangular bit held by a carpenter's brace. Dutch surgeon Matthia Narvatio's attempt to improve on the brace and bit with a gear-driven device was generally thought too complicated and was not widely adopted until several centuries later. Ambroise Paré used a triangular bit and a circular saw held by a brace, both of which he recommended be "anointed with oyle, that they may runne more glib and glad, and cut more sweetely" (Crooke 1634). The French battlefield surgeon recommended performing the surgery next to a fire of hot coals, lest the brain be exposed to cold air, and also suggested plugging the patient's ears with lint so he would not hear the drill's grinding and become unduly frightened. Paré and his contemporaries recognized the dangers of opening the skull over one of the large draining veins that lie within the dural layers and knew that opening over the frontal sinus could result in a spinal fluid leak. (English surgeon Helkiah Crooke described one patient with a nonhealing hole in the frontal sinus who could hold his nose and blow out a candle through his forehead.)

Exploratory opening of the skull to remove bone fragments or to search for blood clots remained common practice through the 19th and much of the 20th century. During the American Civil War, Union doctors reported trephining 196 patients for gunshot wounds. Forty-six of these operations were done as primary procedures in field hospitals. Of the 196, 110 died. The availability of X-ray in World War I lessened the incidence of trephine for exploration but did not eliminate it. Exploratory trephine has essentially vanished with availability of computed tomography (CT) scanning and magnetic resonance imaging (MRI), but the trephination is still used as part of removing bone fragments and foreign bodies and to drain intracranial blood clots. Modern drills and saws are powered by either batteries or high-pressure air, but most neurosurgical operative sets still contain triangular bits, circular saws, and braces that would be entirely familiar to a 16th-century French military surgeon to be used in case the high-speed instruments fail.

See also Celsus, Aulus Cornelius; Civil War in the United States; Classical Greek Military Medicine; Cushing, Harvey Williams; Fabrizio d'Aquapendente, Geronimio; Head Injury and Cranial Surgery; Paré Ambroise; Prehistoric Military Medicine

References

Bennion, Elisabeth. *Antique Medical Instruments.* Berkeley: University of California Press, 1979.

Crooke, Helkiah. *An Explanation of the Fashion and Use of Three and Fifty Instruments of Chirurgery Gathered out of Ambrosius Pareus, the Famous French Chirurgien, and Done into English, for the behoose of Young Practitioners in Chirurgery.* London: Michael Sparke, 1634; reprinted in facsimile, Edinburgh: West Port Books, 1982.

Kirkup, J. R. 1981. "The History and Evolution of Surgical Instruments." *Annals of the Royal College of Surgeons of England* 63: 279–285.

Thompson, C. J. S. *The History and Evolution of Surgical Instruments.* New York: Schuman's, 1942.

Wangensteen, Owen, and Sarah D. Wangensteen. *The Rise of Surgery from Empiric Craft to Scientific Discipline.* Minneapolis: University of Minnesota Press, 1978.

Triage

Triage is the process of sorting patients according to urgency or importance of treatment.

The practice probably originated—at least as a formalized procedure—with Baron Dominique-Jean Larrey, surgeon to Napoleon Bonaparte's army, whose *ambulances volantes* ("flying hospitals" modeled after the French military's highly mobile artillery) brought medical care to the front lines where it was necessary to choose who would be treated first. Larrey allocated 40 physicians and 250 support personnel, including nurses, surgical assistants, and stretcher bearers, to each mobile unit. In the large-scale battles occasioned by the French *levée en masse*, those medical resources were often overwhelmed. Larrey said, "Those who are dangerously wounded must be tended first, entirely without regard to rank or distinction. Those less severely injured must wait until the gravely wounded have been operated on and dressed" (Larrey 1832, 27). The practice, which combined an egalitarian revolutionary philosophy with preservation of much-needed manpower, became standard in the imperial armies.

At the inception of the American Civil War, neither the Union nor the Confederate armies were prepared to deal with the volume of casualties occasioned by the juxtaposition of powerful defensive weapons and overly aggressive offensive tactics. The week it took to clear casualties from the field after the first Battle of Bull Run was the proximate cause of Jonathan Letterman's reform of the Union Army medical corps. Rapidly removing the wounded and delivering them to aid stations and hospitals made triage essential. At the 1863 Battle of Antietam, all the Union casualties were off the field in less than 24 hours, but the medical corps was drowned in the resulting flood of wounded soldiers. Walt Whitman, who witnessed the scene, said, "The men, whatever their condition, lie there, and patiently wait till their turn comes to be taken up" (Whitman 1910, 28). The wounded were sorted, but the sorting was more often based on who arrived first than on who most needed care.

The greater number of casualties, the stationary front, and better transport in World War I led to a fundamental change in allocation of medical resources. The word "triage"—from the French *trier*, or "to sort," and originally applied to picking out defective coffee beans—first achieved currency in that conflict. Military medical services on both sides of the war used staged evacuation systems beginning with forward dressing stations, or *postes de secours*, from which the wounded were taken to casualty clearing stations, where minor surgery could be done or the patient could be stabilized before being sent on to evacuation hospitals and then, if necessary, to rear-area base hospitals for complicated procedures or prolonged recovery.

There were two general triage systems. The first, initially employed by the British Royal Army Medical Corps, sorted men into those too severely wounded to be transported, those wounded but requiring transport, and those capable of walking. A later system divided men into those to be evacuated immediately, those needing minor surgery or wound dressing that could be done at the dressing or casualty clearing station, those needing major surgery, and those needing immediate resuscitation. Much of

this system was based on the availability of transport, but preservation of manpower was also a primary consideration. To that end, as much care as possible was provided close to the front, and men were not evacuated to a rear area unless transport was absolutely necessary. Physicians on both sides realized that, once a man was away from the front, his chances of returning to combat were markedly reduced.

World War II's moving fronts and the availability of fixed-wing air transport again changed the nature of triage. Early resuscitation with blood and plasma made survival from more severe injuries possible and transport to facilities capable of performing transfusions more important. The scarcity of some effective new treatments also posed ethical triage dilemmas. The U.S. Army in North Africa decided to use hard-to-come-by penicillin for soldiers with venereal disease rather than for those with severe wounds under the theory that the former were more likely to return to combat than the latter. The Royal Air Force made a similar decision with regard to its bomber pilots.

Air evacuation by rotor craft in Korea and Viet Nam combined with better resuscitative and surgical techniques returned the emphasis in triage to treating the more severely injured and to attempting to salvage injured soldiers who would not have survived in earlier wars. Continued advances have led to a practice of emergency stabilization followed by long-distance air transport of patients still under anesthesia to base hospitals or even rear-area facilities thousands of miles away for completion of their operations.

Triage, one of military medicine's most significant contributions to civilian trauma care, is now a standard practice in emergency rooms around the world.

See also Civil War in the United States; Iraq and Afghan Wars; Korean Conflict; Larrey, Baron Dominique-Jean; Viet Nam War; World War I Medicine; World War II Medicine

References
Blagg, C. R. 2004. "Triage: Napoleon to the Present Day." *Journal of Nephrology* 17: 629–632.
Larrey, Dominique-Jean. *The Surgical Memoirs of the Campaign in Russia*. Philadelphia: Cowey and Lea, 1832.
Whitman, Walt. *Complete Prose Works*. New York: Appleton and Company, 1910.

Trotter, Thomas (ca. 1760–1832)

A British naval surgeon and an advocate of improved sanitation and living conditions in the Royal Navy, Thomas Trotter was born in Melrose, Roxburghshire, Scotland, the second son of a local baker. He attended Edinburgh University, where he took classes in anatomy and surgery from Alexander Monro secundus, although his education was frequently interrupted and he did not actually receive his medical degree until 1788. He joined the Royal Navy in 1779 and was assigned to the Channel Fleet. During a 1780 voyage to the West Indies, Trotter's ship was struck by a hurricane and was dismasted. The crippled ship then lost a large part of its crew to scurvy and dysentery as it struggled back to Britain.

Trotter's voyage on a slaving ship early in his career made him one of Britain's most ardent opponents of the practice. While serving as fleet surgeon to Lord Howe, Trotter campaigned to remove the "venereal fee" that British sailors had to pay when diagnosed with the disease, contending that the practice made it less likely that the men would seek treatment. In the belief that drunkenness was a main cause of venereal infection while ashore and of accidents at sea, Trotter led the effort that saw the number of "gin shops" in Portsmouth decrease from 300 to 140. He thought impressments led to bringing the physically unfit into the navy and that flogging was cruel and ineffective, and he promoted a regular program of exercise and entertainment to promote health among the crews.

Trotter published *Medicina Nautica*, a three-volume, 1,400-page encyclopedic treatment of naval medicine between 1797 and 1803. The book played a major, though largely forgotten, role in the Royal Navy's accepting James Lind's proof that citrus juice could prevent scurvy and helped promote Edward Jenner's smallpox vaccine for all British sailors.

Trotter retired from the navy in 1802 and settled in Newcastle-upon-Tyne, where he practiced and continued to publish books and pamphlets on drunkenness and occupational disease and books of poetry. He retired in 1827 and eventually returned to Edinburgh, where he died five years later.

See also Alcoholism; Blane, Sir Gilbert; British Military Medicine; Lind, James; Napoleonic Wars; Naval Medicine; Scurvy; Vaccination and Variolation

Reference
Porter, Ian Alexander. 1963. "Thomas Trotter, M.D., Naval Physician." *Medical History* 7 (April): 154–164.

Tularemia

Tularemia is a systemic disease caused by the gram-negative rod *Francisella tularensis*; the disease is primarily important militarily for its potential as a biological weapon.

Tularemia is endemic in small mammals, especially rabbits but to a lesser extent in squirrels, dogs, and cats, and is common to those animals in the Rocky Mountain states, California, and Oklahoma. It is also endemic in Eastern Europe and Siberia and is transmitted to humans by ticks and biting flies. The disease is unusual in that it can enter the human body through multiple portals other than insect bite, including inhalation and ingestion, and a very small number of bacteria can cause clinical illness.

Tularemia transmitted by insect bite begins with a skin lesion characterized by a raised red edge around an ulcerated center and is accompanied by swelling in nearby lymph nodes. If ingested, the bacteria can cause tonsillar ulceration and, if inhaled, can cause pneumonia. When the organism enters the bloodstream, it causes fever, chills, muscle aches, and headache. Without treatment, tularemia has only about a 5 percent mortality rate, but it can disable its victims for two to four weeks and, in rare cases, for several months.

After World War II, American, British, and Canadian military scientists all initiated active research into weaponizing tularemia. The U.S. program was centered at the Pine Bluff Arsenal in Arkansas after 1956. Tularemia was one of the first organisms tested as a bioweapon by the Soviet Union, and there is some evidence that the Red Army deployed it against the Germans in 1941 but abandoned the experiment after an outbreak in its own forces. After the war, the Soviet research program was moved to the facility at Vozrozhdeniye Island, where a vaccine-resistant strain was tested on primates in 1982.

Tularemia can be treated with antibiotics and is one of the few diseases for which streptomycin remains a first-line agent.

See also Chemical and Biological Warfare; Vozrozhdeniye Island

References
Alibek, Ken, with Stephen Handelman. *Biohazard*. London: Arrow Books, 2000.
Miller, Judith, Stephen Engelberg, and William Broad. *Germs: Biological Weapons and America's Secret War*. New York: Simon & Schuster, 2001.

Typhoid Fever

Typhoid fever is a fecally transmitted bacterial disease responsible for large numbers of deaths among soldiers, particularly in the 19th century.

Typhoid fever is caused by *Salmonella typhi* (originally *Bacillus typhosus*) and results in fever, diarrhea, abdominal pain, and a typical rose-colored skin rash. It can progress to prostration, temperatures as high as 107ºF, and death, and it was the major cause of mortality among American troops in the Spanish-American War.

Although the disease was shown to be distinct from louse-borne typhus in 1836 and was also known to be separate from mosquito-borne malaria, clinicians continued to confuse it with those diseases almost to the turn of the 20th century. Differentiation was important both because methods of control for a disease caused by fecal contamination were different from those for an illness carried by insects and because quinine, which was the staple treatment for malaria, was of no use in typhoid.

By the mid-19th century, typhoid was endemic in the United States, largely because growth of cities had led to the concentration of populations and widespread contamination of water supplies with sewage. This was a particular problem with typhoid

An invalid camp for the 15th Minnesota Regiment from Camp Ramsey. The hospital camp was set up away from the main camp to isolate typhoid sufferers during an epidemic. (Minnesota Historical Society/Corbis)

because the organism occasionally takes up residence in the gallbladder, where it causes no symptoms but is repeatedly shed into the environment. The carrier state was unrecognized through much of the 19th century, leading many practicing physicians to misdiagnose epidemics of febrile disease.

Bringing large groups of urban men together in camps without sanitary facilities or adequate drainage, as was done at the beginning of the Spanish-American War, virtually guaranteed typhoid outbreaks. It is estimated that 60,000 men—approximately the number stationed at Camp Thomas in Georgia in 1898—shed about 9.4 tons of feces a day. It was also estimated that, for every

1,300-man volunteer regiment, there would be three or four asymptomatic typhoid carriers contaminating that fecal matter.

James Widal developed a serologic test for typhoid in which a small amount of serum from a patient who had been infected with the disease would cause clumping of typhoid organisms that could be seen under the microscope. The test was both highly sensitive and highly specific and allowed retrospective study of the camp epidemics by the Typhoid Board after the Spanish-American War. The board incorrectly concluded that typhoid was carried by flies and that contaminated water had little to do with the disease. It also concluded that sanitation in large groups of new troops could never be adequate and that a vaccine was the only solution to military outbreaks of the disease. This opinion was pressed in Britain by Sir Almroth Wright, who convinced Lord Kitchener to require vaccination for all British troops serving outside the country. The British Expeditionary Force was subsequently supplied with 2 million doses of typhoid vaccine and, as a result, suffered only 1,191 deaths from the disease during all of World War I.

See also Spanish-American War; World War I Medicine

References

Cirillo, Vincent. *Bullets and Bacilli: The Spanish-American War and Military Medicine.* New Brunswick, NJ: Rutgers University Press, 1999.

Gillet, Mary. *The Army Medical Department, 1865–1917.* Washington, D.C.: Center of Military History, 1995.

Typhus

Typhus is a systemic disease caused by *Rickettsia prowazekii*, a small, rod-shaped bacterium that can live only inside a host's cells.

Rickettsia prowazekii was named for Howard Ricketts and Stanislas von Prowazek, both typhus investigators and both of whom died from the disease. Typhus is a zoonosis—an infection transmitted from an animal reservoir to a human host by a third organism. That organism is most often an arthropod such as a chigger, tick, flea, mite, or, in the case of typhus, *Pediculus humanis*, the human body louse. The louse feeds on an infected animal and defecates infected material onto the skin of the next host. Humans will scratch the contaminated area, injecting the louse feces beneath the skin and ultimately into the bloodstream.

The disease starts with a fever, typically around 103°F, but occasionally as high as 105°F. A rash usually breaks out by the fourth or fifth day, at first pink then fading to the small brown patches mistakenly called petechiae in older descriptions. The rash typically starts on the back and shoulders and spreads to the extremities, hands, and feet. It can progress to gangrene accompanied by the characteristic foul odor of typhus patients who are literally rotting. Severe headache and delirium mark the final stages of the disease before a crisis results in either recovery or death. The disease typically occurs in debilitated victims who live in closely crowded conditions and who lack facilities to wash either their bodies or the clothes in which lice preferentially reside.

Less severe forms of typhus are also seen. *Rickettsia tsutsugamushi*, endemic in the South Pacific, caused the similar but less severe scrub typhus (tsutsugamushi fever), which infected 18,000 American soldiers in World War II and was a leading cause of hospitalization for febrile illness in Viet Nam. Scrub typhus resides in rodents and is transmitted by chiggers. A second less severe form, caused by *Rochalimaia quintana* and also transmitted by body lice, is trench fever, which infected from 20 to 33 percent of British and German troops in Flanders during World War I.

True typhus is difficult to diagnose prior to reaching full epidemic proportions because the early symptoms are vague, the rash does not always appear, and no reliable laboratory test can detect it in the disease's initial stages. Once diagnosed, the disease can be successfully treated with antibiotics such as doxycycline, tetracycline, and chloramphenicol, although sulfa drugs paradoxically aggravate the illness. There is also an effective vaccine available. Epidemics can be most effectively controlled by delousing with DDT, lindane, or Malathion.

Typhus probably originated in Asia and came to Europe relatively late. There may have been an outbreak in a Sicilian monastery as early as A.D. 1083, but the first well-documented epidemic was in Ferdinand of Aragon and Isabella of Castile's troops in 1489. The Iberian monarchs hired Cypriot mercenaries who had recently fought with the Turks, and the hired soldiers brought typhus with them. During the Granada campaign, the Spanish lost 3,000 troops to injury and 17,000 to disease, almost exclusively typhus. The Spanish subsequently brought the disease to the New World; Columbus had the disease himself in 1494.

Typhus broke out with the 16th-century wars with the Turks, which for the first time led to pan-European epidemics. In 1542, typhus killed 30,000 Christian soldiers in Hungary, and, 24 years later, it forced Emperor Maximilian II to abort his advance against Sultan Suleiman. Typhus was a constant problem for both soldiers and civilians during the entire Thirty Years War. In 1643, Charles I of England was forced to give up his advance on London when typhus rendered his army ineffectual.

Perhaps the most notorious epidemic of military typhus was that which decimated Napoleon Bonaparte's Grand Army in its 1812 Russian campaign. The French emperor crossed the Nieman River from Prussia into Poland with half a million men, 265,000 of whom constituted his core army. They entered Vilna in the middle of a hot, dry summer and found neither enough food to eat nor enough clean water to drink. The soldiers were weakened by dysentery and unwashed because there was no water with which to bathe. The city itself was crowded and filthy, and it harbored endemic typhus, which became epidemic in the debilitated occupying army. By the third week in July the French army, still 300 miles from Moscow, had 80,000 men either dead from disease or too sick to fight. By the Battle of Borodino, Napoleon's army was reduced to only 130,000, and another 10,000 were lost to typhus in the week between the battle and the entry into Moscow. Typhus continued to rage through the army during the retreat, and 20,000 sick were abandoned in Smolensk. By the time the Grand Army returned to Prussia, there were only 35,000 survivors, the rest lost to hunger, cold, and dysentery, but mostly to typhus. In retreat, the soldiers spread the epidemic and devastated the communities through which they passed.

Typhus was again a severe problem in the Crimea and in World War I. Epidemic typhus did not occur on the Western Front, although the less severe trench fever was common. On the Eastern Front, however, typhus was rampant during and after both the war and the Russian Revolution. In Serbia, 150,000 soldiers contracted the disease, effectively removing that country from the war. The worst typhus epidemic in history occurred in Russia between 1917 and 1921, resulting in 25 million cases and 3 million deaths. Because insecticides allowed effective delousing, typhus was not an especially severe military problem during World War II. A brief epidemic in Naples in 1943 was readily controlled with DDT delousing. Typhus was, however, a severe problem in German concentration camps. Virtually every survivor of Bergen-Belsen either had or had recovered from typhus, and the disease typically carried a 60 percent mortality rate in the camps.

Because of effective antibiotics and insect control, typhus is no longer a significant military problem, but in the years between 1500 and 1813 it played a major role in virtually every European war.

See also Napoleonic Wars; Scrub Typhus; Trench Fever (Volhynian Fever); World War I Medicine

References

Cartwright, Frederick, and Michael Biddiss. *Disease and History.* New York: Dorset Press, 1972.

Cornebise, Alfred. *Typhus and Doughboys: The American Polish Typhus Relief Expedition, 1919–1921.* Newark: University of Delaware Press, 1982.

Karlen, Arno. *Man and Microbes: Disease and Plagues in History and Modern Times.* New York: Simon & Schuster, 1995.

Zinsser, Hans. *Rats, Lice and History.* Boston: Little, Brown and Co., 1934.

U

Unit 731

Unit 731, the Japanese chemical and biological warfare unit based in Manchuria during World War II, was infamous for its experiments on human subjects.

The abysmal performance of the Japanese military medical system in the 1894 war with China led to major reforms, including sending a number of Japanese army physicians to Europe for advanced training. By the time of the Russo-Japanese War, Japanese military medicine may have been the best in the world, especially in its management of infectious and epidemic disease. After 1918, Japanese interest in bacterial disease turned to the potential use of infection as a weapon.

The Japanese chemical and biological warfare program escalated after the invasion of Manchuria and the country's 1932 withdrawal from the League of Nations. The euphemistically named Epidemic Prevention Laboratory in Tokyo was moved to a 6-square-kilometer site in Pingfang outside the Manchurian city of Harbin and was eventually renamed Unit 731. The unit was placed under Kyoto-trained bacteriologist and phy-sician Shiro Ishii. Several other camps were later constructed in China, including the Department of Veterinary Disease Prevention of the Kuantung Army (the Wakamatsu Unit, or Unit 100) outside Changchun, and a small unit near Mukden, where American, British, and New Zealand prisoners were held.

All of the units engaged in experiments using human prisoners, although by far the majority of victims were Chinese delivered by the *Kempeitai*, the Japanese military secret police. Experiments using chemical agents and environmental extremes were carried out, but Unit 731 concentrated especially on weaponizing biological agents including typhoid, glanders, epidemic hemorrhagic fever, and plague. Ishii's unit developed porcelain bombs stuffed with cotton wadding, rice, wheat, and plague-infested fleas that were dropped over cities in Chechiang Province, causing about 24 deaths but failing to precipitate an epidemic.

In 1945, the Unit 731 research facilities were destroyed in advance of Allied capture. Ishii negotiated immunity from war crimes prosecution in return for delivering information that American biowarfare experts deemed important in the developing struggle with the Soviet Union. Many of the senior physicians involved in the Japanese programs went on to successful academic and business careers after the war. Ishii, however, never regained his prewar stature and died of throat cancer in 1959.

See also Chemical and Biological Warfare; Human Experimentation; Ishii, Shiro; Japanese Military Medicine; World War II Medicine

References

Gold, Hal. *Unit 731 Testimony.* Boston: Tuttle Publishing, 1966.

Harris, Sheldon. *Factories of Death: Japanese Biological Warfare 1932–45 and the American Cover-up.* New York: Routledge, 1994.

Williams, Peter, and David Wallace. *Unit 731: Japan's Secret Biological Warfare in World War II.* London: Hodder and Stoughton, 1989.

V

Vaccination and Variolation

Vaccination refers to inoculation with live *Vaccinae variolae* (cowpox) virus. Variolation refers to inoculation with live *Variolae major* (smallpox) virus.

Both variolation and vaccination are efforts to generate immunity against smallpox. Variolation was employed by practitioners in China and the Middle East for centuries and by farmers and laborers in rural England, where it was referred to as "buying the pox." The assumption was that one could harvest virus from a patient suffering a mild form of the disease and transmit it and the associated immunity with less risk than random exposure to a possibly more virulent case. In fact, mortality from variolation was only 2–3 percent as compared with 20–30 percent from naturally acquired smallpox.

Variolation was popularized in Europe by Lady Mary Wortley Montague, the wife of the British ambassador to the Ottoman Empire. Lady Montague had been famous for her beauty until 1715, when she was permanently scarred by smallpox in an outbreak that also took the life of her 20-year-old brother. She encountered the practice of variolation when her diplomat husband was posted to Constantinople. While there, she arranged to have her young son inoculated. On her return to London in 1718, she had her daughter inoculated as a demonstration for the royal family. After further successful experiments on prisoners, Charles Maitland variolated the Princess of Wales's two daughters. Interest in variolation was piqued among Europe's ruling families by the death of France's Louis XV from smallpox, and the practice was widely adopted by Continental royalty in the early 18th century.

By 1775, both the Dutch and Prussian armies had variolation programs for their armies, but it was the American Continental Army that first made the practice mandatory. Gen. George Washington required that all new recruits and all veterans about to start a campaign be variolated. The precipitating event for his order was the Quebec invasion of 1775, which failed when half of Gen. Horatio Gates's troops acquired smallpox. The British defenders, many of whom had been variolated, suffered minimal losses; it is likely that, absent smallpox,

Canada would have fallen to the Americans. Washington's order was carried out over the objection of Patrick Henry and the Virginia House of Commons, but, in spite of those objections and the fact that as many as 8 percent of those inoculated died, variolation was repeated at Valley Forge in 1778.

The picture changed in 1798 when English country physician Edward Jenner, acting on the folk medicine conviction that milkmaids did not get smallpox, inoculated a young patient with material from bovine pocks and then deliberately exposed him to smallpox and proved that the practice resulted in immunity. Vaccination was accepted with remarkable alacrity throughout the Western world. The same year as Jenner's experiment, the British Sick and Wounded Board authorized mandatory immunization for the Royal Army. Napoleon Bonaparte became a staunch advocate of immunization and an admirer of Jenner, whom he allowed to issue passports under his own signature that were good for travel throughout the continent in spite of the ongoing war between France and Great Britain. He is said to have commented that he could refuse nothing Jenner asked.

In 1802, Thomas Jefferson signed the Act to Encourage Vaccination requiring the U.S. Post Office to transport vaccine without charge. In 1803, Spain sent vaccination teams first to Mexico, then throughout its empire to inoculate its soldiers and administrators. Prussia made vaccination mandatory, but post-Napoleonic France did not. As a result, 14,178 French prisoners were infected with smallpox after the 1870–1871 Franco-Prussian War, and 1,963 died. The German armies, on the other hand, suffered only 4,835 cases and 178 deaths.

By the 20th century, vaccination had removed smallpox from most of the world, and, in 1959, the Soviet Union proposed a campaign to eliminate the disease worldwide. The effort culminated in the final case of naturally occurring smallpox being recorded on October 16, 1975.

Stores of the virus were, however, retained in research facilities in the United States and the Soviet Union, and programs continued to turn the organism into a biological weapon. It is estimated that the Soviet Union produced as much as 20 tons of virus for delivery by long-range missiles. In an accidental 1971 release in Kazakhstan, a number of people caught the disease, including seven who had previously been vaccinated. The possibility that weaponized smallpox might be resistant to immunization, together with the fact that routine smallpox vaccination has not been practiced since the 1980s, raises the possibility of an intentionally created epidemic in the future.

See also Chemical and Biological Warfare; Franco-Prussian War; Smallpox

References
Benenson, Abram. 1984. "Immunization and Military Medicine." *Review of Infectious Diseases* 6 (1): 1–12.
Bowen, John Z. 1981. "The Odyssey of Smallpox Vaccination." *Bulletin of the History of Medicine* 55 (Spring): 17–33.
Duffy, John. *Epidemics in Colonial America*. Baton Rouge: Louisiana State University Press, 1953.
Gillet, Mary. *The Army Medical Department, 1775–1818*. Washington, D.C.: Center of Military History, 1981.

Vesalius, Andreas (1514–1564)

Andreas Vesalius made anatomy a science. He was born in Flanders to German parents, and his father served as apothecary to

Holy Roman Emperor Charles V. Vesalius received a degree in arts from the University of Louvain in 1529 and attended the University of Paris from 1533 to 1536. He received a medical degree from the University of Padua in 1537, where he remained as a lecturer in surgery. Early in his career, he abandoned classical authorities in favor of direct knowledge obtained in the dissecting room. He began haunting local cemeteries, and his fervor for acquiring anatomic material led to his being brought before the Inquisition on charges of having performed an autopsy on someone not yet entirely dead.

Vesalius's five years as a teacher at Padua culminated in publication of *De Fabrica Humani Corporis* in 1543. Although the *Fabrica* would become the most important medical work between Galen and William Harvey, it was initially condemned by traditionalists. The criticism was so severe that Vesalius burned his other manuscripts and abandoned Padua for Spain and accepted an appointment as court physician to Charles V.

Vesalius settled in Madrid, married, and adapted to court life. He joined the emperor in his wars against the French but treated the wounded with only mixed success. He traveled with the army to Ghent, Brussels, Cologne, and Nijmegen and eventually settled in Brussels, where he opened a lucrative private practice and acquired a considerable fortune. In 1558 he was called to France to join Ambroise Paré in treating King Henry II, who had suffered a lance wound to the eye during a tournament. The king died, and Vesalius's main service was performing the royal autopsy.

In 1564, Vesalius was invited back to be a professor at the university at Padua, a position he intended to accept after completing a pilgrimage to the Holy Land, which may have been ordered by the Church as atonement for accusations of vivisection. On the way back to Italy, he died in a shipwreck off the island of Zante.

See also 16th-Century Military Medicine

References
Cushing, Harvey. *A Bio-Bibliography of Andreas Vesalius*. New York: Schuman's, 1943.
Garrison, Daniel, and Malcolm Hast. *On the Fabric of the Human Body: An Annotated Translation of the 1543 and 1555 Editions of Andreas Vesalius' De Humani Corporis Fabrica*. Evanston, IL: Northwestern University Press, 2003.
O'Malley, C. D. *Andreas Vesalius of Brussels, 1514–1564*. Berkeley: University of California Press, 1965.

Viet Nam War (1964–1973)

Because of the tropical climate, the distance from North America, and the insurgent nature of the conflict, the Viet Nam War was one of the most difficult medical challenges faced by U.S. military physicians.

The Republic of Viet Nam (South Viet Nam) was 700 miles long and, at most, 125 miles wide, had a year-round hot climate with a wet and a dry season, and had very poor roads, making ground transport from one area to the next difficult in the best conditions and occasionally impossible. Viet Nam was 1,000 miles from the nearest U.S. Army base hospital (Clark Air Force Base in the Philippines), 2,700 miles from the nearest complete American medical center in Japan, and 7,800 miles from the evacuation hospital at Travis Air Force Base in Nevada. The war was a combination of large battles and an ongoing counterinsurgency with no clear front lines and was fought, for the most part, as limited actions by small tactical units.

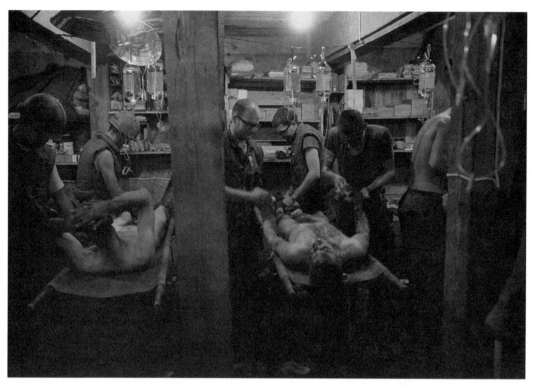

Casualty treatment facility at the Khe Sanh field hospital, South Viet Nam, in 1968. (Christian Simonpietri/Corbis)

While still in an advisory role, the U.S. Army opened the 100-bed 8th Field Hospital in the coastal city of Nha Trang in 1962. That remained its only major medical facility in Viet Nam until the 3d Field Hospital opened in Saigon in 1965 in response to the rapid American military expansion after the August 1964 Gulf of Tonkin incident. The 44th Medical Brigade was dispatched from Fort Sam Houston in San Antonio in January 1966 and grew to 7,830 members by the end of that year. The brigade remained the primary medical organizational unit in Viet Nam until it was superseded by the U.S. Army Medical Command, Viet Nam in 1970. In addition to the two field hospitals, the army medical corps deployed a series of smaller surgical hospitals, several evacuation hospitals, and a convalescent center at Cam Ranh Bay that totaled 5,283 beds by the end of 1968.

Largely because of the tropical climate, disease was the greatest problem for American military physicians throughout the war. Between 1965 and 1969, 69 percent of hospital admissions were for disease and only about 16 percent were for battle-related injuries. The latter, however, accounted for just over half of the hospital days because trauma required longer inpatient stays. Even so, the admission rate for disease in American troops in Viet Nam (351/1,000/year) was significantly less than had been the case in the Pacific Theater during World War II (890/1,000/year), an improvement that is probably best attributed to better preventive medicine in the later war.

The main disease problems were malaria, neuropsychiatric disease, viral hepatitis, skin diseases, acute respiratory infections, diarrheal disease, and venereal disease. Drug-resistant falciparum malaria and drug-resistant venereal disease were particularly serious problems, and the Army worried throughout the conflict that both would be brought back to the United States by returning soldiers. That did not occur. The incidence of psychiatric disease increased steadily through the conflict and was, by 1970, the second most common cause of hospitalization, with drug abuse being particularly problematic. Marijuana, heroin, opium, barbiturates, and amphetamines were all readily available and relatively inexpensive. One study of exiting soldiers revealed that 21.5 percent of those leaving Viet Nam had used marijuana and 17.4 percent had used opium or heroin.

Better transport and better care of serious injuries were hallmarks of the conflict. A total of 8,744,000 American troops served in the Viet Nam War between 1964 and the cease-fire in 1973. Of these, 47,424 were killed in action and 153,303 suffered wounds severe enough to require hospitalization. The ratio of dead to wounded was 1:3.1 in World War II, 1:4.1 in Korea, and 1:5.6 in Viet Nam. Mortality from wounds in those who reached a hospital was 4.5 percent in World War II, 2.5 percent in Korea, and 2.6 percent in Viet Nam. Unlike the earlier wars, artillery injuries were relatively rare. The majority of wounds were from high-velocity small arms such as the AK-47 and from mines and booby-trap bombs. By 1970, 80 percent of wounds were from explosives. Because many wounds were inflicted in heavily fertilized rice fields, bacterial contamination was a serious problem.

The front line was neither movable nor even identifiable, so hospitals in Viet Nam were in fixed locations with helicopter transport from the battlefield to those facilities. The favorable Viet Nam experience with aeromedical evacuation led to its being adopted in American civilian practice in the decade immediately following the war. At the war's apogee in 1969, 206,229 wounded soldiers were transported in army helicopters, and American medivac pilots flew 78,652 combat hours.

Treatment of major wounds and related shock improved significantly during the Viet Nam War. Whole blood was routinely available and used to a much greater extent than had been the case in prior conflicts. Techniques of vascular reconstruction led to an amputation rate for injury to major vessels that was one-fourth of that in World War II. The improvements in surgical management of multiple trauma were, like helicopter evacuation, subsequently transferred to civilian practice.

See also Aeromedical Evacuation; Drug Addiction; Field Hospitals; Gonorrhea; Malaria; Shock

References

Neel, Spurgeon. *Medical Support of the U.S. Army in Vietnam, 1965–1970.* Washington, D.C.: Department of the Army, 1973.

Sun, Sue. 2004. "Where the Girls Are: The Management of Venereal Disease by United States Military Forces in Vietnam." *Literature and Medicine* 23 (1): 66–87.

Vozrozhdeniye Island

Vozrozhdeniye Island was the primary test site for the Soviet Union's biological warfare program.

Vozrozhdeniye Island lies in the Aral Sea between Kazakhstan and Uzbekistan, which currently share its ownership. Stalin began bioweapons testing on the island in the 1930s, abandoned the program to concentrate on nuclear weapons, and reopened the facility in 1954. Until its closure in 1992, Vozrozhdeniye housed a small city of 1,500 occupants and an extensive laboratory complex and test range.

Experiments at the laboratory were carried out on small animals (guinea pigs, hamsters, rabbits), large animals (horses and donkeys), and nonhuman primates. According to Gennadi Lepyoshkin, who directed the facility until its closure, about two-thirds of the research was defensive, such as development of vaccines against anthrax and plague and design of protective clothing, and one-third was offensive, concentrating on bacterial agents such as plague and anthrax.

When the facility was closed, large volumes of infected material were buried and left on the island. The American government, in concert with Uzbek officials, has destroyed some of the island's facilities in an attempt to prevent disease spread, but it is widely believed that the island remains contaminated.

See also Anthrax; Chemical and Biological Warfare; Plague (Bubonic Plague, Black Death); Smallpox

References

Miller, Judith, Stephen Engelberg, and William Broad. *Germs: Biological Weapons and America's Secret War*. New York: Simon & Schuster, 2001.
Pala, Christopher. "Anthrax Island." *New York Times Magazine*, January 12, 2003.

Warren, John
(1753–1815)

An American Revolutionary War surgeon and founder of Harvard Medical School, John Warren was born in the Boston suburb of Roxbury, the descendant of John Warren, who had accompanied John Winthrop on the *Arabella* and had settled with him in the Massachusetts Bay Company colony at Salem. He was the younger brother of Joseph Warren, a physician and general in the Massachusetts militia who died at Bunker Hill.

John Warren entered Harvard College in 1767 at the age of 14, although he had not learned to read until he was 10. He graduated in 1771 and entered a medical apprenticeship under his brother, opening his own practice in Salem in 1773. That same year, he participated in the Boston Tea Party and subsequently became physician to Salem's militia regiment. He suffered a bayonet wound while retrieving his brother's body after the Battle of Bunker Hill.

In July 1775, Warren was appointed senior surgeon to Gen. George Washington's Continental Army. In that position, he furthered his anatomic education by performing autopsies whenever possible on deceased soldiers. Warren created a stir when he announced that the British, on retreating from Boston, had left behind medicine vials contaminated with arsenic. He went to New York with Washington in 1776, where he introduced a system in which the regimental surgeon was placed 300–500 yards behind infantry lines so he could quickly apply lint and ligatures to stop bleeding, splint fractures, and remove foreign bodies.

Warren, forced to leave the army in 1777 because of a variety of personal medical problems, returned to Boston and opened a private hospital at what is now the site of Massachusetts General Hospital. He began a series of public anatomy lectures and was invited to teach upperclassmen at Harvard. His course was so popular that the Harvard College Corporation established formal professorships in anatomy and surgery, theory and practice of physic, and chemistry and *materia medica*, from which eventually came a full-fledged medical school. Warren took the initial appointment in anatomy and surgery and became New England's leading surgeon.

345

He went on to have 17 children, including surgeon John Collins Warren, before dying of pneumonia at age 62.

See also American Revolutionary War; Warren, Joseph

References
Packard, Francis. *History of Medicine in the United States*. New York: Paul B. Hoeber, 1931.
Reiss, Oscar. *Medicine and the American Revolution: How Diseases and Their Treatments Affected the Colonial Army*. Jefferson, NC: McFarland & Co., Inc., 1998.

Warren, Joseph
(1741–1775)

Joseph Warren was a Boston physician who abandoned medicine for a brief military career in the American Revolution.

Warren was born in Roxbury, Massachusetts, and graduated from Harvard College in 1759. He served briefly as master at the Roxbury grammar school before entering an apprenticeship under Dr. James Lloyd. At 23 years of age, Warren opened his own practice in Boston and acquired local fame for his management of epidemic smallpox in that city, including successful treatment of John Adams, for whom he subsequently served as family physician.

Warren became politically involved with the rebellious Bostonians when British troops occupied the city in 1768, and he later helped write the Suffolk Resolves in response to the Intolerable Acts of 1774. In 1775, he was elected president of the Provincial Congress, and he was named major general of the Massachusetts colonial forces later that year. In that capacity, he went to Bunker Hill upon hearing that the British had crossed Boston Harbor and landed at Charlestown. He survived most of the Battle of Bunker Hill but was struck in the head by a musket ball and killed during the retreat. His brother John, also a physician, was wounded by a British bayonet the following day while attempting to recover the body.

See also American Revolutionary War; Warren, John

Reference
Kelly, Howard A., and Walter L. Burrage. *Dictionary of American Medical Biography: Lives of Eminent Physicians of the United States and Canada, from the Earliest Times*. Boston: Milford House, 1928.

Wiseman, Richard
(1622–1676)

Richard Wiseman played a role as important to the development of English surgery as did his contemporary Thomas Sydenham to English medicine.

Wiseman began his career as a surgical apprentice at age 15, but, like Ambroise Paré, most of his learning came from treating wounded soldiers. After completing medical training, he joined the Dutch Navy. During the war between Oliver Cromwell's rebels and the Stuart monarchy, Wiseman escaped to France. He returned to England to fight with the Loyalists but was captured in 1651. Although confined in the Old Bailey, he was allowed to continue to practice and, in 1654, escaped England and served as a surgeon in the Spanish Navy until the restoration of the British monarchy.

The Stuarts rewarded Wiseman's loyalty by appointing him surgeon in ordinary to the king and, in 1672, principal surgeon to the Crown. In that role, he became the paradigm for the consulting surgeon, operating only on patients referred to him by other physicians. In 1672, he published *Several Chirurgicall Treatises*, which described more than 600 of his own cases. Wiseman was an unusually skillful surgeon and an astute medical observer. He recognized that syphilis and gonorrhea were separate diseases. He preferred oil of turpentine for hemostasis, although admitting that he occasionally fell back on the hot cautery "in the heat of fight." He also recognized that gunshot wounds of a joint almost inevitably led to infection and, consequently, thought they required early amputation.

See also Amputation; 17th-Century Military
  Medicine; Sydenham, Thomas

References

Bakay, Louis. 1987. "Richard Wiseman, a Royalist Surgeon of the English Civil War." *Surgical Neurology* 27 (May): 415–418.
Hull, G. 1996. "Richard Wiseman, 1622–1676." *Annals of the Royal College of Surgeons of England* 78 (4 Suppl., July): 193–195.

World War I Medicine

World War I was the first multifront war fought with the full benefit of anesthesia, antisepsis, and motor transport.

World War I was fought just as a number of advances in medicine and surgery were coming into general use. Routine use of anesthesia had been followed, late in the 19th century, with the recognition of the microbial origin of disease and associated techniques of surgical antisepsis and asepsis. The use of litter companies and "field ambulances" ("ambulance" in the terminology of the time is from the French and referred to an entire transport and hospital system) dated to reforms following the Boer War, and sequential triage through mobile casualty clearing stations and rail transport to rear-area general hospitals dated only to 1907. The Japanese had developed intermediate evacuation hospitals between forward and rear areas and had used hospital ships to facilitate early stabilization and wound management, both techniques imported from the German hospitals in which the majority of Imperial Army physicians had trained.

Mass mobilization at the beginning of the war necessitated incorporation of virtually the entire medical manpower pools of both France and Germany. Young physicians were sent to the front while more experienced doctors were assigned to manage the complicated cases referred to rear-area hospitals. None of the warring European powers had enough physicians to satisfy both their military and their civilian needs, so the first Americans to officially participate in the war were medical personnel assigned to the British Army within a month of President Woodrow Wilson's declaration of war (although volunteer medical units—usually recruited from individual medical schools and operating under the aegis of the American Hospital of Paris—had served in France since 1915). Before the first American combatant reached Europe, 1,400 physicians, 1,000 nurses, 2,600 enlisted personnel, and six base hospitals had been deployed. After the United States entered the war in 1917, the Army medical corps rapidly expanded. In June 1916, there were only 443 American medical officers; by 1918, there were 30,951, more than had been in the entire army before the war started.

The British Army had proven the usefulness of female military nurses during the Crimean War, but no European army had an adequate number of trained nurses when the war started. Queen Alexandra's Imperial Military Nursing Service, the nursing unit of the Royal Army Medical Corps, had

First aid nurses of the British Yeomanry Corps help a wounded soldier onto a stretcher, January 1915. (Underwood & Underwood/Corbis)

fewer than 300 nurses in 1914. That number increased to 10,404 by 1918 and was supplemented by more than 9,000 partially trained volunteer nursing personnel in voluntary aid detachments.

Beginning in 1914, a significant portion of the ambulance transport on the Western Front was provided by American volunteers, mostly under either the American Field Service or the American Field Ambulance Service. The American Red Cross initially provided volunteer services to both sides in the conflict but restricted its aid to the Entente powers after the SS *Lusitania* was sunk.

The number of hospital beds increased as dramatically as did the number of personnel.

When the war started, there had been only 18,000 hospital beds in the entire British Empire; by the war's end, there were 637,000.

The chief medical administrators of the various combatants were Gen. Sir Alfred Keogh and Gen. Sir John Goodwin of Great Britain; Gen. William C. Gorgas of the United States; M. Justin Godant of France; and Lt. Gen. Otto von Schjeming of Germany.

Improved survival from trauma during World War I started with improved organization and transport. *Postes de secours*, or forward aid stations, were established soon after the war settled into static trench warfare. These stations were situated just behind the front lines and were the first stop for litter bearers who retrieved wounded from the field. After initial bandaging and control of hemorrhage, the men were transported (usually by motor ambulance after the war's first months) to casualty clearing stations (CCSs) located just out of artillery range. There wounds were débrided (dead tissue removed) and redressed, fractures were stabilized, and men with minor injuries were definitively treated and returned to the front. From the CCS, the wounded were evacuated to field hospitals where specialty surgical teams could perform definitive operations. The field hospitals were usually adjacent to rail lines so men who needed more complex surgery, convalescence, or rehabilitation could be moved to large institutions in the interior.

Motorized ambulance transport was facilitated by a relatively stationary front and the general availability of usable roads just behind the battle lines. Prior to 1917, ambulance services on the Western Front were under combat rather than medical service command and were used for transport only. The drivers were not trained to treat the wounded, and nurses and physicians did not accompany the ambulances. Drivers came both from troop transport divisions and from various volunteer organizations such as the St. Johns Ambulance, the Society of Friends, and the American Ambulance Field Service. John Dos Passos, Ernest Hemingway, and e. e. cummings were among those who served as volunteer drivers, and each described his experience in postwar works.

In the war's first months, it was not uncommon for the wounded to wait one or two days before being treated, but the establishment of CCSs made treatment typically available within minutes to hours, with consequent decreases in blood loss and infection and dramatic improvements in survival.

Much of the war on the Western Front was fought in French fields that had been cultivated and fertilized for centuries and were heavily contaminated with *Clostridium perfringens*, the organism responsible for gas gangrene, and the related *Clostridium tetani*, responsible for tetanus. Early débridement helped with the first problem, and the general use of tetanus antiserum (a total of more than 11 million doses by war's end) after 1915 virtually eliminated the second.

Several methods of chemical wound sterilization were developed during the war. Direct application of chlorine was replaced by continuous irrigation with a combination of hypochlorites and boric acid from an apparatus designed by French physician Alexis Carrel and British chemist H. D. Dakin. In spite of the contaminated soil in which the war was fought, the hospital death rate for wounds was 4.5 per 1,000, less than half that of the American Civil War.

Technical improvements during the war included general use of hypodermic syringes, better retractors and forceps, general use of sterile rubber gloves, routine use of thermometers, use of sterile gauze instead of lint, mobile laboratories and X-ray units, and routine vaccination against several infectious diseases.

Trench warfare and the widespread use of machine guns, shrapnel, high explosives, land mines, grenades, and mortars resulted in an assortment of previously uncommon injuries. Wounds to the head and face were especially common in men who peeked over trench rims and became targets for weapons on the other side. Land mines in the area between the trenches were responsible for large numbers of blast injuries to the extremities. Earlier and more effective surgery allowed more men with these injuries to survive than had been the case in previous wars but also necessitated improvements in rehabilitation and prostheses and in the management of bone and nerve injuries. Improvements in anesthesia and antiseptic surgery resulted in decreased case mortality rates in head, chest, and extremity wounds, but the lack of antibiotics still hampered survival rates, especially from wounds that penetrated an abdominal viscus.

For the first time in a major war, the death rate from injury among combatants in World War I was more than twice that from disease, even when the mortality from the influenza epidemic of 1918–1919 is taken into account. Nonetheless, disease remained a significant problem. Many recruits came from sparsely populated rural areas and had not acquired the immunity to communicable disease enjoyed by their urban counterparts. When the two groups were put together in close quarters, epidemics of childhood diseases such as measles, mumps, meningitis, and scarlet fever were inevitable. Other diseases, including smallpox, typhoid, tetanus, diphtheria, and some forms of dysentery, that had plagued previous armies were controlled with vaccines. Arthropod-borne diseases such as typhus and trench fever were partially controlled by insecticides, especially the newly developed DDT. The Germans on the Western Front suffered less from infectious disease than the French and British, largely because their sanitation was more effective. The French were convinced the trench lines were temporary, so they did little to improve them. The Germans anticipated staying in France, so they built more elaborate trenches and lined them with concrete, which could be washed down and sanitized.

Infectious diseases were even more problematic in Africa and the Middle East than in Europe. The East African campaign saw the highest incidence of disease of any theater in the war, with malaria being especially common. Dysentery and malaria crippled the British in Mesopotamia, with 10 percent of the army reporting sick every day during the siege of Kut. At Gallipoli, 85,000 men were hospitalized (and most were evacuated to Egypt) for disease, mostly dysentery.

The Germans introduced gas as a weapon at Ypres nine months into the war. At first the irritant chlorine was used; it was later replaced by mustard gas and phosgene. Effective gas masks were available by July 1915, and 27 million were produced by the end of the war. Gas as a weapon was paradoxically humane, compared with other types of war injury; of 185,000 British gas casualties, only 9,000 died.

See also Ambulances and Transport; American Field Service and Other World War I Volunteer Ambulance Services; Anesthesiology; Antisepsis; Asepsis, British Military Medicine; Carrel, Alexis; Carrel-Dakin Irrigation; Casualty Clearing Stations and Staged Evacuation; Chemical and Biological Warfare; Cushing, Harvey Williams; DDT (Dichlorodiphenyltrichloroethane); Débridement; Dysentery; Field Hospitals; Gas Gangrene; Gorgas, William Crawford; Head Injury and Cranial Surgery; Influenza; Ireland, Major General Merritte Weber; Malaria; Nursing in the Military; Prussian and German Military Medicine; Queen Alexandra's Imperial Military Nursing Service; Rehabilitation and Reconstructive Surgery; Royal Army Medical Corps; Tetanus; Trench Fever (Volhynian Fever); Trench Foot; Typhus; X-Ray

References

Bayne-Jones, Stanhope. *The Evolution of Preventive Medicine in the United States Army, 1607–1939*. Washington, D.C.: Office of the Surgeon General, Department of the Army, 1968.

Fauntleroy, A. M. *Report on the Medico-Military Aspects of the European War from Observations taken behind the Allied Armies in France.* Washington, D.C.: Government Printing Office, 1915.

Gillet, Mary. *The Army Medical Department, 1865–1917.* Washington, D.C.: Center of Military History, 1995.

Ireland, M. W., ed. *The Medical Department of the United States Army in the World War, 1917–1918.* 15 vols. Washington, D.C.: Government Printing Office, 1921–1929.

Lovegrove, Peter. *Not the Least Crusade: A Short History of the Royal Army Medical Corps.* Aldershot, UK: Gale & Polden, Ltd., 1952.

MacDonald, Lyn. *The Roses of No Man's Land.* New York: Atheneum, 1989.

World War II Medicine

World War II was a conflict marked by advances in triage and transport, management of shock, and treatment of infectious diseases, as well as the emergence of aviation and submarine medicine and the misuse of human experimentation which led to new standards for medical research.

Better transportation and triage were made possible by improvement in systems first tried in World War I. By 1939 military surgeons recognized the importance of early management of battlefield trauma, and medics trained and equipped to control blood loss and administer analgesics at the initial site of injury were regularly attached to individual combat units. Injectable morphine dispensed on the battlefield lessened both pain and shock during evacuation. Taking the model adopted by the Royal Army Medical Corps during the previous world war, transport from the field was organized in stages, with each step assigned a specific range of duties.

The first stop after field stabilization was the regimental collecting station, where hemostatic bandages and splints could be applied. The collecting stations also had plasma or blood available to manage shock and could secure adequate ventilation, including tracheotomy if needed. From the collecting station, men could be moved to semi-mobile field hospitals equipped to perform emergency surgery. The field hospitals were the first stage fully staffed with physicians. From the field hospital, men could be moved to fixed-station or general hospitals where more complex procedures (neurosurgery, chest surgery, orthopedic reconstructions, and the like) could be performed and where men expected to return to duty could convalesce. General and rehabilitation hospitals in the zone of the interior provided major reconstruction (predominantly orthopedic and plastic surgical procedures) and long-term rehabilitation if necessary. Depending on the severity of injury, a wounded man could exit the system and return to duty at any point in the chain.

Semi-mobile medical units were linear descendants of the French "auto-chir," a World War I attempt to create motorized field hospitals. A high level of mobility was less important in that relatively stationary war, and development of the freely moveable hospital only blossomed in World War II. These "auxiliary surgical teams" remained somewhat difficult to transport and limited in the services they could provide but were an important interim step toward the mobile army surgical hospitals of Korea and Viet Nam.

Aeromedical evacuation, although tried in a crude way in World War I, came into its own in World War II. It largely involved use of fixed-wing aircraft (mostly C-47s, C-54s, and C-54As) to move men from field or general hospitals to facilities in the zone of the interior. Medical air transport became especially sophisticated in the long distances of the Pacific war where the Army Nurse Corps developed the expertise in managing patients during prolonged transit that presaged current civilian and military flight nurses.

The island war in the Pacific presented unique problems in medical evacuation; the distances were inordinately long, and there was almost never an accessible general hospital to augment basic field hospital care. Although hospital ships had been used since the mid-1800s and had reached a high degree of sophistication under the Japanese in their war with Russia, the U.S. Navy employed them to unprecedented advantage in World War II. At the beginning of the war, the Navy had only two hospital ships (the USS *Relief* and the USS *Solace*), and only one of these was in the Pacific. During the war, the United States commissioned an additional eight hospital ships and developed an entire class of troop transports equipped to provide limited hospital services. The Navy also deployed a series of adapted landing craft—LST (H)s—manned with four surgeons and 27 corpsmen and capable of serving as field hospitals for up to 350 wounded. Hospital ships were held well back from areas of direct combat and served essentially the same role as land-based general hospitals.

Although some new surgical techniques, particularly in vascular surgery, were developed during World War II, the primary advances were in early management and treatment of physiologic effects of trauma. As noted above, medics made almost immediate hemostasis and pain management a standard. Better understanding of the mechanisms and treatment of shock came early in the war. Shock is clinically char-acterized by a fall in blood pressure, a rise in the pulse, coolness and discoloration of poorly perfused extremities, and mental changes ranging from anxiety through confusion to coma. The syndrome's common denominator is failure of the heart and circulatory system to supply adequate blood to the body's organs. In the early years of the war clinicians realized that poor perfusion was the common factor in a variety of types of shock. Blood loss, loss of body fluid such as that caused by weeping burn wounds, sepsis with its toxic bacteriologic by-products, and extreme cold can all cause the circulatory system to fail. The physiologic effects of that failure can (at least temporarily) be ameliorated by increasing the amount of fluid in the system.

Soviet scientists in the 1930s had shown that plasma—blood with red cells removed—could be effectively used to treat shock. Plasma had two signal advantages: unlike whole blood, it was not type specific, and it could be readily stored for long periods. Plasma could be started by medics at the front, and it was widely administered from the early days of the war.

Recognizing the need for blood and plasma, the British started a national blood banking program early in the war, a collection and storage system the Americans later enlarged and improved. As the war progressed, plasma's limitations as a replacement for lost blood became evident, and use of whole blood to treat shock became more prevalent. Although civilian donors played a major role in supplying the blood banks, most donations came from combatants themselves, with medics providing a disproportionate share. In addition to whole blood, military surgeons had cardiac stimulants and vasoconstrictors such as adrenaline and ephedrine to augment perfusion.

Military medicine also saw significant advances in management of infectious diseases during World War II. These improvements primarily involved treatment and control of tropical diseases, control of diseases resulting from poor sanitation aggravated by dietary deficiency, and chemical treatment of infections.

The Pacific war forced Japanese and Allied soldiers to fight in areas where tropical infections, especially malaria, were endemic. In the latter part of 1942 and early 1943, American soldiers in the Solomon Islands were hospitalized for malaria at a rate of 970 per 1,000 per year, with 100,000 men ultimately contracting the disease. The unacceptable loss of fighting men led Gen. Douglas MacArthur to form the Combined Advisory Committee on Tropical Medicine, Hygiene, and Sanitation. The committee instituted preventive measures that brought an 85 percent decrease in the hospitalization rate within six months.

Quinine was the agent of choice in treating malaria at the beginning of the war, but the Japanese captured the drug's major sources of supply. The antimalarial Atabrine was developed as a synthetic substitute, and, although soldiers had to be forced to take it because of its bitter taste and tendency to turn the skin yellow, 2.5 billion doses had been dispensed by war's end.

Vigorous efforts were used to control the Anopheles mosquito that carried the disease, including oil coating of breeding ponds and spraying with the newly developed chemical insecticide DDT. As a result of these preventive measures, less than 1 percent of hospitalized American personnel had malaria by the end of 1943. The Japanese did not do as well. They had access to quinine but were ineffective in distributing it. In addition, their soldiers were often underfed, and their rice-based diet resulted in vitamin deficiencies, particularly B1 deficiency or beriberi, which increased susceptibility to infectious disease.

Besides malaria, soldiers in the Pacific Theater suffered from dengue fever (an untreatable, incapacitating, but usually self-limited viral disease), various forms of infectious diarrhea, and fungal skin diseases (collectively termed "jungle rot").

Typhus, a louse-borne rickettsial disease, was the most threatening infectious disease in the European Theater. When the Allies launched the North African offensive, the area was in the midst of a typhus epidemic that ultimately infected more than 500,000 civilians. The U.S. Army received a vaccine mass-produced by a process developed in the U.S. Department of Agriculture, and only 11 men out of a force of nearly half a million contracted typhus. Allied troops arrived in Europe vaccinated against typhus, typhoid, paratyphoid, and smallpox, but malaria remained a significant problem, especially in Italy, because Allied soldiers resisted taking Atabrine.

In addition to preventive vaccination, DDT was used to kill body lice that carried typhus. The new chemical agent stayed in clothes, so people could be dusted without removing their clothes (an important factor in the North African Muslim culture), and the clothing no longer had to be sterilized or destroyed. Effective delousing was also important in limiting typhus outbreaks in Russia, Eastern Europe, and Germany as the war ended. It was especially useful in controlling epidemics among concentration camp survivors when those facilities were liberated.

One of the most important advances in treatment of wartime trauma was the use of antibiotics. German scientist Gerhard Domagk, working at I. G. Farbenindustrie, had synthesized Prontosil in 1935, and scientists at the Pasteur Institute in Paris had adapted that chemical into the more effective sulfanilamide, an antimicrobial that could be applied directly to a wound or taken orally. Sulfa drugs were used prophylactically and therapeutically from the first months of the war. Sir Alexander Fleming had accidentally discovered the antibacterial properties of penicillin in 1929, but the drug was difficult and expensive to produce and was not widely used until 1940, when scientists at Oxford University produced a concentrated form suitable for clinical applications. The drug remained so expensive that it was routinely recovered from patients' urine, purified, and reused.

Improvements in aviation and submarine technology outstripped the ability of humans to adapt to newly accessible environments. Frenchman Paul Bert had described the physiologic effects of extreme altitude on balloonists in the previous century, but the extremes of temperature, pressure, and oxygen tension became acute concerns as great depths and nearly stratospheric altitudes were reached. Warplanes had service ceilings well beyond the survival capabilities of humans without artificial pressurization. Supplemental oxygen was required above 10,000 feet, and daytime bombing missions at altitudes in excess of 25,000 feet were the rule in the European Theater. At these altitudes, temperatures ranged as low as –50ºF, posing significant risk of frostbite or even hypothermic shock. A dive-bomber could descend at 30,000 feet per minute (compared with a commercial airliner's 400 feet per minute), a rate that introduced serious risk of barotrauma to the middle ear, sinuses, or intestines. Pooling of blood in the extremities due to extreme gravitational forces from rapid acceleration caused loss of vision and unconsciousness. Allied pilots taped their

legs and abdomens to protect against blackouts, and the Germans manufactured the first pressurized body suit with the same goal. Rapid ascent either from the ocean to the surface or the surface to high altitudes produced intravascular nitrogen bubbles leading to the syndrome of joint pain and stroke, collectively referred to as the bends.

Human experimentation carried out by the German and Japanese military medical establishments led to permanent changes in standards for scientific research. The Japanese used Russian and Chinese prisoners of war and civilians in biowarfare experiments in Manchuria and performed anatomy experiments on living American prisoners in Japan. Germans used concentration camp inmates to perform experiments on pressure and cold tolerance that, although undeniably inhumane, provided information that remains unique. Allied military surgeons were called on to help assess the Axis physicians' behavior after the war, and the resulting Nuremberg Code still sets the standards for ethically appropriate human experimentation.

See also Aeromedical Evacuation; Ambulances and Transport; Aviation Medicine; Baromedicine; Field Hospitals; Hospital Ships; Malaria; Quinine; Shock; Transfusion; Triage

References

Cowdrey, Albert. *Fighting for Life: American Military Medicine in World War II* (New York: Free Press), 1994.

Herman, Jan. *Battle Station Sick Bay: Navy Medicine in World War II.* Annapolis, MD: Naval Institute Press, 1997.

MacNalty, Arthur. *Medical Services in War: The Principle Medical Lesson of the Second World War.* London: His Majesty's Stationery Office, 1968.

Rawicz, Jerzy. *Nazi Medicine: Doctors, Victims and Medicine in Auschwitz.* New York: H. Fertig, 1986.

Talliaferro, William. *Medicine and the War.*
　Chicago: University of Chicago Press, 1944.
U.S. Army Medical Service. *Preventive Medicine
　in World War II.* Washington, D.C.: Office of
　the Surgeon General, 1955.

Wright, Almroth
(1861–1947)

Almroth Wright was a physician who exerted a major influence on sanitation and wound care in the World War I–era British medical service.

Wright graduated from Trinity University in Dublin with a degree in the arts in 1883. Short of money, he took a job as an admiralty clerk and then as an instructor at Cambridge before emigrating to Sydney, Australia, where he obtained a medical degree in 1892. After graduation, he returned to England as professor of pathology at the army medical school at Netley, where he became a bacteriologist. In 1902, Wright moved to St. Mary's Medical School on Praed Street, where he spent the balance of his career.

He was knighted in 1906 and was, at the outbreak of World War I, one of Britain's most respected research physicians. In 1914, he pressed Lord Kitchener to mandate typhoid vaccination for all British troops and began production of 10 million doses of vaccine, most of which were prepared in his laboratories at St. Mary's. As a result, the incidence of typhoid, which had been a major problem in the Boer War 15 years earlier, was negligible among British forces in France. He then turned his attention to the problem of wound sepsis and, with his junior associate Alexander Fleming, established a laboratory at the base hospital in the Bois de Boulogne in Paris. He adamantly opposed Alexis Carrel's wound irrigation with antiseptics, favoring instead wide débridement and irrigation with sterile saline.

Wright was a difficult personality who would not allow women to work in his laboratories, taking the public position that they were physiologically inferior to men. He earned the nickname "Sir Almost Right" and was satirized by his friend George Bernard Shaw in the play *The Doctor's Dilemma.* His scorn for antibiotics and preference for vaccines and prevention in the control of wound infection are ironic considering the fact that he was succeeded at St. Mary's by his former associate, Fleming, the discoverer of penicillin.

Wright died of heart failure in London at the age of 86.

See also Carrel-Dakin Irrigation; Typhoid
　Fever; World War I Medicine

References
Colebrook, Leonard. *Almroth Wright: Provoca-
　tive Doctor and Thinker.* London: Wm.
　Heinemann Medical Books, 1954.
Dunnill, Michael. *The Plato of Praed Street: The
　Life and Times of Almroth Wright.* London:
　Royal Society of Medicine Press, Ltd., 2000.

Würtz, Felix
(1518–1575)

Felix Würtz was a Swiss military surgeon best known for wound treatment and surgery of children.

Würtz trained in Zurich as a barber-surgeon before going to Nuremberg for further training, where he became an admirer and follower of Paracelsus. He also studied in Rome and Padua, where he may have encountered Andreas Vesalius. He spent his professional career in Basel and Zurich. His *An Experimental Treatise of Surgery* departed from earlier texts in that it was written in the vernacular German. The book described Würtz's experience treating gunshot wounds, fractures, and dislocations. Unlike his contemporaries, Würtz recommended letting open fractures heal rather than immediately resorting to amputation. For this, he has been called the father of conservative surgery.

Like Paracelsus, Würtz favored clean hands for wound surgeons and advised against overuse of poultices and plasters. However, like Ambroise Paré, he recommended irrigating wounds with turpentine. He was one of the first to suggest that droplets from surgeons' mouths might be a source of contamination that would cause "rottenness" in wounds and suggested that operators avoid breathing into wounds or cover their mouths with cloth. Like his contemporaries, Würtz believed pus was necessary to wound healing, contending that drainage removed foreign material.

Würtz also wrote the first text dealing specifically with the surgery of children, possibly inspired by the fact that his oldest child was crippled.

Details of Würtz's life and death are sketchy, but it is likely that he died in 1575, as the 1576 edition of his multivolume text on wound surgery was edited by his brother Rudolf.

See also Asepsis; Fractures; Paracelsus (Aureolus Theophrastus Bombastus von Hohenheim); Paré, Ambroise

References
Pilcher, James E. 1896. "Felix Würtz and Pierre Franco—A Glimpse of Sixteenth Century Surgery." *Annals of Surgery* 24 (October): 505–534.
Seror, D., A. Szold, and S. Nissan. 1991. "Felix Würtz: Surgeon and Pediatrician." *Journal of Pediatric Surgery* 10 (October 26): 1152–1155.

X-Ray

X-ray is short wavelength, high-energy radiation that can be used to visualize internal body structures.

German physicist Wilhelm Conrad Röntgen first noted on December 28, 1895, that a wave form different from electrons could be generated from a cathode ray tube. Shortly thereafter, he noticed that those rays penetrated skin more easily than bone and would leave a shadow of the bone on a photographic plate. He described the finding to a friend, who communicated it to a relative who edited *Die Presse* in Vienna, and the newspaper ran a front-page story about the discovery on January 5, 1896. Within days, the story was repeated in newspapers around the world.

Both the public and medical professionals realized almost immediately the medical potential of X-rays in defining fractures and locating foreign bodies. On February 3, the first clinical X-ray image in the United States was produced at Dartmouth College on a child with a fractured forearm. Two days later, scientists at the U.S. Military Academy at West Point experimented with the penetration of X-rays through steel, bronze, and copper. Within the following month, Giuseppe Alvaro used X-rays to find bullets in two soldiers who had fought at the Battles of Mai-Maret and Adowa, although he did so well after the battle at a facility in Naples. Both bullets were successfully located and removed. During the Greco-Turkish War of 1897, the German Red Cross put an X-ray machine at the Turkish Yildiz Hospital in Constantinople, and the British put a machine near Athens to use on Greek wounded. Both were restricted to rear-area facilities because of the delicacy of the X-ray tubes and difficulty getting reliable power sources.

Although the British Surgeon Major Walter C. Beevor managed to haul an X-ray machine and a hand-operated dynamo to the front during the 1897–1898 Tirah campaign in India, military surgeons continued to take the point of view that X-rays were best used in a delayed fashion. There was widespread feeling that making it easy to locate bullets inside the body might encourage young surgeons to operate more often than was actually necessary. Still, X-ray imaging made it much less necessary to probe deep in body cavities for lost projectiles, and X-rays were regularly employed during the British Nile expedition in September 1898. During the Spanish-American War, U.S. Army and Navy surgeons used a total of 17 X-ray machines manufactured by the Edison Company and General Electric, among others, which were kept on the hospital ships USS *Relief*, USS *Missouri*, and USS *Bay State*. Physicians on these vessels were also the first to describe burns from X-ray overdose.

By World War I, X-ray had become a standard tool in the military surgical armamentarium, and Marie Curie personally operated a unit near the French lines. Interestingly, forward surgical teams in Iraq and Afghanistan have forgone X-ray in advance surgical units under the assumption that fractures can be treated based on physical examination and surgery extensive enough to require X-ray diagnosis is best done elsewhere.

See also Boer War; Spanish-American War

References
Bruwer, André, ed. *Classic Descriptions in Diagnostic Roentgenology*. Springfield, IL: Charles C. Thomas, 1964.
Cirillo, Vincent. *Bullets and Bacilli: The Spanish-American War and Military Medicine*. New Brunswick, NJ: Rutgers University Press, 1999.
Eisenberg, Ronald. *Radiology: An Illustrated History*. St. Louis: Mosby Year Book, 1992.

Y

Yellow Fever

Yellow fever is an arbovirus (arthropod-borne) disease transmitted among primates by female mosquitoes, primarily of the species *Aedes aegyptii*.

The disease can live in several generations of mosquitoes and can be transmitted among monkeys and men, but is most virulent when passed from mosquitoes to humans in densely populated environments. The Aedes species has become remarkably domesticated, preferring to reproduce in still water held in artificial containers such as ships' water barrels.

The illness begins with headache, fever, and malaise, which progress within hours to chills and vomiting. Within five days, patients may exhibit the internal bleeding, liver failure, and jaundice that give the disease its name. Yellow fever is fatal in 50 percent of those who contract it.

Because of its short course and high mortality, yellow fever was largely confined to Africa until sailing ships and improved navigation made long sea voyages possible. When men were confined in closed spaces with an ample supply of stagnant water,

the Aedes mosquito could reproduce and the disease spread serially among the crew as the voyage progressed. Consequently, ships transported the mosquitoes and virus from Africa to virtually every port visited by merchant and military navies.

Having had yellow fever confers lifetime immunity, a fact leading to two geopolitical effects. Britain and France were never able to establish effective control of West Africa between the 16th and 19th centuries—West African school children still sing songs in praise of yellow fever as a protector against white men. In addition, when disease almost eliminated Native Americans in the century after the European encounter, they were replaced by African slaves who were relatively immune to infectious diseases—especially yellow fever—introduced by European sailors.

Yellow fever came to the New World in 1647–1648 when nearly simultaneous epidemics ravaged Barbados, Havana, and the Yucatan. For the next 200 years, the disease devastated coastal cities throughout North America from New Orleans to Halifax. In 1800 Thomas Jefferson opined that yellow fever would preclude development of any great cities in the United States. In 1802 Napoleon dispatched 25,000 men to quell Toussaint-Loverture's slave revolt in Haiti; 22,000 of the soldiers died, leading the French not only to abandon Haiti but also to sell the Louisiana territory and give up their interest in North America.

American imperialism finally furnished a combination of the impetus and the means to control yellow fever. After the Spanish-American War, it became imperative to make the Caribbean safe for U.S. military personnel. Walter Reed's Yellow Fever Commission (with the essential help of Cuban physician Carlos Finlay) proved that yellow fever was transmitted by mosquitoes and undertook to eradicate its breeding places and to control the disease in Havana. Understanding how to control yellow fever made it possible to dig the Panama Canal without the disastrous personnel losses suffered by Ferdinand de Lesseps's earlier attempt. In 1914, largely due to efforts of William Gorgas, the canal was completed and the U.S. Navy became a legitimate two-ocean force.

See also Gorgas, William Crawford; Reed, Walter; Spanish-American War

References

Cartwright, Frederick. *Disease and History*. New York: Dorset Press, 1972.

Garrett, Laurie. *The Coming Plague: Newly Emerging Diseases in a World out of Balance*. New York: Farrar, Straus & Giroux, 1994.

Gillet, Mary. *The Army Medical Department, 1865–1917*. Washington, D.C.: Center of Military History, 1995.

McNeill, William. *Plagues and Peoples*. New York: Anchor Books, 1976.

Truby, Albert. *Memoir of Walter Reed: The Yellow Fever Episode*. New York: Paul B. Hoeber, Inc., 1943.

ANNOTATED BIBLIOGRAPHY

Adams, Francis. *The Genuine Works of Hippocrates.* London: Baillière, Tindall & Cox, 1939. Adams's selection of the works attributed to Hippocrates of Cos in an excellent translation.

Adams, Ruth, and Susan Cullen, eds. *The Final Epidemic: Physicians and Scientists on Nuclear War.* Chicago: Educational Foundation for Nuclear Science, 1981.

Adamson, P. B. "The Military Surgeon: His Place in History." *Journal of the Royal Army Medical Corps* 128 (1982): 43–50. A nice, short summary of military surgery.

Alibek, Ken, with Stephen Handelman. *Biohazard: The Chilling True Story of the Largest Covert Biological Weapons Program in the World Told from Inside by the Man who Ran It.* New York: Random House, 2000. A bit overwrought but written by a former leader of the Soviet bioweapons program and authoritative for that reason.

Ashburn, P. M. *The Elements of Military Hygiene Especially Arranged for Officers and Men of the Line.* Boston: Houghton Mifflin, 1900.

Ashburn, P. M. *A History of the Medical Department of the United States Army.* Boston: Houghton Mifflin, 1929. A fine survey from the American Revolutionary War through World War I.

Barnes, Joseph K., and others, eds. *The Medical and Surgical History of the War of the Rebellion.* Washington, D.C.: Government Printing Office, 1870–1888. A monumental compilation of the medical and surgical experience of the Union Army.

Baylen, Joseph O., and Alan Conway, eds., *Soldier-Surgeon: The Crimean War Letters of Dr. Douglas A. Reid, 1855–1856.* Knoxville: University of Tennessee Press, 1968.

Bayne-Jones, Stanhope. *The Evolution of Preventive Medicine in the United States Army, 1607–1939.* Washington, D.C.: Office of the Surgeon General, Department of the Army, 1968. Covers the nonsurgical aspects of military medicine in America from the colonial era to the early 20th century.

Bennion, Elisabeth. *Antique Medical Instruments.* Berkeley: University of California Press, 1979. Descriptions and photographs of medical instruments compiled from museums and collections throughout Europe and America.

Bernadac, Christian. *Les Médicins Maudits: Les Expériences Médicales Humaines dans les Camps de Concentration.* Paris: Éditions Famot, 1967.

Bettman, Otto. *A Pictorial History of Medicine.* Springfield, IL: Charles C. Thomas, 1956.

Bowers, John Z. *Western Medical Pioneers in Feudal Japan*. Baltimore: Johns Hopkins University Press, 1970.

Bowers, John Z. *When the Twain Meet: The Rise of Western Medicine in Japan*. Baltimore: Johns Hopkins University Press, 1980. The events that led to Japan's rapid adoption of Western medical and surgical techniques in the years leading up to the Russo-Japanese War.

Breasted, James Henry. *The Edwin Smith Surgical Papyrus Published in Facsimile and Hieroglyphic Transliteration with Translation and Commentary in Two Volumes*. Chicago: University of Chicago Press, 1930. Quite possibly from an Egyptian manual of military medicine and the primary source on Egyptian medicine and surgery.

Cartwright, Frederick, in collaboration with Michael Biddiss. *Disease and History*. New York: Dorset Press, 1972.

Chamberlain, Weston. "History of Military Medicine and Its Contributions to Science." *Annual Report of the Smithsonian Institution*, 1918: 235–249. Reprinted from *Boston Medical and Surgical Journal*, April 5, 1917.

Cirillo, Vincent. *Bullets and Bacilli: The Spanish-American War and Military Medicine*. New Brunswick, NJ: Rutgers University Press, 2004.

Coates, John Boyd, ed. *Medical Department of the United States Army: Surgery in World War II*. Washington, D.C.: Office of the Surgeon General of the Department of the Army, 1958. The multivolume recapitulation of the history of the Army Medical Department in World War II.

Cohen, Mark Nathan. *Health & The Rise of Civilization*. New Haven, CT: Yale University Press, 1989.

Comrie, John. *History of Scottish Medicine*. London: Baillière, Tindall & Cox, 1932.

Cornbise, Alfred. *Typhus and the Doughboys: The American Polish Typhus Relief Expedition, 1919–1921*. Newark, DE: University of Delaware Press, 1982.

Courville, Cecil. "Prehistoric Trepination." *Bulletin of the Los Angeles County Medical Society* 1 (1937): 42–46.

Cowdrey, Albert E. *United States Army in the Korean War: The Medics' War*. Washington, D.C.: Center of Military History, 1987. The most readable and complete summary of American military medicine in Korea.

Cowdrey, Albert E. *Fighting for Life: American Military Medicine in World War II*. New York: Free Press, 1994. The only accessible single-volume study of American military medicine in World War II.

Cunningham, H. H. *Doctors in Gray: The Confederate Medical Service*. Baton Rouge: Louisiana State University Press, 1958. A compilation of the Confederate medical experience, although, unlike those of the Union Army, most Confederate records were lost when Richmond burned at the end of the war.

Curtin, Philip D. *Disease and Empire: The Health of European Troops in the Conquest of Africa*. Cambridge: Cambridge University Press, 1998.

Cushing, Harvey. *From a Surgeon's Journal*. Boston: Little, Brown and Co., 1937. Firsthand stories from the Western Front in World War I.

Daremberg, Charles. *État de la Médecine entre Homère & Hippocrate: Anatomie, Physiologie, Pathologie, Médecine Militaire, Histoire des Écoles Médicales pour faire suite à la Médecine dans*

Homère. Paris: Librairie Académique Didier et Cie., 1869. An excellent presentation of ancient Greek medicine, although based on unavoidably limited sources.

Farmer, Malcolm. "The Origins of Weapon Systems." *Current Anthropology* 35 (December 1994): 679–681.

Fauntleroy, A. M. *Report on the Medico-Military Aspects of the European War*. Washington, D.C.: Government Printing Office, 1915. Descriptions of medical organization and treatment early in World War I.

Ferguson, R. Brian. "The Causes and Origins of 'Primitive Warfare': On Evolved Motivation for War." *Anthropological Quarterly* 73 (July 2000): 159–164.

Ferrill, Arther. *The Origins of War: From the Stone Age to Alexander the Great*. London: Thames and Hudson, 1985.

Fink, Sheri. *War Hospital: A True Story of Surgery and Survival*. New York: Public Affairs, 2003. Descriptions of medical care in the Bosnian conflict.

Freemon, Frank R. *Gangrene and Glory: Medical Care during the American Civil War*. Urbana: University of Illinois Press, 2001.

Gabriel, Richard A., and Karen S. Metz. *A History of Military Medicine from the Renaissance through Modern Times*. New York: Greenwood Press, 1992. A two-volume history of military medicine particularly strong in its treatment of ancient military medicine.

Gallagher, Hugh Gregory. *By Trust Betrayed: Patients, Physicians, and the License to Kill in the Third Reich*. New York: Henry Holt, 1990.

Garrison, Fielding. *An Introduction to the History of Medicine with Medical Chronology, Suggestions for Study and Bibliographic Data*. Philadelphia: W. B. Saunders Co., 1929. Still the standard one-volume history of medicine.

Garrison, Fielding. *Notes on the History of Military Medicine*. Washington, D.C.: Association of Military Surgeons, 1922. By far the best short study of military medicine. Long out of print but without peer in its completeness and scholarship.

Gillett, Mary C. *The Army Medical Department, 1775–1818*. Washington, D.C.: Center of Military History, 1981.

Gillett, Mary C. *The Army Medical Department, 1818–1865*. Washington, D.C.: Center of Military History, 1987.

Gillett, Mary C. *The Army Medical Department*. Washington, D.C.: Center of Military History, 1995. A fine and complete study of the Army Medical Department.

Goliszek, Andrew. *In the Name of Science: A History of Secret Programs, Medical Research, and Human Experimentation*. New York: St. Martin's Press, 2003.

Gordon, Maurice Bear. *Naval and Maritime Medicine during the American Revolution*. Ventnor, NJ: Ventnor Publishers, 1978.

Greenblatt, Samuel H., ed. *A History of Neurosurgery in Its Scientific and Professional Contexts*. Park Ridge, IL: American Association of Neurological Surgeons, 1997.

Gurdjian, E. S. *Head Injury from Antiquity to the Present with Special Reference to Penetrating Head Wounds*. Springfield, IL: Charles C. Thomas, 1973. A brief but comprehensive study of head injury, although somewhat dated now.

Haller, John S. *Farmcarts to Fords: A History of the Military Ambulance, 1790–1925*. Carbondale: Southern Illinois University Press, 1992. A well-researched, well-written, and nicely illustrated study of military transport. There is no other comparable study.

Heller, Charles E. *Chemical Warfare in World War I: The American Experience, 1917–1918*. Washington, D.C.: Government Printing Office, 1984.

Herman, Jan K. *Battle Station Sick Bay: Navy Medicine in World War II*. Annapolis, MD: Naval Institute Press, 1997.

Horrax, Gilbert. *Neurosurgery: An Historical Sketch*. Springfield, IL: Charles C. Thomas, 1952.

Ireland, M. W., ed. *The Medical Department of the United States Army in the World War, 1917–1918*. 15 vols. Washington, D.C.: Government Printing Office, 1921–1929. Like the American Civil War and World War II compilations, this is a comprehensive collection of statistics from the American World War I experience.

Jones. W. H. S. *Philosophy and Medicine in Ancient Greece*. Baltimore: Johns Hopkins University Press, 1946.

Keegan, John. *A History of Warfare*. New York: Alfred A. Knopf, Inc., 1993.

Keen, W. W. *The Treatment of War Wounds*. Philadelphia: W. B. Saunders Co., 1918. A good summary of the theory of wound management as of the latter part of World War I.

Keevil, J. J. *Medicine and the Navy: 1200–1900*. Edinburgh: E. & S. Livingstone Ltd., 1957. A two-volume study of medicine in the Royal Navy.

Kelly, Howard A., and Walter L. Burrage. *Dictionary of American Medical Biography: Lives of Eminent Physicians of the United States and Canada, from the Earliest Times*. Boston: Milford House, 1928. Entries written by many of the most prominent academic physicians of the time. A number of the entries are written by men who knew their subjects personally.

Kimura, S. *The Surgical & Medical History of the Naval War between Japan & Russia*. Tokyo: Bureau of Medical Affairs, Navy Department, 1911. A hard-to-find volume that has a wealth of information and affords a good picture of the state of Japanese medicine at the time of Japan's war with Russia.

Klawans, Harold L. *The Medicine of History from Paracelsus to Freud*. New York: Raven Press, 1982.

Lada, John, ed. *Medical Statistics in World War II*. Washington, D.C.: Office of the Surgeon General, Department of the Army, 1975. The statistical volume from the larger series on military medicine in that war.

Laffont, Robert. *The Ancient Art of Warfare*. Greenwich, CT: New York Graphic Society, Ltd., 1966.

Lafin, John. *Surgeons in the Field*. London: J. M. Dent & Sons, Ltd., 1970.

LeClerc, Daniel. *The History of Physick or an Account of the Rise and Progress of the Art and the Several Discoveries therein from Age to Age*. London: D. Brown, 1699. The prototypical history of medicine.

LeClerc, Lucien. *Histoire de la Médicine Arabe*. New York: Burt Franklin, 1971; originally published 1876. Still considered the best history of Arabic medicine.

Lelean, P. S. *Sanitation in War*. Philadelphia: P. Blakiston's Son & Co., 1915. Nonsurgical practice at the beginning of World War I.

Levin, Simon S. *Adam's Rib: Essays on Biblical Medicine*. Los Altos, CA: Geron-X, Inc., 1970.

Lovegrove, Peter. *Not Least in the Crusade: A Short History of the Royal Army Medical Corps*. Aldershot, UK: Gale & Polden, Ltd., 1952. A very good short study of the Royal Army Medical Corps.

MacDonald, Lyn. *The Roses of No Man's Land*. New York: Atheneum, 1989.

MacKinney, Loren C. *Early Medieval Medicine with Special Reference to France and Chartres*. Baltimore: Johns Hopkins University Press, 1937.

Majno, Guido. *The Healing Hand: Man and Wound in the Ancient World*. Cambridge, MA: Harvard University Press, 1975. A quirky but engaging and remarkably well-researched study of wound care in the ancient Middle East, Egypt, and Greece.

Makins, George. *Surgical Experiences in South Africa, 1899–1900*. Philadelphia: P. Blakiston's Son & Co., 1900.

McGrew, Roderick E. *Encyclopedia of Medical History*. New York: McGraw-Hill, 1985.

McHenry, Lawrence C. *Garrison's History of Neurology, Revised and Enlarged with a Bibliography of Classical, Original and Standard Works in Neurology*. Springfield, IL: Charles C. Thomas, 1969.

McLaughlin, Redmond. *The Royal Army Medical Corps*. London: Leo Cooper, Inc., 1972.

McNeill, William H. *Plagues and Peoples*. New York: Doubleday, 1977.

Miller, Judith, Stephen Engelberg, and William Broad. *Germs: Biological Weapons and America's Secret War*. New York: Simon & Schuster, 2001.

Mitchell, Piers D. *Medicine in the Crusades: Warfare, Wounds and the Medieval Surgeon*. Cambridge: Cambridge University Press, 2004.

Moodie, R. L. "Studies in Paleopathology: A Prehistoric Surgical Bandage from Peru." *Annals of Medical History* 8 (1926): 69–72.

Moodie, R. L. "Studies in Paleopathology XXI: Injuries of the Head among the Pre-Columbian Peruvians." *Annals of Medical History* 9 (1927): 277–307.

Mullins, William S. *A Decade of Progress: The United States Army Medical Department, 1959–1969*. Washington, D.C.: Office of the Surgeon General, Department of the Army, 1971.

Neel, Spurgeon. *Medical Support of the U.S. Army in Vietnam: 1965–1970*. Washington, D.C.: Department of the Army, 1973. The best short presentation of the American military medical experience in Southeast Asia.

Nicholls, T. B. *Organization, Strategy and Tactics of the Army Medical Services in War*. London: Baillière, Tindall & Cox, 1937.

O'Connell, Robert L. *Of Arms and Men: A History of War, Weapons, and Aggression*. New York: Oxford University Press, 1989.

Ogston, Alexander. *Reminiscences of Three Campaigns*. London: Hodder and Stoughton, n.d. Personal recollections of a surgeon who served in the Egyptian Campaign, the Boer War, and in Eastern and Western Europe during World War I.

Oman, Charles M. *Doctors Aweigh: The Story of the United States Navy Medical Corps in Action*. Garden City, NY: Doubleday, Doran and Co., Inc., 1943.

Oppenheim, A. Leo. "Mesopotamian Medicine." *Bulletin of the History of Medicine* 36 (March–April 1962): 97–106.

Packard, Francis R. *The Life and Times of Ambroise Paré*. New York: Paul B. Hoeber, 1921. A study of both Paré and his era.

Packard, Francis R. *History of Medicine in the United States*. New York: Paul B. Hoeber, 1931. History of American medicine from colonial times forward with an emphasis on biographies of the major participants.

Paré, Ambroise. *An Explanation of the fashion and use of Three and Fifty Instruments of Chirurgery by Helkiah Crooke from Ambroise Paré*. Originally published 1631; reprinted in facsimile by Edinburgh: West Port Books, 1982.

Piggott, Juliet. *Queen Alexandra's Royal Army Nursing Corps*. London: Leo Cooper, Ltd., 1975.

Plumridge, John H. *Hospital Ships and Ambulance Trains*. London: Seeley, Service & Co., 1975.

Porter, Roy. *The Greatest Benefit of Mankind: A Medical History of Humanity*. New York: W. W. Norton & Co., 1997. Porter brings his formidable talents as a historian to bear on a general summary of medical history that frequently touches on topics of significance to military medicine.

Reiss, Oscar. *Medicine and the American Revolution: How Diseases and Their Treatment Affected the Colonial Army*. Jefferson, NC: McFarland & Co., Inc., 1998.

Reverby, Susan M. *Ordered to Care: The Dilemma of American Nursing, 1850–1945*. Cambridge: Cambridge University Press, 1987.

Roddis, Louis. *A Short History of Nautical Medicine*. New York: Paul B. Hoeber, Inc., 1941. There has not been a comparable subsequent comprehensive history of naval military medicine.

Roddis, Louis. *James Lind, Founder of Nautical Medicine*. New York: Schuman's, 1950.

Ryan, Charles. *With an Ambulance during the Franco-German War: Personal Experiences and Adventures with Both Armies*. New York: Charles Scribner's Sons, 1896.

Salazar, Christine F. *The Treatment of War Wounds in Graeco-Roman Antiquity*. Leiden, the Netherlands: Brill, 2000.

Saunders, J. B. de C. M. *The Transitions from Ancient Egyptian to Greek Medicine*. Lawrence: University of Kansas Press, 1963.

Sigerist, Henry. *A History of Medicine: Primitive and Archaic Medicine*. New York: Oxford University Press, 1951.

Sigerist, Henry. *A History of Medicine: Early Greek, Hindu, and Persian Medicine*. New York: Oxford University Press, 1961. The first two of an anticipated but never completed multivolume history of medicine. Sigerist did not live to see the project completed.

Taliaferro, William H. *Medicine and the War*. Chicago: University of Chicago Press, 1944.

Thompson, C. J. S. *The History and Evolution of Surgical Instruments*. New York: Schuman's, 1942. This, with Bennion (1979), comprises most of what has been published in book form on the subject of medical instruments.

Thompson, R. C. *Assyrian Medical Texts from the Originals at the British Museum*. London: Oxford University Press, 1923.

Wangensteen, Owen, and Sarah Wangensteen. *The Rise of Surgery from Empiric Craft to Scientific Discipline*. Minneapolis: University of Minnesota Press, 1978. The famous Minnesota surgeon and his daughter wrote a well-researched and quite complete discussion of the history of medicine. The book is a rich source of bibliographical source material.

Wilbur, C. Keith. *Revolutionary Medicine*. Guilford, CT: Globe Pequot Press, 1980.

Williams, Peter, and David Wallace. *Unit 731: Japan's Secret Biological Warfare in World War II*. London: Hodder and Stoughton, 1989.

Williams, Peter, and David Wallace. *Civil War Medicine*. Guilford, CT: Globe Pequot Press, 1998.

Zajtchuk, Russ, and Ronald Bellamy, eds. *Textbook of Military Medicine: Medical Aspects of Chemical and Biological Warfare*. Washington, D.C.: Office of the Surgeon General, Department of the Army, 1997.

Zimmer, Henry R. *Hindu Medicine*. Baltimore: Johns Hopkins University Press, 1948.

Zimmerman, Leo M., and Ilza Veith. *Great Ideas in the History of Surgery*. Baltimore: Williams & Wilkins Co., 1961. An excellent collection of biographical essays of men key to the development of surgery.

Zinsser, Hans. *Rats, Lice and History: The Biography of a Bacillus*. Boston: Little, Brown and Co., 1934. A dated but interesting study of typhus.

INDEX

ABOUT THE AUTHOR

Jack E. McCallum practiced adult and pediatric neurosurgery in Fort Worth, Texas, from 1977 to 2005. He earned a doctorate in history in 2001 and has taught American history, history of medicine, and the ethics of science at Texas Christian University since that time. He has recently published a biography of Leonard Wood and has contributed to a number of books on military history. He lives on a small farm outside Fort Worth with his wife and daughter.